SITE OF OLD FORT PIERRE (S. DAK.)

where Chardon sleeps in "*one of those lonely graves,* * * * * *on the upper Missouri, unmarked, and, today, unknown*"

The Miller Studio, Pierre, S. Dak.

CHARDON'S JOURNAL AT FORT CLARK

1834–1839

*Descriptive of Life on the Upper Missouri; of a Fur
Trader's Experiences Among the Mandans,
Gros Ventres, and Their Neighbors;
of the Ravages of the Small-
Pox Epidemic of 1837*

Edited with Historical Introduction and Notes by
ANNIE HELOISE ABEL

*Introduction to the Bison Books edition by
William R. Swagerty*

University of Nebraska Press
Lincoln and London

⊛ The paper in this book meets the minimum requirements of
American National Standard for Information Sciences—Perma-
nence of Paper for Printed Library Materials, ANSI Z39.48-1984.

First Bison Books printing: 1997
Most recent printing indicated by the last digit below:
10 9   8   7   6   5   4   3   2   1

Library of Congress Cataloging-in-Publication Data
Chardon, Francis A., d. 1848.
[Journal at Fort Clark]
Chardon's journal at Fort Clark, 1834–1839 / edited with historical
introduction and notes by Annie Heloise Abel.
p. cm.
"Descriptive of life on the upper Missouri; of a fur trader's experi-
ences among the Mandans, Gros Ventres, and their neighbors; of
the ravages of the small-pox epidemic of 1837."
Reprint of the 1932 ed.
Half title: Fort Clark journal of F. A. Chardon.
Includes bibliographical references and index.
ISBN 0-8032-6375-9 (pa: alk. paper)
1. Misouri River Valley—Description and travel. 2. North
Dakota—Description and travel. 3. Chardon, Francis A., d.
1848—Diaries. 4. Fur traders—Missouri River Valley—Diaries.
5. Fur trade—Missouri River Valley—History—19th century.
6. Fort Clark (N.D.) 7. Frontier and pioneer life—Missouri River
Valley. 8. Indians of North America—Missouri River Valley—
History—19th century. 9. Mandan Indians—Missouri River
Valley—History—19th century. I. Abel, Annie Heloise,
1873–   . II. Title.
F598.C48   1997
978.48843—dc21
96-29657   CIP

Reprinted from the original 1932 edition published under the
auspices of Lawrence K. Fox, Superintendent, Department of
History, State of South Dakota, Pierre, South Dakota.

To the Memory

of

Judge Walter B. Douglas and Dr. Howard
M. Hamblin, two men, who, though widely
disassociated, had this in common : an appre-
ciation of the worth of even the humblest
VOYAGEUR in the opening up of the

Great West

CONTENTS

ILLUSTRATIONS

INTRODUCTION

William R. Swagerty

On the west bank of the Missouri River six miles southeast of the town of Stanton, North Dakota, not far from Knife River and Fort Mandan historic sites, lies a wind-swept terrace that once was home to several thousand Mandans and Arikaras and a dozen or so whites who lived among them for a generation. Located in a transitional ecotone between the Missouri River floodplain and the Dakota prairie, this settlement landscape, like others in the Knife River and Missouri River confluence area, proved ideal for establishing towns. Combined with fishing, hunting, and gathering, horticulture provided Middle Missouri village Indians with well-rounded diets and surpluses for trade with neighboring tribes.[1]

The occupation of this bench by the Mitutanka Mandans in the early 1820s attracted white traders who built posts adjacent to the large earth mound village. By the 1830s, Mit-tutta-hang-kush, the main village, housed over 1,000 inhabitants and was a noted landmark for Indians and whites alike on the middle stretch of the Missouri. Its founding and abandonment are directly linked to the story that unfolds in the *Journal at Fort Clark*.[2]

FORT CLARK IN HISTORICAL CONTEXT

Fort Clark dates from 1831 through 1860, the era of near-domination of the American Fur Company (AFC) on the Missouri River. It overlaps Mandan occupation from about 1822 to 1837. In 1837, the entire high plains suffered a smallpox epidemic that halved the native population, killing larger numbers of village peoples than those less sedentary. The Mandans suffered a loss of more than 90 percent of their population during the summer of that year, only 138 individuals remaining from a pre-epidemic population estimated between 1,600 and 2,000—the highest historic decline in a single epidemic episode in North American history.[3] In the fall of 1837, the few Mandans who survived packed up and moved away to live with the Hidatsas. Their village became home to the Arikaras, newcomers to the area, also hard hit by the smallpox, who migrated up from the south, possibly in need of cached food and seed to start over. The Arikaras remained in the older Mandan village, reshaping it to suit their needs. They remained there until the end of 1861.

The fort served as the principal trading post for the sedentary Mandans and Hidatsas (1831–37) and later the local Arikaras (1837–62). It was also visited by traders from the Crows and by groups representing major divisions of the Lakota Sioux, including Yanktons, Yanktonais, and Tetons. The Tetons were subdivided into Brulés, Oglalas, and Saones. In the mid-nineteenth century, the Saones (often spelled "Saons" or "Sawons" in the journals) developed into the Minneconjous, Hunkpapas, Sans Arcs, Two Kettles, and Blackfoot Sioux. Each of these buffalo-hunting groups moved about in extended families or bands, which worked independently but traded with each other and with Middle Missouri Indians prior to and during the early decades of the nineteenth century.[4] Their frequent presence in and out of Mandan-Hidatsa-Arikara country was noted by chroniclers of the day, who often saw more conflict than cooperation among Indians as competition for wildlife resources increased with new demands for furs and hides.[5] The Arikaras suffered periodically from Sioux intruders, who burned their village in 1839, and their misfortunes were compounded by further episodes of cholera in 1851 and smallpox in 1856.[6]

Fort Clark also shared the terrace from the late 1850s to 1861 with an opposition firm headed by Charles Primeau.[7] Following a fire in 1860, which burned the south half of the fort and forced its abandonment, Primeau's Post was bought out, serving the AFC for a year or so more. By the end of 1861, the last Arikara had moved to nearby Fort Berthold, ending the need for a trading post at this location. Ground that had once supported the first farmers of the Missouri reverted to prairie.[8]

Prior to 1931, when the State Historical Society of North Dakota assumed jurisdiction of Fort Clark, the 231-acre site was unmanaged state property at times subject to pot-hunting. Some mapping was undertaken before the 1960s, but serious archaeological excavations did not begin until the 1970s. Only recently have summaries of the archaeology at Fort Clark been made available. Today there are no historic structures remaining, no reconstructions, and almost no physical evidence that there ever was a major village and fort at this place. Visitors can take a self-guided tour through land reclaimed by pocket gophers, whose mounds are scattered among depressions marking the locations of historic structures. To the discerning eye, the fortification ditch that once enclosed a large earth lodge village is still visible, as are circular rings of eighty-six Mandan and Arikara lodges. Many pits and holes, mapped in minute detail, make this site the largest and potentially the most important for combining archaeological and historical data in the entire Plains culture area.[9]

The central plaza, once filled with ceremonial and social gatherings, is now empty, but it is possible to imagine the excitement that visitors such as Prince Maximilian of Germany and the artists George Catlin and John James Audubon experienced as they toured the Missouri River country in the 1830s and 1840s. The outline of the walls of Fort Clark, once visible for many miles to travelers on the Missouri River, reveal a trading post that exerted a regional influence disproportionate to its modest size and ignominious ending.[10]

Of the three most important AFC forts of the Upper Missouri River fur trade, Fort Union (1829–65) is the best documented and studied and is now partially reconstructed as a major interpretive site within the National Park System.[11] Fort Pierre Chouteau (1831–55) has a secure place through literature connecting that pivot point on the river with the development of the city of Pierre, South Dakota.[12] Except for archaeologists who have worked at the site and historians of the fur trade, few will have heard of the Mitutanka Mandan Indians or of Fort Clark itself. Yet the story of what took place midpoint between Fort Union and Fort Pierre from 1822 to 1861 encapsulates the larger history of Indian-white contact throughout

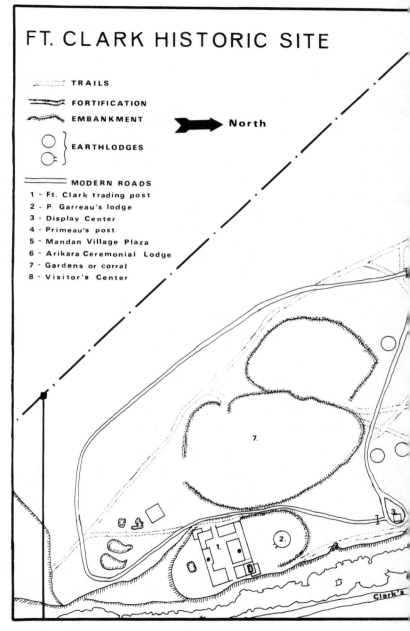

FT. CLARK HISTORIC SITE

TRAILS

FORTIFICATION

EMBANKMENT   North

EARTHLODGES

MODERN ROADS

1 - Ft. Clark trading post
2 - P. Garreau's lodge
3 - Display Center
4 - Primeau's post
5 - Mandan Village Plaza
6 - Arikara Ceremonial Lodge
7 - Gardens or corral
8 - Visitor's Center

7.

1.

2.

Clark's

State Historical Society of North Dakota, by C. L. Dill, 1974

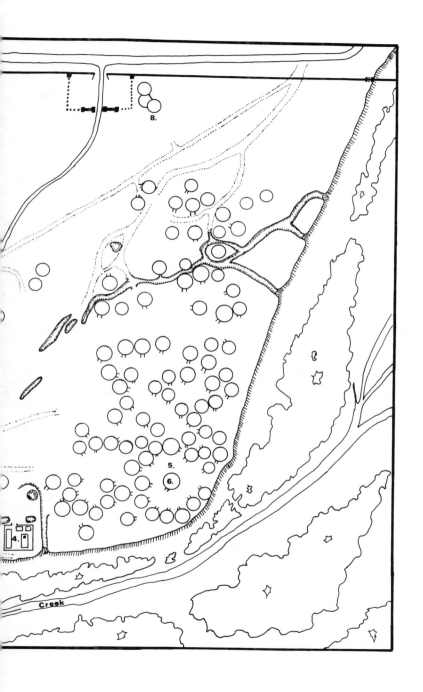

8.

5.
6.
4.

Creek

North America. Within three decades of occupation, the local native landscape underwent cultural, material, and demographic shifts that depopulated major tribes such as the Mandan-Hidatsa and led to consolidation of survivors at Fort Berthold and elsewhere.[13]

THE *JOURNAL AT FORT CLARK* AND ITS AUTHOR

The day-by-day narrative recorded in the journal kept by Francis A. Chardon from 1834 to 1839 at Fort Clark is a rare source for the dynamics of diverse cultures meeting in "Indian country" on unwritten but well-understood diplomatic terms. The story properly begins a century earlier in 1738 when Pierre Gaultier de Varennes, the Sieur de la Vérendrye, under authority from the king of France, crossed what is now the border between Canada and the United States into present-day North Dakota. Quick to see the potential of profits and eager to promote friendship with native peoples, La Vérendrye worked his way to the center of the Middle Missouri Trade System, a network of economic and kinship relationships stretching from the summer villages of the Mandan, Hidatsa, and Arikara tribes on the Missouri and its tributaries to the Rocky Mountains.[14] Between 1785 and 1812, the French success in building small posts and in trafficking with Missouri River tribes attracted British and Spanish traders to do the same.[15]

Beginning with Lewis and Clark, American explorers contacted these same village peoples and reported back the prospects for successful trade in the trans-Missouri West, thus promoting an industry that has been known ever since as the fur trade of the Far West. Earliest American efforts are associated with the Missouri Fur Company, organized in 1809 by Manuel Lisa of St. Louis.[16] Lisa employed whites to tap the lucrative Crow and Blackfeet country of the northern Rockies, thus bypassing the middleman tribes living along the Missouri. This strategy violated Indians' territorial boundaries of hunting and trading and damaged Indian-white relations, forcing Lisa and his trappers to compete with rather than trade peacefully with resident tribes. Despite heavy losses of traders' lives and property, several hundred whites, especially those associated with the Rocky Mountain Rendezvous System (1825–40) continued this selective approach and some lived to tell about it. Even the most successful of these "mountain man" associations, the Rocky Mountain Fur Company, organized in 1822 by William H. Ashley and Andrew Henry, suffered heavy losses of men and property wherever the protocol of preexisting Indian trade was avoided or confronted, especially in the homeland of the Blackfoot.[17]

The lesson of the need to stick to Indian trading protocol was learned early by companies that were to succeed on the Missouri. In 1822, in addition to Ashley's St. Louis–based Rocky Mountain Fur Company, two additional major fur trading companies formed partnerships to compete for the Indian trade of the trans-Missouri West. The Columbia Fur Company was a new association of old Nor'westers, former Montreal-based North West Company men who became independent after the merger of their parent company with the Hudson's Bay Company in 1821. Operating along the Red River, from 1822 to 1827 they infiltrated "American" territory along the Missouri, establishing posts at crossroads to attract intertribal trade. By adhering to the old Indian system of using native middlemen traders to collect and distribute furs and goods, Columbia Fur experienced local success but had difficulty moving furs out and goods into their posts due to competition with the larger companies. Consolidation with the American Fur Company resulted in 1827.[18]

Because of its association in name and in business arrangements with John Jacob Astor's New York office of the original American Fur Company (founded in 1808), many students of the fur trade have assumed that Astor directed the trade of the Missouri region as well.[19] Such was not the case. The St. Louis–based Western Department of the AFC, also formed in 1822, was a separate operation that cooperated with Astor by using his purchasing power to order goods in Europe and along the Atlantic coast and his marketing agents in London and on the Continent to dispose of furs on a percentage of profit basis. The Western Department lasted until 1865 and underwent several reorganizations and changes in legal title but was always known as Pierre Chouteau Jr.'s operation. The House of Chouteau, like that of Astor, held great clout and sway on waterfronts, in banks, and in factories that turned raw furs into fashionable apparel and supplied the white traders with the beads, blankets, guns, and hardware needed to sustain trade with Indians.[20]

This Western Department separated from Astor in 1834 but retained the acronym, AFC, as symbol of near-control of trade wherever it operated. Despite strong opposition of rivals, the AFC prevailed in the long run, absorbing or driving them out. In the process, a string of depots, forts, and wintering posts was constructed from Bellevue in present-day Nebraska as far west as Fort Benton in the heart of Montana. By the end of 1827, the AFC had bought out the major posts of Columbia Fur and enlisted most of its partners as officers of Pierre Chouteau and Company under a newly formed subdivision, the Upper Missouri Outfit (UMO).[21]

The journal that follows begins on 18 June 1834, in the third year of Fort Clark's existence, and ends rather abruptly on 6 May 1839, almost five years later. The post was constructed by James Kipp, a former Columbia Fur partner who had become a prized trader with the UMO. Kipp was quite familiar with the area, having established Tilton's Post, a Columbia Fur Company enterprise, somewhere nearby a decade earlier. The structure was typical of a middle-sized fur post of its day, with picketed walls 120 by 160 feet, two gates, and blockhouses at two corners. Within this garrison-like compound, a handful of employees on payroll labored to collect, sort, pack, and transport the furs and hides brought out of Indian country. They were joined periodically by workers and company directors from other posts up and down the river.[22]

Part of the larger UMO workforce of three hundred or so men, these traders, craftsmen, and engagés (day laborers) led lives typical of Jacksonian-era workers in the new "factory system" of the United States. Although their time in Indian country had episodes of danger and adventure, long cold winters and hard physical work during spring, summer, and fall were the rule. Men suffered daily monotony, stress, and depression leading to over-drinking. Lonely for family life and affection, they contracted successive common-law marriages with Indian and mixed-blooded women, most of whom had been sold or traded by male relatives.[23]

Although marriage practices were far less formal than those in "white civilization," wages and conditions were very similar to those of the United States or eastern Canada. But the distance from relatives and isolation of these posts from each other created distress that overwhelmed even the stronger among fur trade employees. Consequently, fur trade careers were short, averaging 15 years with the UMO for owners and officers, 6.3 years for mid-level managers including clerks and traders, and 2.7 years for servants in the rank and file. Desertion, premature death, and early retirement are common in the documentary record. [24]

The daily lives of AFC workers on the Missouri River were first analyzed by Hiram M. Chittenden, the earliest historian to gain access to the papers of Pierre Chouteau and Company, now housed at the Missouri Historical Society in St. Louis.[25] Other scholars have delved into the myriad documents now available, but social scientists have yet to give a sequential account of the American Fur Company and its Upper Missouri Outfit. Successful studies of fur traders and their activities utilize a variety of sources in reconstructing narrative and analytical histories. The most familiar are travelogues by visitors, dignitaries, and the occasional artists or naturalists who ventured into the West. Letters to and from fur trade field personnel and the financial ledgers are also essential documentary tools for evaluating chronology, economy, and the relative stability or importance of a fur trade enterprise, but seldom do we have a candid, personal account that only a diary or an unaltered journal renders.[26]

For the Missouri River country during the American period, published journals kept by fur trade personnel include that of John C. Luttig, a clerk with Lisa's Missouri Fur Company (1812–13); that of Charles Larpenteur, a fellow Upper Missouri Outfit trader, active from 1833 to the dissolution of the AFC in 1865; that of Swiss artist and AFC clerk Rudolph Friederich Kurz during his short time in America (1846–52); and that of Missouri River trader Henry A. Boller, who worked for companies in opposition to the Upper Missouri Outfit from 1858 to 1863, at one time in partnership with Charles Larpenteur. Each is invaluable as a candid, detailed account of daily life.[27]

The value of the Fort Clark journal is heightened by the fact that its author, Francis A. Chardon, probably never intended it to become a public document, whereas Larpenteur prepared his autobiography, *Forty Years a Fur Trader on the Upper Missouri* (also a Bison Book), from the still-unpublished "journal," a transcript of which is now housed at the Minnesota Historical Society.[28] Chardon never got that chance.

Chardon's early life remains obscure. He was born in Philadelphia, most likely as "François Auguste," to a family of French extraction. He first turns up in the West soon after the end of the War of 1812, having participated in that conflict, possibly as a soldier with Andrew Jackson at the Battle of New Orleans, whose name he celebrates several times in the journal.[29] Between 1815 and 1827, Chardon spent time with the Osage, intermarrying and having one son, Francis T. Chardon, whose formal acceptance of land under the Osage Treaty of 1825 was witnessed by his father.[30] According to biographer Ray H. Mattison, Chardon entered the service of the UMO "about 1827–1828."[31] His first assignment was among the Teton Sioux at the forks of the Cheyenne River in present-day South Dakota, an appropriate posting, for he spoke Osage, a Siouan language.[32] He is listed on the 1830 UMO roster as "Clerk & Trader," assigned to the "Sawons" (Saones), number 248 of 287 employees, at the very high annual salary of $800.[33]

In 1832 Chardon was at Fort Union, and in 1833 he was in Blackfoot country where in December he built a post with the help of twenty men at the junction of Popular (or Porcupine) River and Milk River for the UMO. The post was named Fort Jackson in honor of the president.[34] From the spring of 1834 through 1842, Chardon was *bourgeois* (manager) at Fort Clark. He was not always happy there, but he was more comfortable than most men of his rank. He enjoyed a good salary that allowed him to purchase a black slave, and, at one point in his life, an Indian woman of fifteen years who probably served as wife-concubine. Chardon had a succession of Indian wives, mostly Sioux. He started a second family with Tchon-su-mons-

ka (the Sand Bar), painted by George Catlin and described by
the artist as "very richly dressed, the upper part of her gar-
ment being almost literally covered with brass buttons; and
her hair, which was inimitably beautiful and soft, and glossy
as silk, fell over her shoulders in great profusion, and in beautiful waves."[35] (See the sketch facing page 110 in the *Journal*.)

Tchon-su-mons-ka and Chardon had two sons, Francis
Bolivar in 1832 and Andrew Jackson in 1835. Young "Bolivar"
accompanied his father on his sole trip "back home" to Pennsylvania in 1835, where the lad remained with Chardon's parents until 1845 or so. On a visit to Philadelphia in the early
1840s, George Catlin described Bolivar as "a fine-looking half-
breed boy, about ten years old."[36] Bolivar attended St. Louis
University and inherited a fairly large sum upon the death of
his father.[37]

Undoubtedly, Chardon's most trying time was the year 1837.
In April, Tchon-su-mons-ka died. That summer Chardon witnessed firsthand the spread of smallpox from the steamboat
St. Peters, which arrived at Fort Clark on 19 June 1837; eventually smallpox took the life of his son, young Andrew Jackson.[38] By the time the steamboat returned from Ft. Union on
12 July, the entire Missouri River region had been infected,
leading Chardon to write in his journal on Thursday, 20 July,
"No News in that quarter [Arikara country], except the Small
Pox" (122). By the end of the month, many of Chardon's trading partners and most of his closest friends and allies, including Chief Four Bears of the Mandan, were dead or dying. The
journal reports the spread of death among the Sioux, Blackfeet,
Gros Ventres, and others near and far. As editor Annie Heloise
Abel remarks, "The day-by-day progress of that [disease] in its
devastating course is the chief single interest of Chardon's Fort
Clark journal" (lvi).[39]

There is much more to the journal than this. No other source
besides occasional candid letters sent by officers to and from
St. Louis gives as much detail on daily life as does Chardon.
Unfortunately, there is no sequel and the only other compa-
rable journal from Fort Clark, kept by Alexander Kennedy in
1834, is a mere fragment (see appendix A).

In May of 1839, after the few surviving Mandans had moved,

Chardon reported in person at Ft. Pierre. Three weeks later, the French scientist Joseph N. Nicollet, in company with American explorer John C. Frémont, arrived at Fort Pierre aboard the AFC steamer *Antelope*. Chardon apparently "loaned" his journal through a fellow trader to Nicollet, who never returned it.[40]

Chardon returned to Fort Clark to serve his new clientele—the Arikaras. His immoderate drinking and confrontational behavior at the fort led to charges of murder against him. In 1843, the UMO transferred him to Fort McKenzie, but his temper seems to have prevailed, and in February 1844 he helped to kill at least six Piegans (Blackfeet) trading at Fort McKenzie in retaliation for the killing of his black servant, Reese. The victims were scalped and the whites held a scalp dance in the fort that night, an event the Blackfeet did not forget or forgive.[41] As John Sunder has written, "Although he was an experienced Company agent from Fort Clark, he was also a hotheaded Frenchman who bartered liquor freely, befriended the wrong people, and left a trail of tension from post to post."[42] The incident forced the closing of Fort McKenzie, and ruined trade with the Blackfeet for years, but Chouteau and Company retained Chardon, allowing him to build a new post nearby in the spring of 1844 at the mouth of the Judith River. Fort Francis A. Chardon was short lived owing to the hostility of the Blackfeet and was soon replaced by Fort Lewis (1846) and Fort Benton (1850).[43]

Chardon ended his days on the middle stretch of the Missouri. He returned to Fort Clark in 1846, where he was ordered out of Indian country by the U.S. Indian Agent Andrew Drips for illegally selling liquor. He worked his way back from St. Louis to end his days an Indian trader, dying at Fort Pierre of a severe case of rheumatism in 1848.[44]

Nicollet died in 1843 without completing his treatise on North America, his effects being placed in a trunk in the Topographical Bureau of the War Department in Washington. In 1921, the contents were discovered by Dr. Howard M. Hamblin. Other scholars, including Frederick Webb Hodge and Milo M. Quaife, learned of the trunk, but it was Dr. Annie Heloise Abel who took time to evaluate and edit the original manuscripts, which were subsequently transferred to the Library of Congress.[45]

Editor Annie Heloise Abel (1873–1947)

By the time Annie Heloise Abel was shown the Nicollet trunk, she had already established herself among historians as scholar and editor. Born in Sussex, England, one of six children, Annie moved to Salina, Kansas, with her family in 1885 at age twelve. After a common school education, she earned a degree at the University of Kansas in 1898 and became a teacher in the rural community of Colby, but within a year she had decided to pursue history as a career. Her master's thesis, completed at Kansas in 1900, was titled "Indian Reservations in Kansas and the Extinguishment of Their Title." From this point on, Abel spent most of her academic life investigating aspects of Indian-white relations.[46]

In 1905 Abel completed her doctorate at Yale. Her prize-winning dissertation, "The History of Events Resulting in Indian Consolidation West of the Mississippi River," was published the following year in the *Annual Report of the American Historical Association*, a tribute to the integrity of her investigation.[47]

That same year Abel temporarily taught at Wells College in New York but moved on to Women's College of Baltimore in 1907 (now Goucher College), where she rose rapidly to full professor and chair of the department of history. She left for Smith College in 1915, where she distinguished herself as head of the Honors Program until 1919. While at Smith, her scholarly interest in Indian affairs led her back to the Indian Bureau files and into a three-volume study for which she is best known. Released as *The Slaveholding Indians*, the trilogy tells the story of the Five Civilized Tribes in the nineteenth century—their progress, betrayal, removal to Indian Territory, and subsequent participation in the American Civil War.[48] It was probably while researching this large work that Abel was shown Chardon's manuscript journal through the office of Frederick Webb Hodge, ethnologist-in-charge of the Bureau of American Ethnology from 1910 to 1918. In addition to the Chardon jour-

nal, Nicollet's trunk contained a manuscript copy in French of
the narrative of St. Louis trader Regis Loisel's 1803–4 expedition up the Missouri, recorded by Pierre-Antoine Tabeau. The
latter commanded her attention first, but she determined to
see both projects completed.[49]

On sabbatical leave to Australia from 1921 to 1922, Abel
met George Cockburn Henderson, a professor of history at the
University of Adelaide. They married, Abel resigned from
Smith, but the union did not last. By 1924, she was back in the
United States, retaining from that point forward the hyphen-
ated surname, Abel-Henderson, which she used in legal matters, including copyrights, but not on title pages.

Abel returned to the University of Kansas in 1928 as full
professor and was the recipient of a Social Science Research
Council grant that same year. This enabled her to continue
editing the Tabeau narrative and the Fort Clark journal, which
was finished in 1930 during her first year of formal retirement
at Hood's Canal, Washington, where Annie had moved to join
her sister, Rose. The book was published two years later, in the
depth of the Great Depression, by the Department of History
of the State of South Dakota in a very limited edition.[50] It has
been reprinted once, but until now, it has never been afford-
able for a general audience.[51]

As editor, Abel was a superb researcher. Her copious endnotes
give the reader a tour of American Fur Company operations
not available anywhere else, not even in Chittenden's more
general history. Moreover, her sleuthing interest in understanding the character and personality of her subjects led her to
biographical details found nowhere else. Abel was not without
her bias, which she reveals immediately in the introduction.
She compared all American Indians to her primary interest—
the Five Civilized Tribes—and used their example as the gauge
for all others. The village tribes of the Missouri thus fared poorly
by her standards.[52]

Abel also did not like the AFC, characterizing Astor's methods in driving out competition as "reprehensible" (xlix), and
the principal owners and partners of the Western Department,
including Chouteau and Kenneth Mackenzie, as "a sorry group."
(lxii). It is clear that she admired some aspects of Chardon's

character, especially his candor. Abel's prejudice against the Mandans, in particular, was undoubtedly influenced in part by Chardon's own bias against the very tribe with which he worked the longest. Her criticisms of Chardon are largely critiques of more general matters associated with the fur trade society which she grew to know through the journal. She especially condemned the casual practice of multiple marriages to Indian women and overconsumption of alcohol, for she was a leader in the suffrage movement and in women's rights. She gives Chardon credit for providing both education and inheritance for his son Bolivar. Abel saw in Bolivar's education and assimilation into white civilization an example of progress, a view shared by many other reformers of her day. Although she does not say so directly, one suspects she agreed with George Catlin's assessment of Chardon when Catlin wrote for his 1841 audience, that "this extraordinary man . . . by his bold and daring nature has not only carried dread and consternation amongst the Indian tribes wherever he had gone; but has commanded much respect, and rendered essential service to the Company in the prosecution of their dangerous and critical dealings with the Indian tribes."[53]

Here then is Chardon's eyewitness account of life as a Missouri River fur trader in the 1830s. Here also is a model of excellent editing, complete with 518 notes, a lengthy appendix, and a useful index. Since its publication in 1932, scholars have revised some of Abel's factual assertions and assumptions about people and places, but on the whole the work reflects the high quality of archival research produced by American public and private universities in the early twentieth century, as well as Annie Heloise Abel's own very high expectations of herself as a scholar.[54]

A NOTE ON THE TERMINOLOGY:

As editor, Annie Abel provides the reader with clear explanation of most terms; however, she was not very interested in nineteenth-century colloquialisms nor in fur traders' systems of accounting for furs and hides. For ease of transportation and to reduce spoilage, both furs and hides were usually pressed and bundled into "packs." A buffalo pack normally contained ten hides or robes. Beaver pelts were weighed by the pound and were also pressed into packs, each one containing between eighty and one hundred furs. A pack of river otter contained around sixty animal furs. Muskrats were usually labeled "rats" and were not very valuable individually but were the most widely trapped animal next to beaver. Chardon reports taking thousands of "Rats" during his stay at Fort Clark, a term derivative of the French-Canadian word for muskrat, *rat musqué.* He also uses the term "Ree" for Arikara and on one occasion confuses the reader with the use of "Minetaree" to mean Gros Ventres or Hidatsas (181, 320 n.517). Mandans called the neighboring Hidatsas "Minitari," which means "cross the water." French-Canadians called the same people Gros Ventres, meaning Big Bellies, not to be confused with the modern Gros Ventres or Atsina of Montana who live at Fort Belknap Reservation. Abel follows Chardon's use of Gros Ventres to mean the Hidatsas.

NOTES

1. See W. Raymond Wood, *An Interpretation of Mandan Culture History,* Bureau of American Ethnology Bulletin 198 (Washington DC, 1967); Donald J. Lehmer, *Introduction to Middle Missouri Archeology,* National Park Service Anthropological Papers 1 (Washington DC, 1971); Stanley A. Ahler, Thomas D. Thiessen, and Michael K. Trimble, *The Prehistory and Early History of the Hidatsa Indians* (Grand Forks: University of North Dakota Press, 1991); and *The Phase I Archeological Research Program for the Knife River Indian Villages National Historic Site, Part II: Ethnohistorical Studies*, ed. Thomas D. Thiessen, Midwest Archaeological Center Occasional Studies in Anthropology 27 (Lincoln: National Park Service, 1993).

On horticultural adaptations of these tribes, see Gilbert L. Wilson, *Agriculture of the Hidatsa Indians: An Indian Interpretation,* University of Minnesota Studies in the Social Sciences 9 (1917; reprinted as *Buffalo Bird Woman's Garden: Agriculture of the Hidatsa Indians,* as told to Gilbert L. Wilson, St. Paul: Minnesota Historical Society Press, 1987).

2. General readers will want to consult Roy W. Meyer, *The Village Indians of the Upper Missouri: The Mandans, Hidatsas, and Arikaras*

(Lincoln: University of Nebraska Press, 1977); specialists should see W. Raymond Wood, "Integrating Ethnohistory and Archaeology at Fort Clark State Historic Site, North Dakota," *American Antiquity* 58(3) 1993:544–59.

3. See Clyde Dollar, "The High Plains Smallpox Epidemic of 1837–38," *Western Historical Quarterly* 8(1) 1977:15–38. Also see Russell Thornton, *American Indian Holocaust and Survival: A Population History since 1492* (Norman: University of Oklahoma Press, 1987), 94–99.

4. On early trade, see John C. Ewers, "The Indian Trade of the Upper Missouri Before Lewis and Clark: An Interpretation," *Bulletin of the Missouri Historical Society* 10(4) 1954:429–46, reprinted in *Indian Life on the Upper Missouri* (Norman: University of Oklahoma Press, 1968), 14–33; W. R. Swagerty, "Indian Trade of the Trans-Mississippi West to 1870," in *Indian-White Relations*, vol. 4 of *Handbook of North American Indians*, ed. Wilcomb E. Washburn (Washington DC: Smithsonian Institution, 1988), 351–74.

On the Mandans, Hidatsas, and Arikaras, see Alfred W. Bowers, *Mandan Social and Ceremonial Organization* (Chicago: University of Chicago Press, 1950; reprint, Moscow: University of Idaho Press, 1991); Bowers, *Hidatsa Social & Ceremonial Organization,* Bureau of American Ethnology Bulletin 194 (Washington DC, 1963; reprint, Lincoln: University of Nebraska Press, 1992).

The introduction to the latter by Douglas R. Parks is especially informative on all three tribes as is the overview in Ahler, et al., *Prehistory and Early History.*

5. See Anthony McGinnis, *Counting Coup and Cutting Horses: Intertribal Warfare on the Northern Plains, 1738–1889* (Evergeen CO: Cordillera Press, 1990); essays in *The Hidden Half: Studies of Plains Indian Women*, ed. Patricia Albers and Beatrice Medicine (Washington DC: University Press of America, 1983); and *The Political Economy of North American Indians*, ed. John H. Moore (Norman: University of Oklahoma Press, 1993).

6. This reconstruction is based largely on C. L. Dill's fine summary in "Fort Clark on the Missouri: Prairie Post and Field Lab, 1831–1990," in *The Fur Trade in North Dakota*, ed. Virginia L. Heidenreich (Bismarck: State Historical Society of North Dakota, 1990), 17–32.

7. Clark, Primeau and Company was formed in 1857 as a subsidiary of Frost, Todd and Company based in Sioux City, Iowa. Most of the employees in the field were former UMO men who were dissatisfied with terms and saw opportunity in the new concern. Frost, Todd

and Company dissolved in 1859, but Malcomb Clark and Charles Primeau continued to oppose the AFC until 1860, when they were bought out by Chouteau. See Thomas D. Thiessen, "Historic Trading Posts Near the Mouth of the Knife River, 1794–1860), in *Phase I Archeological Research Program,* ed. Thiessen, 67–68.

8. For chronology of this region, see W. Raymond Wood, "Early Fur Trade on the Northern Plains," in *The Fur Trade in North Dakota,* ed. Virginia L. Heidenreich (Bismarck: State Historical Society of North Dakota, 1990), 2–16.

9. For a description of the site and the history of archaeology associated with it, see C. L. Dill, "Fort Clark on the Missouri"; C. L. Dill and Erik L. Holland, "Fort Clark Research Reports," vol. 1, (Bismarck: State Historical Society of North Dakota, 1983), typescript on file, North Dakota Heritage Center; and W. Raymond Wood, "Integrating Ethnohistory and Archeology at Fort Clark State Historic Site, North Dakota," *American Antiquity* 58(3) 1993:544–59.

10. From 1973 to 1990, the State of North Dakota staffed the site with a supervisor. In 1986, Fort Clark was nominated and added to the National Register of Historic Places. Today there is a small stone structure with maps and brochures for self-guided tours.

11. The starting point for all overviews of Upper Missouri fur trade history is Hiram Martin Chittenden, *The American Fur Trade of the Far West,* 3 vols. (New York: Francis P. Harper, 1902; reprint, 2 vols., New York: Press of the Pioneers, 1935; reprint of 1935 ed., 2 vols., Lincoln: University of Nebraska Press, 1986). Also see David J. Wishart, *The Fur Trade of the American West, 1807–1840: A Geographical Synthesis* (Lincoln: University of Nebraska Press, 1979).

For specialized studies of Fort Union, see Erwin N. Thompson, *Fort Union Trading Post Historic Structures Report,* part 2 (Washington DC: National Park Service, 1968; reprinted as *Fort Union Trading Post: Fur Trade Empire on the Upper Missouri,* Williston: Fort Union Association, 1994). See Thompson's useful appendix for a chronology from 1673 to 1966, when Fort Union was added to the National Park System. Also see William J. Hunt Jr., et al., *Fort Union Material Culture Reports*, 9 parts (Lincoln: National Park Service Midwest Archaeological Center, 1986–96).

12. The best summary of the role of the forts is provided in John E. Sunder, *The Fur Trade on the Upper Missouri, 1840–1865* (Norman: University of Oklahoma Press, 1965); and Robert G. Athearn, *Forts of the Upper Missouri* (Englewood Cliffs NJ: Prentice Hall, 1967). On Fort Pierre see Harold H. Schuler, *Fort Pierre Chouteau* (Vermillion: University of South Dakota Press, 1990).

13. This story is summarized by Roy W. Meyer, *The Village Indians of the Upper Missouri* (Lincoln: University of Nebraska Press, 1977) and by Mary Jane Schneider, *The Hidatsa* (New York: Chelsea House, 1989).

For the material impact of the fur trade on the Missouri River tribes, see Dill and Holland, "Fort Clark Research Reports"; Hunt, et. al., *Fort Union Research Reports*; G. Hubert Smith, *Like-A-Fishhook Village and Fort Berthold Reservoir, North Dakota*, National Park Service Anthropological Papers 2 (Washington DC, 1972); and J. Daniel Rogers, *Objects of Change: The Archaeology and History of Arikara Contact with Europeans* (Washington DC: Smithsonian Institution Press, 1990).

14. See W. Raymond Wood, "Plains Trade in Prehistoric and Protohistoric Intertribal Relations," in *Anthropology on the Great Plains*, ed. W. Raymond Wood and Margot Liberty (Lincoln: University of Nebraska Press, 1980), 98–109.

15. See *Early Fur Trade on the Northern Plains: Canadian Traders among the Mandan and Hidatsa Indians, 1738–1818*, ed. W. Raymond Wood and Thomas D. Thiessen (Norman: University of Oklahoma Press, 1985).

16. Richard Oglesby, *Manuel Lisa and the Opening of the Missouri Fur Trade* (Norman: University of Oklahoma Press, 1963).

17. For this story see Chittenden, *The American Fur Trade*; LeRoy R. Hafen, "A Brief History of the Fur Trade of the Far West," in *Mountain Men and the Fur Trade of the Far West*, ed. LeRoy R. Hafen, 10 vols. (Glendale CA: Arthur H. Clark, 1965–1972), 1:17–165; and *The West of William H. Ashley*, ed. Dale L. Morgan (Denver: The Old West Publishing Co., 1964).

18. See Wood, "Early Fur Trade," 7–12; and Thiessen, "Historic Trading Posts," 47–61.

19. John Denis Haeger, *John Jacob Astor: Business and Finance in the Early Republic* (Detroit: Wayne State University Press, 1991).

20. The best summary of the St. Louis–based American Fur Company operation is Janet Lecompte, "Pierre Chouteau, Jr.," in *Mountain Men and the Fur Trade*, ed. Hafen, 9:91–123. Also see Lecompte, "The Chouteaus and the St. Louis Fur Trade," in A *Guide to the Microfilm Edition of Papers of the St. Louis Fur Trade*, ed. William R. Swagerty (Bethesda: University Publications of America for the Missouri Historical Society, 1991), xiii–xxii.

21. No separate history of the Upper Missouri Outfit has been written. The best summaries remain those of Chittenden and Sunder. Works in progress on this subject are being undertaken inde-

pendently by Barton Barbour, Melvin Thurman, and W. R. Swagerty.

22. See Thiessen, "Historic Trading Posts," 58–62.

23. No authoritative labor history of this fur trade frontier has been written. See W. R. Swagerty, "A View From the Bottom Up: The Work Force of the American Fur Company on the Upper Missouri in the 1830s," *Montana: The Magazine of Western History* 43(1) (1993):18–33; and papers in the *Fort Union Fur Trade Symposium Proceedings, September 13–15, 1990*, ed. Paul Hedren (Williston SD: Friends of Fort Union Trading Post, 1994).

24. The average of fifteen active years in the fur trade for owners and officers is consistent with a much larger sample group including HBC, North West Company, and free trappers and traders. See W. R. Swagerty, "Marriage and Settlement Patterns of Rocky Mountain Trappers and Traders," *Western Historical Quarterly* 11(2) (1980):159–80.

For a study testing the statistics in the above as applicable to the UMO, see W. R. Swagerty and Dick A. Wilson, "Faithful Service under Different Flags: A Socioeconomic Profile of the Columbia District, Hudson's Bay Company and the Upper Missouri Outfit, American Fur Company, 1825–1835," in *The Fur Trade Revisited*, ed. Jennifer S. H. Brown, et al. (East Lansing: Michigan State University Press, 1994), 243–67.

25. See Peter Michel, "The St. Louis Fur Trade: Fur Company Ledgers and Account Books in the Archives of the Missouri Historical Society," *Gateway Heritage* [Missouri Historical Society, St. Louis] 6(2) (1985):10–17; and W. R. Swagerty, "General Introduction," in *Guide to the Microfilm Edition*, v–xi.

26. Several "Letterbooks" (duplicate or "carbon" copies of letters sent from fur posts) have survived and these are second only to journals for an inside view. The most important of these are the "Fort Tecumseh and Fort Pierre Journal and Letter Books" abstracted by Charles Edmund DeLand, notes by Doane Robinson, *South Dakota Historical Collections* 9 (1918):69–239, available in manuscript on microfilm from the Chouteau Collection of the Missouri Historical Society, St. Louis, on reels 16, 17, and 19 of "Papers of the St. Louis Fur Trade," ed. W. R. Swagerty; and the "Fort Union Letterbook, October 29, 1833–December 10, 1835," available on reel 22.

27. John C. Luttig, *Journal of a Fur Trading Expedition on the Upper Missouri, 1812–1813*, ed. Stella M. Drumm (St. Louis: Missouri Historical Society, 1920; reprint, New York: Argosy-Antiquarian, 1964); Charles Larpenteur, *Forty Years a Fur Trader on the Upper Missouri: The Personal Narrative of Charles Larpenteur,*

1833–1872, ed. Elliott Coues, 2 vols. (New York: Francis P. Harper, 1898; reprint, Lincoln: University of Nebraska Press, 1989); *Journal of Rudolph Friederich Kurz: An Account of His Experiences among Fur Traders and American Indians on the Mississippi and the Upper Missouri Rivers during the Years 1846 to 1852*, trans. Myrtis Jarrell, ed. J. N. B. Hewitt, Bureau of American Ethnology Bulletin 115 (Washington DC, 1937; reprint, Lincoln: University of Nebraska Press, 1970); *Henry A. Boller: Missouri River Fur Trader*, ed. Ray H. Mattison (Bismarck: State Historical Society of North Dakota, 1966).

28. See Louis Pfaller, "Charles Larpenteur," in *Mountain Men and the Fur Trade*, ed. Hafen, 1:295–311. Erwin N. Thompson has done a partial editing of the original Larpenteur manuscript, which is now at the Minnesota Historical Society. His "White Man Bar (Mato Washejoe), Upper Missouri Trader; Journals and Notes of Charles Larpenteur between 1834 and 1872," transcribed by Erwin N. Thompson, n.d., is on file at Fort Union Trading Post National Historic Site.

29. No record of Chardon's birth has surfaced. See Annie Heloise Abel's discussion of Chardon's early years and his possible service at the Battle of New Orleans with Jackson, xli, 208 n.35 n.36, 209 n.37 n.38.

30. Abel, 209 n.44.

31. Ray H. Mattison, "Francis A. Chardon," in *Mountain Men and the Fur Trade*, ed. Hafen, 1:225–27; reprinted in *Fur Traders, Trappers, and Mountain Men of the Upper Missouri*, ed. LeRoy R. Hafen, introduction by Scott Eckberg (Lincoln: University of Nebraska Press, 1995), 61–64.

32. See Abel, xlvi–xlviii.

33. "Persons Employed for the Upper Missouri Outfit for the Year 1830," Chouteau Collection, Missouri Historical Society. Several others at Chardon's rank were making an average of $371.94 that year. See Swagerty, "A View from the Bottom Up," 30–31 and Abel, 227 n.81.

34. See Chittenden, *The American Fur Trade*, 2:935 (1935 ed.). Also see Abel's reconstruction, pp. xlviii–xlix.

35. George Catlin, *Letters and Notes on the Manners, Customs, and Conditions of North American Indians* (New York and London, 1841; reprint of 1844 London ed., intro. by Marjorie Halpin, 2 vols., New York: Dover, 1973), 1:224.

36. Catlin, *Letters and Notes*, 1:225.

37. Abel has pieced this together for her readers, but it is hidden in her endnotes. See xliii–xliv, 213 n.51 n.52, 214 n.53.

38. Tuchon-su-mons-ka died 24 April 1837; Andrew Jackson on 22 September at the height of the epidemic (109, 137).

39. Milo M. Quaife gained access to the Chardon manuscript journal and published excerpts from it in his "The Smallpox Epidemic on the Upper Missouri," *Mississippi Valley Historical Review* 17 (June 1930–March 1931):278–99.

40. Abel makes a good case that Nicollet obtained the journal through trader Pierre D. Papín (lxv–lxvi, and esp. 270 n.257). Nicollet did not mention this in his diary, but it seems plausible. See *The Journals of Joseph N. Nicollet: A Scientist on the Mississippi Headwaters with Notes on Indian Life, 1836–37*, trans. André Fertey, ed. Martha Coleman Bray (St. Paul: Minnesota Historical Society, 1970), esp. 27–28; and *Joseph N. Nicollet on the Plains and Prairies: The Expeditions of 1838–39, with Journals, Letters, and Notes on the Dakota Indians*, trans. and ed. Edmund C. Bray and Martha Coleman Bray (St. Paul: Minnesota Historical Society Press, 1976), 34–35.

41. See John C. Ewers, *The Blackfeet: Raiders on the Northwestern Plains* (Norman: University of Oklahoma Press, 1958), 66–68, for an authoritative discussion of this affair. Also see Lieut. James H. Bradley, "Affairs at Fort Benton from 1831 to 1869," *Contributions to the Historical Society of Montana* 3 (1900):201–87. Bradley claims that at least twenty-one Blackfeet died when a cannon was discharged by Alexander Harvey, aided by Chardon (237).

42. Sunder, *Fur Trade on the Upper Missouri*, 61. Also see Abel, 246 n.186.

43. Bradley, "Affairs at Fort Benton from 1831 to 1869," 237–39; and documents in the Chouteau Collection, Missouri Historical Society.

44. See Abel's discussion (lxiv–lxv); Mattison, "Francis A. Chardon," in *Mountain Men and the Fur Trade*, ed. Hafen, 1:226–27; and Sunder, *Fur Trade on the Upper Missouri*, 61–62.

45. See Abel, 270. On 1921 as the date of discovery of the manuscript see Bray and Bray in *Joseph N. Nicollet on the Plains and Prairies*, 34.

46. See Harry Kelsey, "A Dedication to the Memory of Annie Heloise Abel-Henderson," *Arizona and the West* 15(1) 1973:1–4; and Dan L. Thrapp, "Abel, Annie Heloise," in *Encyclopedia of Frontier Biography*, 3 vols. (Glendale CA: Arthur H. Clark, 1988), 3:2–3.

47. Annie Heloise Abel, "History of Events Resulting in Indian Consolidation West of the Mississippi River," *American Historical Association Annual Report, 1906*, 1:235–450. Abel won the Justin Winsor Prize in History for 1906.

48. Annie Heloise Abel, *The Slaveholding Indians*, 3 vols. (Cleveland: Arthur H. Clark, 1915–25). All three volumes have recently been reprinted by the University of Nebraska Press, with introduc-

tions by Theda Perdue and Michael D. Green, as *The American Indian as Slaveholder and Secessionist* (1992); *The American Indian in the Civil War, 1862–1865* (1992); and *The American Indian and the End of the Confederacy, 1863–1866* (1993).

49. Abel briefly describes the discovery and history of both projects in her preface to *Tabeau's Narrative of Loisel's Expedition to the Upper Missouri*, ed. Annie Heloise Abel (Norman: University of Oklahoma Press, 1939) and in the historical introduction to Chardon's *Journal*, lxvi–lxvii.

50. The copyright was retained by Abel-Henderson, but the book was published under the auspices of the State of South Dakota through Athens Press in Iowa City.

51. The facsimile reprint was made available by Books for Libraries Press of Freeport, New York, in 1970.

52. See the discussion of Abel's interest in the Five Civilized Tribes in the introductions by Perdue and Green to the aforementioned Bison Books edition of *The Slaveholding Indians*.

53. Catlin, *Letters and Notes*, 1:224.

54. The most serious factual error concerns Abel's association of Fort Floyd as the original Fort Union (xxxviii–xxxix). Recent archaeological and historical work by the National Park Service has proven that the two were quite separate. See William J. Hunt Jr., "Fort Floyd: An Enigmatic Nineteenth-Century Trading Post," *North Dakota History* 61(2) (1994):7–20.

One oddity of the *Journal* which reads as an awkward insertion is Chief Four Bears' death speech, "(Small Pox talk)," purportedly recorded by Chardon and found with the journal but not in it and not actually entered into the journal at the time of the Mandan chief's death from smallpox on 30 July 1837. In it we read, "One of our best friends of the Village (The Four Bears) died today, regretted by all who Knew him" (124). Although the speech has become famous as an Indian view of the smallpox epidemic, some scholars doubt its authenticity (see Milner, "The High Plains Smallpox Epidemic of 1837–38," 31). Abel obviously believed it to be in Chardon's hand and therefore placed it in chronological order where it belonged, following the entry on 31 July (124–25). Also see 316 n.486.

EDITOR'S PREFACE

LITTLE did I think when I began the editorial work on
Chardon's Fort Clark journal, which, by the by, was almost immediately after its discovery, that so long a time
would have to elapse ere the publication could be regarded as a certainty. The interruptions, the frustrations of
apparently well-conceived plans, the obstacles in the way,
generally, have been so many that, if at all superstitious-
ly-inclined, one might well think an adverse fate pursued. And doubts have assailed as to the best way to
proceed. One tentative *Introduction* was a discourse on
the United States Indian policy, policies, or lack of policy, from the beginning of things national to the middle of the century; another, such an account of the peltry
traffic as would make Chardon and his diary fit into a
series that others had then in contemplation, dealing with
fur traders of the West; yet one other — and this when
Canadian publication seemed less than a remote possibility — was a history of the Upper Missouri Outfit as a
development out of the Columbia Fur Company and the
Selkirk Colony on Red River of the North. The circumstances that ultimately made one of the Dakotas, where
all the scenes were laid, as it happened, a sort of patron
saint of the undertaking seemed singularly opportune.

The protracted preparations have brought in their
train both advantages and disadvantages. Among the
latter, have been the wasting of time in the going over
the same ground again and again, the losing of the
thread of one's discourse, and the stealing of one's thunder by others; but all such have been more than counterbalanced by the thoroughness of research that delay
has rendered possible. Possible, too, has it made the

resort to friends, more fortunately placed than I with respect to libraries and records. Of these I would like particularly to mention Miss Emily Hardy Hall of the Yale Library staff; Dr. Eleanor L. Lord, accessible to the church and other records of Philadelphia; and Dr. Elizabeth F. Rogers, who, at Wilson College, Chambersburg, Pennsylvania, is within reach of the Culbertson family archives. To these three friends and erstwhile students or colleagues I am indebted in varying degrees as well as to the following: Miss Charlotte Lois Dodge, Mr. Kingsmill Commander, and my sisters, Dr. Wright and Lena M. Abel, for very real assistance in verifying, transcribing or collating; also to Mrs. J. A. Wilson of Ottawa, who has lent me rare travel narratives from the library of her father, Dr. Henry A. Tuzo of the Hudson's Bay Co. and to Father G. J. Garraghan, S. J., of St. Louis University, who generously furnished me with a transcript of one of Father Point's journals.

My greatest debt by far, however, is to individuals of the staff of each of the three places where I have been privileged to conduct a greatly-extended personal research and I herewith name them in the order of time rather than of service; for all have been most kind: — Mr. Charles Hawke, Chief Clerk, and Mr. J. Kinney of the Forestry Division of the United States Indian Office at Washington; Mrs. Nettie H. Beauregard, Archivist, and Miss Stella M. Drumm, Librarian, of the Missouri Historical Society at St. Louis; Dr. Arthur G. Doughty, Deputy Minister, and Miss Magdalen Casey, Librarian, of the Canadian Dominion Archives at Ottawa. In her facile reading of faded and, to me, almost illegible French script, Mrs. Beauregard has been very helpful and very labor-saving. Furthermore, both she and Miss Drumm, knowing their own records so well, have been able to make me aware of undreamed-of possibilities and five months or more spent in almost daily toil at the *Jefferson Memorial Building* I count among the most enjoyable and profitable of my many research experiences. The liberal aid given by Miss Drumm in the matter of both biographical and bibliographical information — not a tenth part of which I have been able to use as yet — was in the nature of an immense relief. Needless to say, her knowledge of local history far exceeds my own.

The late Dr. H. M. Hamblin, who unearthed the Nicollet chest and brought to my attention its valuable contents before he had taken the time to examine them himself, I have remembered in my dedication; but even that is but a poor recognition of his unquestioned worth. Year by year since his death I am appreciating more and more what it must have meant to me, who had no roots in the American past myself, to have at hand, in the United States Indian Office, where I was then spending all my leisure time, someone like Dr. Hamblin, who, coming from New England originally, had actually participated in the *Westward Movement*, known red men intimately, white politicians more so, and could suggest lines of research because of a former contact with the persons or events involved.

ANNIE HELOISE ABEL-HENDERSON

HOOD'S CANAL, WASHINGTON, SEPTEMBER, 1930.

HISTORICAL INTRODUCTION

FORT CLARK,[1] the scene of most of the events described in the fur trader's journal here edited, was one of three[2] principal posts of the American Fur Company on the upper Missouri. It belonged, specifically, to what was called, the *Upper Missouri Outfit,* the organization of which had followed immediately upon the union of the Columbia Fur Company with the American, in 1827. That union, as negotiated, after untold interruptions and delays,[3] by Ramsay Crooks,[4] John Jacob Astor's[5] very capable agent, with Kenneth Mackenzie,[6] the equally capable representative of Tilton[7] and his associates, was in the nature of an absorption, whereby Mackenzie and his friends, Daniel Lamont and William Laidlaw, passed over to the Astor concern but upon the understanding, most definitely expressed, that they, collectively, should constitute a separate and distinct branch of its Western Department, at the head of which stood Pierre Chouteau, Jr.,[8] Bernard Pratte, and other merchants of St. Louis.

Thus had come into being the famous Upper Missouri Outfit, which, in all its essentials, was but the old Columbia Fur Company in another guise, Tilton gone, Renville gone, but the rank and file of its personnel retained. Retained, likewise, were its ideals and its ambitions, though operating, henceforth, in one respect, in a restricted area; for Astor's new recruit, retiring altogether from the St. Peter's,[9] once its richest field, was to confine its energies to the development of the fur trade of the upper Missouri and across the mountains towards the Far West.

The consolidation with its late most energetic rival was a signal triumph for the American Fur Company, the consummation of a long effort, tirelessly expended. Since about 1816, it had dominated in the region of the Great Lakes and could now just as effectively impose itself upon the Mississippi and her mighty affluent, the Missouri. Its power and prestige at Washington had grown with the years especially after the admission of the State of Missouri to the American Union and the election of the masterful Thomas Hart Benton to the United States Senate.[10] Useless quite had it already proved for friends of the Indians, notably Thomas L. McKenney in his defense of the *Indian Factory System,* to declaim against so pernicious a combination.[11] More and more were their protests disregarded as Astor, professing a patriotism he never at any time in the whole of his career sincerely felt, built up his gigantic monopoly, reaping where others had sowed and riding rough-shod over reds and whites alike. Not for nothing had he drawn to himself and into the vortex of his great combine the powerful Chouteau interests of St. Louis, which, from that time on and under the name of the ''Western Department of the American Fur Company,'' continued in the way the original emigrants from New Orleans had directed. Between the Chouteaus and Astor there had never been any really appreciable difference, any dissimilarity of methods or of public morals. All of them were resourceful, eternally vigilant, unscrupulous, notoriously selfish, adept at the shaping of national policies to private ends, brazen in their defiance of the law, remorseless in their exploitation of the Indians.

Once organized, the Upper Missouri Outfit threw itself enthusiastically into the work outlined for it, utilizing what posts from the Poncas northward its predecessor had erected and projecting others beyond. In 1829 was begun the building of Fort Union[12] near the mouth of the Yellowstone and this under Mackenzie's personal supervision. ''Fort Floyd'' it is said to have been christened, tentatively,[13] in honor, we may suppose, not of the obscure Charles Floyd, whose only title to fame rests on the accidental circumstance of his having died prematurely when serving as one of the several sergeants of the Lewis and Clark expedition, but of his cousin, Dr. John Floyd,[14] United States congressman from Virginia, who had endeavored, in season and out of season and, at first, from very questionable motives,[15] to establish an exclusive American title to Oregon by arousing in the United States Congress sufficient interest to accomplish its military occupation and eventual settlement.[16]   To control the trade of the Far West, thus out-witting the Hudson's Bay Company, had long been Kenneth Mackenzie's dearest wish and the very name of the Columbia Fur Company, of which he was reputed to be the real head,[17] had been as significant in its day as was that now bestowed upon the establishment near the mouth of the Yellowstone.   In joining forces with Ramsay Crooks, an ex-Astorian and therefore presumably committed to an interest in Oregon, Mackenzie had done the wisest thing possible in the furtherance, at long range, of his own pet ideas, especially as Crooks had long since demonstrated what a telling influence he, individually, could exert, not alone over Floyd, but over Benton as well.[18]

And everywhere that Mackenzie went, went Astor's reprehensible methods.[19]   Being so nearly identical with those of the North West Company of Montreal, in whose service Columbia Fur Company employees almost to a man had had their training, they were easily adopted.   Chief among them was the ruthlessness displayed towards an *Opposition,* no matter how, when, or where encountered.   Contesting any and every advance up the Missouri or pretensions to exclusive control, appeared numerous traders, acting singly or in combination.   On the lower reaches of the stream but above the Poncas, the opponent most to be withstood was the P. D. Papin Company, called, in criticism or derision, the "French,"[20] precisely as the Upper Missouri Outfit was called, not infrequently, the "English."[21] Farther up, were the successive offshoots of the old Ashley-Henry concern,[22] the Sublette brothers and their colleagues. With the French Company, Mackenzie made short shrift, eliminating it utterly in 1830; but not until 1834 did he even measurably dispose of the Rocky Mountain men.   In the interval between the two events, transpired several things that were destined to affect, although in varying degrees, the fortunes of the Upper Missouri Outfit.   Larger and better establishments were created, Fort Clark replacing what remained of Tilton's post at the Mandans[23] and Fort Pierre,[24] Fort Tecumseh[25] at the Bad River;[26] steamboat transportation was introduced on the upper Missouri and, following that, as a necessary consequence, extensions in the traffic were made beyond the mouth of the Yellowstone; spirituous liquors were more rigidly prohibited from the "Indian country"[27] and, to supply their possible lack, a still was set up at Fort Union;[28] last but not least that obnoxious obstruction to commerce,[29] the Arikaras, was removed, they voluntarily departing for the Platte,[30] to a new residence among the Pawnees, their near of kin.[31]

The strict chronological sequence of the foregoing is not so material as is the fact that they one and all ante-dated 1834; since, in that year, came, besides the adjustment with the Sublette people that signified their withdrawal as competitors on the Missouri, a serious crisis in the affairs of the American Fur Company itself, a crisis precipitated by the retirement of its founder, John Jacob Astor.[32] The first great result of this was an ostensible disintegration of the monopoly. Out of the ruins, however, if ruins they were, emerged two companies, professedly independent but so intimately bound together, in reality, that they could, on occasion, present a united front to the outside world and, in them, the American Fur Company lived again, still interfered at Washington, still exploited right and left in the Indian country. At the head of the one subsidiary enterprise and the virtual successor of Astor was Ramsay Crooks, while, in the other, the senior partner was Bernard Pratte, his father-in-law, notwithstanding that the most active, first, last, and always, was Pierre Chouteau, Junior, by whose name, indeed, the company at St. Louis was usually designated.

To the Pratte, Pierre Chouteau Jr. & Company, the Upper Missouri Outfit was to sustain much the same relation that it had borne to the Western Department. None the less, the changes of 1834 forced a certain re-organization upon it. Interestingly-enough, it is from that event that the *Fort Clark Journal* dates its beginning.[33] The arrangement with Sublette as well as the changes incident to re-organization entailed a considerable shifting of men and brought to the Mandans Francis

A. Chardon. The covering page of his journal supplies these
particulars:

"FORT CLARK

JOURNAL

Mandan Village

June 18th 1834[34]

F. A. Chardon"

Of Francis A. Chardon, biographically, considerable has been
ascertained by dint of diligent research, and something con-
jectured. He was of French extraction, his full baptismal name
being probably François Auguste[35] Chardon and he the son of a
certain Anthony, or Antoine, Chardon of Philadelphia.[36] Exactly when or under what circumstances Francis Chardon left
that place or any other in Pennsylvania it is not possible to say.
From his extravagant admiration of Andrew Jackson, more
than a mere party loyalty would seem to demand, and from a
further personal reference[37] in his journal to the Battle of New
Orleans on the occasion of its twentieth anniversary, the inference might be drawn that he had seen service in the second
American war with Great Britain and actually under the man
whose martial exploits and personal qualities so greatly appealed to him; but an examination of the extant records of that
war, the national, at Washington and the local, in Pennsylvania,
has revealed no trace of a soldier or sailor of his name.[38]

Another conjecture, based upon Chardon's apparent and more
than ordinary intimacy[39] with the Berthold family, is, that he
was attracted to the American West by Bartholomew Berthold,
who, an émigré from France in the suite of General Willot,[40] had
become a naturalized citizen of the United States in Philadel-

phia, had journeyed westward in 1809 to St. Louis, had married into the Chouteau family there, and had formed in 1812 an Indian trade partnership with his brother-in-law, Pierre Chouteau, Jr.[41] From that time on these two men, either alone or in combination with some of their numerous and ever-increasing relatives and family connections, constituted one business concern after another or several concerns simultaneously and, of whatever one it was that operated in the Osage country, Chardon was, after about 1817, when the first Berthold-Chouteau partnership underwent dissolution, an employee.[42]

Writing in his journal, on New Year's Day, 1837, Chardon recorded the fact that ''This day last year, I had the pleasure, (after an absence of twenty years), of dineing with my Old Father & Mother.'' The score of years may have been approximate only and, if he fought at New Orleans in January of 1815, he might very easily have loitered in the West afterwards, passing upward from Louisiana, as many others were doing, into the valley of the Arkansas, where the acquaintance with Bartholomew Berthold had its beginning or its renewal, the latter, if, as is most likely, Berthold had had dealings with Anthony Chardon in the Quaker City and if Anthony were the father of Francis.

The stay of Francis Chardon in the Osage country was a relatively long one, long enough at any rate for him to gain considerable familiarity with the Osage language, a familiarity that Maximilian remarked upon and took advantage[43] of when, in the summer and autumn of 1833, he came to know Chardon at Fort Union on the upper Missouri. It was long enough, also, for Chardon to form the usual family connection with a squaw and to have an Indian progeny. His Osage son, Francis T. Chardon, was one of the half-breed beneficiaries under the Osage treaty of 1825, which Chardon himself, the trader and the father, witnessed.[44]

Soon thereafter, presumably, he was transferred to the upper Missouri. At all events, he was there from the time of the establishment of the Upper Missouri Outfit.[45] What became of his Osage son and of that son's mother is problematical. In the winter of 1833, he tried to recover possession of the former[46] and paid for an *express*[47] to go after him; but nothing has been forthcoming to warrant the supposition that he ever saw him again. Francis T. Chardon[48] was not remembered in his father's will, nor is he or his Osage mother ever alluded to in the present journal, although there are recorded there many very personal and private matters.

As far as the journal entries go, quite otherwise was it with most of this woman's successors, and they were not limited to two or three. Leaving out of account a "Ree wife"[49] and a girl of fifteen, whom Chardon bought for one hundred and fifty dollars after the former had left him, possibly also another, whom he confesses he stole from his friend Jacob Halsey,[50] when at Fort Pierre in 1838 and to whom, on occasion, he gave "a good whipping,"[51] once, indeed, for the heinous offense of not mending his moccasins, three are noted that seem to have had a regular standing and a stay of some duration in his household. All three, as it happened, were of Sioux origin. The first of the three, *Tchon - su - mons - ka,* the Sand Bar, was the mother of two boys, Francis Bolivar[52] and Andrew Jackson,[53] and she was one of the "two very pretty Sioux women," of whom George Catlin undertook to make portraits.[54] Hers was the elaborate native dress that Chardon sent to Catlin,[55] after her death most likely, which took place, April 24, 1837.[56] Her baby boy, the little Andrew Jackson, died in the September following, when the smallpox epidemic was at its height and doubtless a victim of it; but Chardon fails so to say. He had sent the child to Fort Pierre to be out of reach of the scourge and a few days subsequently recorded his death without mentioning even his name. By such an omission may not a father's grief be measured?

Chardon's second Sioux wife was a Marguerite Marie and, possibly, the same as the woman he stole from Halsey at Fort Pierre in the country of the Tetons, to which *Tchon - su - mons - ka* had belonged. Marguerite Marie was twenty-five years of age in 1840 and, on July 4th of that year, was baptized by Father Hoecken at Fort Clark.[57] What became of her is not known. The third Sioux wife was a certain Ellen, a half-breed, who long outlived Chardon.[58] The two boys, ''Manzaischata and his brother Mankezeeta,'' named with her in Chardon's will and provided for, may have been his children by her and one of them, perhaps, the Jean Baptiste Chardon that Father De Smet speaks of as being, in subsequent years, a Sioux interpreter.[59]

In these many marriages of Chardon, regular or irregular and mostly the latter, there was really nothing peculiar.[60] They were typical of life beyond the settlements, no more numerous, no more ephemeral, than were those of traders and trappers generally in the ''Indian country.'' Their only significance comes in the realization that they can be multiplied for the trading fraternity and the tribes as a whole a thousandfold without any exaggeration. From the *bourgeois*[61] down to the meanest of the *mangeurs du lard*[62] the relationship existed, becoming more gross as it descended. In the days of the fur trade, Indian women were exploited just as surely as were the animals hunted and slain and they were exploited, not alone by white men, but by men of their own families, by brothers, fathers, and husbands. If not promiscuous in their sexual relations before the advent of the trader, the less prominent of them inevitably were after. The unions of the daughters of chiefs, made for purely business reasons oftentimes, were slightly more nearly permanent but no more truly real. They all lasted, even among the Roman Catholics, only so long as the dominant partner found it convenient or remained in the ''Indian country.''

Individually, marriages with Indian women in the ''Indian country'' were not an impediment to an additional contemporaneous marriage in the settlements; but were sufficiently irregular for it to be necessary, should a white wife threaten a visit to a trading post, for the word to be passed along so that any red companion might be, betimes and for the time being, hidden safely away.[63] Genuine affection between the sexes of the differing races there frequently was. It was sometimes born, as was the case with Daniel Harmon[64] and his half-caste squaw, of long association, faithfulness, and a common sorrow. Its presence to a degree was the rule, no doubt, and its utter absence, the very great exception, although neither the display of jealousy nor the indulgence in resentment to the point of fiendish cruelty was, of that, any criterion. Affection for the offspring there almost invariably was and on the part of both parents. Chardon's solicitude for his boys — he apparently had no daughters — , his provision for the education of the youthful Bolivar, constituted a markedly redeeming trait in his rough and ready and sometimes brutal character. It was not the only one, but, on that subject, there will be ample opportunity to enlarge presently.

Excepting Chardon and a few others, the middle-rank men, the traders, the book-keepers, the clerks, of the Upper Missouri Outfit were all, as has been already intimated, ex-employees of the Columbia Fur Company, as were the three brilliant young Scotsmen, Kenneth Mackenzie,[65] William Laidlaw,[66] and Daniel Lamont,[67] who were its agents and in immediate control. Though young, these three, the eldest of them only thirty, they were all as experienced in the ways of the fur trade and of the wilds beyond the frontier as was Ramsay Crooks himself or Astor; and, if, because of them, a picturesque trio, and especially of their leading member, Kenneth Mackenzie, ''King of the Missouri,''[68] ''Emperor of the West,''[69] a glamor has been thrown over that part of the Indian trade that came under their supervision, relieving it, somewhat, of its sordidness and of its utter viciousness, that glamor must not be allowed to blind us to the evils of great magnitude that they condoned and tacitly fostered.

It is true they introduced into the American traffic of prairie and mountain something of the pomp and dignity[70] that it had lacked before and still lacked elsewhere and that had always more or less characterized the British fur trade in which they had all gained their experience; true also that they were able by their superior intellectual attainments and their regard for the amenities of life[71] to make the Missouri posts,[72] where they personally held sway, attractive, not alone to sportsmen,[73] who came thousands of miles to indulge in buffalo-hunting, but to scholars of scientific bent.[74] At these posts, over a sumptuous repast, at as well appointed a table as could be boasted at any factory of the Hudson's Bay Company, or in the long evenings beside the fire, conversation of a high order could be enjoyed.[75] Good cheer abounded; but, necessarily, it was of the sort that is dependent upon the flow of ardent spirits, of which there was never any lack in those days on the upper Missouri,[76] notwithstanding that, for some short periods, when there happened to be a spurt of vigilance visible[77] among those entrusted with the execution of the trade and intercourse laws[78] of the United States government, home products had to be resorted to that were not of the best and concoctions drunk that only too obviously failed to pass muster.[79]

Into this charmed circle came Francis A. Chardon and within it he stayed, spending the remainder of his days, except for short holidays and the one vacation year already mentioned, on the upper Missouri, continuing there after the circle was broken, Mackenzie withdrawn, Lamont and Halsey dead. And his services were esteemed highly from the start, his salary, at one time, being eight hundred dollars a year, when that of James Kipp[80] was only six hundred and that of others, seemingly far more prominent than he, in like proportion, though on a downward scale.[81] From the summer of 1829,[82] his movements for almost all of the remaining period of his life can be determined with more than a fair approach to definiteness and accuracy. His acquaintance with Laidlaw, the first of the three Scotch partners whom he came to know and to regard and to esteem as a friend, began at the Forks of the Cheyenne,[83] where he was trading with the Saones and Laidlaw with the Yanctonais. The acquaintance between them, when it did begin, was a pleasant one and their experiences together were such that, in after years, they liked to refer to them often and to dwell upon them lingeringly.

The custom was for the individual traders to repair to their "wintering ground" when the season opened about October or, possibly, late September and not to return to headquarters, which in the case of these two men was Fort Tecumseh, until it closed in April. Fort Tecumseh was for the Upper Missouri Outfit at first what it had been for the Columbia Fur Company

— its most important post. It was the Teton post and continued so to be until Fort Pierre was built and ready for occupancy.[84] Both were a short distance above the mouth of Bad River, and there, after 1829, Laidlaw held sway for many years, presiding first at Fort Tecumseh and then at Fort Pierre as did Kenneth Mackenzie at Fort Union. Between these two principal posts and back and forth to St. Louis, passed Lamont, taking note of conditions, having charge of supplies, and examining accounts. Sometimes, too, he substituted at a principal post[85] or conducted the trade, as Laidlaw did at the Forks of the Cheyenne, at a minor. Among the three Scotsmen circulated letters, delightful in their little touches of friendliness, reminders of home, messages to one another of cheer and affection, hopes expressed of early re-unions.

There were others to gather around the festive board at Fort Tecumseh, while Chardon had residence there, besides those belonging regularly to the post. Occasional visitors were James Kipp, Lewis Crawford,[86] Colin Campbell,[87] William and Thomas Dickson,[88] Richard T. Holliday[89] and his brother, J. M. Holliday, all old associates of other days, spent in similar ways on the Red River of the North, on the St. Peter's, and even on the Missouri itself. The most distinguished visitor outside the trade was Prince Paul of Württemberg[90] and, since he, on the occasion of a previous visit to the United States,[91] had gone down as far as the country of the Osages and that in 1823, when Chardon was presumably yet there, the two men, despite differences in rank and cultural endowment, must have had a common knowledge of a different section of the "Indian country" to discuss and to bring them together. In early September of 1830, which was after Prince Paul had departed, came James Archdale Hamilton,[92] an English gentleman of refinement and cultivated tastes, who, for some reason or other never explained, had chosen to suppress his family name of Palmer and to limit himself to the use of his Christian.[93] Between Hamilton and Chardon there could have been very little in common and it argues well for the general amiability and trustworthiness of the latter that the former, like Laidlaw and Halsey, manifested nothing but a cordial friendship for him. Chardon was, apparently, one Frenchman on the Missouri between whom and the Anglo-Saxons no invidious distinction was ever made.

And there was a distinction made, ordinarily. Not far from Fort Tecumseh was the principal establishment of the French Company and it is very noticeable, from the records, that, in the intercourse rendered necessary by business relations and revealed in a pretty regular and constant correspondence, there was little room for anything but the fur trade as a subject of discussion. Moreover, even after the "Opposition" had been eliminated and Papin's clientele taken over by Mackenzie, as was the case in this year of 1830, matters were not greatly altered. Laidlaw did not send his affectionate greetings to Picotte or to the Cerré brothers as he did to Hamilton, to Crawford, to Kipp, and, most of all, to Mackenzie, to whom he was devotedly attached; neither did Lamont. It is interesting to observe, however, that, while the P. D. Papin & Co. remained the "Opposition" but was being approached with an eye to its own absorption, the exchange of civilities was an almost daily event and such as promised full concord. Competition in the trade, keen and bitter though it still was, did not preclude dining together and hunting together.[94] That it should ever have been otherwise would seem to have been a pity. The days and the evenings must have been very long at times, intolerably so, especially when the weather was inclement and reading matter exhausted. To relieve an almost insupportable tedium race antipathies and trade jealousies might surely have been set aside; but they very rarely were.

The consolidation of interests effected between the Upper Missouri Outfit and the French Company necessitated certain readjustments in the placing of equipments for the approaching winter's trade; but Laidlaw and Chardon returned, as usual, to the Forks of the Cheyenne, where the former could supervise the work of the men who were felling timber for the erection of the Fort Pierre that was to be.[95] Lamont, meanwhile, took charge at Fort Tecumseh; Papin and Emilien Primeau[96] went to the White River; Frederick Laboue[97] to the Moreau River;

and Richard T. Holliday to the Arikara village, which was not far from the Mandan, in the vicinity of which, James Kipp was preparing to build Fort Clark and where John McKnight[98] was stationed and where David D. Mitchell[99] had recently come to spend his first winter on the upper Missouri. Laidlaw returned to Fort Tecumseh to spend Christmas and New Year's with Lamont and, most likely, the others, including Chardon, came also. In early spring, the best of the trade being over, Laidlaw left the Forks of the Cheyenne, his Indian family with him, and allowed Chardon to follow after with the results of their winter's labors, "11 skin canoes containing 1440 packs Robes." His post had been reported by Lamont as doing better than any other.[100]

This was Chardon's last wintering in Laidlaw's company and among the Saones; for, quite early in 1832 for a certainty, he was at Fort Union, where Hamilton also was. Writing to Mackenzie the middle of February, Laidlaw sent to each of the three some little personal message, as was his wont, to Hamilton, his "best love," to Chardon, his remembrances, and to Mackenzie, who had recently lost an infant half-breed son, his sympathy and his "best love" as well.[101] Chardon's transfer to Fort Union had probably been resolved upon by Mackenzie as a part of his scheme for expansion in the trade, incident to the introduction of steamboat transportation on the upper Missouri.[102] The summer previous he had arrived at Fort Tecumseh the first days of June to find Chardon and Halsey practically alone and to learn that Lamont had been "obliged to descend the river to the Poncas with two of our largest Keel boats for the purpose of assisting the Steam boat."[103] The steamboat was the *Yellowstone*[104] and her detention below was a matter of great concern to Mackenzie; for the idea of introducing the change in navigation was almost entirely his and had been strenuously opposed by Pratte and Cabanné, two of the most influential of the firm of Pierre Chouteau Jr. & Co., they deriding it as all an expense for nothing.[105] He therefore awaited the arrival of the *Yellowstone*[106] most anxiously and was keenly disappointed to hear that she had had to have her cargo reduced at the Niobrara and would not be able to proceed beyond the Little Missouri [Bad River] for that season.

How Chardon travelled to Fort Union must be surmised. The journey overland was the one Mackenzie himself usually made; for he was a splendid horseman and greatly enjoyed a canter across the spacious prairies.[107] We may well suppose that the two men went together, Mackenzie's enthusiasm enlivening the hours and all the charm that new surroundings have, anywhere, attracting his companion as it was to attract Palliser[108] taking the same route for the first time sixteen years afterwards. Once at Fort Union, Chardon entered upon a new phase of his experience as a trader. Previously, his dealings had been solely with Osages and Sioux, branches both though widely separated, of the Dacotah. Now he was to know a third branch, the Assiniboines, separated more widely still, and to know, in addition, the Crees, the Crows, and the Blackfeet.

Under circumstances so diverting, Chardon must have found life at Fort Union[109] anything but monotonous and, because for him, it was to terminate comparatively soon, lasting at best a bare two and a half years, its interest could never have waned, particularly as his period of sojourn there happened to include the time when visitors from the outside world were slightly more numerous and interesting than usual. In 1832, came George Catlin, travelling by the *Yellowstone* on the first trip she made to her real destination; in 1833, Nathaniel Wyeth[110] and Maximilian, the former from the west and overland, the latter from the east, first, by the *Yellowstone* as far as Fort Pierre and, then, by her sister boat, the *Assiniboine*.[111] From Catlin, impressionable, imaginative, verbose, come some of our earliest glimpses into the character and temperament of Chardon, in whose company, he evidently spent a considerable portion of his time, enjoying, indeed, his first buffalo hunt[112] with him, on which occasion, Chardon "tossed the feather," as a signal for the sport to commence. Newly initiated, though Catlin was, into the mysteries of big game shooting, it was not he who met with the disaster expected of beginners; for, not he, but the experienced Chardon took the "famous leap," which Catlin, witnessing with great glee after his first alarm had subsided, commemorated in one of his all-too-realistic paintings.[113] Maximilian, though somewhat less interested than was Catlin in sporting aspects of life at a remote post, yet hunted at Fort Union also and in the company of Chardon, whose cheerful disposition[114] impressed him as it did all the well-known wayfarers with whom this particular trader came in contact and who have left us a record.

As Fort Pierre was the distributing center for the various posts and wintering grounds in its vicinity, so was Fort Union to be for those to the westward of itself. At the time of Maximilian's arrival[115] on the upper Missouri, two of those posts had already been established, one for the Blackfeet in the neighborhood of the Marias River, the other for the Crows at the mouth of the Bighorn.[116] In June, 1831, being then at Fort Tecumseh, Mackenzie had notified[117] Pierre Chouteau, Jr. of a promise he had made to the Blackfeet that they should have a fort of their own the succeeding fall.[118] Almost immediately thereafter, James Kipp had been despatched from Fort Clark to begin its construction and to open the trade. By the sixteenth of September, he "had got up safe, as far as the mouth of the Musselshell River,"[119] the "Coquille of the Canadians."[120] Late in November, a delegation of Blackfeet made their way to Fort Union and, "On the vigil of the feast of St. Andrew," an auspicious date for Mackenzie the Scot, signed with him a convention of amity and commerce and, if due allowance be made for a possible mis-interpretation of an initial or the merging of two initials by reason of illegibility or some other cause, it can be taken for granted that Chardon shared with Hamilton the honor of witnessing it. [121] That being the case, his departure from Fort Tecumseh had already taken place.[122] He may even have been of Kipp's party; but, if so, Fort Piegan knew him for a brief while only and he may have been the one who brought back to Fort Union the news from that ill-fated place; for ill-fated it was and, being first left neglected[123] by the whites and then burned by the Indians, was replaced, as far as the service intended was concerned, by Fort McKenzie on the edge of the

Mauvaises Terres. This was in 1833 and it was to Fort McKenzie that Maximilian was bound when he left Fort Union in D. D. Mitchell's[124] company, July 4th, 1833. He had tarried at the Yellowstone post a fortnight.

Towards the end of September, the twenty-eighth to be exact, Maximilian returned;[125] but it was to find Mackenzie gone to the Bad River to await at Fort Pierre the arrival of Lamont bringing dispatches from St. Louis and to discuss with Laidlaw the next season's trade. At Fort Union, he had left Hamilton in charge with three clerks, "Messrs Chardon, Brazeau,[126] and Moncrevier,"[127] to assist him.[128] The returns for 1832 had been much below the average, fur exceedingly scarce, the Opposition keen. To circumvent it all along the line was Mackenzie's avowed determination. His mettle was up and with reason; for he was convinced in his own mind that "Sublette & Co." were being favored in the matter of alcoholic beverages. While his own freight was all too thoroughly examined, that of Congressman Ashley's successors was only perfunctorily so.[129] Mackenzie was beloved of the Indians[130] and his faith in them was implicit. Though they might flirt with his enemies he was confident that they would return ere long to their first allegiance, "saying the new people are only come for a day."[131]

Both going and returning on the occasion of his visit to Mitchell's post, Maximilian had remarked upon the environs of *La Rivière aux Trembles,* the same that Lewis and Clark had designated Martha's River[132] and the Poplar of today. The hunters of his party had landed and, though their particular luck had not been anything out of the ordinary, the possibilities of the locality were quite evident. This was fortunate since Mackenzie had already decided that it would be advisable to establish a post to the westward of Fort Union, preferably near the mouth of Milk River; in order to compel his "opponents to divide their forces."[133] Scarcely had he returned to Fort Union — and he did hasten back there, November eighth, fearing the approach of winter weather and having waited in vain for Lamont[134] — before he prepared to execute his plan, strengthened in it, no doubt, by the sanguine reports, still echoing, of Maximilian's experiences. Chardon was his choice of a trader and him he sent forth within a few days of his own return "with a snug equipment & 20 men,"[135] instructing him to proceed up stream "as near to [the] Mouth of R. au Lait as the ice then running fast in the river would permit." "After 10 days heavy work he came to anchor on this side La R^{re} au tremble,[136] where" he built "a comfortable fort ab^t 80 ft. square,"[137] which he called Fort Jackson[138] in recognition of the fact that he and his companions were "all Jackson men."[139] In Chardon's wake and in hot pursuit of him had gone the ubiquitous Opposition. Mackenzie's ruse had succeeded.

The day before Chardon had set out,[140] Robert Campbell, Sublette's junior partner engaged in superintending the construction of a large opposition post[141] near Fort Union, had made tentative offers of a closing-out sale to Mackenzie, who, duly considering the proposition over-night, rejected it summarily, affecting to believe the price demanded preposterously high.[142] To his clerks, whom he had taken into his confidence and who had pledged him loyal support, he confessed that he intended to pursue a temporizing policy because he believed in driving out rather than in buying out a rival.[143] Throughout the winter, competition waxed keener and keener, yet, from time to time, Campbell renewed his offers, meeting with rebuff after rebuff, until, finally, Mackenzie, having brought him to a place where his proposals were compatible with Mackenzie's scheme, consented to negotiate. After that, a bargain was soon struck, the details of which are not pertinent here except in so far as they conditioned a re-distribution of men on the upper Missouri, where, in return for a temporary abandonment of a projected trans-montane venture, Mackenzie secured an unfettered trade.[144] It was well that this compromise had been possible; for it was now the spring of 1834 and the drastic re-organization of the American Fur Company itself already impending. For the Upper Missouri Outfit the changes in prospect were relatively inconsiderable, yet, for our purpose, were not without significance. Mitchell was withdrawing altogether, going back to Virginia; but only for a time, as it developed, while Alexander

Culbertson[145] who had been with him at Fort McKenzie, was being spoken of as his sole successor there. That was Mackenzie's plan; but Culbertson, distrustful of his own competency for single-handed control at so hazardous a post as the Blackfeet, so hazardous that engagés had been unwilling to return to it, declined the honor.[146] Mackenzie, demurring, was yet obliged to acquiesce and this he did by selecting Kipp in Mitchell's stead, leaving Culbertson as the assistant, and sending Chardon to the vacant post at the Mandans.

At Fort Clark among the Mandans, Maximilian had been spending the winter, though none too pleasantly,[147] notwithstanding that Kipp had done his best to make him comfortable. He was now awaiting the arrival of engagés from Fort Union, who, under instructions from Mackenzie, would accompany him to St. Louis. On April 14th, they arrived and with them Chardon,[148] who decided to go on with Maximilian as far as Fort Pierre, where, presumably, his wife, *Tchon-su-mons-ka,* was yet staying[149] and where he, too, must have stayed until the time came for him to assume charge at Fort Clark. That time was June, the date of the beginning of his journal, which may be left to tell its own story.

And if the reader has waited until now to get any other idea of the Mandan Indians than the almost fanciful one that Thomas Jefferson with no first-hand knowledge whatsoever entertained or that Catlin so assiduously propagated, the story will be replete with disillusionment. Chardon's idea of the Mandans, so very different a one, was gained from an actual residence of several years among or near them and, on examination, will be found practically identical with that that the North West Company men, David Thompson,[150] Charles MacKenzie,[151] and Alexander Henry,[152] had had—and it was not a flattering one. In the long history of Indian wrongs, so seldom righted, there are tribes that are outstanding because high-minded in an Indian way, noble even by any standard, dignified, tenacious of what was justly their due, fierce if the occasion called for ferocity; but of none of these were the Mandans. Instead of standing alone, apart as it were, because superior to all or most, they really belong, not with the Cherokees, the Sioux, the Northern Cheyennes, and others like them, the proud, the valiant, the dauntless ones, but with their nearest neighbors, the rascally, the cowardly Arikaras[153] and the lascivious Gros Ventres,[154] to whom they, the Mandans, were not one whit superior. Although an interval of about half a century intervened between the visit of Verendrye in 1738[155] and the first[156] made by British traders, the latter made several such visits, a few of them quite protracted, and it was certainly not from them that the absurd notions respecting Mandan superiority to other Indians arose. They had discovered no reason for idealizing them. As agriculturalists even, the Mandans were not alone and peculiar. All their near neighbors were cultivators of the soil as were also far distant tribes towards the east.[157]

For white people, however, there is something of comfort to be found in the knowledge that the depravity of the upper Missouri tribes as it existed in Chardon's time was not chargeable against civilization. They were, from all accounts, singularly temperate, not given, in the least, to drunkenness. Lewis and Clark noted this fact,[158] so did Maximilian eight-and-twenty years later.[159] Though Chardon himself may have had a perennial thirst and, as Larpenteur intimated,[160] indulged it, at times, to excess, there is no trace in his journal of his distributing firewater to the Indians whose peltries he coveted. This is noteworthy; because Laidlaw at Fort Pierre, Mackenzie at Fort Union, and Mitchell at Fort McKenzie[161] were, in the same period of time, in this respect exceedingly culpable. The depravity of the upper Missouri tribes was inherent. It was what was to have been expected of their stage of development and that, being so, the unreality of many of the preconceived notions about them is apparent.

But the knowing the truth about their character and degree of ascent upward does not preclude a genuine sympathy for them in the scourge that depleted their ranks and well-nigh exterminated them — the small-pox epidemic of 1837. The day-by-day progress of that in its devastating course is the chief single interest of Chardon's Fort Clark journal. Previously, what was

known of it had come from Halsey's report[162] to headquarters;
from an unsigned letter, published as an appendix to Maximilian's narrative;[163] from the meagre information imparted
by Mitchell to Schoolcraft and incorporated by him in his work
on the Indians;[164] and, finally, from the very general account to
be gleaned from Audubon,[165] based upon his conversations with
Chardon, sufficiently long after the events for some of the facts
to be hazy in the original eye-witness's mind. However, the
main facts were kept permanently fresh, no doubt, by the constant reminders before his eyes; for Chardon's acquaintance
with the Mandans, the Gros Ventres, and the Arikaras was not
limited, by any means, to the five years of his journal. This
will be evident if his biography be now resumed.

Strange to relate Chardon's Fort Clark journal was brought
to an end very abruptly in early May of 1839,[166] when he was
on one of his periodical visits to Fort Pierre; but there is no
reason for thinking that his stay at the former Mandan post
was at the same time terminated. Forasmuch as the Pierre Chouteau, Jr. & Company journals and ledgers show that he had accounts there in the three succeeding years[167] and it is known
positively that he was in charge in 1843, it seems a fair assump-
tion to make that he was at Fort Clark through all the inter-
vening time, except for occasional visits elsewhere; for example,
to St. Louis in both 1841[168] and 1842,[169] and except for a stay
through the trading season at what the *Sire Log* designates
"*l'ancien hyvernement de Chardon*," which was in the vicinity
of *Rivière au Castor*.[170] If this were the case, he continued in
touch with the Mandans, who, however, were no longer occupying their old villages, the ones, where Lewis and Clark had found
them; for, after the thinning out of their numbers by the small-
pox, they had, in horror and desperation, abandoned the scene
of the terrible disaster and taken up their residence, in the first
instance, with the almost equally afflicted Gros Ventres and,
next, in new quarters of their own near by. The Arikaras,
meanwhile, had come to take possession of the Mandan village at
Fort Clark.

The conviction regarding the whereabouts of Francis Chardon

in 1843 comes from the *Sire Log* and from Audubon's *Missouri River Journals*,[171] strictly contemporary and mutually substantiating. Audubon was travelling up the river in the steamboat *Omega*, of which Joseph Sire was captain,[172] and, although he fell in with Chardon before he reached Fort Pierre and counted him one of his hosts while there, one of those who were "very kind and affable,"[173] it was yet at Fort Clark that he made his more intimate acquaintance, "entered Mr. Chardon's own room,"[174] and was presented with various objects of interest.[175] It was at Fort Clark, also, that Chardon showed yet other favors to Audubon, such as would have been within the province of none but the chief factor. Figuring in that capacity, Chardon had Audubon conducted by an Indian to the Arikara village, "particularly to show us the 'Medicine Lodge,'"[176] and gave him "full control" of Alexis Bombarde, a hunter, "till we reach the Yellowstone."[177]

And to the Yellowstone Chardon was himself going, *en route* for Fort McKenzie.[178] He left Fort Clark when Audubon did and proceeded up the river by the *Omega*, reaching Fort Union, June 12th,[179] where he, somewhat unexpectedly, found Culbertson,[180] whose place at the Blackfeet post he was to take. He resumed his journey on the 22nd;[181] but, in the interval, saw much of Audubon and it was then that he related, at Audubon's special request, his personal experiences with the small-pox epidemic of 1837.[182] There was much excitement at Fort Union, pending the departure of Chardon, and great bustle. A ball was given in his honor;[183] but the day of his leaving finally came and Audubon with the others bade him adieu.[184]

In the estimation of many who have come after him this transfer of Chardon to Fort McKenzie was his undoing.[185] All seems to have gone fairly well, however, until the beginning of the next year; but, on February 19th,[186] came, as far as his reputation is concerned, the great catastrophe. This was the Blackfeet massacre with which his name and Alexander Harvey's have been ever since most unpleasantly connected. That it was a horrid affair there is no gainsaying; but it was unquestionably made more so in retrospect than it was in reality, it having been dealt with by those who reported it years and years afterwards as if it were an isolated case of outrage and, in the calendar of crimes against the Indians, almost without a parallel. These reporters were chiefly Larpenteur and Culbertson; but, in the weighing of their incriminating evidence against Chardon and Harvey, there are various circumstances that must be taken account of. First of all, care must be taken to deal individually with the two who are accused.[187] Because Harvey had come to be a desperate character is no sound reason for denouncing Chardon as like unto him. It must be remembered, too, that not until Harvey had joined a rival concern[188] was he so generally execrated.[189] Furthermore, both Larpenteur and Culbertson would be in a position of being more than ordinarily resentful and of giving in the premises *ex parte* evidence, the latter, because from being intimidated by the Blackfeet he had passed to a genuine attachment for them, marrying among them;[190] the former, because he had been much with Culbertson and had served at Fort McKenzie with him.

Regardless of how much blame attaches to Chardon and Harvey jointly or to either alone for the affair of February 19, 1844, there can be no question that that event had more than a little to do with Chardon's next migration. "Reasons of prudence," declares Father Point dictated the dismantling of Fort McKenzie,[191] which, none-the-less, had survived very much longer than any other Blackfeet post to date; but not for one moment was any idea entertained of abandoning the region completely. On the contrary, a new site was at once selected and that, curiously enough, by Chardon. This of itself would argue against his conduct having seemed, according to the standards of the time, so dreadfully reprehensible. The wonder is that he was not recalled and severely reprimanded instead of being continued in the Blackfeet trade and made the judge of a suitable location for it. In his choice of a site was the origin of a fort, named after him, *Fort F. A. C.*,[192] at the mouth of the Judith,[193] a beautiful spot; but too exposed, too accessible to enemies, to be perfectly eligible and it was soon condemned. Before long, too, Culbertson returned to resume his old duties and he, nothing loath to see the last of Fort F.A.C., had it destroyed.[194] This was in 1845.[195]

But Chardon had already gone away. He had gone back to Fort Clark.[196] It was not to be for long, however.[197] The trade there was not sufficient. Chardon, accordingly, moved up to where the Gros Ventres[198] were located and prepared to winter with them, to the great indignation and threatened vengeance of the Arikaras,[199] who were still at Fort Clark and who were only mollified when promised a trader of their own,[200] Desautels, the nephew of James Kipp.[201] Meanwhile, at the place, "l'ours qui danse,"[202] Chardon established himself, giving his post the name of Fort James.[203] In February of 1846 that name was still being used;[204] but, in March, for some reason or other, that of Berthold[205] had been substituted.[206] With the removal to the neighborhood of the Gros Ventres Picotte was much gratified,[207] the results soon justifying it, as he had anticipated. He was equally gratified with changes effected by Culbertson farther west.[208] Culbertson, too, had constructed a new post, upon which he had bestowed the name of Honoré; but, at the suggestion of Picotte himself, it gave way to Lewis.[209]

To all appearances the year 1846 opened auspiciously for the Upper Missouri Outfit and for P. Chouteau, Jr. & Company in St. Louis, particularly as the Pratte-Cabanné opposition had recently been eliminated.[210] Yet many things to those watchful of events presaged a storm and soon clouds were distinctly lowering. The storm burst; but, before the havoc it wrought can be adequately gauged, it behoves us to consider a phase of our subject that, heretofore, we have found it convenient to slight, if not utterly to ignore — at all events, in its fullest bearings — the United States Indian policy beyond the frontier.

If the Lewis and Clark expedition be left out of account, the United States government, prior to the sending forth of the much-discussed Yellowstone expedition,[211] had not concerned itself in any appreciable way with the Indians of the upper Missouri; and it is worthy of note that, in urging that project upon Congress, the Secretary of War, John C. Calhoun, was moved, not by any sense of responsibility for the aborigines, but simply and solely by the desire to advance American trade, which then appeared to be the only sure road to national wealth and increased dominion. To ignore the Indians, however, was impossible; for they lay across the path of permanent progress. This was only too evident after Ashley and Jedediah Smith had added their experiences, cumulative and depressing, to those of men like Manuel Lisa, who, as a matter of fact, was more fortunate than most.

Not peace-loving Indians, making their own appeal to a self-appointed guardian by virtue of their obvious capacity for civilization, but hostile ones, challenging the white man's advance into their hunting grounds, were the direct cause of the inception of a *Native Policy* that stretched beyond the area of settlement and the inception was made manifest when, in June, 1824, George H. Kennerly and Peter Wilson were "appointed under the 3rd section of the Act of 25th Ultimo, Sub-Agents to be employed among the Indian tribes on the waters of the Upper Missouri."[212] In the subsequent allotment of service, the nearer tribes were made Kennerly's peculiar charge and the more remote, Wilson's,[213] particularly, the Mandans, who, in the minds of many, had still a name to conjure with and so eager, apparently, was Wilson to test this, in so big a hurry was he to be off, that he neglected to wait to receive his instructions.[214] He, ultimately, went up with Atkinson's expedition; but, aside from playing a minor part in some of the trade treaties, negotiated at that time, contributed little to the service.[215] In fact, his days were already numbered. He reached the Mandans and sickened there, dying, after his removal to Fort Atkinson, May 15, 1826.[216]

In the same letter that he announced the death of Sub-Agent Wilson, Superintendent Clark recommended John F. A. Sanford as his successor and he was duly appointed.[217] The new sub-agent was a Virginian, from Winchester;[218] but, for about a year, he had been employed in Clark's office in St. Louis.[219] Historically, he is best known because of his connection with the Dred Scott case,[220] a connection that would be better comprehended, perhaps, were fuller cognizance taken of his career as Indian Agent and fur trader. He served in the former capacity from 1826 to 1834; but never were his charges his first concern. So zealously did he work for the advantage and profit of the American Fur Company that one might well have thought he was its agent, especially after his marriage, which occurred in 1832 and which made him a son-in-law of Pierre Chouteau, Jr.[221] In the career of this man, Sanford, as sub-agent for the Mandans and other Indians of the upper Missouri, is to be seen most pointedly the subordination of a public trust and a public duty to personal convenience and aggrandizement. His was a most glaring case of the exploitation of the Indian service in the interest of the American Fur Company. Why he was tolerated so long passes our comprehension except when we remember that he was the intimate friend of Superintendent Clark and that Senator Benton was still "the distinguished representative of the fur-trading interests in Congress."[222] When Sanford was at last ousted it was because of the counter-influence of General Ashley.[223]

But that "consummation devoutly to be wished" was not achieved until 1834 and, in the meantime, Indian affairs on the upper Missouri were conducted after this wise: — Between the agents of the Upper Missouri Outfit, especially Mackenzie, and Indian sub-agent Sanford there was a continual exchange of favors and Sanford's annual visit — for he was never really in residence among his charges[224] — was so timed that he and Mackenzie travelled together,[225] he distributing with lavish hand the presents that public funds had paid for, while Mackenzie looked benignly on, deriving for himself and for the fur company he represented full credit for a munificence that cost him nothing, except, perhaps, a gift of buffalo tongues[226] or a free transportation. On the occasion of these annual visits, moreover, Sanford busied himself in collecting evidence in order that the traders might get indemnity for alleged Indian depredations.[227] To all appearances, it was very much more his duty to increase the gains of traders, well or ill-begotten, than to protect the Indians from trumped-up charges, aggression, spoliation, and extortion.

Such a course as his was bound to over-reach itself at last, however.[228] Identified as he was with the American Fur Company, connected by marriage with one of its principal agents, he was a fair target for the Opposition and, through Ashley, his absenteeism and his general neglect of duty were brought to the attention of the Indian Office.[229] Not even Superintendent Clark could longer excuse or defend him. His own impertinent letters but aggravated his offense and Clark was instructed to inform him that he must immediately repair to his agency or be superseded.[230] Without a doubt he was already engaged for the service of the American Fur Company and he now came out openly as its employee. He had cast his duty, for the faithful performance of which he had pledged his honor, to the winds.

Sanford's successor was William Neil Fulkerson[231] of St. Charles, Missouri, Ashley's brother-in-law,[232] who, while not a forceful agent, yet did manage to sustain himself creditably in his office and held it until the year of Ashley's decease.[233] He made no particular study of the Indians under his care. His reports were commonplace. The supreme importance of the fur trade pervaded them as it had pervaded Sanford's; but with a difference; for Fulkerson declined to cater to the American Fur Company. The government gratuities he dispensed independently and Mackenzie, coming back from an extended absence abroad and realizing this, took umbrage.[234] How quietly and unassumingly Fulkerson conducted himself as sub-agent for the Mandans and their neighbors can be inferred from the Fort Clark journal, in which Chardon had only very rarely an occasion to refer to him. He lived through the period of the small-pox epidemic; but was, apparently, not fully in residence and, in 1838, he resigned. His place was not filled, so few were the Indians who were left. To all intents and purposes, the upper Missouri sub-agency had ceased to exist.

In 1842, it was resuscitated and in a manner that, judge it as leniently as we may, can only serve to cast ridicule upon the Indian Office for allowing itself to be so easily hoodwinked or a suspicion of downright knavery and deception upon Senator Benton and his self-seeking friends[235] of the American Fur Company, Chouteau, Sanford, Sarpy, and Clapp, a sorry group, to whom, undoubtedly, both Mackenzie and even Mitchell should be added.

The years after 1838 were lean years for the fur trade everywhere. It was an era of diminishing returns in the peltry traffic and this on account of no single cause, although it be generally conceded that by 1838 the great day of trapping was over. With a falling supply came an increased demand and a consequent increase of effort. Opposition was multiplied and, as Davidson says had been the case in Canada,[236] the keenness of the competition could be measured by the amount of liquor distributed. Not that it was ever distributed south of the line, if by that be implied given away for nothing. Quite the contrary; for it was sold at almost fabulous prices and the American Fur Company had its usual full share of receipts, having done its usual amount of introducing into the Indian country and of adulterating.

Then, all at once, seemingly, it presented a complete change of front, became humanitarian, recommended, even pleaded, that the upper Missouri sub-agency be revived and restored in order that the drink evil, so awful to contemplate in its demoralizing effects upon the Indians, might be eradicated. The implication was, of course, that others than American Fur Company men were the violators of the trade and intercourse laws. Here let it not go unremarked that the Superintendent of Indian Affairs at St. Louis at the time was none other than David Dawson Mitchell, the builder of Fort McKenzie, ex-partner of the Upper Missouri Outfit, who had been appointed in 1841 as successor to Joshua Pilcher, another ex-employee of the American Fur Company and the same who had been the incumbent of the superintendency office in succession to General Clark.[237] The most likely candidate in 1838 had seemed, for a while, to be John Dougherty[238] of the Ashley-Sublette persuasion, a strong Missouri Whig. Of that fact he had been given assurance[239] and grievous was his disappointment when it proved otherwise and his old enemy, Pilcher, was preferred.[240] Again, in 1841, Dougherty was a candidate, although scarcely an applicant. George C. Sibley was another.[241] Indeed, there were several candidates; but, as it developed, not one had the ghost of a chance with Mitchell in the field; for behind Mitchell stood Senator Benton. Had the choice only fallen upon Sibley, a man, like his maternal grandfather, the Reverend Samuel Hopkins, of genuine humanitarian and philanthropic impulses, how radically different might have been the course of events!

But Fate had ordered it differently and, in 1842, when there was a prospect of restoring the upper Missouri sub-agency, Mitchell, installed in St. Louis, hand-in-glove with Chouteau, Sarpy and all the rest, came forward, having a good man handy, none better, whom he urged might be appointed in Fulkerson's long vacant place. The plea prevailed, the prayers of the American Fur Company[242] were answered, and, a special agency being arranged for, with no other object in immediate view than the enforcement of the prohibition law, Andrew Drips was appointed to it. He was of the Upper Missouri Outfit and he passed from one service to the other without so much as the interval of a single day. In point of fact, it was expected that he should serve two masters and he did. The great farce had begun.

That it was a great farce and one staged down to the minutest detail by the chief aggressors, the chief violators of the prohibition law, who can dispute, knowing all the facts as they stand revealed in personal, business, and official letters of the time? Surely, never was so much disinterested zeal in a public cause displayed before or since, never at all events, so great a pretense of it. And expedited on his way was the chief actor; for, unless his work could begin at once, the desired effect, the heading off of Opposition traders would be lost. Once started, Drips proceeded to Fort Pierre and there, at what was now most certainly the principal post of the Upper Missouri Outfit, halted, making it his headquarters, accepting its hospitality.

The play had a long run; for this was 1842 and not until 1846 was the great exposure that brought it to its conclusion made. And, when it was made, it was made through the agency of that "desperado," Alexander Harvey, and because of a bitter animosity that had developed in his mind towards Chardon and certain others of his associates on the upper Missouri, who had plotted against his life, so he claimed.[243] All attempts to propitiate Harvey failed, notwithstanding that Picotte, now the chief agent of the Upper Missouri Outfit, was willing to see conferred upon him, as a peace-offering, the Blackfeet post.[244] Obdurate and revengeful, Harvey went down to St. Louis, filed charges of felonious assault against three men, Jacob Berger, James Lee, and Malcolm Clark, and lodged information respecting alleged violations of the prohibition law against various employees of the American Fur Company, the upshot of which was that Chardon and others were ordered deported[245] from the Indian country straightway,[246] Andrew Drips was removed,[247] and Pierre Chouteau, Jr. was suited on his bond.[248] Quite a number of suits-at-law in the Circuit Court of the United States for the District of Missouri resulted from this. Among them was one against Pierre Chouteau, Kenneth Mackenzie, and John Sarpy; another against Sarpy, Mackenzie, and Sylvestre Labbadie; also individual suits against Culbertson, Kipp, Picotte, and Chardon.[249] Delays and delays came, however; material witnesses disappeared, were spirited away, seemingly; and, although some cases were disposed of with damages awarded of one cent, the more important were continued from year to year.

Meanwhile, Francis Chardon went back to the Indian country and was at Fort Berthold again in 1847.[250] There Palliser came across him and, in the spring of 1848,[251] spent quite a little time with him, finding him, as others had found him earlier, kindly, obliging, and hospitable. From Palliser, we get our last account of him, the last, that is, of any detail and sympathetic; for Chardon was dying. He had been suffering agony from rheumatism and, when Palliser came back after going away on a somewhat extended hunting excursion, the end was very near.[252] To Palliser, Chardon unburdened his conscience and dictated his will,[253] then died. Culbertson buried him at Fort Pierre, where, long before, he had spent what we may suppose were some of his happiest years and his became one of those lonely graves, of which there have been many on the upper Missouri, unmarked and, today, unknown.[254]

A word or two in conclusion about his journal, its hiding-place, its present resting-place, and its literary, scientific, or historical value. It ended abruptly, as has been said, and then it disappeared, coming again to light only about a decade ago.[255] Where had it been in the long interval? Because, when found, it was in a cloth bag, addressed to

"Mr Nickolet

St Louis

Care of P.D.Papin"   ,

the supposition is, that from Chardon it passed, through Papin's hands, to J. N. Nicollet's, being added to the collection of source material that that famous expatriated French explorer is known to have been making with the object in view of writing an exhaustive treatise on the country through which flow the Mississippi and her tributaries.[256] When, at length, re-discovered, it was reposing in the Topographical Bureau of the United States War Department and in an old-fashioned chest that bore the name of Nicollet. Other things of like significance were with it and all point to the one conclusion that they had been brought together for a specific purpose, the one just referred to. This theory, or whatever it be, is strengthened by the fact that Nicollet was up the Missouri in 1839 and at Fort Pierre shortly after Chardon's own arrival there.[257] If he met Chardon, he very likely questioned him, as Audubon did four years afterwards, about the small-pox epidemic of 1837 and, hearing of the journal that was bound to be a contemporary record of facts, however gruesome, solicited Chardon for it, either as a loan or a gift, the former in all probability; but, with the lapse of time, that circumstance being overlooked, the transaction became one of those borrowings, of which many of us are victims sooner or later, that merge imperceptibly into permanent possession. Nicollet died in 1843 without having written his treatise, whereupon, presumably, such of his effects as had a bearing upon his professional tasks passed into the custody of the government and were lost to memory.

A very cursory glance at the Fort Clark journal will show

that it can make no pretensions to literary merit. Neither does it contribute anything of moment to anthropological or ethnological knowledge. In this it is disappointing and, inasmuch as it was kept at a time when the scientific world was seeking a more intimate acquaintance with the very Indians among whom Chardon passed his days, very surprising. Think what Chardon might have told, had he wished, of Mandan customs, either in refutation or substantiation of what observers and investigators like Catlin and Maximilian had set forth; but on all such points he was most exasperatingly silent. Obviously, his journal was intended as a business record merely and the human interest it displays is incidental and accidental. However, it does have that human interest and in no slight degree. This was because of Chardon's own personality, which impressed itself, in little ways not always the most delicate, upon even very mundane accounts. In his pages, we find Toussaint Charbonneau[258] again, though not the more worthy Sacajawea, and, more interesting still, we find that strange fantastic figure, the "Liberator of All the Indians," as he called himself, James Dickson,[259] whose projects, vague and quixotic though they were, aroused in their time, some faint international apprehension. Of his obscure and tragic end, Chardon seems to give us contemporary and certain information. Equally certain, though indirect, is the information he gives of the typical fur trader's disdainful attitude towards the objects of Dickson's compassion. In the very year that Chardon took up his quarters at Fort Clark, Protestant missionaries began their organized labors among the Sioux of the upper Mississippi,[260] but the tribes of the upper Missouri were to remain neglected by the agents of civilization for many a long day yet, even by the Roman Catholics, who were usually the more forehanded. Unlike the Hudson's Bay Company, the American Fur Company did nothing, anywhere, for the evangelization of the aborigines it exploited. Chardon's journal belongs, therefore, in the class with Larpenteur's and Culbertson's and is, like them, reminiscent of a period that some profess to find romantic but that has positively nothing to say for itself when considered from the standpoint of Indian advancement.

Rather did the white men, traders, trappers, and engagés, relapse into barbarism than do aught to assist the red in emerging from it. Not the virtues but the vices of the superior race were propagated and diffused. Repeated so often, this has become a platitude, perhaps, but it is, none the less, most terribly true. Who of us dares to say that, in the face of an inevitable deterioration, physical, moral, and mental, coming to them from mere contact with whites, the small-pox epidemic was the greatest calamity that could have befallen the Mandans?

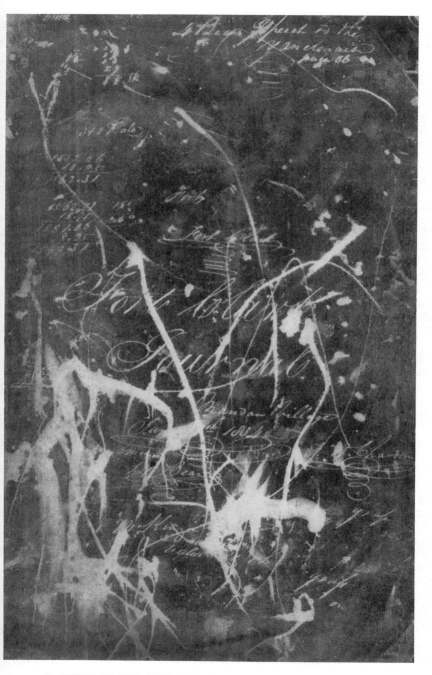

FACSIMILE OF THE COVER PAGE OF THE ORIGINAL MANUSCRPT

THE JOURNAL

JOURNAL FOR FORT CLARK, MANDAN VILLAGE, U. M. O. JUNE 19th — 1834 — F. A. C.

June 18th — Steam Boat Assinniboine arrived[261]

19 — Steam Boat started for the Yellow Stone.[262]

July 6th — Keel & MacKinac Boats[263] arrived from Fort Union on their way to St. Louis ; left this place the same day ½ past 4 o'Clock —

July 11 — Cambell[264] & Co arrived from Fort William[265] and continued on the same day, left one of passengers Mr Winter —[266]

July 14 — Commenced Makeing hay

July 23 — Battle with the Yanctons and Mandans , 1 Scioux - 1 Mandan — 1 Gros Ventre Killed — 5 Mandans wounded

July 30 — K. M. K.[267] and Suitte[268] arrived from Fort Union

July 31 — K. M. K. and Suitte started for St. Louis.

Augt. 2 — May[269] & Winter started for their beaver hunt —

Augt 3 — Buffaloe chase on the hill — Chardon[270] Killed 1 in 300 yards of the Village[271] — Opened Barril flour —

Augt 4 — Windy — Cleared out the ice house, Indians around the Fort in the night , heard several gun's fire —

Tuesday 5 — Finished hauling the hay — from the little riviere qui barre[272] — rain in the evening —

Wednesday 6 — Started L. Bijoux[273] for the Yancton camp on the riviere au Boulet[274] — to trade Beaver. Winter came in today, haveing been pursued by the Indians on his way out Beaver hunting.

Thursday 7 — False alarms in the Village since 3 or 4 nights past — heavy rain in the Morning

Friday 8 — Pleasant weather — there has been no rain since the 23 of last Month — the Indians were Complaining about their crops, but the shower of this Morning has put them again to rights. May arrived from the Gros Ventres, with news of the Death of Rotten Belly — (cheif of the crows) who was Killed by the Black feet —[275]

Saturday 9 — Durant[276] started for the Gros Ventres in quest of News — Horse race, between Black Hawk & Old Swan — Blakey took the lead and Kept it, to the great surprise of some of the spectators —[277] Finished hauling hay   60 Loads —

Sunday 10 — Race between Black Hawk, Old Swan, and two of the best Mandan horses — Black came out Master of the field — Old Swan Next — Purse amounted to One Hundred and thirty Dollars — which was divided between the Whites & Reds.

Monday 11 — Rain, disagreeable weather — Old Bijoux arrived from the Yanctonais camp[278] — traded 23 Beaver skins, left their camp yesterday at the cannon Ball river   350 Lodges — Saw Buffaloes on his way at the square hills[279] — he says the Yanctons are not disposed to Make peace with the Mandans, & Gros Ventres — distributed out traps to the Hunters, arrainged with Old Charbonneau[280] for provisions, &c &c —

Tuesday 12 — Cloudy — disagreeable weather — Went out to run Buffaloe, with the Indians — Killed two cows. I almost broke my leg,[281] from a fall from my horse — The Indians Killed upwards of a hundred — there seems to be an abundance of them at the square hills,   Sent down the flat boat, to bring up the wood for my wintering —

Wednesday 13 — Strong N.E. wind,   the effects of the fall I got yesterday is very painfull Not being able to get out of bed untill 8,O'Clock — a circumstance which has not happened to me these 10 years past — Bullé[282] & Lacroix[283] after remaining in the Mandan Village, since the departure of the Steam Boat - has at length started for Fort Pierre![284]   May success attend them.   The Indians have commenced eating their new crop of corn —[285]

Thursday 14 — Cool and pleasant — continue hauling wood , Grande Parade and sham fight with the Mandan's —

Friday 15 — Cloudy — every thing still to day —

Saturday 16 — Smoaky weather – Sent Bellehumeur[286] in quest of fresh meat – 1 cow   Winter & Digueire[287] left here for below — Went out to take a pleasure ride, and as fortune would have it, met a band of cow's - 10 miles from the fort — run them and Killed 3 Cows —

Sunday 17 — Thick fog — the Indians went out to run Buffaloe, after haveing run a band of cows, and Killed a quantity, on their way home saw enemies , they immediately threw away their meat, and arrived at their Village, as they left it, with nothing — the Sioux had been in the corn fields the night previous, and carried off some corn —

Monday 18 — Cloudy — 2 Men Sick — No work going on except the Carter, who still continues hauleing wood — Durant left here to day for his fall hunt, in company with May — Feast to the Cheifs and Soldiers of the Mandan Village — &c &c &c —

Tuesday 19 — Cool pleasant weather , the Mandans still continue to keep watch at night, for fear of Enemies, as they have had several allerts lately —

Wednesday 20 — Cloudy – and appearance of rain,   finished hauleing wood , and to my surprise instead of 60 cords which I ought to have had, only found 28 — so much have I been duped for not keeping a good and watchfull eye over Men, who will take every opportunity they can to deceive their employers, however I am in hopes, that all will go on better!   rain and thunder —

Thursday 21 — Fine weather in the morning — rain and thunder storm in the evening — Went out to run Buffaloe, and Killed one fat cow — Mitchel also Killed one —

Friday 22 — Cloudy - and appearance of rain —

Saturday 23 — Garreau,[288] Tabot[289] — Dusseau[290] and Joy-aille[291] left here for their fall hunt — Enemies supposed to be

Yanctonnais made their appearance on the opposite side of the river, after exchangeing a few shots disappeared, the Mandans did not think it prudent to cross the river, An old Man and his wife, who crossed yesterday in quest of Berries, have not yet returned — it is thought that they have fell Victims to their enemies, (Poor Devils) Molleur[292] came in from the woods with his foot badly cut — Some young men who went out in search of the two old Couple, came in in the evening and brought word of the Death of them both — that they were Killed, scalped, and butchered, *So Much for Berries* —[293]

Sunday 24 — Cool and pleasant — News of a band of Buffaloe, *below* — Mandans went to run them — Accompanied them to the chaise and Killed one — On our way home we were overtaken by a shower of rain, and thunder , the Indians say that we Killed all the band amounting to 27 Bulls —

Monday 25 — Cloudy disagreeable weather, a Gros Ventre informed me, that 2 men in a canoe passed their Village yesterday. It is presumed they are disserters from above —[294]

Tuesday 26 — Cloudy — I was informed by the Indians that the day Garreau & Co. started for their hunt, they heard several reports of guns in the direction they went — I thought perhaps the Sioux might of Killed them, this morning I went out to discover, and from the hill opposite the Village discovered a band of cows. I immediately gave the alarm to the Village, who hurried out, all prepared for the chaise — We nearly distroyed the whole band amounting to 100 head — I myself Killed 3 — Mitchel 2 —

Wednesday 27 — Last night we had a thunder storm accompanied with rain and wind from S. W. — on opening the gates of the Fort early this morning the first object that struck our View, was a Buffaloe Bull on the hill, walking deliberately towards the Village , two horsemen went in pursuit of him, and Killed him near the Village —

Thursday 28 — Pleasant day — The Mandans are preparing for their fall hunt — distributed out traps to them.

Friday 29 — All tranquill to day —

Saturday 30 — Strong South Wind — Weather smok'y — nothing worth recording to day —

Sunday 31 — Cool pleasant weather — As I keep a dayly a/c of Rats[295] Killed at the Fort, since my arrival I must announce the Death of ninety seven.

[1834]   [SEPTEMBER]

Monday 1 — Went out in search of fresh meat — took 3 Men & 6 Horses in hopes of finding Cattle close at hand, but to my great surprise, after travelling all day, met with nothing except a small band of Bull's — Killed one and took the choise[296] parts for supper — Camped opposite the square hills —

Tuesday 2 — Left camp before daylight — at sunrise saw 1 cow that had been wounded some time past - in company with 3 calves — run them and Killed one calf — arrived at the Fort ¼ past 6 O'clock — Much fatigued —

Wednesday 3 — Weather continues very smokey — a war party of Gros Ventres who had been out in search of the Yanctons, arrived to day, haveing seen the camp at Heart river.[297]

Thursday 4th — Pleasant day —

Friday 5 — Strong wind from the north — finished hauling the Steam Boat wood — rain in the afternoon —

Saturday 6 — Frost for the first time made its appearance this morning —

Sunday 7 — An Indian who went out in quest of Plumbs yesterday has not yet returned — No doubt he has shared the same fate as the old couple did on the 23rd of last month — Oh! Plumbs & Cherries ! May success attend you — In the afternoon I went out in company with some Mandans in search of the lost Man, and found him dead — and scalped, in one mile of the Fort —

Monday 8 — Enemies around the Fort last night — they Knocked at the gate several times, and hollowed for us to go out to them — a Gros Ventre who was in the Fort, did not close his eyes all night — J. B. Joncá[298] arrived from the Gros Ventres, and said that the Assinneboines had arrived with their Lodges opposite their village[299] — Joncá promised that he would bring me some beaver, skins and robes, that he has at his lodge —

Tuesday 9 — Pleasant day — Feast and council with the heads of Departments —[300]

Wednesday 10 — The Mandans crossed the river to run Buffaloe — sent Mitchel with four horses — the men came in from the woods, haveing seen Indians.

Thursday 11 — Cool morning — in the evening the Indians all returned from the chaise , with an abundance of meat — Mitchel arrived with four Cows —

Friday 12 — The weather continues smokey — Charboneau gave a feast to the Indians, and distributed out Knives & Tobacco —

Saturday 13 — Cloudy — I forgot to mention that the Indians, on the 11th inst, Killed a White calf[301] the skin of which is valued at 4 Horses — Medicine feast at the Village to day — A Yanctonnais slipped in the Village unperceived and brought information that the Sioux Camp will be here tomorrow , that he stole away from their camp, contrairy to the orders of the Soldiers,[302] , he will be detained close Prisoner untill further news —

Sunday 14 — This Morning early 2 more Yanctons arrived and affirmed what the Prisoner said — they sent him off with some tobacco — I also sent some tobacco to the Soldiers — The Mandans are all upon their guard, expecting *traihison* — rain in the afternoon.

Monday 15 — The Sioux camp has not yet arrived on account of the rain yesterday — a band belonging to the *Bande des Chein* — or dog band[303] — came and gave us a dance — after given them a small present, they went to the Village expecting to get something there but no one was disposed to give them anything — they left the Village as they said, with their hearts bad — I am inclined to believe that all will not go on strait —

as they do not appear to be friendly to each other — The Principal Men of the Yanctons advised me to Keep my horses penned up in the Fort — The Sioux camp arrived in the evening —

Tuesday 16 — Preparations for feast — gave a small present to the Sioux and commenced tradeing Robes & Beaver — Sold three horses — four dogs lost their lives to day for the soldier feast — rain in the afternoon —

Wednesday 17 — Clear and pleasant — the Sioux begins to be troublesome — trade begins to be at an end with us , but very brisk at the Village — a bande of Gros Ventres about 60 in number came to smoke with the Sioux, but the Sioux do not seem disposed to smoke — if any disturbance takes place between the Sioux & Gros Ventres, the Mandans say they will help the latter — they are only waiting for them to begin the fun —

Thursday 18 — Pleasant day — the Sioux camp talk of starting tomorrow — Yesterday a grand feast was given to the Cheifs & Soldiers of the Gros Ventres — The *Par Fleche Rouge* at the head — the Sioux gave him 4 Guns, 2 Blks Scarlet — 4 Blue Blkts, and a quantity of other articles — he left their camp as he said with his heart good —

Friday 19 — Cloudy and appearance of rain — early this morning to my great comfort — the Sioux camp started — cleared out the retail store, and found I had traded 128 lb Beaver — 96 Robes — 76 calf skins — 80 pieces meat — Cords[304] Siniews &c &c — at 4 P.M. we had a shower of rain and hail — Joncá arrived to day with his six beaver skins —

Saturday 20 — Haveing kept the horses in the Fort since Sunday last — I thought it safe to let them out this Morning — ½ hour afterwards we had an alarm, saying that the Gros Ventres were attacked — I immediately had the horses sent for — some time after the report of a cannon was distinctly heard , the Mandans rushed to the field of action, and arrived there in time to succor the Gros Ventres — after some skirmishing the two parties withdrew — the Mandans lost 1 Killed and six wounded — the Gros Ventres 2 Killed and twelve wounded — that of the enemy is not known — in the afternoon a Yancton who left this place on the 19th inst made his appearance on the hill — he came in quest of a lost Man — 5 or 6 Mandans went out to meet him with intention to Kill him, but much to their credit they told him to depart immediately —

Sunday 21st — Strong wind from the north, rain in the afternoon — Joncá left here to day for his fall hunt —

Monday 22 — Commenced daubing[305] the houses — the wind continued strong all day — Went to the Pond to shoot ducks — found a stray horse belonging to the Mandans, supposed to have been stolen by the Sioux 5 days since.

Tuesday 23 — Cloudy and appearance of rain — late in the evening the Macinaw boat from Fort Union bound for St Louis arrived[306] — Francis[307] the Patron[308] with 15 Men —

Wednesday 24 — The Mackinaw boat left here early — they being out of Provisions, I was obliged to let them have what corn I had amounting to 7 Bushels — disagreeable weather throughout the day — Some few Mandans crossed the river in quest of buffaloe —

Thursday 25 — Snow for the first time this year made its appearance to day — the Mandans arrived from the chaise with an abundance of meat — Cattle very scarce —

Friday 26 — Pleasant day —

Saturday 27 — The crops of corn has turned out very bad — therefore I do not expect to trade much of that article, however, to day I cannot complain, as I have traded twelve bushels — They harrangued in the Village to trade but little Corn, as starveing times are near at hand — I hope Not. *O. B. F.*[309]

Sunday 28 — Pleasant day — No News to day —

Monday 29 — Continued daubing the houses — Sent Bijoux up to the Gros Ventres for news &c &c — an Indian who was wounded in the battle of the 20th died last night — Bijoux arrived in the evening with no news of any importance — Strong wind and rain in the night —

Tuesday 30 — Cloudy — 2 more of the Wounded died today —

[1834]   OCTOBER

Wednesday 1 — Cloudy — strong North wind — Number of Rats Killed last Month 28 — the Mandans has been busily engaged since yesterday in crossing the river on an excursion for fresh meat &c —

Thursday 2 — Cloudy — strong North wind — busy tradeing Corn to day as the Indians are Preparing to leave their Village for their winter quarters —[310]

Friday 3 — Rain and hail — No News —

Saturday 4 — Pleasant weather — Went out in search of cattle — returned in the evening unsuccessfull —

Sunday 5 — Pleasant day —

Monday 6 — Strong North east wind — Rain

Tuesday 7 — Finished white washing the Fort — Charbonneau arrived from the Gros Ventres with fresh meat — Cattle scarce —

Wednesday 8 — No News —[311]

Thursday 9 — The Gros Ventres talk of Moveing up to their winter quarters — 2 young bucks came after Old Bijoux —

Friday 10 — Prepared the Equipment[312] for Bijoux — the water rose to day 4 inches —

Saturday 11 — Bijoux left here to day for his winter quarter's — the water continues riseing. Strong North West Wind throughout the day —

Sunday 12 — Pleasant day — No News —

Monday 13 — Cloudy — the 2 carts that went up to the Gros Ventres with Old Bijoux arrived to day — No News in that quarter —

Tuesday 14 — No News —

Wednesday 15 — Same as yesterday —

Thursday 16 — Cloudy — Joncà arrived to day with fourteen beaver skins — Molleur also arrived from Bijoux's camp — to get horses to convey his plunder to his Wintering quarters — Garreau, Bullé, Joyaille and Tabot arrived from their hunt, with but few beaver skins, saying for an excuse that the Yanctons has ruined the whole Country, the Amount of all their furs will not pay their debts to the Company — if they had continued to trap one Month more, as most trappers would of done in all probability they would of made good returns —

Friday 17 — Moleur & Joncá started for the Gros Ventres, with 2 horses for L. Bijoux — Settlement and quarrel with the hunters —

Saturday 18 — Strong north Wind.

Sunday 19   Tabot and Joyaille left here to day for St Louis. Bullé also started out trapping — the Mandans crossed the river, to camp in the Point of Woods[313] opposite the Fort —

Monday 20 — No News —

Tuesday 21 — The Indians arrived to day from their dry meat excursion .

Wednesday 22 — Pleasant day — Charboneau and his Lady[314] started for the Gros Ventres, on a visit — (or to tell the truth,) in quest of one of his runaway Wives - for I must inform you he has two lovely ones — Poor old Man. Molleur arrived from Bijoux camp. All well.

Thursday 23 — Molleur left here for Bijoux camp — enemies supposed to be the Assinniboines fired on the Mandan Camp last Night —

Friday 24 — No News —

Saturday 25 — Rain and disagreeable Weather — May and Durant arrived late in the evening — haveing made an excellent hunt —

Sunday 26 — Charboneau arrived from the Gros Ventres — No News in that quarter except that Buffaloe are plenty.

Monday 27 — Last night — 11 O'clock enemies around the Fort, and Knocked several times at the gate — Set 2 Men chopping wood for coal — Miller with 2 free trappers arrived from Fort Union[315] — No News in that quarter —

Tuesday 28 — No News — put the horses in the Point.[316]

Wednesday 29 — Miller, and the two hunters started for below — takeing with them 54 Beaver skins.

Thursday 30 — No news—

Friday 31 — As yesterday ! Number of Rats this Month 97 —

[1834]   NOVEMBER

Saturday 1 — Thick foggy Weather —

Sunday 2 — Started out in company with Mr May & an Indian in quest of Meat on Knife river[317] — arrived there late in the evening — run a bande of Cows and Killed one, started in search of an encampment — Proceeding along the river to find out a good camping place, we were hailed from the bushes, *Hollow* ! Hollow was the answer, and out rushed one of the largest Kind of Americans, with his rifle in his hand, ready to drop one of us — however, We camped with him that night — his name was John Newman,[318] a trapper, who had left the little Miss°[319] — in September last, with an associate, who left him on the Cheyenne river — Newton [*sic*] mistook Knife river, for Cherry river[320] —

Monday 3 — Left camp early to Kill Meat and arrived late at the Camp —

Tuesday 4 — Started for the Fort with our horses loaded with Meat, in company with Newton, [*sic*] who has made up his mind to go down by the way of the Miss° — in a canoe —

Wednesday 5 — Pleasant weather — Legris[321] and suitte - arrived from Fort Union — finished hauling wood for the coal.

Thursday 6 — May and Newman started for the Fort[322] below. O. B. F.

Friday 7 — Two Mandans started for the Sioux Camp on

Cannon ball river, as deputys for the Village — Bought - & settled with Legris and Villeandré[323] for their beaver, they disputed the goodness of the steel yards, saying that they were the damdest rascally pair that ever was in the Miss° — however I got along well enough with them, finished covering the coal pit —

Saturday 8 — Legris and Dupuis[324] started for Fort Union, with a Black foot wife,   set fire to the coal Kiln —

Sunday 9 — Pleasant fall weather — a bande of Gros Ventres arrived yesterday from War, haveing stolen 20 horses from the Saons[325] —

Monday 10 — The Black foot wife who - left here on the 8th inst, deserted and arrived here last evening — Charboneau arrived from the Gros Ventre Village with all sorts of talk —

Tuesday 11 — A small party of Mandans left here early this Morning on a war excursion to the Sioux Camp — Durant, Villeandré, and Màntá[326] started out trapping on Knife river. Lacroix arrived from below, haveing been sent by Primeau & Co.[327] to administer to the Indians, he says on arriving at the Yanctonais Camp they made him present of 500 Pcs Meat - 60 Robes , & some Beaver which he sent down in a skin canoe by a Man that was in company with him —

Wednesday 12 — Pleasant fall weather — sent Michel out after fresh Meat — the Mandans in fine spirits, on account of the Opposition[328] this Winter, some few beaver skins that I traded of them some time past - they begin to regret them, however they are safe —

Thursday 13 — Cloudy — the two plenipotentiaries that went to the Yancton Camp arrived this Morning - with News of the arrival of the Opposition boat at the Yancton Camp — (Picotts[329] Wintering ground) — the war party who left here on the 11th inst came back to day, haveing seen enemies !

Friday 14 — Light fall of snow last night — Mitchel arrived with the Meat of 5 cows — Cold throughout the day — 5 Mandans who started a beaver hunting some time last Month arrived to day with 50 or 60 Beaver — Molleur also arrived from Bijouxs Camp —

Saturday 15 — Molleur started for the Gros Ventres — the ice for the first time this year begins to run in the river — traded all the beaver that the Indians brought yesterday — the Opposition being so near at hand, made me very anxious to get the skins before their arrival —

Sunday 16 — The ice continues running very thick in the river —

Monday 17 — Fine pleasant weather — Durant and Co. arrived to day with 5 Beaver sks — Ice stopped running —

Tuesday 18 — Finished the coal pit — Lacroix started for the Yanctons, with several Mandans to bring up goods — the horses that I had put in the Point of Woods below, on the 28th of last Month — came back to day in good order.

Wednesday 19 — Dreams, begin to Make their appearance in the fort —

Thursday 20 — The time appointed for the arrival of the *Emperor* of the West,[330] is almost expired — We are all in hopes that he will soon arrive and bring us good tidings from below — Durant started out after Meat — at 10,A.M. - rain —

Friday 21 — Cloudy & Cold, Wind from the west —

Saturday 22 — Cloudy weather — Durant arrived with the Meat of two Cows and one calf — Cattle are plenty 30 Miles from the Fort —

Sunday 23 — The Mandans crossed the river to go to *Cérne*[331] Buffaloe —

Monday 24 — Pleasant day — Commenced working in the Black smith shop —

Tuesday 25 — The Mandans arrived from the cerne with a quantity of Meat —

Wednesday 26 — News from the Yancton camp, stateing the

arrival of Dickson[332] at that Post — J. Howard[333] arrived from Fort Union, with letters ~~from~~ for K. McK.

Thursday 27 — Pleasant fall weather — No News —

Friday 28 — Cloudy — Molleur arrived from the Gros Ventres for Medicine for Bijoux —

Saturday 29 — Snow last night — Wind from the North West — Charbonneau started for the Cheyenne Camp in company with some Gros Ventres - and Mandans — sent after the horses that remained in the point below —

Sunday 30 — The Indians on the opposite side Killed Buffaloe close to their camp — several Yanctons arrived with robes, from Hart river — Eclipse of the sun —

[1834]   DECEMBER

Monday 1 — Cloudy — Number of rats Killed last Month 87 — News from the Gros Ventres, stateing a battle between them and the Assinniboines, in which the former lost 4 in Killed, and the latter 18 — the Assinniboins took away with them several horses —[334]

Tuesday 2 — No News —

Wednesday 3 — As yesterday —

Thursday 4 — My larder being nearly out, sent Mitchel with 5 horses in search of Cattle —Mr D. Lamont[335] and Lafarriere[336] arrived —

Friday 5 — Cold Stormy day —

Saturday 6 — Same as yesterday — Prepared the Eqpt. for the Yanctonais —

Sunday 7 — J. Andrews[337] with a dog train left here for Dickson's Post with goods for that place —

Monday 8 — Legris arrived from Fort Union —

Tuesday 9 — Fine Pleasant day —

Wednesday 10 — D. Lamont and suitte left here for Fort

Union — Accompanied them as far as the Gros Ventres — Arrived there late in the evening much fatigued —

Thursday 11 — D. Lamont left the Gros Ventres at 10 A. M. — Accompanied him a few Miles and arrived at the Village ½ past 3 P.M.

Friday 12 — Started for the fort at sun rise and arrived at 2 O'clock — found all well —

Saturday 13 — Run a bande of Bulls on the hill, and Killed one — Yanctons arrived from heart river with some few robes — and Beaver.

Sunday 14 — Fine Pleasant day — it appears that the Sioux from below carries on trade with the Mandans, tradeing corn for robes —

Monday 15 — Set the Men at work to make dog trains —

Tuesday 16 — The weather continues Mild, haveing had no snow of any consequence this season — and cattle scarce owing to the warm weather — a White Cow skin that I have had in the store for some time past sold to day for the enormous Price of six Horses —

Wednesday 17 — Cloudy — appearance of snow — Wind from the North West — Durant arrived from below with wood for makeing dog trains —

Thursday 18 — Light fall of snow last night — finished sawing wood for Dog trains —

Friday 19 — Quarreled with my Horse guard for Neglect of his Horses — sent him off — snow —

Saturday 20 — Cold Windy day —

Sunday 21 — Snow — Stormy Weather —

Monday 22 — One of the coldest days this year —

Tuesday 23 — No News —

Wednesday 24 — A Yancton arrived this Morning from the Camp on Hart river, brought information that 2 horses belonging to the Mandans — that was missing some time since, was stolen by the *Onk pa Ta* and that the soldiers has went in search of them, and that they will be here, in 3 or 4 days — Bijoux arrived from the Gros Ventres, to spend the Christmas day with us, Charboneau is busily employed in Makeing a grand feast —

Thursday 25 — Christmas comes but once a year, and when it comes it brings good cheer. But not here! As every thing seems the same, No New faces, No News, and worst of all No Cattle, last Night at ½ past 10 O'Clock we partook of a fine supper Prepared by Old Charboneau, consisting of Meat pies, bread, fricassied pheasants Boiled tongues, roast beef — and Coffee — the brilliant assembly consisted of Ind[ns] Half Breeds, Canadians, Squaws and children, to have taken a Birds eyes view, of the whole group, seated at the festive board, would of astonished any, but those who are accustomed to such sights, to of seen in what little time, the Contents of the table was dispatched, some as much as seven to nine cups of coffee, and the rest in like proportion, good luck for the Cooks that they were of the Number seated at the table, or their share would of been scant — as every one had done Honour to his plate —

Friday 26 — Bijoux started for the Gros Ventres — The Dog bande gave us a dance — they went off well pleased, as both the Whites & Reds, were very liberal towards them,   the French Boys will return them the dance on New Year's day —[338]

Saturday 27 — Thick foggy weather — We were honoured to day with a dance, by the Old Ladies of the Village, the White Buffaloe Cap dance[339] — it is reported that the Sioux will be here to morrow —

Sunday 28 — For some time past the weather has been threatening, and to day we have had some rain, and hail —

Monday 29 — No News to day — Pleasant weather,   the Sioux that was expected to arrive yesterday, has not yet arrived —

Tuesday 30 — Stormy disagreeable weather — Garreau started out in search of cattle — the Yanctons are at length arrived, between 2 and 3 hundred, Men and Women, bringing with them some few Robes to trade corn — cattle scarce in their neighbourhood.

Wednesday 31 — Number of Rats Killed this Month 34 — This Morning a Sioux was Killed in the Village - by a Gros Ventre, who made his escape after committing the deed,   in the afternoon the Sioux all left the Village for their camp.

ADIEU 1834

1835

FORT CLARK—1ST JANUARY 1835

Thursday 1st. — New Year's day — Mitchel Bellehumeur's Wife was delivered of a Boy, who was christened *Baptiste* — Garreau arrived with fresh Meat — Cattle scarce —

Friday 2 — Cold, and appearance of snow. One of my Carters frose his nose, comeing from the Point of Woods, to the Fort —

Saturday 3 — Mr. May — who left here the 6th of November for the Little Missouri, [Bad River], and was to be back in 20 Days, has not yet returned, nor any news of him. I begin to fear that some accident has happened to him.[340] The Mandans started out to cerne Buffaloe on the west side of the river.

Sunday 4 — Sent Mitchel with 6 Horses and 3 Men in search of Cattle on Knife river.

Monday 5 — Last Night the rats were very thick   we Killed 18 — The Mandans commenced entering in their summer Village,   they fear the Scioux, on account of the fellow that was Killed in their Village the 31st of December last — the Mandans arrived with fresh Meat —

Tuesday 6 — Molleur arrived from the Gros Ventres to get corn for Bijoux, as they are all starveing in that quarter. I do not believe the Gros Ventres will Make 20 packs of Robes — as Bijoux has only traded 14 Robes since last October.

Wednesday 7 — Warm and Pleasant weather — Died this day three years, the Old Mandan Cheif (The White Head)[341] regretted by all Who Knew him.

Thursday 8 — Dull and Lonesome,[342] Not so brisk as at this day 20 Years ago, at New Orleans. Mr May arrived from Little Miss⁰ — No News in that quarter, Buffaloe scarce all over that country. J. Andrews with 2 dog trains and one Horse train arrived from Dickson's Camp,[343] in quest of Merchandises —

Friday 9 — Put up an Eqᵗ for the Yanctons. Express[344] arrived from the Yellow Stone, Out 11 Days — No News —

Saturday 10 — Started the Men for the Yanctonais — with 1 Horse, and 2 dog trains — loaded with Merchandises — for that Post —Mitchel arrived with fresh Meat Out 7 Days —

Sunday 11 — Molleur with one dog train, with Provisions, started up to the Gros Ventres —

Monday 12 — May it be so —

Tuesday 13 — Commenced cutting ice — cleared out the ice house - Dauphin[345] arrived from the Gros Ventres, with 1 dog train, with robes and beaver, all starveing in that quarter. *O. B. F.*

Wednesday 14 — Disagreeable Weather, the Gros Ventres gave us a dance — the Mandans are busily engaged in moveing into their summer Village —

Thursday 15 — Started to the Gros Ventres, driven back by a storm.

Friday 16 — Commenced filling the Ice house — P. Garreau who left here 3 days ago for Heart River, arrived to day, bringing with him the Opposition, headed by Primeau,[346] with 2 horses loaded with Merchandises —

Saturday 17 — Pleasant Weather. Mandans started Out to Make Meat &c —

Sunday 18 — Started up to the Gros Ventres in company with Mr May — found the Village abandoned by all, except a few Old Men and Women — Cattle in abundance in their Neighbourhood.

Monday 19 — Spent the day with Old Bijoux —

Tuesday 20 — Started for the Fort at 9 A.M. — and arrived at 2 P.M. — found all well —

Wednesday 21 — Tout la Meme chose —

Thursday 22 —Two Yanctons arrived from Heart River to settle some difficulty between them and the Mandans, on a/c of a Horse stolen by the former —

Friday 23 — No News —

Saturday 24 —As Yesterday —

Sunday 25 — Ditto

Monday 26 — Ditto

Tuesday 27 — The two Yanctons that arrived the 22nd, left here to day for their camp,   several Mandans arrived to day with fresh Meat, from their Camp about 20 Miles from the Fort —

Wednesday 28 — Snow,   Started for the Mandan Camp for Meat,   arrived there in the afternoon,   succeeded in getting 4 horse loads —

Thursday 29 — Remained at Camp all day, on a/c of the bad weather —

Friday 30 — Started for home, and arrived at ½ past 2 — Emelien went up to pay a visit to his old friends the Gros Ventres — the pack horses arrived at sun down —

Saturday 31 — Number of Rats Killed this Month 91 —

FORT CLARK — 1ST FEBRUARY 1835

Sunday 1st — Cold windy day — the Mandans arrived from Makeing dryed Meat —

Monday 2 — The Weather Continues cold ,

Tuesday 3 — Sent a dog train to the Gros Ventres for robes —

Wednesday 4 — Fine pleasant weather, 1 dog train arrived from the Gros Ventres with Robes — 3 others arrived from the Yanctons in search of corn as they are all starveing in that quarter. Newman arrived in the afternoon.

Thursday 5 — Cold Windy day —

Friday 6 — 3 Dog trains left here for Beaver River[347]

Saturday 7 — The Weather continues cold — North Wind —

Sunday 8 — Fine pleasant day —

Monday 9 — Sent a dog train to the Gros Ventres, feast and Council with the heads of Departments —

Tuesday 10 — Warm pleasant day

Wednesday 11 — The Mandans went out on discovery, came back with news of cattle, being in abundance 15 Miles distant — Preperations for the Cerne tomorrow —

Thursday 12 — Started out early to run Buffaloe — Arrived in the evening with 4 cows — rain during the day —

Friday 13 — Appearance of bad weather.

Saturday 14 — The 4 Bears[348] arrived to day , he gave me one horse load of fresh Meat — shod the two cart horses —

Sunday 15 — Pleasant day — 1 Horse train with Merchandises belonging to the opposition arrived from below —

Monday 16 — The Mandans went out on discovery —Commenced makeing packs — Since last June, I have only traded 40 packs — Snow storm in the afternoon — M.C.W.

Tuesday 17 — Last night the snow for the first time fell 6 or 8 inches — Put up the press for pressing packs — As we were sitting quietly by the fire, our attention was all at once drawn from a squake in the other room — I have been informed since that it was ocassioned by Durant's Woman, Who gave birth to a Boy — resembling his father, excepting the face not haveing so many holes —But red headed and Pock Marked — The Gros Ventres gave us a dance —

Wednesday 18 — Sent a dog train to the Gros Ventres, Commenced pressing packs —

Thursday 19 — Fine pleasant day — Primeau's horse train and two Men started for the Yanctonais Post — Dog train arrived from the Gros Ventres.

Friday 20 — Stormy Weather.

Saturday 21 — Ditto   Ditto

Sunday 22 — Pleasant day —

Monday 23 — Sent a horse train to the Gros Ventres — Charboneau arrived — No News — Buffaloe scarce

Tuesday 24 — Snow   storm — Weather   cold,   and   windy — horse train arrived from the Gros Ventres —

Wednesday 25 — One of the coldest days this year —

Thursday 26 — Weather continues cold — An other half breed made its appearance in the World last night — the snow blew at a great rate all day —

Friday 27 — Yesterday the horse guard came back without finding the horses — this Morning found my Black Mule frose — haveing been out in the storm of yesterday —

Saturday 28 — Cold — Number of rats this Month 34 —

Robes left for Horses[349]

~~The Womans Blanket   10~~-[*Sic*]
The Big Soldier   14
~~The Broken Kettle   10~~-[*Sic*]
The Son of old Sioux — 3
The Bear Tooth — 7
Gouche Cr by   5 Robes
The Son of the Wolf Chief 5

Jackson   16
The fool Chief   6 Robes — 3 calf Skins —

Bloody Knife

1 — 3 pt Blks — 3
   2 yds stroud — 2
1 — 1 pt Blks — 1 —
1 — 3 pt Scarlet 4 —
1 — 3 pt Blks   3 —
   Tobacco   1 —

Fort Clark — 1st March 1835

Sunday 1st — The first fine day we have had since several days past — 3 Dog trains arrived from Dixons Camp in quest of something to eat — No cattle in their neighbourhood —

Monday 2 — Sent two trains to the Gros Ventres to bring down Bijoux and his Merchandises to the summer Village —

Tuesday 3 — The Dog trains left here to day for Apple Creek[350] — The Mandans went out in search of Cattle — Came back without finding any —

Wednesday 4 — Pleasant day —

Thursday 5 — Train arrived from Gros Ventres with Robes —

Friday 6 — Sent 1 dog train with Merchandises to the Gros Ventres — Snow — One of Dicksons Men (Lenfant[351]) who deserted from below arrived to day with news of Buffaloe at the square Hills —

Saturday 7 — Dog train arrived from Gros Ventres — No news in that quarter except that Old Bijoux is still lodging Complaints. Mandans started out to make dryed Meat — Primeaus horse train with goods arrived —

Sunday 8 — Sent 4 horses out after fresh Meat — appearance of falling weather —

Monday 9 — Foggy Morning — Primeau's men started for below — himself for the Gros Ventres — One of my horses died last Night —

Tuesday 10 — May and Newman started out for their spring hunt — My horses arrived with fresh Meat — cattle plenty in 15 Miles from the Fort —

Wednesday 11 — Weather fine — some appearance of Spring — Mantá arrived from the Gros Ventres, Durant arrived with fresh Meat —

Thursday 12 — Strong N.W. Wind —

Friday 13 — Last Night we had a shower of rain — the snow is fast disappearing — some appearance of Spring — set 2 Men to cutting the Flat Boat out of the ice, Wind S.W. Rained several times in course of the day — Made packs, of Robes, and Beaver — Durant went up to the Gros Ventres —

Saturday 14 — Pleasant day — Pressed Packs — Durant arrived from the Gros Ventres — May and Newman left here the 12th inst in Company with several Gros Ventres, the latter bound for the Crow Camp —

Sunday 15 — Sent 1 Horse load of Merchandises up to the Gros Ventres — Chapman[352] started for below — Strong S. W. wind — rain in the afternoon — 1 horse arrived with robes from the G. V.

Monday 16 — Sent 1 horse load of Merchandises to the Gros Ventres — Set the Black smith to work in the shop — Went up to the G.V. Came back in the evening — 2 Mandans arrived with news of the death of the Saon Blessé — Killed by the Yanctons yesterday —

Tuesday 17 — Sent 1 horse load of Merchandises to the Gros Ventres — Shower of rain last night — Cloudy, disagreeable weather, strong S .W. wind — the Mandans preparing for War — a Bande of Elk made their appearance on the other side of the river — the Mandans all crossed, thinking it was a band of Sioux —

Wednesday 18 — Prepared the express for Fort Union, a bande of Yancton's arrived with Robes — 140 —

Thursday 19 — Finished tradeing with the Sioux — Started the Express for Fort Union - Charboneau and Bullé[353] — Snow in the afternoon —A Flock of Ducks passed to day — the first this year — Put up an Eq[t] for to start to the Yancton Camp —

Friday 20 — Yancton started for their camp — Snow — Started for the Yancton camp with 2 Carts and 4 pack Horses - to trade Robes and Meat — A War party of Mandans started for War against the Yanctons - at Lachapells camp[354] —

Saturday 21 — Commenced tradeing with the Yanctons traded 180 Robes and 100 pcs Meat —

Sunday 22 — Started for home early in the Morning Accompanied the Sioux to Surround[355] Buffaloe — Killed two — left the Carts at 4 P. M. - at the little river 10 Miles from the Fort — Arrived at the Fort at sun down — the Carts arrived late in the evening — 180 Robes

Monday 23 — Troubled with sore eyes — or as it is called in this Country - Snow Blind[356] — Primeau arrived from the Gros Ventres, expecting to Make a haul of some Robes, from the Sioux that came in with me yesterday — several small war parties have started since the 20th inst —

Tuesday 24 — Garreau and Lacroix started for the Yancton Camp with 2 horses and Merchandises, Ducks comeing from all quarters, appearance of Spring — The express that started for Fort Union the 19th inst - Came back to day - on account of the high waters — River commenced rising — had a Duck for supper, the first this year —

Wednesday 25 — Cloudy — Wind S.W — Sent 2 Carts, and 2 pack horses to the Yancton Camp - to bring in the Robes and Meat, that I left there the 22nd inst —

Thursday 26 — The water rose 4 feet last Night — Ice commenced breaking — the Flat Boat broke its cable, and went adrift — Sent 2 Men to the Gros Ventres - laden with Merchandisès for Bijoux — Several of the War party who left here the 20th inst came back to day — left the party at Lachapelle's — A Bande of Cows passed the Fort, on the ice — Garreau and Lacroix arrived with fresh Meat —

Friday 27 — Light fall of snow last Night — Made packs — the carts that I sent to the Yancton Camp the 25th inst, to bring in the Robes that I left there the 22nd arrived last Night with 220 Robes and 50 pcs Meat — the War Party which left here the 20th came back to day - without Makeing a *Coup*

Saturday 28 — Continued Makeing packs — This day has been one of the pleasantest days that we have had this year ! — Medicine feast[357] at the Village — finished Makeing packs 56 —

Sunday 29 — Fine spring Weather — Pressed packs — Mandans went out to run Buffaloe,

Monday 30 — Durant and Joncá started for their spring hunt — Sent 2 Carts to the Gros Ventres for Robes — 195 — Cleaned out the Fort — &c &c —

Tuesday 31 — Made packs — The Opposition Hunters Garreau & Co - started for their spring hunt — Sent a Horse load of Merchandises to the G.V. — Trade begins to be brisk in that quarter — Number of Rats Killed this Month 110 —

FORT CLARK 1ST APRIL 1835

Wednesday 1 — Rain last Night — Strong South West Wind — Sent a cart to the Gros Ventres for Robes *90* — Put a Man in the place of Old Bijoux - the old man being very sick —

Thursday 2 — Pressed packs — the Wind continues very strong — the Mandans report the arrival of some White Men at the Gros Ventres —

Friday 3 — A dog who passed the winter with Lachapelle at the Yanctonais, came to the Fort last Night — Sent a cart to the Gros Ventres for Robes, 100 Robes — Durant Jonca, Garreau & Co. arrived to day — the Yanctonais pillaged them on Knife river ,

Saturday 4 — Sent a Man to the Gros Ventres, with goods — Made packs — Villeandré, and Mantá, started for to trap beaver, up the river — in a canoe —

Sunday 5 — Pleasant weather, Allert in the Village —two Bulls that hove in sight, was the occasion .

Monday 6 — Sent a cart to the Gros Ventres for Robes 110 — Made packs — the Mandans gave us a dance, in fireing they broke 3 pains of glass —

Tuesday 7 — Pressed packs 49 — Dauphin and an Indian quarrelled — in the affair Dauphin pushed him — in the afternoon as Dauphin was hunting his horses, the Mandan approached him from behind a hill — before he was perceived, he shot, the contents, struck poor Dauphin, in the arm, just below the sholder, entered his body — above the Heart — on the left side, and came out on the right side of his back bone — the Mandans appear to say Nothing about it —

Wednesday 8 — Poor Dauphin is very low, haveing passed the Night without sleep — I have offered a reward to any one that will Kill the Mandan, either secretly, or openly[358] — several has promised to do it, but I have but little faith in them — they are without any exception (except the Crees) the meanest, dirtiest, worthless, cowardly set of Dogs — on the Missouri[359] — the heads of Departments came to day with Robes — and a *Pipe* to make me smoke — which I refused to do — they gave poor Dauphin 14 Robes.

Thursday 9 — Sent a cart to the Gros Ventres for Robes 50 — The Indians came in with fresh meat —

Friday 10 — Cloudy — Made packs 15 — rain and hail during the day — the Prairies are again covered with snow — and hail —

Saturday 11 — Cold, Snow and rain. Durant's child died last Night — North Wind all day, very cold and disagreeable .

Sunday 12 — Weather, clear and cold — Strong North Wind

— trade goes on but slowly — but I am in hopes it will be brisk again in a few days —

Monday 13 — Primeau started for the Gros Ventres, takeing with him, all the Merchandises he had at the Mandan Village. As soon as Primeau starts for below, I intend to raise the trade — Durant and Bullé, started down the river, to trap Beaver as far as the Little Miss⁰ [Bad River] — set fire to the *Hay-stack* to prevent the Mandans from stealing it —

Tuesday 14 — Cloudy and cold — at 10 A.M. - Snow-storm — Made Packs — 7 —

Wednesday 15 — The Weather continues cold — Sent a Man to the Gros Ventres for news — Dauphin is on a fair way of getting better,   his Indian Doctor is very attentive, both Night & Day — the Mandans are all out, hunting something to eat,   they are encamped between Hart river and the Square hills —

Thursday 16 — Weather continues cold — Wind S.W — trade goes on but slow — oweing to the cold, the squaws not being able to dress their Robes .

Friday 17 — Cloudy — for several days past - the children of the Village die off 2 and 3 every day — it is my opinion that they are Killed by the Indian Doctors —Dauphin walked out of the Fort, the first time that he has been on his feet, since he was wounded —

Saturday 18 — Started out early to hunt Cattle — at 10 A.M - Run a bande of bulls — Killed 2 — Camped in 10 Miles of the Fort,   Primeau passed here in the afternoon, in a skin canoe, bound for St Louis. Mantá and Villeandré, arrived, from their spring hunt, haveing been fired on by the Assinneboins, and made a very narrow escape — Made Packs 28 —

Sunday 19 —Left Camp before day light and arrived at the Fort at 9 OClock — half frose, haveing passed the Night in the prairie without fire,   the Mandans report Cattle plenty on the east side of the river — *O. B. F.* the last.

Monday 20 — Shower of rain last Night — Strong N. West Wind — Made Packs 10 —

Tuesday 21 — The wind continues strong — sent a Man to the Gros Ventres for news — came back in the afternoon,   No News in that quarter,

Wednesday 22 — Pleasant weather — Set the Blacksmith to work in the shop —

Thursday 23 — The Mandans arrived from their Camp at the square Hills — brought several horses laden with fresh Meat —

Friday 24 — Weather unsettled — No News from any quarter since last 4th of February — shower of rain in the afternoon — A Mandan by the Name of *Old Sioux* has been missing since 6 day — is thought to have been Killed by Sioux —

Saturday 25 — Fine   day — Smoky   Weather — Made   two Soldiers for the Fort —

Sunday 26 — Strong S. East Wind — An Indian arrived from the Gros Ventres — reports the arrival of May & Newman at that place, haveing been robed by the Sioux, out beaver hunting .

Monday 27 — Commenced hauleing wood — went up to the Gros Ventres,   the report of yesterday is not true,   strong S.W. Wind —

Tuesday 28 — Thick fog — Covered the ware house and store with dirt —

Wednesday 29 — A bande of Mandans who had been out beaver hunting arrived last Night — with but few beaver skins — they report that the Saons are comeing in a large body against the Gros Ventres — and that they saw a party of white hunters, near the Black Hills — they say that Mitchel Gravelle,[360] was of their Number — The Gros Ventres that left here with May and Newman, for the Crow Village - arrived to day —

Thursday 30 — Fine pleasant day, the first we have had since several days past — the Mandans crossed the river in search of Buffaloes — the squaws are busily engaged in picketing in their

Village, they fear an attack from the Sioux — Charboneau arrived from the Gros Ventres with an over stock of Indian News - from all quarters — Number of Rats this Month 130 — 270 Packs Robes in the ware house (Pressed)

FORT CLARK — 1ST MAY 1835

Friday 1st — Cloudy — Parade dance at the Village — slight rain in the afternoon — the water rose last Night 6 inches —

Saturday 2d — Cold East wind — slight rain all day — Weather disagreeable —

Sunday 3 — Weather same as yesterday — Wind N. East — Snow in the afternoon — water riseing —

Monday 4 — The Snow is laying on the ground two inches deep — Severe snow storm,   I fear for my Indian horses — as they are in a very poor condition - and no grass for them to eat — Eat a Rat this evening for supper — We are almost as bad off as the Horses —

Tuesday 5 — Started out at Day-light to hunt Buffaloe — Discovered a bande at 10 A.M — Run them at 12 — Killed three , started for Home at 3 P.M. - and arrived at 9 - found my family increased to one more Boy[361] — the Mandans started out to dry Meat —

Wednesday 6 — Mr Crawfor[d],[362] in a dug-out arrived from Fort Union — left the Steam Boat Assinneboine at White Earth river, detained by the Water —[363]

Thursday 7 — Sent a cart to the Gros Ventres for Robes — the Yanctons has Killed up a small war party of Gros Ventres — amounting to 11 — they were in all 18 — 7 of which made their escape —

Friday 8 — Calm, pleasant day — allert in the Village last night —

Saturday 9 — Water riseing — Made packs - 11 —

Sunday 10 — Warm pleasant day — Quarrelled with the Balle

dans le Coup - On account of a Horse, and divers other rumors —

Monday 11 — The Water continues riseing slowly — Mr Balle dans le Coup, came to day — rigged off like a second Don Quixotte, alone, to attack the Fort, luckily for him the Indians turned him back, before he approched too near to us —

Tuesday 12 — The water fell last Night — the Mandans arrived from makeing dryed Meat, very unsuccessfull. Strong south East Wind all day — allert at the Village —

Wednesday 13 — Raind all last Night — took an Inventory of goods —

Thursday 14 — The Weather continues unsettled — the water rose to day 18 inches —

Friday 15 — A war party of Gros Ventres left here to day — in search of the Yanctons —

Saturday 16 — Cloudy — Thunder for the first time this season — sent a Man to the Gros Ventres with Merchandises —

Sunday 17 — Went up to the Gros Ventres — Met 3 Boats on the way — Mr Lamont[364] and Kipp — returned back to the Fort — loaded one Mackinaw Boat 203 packs Robes — 11 packs Beaver .

Monday 18 — Boats detained by the Wind — heavy rain last Night — thunder & Lightning — Bijoux returned to the Gros Ventres.

Tuesday 19 — Three Mackinaw Boats[365] — with Mr Lamont, Kipp and Crawford on board started for St Louis — saluted them with six shots from my cannon — Sold a White Cow skin 5 Horses and twenty Robes to the Mandans — *le coup de Boeuf*

Wednesday 20 — Strong south East Wind — continued all day —

Thursday 21 — Same as yesterday — strong S.E. Wind.

Friday 22 — Wind as usual — throughout the day —

Saturday 23 — During the whole of this Month, the weather has been remarkably cold — Strong Wind since 4 days —

Sunday 24 — Appearance of fine weather — the water riseing rapidly — 5 Bulls hove in sight of the Village, the Mandans prepared for the fight — and succeeded after a race of six Miles in Killing them all —Went out on discovery — No cattle — in returning home - Garreau Killed a Cabrie,[366] in the act of cutting it up - Our Horses who were tied close along side of us - took fright and run off — We pursued them for about 10 Miles, but without overtakeing them — Arrived at the Fort late — Much fatigued — I intend to start early tomorrow in search of them — the Mandans all started out to make dryed Meat —

Monday 25 — Rain — the water continues riseing — Just as I was in the act of setting out in search of my two lost Horses, to my great Comfort, and good luck, they made their appearance, with the loss only of both their bridles —

Tuesday 26 — The water continues riseing. No doubt but the Anual rise has commenced.   Weather Cloudy - and cool — rain in the afternoon — the Steam Boat Assinneboine arrived in the evening —

Wednesday 27 — Loaded the Steam Boat 104 pack — She left this place at 8 'OClock A.M — the water rose six inches last Night —

Thursday 28 — The water fell last Night as much as it rose yesterday — rainy disagreeable weather —

Friday 29 — Started Out early with 4 pack Horses, in search of Cattle , found one Bull in 40 Miles from this place — Pursued and Killed him — struck my Course to the Mandan Camp, Arrived there in the evening — they gave me a suply of fresh Meat —

Saturday 29 — Left Camp early for the Fort — and arrived at 2 O'clock — the Water since 2 days has fell considerable — it has commenced riseing again to day — Several of the Mandans arrived with fresh Meat —

Sunday 31st — Fine pleasant day — the water continues rise-ing — Number of Rats Killed this Month 139 —

FORT CLARK — 1ST JUNE 1835 — MONDAY

Monday 1 — Durant & Bonaventure,[367] arrived from Fort Pierre with 4 Horses — No News —

Tuesday 2 — The Mandans arrived from their dried Meat excursion very successful — Made butter to day - the first that has ever been made at this Post — I had almost forgotten to mention that the Steam Boat left us a Cow & Calf —

Wednesday 3 — Arrainged the goods in the ware house — in the afternoon we had a strong N.W Wind — Accompanied with rain and hail — at sundown we had clear weather —

Thursday 4 —Cool and pleasant —

Friday 5 — Rain all last Night — with heavy thunder — the Mandans are prepareing for war —

Saturday 6 — A small war party started out — all on Horse Back — (on the opposite side) — in search of the Yanctons — May they never return to their Village, is the Wish of Your Humble Servant — 6 Cows came in sight of the Village — after a race of 4 Miles they succeeded in Killing 3 of them —

Sunday 7 — The water rose last night 2 feet — rain, strong S.E. wind —

Monday 8 — The water rose last night 3 feet — a bande of cows (100) — was discovered from the hill — We all prepared for the chaise. We Killed almost the whole bande, after Killing one - my Horse fell and unfortunately broke my gun — started for home immediately, on my way to the Fort - I Killed an-other — rain

Tuesday 9 — Bullé arrived from the Gros Ventres , all quiet in that quarter —

Wednesday 10 — All's well —

Thursday 11 — The water continues riseing — it is much high-

er at present - than it was at the spring rise, March 26th. The
Steam Boat arrived from St Louis this day three years[368] — May
& Newman arrived from Hunting —

Friday 12 — Busily employed in catching drift wood —

Saturday 13 — The water commenced falling —

Sunday 14   Same as yesterday —

Monday 15 — Planted the Flag Staff — and hoisted the flag
in Honour of General Jackson - [369]

Tuesday 16 — The war party that left here the 6th inst arrived to day — Without Makeing a *Coup* —

Wednesday 17 — A Deer came running through the prarie —
entered the Mandan Village — and jumped off the Bluff - without any injury — and made his escape on the other side — Went
Out hunting, saw enemies, and returned —

Thursday 18 — Rain — one of the heaviest we have had this
season — the Steam Boat arrived this day, one year —

Friday 19 — A small war party that left here ten days ago -
arrived to day — haveing discovered enemies — and run away
from them —

Saturday 20 — The river is riseing since yesterday — Durant
and Venture started out hunting—

Sunday 21 — Run a Bande of Buffaloe (20) on the hill —
Durant and Venture arrived with plenty of fresh Meat —report
Cattle in abundance 40 Miles Off —

Monday 22 — For several days past the weather has been cold,
cloudy, and Windy — rain —

Tuesday 23 — Rain — all Day

Wednesday 24 — Ditto — Do — Do —

Thursday 25 — Ditto — Do — Do — the powder house caved
in —

Friday 26 — Ditto — D[o] — D[o] — the water rose last Night 2
feet

Saturday 27 — Ditto — D⁰ — D⁰ ,,   ,,   ,,   ,,   ,,   ,,
,,—

Sunday 28 — Ditto — some appearance of fine weather —

Monday 29   No News —

Tuesday 30 — Started out hunting returned in the afternoon with 6 Bulls — May started for Fort Pierre — the river fell to day 2 feet — Number of Rats Killed this Month 104 —

FORT CLARK 1ST JULY 1835 — WEDNESDAY

Wednesday 1 — Pleasant weather — Sent up to the Gros Ventres - for the Merchandise &c &c - trade being at an end — the Mandans gave us a dance — they went off displeased —

Thursday 2 — The water continues falling — had my young Bull cut —

Friday 3 — Covered the powder house —

Saturday 4 — The 60th of American Independence —

Sunday 5 —- Feast at the Village —

Monday 6 — Three Yanctons arrived from their camp on Canon Ball river — to smoke with the Mandans — they say that the Soldiers have taken the Horses, that was stolen from the Whites last spring, and have delivered them up to Mr Laidlaw —

Tuesday 7 — The Yanctons that arrived yesterday, started early this Morning — as several of the Mandans and Gros Ventres talked of Killing them — the weather for 3 or 4 days past has been very cold for the season —

Wednesday 8 — The water rose since yesterday 2 feet —

Thursday 9 — The water continues riseing — A war party of Gros Ventres arrived with 2 Assiniboine scalps — two Men arrived from Fort Union in quest of News[370] — Nothing New in that quarter —

Friday 10 — The Water rose last Night 18 inches — The Mandans arrived with fresh Meat, out 4 days — Rain —

Saturday 11 — Rain — the little Mandan Village danced —

Sunday 12 — Weather smokey — Went out on discovery — Came back without seeing any thing —

Monday 13 — Started out hunting — Killed three Bulls — Camped Out —

Tuesday 14 — Left Camp early and arrived at the Fort at 10 A. M —

Wednesday 15 — Went to the Medicine dance last Night — Came back late and got a whipping from my Wife for my bad behaviour —

Thursday 16 — The Soldiers came to day to ask permission to stop the trade from the little Village on account of some dispute among themselves — Which I refused to do — The Gros Ventres gave us a dance —

Friday 17 — No News —

Saturday 18 — Buffaloe race (4) on the hill —

Sunday 19 — Started out hunting with 3 pack horses — Camped in 15 Miles of the Fort —

Monday 20 — Left Camp early — saw Buffaloe at 10 A. M — run them and Killed three fat Cows — started for home and arrived at the Fort at 5 P. M — Commenced Makeing Hay —

Tuesday 21 — Cloudy — Mosquetoes in abundance[371] — the Gros-Ventres gave us a dance — 4 Boats arrived from Fort Union bound to StLouis[372] — no News in that quarter —

Wednesday 22 — The MacKinaw Boats (Mr. Brazeau[373]) left here this Morning early —

Thursday 23 — Rain — the Mandans gave us a dance —

Friday 24 — Major Fulkinson[374] (agent for the Mandans) and Mr May, arrived from Fort Pierre — the Steam Boat Assinniboine[375] was burnt a little below Heart river,[376] and all her cargo— 1100 Packs and some Beaver, distroyed —

Saturday 25 — Rain — Mr Grosclaude[377] and Labombarbe[378] started for Fort Union —

Sunday 26 — The Indians run a bande of cows close to the Village — and nearly distroyed all of the band — shower of rain and hail in the afternoon —

Monday 27 — The Indians arrived with fresh meat from the other side of the river — out 4 days —

Tuesday 28 — Several Yanctons arrived from their Camp on Heart river — report Cattle plenty in 50 Miles of the Fort — rain —

Wednesday 29 — Cloudy —

Thursday 30 — The Yanctons started for their Camp — several Gros Ventres accompanied them — Newman & Mantá left here for their fall hunt — Finished my last barril of Flour —

Friday 31 — Went out in search of Buffaloe , came back without finding any — Discharged my Cook for negligence — Number of Rats Killed this Month 88 —

FORT CLARK — 1ST AUGUST 1835 — SATURDAY

Saturday 1st — Cool and pleasant — Several Mandans arrived to day with fresh Meat — report Cattle far off —

Sunday 2nd — All's Well —

Monday 3 — The praries are on fire below

Tuesday 4 — No News —

Wednesday 5 — The Gros Ventres who left here the 30th of last Month for the Sioux Camp - arrived to day — they were well received at the Sioux Camp —

Thursday 6 — May and Durant started for Red River[379] —

Friday 7 — Pleasant Weather — Commenced hauleing hay —

Saturday 8 — The Yanctons started for their Camp —

Sunday 9 — Indian ceremonie at the Village —

Monday 10 — Rain — We had to day for the first time a Jackson dinner of squashes[380]

Tuesday 11 — Rain — disagreeable Weather — the Medicine dance of 4 days, finished to day —

F. A. Chardon

See # 2   [381]

FORT CLARK JOURNAL

Mandan Village

2

1835

August 12th 1835

Francis A. Chardon

Francis A. Chardon

Fisher Ames   Satan

FORT CLARK 12TH AUGUST 1835

I arrived at this place on the 18th of June 1834 — from that date up to the present — I have traded 340 packs Buffaloe Robes — 1100lb Beaver — Killed 39 Buffaloe — 1056 House Rats, and have Made a Fine Boy,[382] who I have Named Andrew Jackson, in Honour of the Old General — Whose health I am in hopes of drinking at St Louis this fall —

F. A. Chardon —

September[383]

1835

September

Wednesday 12 — Indians all out after Berries — Rain in the afternoon ,

Thursday 13 — Garreau arrived from hunting — reports the Boat close at hand, sent a canoe, with some corn to Meet the Boat as he informed me they were short of Provisions, Several Yanctons arrived from their camp — to smoke with the Mandans —

1837

But I am sick [*Sic*]
Dauphin arrived from the Boat —

Friday 14 — The Boats arrived in the afternoon — 28 Days from Fort Pierre —

Saturday 15 — Packed up some few goods for Fort Union —

Sunday 16 — Started to the Sioux Camp in Company with some Sioux after meat, Mandans went over the river to surround — The 2 Mackinaw boats started for fort Union, Cotá[384] went with them, Kept David Ewing in his place — rained in the evening

Monday 17 — The agent of the Mandans[385] &c went to the Gros Ventres Villiag [*Sic*] to give them their presents, returned in the evening — arrived whilst he was there, from Fort Union Messrs Samuel Tulleck,[386] and Labombard, in quest of the boats and news,   they bring none themselves.

Tuesday 18 — The Indians that went over the River yesterday to Surround, came in to day with plenty Buffalo —

Wednesday 19 — The agent made the Mandans their presents, — Sprinkled with rain several times during the day, — I returned to day from the Sioux ~~lodge~~ camp — the carts will return tomorrow with about 800 p^s. meat — comeing in saw *Bully and Venture,* who started last Sunday to make their fall hunt   they had Caught One BEAVER — A Gros Ventre, endeavoured to kill a Sioux but failed, and took his horse in pledge for the scalp the Sioux carried off

Thursday 20 — Duronts wife died on the 18th Inst: — breakfasted about sun rise — Carts arrived with meat — A Grovont Chief, (the red Shield) took from the Gros Ventre, the horse mentioned on yesterday and has gone to the *Yanktona* Camp with it, loaded with pumpkins, a Gun & Chiefs coat to give to the owner — made our supper of bread & milk —

Friday 21 — Breakfasted as yesterday , — good fish for dinner Feasted the Mandan Soldiers — fine day   little windy — a fieu Rees arrived from the Sioux camp (*squaws*)

Saturday 22 — Breakfasted between day light and Sun up — Morning cloudy and windy — Started three carts back to the Sioux camp after meat about 6 OClock, A.M.   some thunder in the fore part of the day and a fieu drops of rain — considerable shower at *one* P. M — *Frost ,* yesterday & day before — Afternoon warm calm and pleasant — Dave[387] (the cook) had great trouble milking his cow —

Sunday 23 — Took a dose of Salts for the Diarrhoea and Breakfasted a little after sun rise — smoky and windy — *The wounded face ,* and *Four Bares* (Mandans) with their partizans started for the Yanktona camp over the River to revenge the

Death of the *wounded Saon*,[388] who was killed by the Yanktonas last Spring — God send them Speed , it is perfectly imaterial how fieu of them return,   I wish both parties a severe conflict and heavy losses — 12 oClock sprinkle of Rain —, considerable shower at 2 O,C. and some thunder — the bal : of the evening rainy and disagreeable — moon changed .

Monday 24 — Morning cloudy — misty till about 10 O.C. A.M. The Squaws who went with the war party yesterday returned to day with plenty of Cherries —smoke all vanished— afternoon pleasant — little cool — clearing off —sun set clear, the wind calm — little fire pleasant,   night fine for sleeping

Tuesday 25 — Heavy fog — My Squaw and the blacksmith's little son both have the Diarrhoea this morning, it is among the Mandans , some have died in 12 hours after its first appearance , gave my Squaw a fieu drops of Lodanum & Camphor, 25 drops of the former and 15 of the latter — 8 oClock, fog disappeared — distributed out traps to the Mandan Indians, to make their fall hunt with — Cool in the shade, and hot in the Sun. This day at St Louis would be a real *fever* and *Ague* breeder — began to haze up in the afternoon— The little dog band of Gros Ventres danced in the Fort, the AGENT made them a small present of knives & tobacco — Caught a Chicken by the head in a trap set for rats, in the office — The Gros Ventre Chief *red arrow fender* (or shield) returned from the Yanktona band of Sioux where he went to return the horse mentioned on the 20th Inst , he came to see the agent — said the Yanktonas hart were good, the agent made him a present of a blanket — as token of his approbation for his conduct in this matter,   also put a new Ribbon in his *meddal*[389] — 6 OClock began to rain, rained moderately all night —

Wednesday 26 — Disagreeable, wet morning, but calm — rained gently until 12 —   2. OClock P.M. Pierre Garrot returned from the Sioux Camp with two carts loaded with meat, the third Cart (Monta's) having broke down a fieu miles from here and *The Bichon*[390] horse gave out — 3 OClock started Algiers[391] (my dutch hand) back with a wheel to repair the remaining Cart and assist in bringing it in — 7 OClock, my *dutch-man,* returned with the wheel of the cart, not being able to find Monta, as he had repaired his cart and gone, God knows where — All the afternoon pleasant over head but disagreeable under foot — Sun set clear —

Thursday 27 — Morning cloudy;   like for rain — 6 OClock started with *Pierre,* one of the hands, in search of *Montá* and his cart — returned, not able to find Montá —10, OClock, Montá returned with his cart having went nearly to the Gros Ventres, and now swears he was not lost, but went 10 miles out of his way for a good road to come home in — 1 OClock, a small sprinkle of rain —

Friday 28 — Still cloudy,   looks like for rain — 7 OClock A.M. raining , 8 OClock, ceased raining, the shower was a gentle one — The Squaws gave us a dance at 4 O.C. P. M. made them a small present, also the Agent made them a small present — it rained and the sun shone alternately through the day — still cloudy but has the appearance of clearing off — *Old Charboneau,* gave us a superb supper of Coffee and *Mince Pie,* the pie was *charming*

Saturday 29 — Morning pleasant,   warm and calm,   rather cloudy — This has been a pleasant day, the Squaws of the Fort practised dancing all the afternoon, in order to honor the Mandans with a dance tomorrow to see if they have *Strong hearts* —

Sunday 30 — Morning pleasant, calm, and clear — it makes the *hens* cackle — Some days since some of the Indians stole a rat trap. I informed the Soldiers of the Village of it, who after ransacking the big Village over, went to the little Village,[392] where they found it, and to day returned it to me — The Squaws of the Fort had their dance at the Village, got a fieu presents from there — such as guns, Robes, and Chiefs Coats;   I must say they were either very poor, or their hearts very *soft* — had tea for supper being Sunday night — The Mandan Indians who left this some days since [to] treat for peace with "*The No Bows*"[393] (Band of Sioux) returned this evening, having met with rather a bad reception;   one returned with his arm broke, it will be 5 or 6 days before the truth can be ascertained.

Monday 31 — Fine morning — The Squaws of the Fort went to the Gros Ventres, to dance, under the direction of Old Manuel,[394] and the Ree — escorted by the Agent, his Interpreter, and the Interpreter of the Fort. They rec^d. as presents some Robes a fieu Guns a horse &c — returned by the little Mandan Village — Danced for them there, rec^d. 2 Robes &c — The greater part of the Gros Ventres were out hunting — About 50 of the Sioux came in this evening — The day has been fine, clouded up this evening — Killed 123 rats this month.

SEPTEMBER

Tuesday 1 — Morning cloudy and windy — hard wind last night — The war party which left on the 23^d. returned this evening done nothing — The Soldiers made a large feast for the entertainment of the Sioux. The Sioux were well rec^d. by the *Mandans,*   the peace concluded, and ratified between them, I have no doubt will last at least, as long as the Mandans corn lasts — The day has been cloudy, and threatened rain all day but had none a little misty about 10 Oclock — The Agent, made the 2 bravs,[395] the *Fool* Chief & Little Sioux a present of a Blanket each, & some powder, lead & tobacco, for their exertions in concluding the peace between them & the Sioux

Wednesday 2 — Morning fine — The Sioux left this,   in company with the Agent, myself, and several of the principal Chiefs and soldiers of the *Mandans,* for the Gros Ventres, to ratify the treaty[396] concluded between them — they were well rec^d. by the Gros Ventres and Saluted by a couple of fires from their Cannon, the treaty was ratified and we called on as witnesses — left there about 5 OClock P.M. and returned to the Fort — arrived to day from Fort Union two *free trapers* on their way to St Louis brought a letter from Mr. Hamilton — Met *Pecot*[397] with the Boats just above the mouth of white River, all was well, they Report there are about 300 Assinneboins and Crees, on their way to attact the Gros Ventres — The day has been fine —

Thursday 3 — Rained last night , — The Sioux returned from the *Gros Ventres* well pleased, the Soldiers were Vigilent all night in protecting them — On the night of the 30th. Augt — some Indians stole *Pierre Garot's*[398] horse — supposed to be Yanktonas on the N. side River — In the evening cleared off — wind calm — The day has been cloudy —

Friday 4 — Beautiful, clear, calm and pleasant morning — Sioux left this morning for their Camp — Afternoon, clouded up — Some Yanktonas arrived about 9 OClk P. M. report the Camp will be here in 5 or 6 days —

Saturday 5th — Morning cloudy, Some wind, — sprinkled with rain last night — More of the Yanktonas arrived — they came by the Gros Ventres, danced there, Gros V- made them presents of Robes, Guns and a horse, — on their way from there here a *Mandan* of the little Village pillaged the horse — one of the Chiefs took the horse brot: him here and delivered him up to the owner again — It in turn has rained, & hailed, the wind blew, the sun shone, been calm, cold and warm to day and the sun set clear — A singular day —

Sunday 6 — Morning extremely fine — nothing of importance took place to day — The day held its own thro'out without change, clear, calm and warm

Monday 7 — Morning, as Yesterday — Set the men to hauling hay — Number of the Yanktons here, have gone to the Gros Ventres to day — The two free trapers who arrived here on the 2nd Instant from Fort Union on their way to St. Louis, this day departed from here for their place of destination; I sent letters by them to Fort Pierre[399] — The day kept fine.

Tuesday 8 — Morning clear and pleasant — The Yanktona & Saon camps arrived, in great pomp, and with much ceremony 400 lodges, — nothing further of importance transpired to day — It has been altogether a fine day —

Wednesday 9 — Another fine morning — The Yanktonas danced the *bull* dance[400] in the fort Yesterday — & gave us a dance again to day, the Agent and myself each made them small present of Tobacco — I differing a little by giving a fieu Knives, but not so much tobacco —

Thursday 10 — The weather changed last night,   morning cloudy and windy — wind from the west — made a feast for the Chiefs and Soldiers of the Sioux Camp — the Agent made them a small present of Powder, Balls and Tobacco — They talked very fine, always taking care however to praise themselves much — love the whites dearly — (at least, till they are refused something) —

— A difficulty took place to day between the Mandan Soldiers, and some Young men of the Yanktonas; which had nearly been a serious thing; as the Y's armed themselves with Guns and their Bows and arrows, and came to the fort to attact them; but fortunately, the One they wanted [to] see had gone to the Village — they went in quest of him, about 8 in number; nothing however was done; I anticipate, the matter is not yet settled — They threatened to shoot any one, which I apprehend they will do if they cannot get revenge out of the Mandans —

Friday 11 — The morning cloudy but calm — Breakfasted by candle light — Had three dances by the Sioux Squaws,   had to make them all small presents, the Agent had to do like wise — Some lads danced also, the Agent gave them a fieu knives and a little Tobacco,   I gave nothing — I wish to God dancing is over — Reported the Assinnaboins had attacted the Gros Ventres, it was handsome to see the Sioux and Mandans - start to their assistance;   but greatly to their mortification, before they had proceeded far, it was ascertained the report was false;   it grew out of the arrival of a fieu Soan Sioux there — The day has been a cloudy one, tho' calm, and by no means disagreeable —

Saturday 12 — Morning cloudy and calm — last night, it lightened, Thunder'd, raind and the wind blew, every appearance of rain to day — Yesterday the Yanktonas stole 4 of the best horses belonging to the Mandan Village and crossed the River with them,   I anticipate h—l among them Yet before they leave this — Shot at one of the Sioux dogs for chasing my chickens,   but unfortunately missed him in consequence of my pistol being too hard in triger — had a little rain at (10) - O.C., fine day from that to (4) O.C. rained again — *M*ʳ *Charboneau* was taken sick yesterday, with something like the Cholic, — the 4 Bear, and two or three others of the Mandans have pursued the Yanktonas who stole the horses —

Sunday 13 — Morning cloudy — Saw a flock of wild Geese — The Sioux danced the bear dance[401] in the fort, we made them a small present; they also danced at the Village: there to imitate the *bear* more thoroughly, they killed a dog and devoured him raw — In the afternoon, another company of the big dog band danced also in the fort — had to make them a small present, Oh! God, but I am tired of dancing — The Mandan Squaws danced at the Sioux Camp, received some pretty good presents, — a horse or two, worth dancing for — The day partially cleared off — The Ree Squaws, married to the *Saons,* have disappeared 7 or 8 in number , there will be the DEVIL to pay about it before they leave this I expect, as they must be secreted at the Mandan Village — The Yanktonas returned to the Mandans two horses in part pay for the 4 they pillaged a fieu days Since — everything appears almost like the Yanktonas were trying to pick a quarrel with the Mandans,   I hardly think it possible they can leave without a fight —

Monday 14 — Morning Clear — killed 38 *rats,*   5 last Knight and 33 this morning — The 4 Bear and his companions returned Yesterday having lost the track — 7 OClock A. M. Sioux Camp commenced moving, lodges all down — 8 OClock, all off except a fieu, beggars, — bought a horse from the Yanktonas — Cleared out the Store , and found I had traded from the Sioux 360 Robes, 102 Calf Skins, 74ᶦᵇ Beaver , 200 pieces of Meat, 12 Sacks of Cords, — They carried off with them, 1½ pack of Beaver to buy horses with — Contrary to all expectations the Soux have gone without a fight with the Mandans, & I believe have Stole no more horses, — to day has been Tolerable windy —

Tuesday 15ᵗʰ — Morning Cloudy and windy,— wind all night — 10 OClock Cleared off , fine day, only moderately windy — One of old Manuel's wives died — I think May is *hamered* —

Wednesday 16 — Morning Cloudy, inclined to be windy — looks cold but cant say it is overly so — 7 OClo'k Peacot[402] with Mackanaw Boats arrived from Fort Union, for St Louis — Making preperations to go down in with them — rained a little in the afternoon — Shipped on them 70 packs of Robes, and 2 packs of Beaver — Pecot Brot 2 Bottle of wine and we fergot to drink it[403] — The Agent distributed the bal. of his presents among the Mandans — powder lead and Tobacco —

Thursday 17 — Ready to Start[404] , morning Cloudy — off at 7 Oclock A.M. (Adieu)

Killed 98 Rats this Month

1836

Disguise thyself as thou wilt,
Oh Slavery, Still thou art a bitter draught,
and though thousands in all ages have been
made to drink of thy cup, it is no
less bitter on that account.[405]

STERNE

FORT CLARK — 1ST JANUARY 1836

I commence[406] the dull, irksome task of recording the petty incidents of this post, on New Years day and if the weather may be considered as emblematic of the Year — It will be calm and pleasant as heart could wish.

2nd — Rode up to the Gros Ventre Village in company with old Charboneau — Indians all absent making Meat,   returned in the Evening,   pleasant day.

3rd — The Sioux all moveing up from below — complain of being in a Starving condition.

4th — Weather continues fine as usual,   no news —

5th — Walked over to where the men were choping wood — found them idle.

6th — Started out our Hunters in quest of Meat our larder being completely empty. D. Ewing[407] commenced cuting Steam Boat wood in the Point below — Many of the Yanctonas passed the Fort on their way out in search of Buffalo — they are all Sta(r)ving.

7th — Slight fall of Snow during the day — walked Several Miles down the river in search of a Suitable point to cut wood for the Steam Boat, concluded to send the choppers to the little lake.[408] The Yanctonas continue moveing up the River.

8th — Cold & Cloudy — frequent Showers of Snow. B. Dufond[409] sent up for Trains to bring his goods & packs to this place, the Indians haveing all left.

Saturday 9th — Old Charboneau returned from the Gros Ventre Village — no news Except that of the Sioux Stealing a quantity of corn from the Gros Ventre? The quarrel however seems to have been amicably Setled. A camp of Yanctonas Moved up from below —

Sunday 10th — Cold Stormy day — The turbulent passions of the Indians seems to have been in accordance with the waring of the elements. The Camp of Yanctonas that passed up Yesterday camped near the Gros Ventre Village where they were attacked this Morning at daylight by the whole force of the Gros Ventres — The only inteligence we have received of the Battle was from a few stragling Sioux who had escaped the general Slaughter — they State that the Sioux Camp consisting of about 40 Lodges — was taken by surprise — and that the Sioux Men, Women, and children were indiscriminately butchered, they istimated their loss at upward of a 100. —

The Sioux who were camped near the Mandans distrusting the friendly talk of their allies, fled during the night, A Young Sioux — who had lost all his relations in the Morning — attempted to Kill a Gros Ventre Boy in the Fort. — Baptist Dufond arrived at night, bringing up his plunder —

Monday 11 — The weather continues cold and Stormy — consequently - there has been no arrivals from the Gros Ventre

Village to give the details of the Great Battle of Yesterday —
The four Bears Started up this Morning to gather news — we
will receive the Budget tomorrow. I am quite uneasy about our
Hunters - who have not as Yet Made their appearance.

Tuesday 12th — No tidings of our Hunters — I am becoming
Seriously alarmed for their Safety, The unseted State of the
country Justifies the worst anticipations   no *official* account has
as Yet reached us of the great Battle of the 10th inst, — But
from the vague information we have received, it appears to have
been even More Sanguinary than was at first reported.   A
Young Mandan who Visited the field — States that he counted
160 — dead bodies; — (*doubtful*)

Wednesday 13th — No News of our Hunters. One of Premeau's
Men came up from below — he States that the Sioux who were
retreating from this Place - robed him on his way up.   (it is
supposed of whiskey),   weather calm — cold, & Clear (we are
all starving .)

Thursday 14th — We still remain in a state of anxious sus-
pense respecting the Hunters. Old Charboneau went up to the
Gros Ventre Village , weather intensely cold — I purpose going
out tomorrow in search of my Men, Provided the weather
Moderates.

Friday 15th — We were highly gratified this morning by the
arrival of the Hunters — whom we had given up for lost. After ten days hard traveling they returned without seeing a
Single cow. This is truly a gloomy prospect. Old Charboneau
returned from the Gros Ventres bringing down 30 Robes — the
proceeds of 2 Months Trade, Adams[410] — who is engaged to
Premeau & Co returned from the little lake — without bringing
up the goods — there are Yet 14 Lodges Sioux remaining at
that Camp ,

Saturday 16th — Weather continues unsettled — Heavy fall
of Snow in the Evening, Sent down the Men to Haul Hay —
But they returned with the distressing report of its all being
burnt for this neighbourly act I suppose we thank our Sioux

friends — Our prospect for the winter is now gloomy in the extreme. I have concluded to send off all my horses & Hunters to make a liveing in the Prairies — or starve as fate May direct , no news from any quarter .

Sunday 17th — Cold Stormy day — One of my Men who Came down from the Gros Ventres — says Buffalo were plenty within 10 Miles of the Village

Monday 18th — Made preparations for sending My Men out to Starve in the Prairies, went up to where the Men were chopping Steam wood, found they had been idle, Cold day,

Tuesday 19th — The Men who had been sent to Cut Steam Boat wood came down in the Morning with a Story that the Mandans had attempted to Kill them. After many enquires amongst the Indians I concluded it was a false report and sent them back. The whole of the Hunters & half Breeds Started up the Missouri to Hunt. Mr. May[411] left the Fort and took up lodgeings in the Mandan Village (A Strange fancy)

Wednesday 20th — Weather intensely cold. Two Men came up from Apple River for corn. They say both Whites and Indians below are Starving. The greater part of the Yanctonas have gone up Heart River in search of Buffalo.

Thursday 21st — We have all been confined to the House by the cold, which seems to have increased at least 10 degrees since Yesterday, it is with great dificulty the Men can prevent themselves from freezing while Hauling a load of wood,

Old Charboneau Started to the Gros Ventres to aid in Moveing the goods to the Summer Village, this being the day appointed by the Indians for that purpose.

Had the Honour of a long visit from Mr Chapman — He speaks of their prospects in a very desponding tone, and seems Heartily to regret ever haveing engaged in the Bussiness.

Friday 22nd — About 2 o clock the Trains from Fort Union arrived — no news of importance, they found Buffalo in great abundance all the way from the Yellow Stone to the little Missouri — They Saw nothing of my hunters haveing past them on

the way. Old Charboneau returned from the Gros Ventres —
without having accomplished the object of his visit which was
to move the goods to the Summer Village. Cold as usual —

Saturday 23rd — Weather moderated very much since Yesterday — no news — Started Ortibise[412] Men down with corn.

Sunday 24th — Wrote letters & prepared to start the Men to
Fort Union in the morning — gave a Dinner to our Opponants
which must have been very welcome as they were in a Straving
[*sic*] State. Cold as usual —

Monday 25th — The Men who came down from F U. started
at daylight this morning. But the weather is so very cold that
that it will be almost impossible for them to travel. An Indian
who came down from the Gros Ventres says that cattle is comeing in.

Tuesday 26th — Cold Stormy day. It is with much dificulty
the Men can furnish wood for the Fort, they are nearly all
frost bit.

Wednesday 27th — Weather moderated very much since Yesterday — Made preparations to go out in search of cattle tomorrow. No news from any quarter — *lonesome*

One Single word *lonesome* — would suffice to express our feelings any day throughout the Year — We might add — discontented — but this would include the fate of all Mankind. It is
a Melancholy reflection when we look forward into futurity —
and know that the remnant of our days *must* be spent in toil-
some and unavailing pursuits of happiness. And that sooner or
later we must sink into the grave without ever being able to
attain the object for which we have toiled and suffered so much.
If we turn with discontent from this ideal picture, and take a
retrospective glance at the past, the scene is no less gloomy. It
is like a dreary expansive waste — without one green verdant
spot on which Memmory loves to linger. The day dreams in
which we used to indulge during our halcyon days of Youth
have long since proved as baseless as Visions ever are. The little experience that time has given only teaches us to Know,
,That Man was Made to Mourn,

Thursday 28th — Wrote letters to Campbell also to M^r. Laid-law and made preparations for starting B. Dufond to Beaver River in the morning. Old Charboneau went up to the Gros Ventres to get meat. Weather mild and pleasant , was disappointed in taking My ride in Search of Buffalo — being obliged to use my riding Horses to haul wood.

Friday 29 — Started B. Dufond to the Yanctonas — haveing abandoned all hopes of seeing any Sioux at this place. Charboneau returned from the Gros Ventres — Weather changeable though mild.

Saturday 30th — Two Young Mandans came down from the Camp, they bring the cheering inteligence of Buffalo being very plenty — cold day.

Sunday 31st — Last day of a long gloomy Month. God send the next may be more agreeable. Heard from our Hunters Cattle plenty, beginning to look out anxiously for the Express from St. Louis.

[FEBRUARY, 1836]

Monday 1st — One of the Men belonging to Premeau & Co came up this Evening who brings the melancholy inteligence of Premeau's[413] death . He was Killed by the Yanctonas a few Miles below Apple River. The Indians pillaged all their goods — and my informant thinks it highly probable that Old Bijou and the other Men who remained behind has been murdered also. But as he recived a blow with a tomahawk on the side of his head — which seems to have unsettled his wits, besides being thoroughly frightened, I am in hopes his Story is Somewhat exagerated. He also States that he found a [man] lieing dead in the road a few miles below this place , he was entirely naked and appears to have been recently Killed. I think it highly probable it may be Baptist Dufond who left this place a few days since for Beaver River.

Tuesday 2nd — Rode down below in search of the Man who was found murdered Yesterday, met two of Campbells Men comeing up for corn who satisfied me it was an Indian and not

Dufond — as I had supposed — they confirm the report of Premeau's death and State more over that the Yanctonas are behaveing in a most outragious Manner — and that there is no security for either life or property amongst them.   Both Indians & whites are Starving below.

Wednesday 3rd — The Express from St Louis arrived late this evening — lots of news — busy making preparations to Send to Ft. Union in the morning.

Thursday 4th — Started the Express to Fort Union — also to Fort Pierre — Two Men of the opposition party came up from below — have not heard the news . Weather remarkably pleasant.

Friday 5th — Day warm and windy — an Indian who came down from the camp States that my Hunters have plenty of meat and will be in tomorrow.

Saturday 6th — No news from any quarter — warm pleasant day — The Hunters are expected in tomorrow.

Sunday 7th — Warm and windy — Mr. May returned to the Fort. Indians report Buffalo plenty on the North Side of the River — I was much disappointed on account of my hunters not returning to day.

Monday 8th — My Hunters arrived late this evening well loaded with Meat. They State that the Cattle was in great abundance near the *l'Ours qui danse*[414] on the north Side of the River — the Indians all broke up their hunting camp and came in to the Village,   Snow Storm in the Evening.

Tuesday 9th — Mr. Chapman made an offer to sell out his Stock to the Company — we could not agree on terms. Halcro[415] returned from the Yellow Stone — No news except the death of Micheal Gravell who was Killed by the Blackfeet near the head waters of Milk River.[416] Boulie came down to get a train to move his goods to the summer Village. Cold day —

Wednesday 10th — Cold Stormy day — nothing new.

Thursday 11 — Mr. May haveing become disatisfied with his

liveing concluded to make one of our family. Slight fall of snow during the day — Evening clear — Bonteur returned from the Gros Ventres no news.

Friday 12th — Made preparations for sending up P. Garrow in the morning with a Small equipment to trade with the Assiniboines — Hoping in the mean time he may not be able to find them.

Saturday 13th — Started P. Garreau to the Assiniboines to trade Snow during the Evening —

Sunday 14th — Mild Beautiful Weather . The Indians went across the River in search of Cattle — but returned late in the Evening without haveing seen any — Extremely lonesome and low Spirited — I hardly know how to account for it, but I have always found Sunday to be the dullest and longest day in the week — that is — the Sundays spent in the Indian Country — I suppose it is because we are apt to contrast the scene with that of civilized life — when Kin and acquaintances all assemble at the sound of the *church going bell* — Although the solemn tolling of a church bell — never possessed much attraction for me, (only so far as Served to announce the time and place - where bright eyes were to be seen.) But I could not help feeling this evening — (Whilst gazing round on this dreary, Savage waste,) That could I at this moment hear even the tinkling of a sheep bell — much less the Solemn toll of the church going bell, that the joyful Sound would repay Me for whole Months of privation. Alas, how little do we suspect during our halcyon days of Youth — Surrounded by all that can cheer our gloomy path through life, what Years of Sorrow are Yet in Store, But I will not repine for joys that is past and gone.

' For joys that is past let us never repine,
, ,Nor grieve for the days of auld lang syne, ,

Monday 15 — Fine day — took a long and solitary walk, I am not however sufficiently melancholy or romantic to agree with the indolent poet, who says —

> *How calm and quiet a delight,*
> *It is — alone to read and meditate and write,*
> *To ride, walk, or sleep at one's ease,*
> *Pleasing a Mans self,*
> *None others to displease,*

Tuesday 16th — Old Bigeau arrived from below late this evening have had no opportunity to hear news — the Indians say he has come up for horses to bring goods to this place , Indians all Started hunting cross the River.

Wednesday 17th — The Hunters Started across the River in search of Cattle . Warm sultry day — rain in the P. M.

Thursday 18th — Two Young Mandans came in from the Hunters Camp. They State that the west wind which has prevailed for several days — and drove the Smoke of the Village to the east have chased all the Cattle out of the neighbourhood, Remarkably warm,

Friday 19th — Warm and sultry Several showers of rain during the day — which is the 2nd time I have ever witnessed such weather at this Season during my residence on the upper Missouri.

Saturday 20 — The Hunters returned — brought in three cows — report Buffalo plenty on on the North Side of the River. Weather continues remarkably warm.

Sunday 21st — Fine Weather continues Same as Yesterday — No news from any quarter — Beaver Hunters preparing to Start out on the Spring hunt.

Monday 22nd — Rode up to the Gros Ventre Village found the Indians all in the Summer Village — the Ice having become too rotten for them to remain longer on the N. Side. Drank a glass of grog to the health of our glorious old Washington, this being his birth day,

Tuesday 23rd — Cold and cloudy — Dean[417] came up from Apple River for corn, all Starving below — neither Cattle or Indians no news from the lower Sioux, —

Wednesday 24th — Can find nothing to record worthy the attention of Posterity — unless the fact of an Indian horse falling down the bank and breaking his neck - may be so considered — This however I leave to be decided by the learned.

Thursday 25th — Sent Dean — Ortibise's Man back with corn, Snow — in the Evening   appearance of cold weather,

Friday 26th — Chapmans Men returned from below — have not been able to collect any news from them,   cold & Cloudy,   I am much surprised at hearing nothing from the Yellow Stone My Men haveing been gone near a Month,

Saturday 27th — The Express returned from Fort Union — No news,   The Men report plenty of Buffalo on the River

Sunday 28 — Wrote letters to send below in the morning   the Opposition started two Men to the Assiniboines,   a party of Gros Ventres paid a Visit to the Fort.   Mandans commenced erecting fortifications round the Village,

Monday 29th — The last day of a long gloomy winter ,   I have Spent many a winter in the Indian Country — and the Monotonous dulness of preciding Seasons have possibly been erased from the tablets of my Memory — But I am certain I never spent a more unpleasant one, take it all in all, than the last.   God send better times for the future,

[MARCH, 1836]

Tuesday 1st — Hail gentle Spring, I greet thee with feelings of the most heartfelt delight,   Although in this dreary region there are no green flowery Meads — or sweet singing birds, no balmy breezes loaded with the fragrant odour of regenerated nature, No romantic or love sick swains, no lovely wood nymphs, or in short anything else to Beautify this favourite Season, But though art no less welcome,

Wednesday 2nd — Rode up to the Gros Ventre Village for the

purpose of giveing a feast. Met the greater part of them comeing down to dance at the Mandans,   the feast was consequently
postponed.

Thursday 3 — Two Beaver hunters Newman and Adams —
Started out on their Spring hunt. The Gros Ventres who came
down Yesterday remained to dance in the Village. Great change
in the weather since Yesterday — remarkably warm and windy
— the water is rising rapidly over the Ice, So that we will soon
be unable to Haul wood from the opposite Side.

(*Friday*) *4th* — Cold Stormy day — the water which rose over
the Ice Yesterday was froze over this morning So as to prevent
the carts from crossing to haul wood

Saturday 5th — Rode up to the Gros Ventres and gave a feast
to the Indians — Delorm[418] arrived from Yanctonas   Still
Stavring [*Sic*] in that quarter.

Sunday 6th — Cold windy day.   Vallie[419] and family left for
Fort Union — with the Intention of hunting in company with
the other half breeds — Indians report Buffalo plenty on the
little Missouri — Very unwell during the day.

Monday 7th — Slight fall of Snow, calm and warm,   no news.

Tuesday 8th — Cold Stormy day — no appearance of Spring.

Wednesday 9th — Our cow had a fine calf — An event that
was celebrated with much rejoicing,   cold as usual — Boulie
came down from the Gros Ventres with news that the whole Village had gone out to make Meat —

Thursday 10th — Sent up Old Charboneau to the Gros Ventre
Village to ascertain the truth of Boulie's report. He in part
corroborated his story, but I concluded to leave the goods in the
Village. Several Mandans Started to join the Gros Ventres in
their hunting excursion. Cold weather still continues.

Friday 11th — No news,   cold as usual.

Saturday 12th — Rode up to the Gros Ventre Village to ascertain the truth of the report that the Indians were all leaving,
concluded to leave the goods.

Sunday 13th — Calm mild day,   Two Men belonging to the Opposition came up from below, report Buffalo in great abundance at Apple River, but no Indians

Monday 14th — Collected Several eggs to day — the first this Season,   weather continues cold and windy.

Tuesday 15th — Settled with one of the few men who purposes Starting out hunting in a day or two,   no appearance of Spring, heartily tired of winter

Wednesday 16th — Tremendious Snow Storm during the day, Engaged Delorm till the arrival of the S. Boat

Thursday 17th — Stormy windy day — one of our horses perished with cold and poverty — had a glass of Milk for supper — and great luxury in this country

Friday 18th — Calm beautiful day — and was it not for the Snow which is now a foot deep — would look something like Spring — no news.

Saturday 19th — River commenced rising — cold & windy — Old Charboneau went up to the Gros Ventres.

Sunday 20th — Cold Snowy day — river continues rising notwithstanding the weather has been very cold for the last 20 days — It must be caused by the breaking up of the ice near the Mountains.

Monday 21st — Old Charboneau returned from the Gros Ventres — Indians still absent making Meat — Weather continues cold as usual

Tuesday 22nd — Warm sun shiny day — no news.

Wednesday 23 — Weather moderately warm — snow melted in the P.M.   Indians came in from hunting camp,   plenty meat.

Thursday 24th — Windy disagreeable day — all appearance of spring has again vanished — Indians report Cattle plenty a few miles below.

Friday 25th — Great change in the weather — a warm South wind has prevailed during the day — the Snow has disappeared from the prairies as if by Magic,   each ravine or gully has become a roaring torrent. Several flocks of ducks passed over in the morning. The Sure harbingers of Spring — we are all delighted with the change. Started Delorm out Hunting with Six poor horses and one Man.

Saturday 26 — Our Hunters returned unsuccessful — haveing found no Buffalo in the S Side of the River — they Saw great quantities on the opposite Side but found the ice too weak to cross the Horses — fine weather.

Sunday 27th — Calm Beautiful day — Sold a white Buffalo robe to a Mandan — (the Wounded face) for thirty robes and two Horses.

Monday 28th — River commenced rising — Several flocks of geese passed over — delightful weather.

Tuesday 29 — fine weather Still continues River rising

Wednesday 30th — River rising rapidly — prospect of the ice breaking up during the night — Weather continues fine,

Thursday 31 — The Ice broke up in fine stile — beautiful day, all in high Spirits, although we have no Meat.

APRIL, 1836

Friday 1st — Calm beautiful day. Ice runing very thick in the River — The Indians had great Sport in catching buffalo that was floating down on the ice — a few were still living having taken their Station on large masses of ice — traveled very quickly down Stream. But the greater part that was hauled on Shore had been previously drowned. It is astonishing the feats of hardy dexterity that was performed by some of the Young Men in pursuit of the loathsome Meat. They would boldly embark on the first piece of floating ice that approached the Shore, and Springing from piece to piece - or swiming when the distance was too great to leap, would generally succeed in fastning a cord round the horns — and towing the carcase to shore.[420] Sent out my hunters and horses in search of cattle.

Saturday 2nd — River rose Several feet during the day,   calm beautiful weather — our Hunters not Yet returned .

Sunday 3rd — Windy disagreeable day — rain at night — Killed Thirty four rats — no news of the Hunters, —

Monday 4th — May Started below in a cannoe intending to trap Beaver between this and St. Louis.   The Hunters returned well loaded having found plenty of Cattle.   Our warehouses having become very leaky - I commenced re-covering them with dirt and straw.   The Indians Killed a great number of Cattle only a few miles below the Fort,

Tuesday 5th — Went up to the Gros Ventre Village,   returned late in the evening much fatigued.   Indians not Yet returned from Making Meat.   The Mandans caught caught [*sic*] a great quantity of Buffalo — that were drowned in the River.

Wednesday 6 — Rain in the forenoon — the wolves eat one of our Mules — cold north wind — finished covering the warehouses.

Thursday 7th — Tremendious Snow Storm during the whole day.   My chimny smoked so bad that it was impossible to have fire in my room - so that I have been shivering with cold since morning,   to complete the unlucky day all of our horses are missing — supposed to be Stolen by the Sioux, this is truly a day of *Malheur* .

Friday 8th — Found our horses this morning, two of which we sold to the Indians,   cold and clear — we have great dificulty in pro curring fire wood the point below the Fort being all under water.

Saturday 9 — Clear and cold — I am much surprised at hearing no news from Fort Union — which is all that detains me at this dreary place — traded a quantity of ducks and geese from the Indians.

Sunday 10th — Halcro arrived from white earth[421] River — bringing down his packs in a skin cannoe.   He was unable to give any news from Fort Union — not haveing seen any of our people since Garrow left him in February.   I still remain impatiently waiting to hear from above previous to my leaving for Fort Pierre.[422] Weather cold and windy.

Lord have mercy on us — Amen —

Monday 11th[423] — Cloudy disagreeable day — appearance of snow or rain — Extremely lonesome.

Tuesday 12th — Warm and windy — put up goods to send to the Gros Ventres tomorrow.

Wednesday 13th — Sent goods to the Gros Ventres — The Indians still absent making meat, Weather Same as Yesterday, no news from above.

Thursday 14 — commenced pressing packs — B. Lebrun Started Hunting — The Mandans danced the Bull dance in the fort. fine day —

Friday 15th — Finished making up our packs — 136 packs of Robes and 4 of Beaver traded up to this date, had a repetition of the Bull dance this Evening.

Saturday 16th — Commenced raining about noon - Strong E. wind and has continued till the present time with unabated violence — broke our press — so that we were unable to finish pressing our packs ,

+*Sunday 17th* — I mark this day with a cross — it being one of the longest and most lonely I ever spent. The rain continued last evening till 10 oclock when it changed to a Snow Storm which lasted till 2 oclock P.M. to day The Snow is now lieing near a foot deep and but little more appearance of Spring than there was three months since, I am out of all patience though it is said all things are for the best and I must try to comfort myself in this Christian belief. no news from above — Thy will be done *Amen*

Monday 18th — The Indians who had been absent since the middle making dry Meat (at the Little Missouri) came down in skin cannoes loaded with Meat Robes &c —

Tuesday 19th — Calm beautiful day — Made preparations for sending out hunting in the morning — no news —

Wednesday 20th — rode up to the Gros Ventre Village in compliance with an invitation of the Indians who purposed making a collection of meat for me — found them rather nigerdly in their contributions.   Sent out Delorm in Search of Cattle,   appearance of more Snow.

Thursday 21st — windy in the morning — calm pleasant P.M. took a long Solitary walk duck hunting   Killed only one.   The Hunters returned found plenty Cattle.   No news, as usual

Friday 22nd — Last night a small party of Sioux came to the Fort and beged to come in — but fearing that I should not be able to protect them from the hostility of Mandans I refused them admitance — they departed without doing any mischief — they even refrained from Stealing horses though their was Several in the prairies.

Gave a feast to the two Mandan Villages   Made a speech[424] of four hours, which amply compensated in length and prolixity what it lacked in force or eloquence,   calm beautiful day,

Saturday 23 — Stormy   disagreeable   day — appearance   of snow,

Sunday 24th — Mr. McKinzie arrived at the Fort in the Evening — having left his boat above the Gros Ventres detained by wind — The boat is expected tomorrow,

Sunday 25th [*sic*] — Stormy disagreeable day — The wind which has prevailed for several days Still keeps us port bound The boat arrived from above about 10 A.M. —

J O U R N A L for

Fort Clark

June 18th 1836

\# 3

June[425]

Saturday 18 — The Steam Boat left here to day for the Yellow Stone with Messrs McKinzie, Mitchell, and the Agent on board — Newman and Co. arrived yesterday from their beaver hunt (1 pack) — report Buffaloe close —

Sunday 19 — Rain — Prepared an equipment for the Gros Ventres —

Monday 20 — Bullé started for the Gros Ventres with a few goods — Delorme and Lady accompanied with Mr Durant left here to day for Red River, in the North — Charboneau left the Fort, prefering to stay in the Village —

Tuesday 21 — Mandans went out after Meat — Cleaned out and arrainged the goods in the ware house — a war party of Mandans arrived from the North — haveing stole one Horse —

Wednesday 22 — Rode up to the Gros Ventres,   they do not seem disposed to trade, as they wish to trade at the Opposition prices, however — (let them sweat)   I have heard to day that Durant gave over the idea of going to the North —

Thursday 23 — Started out early with 2 Men and 4 Horses in search of meat,   found cattle in abundance in 20 miles of the Fort, arrived at home late in the evening with 2 fat cows — and one Bull,   got a fall from my horse, and broke my gun —

Friday 24 — Strong wind from the S.W. all day — The Gros Ventres gave us a dance — One of My Men sick —

Saturday 25 — Had a talk with the Principel Men of the Gros Ventres &c. — the Mandans started out in the evening after Meat — since the departure of the Steam Boat the water has fallen three feet —

Sunday 26 — Sent Lachapelle up to the Gros Ventres for News — Mandans arrived loaded with Meat — Lachapelle arrived   No News in that quarter,   trade going on slow —

Monday 27 — Strong S. East wind since 4 days — Water continues falling — a Bull Made his appearance on the sand bar opposite the Fort —

Tuesday 28 — Strong wind from the S. East all day — slight rain in the evening .

Wednesday 29 — The water riseing fast — windy —

Thursday 30 — Morning clear,   Steam Boat Diana arrived about breakfast time from Fort Union, Report the death of the Deshaw family and *Jack Ram,*   which took place on the 26th Inst, by way of worshiping the *Lords Day* ,[426] — Shipped 302 Packs of Robes & 4 Packs of Beaver on the Dianna, — Steam Boat Departed about 11 oClk for St. Louis,   Lachappell embarked on her for the Little Missouri, [Bad River] Sprinkled with rain about 8 O,Clk, bal: of the day fine & Pleasant

Killed *82* Rats this month.

— July 1836

Friday 1 — Morning clear and fine , — sprinkled with rain at 2 P.M. — The Indians went out to hunt for Buffalo, but returned in haste, and report a war party of Soux — It is doubted by some — after the sprinkle of rain, the balance of the evening was fine and pleasant —

Saturday 2 — Morning clear and warm — the war party discovered on Yesterday was a band of Buffalo — All hands out surrounding to day - returned again   killed as many as they wanted. Buffalo in abundance — Michael Belhumeres horse fell with him, had like to have broken his neck, but fortunately, no mischief done him — they left soon in the morning, and returned again at 10 OClock — 4 OClock P.M. some wind and small shower of rain,   before oppressively warm, now pleasant — sun set clear — Newmas[*sic*] wife run off , he went to the Village armed like a Don Quixotte, determined to bring her back dead or alive brot her and the whole family down, had a talk when she concluded to stay at least one night more —

Sunday 3 — Morning Clear, windy, and cold for the Season —

12 OClock Cloudy and windy — River falling — the Rise being from the Yellow Stone — The Village is getting uneasy about the war partizans which have been absent about 33 days — Newmas wife has now left him positively he seems to think that marrying here, is not the thing it is cracked up to be.   only married 15 days and his wife deserted him —

July 4 — All out to surround again. Morning Clear and calm. The Agent went to the Gros Ventres to make them their presents,   sent with him Monto, and Bazil[427] rigged off with cart and bull — all went on well until they came to the first hollow, there the Bull refused positively to pull up the hill, they had to unload and *portage* the presents up and hall the cart themselves — this was the case at every one from that out — at the last however, the fellow became so very obstinate, as to fall on his neck and it was near twenty minutes before he could be got off it — after extricating him, he lay with his head down the hill untill the whole *"jolly crew"* Cordelled the Cart to the top, and again returned to him; when, after a handy use of the cudgel by Montó, he was again on his feet, and after cordilling him up, they proceeded without any further difficulty, they and these that went to surround all returned again, about 4 OClk, the hunters having had good luck — Mandans of the little Village also out Surrounding, returned and reported having seen 5 Sioux, which was a lie - I have no doubt — Prairie a fire at the point of the timber — We had our bitters to day which is more than we had 12 months ago —

July 5 — Morning clear and warm — Agent made his presents to the Mandans — Five boats arrived from the Yellow Stone for St. Louis — No News in that quarter —

Wednesday 6 — Last Night between 11 and 12 oclock, I was allarmed by some one Knocking at the gate. I immediately got up and found it to be 4 Sioux, come in quest of a Straggling scalp — I gave them a few balls and powder and desired them to depart, which they did — this Morning the praries are all on fire, made by the war party of last night — The Boats from Fort Union left here at 7 O'clock, with the Agent on board bound for St Louis — May success attend them — the Mandans from the little Village moved their camp — for fear of an attack from the Sioux —

Thursday 7 — Rain — News from the Gros Ventres of a small bande of Men and Women, out after berries haveing been Killed — two young Men arrived in the evening from the Gros-Ventres, false report —

Friday 8 — All the Mandans of the little Village and some few from the Gros Ventres, have come to settle themselves in the lower Village anticipating an attack from the Sioux — Started out early on discovery — came back at 12'O'clock with out success —

Saturday 9 — Pleasant and Cool for the season — No News from any quarter —

Sunday 10 — Weather cold — so much so that winter clothing we find very comfortable, rain at 12 O'clock — with a strong north east wind — a bande of Cows showed themselves on the hill below — all hands out to surround — the Mandans returned in the evening with plenty of Meat —

Monday 11 — Commenced makeing hay — arrainged the Hay Carts — Discovered enemies on the opposite side of the river, supposed to be horse thieves.

Tuesday 12 — Indians all out after berries — News of cattle being plenty in the neighborhood —

Wednesday 13 — Cold for the season — Rain — Gave a feast to the Old Bull band in hopes of getting them to go out after meat — a bande of Cows hove in sight — sent Mitchel and Garreau with 4 pack horses to run them, the hunters arrived late with the meat of two fat Bulls —

Thursday 14 — Cloudy — Some few Mandans who went out after berries, came back at full speed — haveing saw enemies — about six miles from the Fort — had my horses in the Fort all day — heavy rain in the afternoon —

Friday 15 — Early this morning I was surprised to hear the report of a cannon at the Village, on enquirey I found that the

Mandans are exercising on a four pounder that they have - expecting an attack from the Sioux — the enemies that have been hovering around the Village since three or four days - have at last made their way off with a Mandan scalp (The Hawk's foot) who was guarding his horse at the mouth of the *Riviere qui barre* —

Saturday 16 — Last night we had a severe storm with thunder and lightning — the weather continues Cloudy — Durant went up to the Gros-Ventres, to day to cheat some one, in the sale of a horse —

Sunday 17 — Weather clear and pleasant — at 9 O'clock A.M. Strong North east Wind — five Bulls hove in sight — the Mandans run them and Killed three — 6 P. M. - Newman and Adams left here for their fall hunt—

Monday 18 — Strong N. E. Wind as usual — Weather clear — trade going on brisk to day —

Tuesday 19 — One of the warmest days we have had this summer —

Wednesday 20 — Started out early in search of cattle,   Arrived at home at 4 O.Clock P.M. without success —

Thursday 21 — Cloudy — In the afternoon we had a fine race between three celebrated Horses of this Country — Grey legs — Laidlaw's Grey — and Kipp — One Mile heat — Grey leg came in 15 feet in front of the Grey — Kipp 60 yards — distanced — sprinkled with rain in the evening —

Friday 22 — Sent the Hunters out after meat — they arrived in the evening with three cows — report Cattle plenty in 20 Miles of the Fort —

Saturday 23 — Fine pleasant day — No news from the war party, which have been out 54 days —

Sunday 24 — Rain — Report of a bande of cattle being close — as some one heard the belowing of some Bulls — all hands out in search — Weather continues cloudy — with frequent drops of rain — false report about Cattle —

Monday 25 — An Indian started out after breakfast on discovery — came back and said that he had saw a bande of cattle close — All hands out after Meat — after galloping from 10 in the Morning untill 3 in the Afternoon, we arrived at home, without Meat — and Much jolted with our ride —

Tuesday 26 — Started out early with 4 horses, found cattle in 25 Miles of the Fort — slept out and caught a heavy rain — J. Beckworth[428] with 2 Men arrived from the Yellow Stone —

Wednesday 27 — Got up at day light — wet to the skin from last Nights ducking — arrived at the Fort at 10 O'Clock A. M. with plenty of good fat Meat — rain in the afternoon —

Thursday 28 — Beckworth & Co. started for St. Louis[429] — sent P. Garreau with them as far as the Little Misso. [Bad River] with letters to Mr Papin[430] — the river riseing — shower of rain in the afternoon — sent Durant up to the Gros Ventres for news &c —

Friday 29 — Clear in the Morning — at 10 A.M. heavy thunder storm — commenced hauleing hay —

Saturday 30 — The Mandans have given up all hopes for the return of the War Party — haveing been out sixty days — 28 in number — a number of Gros-Ventres arrived for the purpose of performing at the cerimony — crying for the dead, cutting themselves &c. &c — rain to day —

Sunday 31 — Several Mandans started out last evening in search of Cattle — at 9 - Strong North east wind — the Mandans returned with plenty of Meat — report Cattle to be in thirty Miles of the Fort — fighting and quarreling with the women of the concern — Number of Rats Killed this month 201 —

June	July
82	201

O there is Colonel Johnson, a Man very dark,
And he pretend to shine, vid old General Clark
                                   Jim Crow[431]

1836, August 1st. 31 Days —

Monday 1st — Fine clear Morning - 8 A. M. — North West wind with rain - 5 P. M — Clear - at sun down   four Mandans started out after Meat — Rain —

Tuesday 2 — Last Night we were visited by a small party of Yanctons consisting of nine Men — after a little parly they asked some tobacco which I gave them, and they departed — the Village are uneasy about those that left here last evening — to day our best friend left us (The Little black) who was bought by a Gros-Ventre for thirty Robes and 10 Beaver Skins 18lbs Rain —

Wednesday 3 — Finished makeing one stack of Hay — 30 Loads — Mandans started out in the evening after Meat — sent two Men and three horses with them — rain —

Thursday 4 — Appearance of fine weather — all the wives out after berries — the Indians arrived with plenty of meat — report cattle far off —

Friday 5 — Strong south wind — sprinkled with rain in the afternoon — Charboneau's Grey horse came back from hauling with a strained ancle —

Saturday 6 — Indians all out after berries — eat sweet corn to day for the first time this year — rain in the afternoon —

Sunday 7 — Heavy rain all last night — Weather unsettled , several showers of rain throughout the day —

Monday 8 — Strong east wind — with rain — Wind and Water is against me this year — as it seems almost impossible to finish my hay — stormy and disagreeable all day — and likely to continue so a week or two — however we must put up with it,   and take it as it comes — good, bad or indifferent — like good Christians.

Tuesday 9 — Weather unsettled — the wind has changed to the North-West —

Wednesday 10 — Heavy rain in the morning — Fine weather

at 10 — Indians all out on the opposite side of the river, after berries — the river riseing —

Thursday 11 — Strong South East Wind — a Mandan found a bar of lead — 70lbs — at the Old Fort,[432] supposed to have been covered over with dirt &c. at the time they abandoned the place — I sell no lead to him this year! rain —

Friday 12 — The first pleasant day that we have had this week —

Saturday 13 — Heavy rain all day — two Mandans that left here the 11th. inst. arrived to day with four horses loaded with Meat — cattle scarce on the North side of the river — Hale in the evening —

Sunday 14 — The bad weather still continues — being out of fresh Meat - I determined sending Mitchel with one Man, and three horses, out after Meat — they left here at 5 O'Clock — the Mandans also started out hunting on the north side —

Monday 15 — Fine Morning — Occupied the Men drying the hay from last week's rain — Mitchel arrived with the Meat of three cows — strong south wind at 1.P.M.

Tuesday 16 — Overhauled all the robes in the warehouse, found several of them wet — strong wind from the south since yesterday — Garreau & Co arrived from Fort Pierre haveing been absent 20 Days — the Mandans arrived from the other side, with fresh Meat — report Cattle far off, and scarce —

Wednesday 17 — Busy all day writeing letters to Fort Pierre — and putting up some few articles for   Do.
Set the Men to Mowing hay — the Mandans are uneasy about the War party, they have paid J. Andrews to Make his Medicine,[433] to Know wether they are dead or alive — they gave him robes, scarlet, and a Kittle,   after being in his Medicine lodge one hour — he informed them that the (party war) was yet alive — that in four days we would have an eclipse of the sun — that Newman and Adams were Killed — and that a large war party of Assinniboines & Crees were to attack the Gros Ventres — and that at New Orleans there was a very distructive fire, or as the

New York papers says — dreadfull calamity — or awfull con-
fligration —

Thursday 18 — A bande of Saons arrived to day to smoke
with the Mandans — two or three of the young Mandans, was
for Killing them, but was prevented by the others — who took
their arms from them —

Friday 19 — Some few Mandans went out hunting, sent 2
Men and 4 Horses with them. C. Brazeau[434] & Co started for
Fort Pierre — the Saons went up to pay a visit to the Gros
Ventres —

Saturday 20 — Rain last Night — Strong North west wind —
the Saons returned from the Gros Ventres well pleased the
Mandans gave them little or nothing, except a great many good
words— Overhauled the ledger in the ware house, and found
they do not agree with the Inventory — Garreau arrived from
hunting — without meat —

Sunday 21 — The Saons left here early for their camp —
Frost for the first time this year —

Monday 22 — A small war party of Yanctons came to the Fort
last night — I let two of them in the Fort — had a smoke with
them — gave them a few twists of tobacco — and they started —
smoky weather — the praries are on fire both sides of the river.

Tuesday 23 — Sent out my hunters with six pack horses —
Allert in the Village last night —

Wednesday 24 — A young Woman died at the Village last
Night — or more properly speaking, was Killed by the *Doctors*
— The hunters arrived at 10. A. M. with the Meat of 5 fat
cows — Finished hauleing hay from the Fountaine,[435]

Thursday 25 — Strong south wind — set two Men to cut axel-
trees for my carts , to be in readiness for the Yancton Camp —
Put up some few goods for the Gros Ventres —

Friday 26 — Sent A. Dasseau up to the Gros Ventres with a
small Eqp^t — to Collect a few Robes — the Mandans arrived

with fresh Meat from the North side of the river — report cattle far off —

Saturday 27 — All's quiet! —

Sunday 28 — To day is the time specified by J. Andrews, for the arrival of the Wounded face, and his party — they have not made their appearance — the Mandans have now given them up' as lost — We hear Nothing at the Village but Men & Women crying — Children squalling — and dogs barking — all Mixed together Makes a first rate Bedlam — Durant arrived from the Gros Ventres — No News in that quarter —

Monday 29 — Sent out my hunters with five pack horses — sent P. Garreau to the Gros Ventres to take the place of Bullé , who wishes to go out Beaver hunting — Bullé arrived from the Gros Ventres,   trade going on slow,   but sure, in that quarter — haveing traded but 23 Robes — the hunters arrived with 3 cows —

Tuesday 30 — Set the Men a chopping fire wood — The Cerimony for crying, and cutting, for the *Dead,*[436] was performed at the Village to day — Men, Women and Children, bellowing like so many Bedlamites, the Mandans arrived with fresh Meat — Committed fortification to day and got a Whipping from my beloved *Wife,* for my trouble — Oh poor Me — the Cerimony at the Village continued all day —

Wednesday 31 — Cool and pleasant weather — A. Dusseau and Durant, started for their fall hunt, on Knife river,   May success attend them — ½ hour after their departure they returned, haveing saw two Mandans on the hill, and took them to be enemies . Bullé has determined to talk no more about hunting — he has taken up his axe and made his way to the woods — As for Durant he is a poor *Devil,* Make the best of him, as he cannot for his life leave his *squaw* — for fear of some one running away with her — 4 Gros Ventres that accompanied the Saons to their camp on the 21st inst arrived to day,   arriveing at the Saon camp, some few Yanctons who are encamped with them, were intent on Killing them, but the timely interference of the Saons,

saved them, they say that the *Boeuf long* wounded a Yancton —
three Saons accompanied the Gros-Ventres to their Village —
Killed 168 Rats this Month — total 451 —

1836 — SEPTEMBER 30 DAYS

Thursday 1st — Two Saons arrived to day, report their Camp
close by — Distributed out traps to the Mandans — Indians all
out after Meat —

Friday 2 — Sent one cart to the Gros Ventres to bring home
Garreau — the Cart arrived in the afternoon with 40 Robes —
put up some few goods for the Saon camp —

Saturday 3 — Sent Garreau with three carts to the Saon Camp
on one of the Forks of Cannon Ball River —Durant started out
Beaver hunting with several Mandans on Mouse River[437] —

Sunday 4 — Cloudy — Weather cool, cleared off at 10 — fine
weather the rest of the day, the Mandans got through with their
cerimony of crying for their departed Friends —

Monday 5 — Strong south wind — The Praries are all on fire,
impossible to see the hills, on account of the thick smoke. No
doubt but the Yanctons are near at hand, as we expect an attack
from them every day — feast to the Mandans

Tuesday 6 — Had green peas, and potatoes for dinner to day,
the Mandans busy gathering their corn, for fear that the Yanctons will gather it for them, Which they have threatened to do —

Wednesday 7 — Cloudy — Strong south west wind — Indians
arrived from hunting on the North side of the river, report cattle in abundance near at hand — at 5 P. M. we had a shower of
rain —

Thursday 8 — Rain continued all night — cold and disagreeable weather, no wood in the Fort, and no prospects of getting
any, until the return of my carts from the Saon Camp.

Friday 9 — Durant and several Mandans, that left here on the
3rd inst to trap beaver - returned last evening - haveing saw
enemies, they Caught but 3 Beavers — Indians all out after

Meat on the North side, Sold my Old White *Mare* for 13 Robes.[438]

Saturday 10 — Strong south wind all day — 24 Rees arrived to day from their Village,   they say they are encamped at the Black Hills,   the Mandans are overjoyed to see them,   they were received with Kissing - crying, and hugging[439] — the Mandans arrived from hunting with plenty of fresh Meat —

Sunday 11 — Rain all last Night,   Feast to the Rees — Strong North Wind, and rain,   traded from the Mandans 19 Fine cat fish — Bought a Mule from the *Aricarees* —

Monday 12 — The Rees started early this Morning to pay a Visit to the Gros-Ventres, Not for the Love they have for them, but on a begging excursion,

Tuesday 13 — Strong North west Wind, and rain — the Rees returned from the Gros-Ventres well pleased!   Garreau arrived from the Saon Camp, with 100 pcs. Meat and 80 Robes — 10 Saons accompanied him — We received the News of the War party of 28 — (the Wounded face) partizans, they were all Killed by the Yanctons, after a well fought battle,   9 Yanctons Killed and a great Many Wounded —

Wednesday 14 — Last Night a young Mandan who was crying out side of the Village, was fired on by a Yancton, but unluckily missed him,   the Gun loaded with three balls passed through his robe.   Rain and disagreeable weather all day.

Thursday 15 — The bad weather still continues,   set two Men to Make balls — Charboneau gave us a feast of Mince pie and Coffee - which was excellent —

Friday 16 — The Saons left here early this Morning for their Camp — Sent with them a Yancton woman that I bought from the Gros-Ventres,   Council with the Rees, gave them a small present of Powder, Ball and tobacco - in the name of the Agent — Sent Bullé up to the Gros-Ventres after Robes — Durant started out Beaver hunting —

Saturday 17 — Mandans prepareing to go to War, against

the Yanctons, the Gros-Ventres will go with them, the Men employed hauleing fire wood — Rain

Sunday 18 — The bad weather still continues, the Mandans arrived with plenty of fresh meat, from the North side of the river, report Cattle far off, Snow fell to-day, for the first time this year — Durant arrived from Beaver hunting, with the Meat of one cow,

Monday 19 — Durant started out for the third time to try to make some sort of a hunt — lost one of my horses in the snow storm of Yesterday, had two Men out all day looking for him, found him in the evening — Rain all day,

Tuesday 20 — The bad weather still continues, rained several times during the day — Cold North Wind, the Men Idle all day —

Wednesday 21 — The weather same as yesterday, the Mandans of the Little Village, Killed and Wounded several of their horses, (on account of their Corn fields) the war party I mentioned on the 17th has concluded not to go, as the Gros Ventres will not join with them, quarreled with the Men, for being idle in the woods —

Thursday 22 — Hard frost last Night, the fine weather has at last made its appearance, the Mandans are all out to day, after Buffaloe, on the North side, Sent one of my horses up to the lake, to spend a week or two, Set the Men chopping Wood,

Friday 23 — Sent my hunters Out, with 4 pack horses, on Knife river, two Rees left here last evening for their camp - at the Black hills, their camp will be here the 21th [*sic*] of Next Month. if not detained by bad weather, Mandans arrived from hunting , report cattle in abundance

Saturday 24 — The hunters arrived with the Meat of two bulls, No Cattle in that section of the Country, they saw but 4 Bulls, 2 of which they Killed,

Sunday 25 — One of the finest days we have had this Month, Went up to the lake in search of a lost horse, 2 Men arrived from Fort Union, on their way to S^t. Louis (J. Dupuis and Poircé)[440] — No News in the upper regions — Dupuis & Co. left in the evening —

Monday 26 — A small war party from the little Village started for the Yancton Camp.

Tuesday 27 — Windy day — the Men employed in hauleing fire wood,   sent a letter up to Fort McKinzie by a Black Foot Indian, who has been with the Mandans since the departure of the Steam Boat.   Some few Mandans Crossed the river, to encamp at the Lake below, to Make dry Meat —

Wednesday 28 — One of the Mandans that crossed the river yesterday, arrived this Morning early, saying that the rest of them,   were all Killed by the Yanctons,   30 or 40 of them Crossed over, to Visit the field of Battle,   this evening we shall learn the truth,   two others arrived in the Morning, at 2 P.M. — one squaw arrived from the field of Battle, brought no certain news, except that she made her escape in the dark, and that she heard the reports of a great many guns — those that went to Visit the Field of Battle arrived here late,   they report that they found three, Butchered and scalped, the fourth a woman, not touched by the Butchers except that she was dead, and that her infant child, was close by her side, yet alive, which they brought home, in the hurry of the fight, the enemies did not perceive her, or they would of taken her scalp with the others —

Thursday 29 — Employed one Man daubeing the house — the rest of them a chopping wood,   strong North West wind all day,

Friday 30 — A young Saon that has been here since the 13th inst - left here today for his camp - on Grand River,   Killed twenty six rats last Night — Durant arrived from hunting,

Killed 226 Rats this Month = 677 —

> *A Captain of a Steam Boat, some time ago*
> *Said dat Capt Buzard, Killed poor Jim Crow.*

1836 — OCTOBER 31 DAYS

Saturday 1st — This Month begins with Wind and rain,   Cold — Arrainged my corn scaffold —

Sunday 2 — Cloudy — the War Party that left here the 26 of last Month, arrived last evening, Without Makeing a *Coup* — Durant started again for the 4th time a Beaver hunting on Knife river —

Monday 3 — Light fall of snow in the Morning — three Mandans started Out Beaver hunting, Charboneau arrived from the Gros-Ventres — No News in that quarter, except that a Saon arrived there with a White Cow Skin to trade with the Gros-Ventres —

Tuesday 4 — Strong south east Wind,   the corn trade not yet commenced, that of Beans,   almost over,   Put up in bags to day 25 Bushels — Pincineau[441] arrived from the Yellow Stone,   No News in that quarter, except that the Assinniboines are comeing to War against the Gros-Ventres —

Wednesday 5 — Sent my hunters out with 4 pack horses, the Mandans shot my Bull for the second time, but fortuneately did not Kill him,   all the wives of the Village out after hay - to Make their Corn *Caches*[442] — traded to day 3 Robes and One Beaver Skin — the hunters arrived late, with the Meat of two Bulls —

Thursday 6 — Cloudy — the Mandans harangued in the Village to not give us any corn - to Keep it for the Rees — 3 Mandans that left here the 3rd inst arrived to day with 5 Beaver skins —

Friday 7 — Hard frost - and thick foggy Morning,   the Mandans crossed in the evening to run Buffaloe on the North side —

Saturday 8 — My Old Cook (Baptiste[443]) bought a Young Wife — Paid in cash for her $60.00 — the balance due at different times,   A visit from the G.V. — traded to day 18 Bushels of Corn —

Sunday 9 — Villeandré and Lebrun arrived from the Yellow

Stone — No News in that quarter — Villeandré returned back to the Gros-Ventres — Durant arrived from Beaver hunting, Mandans arrived from hunting,   plenty of Meat,

Monday 10 — Commenced daubeing the Fort — Settled with the Hunters for their Beaver

Tuesday 11 — Allert in the Village last Night — Alcro and his family, with 9 horses and 2 Men, arrived from the Little Misso. — got Drunk to Day in spite of myself — so glad to see one of my old friends, a Keg of two gallons — full[444] —

Wednesday 12 — The two Men that arrived yesterday — started this Morning early — in company with four others — bound for Fort Pierre — The Praries are all on fire on the North side of the River — removed in to my Winter quarters — Cut my young Bull calf —at 11 A.M. Strong North wind —

Thursday 13 — Indians all out after berries —

Friday 14 — Started out hunting with 2 Men and 6 pack horses Killed 2 Cows for supper and camped in 20 Miles of the Fort,   supped on the choise pieces —

Saturday 15 — Left camp early in the morning at 7 A.M. saw a bande of cows, between 50 and 60 — run them and Killed 4 — Started for Home at 3 P.M. — encamped in 15 Miles of the Fort —

Sunday 16 — Last Night we experienced a very severe snow storm,   a heavy rain commenced, after that a snow storm, with a North Wind,   We came very near freezeing — as we got up in the Morning entirely covered with snow, and no fire to warm ourselves,   all the Meat froze as hard as rocks, and ourselves hardly able to move,   started for home at 7 - O Clock and arrived at 3 P.M. — found all well,   arriveing at home, we took a glass of *Milk,* and a Cup of hot coffee which put us all to rights again —

Monday 17 — A small war party from the Little Village started for the Yancton camp — A Black horse that was missing some time past, was found to day,   Dead — Killed by the Mandans of the little Village

Tuesday 18 — Snow fell last Night 4 inches — feast to the Mandans, dressed the 2 Crows — (Gros Ventre.   all the wives turned out to day - and cleaned out the Fort, Mirracles [*sic*] will happen some times.

Venture arrived from the Gros-Ventres, No News in that quarter,   Durant arrived to day from hunting with 7 Beaver skins and two Otters,

Wednesday 19 — Weather clear but cold — snow last Night strong North Wind all day, — bought a Mule from the Gros Ventres,

Thursday 20 — Hunger Makes the Wolf Move — Mandans all out after Buffaloe,   traded yesterday a robe from them for Meat — the Ice commenced running in the river to day — News from the Gros-Ventres of two Beaver hunters that arrived with 40 Beaver skins, it is reported that they have pillaged the Whites —

Friday 21 — The ice running very thick in the river — Durant arrived from the Little Lake — brought with him 8 Beaver skins, and 2 Otters.

Saturday 22 — The Mandans arrived with plenty of fresh Meat — sent 5 of my horses in the Point of Woods below, traded a few Beaver skins from the Gros-Ventres, (marked M.C.) No doubt they have Kill'd and pillaged Old Carriere,[445] who was hunting on Powder river[446] — discharged my Indian horse gard.

Sunday 23 — Shower of rain last night. This Morning early the Mandans found 4 prs Moccossins at the Little River, suposed to have been left there by a war party of Yanctons,   the war-party that left here the 17th inst arrived to day haveing saw no enemies. Snow & rain all day.

Monday 24 — Weather Cloudy — 2 Beaver hunters (Indian) arrived to day with   Beaver skins — sold one of my Indian Poney's for 10 Beaver —

Tuesday 25 — Sent my hunters Out with 6 pack horses , strong south wind at 3 P.M.   Durant started Out for the sixth time a Beaver hunting on Knife river,   the Mandans Killed one of my Dogs —

Wednesday 26 — Two young Men (Rees) left here last evening to hunt for the Ree camp, which is on the way to this place since last Month —

Thursday 27 — The Gros Ventres moved up to their Winter quarters,   the two (Rees) that left here the 25th inst. returned back to day — Durant arrived from hunting with three Beaver skins (6th time)

Friday 28 — Cleared Out the retail Store, Weighed my Beaver — 150*lbs* — My hunters arrived with the Meat of 4 Cows and 1 Bull — Cattle far off —

Saturday 29 — Cold North West Wind — the Mule that I bought the 19th inst, was taken back by its owner to day — (Indian fashion,)   Sold one of my Indian Poneys for 10 Beaver sks - and 2 Robes,   News from the Gros-Ventres,   Battle between them and the Assinniboines, One on each side Killed —

Sunday 30 — Received as a present to day from Mitchel, a Bottle of good Old *Baptiste,*

Monday 31 — The wives of the Village all busy in crossing to the other side, to build their winter huts,   several Lodges will also winter in the Point of Woods below — and some in their summer Village , Killed 294 Rats this Month = 971 —

> *Ov all de Black Niggars, I want you for to No*
> *Dat I am de Nigger, to jump Jim Crow* —
>
> *I wheel about, I turn about, I do just so,*
> *O Never Mind de Vedder, so de wind dont Blow.*

1836   NOVEMBER 30 DAYS

Tuesday 1st — One of the finest days we have had since the 20th of last Month — No News from any quarter — 3 Beaver hunters arrived from below — No Cattle in that section of the

Country — This day[447] being a Holliday with the French, nothing in the way of work going on to day —

Wednesday 2 — Several Mandans that left here three days ago, in search of cattle, arrived last night — haveing saw but six Bulls which they Killed .

Thursday 3 — One of my horses that has been lost since 20 days, was found to day by the Mandans , they refuse to give him up —

Friday 4 — An axe that was stolen from the Men, two days ago, was brought back this Morning — Durant started for the 7th time a Beaver hunting — Mandans Out after Meat — the Indians delivered me my lost horse — Rain at 1 P.M.

Saturday 5 — Sprinkled with rain in the afternoon — Mandans arrived with Meat — it is rumoured in the Village that the Assinneboines have stolen all the Horses of the Gros Ventres — Rain —

Sunday 6 — Mandans arrived with fresh Meat,   report Cattle scarce,   Durant, as usual arrived with a little fresh Meat (a Bull) that he Killed on his way Out Beaver hunting

Monday 7 — Sent Out my hunters with 6 pack Horses on Knife River, Wind changed to the North West,   appearance of bad Weather —

Tuesday 8 — This day had the appearance of bringing News from some quarter, but contrary to my hopes No One arrived, all quiet in the Village — Exchanged horses with Durant —

Wednesday 9 — Last night we were visited by a war party of Yanctons,   after a little *parly,* and a few plugs of tobacco, they departed — Durant started Out for the eighth time a Beaver hunting — (returned back ½ hour after,)

Thursday 10 — Reports says, that the war party of the 8th has stolen several of the Mandan Horses — The Prairies are on fire on the North side ,

Friday 11 — News from the Gros Ventres, of five Crow Indians haveing arrived there from their camp on the *Horn*[448]

River. My Hunters arrived with the Meat of five cows — Cattle far off —

Saturday 12 — Appearance of bad Weather — arrivals from the Gros Ventres, No News in that quarter - and no Cattle, which is worse than all, traded three Beaver skins Marked M.C.[449] —

Sunday 13 — Put up some few goods for the Gros Ventres. Venture Lebrun arrived from above — No News in that quarter —

Monday 14 — Strong North West Wind — a few drops of rain in the Morning. Sent two Carts with with [*sic*] the Merchandise to the Gros-Ventres, Wind Continued all day — Weather smoky —

Tuesday 15 — Last Night was one of the Coldest that we have had this Season, Wind as yesterday, a band of *Rees* (60) arrived from their Camp on one of the Forks of the Little Missouri. Grand feast at the Village, the Wind fell at sun set.

Wednesday 16 — The ice running thick in the river. Pleasant Weather. Mandans busy in feasting their friends the Rees — the two Carts arrived from the Gros-Ventres. No News in that quarter, and no Buffaloe, Which is Worse.

Thursday 17 — Mandans Out after Meat — some few Gros Ventres arrived, to smoke with their Friends the Rees — turned my young Calf out with the other Cattle.

Friday 18 — The Rees left here to pay a visit to the Gros Ventres. Feast to the Mandans. Dressed the Yellow Knife, a Mandan Soldier — the ice continues running thick.

Saturday 19 — Morning Cloudy with the Wind from the south Skated to day for the first time this 12 years past — Came off better than I expected, with only two falls —

Sunday 20 — Strong North West wind all day — No news from any quarter, the hunters of the 17th inst not yet arrived

Monday 21 — Mandans arrived with fresh Meat, from the

north side , report Cattle plenty , the Dummy[450] Killed a White Cow — the skin of which is worth five or six Horses —

Tuesday 22 — The river closed up last Night,   the hunters of the 17th arrived last night — cattle scarce,   the Rees arrived from their Visit to the Gros Ventres,   the Assinneboines stole two horses from the hunters of the 17th inst on Knife river,

Wednesday 23 — Nothing going on to day except my men are hard at Work, hauleing fire wood, Charboneau gave us a feast —

Thursday 24 — Feast and Council with the Rees,   *Great* promises on both sides,

Friday 25 — The Rees left here in the evening for their Camp, they say they will be here with all their Lodges the 15th or 20th of Next Month,   Alcro arrived from the Gros-Ventres,

Saturday 26 — Last Night several articles was stolen from the store,   Snow storm,   it appears that two Gros Ventres that was turned out of the Council of the 24th was the theives that plundered the store,   the Mandan Soldiers are in persuit of them, I have but little hopes of recovering the stolen property,

Sunday 27 — Sent Out by hunters with 6 pack Horses, the Soldiers returned last Night Without success,   the 2 Gros Soldiers returned last Night Without success , the 2 Gros Ventres haveing proved their innocence,

Monday 28 — Alcrow started up to the Gros Ventres,   South Wind all day. No News of my stolen goods, in time to come I may perhaps hear something of them.

Tuesday 29 — Strong West Wind,   Mandans Out after Meat on the North side

Wednesday 30 — This Month finishes with a very cold day, Wind from the North, all quiet at the Village, No News from any quarter,

Killed 168 Rats this Month — Total 1139,

> *I play de Jews harp, Likewise de fiddle*
> *I like de United States, But Not Mr. Biddle.*
> *Jim Crow*

Thursday 1 — Last Night at ½ past 6 — We Were Visited by a small war party from the Yancton camp, they brought one beaver skin with them, at 10 they started, sent a few twists of tobacco to some of the Principel Men of their band,

Friday 2 — Venture arrived from the Gros Ventres, No News in that quarter, Cattle scarce, the hunters arrived late last Night, With the Meat of Seven cows, Out six days —

Saturday 3 — Sent Charboneau up to the Gros Ventres, Mandans starveing , the Fort full of Men, Women & Children a begging Meat; the Mandans arrived from the North side with fresh Meat, Out five days, Cattle scarce,

Sunday 4 — Strong Wind from the North West since several days — the Mandans are on the Watch for the Yanctons, they dug a deep hole in the ground opposite the Fort door, they set up all Night watching,

Monday 5 — Cold, &c &c

Tuesday 6 — Pleasant Morning , some few Mandans that left here three days ago, in search of Cattle, arrived last night, haveing been pursued by enemies, report Cattle far off —

Wednesday 7 — Allert at the Village last Night, Cloudy all day, sent Garreau in serch of a lost horse, Prepared my dog harnesses —

Thursday 8 — The Mandans arrived with fresh Meat from the North side, report cattle near Prepareing to send Out to morrow —

[⊕ New Moon [*sic*] in Margin for this entry.]

Friday 9 — Sent out my hunters with 4 pack horses — Mandans out with them, quarreled with One of my Men, a squaw died at the Village, an Indian arrived from the Gros Ventres, he stated that Cattle are plenty in their Neighborhood ,

Saturday 10 — Filled the Stable with hay 6 loads, appearance of bad Weather,

Sunday 11 — Snow storm last Night,   some few Mandans that left here the 9th inst arrived last Night, without Meat, haveing saw no cattle,   My hunters not yet returned,

Monday 12 — The hunters arrived late last Night with the Meat of three cows —

Tuesday 13 — Light fall of snow last Night,   My cart horses have at length refused to pull up the hill, they are tired, and fatigued. I have sent to serch for my yoke of Oxen as a last resource,   if they refuse, I do not Know what we shall do for fire wood,   the Men came back without finding the Oxen.

Wednesday 14 — Alcrow & Co arrived late last night from the Gros Ventres,   Indians starving in that quarter.   Sent Out again to serch for my Oxen.   An Indian brought back a horse that has been lost since last Month,   Paid him well for his trouble,   Snow storm all day —

Thursday 15 — Cold stormy weather , Mandans arrived with fresh Meat, from the North side   Out 4 days — Cattle scarce.

Friday 16 — Arranged my horse traines,   employed the day makeing Coals to shoe my horses.

Saturday 17 — One of the Coldest days we have had this Month,   Sent Alcrow in serch of the Yancton Camp, for news from below — Prospects of starvation,   No Cattle —

Sunday 18 — Sent Charboneau up to the Gros Ventres, to take the place of Bullé, for a few days.   Sent Garreau to hunt for my Cattle,   the Wolves Killed my Young Calf — refused to make any advances to Durant,   he went off in a great flush —

Monday 19 — Cold day — Snow,   Bullé arrived from the Gros Ventres,   starveing in that quarter, 7 Rees arrived from their Camp,   their Camp will not be here untill spring — Cattle in abundance at their camp —

Tuesday 20 — A Gros Ventre arrived from above, says that 2 White Men arrived at their Camp from Fort Union,   the 2 Men Mentioned by the Indian arrived in the evening — bringing the express for St Louis - from Fort Union.

Wednesday 21 — Busy Writeing letters,   News of a bande of Cows on the opposite side,   Preparations to give them a chace, Alcro arrived without finding the Yancton Camp — he was 4 Days out without eating,   brought the news of a bande of Cows close —

Thursday 22 — Cold and Windy — Snow storm,   which prevents the Mandans from going out after a Bande of cattle that was discovered yesterday, close to the Village. My hunters arrived last evening with the Meat of three Bulls,

Friday 23 — Finished Writeing letters to F. U. — sent out my hunters, with 3 pack horses — Snow in the evening,   My hunters arrived with the Meat of two Cows —

Saturday 24 — The two Men that brought the express from Fort Union started back to day — Bullé started for the Gros Ventres —

Sunday 25 — Christmas day — the Men fired a salute this Morning early — gave them a feast, of eatables but no drinkables to give them,

Monday 26 — Sent two Men with letters to Fort Pierre. My Cattle paid us a visit today — Charboneau arrived late in the evening from the Gros Ventres, No News in that quarter. Indians all starveing, the Mandans sent out on discovery, they came back without discovering any thing — Warm.

Tuesday 27 — South wind, snow melting fast — set the Men chopping fire wood, on the north side —

Wednesday 28 — The Mandans that accompanied the Rees to their camp, arrived last night — on their way to the Ree camp, a young Mandan was Killed by the Yanctons.

Thursday 29 — Mandans all out in serch of cattle on the north side — the Dummy arrived with fresh Meat,   out three days,   2 Bulls —

Friday 30 — Mantá arrived late last Night from the Little Misso. Out 15 days —

Saturday 31 — Early this Morning, six young Men were sent out on Discovery, as far as the Square hills.

Killed this Month 134 Rats — total 1,273.

> *O, 18-36 — is gone to my sorrow,*
> *But 18-37 — will be here to morrow —*
> *Jim Crow*

1837   JANUARY 31 DAYS

Sunday 1st — This day last year, I had the pleasure, (after an absence of twenty years) of dineing with my Old Father & Mother — I Commence this year with 100 packs of Robes, and three packs of Beaver —

Monday 2 — Sent Charboneau up to the Gros Ventres to bring down some robes that I have at that post — the Mandans arrived with fresh meat,   out five days —

Tuesday 3 — Cold and Windy — appearance of snow — Newman arrived with 2 horses, bringing with him a letter from Jos Jouet[451] — dated the 23rd-Oct-1836, from the Cheyenne River —

Wednesday 4 — Pleasant day — Charboneau arrived from the Gros Ventres — With 38 Robes and 9lbs Beaver,   the proceeds of two Months,   all starveing in that quarter.

Thursday 5 — Bellehumeur wife was delivered of a daughter, an eight months child — Cold and appearance of snow — Squaw dance —

Friday 6 — This being a Holliday[452] with the French Old Charboneau gave us an excellent dinner of Pudding, Pies, fryed & Roasted Meat &c &c

Saturday 7 — Light fall of snow last Night — filled the Stable with hay — the Mandans sent out on discovery, they returned in the evening without seeing any thing —

Sunday 8 — Sent out My hunters with two pack horses — Strong wind all day —

Monday 9 — Sent Newman and Charboneau,   with 4 of my

poor horses, down to the little lake to spend a few days — Alcrow & Benture, arrived from below.   Fine prospects of cattle in that quarter .

Tuesday 10 — Cold and Windy,   the Mandans went out in serch of cattle,   on the north side —

Wednesday 11 — Put up some few articles to send to the Yancton Camp,   to trade Meat — the hunters arrived with the Meat of two cows —

Thursday 12 — Sent Alcrow, with one horse, and one dog train to the Yancton Camp —

Friday 13 — The Mandans after three days council among themselves, have concluded to send a Plenipotentiary to the Yanctons , he started at ½ past 4 P.M. — it is the idea of Many that he will reach the Yancton Camp — but not return —

Saturday 14 — Went down to the little Lake, with the intention of leaveing the rest of my poor horses,   on arriveing there I found that my Camp Keepers had started for the Fort, haveing Nothing to eat — Killed a Bull for supper, and camped in the woods —

Sunday 15 — Left Camp early and arrived at the Fort at 1- P.M., found all well,   the Mandans arrived with fresh meat — out 6 days —

Monday 16 — Set Durant to make Coales for the Blacksmith, Went over to see the Men at work,   found them hard at work — *O. B. F.*

Tuesday 17 — Sent Charboneau up to the Gros Ventres to take the place of Bullé for a few days — Bullé arrived in the evening, report Cattle in great abundance near the Little Missouri —

Wednesday 18 — Water riseing,   impossible to cross with the Carts — Set the Blacksmith to work in the shop — Snow , the Plenipotentiary that was sent to the Yancton Camp on the 13th inst arrived to day, bringing with him five of the Principal Men of the Yanctons, also a squaw — on arriveing within a few hundred yards of the Fort, they were all inhumanly murdered by the Mandans, and a few Gros Ventres — that came down from their Village Yesterday for the purpose of aideing in the Butchery — the Yanctons were decoyed up, by the Mandans, sending them some tobacco, by the Plenipotentiary, saying to them that the Mandans were inclined to Make Peace, they took the squaw Prisoner —

Thursday 19 — Sent two Men with one horse, to Meet Alcrow, on his way from the Yancton Camp, his horse haveing give out — Frolic at the Village,   they were up all Night, dancing the scalps[453] of those that were Killed Yesterday — Snow all day — Alcrow arrived from the Yancton Camp, brought no Meat —

Friday 20 — Sent after my horses that I have in the Point of Woods below,   the Wolves eat one horse belonging to Newman— Weather unsettled since several days — Snow in the afternoon —

Saturday 21 — Thick fog,   the Mandans of the little Village arrived from their dried Meat excursion , they have dragged one of the Dead Yanctons up to their Village, to have some fun a danceing around him —

Sunday 22 — Sent Alcrow & Garreau out on discovery. Bullé went up to the Gros Ventres,   Snow storm all day — Alcrow came back without seeing any thing — Kept my horses in the Fort all day — the Mandans are on the look out for the Sioux —

Monday 23 — Charboneau arrived from the Gros Ventres. No News in that quarter. Cattle scarce.

Tuesday 24 — Fine day — sent out on discovery , they came back without seeing any thing.   We are in a fair way of starveing, as cattle are scarce in all directions;   the squaws of the Little Village gave us the scalp dance,   they went off displeased, as I gave them Nothing.

Tuesday [sic] 25 — Sent out My hunters to live or starve in the prairies,   the Men Came back from the Woods haveing saw enemies.

Thursday 26 — Wind and snow all day,   the chickens Commenced laying eggs,

Friday 27 — Pleasant day, the Mandans discovered the tracks of enemies on the opposite side,   supposed to be about twenty, to day a young Mandan came, either with the intent to Kill or scare Me. I left him approach in graspe length, when I disarmed him of his gun and Tomahawk, and sent him back to the Village with his tail between his legs. My Woman and her child being at the Village (at a dance) Prevented me from strikeing him to the earth. No doubt it is better as it is.

Saturday 28 — Sent two Men Out on discovery,   they Came back late in the evening Without seeing any thing. News from the Gros Ventres of Cattle being plenty in their Neighbourhood —

Sunday 29 — Mild and pleasant Weather, Mandans all starveing,   the Mandans gave us a splendid dance (the Bull dance) gave them a small Present and they went off well pleased —

Monday 30 — Set two men to Make balls,   two others to fill the Stable with hay — Settled with an Indian for twenty Beaver Skins that I have of his since last October,   snow storm in the afternoon.

Tuesday 31 — One of my Men sick,   My hunters have not yet returned,   they have been absent seven days. Since My stay at this place I have not been so short of Provisions, as We are at Present. We have not tasted a Morsel of fresh Meat since fifteen days,   the Mandans Much longer,   but I am in hopes that the Month to come, will be accompanied by Mr. Providence, Who has been absent from this place since some time.   I put My trust in him, time Will decide what he will do for us. My Hunters arrived in the evening with the Meat of two Poor Cows,   report the Indians above, in a fair way to starve,   as cattle are scarce in all directions, bad prospects for a good trade this year, however I am in hopes that the *Rees* Will Make up all deficiencies on that score.

Killed this Month 61 Rats — total 1334

Gentlemen, men, and Ladies I have come to let you know
That Jackson is elected, to Jump Jim Crow —
For more particulars apply at the Blacksmith shop.

[1837] FEBUARY 28 DAYS

Wednesday 1 — This Month begins with cold and appearance of bad weather.

Thursday 2— Sent four of my poorest horses to be cached in the hills, as they would in all probability have starved at the Fort, as my hay is almost all distroyed, Some few Mandans started out after cattle, they returned two hours after, being afraid of the bad Weather, a few drops of rain fell to day, Wind from the South.

Friday 3 — Sent my hunters Out with six pack horses, on the North side, several of the Mandans went with them, Others out on this side. I almost forgot to Mention, that this Month, for the first time, I have Commenced a New Article of trade, Which is Rabbit Skins, I am in hopes they will be worth something below —

Saturday 4 — Snow storm last Night, thick fogy in the Morning, Weather mild and pleasant in the afternoon, two Mandans arrived with fresh Meat, report Bulls, plenty in 30 Miles off —

Sunday 5 — One of Sam Patch's[454] leaps, was performed by an Old Woman at the Village this Morning, Who, to Out-do-Sam, instead of Jumping, over the Falls into the water, Made a pitch from the bank of the Village on to the rocks below — Sam beat that if you can —

Monday 6 — Fine pleasant day. No news from any quarter. Indians not yet arrived — the Mandans on the Look Out, day and Night.

Tuesday 7 — The Indians arrived late last night, loaded with

Meat. Jos Desnoyé[455] arrived from the Little Miss⁰. Prospects of a good trade in that quarter. My hunters not yet arrived , the Yanctons moved their camp up hart river — they fear the Mandans —

Wednesday 8 — My hunters arrived late last Night without Meat, haveing been pillaged by the Assinneboines of four horses , they were attacked early in the morning of the 6th by a War party of fourty, Who fired on them (Mistaken them for Mandans,) and unfortunately Killed N. Durant — a free hunter Who has been in this Country several Years, his wife left the Fort this Morning, to take up her quarters in the Village. She appears to not care much about it. What affectionate Wives We all have in this Country !

Thursday 9 — Sent two Men and four horses down to the Square hills in quest of Cattle, as We have Nothing to eat but Corn and beans.

Friday 10 — Sent a horse train to the Gros Ventres to bring down robes,   Mild pleasant Weather. News from the Gros Ventres, of two of them being Killed by the Assiniboines, also of a bande of Rees, haveing arrived at their Camp on the Little Missouri,

Saturday 11 — Allert at the Village last Night, they all Made a rush to the Fort, thinking that the Yanctons had came in, tracks of enemies discovered at the Mouth of the little river, Sent Alcrow to look after the Horses, that I have Cached in the hills, Alcrow Came back Without finding the Horses,   Light fall of snow. Grande feast at the Village. Bullé arrived from the Gros Ventres, bringing With him sixteen Robes, My hunters are Not Yet arrived,   I begin to think that something has happened to them, as they were to be only two nights absent from the Fort —

Sunday 12 — Cold stormy day — strong Wind from the S. E. Snow — drifting all day — left Philadelphia 1 year to day. *O. B. F.*

Monday 13 — Weather same as Yesterday,   at 10 A. M. fine

weather. Bullé returned to the Gros Ventres with 1 horse train. Sent Garreau to look after the Horses I have *cached* in the hills. Garreau came back in the evening, haveing found the horses, the Rees gave us a dance, gave them some tobacco in the place of it, the hunters arrived from the square hills, with the Meat of two Bulls,   report Cattle scarce,   Benture found a horse belonging to the Mandans, who lost him on their way from the Yancton Camp.

Tuesday 14 — Mandans all starveing , although cattle are in 30 miles of the Fort. Fear Makes them Keep at home,   sent two More of My horses in the hills With the Others,   Snow, in the Morning.

Wednesday 15 — Calm, pleasant day. Nothing worth recording to day —

Thursday 16 — Snow— Preperations for sending out after Meat,   the Mandans will also start Out tomorrow,

Friday 17 — Snow drifting,   Wind from the South,   the bad Weather continued all day,   the Men are all Idle to day, haveing Nothing for them to do - about the Fort —

Saturday 18 — Indians all out after Buffaloe. Sent Mitchel With three Horses with them. Sent Alcrow with five Horses down to the square hills — the Mandans gave out going after Buffaloe on account of an Old Woman, Makeing her Medicine[456] and found Out, that enemies are close,   Mitchel started down after Alcrow. Weather Mild and pleasant —

Sunday 19 — Dull lonesome day — enough to give a Man the *Gous* [*Sic*] No News from any quarter, left Wheeling, Virg[a]. to day one Year, on My Way to S[t]. Louis.

Monday 20 — The Mandans of the Little Village arrived With fresh Meat — report Cattle plenty on Knife river,   those of this Village have gone up to pay them a Visit, in the hopes of comeing back With their bellies full — thick foggy Weather —

Tuesday 21 — Fine pleasant weather. Some few Mandans

started Out after Cattle, on the North side,   they all returned in the evening, haveing saw Nothing.

Wednesday 22 — Passed this day one Year at Cincinnati, great rejoicings at that place, the City all alluminated in the Night,   the Canons fireing on both sides of the the River,   the hunters arrived With the Meat of three Bulls and two Cows — lost one Mule on the road ,

Thursday 23 — Several Rees that have been here since last October, started for their camp on the Little Missouri. Mandans out after Meat — the Mandans Killed one of Bentures Horses —

Friday 24 — Fine weather still continues,   four Rees that started Yesterday - came back today — No News from any quarter , the Fort full of Women and Children, begging Meat —

Saturday 25 — The fine weather still continues, the snow Melting fast — hauled sixty loads of Wood to the Fort this Week, Mandans Not Yet returned from hunting —

Sunday 26 — Change in the weather, cold North Wind, with snow — Cleared off at 12 — pleasant the rest of the day — the Dummy arrived with two horses loaded with Meat — report cattle far off — Mandans not yet arrived —

Monday 27 — Cold South West Wind , Two Gros-Ventres arriver from above,   brought the News of the Death of Bullé, Who died Yesterday, at their Village. Sent Alcrow with two Men, and a Horse train to bring down the Merchandise that I have at that place,

Tuesday 28 — Mandans arrived with fresh Meat, out six days, report cattle scarce, the squaws of the Little Village gave us a dance. Alcrow arrived from the Gros Ventres bringing with him the rest of the goods,   brought the *corpse* of Bullé,   had him entered at 4 P.M. —

Killed 89 Rats this month — total 1423 —

116 Packs the beginning of this Month,   March 1st 1837
6 packs pressed April 8th
Loose Robes

FORT CLARK JOURNAL

March 1st 1837

Wednesday 1st — Hail gentle Spring, I greet thee with feelings of the Most heartfull delight[457] — A Gros Ventre arrived from the Ree Camp, he says they are encamped at Turtle Mountain[458] about ninety Miles from this place — The *Par fléche Rouge* a Gros Ventre cheif, with forty Lodges, are encamped with the Rees —

Thursday 2 — Thick foggy Morning, The Gros Ventres moved down to their summer Village. Several Rees arrived from their camp, they say that the camp are on their way to this place, and will be here in ten or fifteen days. Put up some few goods for the Gros Ventres.

Friday 3 — Fine pleasant day — Sent Garreau with a few goods up to the Gros Ventres, great change in the weather since Morning, cold North West Wind, appearance of snow — arrainged my Retail Store, in hopes that trade will be brisk this Month — Mantá came in from the woods with his foot badly cut — The Little Village gave us a dance, gave them some tobacco in the place of it — The Gros Ventres also gave us a dance, but being the scalp dance they got nothing —

Saturday 4 — Light fall of snow last night. The Fort full of Gros Ventres, troublesome times, hauled 46 Loads of Wood this Week, Put up some Tobacco, to send to the Ree camp —

Sunday 5 — Snow — Mandans started Out to Make dried Meat, on the Little Missouri, dull lonesome day — No News from any quarter, the express from St Louis not yet arrived

Monday 6 — The Mandans are makeing Buffaloe Medicine,[459] they are to be very plenty here in five or six days. Newman and

Desnoyé started for their spring hunt,   a few Mandans started Out to make dried Meat, in Company with the Gros Ventres —

Tuesday 7 — Cold, Wind from the North,   the Men all idle on account of the bad Weather,   snowed three times during the day,   four Rees arrived,   bringing With them six horses that they stole from the Yanctons on the Head of Canon Ball river.

Wednesday 8 — The Horse thieves that arrived yesterday, report cattle in abundance in 40 Miles of the Fort — Yesterday and to day are the two Coldest days, that we have had since last January, I expect that it is the Medicine that they are Makeing at the Village to Make Buffaloe approach — the Mandans that started out the 6th inst to Make dried Meat — returned back to day — Fear overtook them on the way —

Thursday 9 — Cold Weather still Continues,   sent Benture up to the Gros Ventres to Collect some News. Benture arrived in the evening, Gros Ventres all out Makeing dried Meat — some old Men and Women that are at the Village,   are in a starving state. The Dummy arrived With fresh Meat, out alone six days. No Prospect of Cattle approaching —

Friday 10 — Cold as usual. Sent Alcrow after the Horses that I have *Cached* in the hills. Alcrow came back in the afternoon,   three of my horses are missing. No News from any quarter. We had something new for supper, 1 doz of eggs[460] —

Saturday 11 — Mandans all out after Buffaloe, sent my hunters with four Pack horses with them, the Weather has Moderated some since Yesterday, rode up to the Gros Ventres, found No One there except a few old Men and Women,   they are all Out Makeing dried Meat and Robes. Garreau has traded twenty five robes since the 3rd inst — bad Prospects of a good trade this Year. Letant[461] arrived from Fort Pierre, bringing the express from St Louis. No News of any importance, except that Van Burin is elected President, of these U.S.

Sunday 12 — Cold as usual — busy writeing letters to Fort Pierre, strong North west wind all day,   No News from any quarter, One of my Men Pilot,[462] wishes to leave me - to go below, thinking to have better times.

Monday 13 — Started Letant to Fort Pierre, with letters to P. D. Papin — Passed the day cutting cords for Makeing Packs, thinking it almost time for my cow to have her calf, had them sent for, but to my sorrow, found out that she was not with calf —

Tuesday 14 — The Cold Weather still continues, snow during the day, the Mandans of the Little Village arrived with some poor Bull meat, out five days, Cattle scarce in all directions — The Medicine Man, that undertook to Make his Medicine, for to Make Cattle approach, has given it up as a bad job — The Indians Killed one of my dogs — retaliated by Killing two others in his place — sweet revenge —

Wednesday 15 — The express from St Louis, for Fort Union, remains here as yet, haveing no person to send with it. Cold North West Wind — the Men not able to haul wood — the wind changed to the south — Commenced thawing in the afternoon —

Thursday 16 — One of the finest days we have had this season — the snow is fast disappearing — The Indians arrived with fresh Meat — at 2 P. M. the weather changed, snow and rain. My hunters are not yet arrived, the Indians that arrived, brought a little poor Bull Meat, haveing saw no Cows —

Friday 17 — Appearance of bad weather, strong south west Wind. Tremendious snow storm during the day — News of the arrival at the Gros Ventres of the Par fleche Rouge and his band. My hunters arrived with the Meat of three Bulls, out seven days. Cattle scarce all over the Country —

Saturday 18 — The bad weather, still continues, Light fall of snow last Night. Sent a cart with a few goods up to the Gros Ventres, Finished hauleing Wood from the opposite side of the river, set the Men to clean Out the Fort — Pleasant in the afternoon, the Cart returned from the Gros Ventres with twenty Robes, Prepared the express for F. U.

Sunday 19 — Started two Men, with the express for Fort Union. Warm south west Wind, the snow has almost all disappeared from the Prairies, The Mandans arrived from Makeing dried Meat, very unsuccessfull — Charboneau arrived from the Gros Ventres. No News in that quarter , all starveing, Discovered the Prairies on fire, supposed to have been done by a War Party of Yanctons —

Monday 20 — Cloudy — Cold North Wind. Set the Men to Cleaning, all around the Fort — Garreau's squaw started up to the Gros Ventres, thinking to fare better in that quarter- Provisions being scarce at this place, No News from the Ree Camp since the 2nd of this Month. Four Men arrived from the North, report that all the Sioux are encamped Within sixty Miles of the Fort —

Tuesday 21 — Pleasant Weather. I was Presented to day with a Sword, from Mr. Dickson — the Liberator of all Indians[463] — Cold in the afternoon — No appearance of the ice breaking up —

Wednesday 22 — Weather same as yesterday —Commenced Makeing Packs. Gardepie[464] Went up to the Little Village, to smoke With the Chiefs, to try to Make peace between them and the Chippaways — A flock of Geese passed to day, the first this Year — I am in hopes that others are Not far behind, to bring us good News of the approach of spring — as it looks nothing like it as yet in this quarter. Gardepie came back from the Little Village, haveing succeeded in establishing a Peace, between them and the Chippaways

Thursday 23 — Distributed out traps to the Mandans and Gros Ventres, the Dummy started out alone on the other side, in serch of Buffaloe — Light fall of snow in the evening —

Friday 24 — Gardepie with one Man started for the North, Mandans arrived from the North side, Came back without seeing any Cattle, Wrote letters to Fort Union —

Saturday 25 — Mr. James Dickson, the Liberator of all Indians, started, with Benture for Fort Union, the Cold Weather still Continues, strong North wind, Some few Mandans started out in serch of Cattle, several flocks of Ducks passed to day - Although No Prospects of Spring. *O. B. F.*

Sunday 26 — The ice broke up this day two years, as yet, it has not the least appearance, Sent up to the Gros Ventres, to Collect some News. Had a Duck for dinner, the first this year —

Monday 27 — Sent out my hunters with six pack horses, the cold weather still continues, Made packs. Gros Ventres arrived from their dried Meat excursion, Very successfull —

Tuesday 28 — Delightful calm day — finished Making packs 118 of Robes, and three of Beaver, Mandans all up at the Gros Ventres a feasting —

Wednesday 29 — Great change in the weather since Yesterday — Cloudy and cold, No appearance of the ice breaking - up — Two of the Horrid Tribe[465] arrived, report their Camp on Knife river, abounding with Meat & Robes My hunters arrived with the Meat of four Bulls —

Thursday 30 — Snow storm last night — the Prairies are again all covered with snow — Cold North Wind — Set the Men to Makeing balls — Mandans arrived with Meat,

Friday 31 — Cold weather still continues, Snow storm at 2 P.M. Charboneau arrived from the Gros Ventres, No News in that quarter, One of my horses died to day —

Number of Rats Killed this Month 87 — Total 1510,

1837 APRIL 30 DAYS

Saturday 1st — The river commenced riseing. Rode up to the Gros Ventres, found all Well, trade going on slow — The snow is fast disappearing from the Prairies. The express that left here the 19th of last Month has not yet returned.

Sunday 2 — Cold Stormy day — strong Wind from the North all day — the river rose to day one foot — but no Prospects of the ice breaking up — it has been later this year, than several

Years past — Owing no doubt to the Mild Winter we have had —
New moon

Monday 3 — Cold as usual — Pressed Packs 31 — The Press
unfortunately broke at 1 P. M. The Dog Bande gave us a splendid dance. Paid them in tobacco. The water continues riseing —

Tuesday 4 — Sent the Men to the woods, to Cut a log thirty
feet in length to Press Packs — Snow — Mandans all starveing,
they are waiting with Patience, hopeing that the ice will brake
up soon, that they May catch the drowned Buff[oe]

Wednesday 5 — An old Woman at the Village tired of this
World hung herself last Night[466] — Cold weather still continues,
Pressed Packs 45 — Jos. Desnoyé arrived from Beaver hunting,
Not being able to continue, haveing caught the Venerial,   left
Newman on Chery creek, eight days ago — Some few articles
that was stolen from the store last 26th of November, was discovered to day — Sent the Soldiers to hunt for the stolen goods ,
they brought back a Part of the stolen articles,   1 1/3 Ps Salampore[467] 4 yds Cloth , 2 Prs Summer Pantloons   10 Yds Check —
1 Green Blkt —

Thursday 6 — Snow storm in the Morning. Weather cold as
usual, the river, same as in January, and No appearance of the
ice Makeing a Move.

The Soldiers has been hunting in the Village all day for the
Stolen Property, without effect as one of the theives is Not returned from hunting .

Friday 7 — Weather same as Yesterday — sent a Cart up to
the Gros Ventres,   the Cart returned at 2 P. M. With 50 Robes.
Nothing New in that quarter —

Saturday 8 — Finished Pressing Packs   118 — traded up to
this date. Calm pleasant day, the first we have had since the 1st
of the Month. News from the Gros Ventres of a small bande of
Rees, Men and Women's on their way to the Ree camp, being
Killed by the Yanctons on Knife river.

Sunday 9 — All the Wives of the Village, Ventured down to

the Point of Woods, the first time they have been there since the Massacre of the 18th of Jan.y — the water rose to day 18 inches. Prospects of the ice breakeing up to Night —

Monday 10 — Covered the warehouses With dirt and straw — Castor arrived from the Gros Ventres for Powder, ball &c.   One of the Warmest days that we have had this season.   Ducks comeing from all quarters.

Tuesday 11 — Sent out my hunters with five Pack horses — sent a Cart with a few goods to the Gros Ventres — Medicine feast at the Village,   the cart returned from the Gros Ventres at 2 P. M. With 24 Robes,   the water fell last Night 10 inches,   ice Not Yet started, although it has the appearance of a Move —

Wednesday 12 — My hunters arrived late last Night, with the Meat of three Bulls, haveing found a small bande of ten, in fifteen Miles of the Fort.   The ice broke up to day at 1 P. M. — in fine stile.   The Mandans are in high spirits, anxiously waiting for the drownded Buffaloe to Pass.   Several of them are encamped on the opposite side of the river, hopeing to Make a quantity of dried Meat — the ice stopped running at 4 P. M. — occassioned no doubt by a *Dig,* formeing somewhere Near the Gros Ventres, the Water rose and fell to day at least 2 feet — a strong North West wind Continued all day —

Thursday 13 — Last night the ice Made a second Move, the water rose at least four feet.   I am in hopes by tomorrow the river will be clear of ice.   Two Rees arrived from their camp, they say that they are encamped in 40 Miles of the Fort.   As they have told me so many lies since last September, I Put no Confidence in What they tell Me,

Friday 14 — The ice Made an other stop last Night.   I was in hopes that it was the last, but this Morning it is running as thick as ever.   Strong south Wind all day — the Mandans have lost all hopes of catching the drownded Buffaloe,   as Not One has passed this year.

Saturday 15 — Snow storm last Night,   the Prairies are again covered with snow, a second Winter has made its appearance, the ice continues running thick in the river — the Indians are all out after a bande of Buffaloe, that was discovered from the hills.   Indians returned in the afternoon haveing Killed four Bulls — Several Rees arrived —

Sunday 16 — Started Jos Desnoyé in a skin Canoe, with Nails &c for Fort Pierre, sent a Cart with a few goods, up to the Gros Ventres,   the Cart returned at 1 P. M. with 43 Robes —

Monday 17 — Set the Men to grinde their axes , as fire wood begins to be scarce, and no appearance of Warm weather.   A drownded Buffaloe Passed this Morning at sun rise,   the Mandans all being abed, Missed their breakfast — Made Packs 10 —

Tuesday 18 — Sent the Men to chop and haule wood at the Riviere qui bar — four Canoes arrived last Night, from the little Misso , loaded with Meat &c — traded two large Beaver skins, the first this year.   Two Rees that arrived the 13th inst started to day for their Camp — Several Mandans started down to the Square hills, to make an encampment —

Wednesday 19 — Warm   and   pleasant — Alcrow   with   two Men, in a dug Out, arrived from Fort Union.   No News in that quarter,   brought with them the Meat of six Antilopes, which they Killed on the way down the river.   Saw no cattle on the river —

Thursday 20 — Rode up to the Gros Ventres , found all well, trade going on slow — several canoes, loaded with robes and meat, arrived there last Night — Mandans all crossed the river, in serch of Buffaloe.

Friday 21 — Started Out at day light on discovery, came back a 2 P. M. without seeing any thing but a few Antilopes, two of which I Killed and brought home, saw the Prairies on fire, in the direction of the Ree Camp,

Saturday 22 — Bourbonné[468] with one Man, arrived late last Night, in a dug out, from the Crow Fort,[469] no News in that quarter.   Bourbonné & Co started for below at 10 A.M.   Five Rees started for their Camp,   sent some Tobacco to the Soldiers.

Sunday 23 — Four Gros Ventres arrived from War — report a large camp of Sioux, on Hart river, left the Ree Camp this Morning at day light — they say that the Ree Camp will be here in 2 or 3 days —

Monday 24 — The Mandans that crossed the River the 20th inst arrived to day with plenty of Meat — report cattle far off, and scarce. My Childrens Mother died[470] this day at 11 OClock — Sent her down in a canoe, to be entered at Fort Pierre, in the Lands of her Parents — Pressed Packs 15 — Trade going on slow —

Tuesday 25 — Last night Alcrows wife was delivered of a Daughter. Sent a Man up to the Gros Ventres in serch of News. The Mandans all started to Meet their friends the Rees, who are to encamp at the Grosventre Village to day — Fight between, Old Baptiste and Farro — Benture started Out a Beaver hunting in a skin canoe to trap as far as Canon Ball River —

Wednesday 26 — Sent two Carts to the Gros Ventres with a few goods — North West Wind all day, smokey Weather. The Carts arrived at 1 P. M. — with 124 Robes — report the Ree Camp at the Gros Ventre Village.

Thursday 27 — Made Packs 18 — Hoisted the Flag, to receive the Ree Camp, as they are to arrive to day — the Rees did not arrive to day as was expected, on account of the Gros Ventres danceing the *Calumet*[471] to them.

Friday 28 — Weather continues smokey — The Ree Camp arrived at 1 P.M. — 250 Lodges, bringing with them three Thousand Buffaloe Robes, and one pack of Beaver — Received them with the Honors of War, fired 10 Salutes from my four pounder, and hoisted the Flag — the Rees are busily engaged in feasting with the Mandans —

Saturday 29 — Sent a Cart up to the Gros Ventres with a few goods — set the Men to Cooking a feast of 10 Kittles for the Rees. Invited to a feast at the Ree Camp — Six dogs lost their lives, for the feast — Gave them a feast in return, of ten Kittles of Corn — and a great deal of good talk, great Promises Made on both sides. The cart returnd from the Gros Ventres with 70 Robes.

Sunday 30 — Commenced tradeing with the Horrid tribe,   the Ree Ladies gave us a splendid dance,   also the Bull Bande, Benture arrived from Beaver hunting, Out six days, Caught 2 Beaver — traded to day 350 Buffaloe Robes —

Killed 68 Rats this Month — total — 1578

1837   MAY 31 DAYS

Monday 1st— Cold south east Wind. Sent all the men with a cart to cut hay for my horses — traded to day 200 Buffaloe Robes —

Tuesday 2 — Sent up to the Gros Ventres for News. Gave a feast to the Ree Soldiers, with a great deal of good talk,   Made four soldiers for the Fort. The Rees are all with the Mandans, excepting twenty Lodges, that went up to the Gros Ventres, on account of the Mandan Village Not being large enough to receive them all.   Manta arrived from the Gros Ventres — no news in that quarter — Traded to day 160 Robes

Wednesday 3 — Fine pleasant weather, Indians all Starveing, Mandans and Rees all crossed the river in quest of Buffaloe. Sprinkled with rain in the afternoon,   traded to day 70 Robes — Thunder for the first time this year —

Thursday 4 — Rain. Cold disagreeable day — set the Men to Make Packs,   Last Night the Cock crowed five times, bad News from some quarter is expected from all the Men[472] — The Rees commenced Makeing their Medicine,   trade going on slow — Traded to day 53 Buffaloe Robes —

Friday 5 — Sent Out my hunters with five pack Horses. The Water rose last night six inches — My hunters arrived at 2 P. M. With the Meat of one Bull — Traded to day 24 Buffaloe Robes —

Saturday 6 — Sent a Cart up to the Gros Ventres with a few goods — Bought a fine Mule from a Ree Indian — The Cart ar-

TCHON-SU-MONS-KA, WIFE OF CHARDON

rived from the G. Ventres with 70 Robes and three Beaver Skins — Indians all returned from hunting, all loaded with fresh Meat, report cattle far off — Storm of rain and wind at 4 P. M. The Indians gave me an abundance of Meat — they were more generous than I thought them to be, after Killing so many Whites,

Sunday 7 — Cold Windy day — the water continues riseing. The Dog band (the Rees) gave us a dance, Which I hope will be the last — several Indians that went Out yesterday on discovery, came back to day without seeing any thing — saw a Grey Horse to day with the stamp of the Compy on him, that was stolen by the Rees last winter from the Yanctons —

Monday 8 — Shower of rain early this Morning, the first we have had this spring — set the Men to Make Packs — The bad weather continued all day— Benture arrived from the Gros Ventres report a small War Party Out in serch of the Yancton Camp —

Tuesday 9 — Three of my horses are missing since yesterday — Race of four Miles, between the Rees and Mandans, a young Buck *Ree* Came Out a head 300 yards — Sent a man with a few goods up to the Gros Ventres —

Wednesday 10 — Two Yancton squaws (Prisoners) that were taken at the Massacre last winter, Made their escape last Night it is rumoured in the Village that I am the cause of their elopement — rain and wind all day — disagreeable Weather, although the weather has been bad, trade has been brisk, sixty five Robes, Benture arrived from the Gros Ventres No News in that quarter. Indians all Out Makeing dried Meat — *O. B. F.*

Thursday 11 — Mandans and Rees all started Out to Make dried Meat, sent two Men with five Pack Horses with them, as we are short of Provisions, haveing sold all my Corn to the Rees — and in a fair way of starveing Myself — however, opposition, the Purse, and the Belly — The Gros Ventres arrived from War, with the scalp of an Assinniboine, traded 70 Robes to day. My stock of Corn is reduced to 22 Bushels —

Friday 12 — All the squaws of the Village out after Fever-ole,[473] as they have Nothing else to eat — Sent Garreau out hunting Antilopes — Wind from the North, weather smokey — Garreau arrived with an Antilope —

Saturday 13 — Hard frost last Night — Put up some few articles for Fort Pierre — One of My hunters arrived with three Horses loaded with Meat — Storm of wind and rain in the evening — The Squaws Commenced makeing their corn fields.

Sunday 14 — Sent a Man up to the Gros Ventres for News — Calm and pleasant in the Morning — Wind and appearance of rain in the afternoon. Council with the chiefs of the Rees — on account of two War Parties that are to start Out against the Saons. Mantá arrived from the Gros Ventres,   No News in that quarter.

Monday 15 — Pressed Packs 50.   a War Party of Rees left here this Morning for the Yancton camp to revenge the Death of those that were Killed the 8th of last Month — Benture arrived With the Meat of one Bull — News from the Gros Ventres of two of them being Killed by the Assinniboines Out Makeing dried Meat —

Tuesday 16 — Pressed Packs - 52 — Cold south wind — The Men at work with their Mittens on — Chaboneau arrived from the Gros Ventres in quest of something to eat, as they are all starveing in that quarter — the report of yesterday is true   one Gros Ventres and two Assinniboines Killed —

Wednesday 17 — Strong Wind from the North east,   Prairies are all on fire on the North side, lit by the War Parties of Assinniboines and Gros Ventres — that are roveing from Camp to Camp, in serch of a scalp — I think there will be hard fighting in this neighbourhood this summer — No News from any quarter —

Thursday 18 — Pressed Packs 33 — Finished Pressing Packs 280 traded up to this date — trade but two Robes to day — as the Indians are all out Makeing Meat — others working at their corn fields —

Friday 19 — Sent Out my hunters with six pack horses — enemies discovered last evening, in the Point of Woods below — supposed to be Yanctons   Allert in the Village, occassioned by several young Men of the little Village, showing themselves on horseback on the opposite side of the river.

Saturday 20 — Cold for the season — appearance of bad Weather.   Sent the Men to the Woods to chop fire Wood — Rees and Mandans not yet returned from their dried Meat excursion,   those that remain are starveing — as their Principal food is roots, that they dig out of the Point of Woods below —

Sunday 21 — Three young Men arrived early this Morning from the dried Meat Camp.   Several of them, with their families will be in to day, with what little Meat they have,   the others have moved Camp further off in serch of Cattle — My hunters arrived with the Meat of four Poor Bulls, which was all they saw —

Monday 22 — Newman arrived from Beaver hunting — he made a tolerable hunt sixty four skins,   he was robed of his gun by a war party of Rees and Gros Ventres on the Little Miss⁰. out five days without eating — Water commenced riseing —

Tuesday 23 — Sent a Cart up to the Gros Ventres for Robes, the water continues riseing — the Cart returned at 2 P. M. with sixty Robes and four Beaver skins — No News in that quarter. Indians all out Makeing dried Meat — The Rees arrived with fresh Meat —

Wednesday 24 — The Indians from the dried Meat Camp, all arrived loaded with Meat,   Cattle scarce. All the Ree Soldiers started up to the Gros Ventres, to Whip those that robbed Newman — The White Horse, one of the Principal Cheifs of the Rees, brought back Newmans Rifle, and some few other articles that was taken from him by the War Party of Rees on the Little Miss⁰. — The Soldiers came back in the evening, after haveing whipped two, one of which they almost Killed.

Thursday 25 — Strong North east Wind all day — Grand feast at the Village.   Indians went out on discovery — came back in the evening without seeing any thing - but a few Antilopes, several of which they Killed —

Friday 26 — The Wind continues to blow from the North East — Made Packs 13 of Robes and 1 of Beaver, Shower of rain, and heavy thunder in the afternoon. The Bull bande of the Little Village, gave us a dance.

Saturday 27 — Six young men that left here the 15th inst in Company with several others, arrived last evening — report Cattle in abundance 50 miles off — Rain. A War Party of Gros Ventres left here to day for the Little Misso in skin canoes —

Sunday 28 — Calm pleasant day — the Rees & Mandans started down the river to Camp, as they have Nothing to eat — hopeing to find something in that direction — Rode up to the Little Village to try to Pursuade them to finish the trade — Four of my horses are Missing, supposed to have been stole.

Monday 29 — Sent Out my hunters with three pack horses — sent the cart up to the Little Village for Robes — sold three horses to day for 10 Beaver sks and 31 Robes — Charboneau arrived from the Gros Ventres, in quest of something to eat — unfortunately I had none to give him — Alcrow & Pilot arrived from the Little Misso.

Tuesday 30 — Several families of Rees started for below — to encamp with those that left here the 28th inst — The water since 3 or 4 days has been falling,   to day it has began to rise. My hunters arrived at 4 P. M., with the Meat of three fat Bulls, report Cattle scarce —

Wednesday 31 — Rode up to the Gros Ventres, found all well, trade beginning to be at an end — the Indians all out Makeing dried Meat — Prepared the Cart &c to start Alcrow and his family to Fort Pierre — A War Party of one hundred Men (Rees) leaves here to Night to War against the Yanctons —

Killed 108 Rats this Month — total 1686

Three Hundred Pack of Robes, and Four hundred Pounds of Beaver, traded up to this date. *F. A. C.*[474]

Thursday 1st — Alcrow and his family started with a horse and cart for Fort Pierre. Sent my Cattle down with him being afraid of the Indians Killing them on account of their corn fields — Sent a cart to the Gros Ventres for Robes. An Indian that left here this Morning a hunting, was brought back almost dead, occasioned by a Bull gorgeing him and his horse — the Cart returned from the Gros Ventres with 60 Robes and 30 Beaver. News from the Gros Ventres of an Indian and his Wife Knocked over by the Assinniboines, out Beaver hunting on Knife river — Quarreled to day with a Mandan for refusing to give him a credit of a kittle —

Friday 2 — The water rose two feet since Yesterday — the Mandans are all Prepareing for War, to revenge the death of the twenty eight, that were Killed last summer by the Yanctons, on the North side of the Misso — The Indians discovered cattle from the hill, all hands out to run them,   they all came back at 3 P.M. with the Meat of 16 cows and two Bulls, the contents of all the Band —

Saturday 3 — Rain in the Morning — Sent Out My hunters with four Pack horses — four young Bucks that left here the 31st of last Month, returned back to day — report Cattle in abundance — 40 miles off — took an inventory of the Goods & Chattles. My hunters arrived with the meat of three Bulls —

Sunday 4 — Sent a Man up to the Gros Ventres to Collect some News, and to hurry them on to finish the trade — Strong south west Wind all day — the water has fell two feet since last night,   it will be almost impossible for the Steam Boat to get up this far unless the river takes an other rise of at least three feet — Bazile arrived from the Gros Ventres. No News in that quarter.

Monday 5 — A War Party of the Mandans all Mounted on horseback (Ball dans le Coup) Partizan[475]) left here last Night to War against the Yanctons — Pressed Packs 29 — Rees &

Mandans all started Out to Make dried Meat — Old Men and Women are all that is left in the Village —

Tuesday 6 — Sent a Cart up to the Gros Ventres to bring down the Merchandises, remaineing at that post, Trade being at an end — the few robes that are left in the Village, will not be Traded untill this summer, the cart arrived at 2 P.M. with twenty six Robes &c — A Bande of Cows came near the Village, the Wind being from the east, they got the scent of us and made off —

Wednesday 7 — Strong wind from the East continues since yesterday — Settled the a/c with the Gros Ventre Post, found they have made but a very poor hunt this year, only six hundred and thirty robes — and one hundred and eighty pounds of Beaver. The Mandans still worse, haveing Made but three hundred and fifty Robes and one hundred Pounds of Beaver — The wind changed to the north West, in the afternoon, with a shower of rain and thunder, No news from any quarter —

Thursday 8 — Shower of rain early this Morning, Strong Wind from the North West all day — sent out four Indians on discovery — came back without seeing any thing — five of the War Party that left here the 15th of last Month arrived to day — they found the Yancton Camp near the Cheyenne river and in the act of stealing horses in the Night, they were discovered, by the Yanctons, they all immediately fled, each taken his own way to save himself — the Others No doubt Will arrive tomorrow — 13 others arrived at sun down;   report the Death of 2 Killed, and 2 Wounded —

Friday 9 — Started out early on discovery — Came back at 1 P.M. without seeing any thing — Four More of the War Party arrived at 4 P.M. — all Naked — as they were obliged to throw away their robes to be as light as Possible, to make head way — all those that arrived yesterday were also Naked,   fourteen are yet missing —

Saturday 10 — Sent Out my hunters with four Pack Horses — The water has been on a stand since four or five days,   to day it has began riseing,   all the squaws of the Village Out after Prairie turnips[476] — Strong wind from the south east in the afternoon,   shower of rain at sun down,   with thunder —

Sunday 11 — Rain continued all last Night,   fine and pleasant this Morning — An Old Mandan Cheif (The White Bear) died to day — regretted by None that Knew him, as for Me, and Many More of the Fort, are glad of his disappearance.

Monday 12 — The rest of the war party of the 15th inst arrived last Night — brought with them three Horses, report the Death of two killed by the Sioux, and One Wounded.   One Sioux Killed — Some few Mandans arrived from below — with several horse loades of dried Meat— report cattle in abundance on the North side of the river, opposite the square hills —

Tuesday 13 — Sent Garreau Out on discovery.   My hunters not yet arrived.   The Rees & Mandans that left here the 28th of last Month, to Make dried Meat — all arrived to day, well loaded, report Cattle scarce,   they saw my hunters two days ago on ~~Heart~~ Hart [*sic*] river.   My hunters arrrived at 4 P. M. with the Meat of 3 Bulls,   they Killed four, but Not haveing enough horses, they were obliged to leave one for the Wolves.

Wednesday 14 — Strong wind from the south east all day — The War Party of Gros Ventres that left here the 27th of last Month, to steal Horses at the Little Misso arrived to day, with ten Horses and two Mules, two of the Horses have the stamp of the Compy on them.   Charboneau arrived from the G. V. — says that eight Boats from Fort Union will be here tomorrow — left the Liberator[477] the other side of the Little Village, as he is tired of Walking, and has laid himself down to die, the boats were Wind bound at the Little Misso — were [*sic*] he got Out to come down by land —

Thursday 15 — Rain all last night,   some appearance of clearing off this Morning — Strong Wind from the south east — No News from any quarter — the Boats are not yet arrived —

Friday 16 — Calm and pleasant in the Morning — Strong

Wind from the South east at 10 A. M. — the Boats arrived at 10
A. M — Prepared to start with them in the Morning[478] —

Saturday 17 — Started early. Wind bound and 10 O'Clock at
the Point of Woods below the square hills — the Wind continued
high all day —

Sunday 18 — Last Night we had a very severe storm of Wind
and rain. We were obliged to onload one of the Boats as she
was sinking and wet a great many robes — The Steam Boat S[t]
Peters hove in sight at 2 P. M. — Cap[t] Pratte,[479] with Mess[rs]
Papin & Halsey[480] on Board, with two Mackinaw Boats that she
was towing up as far as Fort Clark to take down the returns of
that Post — I returned back to Fort Clark on board of the S[t]
Boat — encamped about thirty Miles below the Fort on the
North side —

Monday 19 — Started at day light and arrived at the Mandans
at 3 P. M., onloaded the Merchandises for the Fort — all hands
a Frolicking, found my hunters Out —

Tuesday 20 — The Steam Boat left here this Morning early
for Fort Union,   the Agent for the Mandans has gone above, as
he has nothing to give his red children — Halsey has went up to
reside at Fort Union[481] — My Hunters arrived with plenty of
fresh Meat —

Wednesday 21 — Loaded the two Mac Boats — 320 Packs
Robes & 5 of Beaver,   the water still riseing — The Boats left
here at 2 P. M. — Garreau arrived from hunting with the Meat
of two cows —

Thursday 22 — The Rees and Mandans that left here the 5th
inst all arrived to day well loaded with dried Meat, — traded a
small quantity from them — 4 of the War Party (Mandans)
that left here the 5th inst arrived to day — they say the rest will
be here tomorrow —

Friday 23 — Shower of rain in the Morning — Feast and
Council with the Mandans & Rees,   a great deal of good talk on
both sides — except one of the Principal Cheifs who swore Death

and distruction if the Agent did not pay him for one of his rela-
tions that was Killed by the Whites at the establishment of M^r
Cabanné, his Wife and children came up on board of the Steam
Boat, and told a fine tale against the Whites —

Saturday 24 — Smokey Weather. The War Party of Mandans
that left here the 5th inst arrived to day — they saw enemies but
had not their harts strong enough to attack them. Brave Warriors as Dayvy Crocrite[482] says, in time of Peace — Traded a
quantity of Meat —

Sunday 25 — Wind from the South west, smokey weather —
Sent Charboneau to the Little Mandan Village to distribute a
few twists of tobacco to the heads of Departments —

Monday 26 — Sent Charboneau up to the Gros Ventres to
Collect some news — a small War Party of Rees left here to
day to steal horses at the Pawnee Village —

Tuesday 27 — An other War Party of Mandans and Rees
started to day, on the North side in serch of the Yancton Camp.
May they never return is the only wish I can bestow on them —

Wednesday 28 — Cold for the season — the S. B. arrived from
above at 6 A.M. and started at 7 A. M. The Agent distributed
out a few Presents to the Rees, and gave them a few words of
good talk, and departed. Charboneau arrived from the Gros
Ventres — No News in that quarter — Shower of rain and hail
with heavy Thunder & Lightning — The War Party that left
here the 31st of last Month all came back to day, Without Makeing a Coup —

Thursday 29 — Newman and Benture started up to Fort
Union, to proceed from thence to the Coquille[483] to trap Beaver
down as far as Fort Clark — sprinkled with rain during the
day —

Friday 30 — Sent the Men in the woods to chop fire Wood —
cold rainy Weather — Traded a quantity of Meat and cords from
the Indians. Explanation with one of the Cheifs of the Little
Mandan Village, a threat that he made in Council, all of which

he denied — Traded since the departure of the S. B. 40 Robes, 12 Beaver.

Killed this Month 31 Rats — total 1717 —

1837   JULY 1ST — 31 DAYS

Saturday 1st — Rode up to the Gros Ventres in Company with Garreau, Mitchel, & Charboneau, Counciled with them about 6 Horses they have belonging to the Comp^y — that they stole at the Little Miss^o — they refuse to give them up — heavy rain, with thunder, Lightning, & haile.

Sunday 2nd — Thick foggy Morning — all the Wives of the Village out after Pomme Blanche. The Rees gave us a dance — Storm of Wind from the North West, with rain —

Monday 3 — Arrainged the Merchandise in the ware house — traded seventy Robes and twenty Beaver skins, since the departure of the Steam Boat—

Tuesday 4 — Drank a glass of good old Monongahela to the health of the Old General (Jackson,) The 62nd of American Independence — Rain. Charboneau gave us a dinner, as a celebration of the 4th of July —

Wednesday 5 — A War Party of Rees left here last Night to war against the Sioux — The War Party that left here the 27th of last Month all came back last night, they discovered a Sioux at Apple River. They pursued him several miles without overtaken him, and then returned back — The Rees gave us a dance —

Thursday 6 — Sprinkled with rain in the Morning — The Bull band from the Gros Ventres gave us a splendid dance. The water has fell two feet since yesterday —

Friday 7 — An other small War Party of Rees all Mounted on Horse back started to day for the Sioux Camp — Allert at the Village — Council with the Rees and Mandans, respecting the removal of the Fort, came to a conclusion to build it, at the Point of Woods below — The Dummy arrived with fresh Meat —

Saturday 8 — Rain — Indians prepareing for a dried Meat excursion — traded thirty Robes — The rain continued all day.

Sunday 9 — Appearance of fine weather — the Rees and Mandans all started Out to Make dried Meat — An Indian that arrived yesterday report Cattle in abundance 40 Miles off.

Monday 10 — Sent Charboneau up to the Gros Ventres to collect news, heavy rain in the Morning — clear and pleasant in the afternoon, Charboneau arrived in the evening — No news in that quarter, Indians all out makeing dried meat —

Tuesday 11 — Thick foggy Morning — More rain — No News from any quarter —My hunters not yet arrived — The Mandans of the Little Village all started to day on a dried meat excursion —

Wednesday 12 — Heavy rain all last Night, Dull lonsesome day — all the Indians of the Village Men, Women - and children, (a few old ones excepted) are all out Makeing dried Meat — Nothing stirring, No News, and worst of all, Nothing to eat but a little poor dried Meat that I got from the Steam Boat, on her way from this place to St Louis —

Thursday 13 — Fine day — Sent Garreau out on discovery — Strong south west wind at 10 A.M. which continued all day — Garreau returned in the afternoon without seeing any thing — My Hunters arrived with the meat of three Bulls —

Friday 14 — One of the warmest days that we have had this summer — Weather smokey — A young Mandan died to day of the Small Pox — several others has caught it — the Indians all being out Makeing dried Meat has saved several of them —

Saturday 15 — Sent Mantá Out to hunt a good place to Make hay — he. returned some time after, Much frightened, haveing as he thought, saw enemies, which proved to be, two small Mounds of dirt, Made by the Indians —

Sunday 16 — Charboneau gave us a Jackson dinner, of Pot pye, and pudding —This day has been one of the warmest that we have had this summer — Two of the war party that left here the 5th inst came back to day — left the others at the Old Ree Village — report Cattle in abundance at Heart river —

Monday 17 — Heavy rain and thunder last Night — Covered the houses with dirt — Strong south west wind in the afternoon. Commenced Makeing hay — An other case of the small pox broke out to day at the Village —

Tuesday 18 — The smoke is so thick, that we cannot see as far as the hills , fine times for the Horse theives — Strong wind from the south west all day —

Wednesday 19 — Started out at day light, on discovery — arrived home late in the evening without seeing any thing — We are in a fair way of starveing, but few provissions on hand, and thirty Mouths to feed —

Thursday 20 — Sent Mitchel with two Men — with a Cart and three Mules — to the Ree Camp, to trade Meat — The war party that left here the 5th inst all came back to day — without seeing enemies — Strong south west wind — Mr May and Yoyo[484] arrived from the Little Misso With two Mules and one horse — No News in that quarter, except the Small Pox.

Friday 21 — Heavy shower of rain, and thunder,   hauled four loads of hay from the little river — the Horse gard came back in the afternoon much frightened, haveing discovered the tracks of a war party of Sioux - in the Corn fields —

Saturday 22 — All hands Out after berries. The few Old Men and Women that remain at the Village are starveing — they have sent out to the dried Meat camp to tell them to come in, gave them four pieces of Meat to Make a feast for their children &c — Two loads Hay —

Sunday 23 — Finished haueling hay from the Little river, 10 Loads — Several Indians went out on discovery — They all came back without seeing any thing — Traded several Robes to day, for Meat —

Monday 24 — Two Young Men arrived late last night from the Dried Meat Camp,   he says that they have a great quantity of Meat, and that they will be in to day — set the Men to cut hay at the *Fontaine* —

Tuesday 25 — Several Young Men arrived from the dried Meat Camp, bringing With them each, one piece of Meat for those that remained at the Village. They will all be in to morrow — they say that the small pox has broke out at the Camp —

Wednesday 26 — The Rees and Mandans all arrived to day well loaded with Meat, Mitchel also arrived with 150 pieces. The 4 Bears (Mandan) has caught the small pox, and got crazy and has disappeared from camp — he arrived here in the afternoon — The Indians of the Little Village all arrived in the evening well loaded with dried Meat — the small pox has broke out among them, several has died,

Thursday 27 — Indians all out after berries. No News from any quarter. The small pox is Killing them up at the Village , four died to day — *O. B. F.*

Friday 28 — Rain in the Morning — This day was very Near being my last — a Young Mandan came to the Fort with his gun cocked, and secreted under his robe, with the intention of Killing me, after hunting me in 3 or 4 of the houses he at last found me, the door being shut, he waited some time for me to come out, just as I was in the act of going out, Mitchel caught him, and gave him in the hands of two Indians who conducted him to the Village,   had not Mitchel perceived him the instant he did, I would not be at the trouble of Makeing this statement[485] — I am upon my guard, the Rees are outrageous against the Mandans, they say that the first Mandan that Kills a white, they will exterminate the whole race. I have got 100 Guns ready and 1000lb Powder, ready to hand out to them when the fun commences — The war party of Rees that left here the 7th inst came back to day — with five horses, that they stole from the Sioux — a lodge that was encamped at the Little Misso — they attacked it in the night, after fireing several shots they departed, takeing with them all the Horses — they think to have Killed 3 or 4 in the lodge— The Mandans & Rees gave us two splendid dances, they say they dance, on account of their Not haveing a

long time to live, as they expect to all die of the small pox —
and as long as they are alive, they will take it out in dancing —

Saturday 29— Several more Mandans died last night. Two
Gros Ventres arrived from their dried Meat Camp, it appears
that it has not broke out among them as yet —

Sunday 30 — An other report from the Gros Ventres to day
say, that they are arrived at their Village, and that 10 or 15 of
them have died, two big fish among them, they threaten Death
and Distruction to us all at this place, saying that I was the
cause of the small pox Makeing its appearance in this country[486] — One of our best friends of the Village (The Four Bears)
died to day, regretted by all who Knew him.

Monday 31 — Mandans are getting worse, Nothing will do
them except revenge — Three of the war party that left here
the 26th of last Month arrived to day, With each of them one
horse that they stole from the Yanctons on White river.

Killed 61 Rats this Month — total 1778 —

(Small Pox talk)
18....''....37
July 30th

Speech of the 4 Bears a Mandan Warrior to the
Arricarees and Mandans, 30th July 1837 —

My Friends one and all, Listen to what I have to say — Ever
since I can remember, I have loved the Whites, I have lived
With them ever since I was a Boy, and to the best of my Knowledge, I have never Wronged a White Man, on the Contrary, I
have always Protected them from the insults of Others, Which
they cannot deny. The 4 Bears never saw a White Man hungry,
but what he gave him to eat, Drink, and a Buffaloe skin to sleep
on, in time of Need. I was always ready to die for them, Which
they cannot deny. I have done every thing that a red Skin
could do for them, and how have they repaid it! Wth ingratitude! I have Never Called a White Man a Dog, but to
day, I do Pronounce them to be a set of Black harted Dogs, they

have deceived Me, them that I always considered as Brothers, has turned Out to be My Worst enemies. I have been in Many Battles, and often Wounded, but the Wounds of My enemies I exhalt in, but to day I am Wounded, and by Whom, by those same White Dogs that I have always Considered, and treated as Brothers. I do not fear *Death* my friends. You Know it, but to *die* with my face rotten, that even the Wolves will shrink with horror at seeing Me, and say to themselves, that is the 4 Bears the Friend of the Whites —

Listen well what I have to say, as it will be the last time you will hear Me. think of your Wives, Children, Brothers, Sisters, Friends, and in fact all that you hold dear, are all Dead, or Dying, with their faces all rotten, caused by those dogs the whites, think of all that My friends, and rise all together and Not leave one of them alive. The 4 Bears will act his Part —

1837   AUGUST 31 DAYS

Tuesday 1st — The three horses that the War Party brought in yesterday they say that they belong to the Comp^y — that they were stole on the Island below the Little Miss^o — the Soldiers was for takeing them from them, but I told them to waite untill the arrival of Lachapelle who I expect to arrive in 4 or 5 days —

The Mandans are Makeing their Medicine for rain, As their Corn is all drying up — to day we had several light showers —

Wednesday 2nd — Yesterday an Indian that was out after berries, discovered a band of Cows — all hands out to run them, they all arrived in the Afternoon well laden with fresh meat — haveing run three Bands —

Thursday 3rd — All quiet, No News from any quarter — the Gros Ventres not yet arrived from their dried Meat excursion —

Friday 4 — Same as yesterday — Nothing new — Only two deaths to day — sprinkled with rain in the Morning —

Saturday 5 — Portrá a half breed from the North started to day — alone, for Red River.

Indians out after berries, others out after Meat — News from the Gros Ventres, they say that they are encamped this side of Turtle Mountain, and that a great many of them have died of the small pox — several cheifs among them. They swear vengence against all the Whites, as they say the small pox was brought here by the S. B.

Sunday 6 — One More Ree died last Night — To day we had a tremendous storm of rain, hale, and wind, which Continued for ½ hour with great Violence,   the Fort came very near blowing down,   40 or 50 Loads of hay that I have Out is much damaged

Monday 7 — Six More died to day — several Rees left the Mandan Village, and Pitched their Lodges Out in the Prairie, rain all day— report from the Gros Ventres say they will be at their Village tomorrow —

Tuesday 8 — Four More died to day — the two thirds of the Village are sick, to day I gave six pounds of Epsom salts in doses to Men, Women, and children, the small pox has broke out at the Little Mandan Village — three died yesterday, two cheifs —

Wednesday 9 — Seven More died to day — the Men came back from the hay — at full speed haveing saw enemies,   all hands out for the fight,   False alarm.

Thursday 10 — All the Ree's that were encamped in the Mandan lodges, except a few that are sick, Moved down to the Island hopeing to get rid of the small pox — the Mandans talk of Moveing to the other side of the river, 12 or 15 died to day —

Friday 11 — Sent old Charboneau up to the Gros-Ventres with some tobacco, and a bag full of good talk, as yesterday they sent a very severe threat to me. Mandans all crossed to the other side of the river to encamp - leaveing all that were sick in the Village, I Keep no a/c of the dead, as they die so fast that it is impossible —

Saturday 12 — Cool and pleasant weather, one of my best friends of the Little Village died to day — (Le Fort) — News of a war party of Gros Ventres and Rees (70) being used up by the Saons, quicker work than the small pox —

Sunday 13 — Several reports from the Gros Ventres that they are bent on the distruction of us all, as yet I do not place Much confidence in what report says, Charboneau will bring us the strait News — The Mandans are dying 8 and 10 every day — an Old fellow who has lost the whole of his family to the Number of 14, harrangued to day, that it was time to begin to Kill the Whites, as it was them that brought the small pox in the Country —

Monday 14 — Charboneau arrived late last night , all the reports from the Gros Ventres, it appears to be without foundation, as they say, they never had any thoughts of Killing the Whites, but that the Rees, have made several threats, Which of the two, to believe, I Know not, however, I will still be on my guard. (The White Cow) a Mandan cheif came early this Morning and appeared to be very angry — telling me that I had better clear out, with all the Whites, that if we did not, they would exterminate us all. I told him that we would not leave the place, and that if they were disposed to Kill us to Come on quick, that we were ready for them at all times. The Rees are Makeing Medicine for their sickness. Some of them have made dreams, that they talked to the Sun, others to the Moon, several articles has been sacrifised to them both — the Principal Cheif of the Mandans died to day— The Wolf Cheif)[487] — An other dog, from the Little Village came to the Fort naked with his gun cocked, to Kill one of us, We stopped him —

Tuesday 15 — Gardepie with an other half breed arrived last evening from the North bringing with them 200 Muskrats and 50lb Beaver, Sold him two horses, they left here early this Morning, the small pox scared them off —J. Be Joncá a half breed Kanza, who has been liveing with the Gros Ventres several years, came on horse back at full speed to inform us that the Mandans went up to the Gros Ventres with a pipe, to Make them smoke, to try to get them to help them to Murder us, the Gros Ventres refused to smoke with them, saying that they were friendly to the Whites and that they would not take part with them.   Joncá started back immediately.

The War Party of Rees and Mandans that left here the 26th of June, all came back to day, haveing Killed seven Sioux, Men, Women and children, two Lodges that were camped at the Mouth of White River,   it appears that the small pox has broke out amongst the Sioux,   as some of the Party, on their way back, was taken sick at Grand River,[488] haveing caught the disease from those that they butchered .

Wednesday 16 — Cold for the season,   fire, very comfortable. May started up to see his friends the Gros Ventres.

Several Men, Women, and Children that has been abandoned in the Village, are laying dead in the lodges, some out side of the Village,   others in the little river not entered, which creates a very bad smell all around us — A Ree that has lost his wife and child threatened us to day — We are beset by enemies on all sides — expecting to be shot every Minute —

Thursday 17 — The powder house caved in, the timber being all rotten,   the Rees started out after Buffaloe,   the Indians dying off every day — Were the disease will stop, I Know not — We are badly situated, as we are threatened to be Murdered by the Indians every instant, however we are all determined, and Prepared for the worst — A Young Ree for several days has been lurking around the Fort, watching a good opportunity to Kill me, but not finding a good chance, this Morning he came, full intent to sit himself down in front of the Fort gate, on the Press, and waited a few Minutes for me to go Out,   in the Mean time one of my Men a Dutchman, John Cliver — stepped Out and sat himself down a long side of the Indian, after setting a few Minutes, he got up to come in the Fort , he only Made five paces, when the Indian, shot him in the back bone and Killed him instantaniously,   he made off immediately — We pursued after him shooting at him, but without effect — he got as far as the little river, w[h]ere one of his Brothers is entered,   on arriving there he made a stop, and hollowed to us that, that was the place he wanted to die. Garreau *Cesar* like approached in 15 paces of him and shot, the contents Knocked him over,   he then rushed on him with his large Knife and ripped his body open.   They were both entered at 2 P. M.   I have hoisted the Black flag — an Indian (The two Bulls) showed himself to day, with several others,   how it will turn Out I Know not, but thus far — Man for Man,   the Rees appear to not say Much about it — Garreau deserves the highest praise from us all,   he acted manfully although against his own nation — he always told me that he would always act as he has done — the Mother of the fellow we Killed, came to the Fort crying, saying that she wanted to die also, and wished for us to Kill her.   Garreau stepped up, and with his tommahawk would of Made short work of the Old Woman, but was Prevented —

Friday 18 — Rain all last Night — and this Morning, an Indian that slept in the Fort last night, was taken very sick with the cramp, the Noise that he Made, gave an allert to all of us in the Fort — I thought we were attacked and jumped out of bed in my shirt-tail and seized my gun — I was pleased to find that it was only occasioned by one sick Man, that was dreaming of a White Bear.   An old Ree started this Morning to pay a visit to the Gros Ventres, the Soldiers would not let him enter the Village,   they have made a quarantine and they will permit no one from this place to come near them.   I have herd no talk about the fellow we Killed yesterday - as his two Brothers are not come in from Buffaloe hunting — Nothing but an occasional glass of grog Keeps me alive as I am worried almost to death by the Indians and Whites, the latter (the men) threaten to leave me,   put up some tobacco to send to the Gros Ventres —

Saturday 19 — Charboneau and his family, started for the Gros Ventres last night, being afraid to trust himself in the day time — a Mandan and his Wife Killed themselves yesterday, to not Out live their relations that are dead — Sent ten Pounds of tobacco to the Soldiers of the Gros Ventres, begging them to Not come to their summer Village, as the disease has not yet broke out amongst them,   if it does I am afraid that they will put their threats in execution,   I was in hopes that the disease was almost at an end, but they are dying off 8 and 10 every day — and new cases of it daily — Were it will stop *God* only Knows — An Old Mandan harrangued from the opposite side, to the few that are remaining in the Village, to Prepare themselves, but for what - I could not find out — Wether it is to come in a body to attack us, or some other reason, time will only tell. I Prefer them to come all in one body and then we will Know what we have to do, but they are so treatcherous, that it is impossible to Know Friend or Enemie, however I consider them all the latter, as an Indian is soon turned, like the wind, from one side to the other. As I was sitting out side of the Fort, an Indian came to me, and told me that I had better go in the Fort, as it was dangerous for me to go out — I took his advice and went in, although ashamed to say so —

In the hurry and confusion on the 17th some dog made way with one of my guns — the disease broke out in the Fort six days ago,

Sunday 20 — Sprinkled with rain. Three more died in the Village last night — The Wife of a young Mandan that caught the disease was suffering from the pain,   her husband looked at her, and held down his head,   he jumped up, and said to his wife, When you was young, you were hansome, you are now ugly and going to leave me, but no, I will go with you, he took up his gun and shot her dead, and with his Knife ripped open his own belly — two young men (Rees) Killed themselves to day, one of them stabbed himself with a Knife, and the other with an arrow — Visited by four young men of the Little Village,   there has been but eight deaths at their Village, gave them a pipe of tobacco, and they went off — Several showers of rain throughout the day — a Ree that has been liveing in the Fort, for some time past, caught the disease to day — sent him to the Village — A young Ree that has been sick for some time with the small pox, and being alone in his lodge, thought that it was better to die, than to be in so much pain,   he began to rub the scabs untill blood was running all over his body,   he rolled himself in the ashes, which almost burnt his soul out of his body — two days after he was perfectly well, it is a severe opera-

tion, but few are disposed to try it —however it proved beneficial
to him — May has not yet arrived from the Gros Ventres,   No
doubt but he has been well received by them, is the reason of
his remaining so long —

Monday 21 — Frost this Morning. Winter clothing very comfortable,   the Indians that left here the 17th inst in serch of
cattle, all came back to day with an abundance of Meat — report
cattle scarce and far off — The brother of the dog we Killed the
17th arrived to day — as yet we have herd nothing from him.
I am in hopes that it will all turn out well — An Indian came
and told me to be on my guard — as the fellow above mentioned
is determined to Act as his brother, to Kill one of us, and then
die, he says that he will do it even if all the Village is against
him,   May he change his notion is the wish of your Humble
Servant —

Tuesday 22 — Cool pleasant weather. The disease still Keeps
ahead 8 and 10 die off daily,   Thirty five Mandans [Men] have
died,   the Women and children I Keep no account of [489] — Several Mandans have came back to remain in the Village. One of
my Soldiers — (Ree) died to day — Two young Mandans shot
themselves this Morning — News from the Little Village, that
the disease is getting worse and worse every day,   it is now two
months that it broke out — A Ree that has the small pox, and
thinking that he was going to die, approached near his wife, a
young woman of 19 — and struck her in the head with his tommahawk, with the intent to Kill her,   that she might go with
him in the Other World — she is badly wounded,   a few Minutes
after he cut his throat,   a report is in Circulation, that they intend to fire the Fort — Stationed guards in the Bastion

Wednesday 23 — May and Charboneau arrived late last night
from the Gros Ventres — all appears to be quiet in that quarter,
The little Sioux a *Mandan* died last Night. We had three allerts to day — all hands under Arms, all false reports — Several
Rees arrived from their camp at the Gros Ventres —

Thursday 24 — Seven More died at the Village last Night,
and Many More at the Ree camp at the Point of Woods below —

The fellow that we Killed on the 17th all his band Came to day to smoke with us and Make Peace, how long it will last I cannot tell, however We Must put up with it, good or bad.

Friday 25 — May and Charboneau started last night for the Gros Ventre Village — sent a few pounds of powder & Bals to the Gros Ventres and Rees — An other Mandan cheif died to day — (The long fingers) total Number of Men that has died — 50. I have turned out to be a first rate doctor St Grādo,[490] An Indian that has been bleeding at the Nose all day, I gave him a decoction of all sorts of ingredients Mixed together,   enough to Kill a Buffaloe Bull of the largest size, and stopped the effusion of Blood, the decoction of Medicine, was, a little Magnisia, peppermint,   sugar lead,   all Mixed together in a phial, filled with Indian grog — and the Patient snuffing up his nose three or four times — I done it out of experiment, and am content to say that it proved effectual, the Confidence that an Indian has in the Medicine of the whites, is half the cure,

Saturday 26 — The Indians all started Out on the North side in quest of Buffaloe, as they have Nothing to eat — A young Ree, the nephew of Garreau, died at the Village last night, Much regretted by us all, as he was one of the foremost in aideing to Kill the dog on the 17th inst — A Mandan of the Little Village came to the Fort to day to sing his Medicine song,   got paid for his trouble and went off — glad to get clear of him — A young Ree that has the small pox, told his Mother to go and dig his grave,   she accordingly did so — after the grave was dug,   he walked with the help of his Father to the grave,   I Went Out with the Interpreter to try to pursuade him to return back to the Village — but he would not, saying for the reason that all his young friends were gone, and that he wished to follow them, towards evening he died —

Sunday 27 — Strong east wind,   rain in the Morning. The Indians came back from the *Cerne* well loaded with fresh Meat, report Cattle in abundance 20 Miles off — News from the Gros Ventres of the disease breaking out amongst them.

Monday 28 — Wind from the North,   rain,   disagreeable

Weather, several more Indians arrived — with fresh Meat — from the North side — gave us a small quantity which we found very good — Three more fell sick in the Fort to day — My Interpreter[491] for one, if I loose him I shall be badly off, the bad weather continued all day — and no prospects of clearing off —

Tuesday 29 — Last Night I was taken very sick with the Fever, there is six of us in the Fort that has the Fever, and one the small pox — An Indian Vaccinated his child, by cutting two small pieces of flesh out of his arms, and two on the belly — and then takeing a Scab from one, that was getting well of the disease, and rubbing it on the wounded part, three days after, it took effect, and the child is perfectly well —

Wednesday 30 — All those that I thought had the small pox turned out to be true, the fever left them yesterday, and the disease showed itself. I am perfectly well, as last night, I took a hot whiskey punch, which made me sweat all last night, this Morning I took my daily Bitters as usual. Indians arrived with fresh Meat, report cattle in abundance opposite the Little Lake below —

Thursday 31 — A young Mandan that died 4 days ago, his wife haveing the disease also — Killed her two children, one a fine Boy of eight years, and the other six , to complete the affair she hung herself —

Month of August I bid you farewell with all my heart, after running twenty hair breadths escapes, threatened every instant to be all murdered, however it is the wish of humble servant that the Month of September will be More favorable, the Number of Deaths up to the Present is very near five hundred — The Mandans are all cut off, except 23 young and Old Men —

Killed 89 Rats this month — Total 1867 .

1837   SEPTEMBER 30 DAYS

Friday 1 — This Morning two dead bodies, wrapped in a White skin, and laid on a raft passed by the Fort, on their way to the regions below, May success attend them. The Rees that are encamped in the Point of Woods below, are moveing up to encamp at the Mandan Corn fields — No doubt with the intention of takeing all from them, as what few Mandans are left are not able to contend with the Rees — Mitchels squaw fell to day.

Saturday 2 — Being out of wood, risqued the Men — to the Point of Woods below,   hauled eight loads.   Several Indians arrived with fresh Meat, out 2 days, but one death to day, although several are sick,   those that catch the disease at Present, seldom die.   One Fellow that I had numbered with the dead, I saw on horseback to day — he looked more like a gohst [*sic*] than a being —

Sunday 3 — A young Mandan came to pay us a visit from the Little Village, he informes us, that they are all Most all used up, and that it is his opinion that before the disease stops, that there will not, one be left, except 8 or 10 that has weathered Out the sickness —

Monday 4 — Commenced for the second time, to haule hay, as I have 50 or 60 Loads in the prairie,   the troublesome times prevented me from haueling it — a young Mandan that was given over for dead, and abandoned by his Father, and left alone in the bushes to die, came to life again, and is now doing well,   he is hunting his Father, with the intent to Kill him, for leaveing him alone, Pellot with 2 Men arrived from the Little Misso [Bad River] — No News in that quarter, Out 15 days haveing lost their way, and travelled up as far as the Little Misso — report that from Grande River up, all the Country is black with Buffaloe,   all comeing in this way.   I am in hopes that we shall have them here soon. *O. B. F.*

Tuesday 5th — Thick foggy morning, Indians all out after Buffaloe on the north side. Set the Men to Make a skin canoe to start to Fort Pierre — Covered the stable with dirt &c.

Wednesday 6 — Same as yesterday — Some few Indians started out, on this side, in quest of Buffaloe, rainey, disagreeable weather. No news from any quarter — The canoe destined for Fort Pierre, detained by the bad weather. The Mandans that were encamped on the opposite side of the river all crossed to day, and camped in the Village, to gether their corn —

Thursday 7 — The bad weather still continues. The disease not yet over,   five and six die off daily — No News from the Gros Ventres since 12 days — The Indians that crossed the river the 5th inst arrived to day well-loaded with fresh Meat — others arrived from this side also loaded,   report Cattle plenty all over the Country — Started the canoe with two Men to Fort Pierre,   sent My Boy down with them being afraid of the disease,[492] Several Rees are yet encamped in the Point of Woods below, taken care of the sick,   although New Cases every day — Garreau appears much better to day —Bellehumeur's Wife and 2 Children has it,

Friday 8 — Rain, disagreeable weather,   those that are sick in the Fort get worse,   there is at present seven sick of the disease. A Son of Old L'étaile[493] died to day — regretted by us all,   as he was one of the formost in Killing the dog on the 17th inst. The rain continued all day —

Saturday 9 — Fine weather untill 10 A.M — Cold and cloudy the rest of the day — Wind N.W. Employed the Men Makeing a road on the bank of the river, to haule wood — This winter, I am badly off, as I have 60 Loads of hay yet to haule, and not one stick of wood in the Fort —

Sunday 10 — Charboneau arrived late last night from the Gros Ventres,   all well in that quarter,   the disease has not yet broke out among them,   except his squaw, who died 4 days ago — Put up a few goods to send to the Gros Ventres to trade Robes &c — Hard frost last night —

Monday 11 — Set the Men to haule hay — Charboneau started late last night for the Gros Ventres, With two Mules loaded with Powder, Ball, & Tobacco — Indians Out after Buffaloe on the North side —

Tuesday 12 — The Rees started down the river as far as Hart River to encamp 4 or 5 days as cattle are plenty in that quarter. The Bloody hand, a Ree cheif arrived from his camp, at the

Gros Ventres,   he reports that the disease has broke out at his camp,   Bought a horse from a Mandan — Finished one stack of hay 35 Loades, Five More enterments to day, One of my horses is Missing, supposed to have been stolen.

Wednesday 13 — Cold and appearance of rain,   Set the Men to haule wood, A young girl, the daughter of the Old Star,[494] died in the Fort — Indians arrived from the North side loaded with Meat, Out three days —

Thursday 14 — The weather continues cold,   Wind from the North,   Cloudy and appearance of snow — Two Rees that has been with the Sioux (Saons) since last summer, arrived from their camp on Cannon Ball river,   haveing been sent by the Saons with a Pipe to Make peace with the Rees and Mandans. The disease has not broke out among them. Two of my horses are Missing — A Ree that arrived from the Gros Ventres with a stolen Horse, reports the arrival of two white Men in a canoe, from Fort Union —

Friday 15 — Two men arrived late last Night in a Canoe from Fort Union. The disease has broke Out at the Assinneboines and Black feet, several had died,   the Rees that left here the 12th inst all arrived loaded with Meat — report Cattle plenty on Heart river — Wrote letters and Prepared the express for F. U.

Saturday 16 — The two Men that arrived from Fort Union started early this Morning, with letters for J. Halsey &c — two more of Bellehumeurs Children Caught the disease to day,   he has at Present his Wife and five children sick —

Sunday 17 — The two Rees that arrived from the Saons Camp the 14th inst left here to day — accompanied by two others, with tobacco, to smoke, and Make peace between the two Nations, set the Squaws to sew a skin Canoe, to haule Wood from the other side of the river,   strong Wind from the North which continued all day — hard frost this Morning,   Which froze all the Corn & Pumpkins.

Monday 18 — The Mandans and Rees Crossed the river in quest of Buffaloe, this Morning and yesterday, we had a very hard frost, Which has frozen all the Corn — I shall be badly off this Winter, as I do Not expect to trade ten Bushels of Corn this Year,   Worked all day Makeing a skin Canoe, to haule Wood from the sand bar opposite the Fort — I have not worked as hard these six years as I have to day, haveing but two Men able to Work, the rest are sick a bed,   finished hauleing my hay 64 Loades —

Tuesday 19 — All quiet to day — Nothing Worth relating has transpired, except that the day was pleasant, and that we have not a stick of Wood in the Fort — Tomorrow I am in hopes of haveing 10 or 12 Loads. I was visited by a young fellow from the little Village, he assures Me that there is but 14 of them liveing, the Number of deaths Cannot be less than 800 — What a bande of RASCALS has been used up —

Wednesday 20 — Appearance of rain, cold and Not a stick of Wood in the Fort,   all the sick in the Fort 14 in Number,   Complains of the Cold last night, haveing passed the Night without fire. Bellehumeurs youngest child died to day —

Thursday 21 — Set the Men to haule Wood from the opposite side with a skin Canoe of 6 Sks, — Made two trips, 16 cart loades. The Mandans fearing their Allies, the Rees should unite with the Sioux, have all fled to the opposite side of the river, what their intention is, I Know not, but the few that are left (41) are Miserable, surrounded on all sides.

Friday 22 — The Rees Crossed the river in quest of Buffaloe commenced tradeing Corn — Strong Wind from the South east Which Prevents my hauleing Wood — Entered into My Winter quarters,   My youngest son died to day[495] —

Saturday 23 — An other of Bellehumeurs children died last Night, a fine boy of six years old, sick eight days. Strong Wind again to day, Which Prevents my hauleing Wood. Passed the day With the men sawing Wood.

Sunday 24 — Rain all last Night, the Ducks, geese and Swans, are Comeing from above, Wholesale and retail,   no doubt but winter has set in above,   Arranged my Corn Scaffold — in hopes of tradeing a few bushels.

Monday 25 — Allert at the Village last Night. Yesterday the Gros Ventres stole six horses belonging to the Rees, War will be declared between the two Nations before long - as the Rees talks of retaliating,   hauled 3 Canoe loads of Wood —

Tuesday 26 — Newman & Benture arrived from hunting Beaver, brought with them 105 Sks — Indians arrived with fresh Meat — Strong Wind from the East at 10 A. M. —

Wednesday 27 — Settled with the Hunters for their Beaver, sold them two Horses. Newman started out to Make a second hunt on Powder River, some few Rees started out after Buffaloe. Charboneau arrived from the Gros Ventres bringing With him 85 Robes, and 4 Beaver Sks — reports that but few of the Gros Ventres have the disease and that but 10 has died,   the Rees also has it amongst them, and die off 2 and 3 every day — all Peaceable in that quarter, no bad talk against the Whites, Cattle scarce in their Neighborhood —

Thursday 28 — Rain,   put up some Powder, Ball, & Tobacco to send to the Gros Ventres. Rain. Indians arrived with fresh Meat — Hauled 41 Loads of Wood from the river.

Friday 29 — Heavy rain, thunder and lightning all last night. Charboneau started up to the Gros Ventres with a small equipt to Trade this Winter. Benture and three Indians Went with him, Sold 2 horses to Benture for thirty Pounds Beaver — The Rees that [left] here the 27 inst arrived to day, loaded with fresh Meat,   report Cattle in abundance, set the Men to saw fire wood —

Saturday 30 — Cloudy — Finished Hau[l]ing Wood 90 Loads — Two More Rees died to day, with the Small Pox, several More are sick at the Village. All the Rees and Mandans, Men's Women's and Children, have had the disease, except a few Old Ones, that had it in Old times, it has distroyed the seven eights of the Mandans and one half of the Rees Nations, the Rees that are encamped With the Gros Ventres have just Caught it. No doubt but the one half of them will die also — as they talk of removeing down to this place if so, they Cannot avoid Catching it, as the peste is at this place. Mr. Mitchel[496] arrived from St. Louis with thirty Men, on his way to Fort Union —

Killed 74 Rats this Month — 1941.

1837   OCTOBER 31 DAYS

Sunday 1 — Mitchel and his party left here for Fort Union. Cloudy in the Morning, fine and pleasant in the afternoon Indians all quiet, talk of starting below, to Make their winter quarters, as Buffaloe are plenty in that quarter —

Monday 2 — I have only two Men in the Fort — Set them to haule Wood,   Foggy Morning,   at 10 A. M. cold North wind, with rain.

Tuesday 3 — Snow and rain all last Night, the Prairies are all covered with snow — had it not rained, we would of had snow 3 feet deep, cleared off in the afternoon,

Wednesday 4 — More rain. A Ree that went from here with Mr. Mitchel, came back to day — reports the Rees that were encamped with the Gros Ventres, have seperated, the former are on their way to this place, the latter are still going further up the Misso.

Thursday 5 — Feast and Council with the Rees — gave them a small Present,   and spoke to them about Moveing to their Winter quarters,   Counciled with the Mandans —

Friday 6 — The Rees all started out after fresh Meat, as cattle are plenty near at hand,   a band of Antilopes (200) Made their appearance on the opposite side, Indians out after them —

Saturday 7 — Several Ree lodges Crossed over the river to Winter with the Mandans — A stray horse made his appearance on the other side supposed to be one that Mitchel and his party lost at the square hills —

Sunday 8 — Cloudy — the Rees that left here the 6th inst all arrived loaded with Meat and skins,   report Cattle in abundance

Council with the Mandans, they all came on horseback on the other side, sent the Canoe and crossed 4,

Monday 9 — Strong North west Wind all day — set the men to saw wood — A bande of (50) Antilopes showed themselves on the other side,   good signe of Buffaloe being Plenty.

Tuesday 10 — The Squaws are all busily engaged in dressing the skins that were brought in the 8th inst, as soon as they are finished, they all Move down to the little lake, to Camp for the Winter. The Rees gave us a dance.

Wednesday 11 — Several Mandans arrived last night from hunting, report the Country black with Buffaloe opposite the square hills.

Thursday 12 — Squaw fight at the Village, two young men also came near fighting, on account of a stolen horse.

Friday 13 — Nothing of any importance has transpired to day — except that an Indian came to take one of my Mules from me, that formerly belonged to him, which I exchanged with an other for a horse.

Saturday 14 — The Mandans all moved up the river, where their place of destination is, we cannot find out — A party of five young Rees started this Morning to steal horses from the Gros Ventres,   the Cheifs sent after them, and made them return.

Sunday 15 — Shower of rain last Night.   Thirty or forty Indians all Mounted on horse back were discovered from the Village,   thought to be enemies.

Monday 16 — The Rees all Moved down to the Point of Woods opposite the Little Lake, to take up their Winter quarters — Several Rees that has been liveing with the Sioux, arrived to day — report that the Small Pox has broke Out amongst them, the Rees decamped in the Night as the Sioux were for Killing them —

Tuesday 17 — Smokey Weather,   set the Men to haul wood

from the Village 25 Loads,   all the Indians have decamped, except one lodge, that has lately Caught the disease.

Wednesday 18 — Rain. Two young Bucks came up from the Camp report Cattle in abundance opposite the Little Lake, the bad Weather Continued all day —

Thursday 19 — Cold and Cloudy,   at 4 P. M. fine and pleasant. No News from any quarter, except that one of my Mens squaw run away.

Friday 20 — An Indian arrived from the Camp below — Cattle plenty near their camp —

Saturday 21 — Started out at day light with two Men and four Mules in quest of something to eat   at 9 A. M. discovered a band of cows   run them and Killed four,   got home at sun down,   With our horses well loaded.

Sunday 22 — Light fall of snow last night — Mr Halsey[497] with three Men arrived from Fort Union, in a small Mackinaw boat — bound to Fort Pierre —

Monday 23 — Haveing Nothing to do I thought I would take a trip down with Mr Halsey,   to see My Old friends at Fort Pierre — off at 10 O Clock,   arrived at Fort Pierre the 31st — passage of nine days —

NOVEMBER 24TH, 1837

I arrived here today in twelve days from the Little Missouri [Bad River]. I passed a band of Yanctons opposite the mouth of Cannon Ball River;   we have been the last four days without any thing to eat except one otter;   and to make our trip more agreeable we were two days and one night in snow to our Knees;   however I found all things right at my arrival,   which compensates for the unpleasantness of my trip

Saturday 25 — Men all employed sawing wood — Garreau started out in serch of 2 lost horses — Prepared the express for Fort Union —

Sunday 26 — Sent down to the Ree Camp for a horse that I

left there,   on my way to their place — Started the Men's with the letters to Fort Union, (May & C⁰)

Monday 27 — Sent out my hunters with 4 Mules — Mitchel & Garreau started out in serch of two lost horses,   Prepared the express for Fort Pierre .

Tuesday 28 — Thick fogg — Started two Men , with letters to Fort Pierre,   (Latress⁴⁹⁸ & C⁰) — two horses that has been lost for several days, came to the Fort to day — Snow storm —

Wednesday 29 — Set the Men to Make balls — Put up an Eqᵗ to send to Ree Village — My hunters arrived with the Meat of 4 Cows —

Thursday 30 — Started the Eqᵗ to the Rees,   1 Cart-load of Merchandises,

Killed 268 Rats this Month —total 2209

1837   DECEMBER 31 DAYS

Friday 1ˢᵗ — The Cart arrived from the Ree Camp — No News in that quarter,   except that they are busily engaged in dancing the scalps of three Sioux, that they Killed a few days ago, in the act of stealing horses.

Saturday 2 — Snow storm last last [night?]   a Buffalo Bull Made his appearance on the sand bar opposite the Fort.

Sunday 3 — Sent out my hunters with 4 Mules,   One of the coldest days we have,   the river not yet closed —

Monday 4 — The river frose over last Night,   it has been later this year , than several years past — 80 to 100 Rees came up to the Fort to day, each of them 3 to 4 horses,   on their way out after Buffaloe, which are in abundance, 10 Miles off —

Tuesday 5 — Men employed in haueling wood, others makeing a cart and sled or train. My hunters arrived late with the Meat of 4 Cows —

Wednesday 6 — The squaws came up from the Village to give

us a dance;   they got Nothing for their trouble, and went off dissatisfied.

Thursday 7 — The Indians all arrived well loaded with fresh Meat,   Gave me the Meat of two cows, and thirty tongues —

Friday 8 — The Indians all started down to their camp — two Indians arrived from the Mandan camp, report cattle in abundance.

Saturday 9 — Sent out my hunters with 6 Mules — Two Men from Fort Union with the Express for St Louis arrived.   Out 7 Days —

Sunday 10 — Snow throughout the day.   Prepared the express for St Louis.   Two Indians was discovered on the other side of the river, as they did not come to the Fort, were supposed to be enemies.

Monday 11 — Three Rees arrived from the camp, below — report cattle in abundance, on the North side,   all hands out to run them —

Tuesday 12 — Started two Men with the Express for St Louis. Set traps to catch Wolves,   My hunters not yet returned.

Wednesday 13 — Caught a fox last night — No news from any quarter —

Thursday 14 — Caught eight foxes, and three Wolves last night —

Friday 15 — Caught 3 Wolves and six foxes last Night — My hunters arrived late with the Meat of six cows —

Saturday 16 — Caught three wolves and seven foxes last night,   the Chimney in the Mens house caught fire —

Sunday 17 — Caught one Wolf and one Fox last Night — A young Mandan and his Wife arrived from the Camp above, reported a fight between them and the Assiniboines,   two Mandans Killed,   the former after a hard fight, and the loss of One Man, succeeded in driving off 35 Horses.

Monday 18 — Sent the old *Star* down to the Ree camp to collect some news —

Tuesday 19 — Sent out my hunters with 4 Mules — The Old *Star* arrived from the Camp below — No News in that quarter, except that Buffaloe are plenty — and that a small war party of Sioux stole fourteen horses, two nights ago —

Wednesday 20 — Caught one Wolf last Night,   sent some Tobacco up to the Mandan camp — My hunters arrived with the Meat of three Cows,   report Cattle plenty in 20 Miles of the Fort,   all travelling this way — I am in hopes, that in the course of 2 or 3 days we shall be surrounded by them —

Thursday 21 — May arrived late last Night from Fort Union, had three of his horses stolen on his way to this place by the Assinniboines —

Friday 22 — Started a small War Party up to the Assinniboine Camp, to steal two horses that they have belonging to Me.

Saturday 23 — An Indian arrived from the Camp below, report Cattle plenty — the Yanctons have stolen twelve horses from them two Nights ago —

Sunday 24 — Mild and pleasant.   No News from any quarter —

Monday 25 — Christmas,   Cold North West wind all day —

Tuesday 26 — Sent out my hunters with 4 Mules,   Same as Yesterday —

Wednesday 27 — All's quiet —

Thursday 28 — Do — Do —

Friday 29 — Ditto —

Saturday 30 — My hunters arrived with the Meat of five Cows — Cattle far off — and travelling to the West —

Sunday 31 — Sent a Man down to the Ree Camp to collect some News — Caught three foxes last Night — Charboneau arrived from the Gros Ventre Camp — he was accompanied by 2

Mandans and One Gros Ventre,   he is encamped with only ten Lodges,   the rest of the Lodges are scattered, on the Little Misso — he has had No News of them, for two Months,   in all probability they are all Dead,   the last News that he had from them was,   that 117 had died, and the disease was still rageing —

Killed 85 Rats this Month — total 2294

1838

1838   JANUARY 31 DAYS

Monday 1 — This year commences with 350 Buff. Robes, and 350 lb Beaver — Foxes &c &c   Rain at 2 P.M.   Hunot[499] arrived from the Ree Camp — brought 60 Tongues with him — report Cattle in abundance — Several Ree Lodges arrived from above, on their way to the camp below —

Tuesday 2 — Sent a train with two Men, to the Ree Camp to bring up Robes &c —

Wednesday 3 — Several Rees arrived from the Camp below, left my Men on the Way — at 10 A. M. Wind from the North east with snow, that continued all day —

Thursday 4 — The horse trains arrived late last Night from below with Robes &c &c

Friday 5 — Sent out my hunters with four Mules,   three Rees arrived from the Camp above —

Saturday 6 — An Old Mandan arrived from the Camp above, in quest of his young Wife, that eloped with a young Ree.

Sunday 7 — Charboneau started for the Gros Ventres   a Squaw died in the Fort last Night of the small Pox — the Old Stars Daughter —

Monday 8 — Last night a Young Ree arrived from the Camp below, with a stolen Wife,   report Cattle in abundance.

Tuesday 9 — Three to four hundred Buffaloe Were discovered from the Fort to day, on the North side.   My hunters arrived late with the Meat of four Cows, Cattle far off towards the West.

Wednesday 10 — Went out after Breakfast to run Buffaloe, returned to the Fort at 1 P.M. with 4 Cows. An Indian arrived from the Camp above — report the Death of one, Killed by the Assinnboine.

Thursday 11 — Went out to run Buffaloe, returned to the Fort at dusk with the Meat of three fat Cows, Cattle in abundance.

Friday 12 — Several Rees arrived from the Camp below, report Cattle plenty — trade going on slow in that quarter — *O. B. F.*

Saturday 13 — Newman started out with five Mules, sent my Black Hawk[500] down to the Ree Village, Wind from the S. West

Sunday 14 — Mitchel Went out to hunt two lost horses, came back at 2 P. M. — haveing been taken Prisoner by a small War Party of Yanctons —

Monday 15 — Strong South West Wind, which continued all day —Water riseing fast —

Tuesday 16 — Sent out my hunters with 4 Mules — and 1 horse, Wind from the North east, snow drifting, cold stormy Weather

Wednesday 17 — My hunters arrived late last Night with the Meat of two Cows — One of my Men (a half Breed from the North) Was taken sick with the Small Pox, Cattle in abundance all arround us, several thousand can be seen from the Fort — Two Indians arrived from the Mandan Camp, they inform me that all the Prairies above are Covered with Cattle.

Thursday 18 — All hands Out to run Buffaloe. Killed two on Our way home. May Killed an Antilope, one of the Coldest days we have had — one of my horses died.

Friday 19 — Enemies around the Fort last Night — Strong North West Wind — Snow drifting — the bad Weather Continued all day. I am afraid that several of my horses have perished from the Cold — A Bull Crossed from the opposite side. We Killed him in 30 yds from the Fort.

Saturday 20 — All hands out to approach Cattle, as they are thick opposite the Fort — The hunters came back haveing Killed two cows —

Sunday 21 — Sent a horse traine to bring in a Cow that we have Cached in the snow— the train came back Without Meat, the Wolves haveing eat it all,   Mitchel came in with the skin of an Old Bull.

Monday 22 — The hunters Out after Cattle,   Sent May with one Mule, down to the Ree Camp for a load of Tongues. Mitchel & the Star arrived with the Meat of two Cows and two Antilopes. One of my Mules died.

Tuesday 23 — The Old Star Killed an Antilope. Killed three Wolves last Night. One of the Coldest days we have had this Winter. Two Rees arrived from the Camp above, report the arrival of 40 Gros Ventres lodges at that place.

Wednesday 24 — Sent all my horses up to the Point of Woods, of the Little Village, to remain a few days. The Old Star Killed an Antilope — Three Indians arrived from below — No News —

Thursday 25 — Sent May up to the Gros Ventres, to collect some News. Two Mandans arrived from the Camp above, report Cattle in abundance. Two Rees arrived from below,   all hands out to run Buffaloe, on the North side. The Old Star Killed an Antilope.

Friday 26 — Snow storm. Several squaws arrived from below, on their way to the Upper Camp — report Cattle scarce below —

Saturday 27 — The bad Weather still Continues. Wind from the North West,   snow drifting — the Men not able to cut fire Wood. May arrived from the Gros Ventres. No News in that quarter except that Buffaloe are in abundance. The Small Pox still raveageing —

Sunday 28 — Two herds of Cattle on the opposite side — the bad Weather prevents us from running them, Several Indians arrived from below — The Wind being Contrary, raised the Cattle —

Monday 29 — The bad Weather still Continues, the snow has been drifting for several days,   which prevents us from getting our daily supply of fire Wood —

Tuesday 30 — Newman Came down from the Meat Camp in serch of two Mules that came to the Fort last Night — he reports Cattle in abundance,   he has Killed six fat cows —

Wednesday 31 — The last day of a Cold Month.   The Bloody Hand a Ree Cheif and two others paid me a Visit to day —

Killed 24 Rats this Month — total 2318

1838   FEBRUARY 28 DAYS

Thursday 1 — The cold Weather still Continues, the Men are not able to go out after fire Wood.   The Old Star and his son started out hunting, Cattle in aboundance.   I have traded but 400 Robes up to this date.

Friday 2 — Mitchel Went Out hunting — Came back with the Meat of one cow — Cold and cloudy in the afternoon.   Cattle came in very plenty to day — The Old Star has not yet arrived.

Saturday 3 — Killed one Wolf last Night — Stormy Weather. May and Mitchel went out hunting.   Mitchel arrived with the Meat of one Poor Cow — May Killed two Antilopes,   the Rees run a band of Buffaloe of at least two thousand,   they Killed a great Number —

Sunday 4 — Sent May down to the Ree camp for a loade of Robes.   Mitchel started out hunting.   Mitchel came back from hunting, haveing found a lost horse, belonging to the Mandans.

Monday 5 — Snow storm.   Mitchel Went Out hunting.   Several Mandans arrived from the Camp above, The Gauche[501] at the Head.   The Old Star arrived with the Meat of two Cows,

Mitchel arrived with one fat Cow — Hunot arrived from the Meat Camp haveing had a quarrel with Newman.

Tuesday 6 — The Mandans had a drunken frolic last Night, they all left here this Morning. Sent Hunot down to the Ree camp, to be cured of the Venerial. More arrivals from above. No News, except that cattle are beginning to be scarce in their Neighbourhood.

May arrived from the Ree Camp, With a load of Robes No News in that quarter. Buffaloe scarce. Pleasant day .

Wednesday 7 — Two bands of Cows showed themselves on the North Side. The half breed that was taken with the small Pox the 17th of last Month is perfectly recovered, sent him up to the Meat Camp to take care of the horses. No arrivals to day —

Thursday 8 — Newman Came down from the Meat Camp, haveing broke his rifle. Mitchel and an Indian Went out to run a band of Cows on the North side. May Went out hunting — Newman started back to the Meat Camp,   haveing repaired his rifle. Mitchel & May came back from hunting, the former Killed one cow, the latter three Antilopes and one fox —

Friday 9 — Cold day — A band of Wolves exceeding two hundred Crossed the river, the running season has commenced,   set the squaws to scrape skins, for Makeing Cords. Four Men and one squaw Mandans arrived from the Camp above.

Saturday 10 — A large band of Cattle on the hills back of the Fort. More arrivals from above. Several Gros Ventres are on their way to the lower Ree Camp, to have a friendly smoke together.

Sunday 11 — Change in the Weather, shower of rain in the Morning, the first this year. Bothered with the Indians that arrived Yesterday, the bad Weather Prevented them from starting. May, Garreau, and the *White Horse,* a Ree Cheif, came up from the Camp, with three horses loaded with Robes and Tongues. Charboneau arrived from the Gros Ventres with two horses loaded with Tongues, trade going on slow in that quarter. An other of My Mules died last Night.

Monday 12 — The coldest day that we have had for the last six Years. Garreau & Co. started down to the Ree Camp. Cattle in abundance on the North side.

Tuesday 13 — Same as Yesterday — An other of My Mules died last Night. Killed a cow and an Antilope.

Wednesday 14 —Cold as usual, the Bloody hand came up from the Camp below — after a smoke he departed for above. Mitchel started out hunting, Came back haveing Killed an Antilope. A Bull paid a visit to the Mandan Village. Buffaloe Comeing in from all quarters. We are completely surrounded by them.

Thursday 15 — Killed one Wolf last Night. The hunters all Out. Buffaloe thick. Several Rees came up from below, on their way to the upper Camp — the hunters came in haveing Killed one Cow —

Friday 16 — Put up a small equipment and sent Old Charboneau to the Gros Ventres. May Killed an Antilope.

Saturday 17 — The Old Star came down from the Meat camp, with the Meat of two Cows. May Killed a fat cow —

Sunday 18 — My Old Cook, and his Indian family had a dispute — No News from any quarter — Strong Wind from the N. W. all day —

Monday 19 — Mitchel and Myself Went Out to run a band of Cows on the hill, Killed two. May started Out hunting on the North side   he killed one fat Cow — Three Rees arrived from the Camp above,   all quiet in that quarter,   Buffaloe still holds out in all directions,   the Indian Horses being Poor, they Kill but few —

Tuesday 20 — May Killed a Cow — Newman came down from the Horse Camp, With the Meat of six Cows,   sent the Horses and Mules back to the camp, to bring in an other load tomorrow.

Wednesday 21 — May Killed three Antilopes, Newman arrived from the Meat Camp with five horses well loaded.   Two Rees arrived from the upper camp — Pleasant day — *O. B. F.*

Thursday 22 — Cold and Cloudy — Wind from the North East Which Makes my Chimney smoke.   Two Gros Ventres arrived from above, on their way to the Ree Camp — an other Mule died last Night.

Friday 23 — Weather same as Yesterday.   Newman arrived from the Meat Camp, bringing all that was left, at the camp —

Saturday 24 — Cold and stormy all day — Wind from the South East — No News —

Sunday 25 — Weather same as Yesterday — Newman and his Wife seperated —

Monday 26 — Mitchel Killed a Cow — An other of my Mules died to day.   I hope it is the last! as I have but three left —

Tuesday 27 — Strong South Wind untill 10 A. M. — pleasant the rest of the day — Mitchel Killed a cow — Several Rees came up from the lower camp —

Wednesday 28 — Thick foggy Weather — The bad Weather continued all day.   Newman Killed a cow — May Killed an Antilope —

Killed 16 Rats this Month — (Total) 2334

1838   MARCH 31 DAYS

Thursday 1 — The first day of Spring commences with snow — Pleasant in the afternoon —

Friday 2 — Newman and his wife, after six days quarreling and Pouting with each other had a seperation,   he started down to the Ree Camp in quest of an other.   O may success attend him, in the Wife line, it is his third since his fall hunt —

Saturday 3 — Newman and his Wife Came back from the Ree Village, haveing settled all difficulties amicably — Grand hunting party of Manta & C⁰ started Out to Kill Buffaloe, they all came back shortly after, tired of their walk.

Sunday 4 — Several Rees arrived from the lower camp with Robes Foxes Tongues &c. Two Gros Ventres arrived from above. Cattle getting scarce in all directions, although Cattle have been in Abundance all winter the Indians have not laid up a Morsel of dried Meat, They will starve before long as they have no Corn —

Monday 5 — Snow — The bad Weather Continued all day — bothered with Indians —

Tuesday 6 — After so Much Cold Weather, this day Might be considered a pleasant day, although far from being Warm — Bonture arrived late in the evening from Fort Union — No News in that quarter

Wednesday 7 — Same as yesterday — The Indians that arrived the 4ᵗʰ inst, Went off to day —

Thursday 8 — Several bands of Cattle in sight of the Fort, hunters all out — Several Rees passed here on their way to the Gros Ventres,   to have a smoke with them and the Mandans — My hunters Killed three Cows — they all being poor, they left the Meat —

Friday 9 — Fine pleasant day,   snow thawing fast,   May started Out Beaver hunting. Four squaws arrived from the Mandan Camp. No News in that quarter. Several bands of Buffaloe showed themselves on the hills, both sides of the Fort —

Saturday 10 —An Other fine day. Wrote letters and Prepared to start Bᵉ Lebrun in the Morning for Fort Union. Garreau arrived from the Rees With 20 Robes — Three Mandans arrived from the Camp above —

Sunday 11 — Started Benture for Fort Union with letters for D. D. Mitchell. The Two Bulls arrived from the lower Camp with 10 Robes —

Monday 12 — Set the squaws to clean out the Fort The snow is fast disappearing, in three or four days I am in hopes it will all be gone,   The Wolf Cheif arrived from the Upper Camp with six Robes —

Tuesday 13 — Set the squaws to Work to cut up and dry a quantity of fresh Meat. The Old Star arrived from the Meat camp.

Wednesday 14— — More snow, the hills and planes are again covered. More arrivals from above — No news in that quarter, the small Pox is still rageing with the Gros Ventres —

Thursday 15 — An other fine day — Snow thawing fast. Several Indians came up from below with Robes —

Friday 16 — The Rees commenced Moveing up from below — Water riseing over the Ice —

Saturday 17 — Sent two mules down to the Ree camp for Tongues — Garreau arrived from below, with 40 Robes, Foxes, Tongues &c — My Negro Boy that I sent to remain with the Rees, came up to day, he speaks the language tolerably well for the short time,

Sunday 18 — The water rose last Night two feet. Garreau started back to the Ree Camp. Last Night I Killed an Indians dog for entering of the Fort gate,   the owner of the dog says that he will retaliate. Since eight Oclock this Morning, the Water commenced riseing — at 10 A. M. the ice broke up in fine stile;   at 3 P.M. the ice stopped running occassioned by a bridge of ice formeing a few miles below — since Morning the water has rose 12 feet —

Monday 19 — Stormy day — the water is Much higher at Present than it has been for the last twelve years, although the Ice has stopped running, the River is clear of Ice opposite the Fort, and for several Miles below —

Tuesday 20 — The Old Star arrived late last Night from the Ree Camp with 16 Robes. The water continues high. Cold and Cloudy. Garreau arrived from below with the rest of the merchandises. Several Ree lodges arrived, the rest will be here to morrow — to take possession of the Mandan Village.

Wednesday 21 — Trade going on slow, traded 40 Robes since Yesterday — The water same as the 18th. Two of the Old Stars horses drowned in the lake above the Village,

Thursday 22 — Ducks passed to day, for the first time this year — Feast and Council with the Rees,   traded 60 Robes —

Friday 23 — Strong North West Wind. Several Ree Lodges started out to Make dried Meat — I had a quarrel which almost ended in a fight with a Ree soldier. At 4 P. M. the ice Made an other start. The fellow that I had a quarrel with brought me a Robe to Make friends. We had a smoke together, and settled the difficulty.

Saturday 24 — Trade brisk to day — the water fell several feet. Garreau turned his Wife off for infidelity, poor thing —

Sunday 25 — Newman started Out Beaver hunting. The Rees started Out to Make dried Meat, on Knife river. The band of Bulls gave us a sple[n]did dance. My Negro Boy made his first appearance. Mr. Christy[502] & Larpeter arrived from the Yellow Stone, on their way to St Louis —

Monday 26 — The water fell last Night 4 feet — All the Rees, except a few Old Women have left the Village.

Tuesday 27 — Mr Christy & Co left here early on their way to St Louis,[503] six Bulls made their appearance on the North side,

Wednesday 28 — Gave a feast to 40 Old Women that has been left behind by the Rees and that are starveing,[504] Several Rees arrived from the dried Meat Camp, With six horses loaded with fresh Meat,   report Cattle plenty.

Thursday 29 — Covered the Warehouses and store with dirt — One of My Men's children died to day, a fine Boy — Charboneau arrived from the Gros Ventres for Merchandises &c.

Friday 30 — The Old *Star*,   started for the Ree camp — Put up a small Equipment for to send to the Gros Ventres, Set the Men to Make balls

Saturday 31 — Bad Weather, rain for the first time this year,

May arrived from hunting Beaver on Knife river, he Killed but few on account of the water being low —

Killed 101 Rats this Month — Total 2435 —

This Month ends With 125 Packs Robes and 3½ of Beaver —

1838   APRIL 30 DAYS

Sunday 1 — Charboneau with two Men and a small equipment of goods started for the Gros Ventre Camp — Sent Mitchelle up to the Mandan Camp, to try and persuade them to come down to the Fort and Make their trade. May started with them.

Monday 2 — Smokey Weather, the Prairies are on fire below — Wind from the South East —

Tuesday 3 — Same as yesterday, No News —

Wednesday — The Wolf Cheif and five Lodges arrived from the Mandan Camp — gave them a feast &c.

Thursday 5 — Traded sixty Robes to day — a few drops of rain fell, thunder towards the West, the first this year — Mitchel arrived from the Mandan Camp, they will all be here to-morrow, or the day after, with six hundred Robes, he left Charboneau two days ago, he had traded four hundred Robes, and half pack of Beaver from the Gros Ventres. *O. B. F.*

Friday 6 — The Mandan Camp arrived in the afternoon, Traded 40 Robes —

Saturday 7 — Feast and Council with the Mandans, sprinkled with rain throughout the day —

Sunday 8 — Sent out my hunters with three Horses — Eight Bulls hove in sight, all hands out for the Race, after a fine chace we Killed them all. I brought one, in a 100 yards of the Village, where I Killed him, and gave him to the Old Women of the Village. Villiandré & Latress arrived from Fort Pierre with the express from St Louis.

Monday 9 — Put up a few goods for Fort Pierre. Several Gros Ventres came down to trade, they brought with them 160 Robes — Mitchel found two of his Horses, that has been lost since 4 Months .

Tuesday 10 — Snow storm last Night, the Prairies are again covered with snow — Started one Man with the Express for Fort Union, a distance of three hundred Miles,

Wednesday 11 — Started two Pirogues loaded with Merchandises for Fort Pierre. The squaws of the Village gave us a dance. Strong wind at 10 A. M. from the North West —

Thursday 12 — Cold day — Strong North west wind — Took a sweat, in the sweat house with several others, a War Party of Rees that are to start to War in the Morning against the Sioux, danced the War dance in the Fort. May they never return is my sincere wish.

The Old *Star* arrived from above, bad news in that quarter, old Charboneau on his way to this Place with his skin Canoe loaded with 600 Robes, perished last Night, by a Gale of Wind from the North east, and lost all his robes.

Friday 13 — Sent two men up, to help Charboneau to save something from the wreck — Mandans out after Buffaloe, they all arrived in the evening well loaded — report Cattle in abundance .

Saturday 14 — A War Party of Rees started out to War against the Sioux — Strong wind from the East all day — smokey weather. May arrived from beaver hunting, with nine Beaver skins.

Sunday 15 — The wind from the East still continues. No news from any quarter, a few drops of rain fell, the Wind continued all day —

Monday 16 — Same as Yesterday, Snow — The Prairies are again covered with snow, a second Winter has set in, the Wind that has been blowing from the east since four days, fell at 4 P. M. No News from old Charboneau since the 12th inst.

Tuesday 17 — Mitchel arrived from Charboneaus Camp, they succeeded in hauleing the Canoe out of the Water, and drying the Robes, they are detained by the wind.

Wednesday 18 — Killed sixteen rats last Night — May started out for the third time a Beaver hunting, with one dog. Sent an Indian out, with three Horses, after Meat — My Indian hunter arrived in the afternoon with the Meat of two Cows —

Thursday 19 — Started out to run a band of cows that hove in sight of the Fort — Killed two Cows. Charboneau arrived with his Canoe, haveing wet 400 Robes —

Friday 20 — Distributed out the Wet robes to the squaws of the Village to dress over, giveing them the one fifth of all they dress. Indians all out after Buffaloe —

Saturday 21 — The Indians arrived late last Night, haveing saw their enemies the Sioux, commenced Makeing Packs —

Sunday 22 — Appearance of bad Weather. May arrived from Beaver hunting, with five skins — Strong Wind from the south east all day .

Monday 23 — Indians all out after Buffaloe. Set the Men to Make Packs — The Indians all came back in the afternoon loaded with Meat —

Tuesday 24 — The Wind, and Cold Weather still continue, rain in the afternoon. A Crow Indian arrived from his Camp, on tongue river, out 14 days.

Wednesday 25 — May started down the river, in a skin canoe, to hunt Beaver as far as Fort Pierre.

Thursday 26 — Started out early with two Men, and four Pack Horses in quest of something to eat, arrived at home at 4 P. M. with the Meat of 4 Cows. Rain in the afternoon —

Friday 27 — Finished Makeing Packs, two hundred of Robes, four of Beaver, four of Foxes and one of Wolves — Rain —

Saturday 28 — The bad Weather still continues. The Mandan Soldiers brought Me three Robes, in Payment for some Liquor that I gave them last Winter. An Indian that went Out on discovery came back in the evening, haveing saw enemies, at the little river back of the hills.

Sunday 29 — Indians all out after Buffaloe, they being plenty in 15 Miles from the Fort — Indians all arrived in the afternoon Well loaded with fresh Meat — The water rose since last Night 18 inches.

Monday 30 — Fine pleasant day,   the first we have had since several days — Took an inventory of Goods — Five Lodges Rees arrived from their dried Meat excursion loaded with dried Meat and Robes, out since the 26th of last Month, report three War-Parties Out against the Sioux, The rest of the Lodges will be in here, in 3 or 4 Days —

Strong east wind in the afternoon, Traded six Beaver skins from one of the Indians that arrived to day —

Killed 217 Rats this Month — Total 2652 —

1838   MAY 31 DAYS

Tuesday 1 — Appearance of bad weather in the Morning — cleared off at 12 — fine the rest of the day.

Wednesday 2 — Strong wind from the South east all day, No News from any quarter —

Thursday 3 — Same as yesterday — Seven Bulls hove in sight, all hands out after them, after a fine chase, Killed them all,

Friday 4 — Started out early with 2 Men and four pack horses in quest of Cattle,   on arriveing on the hills back of the Fort, discovered a band of Cows 50,   ran them and Killed four,   arrived at the Fort at 1 P. M — with our Horses well loaded —

Saturday 5 — No News from any quarter, except a a report is in circulation that the Ree Camp, will be here in two days —

Sunday 6 — Started out early with two Men, and three pack Horses, to run a band of cows, that was discovered last eveneing from the hill,   Came back in the afternoon, with my horses well loaded, haveing Killed two fat Bulls — *O. B. F.*

Monday 7 — Four young Bucks arrived from the Ree Camp, they say they will all be here tomorrow,

Tuesday 8 — The Ree Camp arrived at 10 A. M with an abundance of dried Meat and Robes. Out 45 Days, Commenced tradeing &c — Traded 106 Robes and a few Beaver sks.

Wednesday 9 — Several Gros Ventres arrived from above with Robes &c &c.   trade going on slow,   a small war party arrived, haveing been pursued by the Sioux, and made a narrow escape, out 34 Days. A band of Cows Discovered from the Fort,   80 Robes —

Thursday 10 — Started out after breakfast with the Indians to run the band of cows, that was discovered yesterday — A young Ree fell from his horse and was Killed, Killed three Buff — 65 Robes —

Friday 11 — A war party of Rees arrived from war, against their enemies the Sioux, Without Makeing a Coup, Out 26 Days — 52 Robes —

Saturday 12 — Two bands of Cows discovered from the Fort, the Indians haveing all a suply of Meat, and their Horses being poor, they will not run them,   75 Robes —

Sunday 13 — All hands out to run the Band of Cows that was discovered yesterday,   after a fine race we Killed at least 3 to 4 hundred — I Killed   three, Mitchel   also   Killed   three — 24 Robes —

Monday 14 — Water riseing fast — Strong Wind from the East all day,   Rain — trade going on slow —

Tuesday 15 — Rain all last Night,   and to day — Splendid dance at the Village (The Calumet) Went up to see the dance. I was presented with five Robes, 1 Old Gun,   and one Race Horse —

Wednesday 16 — A war Party left here for the Sioux Camp, to steal horses — No News from any quarter, except a drowneded Buffaloe passed here at 2.P. M.

Thursday 17 — The water is riseing fast. Fine day, the Indians all engaged playing Billiards,[505] News from the Gros Ventres that a small party of sioux, Made a Rush on the Village. Killed one, and drove off 35 Horses —

Friday 18 — Last Night just after I had got to bed, I herd an allarm, of to Arms, to Arms, and all the Indians of the Village a Yelling and shouting. I seized My gun and rushed out, the Night being dark we could Not discover our enemies, who had fled, after fireing in one of the Lodges, and Killing one of the principal cheifs (The long Horn) — and Wounding an other in two places — A large piece of ice passed in the river — Seperated from My dear Ree Wife, after a Marriage of one Year[506] —

Saturday 19 — Wind from the West all day — rain in the afternoon —

Sunday 20 — The War Party of Rees that left here the 14th of last Month, arrived to day, haveing Killed one squaw at the Little Miss⁰,   heavy rain all last Night,   all the squaws of the Village are singing and dancing the scalp that was brought in by the War Party,   they report Cattle plenty in ten Miles of the Fort — Water riseing fast —

Monday 21 — Severe snow storm last Night, the Plains are again covered with snow —a second Winter has again put in .

Tuesday 22 — All hands out to *cerne*. We were overtaken by a severe snow storm, and a cold North Wind, and came very near perishing, however we succeeded in getting our suply of good fresh Meat, and arrived at home in the evening, almost frose.

Wednesday 23 — Allert at the Village, enemies suposed to be hovering about the Corn fields. The Indians gave us a splendid dance.

Thursday 24 — Strong south Wind all day — No News from any quarter,   trade going on slow,   260 packs traded up to this date, and four of Beaver.

Friday 25 — Wind same as Yesterday all day.   The Mandan Squaws gave us a dance, Which I hope will be the last —

Saturday 26 — Sent Mitchel out on discovery, came back two hours after, haveing saw six Bulls, one of Which he Killed, sent a Man with two Mules to bring in the Meat —

Sunday 27 — An other case of the Small Pox showed itself Yesterday, on a Young Buck that passed the Winter with a small band of Gros Ventres, and came down a few days ago, to pay a Visit to his friends the Rees — Several Indians Went out on discovery, came back without seeing any thing but a few anti- lopes —

Monday 28 — Strong North east Wind all day — an Indian died at the Village of the Small Pox.   No News from any quar- ter.

Tuesday 29 — Rain last Night — A large band of Cows showed themselves on the hill, all hands out to run them.   My horse haveing a sore foot I could not go, but sent two Men with three Pack Horses, in hopes of getting some from the Indians,   Wind all day.

Wednesday 30 — The Indians arrived late last Night with an abundance of Meat, others still arriveing,   this Morning, they Must have Killed in the least Calculation three to four hundred Buffaloe,   they report the Country below black with them.   Wind all day.

Thursday 31 — An other large band of cows on the hill, all hands out to run them.   Charboneau went up to the Gros Ventre Village, 4 lodges that are encamped there.   No News from the rest of the band since 52 days — The Indians all arrived in the afternoon with an abundance of fresh Meat, haveing Killed at least three hundred Buffaloes.   Charboneau arrived from the Gros Ventres.   No News from that quarter.   Traded 270 Packs of Robes up to this date, and 4½ Packs Beaver.   I am in hopes of finishing the 300 Packs at the arrival of the Gros Ventres as they have a quantity of Robes on hand since last Winter.

Killed 146 Rats this Month — total 2798 .

1838   JUNE 30 DAYS

Friday 1 — Grand dance at the Village (The Calumet) in which several horses was given, with 20 or 30 Guns, Kittles, Blankets &c

Saturday 2 — Thick fogg, the first we have had this year. Water riseing fast, two feet since this Morning —

Sunday 3 — News of the arrival of the Gros Ventres at their summer Village,   Out 55 Days — Shower of Rain,   the Water Continues to rise.   Indians arrived with fresh Meat.

Monday 4 — Started out early with several Indians to run Buffaloe, on our way we were overtaken by a tremendous rain We arrived at the Fort Wet to the skin, with the Meat of three Cows.   The Indians Killed a great Number.

Tuesday 5 — No News from any quarter.

Wednesday 6 — Sent Charboneau up to the Gros Ventres with a few Twists of tobacco, and a bag full of good talk.   Several Gros Ventres arrived bringing with them two letters from Fort Union,   two different War Parties that was in quest of the Assinneboines, but finding none went into the Fort, where they were well received, and all vacinated by Mr. D. D. Mitchel.[507]

Thursday 7 — Heavy rain, with thunder, lightning and hail. Several Gros Ventres Came down to trade a few Robes &c.   A Sioux entered the Ree Village unperceived, he was very near being Killed by a Gros Ventre, but was Prevented by a young Ree, who disarmed him, he says that several hundred Sioux will attack the Gros Ventre Village, early to morrow Morning and that he eloped last Night to Come and tell the Rees to be on their guard, and not to stir out of their Village to help the Gros Ventres — he departed in the Night haveing received 2 horses for his trouble —

Friday 8 — Early this Morning the cry of to Arms was again echoed from the Village, a few Minutes after, the report of several hundred guns were herd in the direction of the Gros Ventre Village,   the report of the Sioux that entered the Village yesterday proved to be true,   he departed last Night.   this evening We shall hear the News of the Battle,   News from the Battle ground of 14 Sioux being Killed and Butchered, and several others that was Killed and carried off — 1 Mandan Killed and six Gros Ventres wounded,   the bodies of the 14 Sioux, after being cut up, was all placed in One heap, and burnt, in sight of their friends,

A half Breed (Vivié[508]) arrived from Fort Union, Out 7 days, as he has brought no letters I am inclined to believe that he has deserted, The Steam Boat Antelope[509] arrived from St Louis — Capt Miller — With Messrs McKinzie, Picotte, Laferriere &c on board,   gave then 10 Shots from my two four pounders, and received the same in exchange,

Saturday 9 — The Antelope started at 8 A.M. for Fort Union, Charboneau went up on board, Shower of rain in the afternoon,

Sunday 10 — Pressed packs 50   the Rees all went up to the Gros Ventres to give them a dance, and to Compliment them for their bravery, in the Battle of the 8th inst Rain in the afternoon.

Monday 11 — Pressed Packs 75 — Several Gros Ventres came down to trade, All hands Out after Buffaloe, Sent two Men with four pack Horses — My two Men arrived in the afternoon with the Meat of two fat Bulls,   the Indians all arrived well loaded with fresh Meat,   Rain

Tuesday 12 — Pressed Packs 106 — The water has been falling since two days,   to day it has again taken a rise of 18 inches

Wednesday 13 — Finished pressing packs 250 — News of a band of Buffaloe Near at hand — The Indians talk of running them in the Morning — they have sent up to invite their friends the Gros Ventres to come down to the race ,   19 packs —

Thursday 14 — All the Rees, Mandans, and Gros Ventres started out early after the band of Buffaloe that was discovered yesterday,   at least 400 horsemen well mounted and equiped for the race,   it was a Most beautiful sight to see them parade in the prairies, each Nation showing themselves on their fleet Horses , they all returned in the afternoon well loaded with good fat Meat — Finished puting up some goods for F P[510]

Friday 15 — Bellehumeur and his family started for the North, to the Colony formerly settled by Lord SelKirk,[511] and at present the tradeing establishment of the *North West Compy* from England.[512]   haveing lived for two Months a single life, and could not stand it any longer, I concluded to day, to buy myself a Wife, a young Virgin of 15 — which cost $ 150 — shower of rain in the afternoon with thunder and lightning —

Saturday 16 — Made packs of Robes — A band of cows showed themselves on the hills below the Island.

Sunday 17 — Shower of rain last night — Indians all out after the Buffaloe that was discovered yesterday — Pressed Packs 32 — at 10 A. M. — several thousand Buffaloe discovered from the Fort,   *O. B. F.*

Monday 18 — The Steam Boat arrived yesterday from above, and departed early this Morning for St Louis, 7 Boats loaded with robes arrived from above, Sunk one of the Boats to have her caulKed in the Morning —

Tuesday 19 — Loaded the MacKinaw Boat 2870, Robes — The Boats detained by the Wind —

Wednesday 20 — The Boats left here at 8 A.M. — arrainged and Cleaned Out the Goods in the Ware House,

Thursday 21 — Strong Wind all last Night — This Morning early We Were attacked by a large War party of Yanctons, after a hard fought battle of 4 Hours, the enemy withdrew, With the loss (only) of their powder and Ball, on both sides.

Friday 22 — Rain all last night,   which continued all day —

Saturday 23 — The river has risen 4 feet since last night,   set the Men to catch drift wood — which is a drifting in abundance, A Band of Elk was discovered from the Fort, the bad weather prevents us from Killing them,

Sunday 24 — This Morning six young Bucks all mounted on horse back went out on discovery,   they were pursued in sight of the Village by a war party of Sioux, who succeeded in Killing one of them, all those of the Village rushed out to the fight, but the Sioux haveing all fleet horses, Made their escape.   The enemies are hovering thick around us,   it is dangerous for us to go Out —

Monday 25 — The Powder house caved in,   set all hands to arrange it — The Gros Ventres came down and traded 120 Robes and a few Beaver skins,   after an absence of 39 Days My Absent Wife thought that she fared better at the Fort, made her appearance,   after a few reproaches on both sides, harmony was restored.

Tuesday 26 — More bad weather,   An other hard fight to day between the Sioux and Rees,   several wounded on both sides, they succeded in driving off several horses,   Traded 40 Robes from the Gros Ventres,

Wednesday 27 — More enemies discovered this Morning — a strange Dog also made his appearance on the other side of the river,   also two bands of Cows,   We had a heavy shower of Rain & hale in the afternoon.

Thursday 28 — The Gros Ventres came down and traded 200 Robes &c — Shower of rain in the afternoon,   Feast to the Cheifs & Soldiers of the Rees —

Friday 29 — A Ree Squaw, that has been liveing with the Sioux, since several years came to the Fort last night, haveing been Out, in the prairies (alone) 19 Days — she reports the Sioux Camp at the Forks of the Hart River.   Shower of rain in the afternoon,   the few remaining Mandans that were liveing with the Rees all started up to remain with the Gros Ventres, as they cannot agree with the Rees, as the latter are continually stealing their Women's — Sent one of my Men out on discovery — he came back two hours after haveing saw a large band of cows.   Preparations to run them in the Morning.

Saturday 30 — Started out early with all the Indians to run the Band of Buffaloe that was discovered yesterday,   after a hard race we succeeded in Killing our load — I Killed three Fat

Bulls — Mr Howick[513] from the Powder river, a Fork of the Yellow Stone arrived to day in a Mackinaw Boat with 700 Robes and a few Beaver skins,   he departed at 4 P.M. - for St Louis — An other fight to day between the Gros Ventres and Mandans several Killed and Wounded on both sides — We also had a Narrow escape,

Killed 68 Rats this Month — total 2866 —

1838   JULY 31 DAYS

Sunday 1 — This Month begins with 400 Robes and some few Beaver sks. traded since the Departure of the Mackinaw Boats for St Louis. The Indians reports the Death of John Newman who left here the 25th March to Make his spring hunt,   he was Killed by the Yanctons.   An other hard fight this Morning, several Killed and Wounded on both sides,   one of my best friends was Killed, We succeeded in getting 3 scalps, the enemy but one,   the Rees burnt the Bodies of their enemies, in sight of their friends.

Monday 2 — Set the Men to cover the houses with dirt.   The Indians are busily engaged in dancing the scalps that were taken in the fight of yesterday.   Drums are beating, squaws singing, children crying, Dogs Barking,   all combined together, Makes a fine Musick, for one that has never been accostomed to such noise,

Tuesday 3 — The Indians of the Upper Village all came down to remain with those of the Lower, in case of an attack from the combined forces of the sioux, that are expected every day — We had an allert to day

Wednesday 4 — The 63rd of American Independence — drank three glass of Old Rye face, on the strength of it, No News to day —

Thursday 5 — Splendid dance at the Village,   Indians discovered on the North side,   supposed to be the Sioux, in quest of a scalp —

Friday 6 — A Deputation of warriors has gone up to the Gros Ventres to have a smoke with them, to invite them down to pass the summer at this place, to help (en masse) in case of an attack from the combined tribes of the Sioux — who are daily expected, News from the Gros Ventres of one being Killed by the Assinniboines, out hunting

Saturday 7 — Pleasant day — No News from any quarter, except report says, that the Gros Ventre Village will be here to morrow, to pass the summer, with the Rees. Fear Makes them join.

Sunday 8 — Started Out early on discovery, came back at 1 P. M — haveing saw a band of cows — Indians all rejoice at the News, as they have Nothing to eat. A Ree that has been liveing with the Sioux, arrived to day, he reports the Death of J. Newman, also the Death of seven that was Killed in the fight of the 1st inst —

Monday 9 — Rain in the Morning,   The Indians decline going after the Band of Buffaloe that I saw yesterday — as they expect the Sioux eney day,   The Gros Ventres has all arrived, and encamped at the little Mandan Village, Two days ago the Assinneboines Killed three of them, and Wounded four others — More enemies (seven) discovered on the hill. They have been in the Point of Woods all day, Waiteing for an opportunity to grasp at a stragling scalp, but fortunately no one ventured out to day —

Tuesday 10 — No News. I was visited from the heads of Departments of the Gros Ventres, after a little sweet talk on both sides they departed —

Wednesday 11 — The Indians that are encamped on the other side, Killed nine Bulls, They brought me a small quantity of fresh meat.

Thursday 12 — An other hard fight to day — the Camp on the other side was attacked by the Assinneboines , Headed by their Old *Partizan* (He that holds the Knife) The Rees rushed to the fight,   swam their horses across the Misso — all eager to help their friends the Gros Ventres,   after a hard fight they Killed 64 and took 8 Women prisoners —

Friday 13 — Great rejoicings at the Village, Scalps flying in all directions, Men, Women and Children singing, crying and dancing, — Started out early on discovery, came back late without seeing any thing. One of the Prisoners that was taken in the fight of Yesterday (A Girl of 12 years) was presented to me to day, by the one that made her Prisoner .

Saturday 14 — Rain last night, Started out early in quest of something to eat, I had not proceeded more than a mile from the Fort, when a War Party of Sioux rushed on us, sent a volly of Balls after us, but as fortune would have it we escaped unhurt. I made a very narrow escape being in advance of all the Party consisting of 14 Indians and 2 Whites.

Sunday 15 — Heavy rain early this Morning. Villeandré with 5 Men arrived from Fort Pierre, out 9 Days — No News in that quarter .

Monday 16 — The Indians all started out in quest of cattle, on Knife River. At 2 P. M. a band of cows was discovered from the Fort, the Indians all being out, I went alone with 3 Men and four pack horses — after a fine race I Killed three fat cows — arrived home late.

Tuesday 17 — All the Indians arrived loaded with fresh Meat, report the Country Black with Buffalo 20 Miles off. A Bull made his appearance on the North side.

Wednesday 18 — Rain all last Night — Cleared off in the evening — The Gros Ventres came down and gave their friends the Rees, a splendid dance.

Thursday 19 — Sent the Men across the river to make a Canoe,

Friday 20 — Set fire to my coal pit — the Men employed a doing - *Nothing,*   Finished Makeing the Canoe for Fort Pierre. Wrote letters for below &c.

Saturday 21 — Rain all last Night, two of the men that arrived the 15th inst started back to day - *Villeandré* — One of the squaws that was taken Prisoner in the fight of the 12th inst deserted to day —

Sunday 22 — Started out after Buffaloe in compʸ with the Indians, as they reported haveing seen a band of Buffaloe last evening, We returned home in the afternoon, *light,* as it was a false report —

Monday 23 — Commenced Makeing hay, The Gros Ventres gave us a dance, I being absent they got Nothing for their trouble.

Tuesday 24 — The Gros Ventres gave the Mandans a dance, in payment of the one they received the 21st inst. *O. B. F.*

Wednesday 25 — Feast and Council with the Gros Ventres, great Promises on both sides. The Rees all started out after meat, in Company with the Gros Ventres,

Thursday 26 — Started out on discovery, Came back without seeing any thing,   bad Prospects, of something to eat—

Friday 27 — The Indians all arrived loaded with Meat, report cattle scarce, Commenced hauleing hay — 2 lods.

Saturday 28 — Heavy shower of rain in the afternoon. Six loads of hay — in the Storm of to day the thunder Killed five of the Gros Ventres Horses —

Sunday 29 — The bad Weather continues, Started out in the afternoon on discovery,   Killed one Bull, which was all I saw — cut him up, and left the Meat in the Prairie.

Monday 30 — Rain all last night —Sent two Men, with 2 Mules to bring in the meat that I left in the Prairie Yesterday. The Gros Ventres gave the Rees an other dance, had a smoke and a long talk with the Gros Ventres.

Tuesday 31 — Finished Makeing coal,   traded 650 Robes since the departure of the Steam Boat —

Killed 137 Rats this Month — total 3003.

Wednesday 1st — A small War Party left here last Night for the Sioux Camp — Finished hauleing hay from the little River thirty Loads —

Thursday 2 — Started out in quest of cattle with six horses and two Men at 1 P. M. — run a band of cows — Killed four, started for home at 4 P. M. — slept out, came very near being eat up by the Mosquetoes.

Friday 3 — Left camp early and arrived at the Fort at 10 A. M — found all Well, except my beloved Ree wife, who has deserted my bed & board,   the Indians all left Yesterday, to Make dried Meat. Finished hauleing hay at the little river 30 loads.

Saturday 4 — Commenced makeing hay at the Fountain. The Old Star started for the Dried Meat camp —

Sunday 5 — Storm of wind and rain last Night. No News from any quarter.

Monday 6 — Hauled two loads of Hay — from the Fountain.

Tuesday 7 — Went out on discovery,   saw Nothing. Storm of rain and wind from the South West —

Wednesday 8 — Put up some few articles to send to the Ree camp.

Thursday 9 — Sent Garreau with two men and six Pack horses to trade Meat at the Ree camp, on Knife river.   Rain at 8 A. M. — which Continued all day .

Friday 10 — The rain Continued all Night, the goods in the warehouse, and all the Robes are Wet.

Saturday 11 — Fine day, arrainged the goods &c in the ware house. Finished one stack of hay 40 Loads —

Sunday 12 — Rain all last night,   cleared off at 10 A.M — all the Old Wives of the Village, and those of the Fort out after berries —

Monday 13 — Appearance of fine weather, hauled two loads of hay, all the Wives out after berries —

Tuesday 14 — Shower of rain in the afternoon.   eat sweet corn, the first this year —

Wednesday 15 — Set two Men to make a Canoe.   Garreau with the two Men, that left here the 9th inst, for the Meat Camp and was to be back in 3 days, has not yet arrived.

Thursday 16 — Finished makeing the canoe   18 feet long —

Friday 17 — Garreau & Co arrived from the dried Meat Camp with 100 Pieces of Meat — in a drunken frolick at the Camp, a Gros Ventre Killed a young Ree,   all the Camp flew to Arms, the Cheifs and Warriors put a stop, or their would of been a bloody fight between the 2 Nations.

Saturday 18 — Started early in the Morning, in a Canoe with two Men's for Fort Pierre,   after a pleasant trip of six days we arrived safe —

[1838]   OCTOBER 31 DAYS

Monday 15 — I left Fort Pierre the 4th of the present in Company with Mr. D. D. Mitchell and his Party Consisting of 24 Men — and after a pleasant trip of 14 days We all arrived safe at this place, and was received by the inmates of the Fort with several shots from their 4 pounder, and the Flag flying at the Mast head.   Nothing of any consequence occurred on our route, we haveing saw but few Indians, and them appeared to be friendly — We Killed Several Buffaloe, Antelopes, Deer, &c &c on our way up, they being in abundance all the way to this place.   We fared sumtuously on the Choice Pieces — On arriveing at the Fort I found all well, and in good order except that one of my Men, a half breed from the North had deserted, and taken with him one of my best Buffaloe Horses —

Tuesday 16 — Mr Mitchell and his Party started at 10 A.M. for Fort Union,   a distance of three hundred Miles from this place. I gave all hands a holliday, and a feast for their good behaviour, in my Absence —

Wednesday 17 — Went up to the Village to see an Old Woman that has been abandoned by the Mandans — I found the Old Woman yet alive, she was glad to see me, after remaining some time with her, she begged of me to depart, saying that she wished to die, that she had not a long time to live, and that my Visite, although glad to see me, was not Welcome, as it would be the means of her liveing 2 or 3 days more, she was very Weak not haveing tasted a Mouthfull since 6 days. I offered the Old Lady all the Assistance in my Power, which she refused, being willing to die, aged at least 100 —

Thursday 18 — Set the Men to Cut Fire Wood on the North side of the river, Killed several Ducks, and one Fox —

Friday 19 — Sent out on discovery for Cattle. The Discoveres returned haveing saw two Bulls, started out in quest of them, after a fine race, I Killed them both.

Saturday 20 — Fine Weather since four days. No News from above —

Sunday 21 — Two Deer made their appearance close to the Fort.

Monday 22 — Sent Old Charboneau up, in serch of the Rees and Gros Ventres.

Tuesday 23 — Sent out on discovery. My discovere came back at 2 P. M. haveing saw three large bands of cows — Preparations to give them a race to morrow —

Wednesday 24 — Started out early to run the band of Cows that was discovered yesterday — after a hard race, against a strong North Wind, and poor horses I succeeded in Killing one fat cow — all the Prairies back of us are Black with them. I am in hopes that in a few days they will be near the Fort. Charboneau not yet arrived.

Thursday 25 — Light fall of snow. Set the Black Smith to make Iron Pipes for the Indians. The Two Bulls, one of the

Principal Cheifs of the Aricarees, came down to pay me a visite, reports Cattle in abundance at their camp, good Prospect of a fine trade this year. May it prove so ! !

Friday 26 — Charboneau arrived late last Night. Put up some tobacco &c for the Gros Ventres & Rees, with the intention of paying them a visit in the Morning —

Saturday 27 — Snow storm last Night, the prairies are all covered Put up two small equipments for the Rees and Gros Ventres, Set the Men to Make balls — Old Charboneau, an old Man of 80, took to himself and *others* a young Wife, a young Assinneboine of 14, a Prisoner that was taken in the fight of this summer, and bought by me of the Rees, the young Men of the Fort, and two *rees,* gave to the Old Man a splendid *Chàrivèree,*[514] the Drums, pans, Kittles &c Beating; guns fireing &c. The Old gentleman gave a feast to the Men, and a glass of grog — and went to bed with his young wife, with the intention of doing his best — The two Indians who had never saw the like before, were under the apprehension that we were for Killing of them, and sneaked off —

Sunday 28 — The Black Smith hard at work, Makeing scrapers for the Indians.

Monday 29 — Started early with two Carts and six Men, with Merchandises for the Rees & Gros Ventres, after a hard day's travel we reached their Camp. I was well received by them all, had a talk with the rees respecting the trade. They have Buffaloes in abundance. I am in hopes they will Make a good haul this year —

Tuesday 30 — Started up to the Gros Ventre Camp, about four Miles above the Rees. I was well received by them also, had a talk with the Principal Cheifs and Warriors, they have all promised to behave well. They presented me with a quantity of fresh and dried Meat, and told me that their Harts were all good, and friendly disposed towards the Whites, that this time last year, they were all fools, and talked bad, that they had lost a great Many of their tribe by the small Pox, and that it was the

Whites that gave them the disease, but since that time they have Killed a great many of their enemies, and that their harts were good, & that they would show by their future Conduct that they would do their best to please me. I slept at their Camp that Night —

Wednesday 31 — Started down to the lower Camp, to be ready to Make an early start for home. The Bull Band gave Me a splendid dance, which lasted untill 10 OClock at Night. We had the ribs of several fat Cows for supper, and passed the evening very comfortable,   a small War party of horse theives arrived to day from the Sioux Camp with 14 Horses —

Killed 346 Rats from the 18th of Aug. — Total 3349 —

[1838]   NOVEMBER 30 DAYS

Thursday 1 — Left Camp at Day-light for home, and arrived at 4 P. M. — found all well,   two Bulls hove in sight —

Friday 2 — Caught 10 Foxes last night. Sent the Men on the other side of the river, in serch of a lost horse,   Came back without finding him.

Saturday 3 — Sent the Men again in serch of the lost horse, Two Bulls hove in sight —

Sunday 4 — Light fall of Snow last Night,   Went out on discovery — saw nothing. *O. B. F.*

Monday 5 — A Band of Cows on the hill.

Tuesday 6 — The Ice commenced running in the river, Snow — A Bull Made his appearance on the other side of the river, Cold Day —

Wednesday 7 — Moved into My Winter quarters,

Thursday 8 — The river closed last night —

Friday 9 — Went out on discovery, saw three Bulls, run them and Killed Two, put up some few articles to send to the Ree Camp —

Saturday 10 — Cold stormy day,   employed the Men, daubing the houses,

Sunday 11 — Snow storm last night —

Monday 12 — Caught two Wolves last Night. Sent two Men with four pack horses to the Ree camp, Shod one of my cart Horses —

Tuesday 13 — No News —

Wednesday 14 — Caught two foxes and one wolf last night. Went to the Village to see the Old Woman, that was abandoned by the Mandans, at their departure for above,   found the Old Lady Dead, and half eat up by the Wolves, Killed a Wolf to day, With a Beaver trap fast to his leg, and has been in that situation since 14 days —

Thursday 15 — Caught five foxes and one wolf last night —

Friday 16 — Caught five wolves and two foxes last night — Cold day — My Men have not yet arrived from the Ree camp, Blacksmith at work as usual,

Saturday 17 — Fine pleasant day. A Bull Made his appearance on the hill — Caught one wolf last night — Gave a good Whipping to my young Wife, the first since our union, as I am united to one, that I stole from my Friend, J. Halsey, on my visit to Fort Pierre last summer —

Sunday 18 — One fox & one wolf last night, Killed a Bull close to the Fort,   sent a cart after the Meat — Men all busy setting traps to catch Wolves &c — My Men arrived from the Ree camp, out seven days — brought with them 100 Tongues, and a quantity of fresh Meat. Cattle in abundance in that quarter. Prospects of a good trade.

Monday 19 — Two wolves & one Fox last night — Squaws all out after Bull Berries .

Tuesday 20 — Two wolves & one Fox last night — Went out on discovery   Saw several Bulls and one band of Cows — ran them and Killed three fat Cows —

Wednesday 21 — One wolf last night — Buffaloes in all directions, and I am sorry to say that I have no good Horse that is able to catch them,   so that we are obliged to eat poor Bull Meat —

Thursday 22 — Four wolves last night — One of my Men sick, gave him a dose of Salts .

Friday 23 — Three wolves last night,   Snow storm, wind from the North East,

Saturday 24 — Three wolves & two foxes last night,   several Buffaloe Bulls near the Fort,   the Men all out after them,   arrived from Fort Pierre, this day one year —

Sunday 25 — Two Foxes last night — A large band of Cows below.   Preperations to give them a race to Morrow —

Monday 26 — Two wolves and one Fox,   Started out with two Men and four horses to run the Band of Cows, that was discovered yesterday,   after a fine chace I Killed three fat cows — the whole country back of us is black with them,   the Indians above have also lots of them near their Camp —

Tuesday 27 — Five wolves last night— A large band of cows on the hill back of the Fort

Wednesday 28 — Two wolves & one Fox.   Killed a Bull Close to the Fort,   Sent the Cart after the Meat —

Thursday 29 — One wolf last night.   Several thousands of Buffaloes discovered from the Fort this Morning,

Friday 30 — Four wolves last night,   Wind from the south west with rain — This Month ends with the Death of 47 Wolves - and 36 Foxes Killed at this place —

93 Skins   total
this Month   Killed 42 Rats this Month — 3391 —

1838   DECEMBER 31 DAYS

Saturday 1st — Three Wolves and one Fox, Wind from the North west,   Snow drifting —

Sunday 2 — Three Wolves last night.   Sent the Men all out hunting, as Buffaloe are very thick all around us.   My hunters arrived with the Meat of four fat cows —

Monday 3 — Two Wolves and one Fox — Sent two Men and five horses up to the Indian camp —

Tuesday 4 — One Wolf and one Fox — One of the Coldest days that we have had,   Men all Idle,

Wednesday 5 — Four Wolves last night,   Went out to run Buffaloe, after a hard race I Killed one Cow — and got my fingers frose in the bargin — My Men arrived late from the Indian camp with 250 Tongues — report cattle in abundance in that quarter, and that the Indians, are quarrelling amongst themselves,

Thursday 6 — Four Wolves,   Sent two Men and five Mules up to the Indian Camp,   Wind from the South,   the Snow has almost all disappeared from the prairies,   Rain,

Friday 7 — Three Wolves and Two foxes — Strong wind all day —

Saturday 8 — Five Wolves and one fox — Went out to run Buffaloe — Killed Two Cows.   My Men arrived from the Camp with Meat & Tongues,   The Old Star came with them —

Sunday 9 — One Wolf and two foxes,   This Morning early a large band of Cows undertook to Cross on the ice,   I called up all the Men and Squaws to surround them, and in so doing they Made a rush for the shore, the ice Not being strong enough broke, and about sixty Bulls, Cows, and calves, remained in the water.   We succeeded in drawing out Seventeen, the rest all went under the ice,   finished butchering at sun down — My larder has quite a respectable look,   With what Meat I had on hand I have at present the Meat of twenty four Buffaloes.

Monday 10 — One wolf and one fox — Sent the Men Out after the meat of a Cow, that I have *cached* in the hills.   Fine summer day — all the snow has disappeared from the Prairies — Two Men arrived from Fort Union with the Express for St Louis,

Out eight days, No News in that quarter except that cattle are plenty —

Tuesday 11 — Four Wolves and one Fox — Busy writeing letters for the express to start tomorrow. Men all Idle, not being able to cross on the ice, as it is covered with water, The Cattle has all disappeared, on account of the Mild weather —

Wednesday 12 — Three wolves last night. Started two Men with the Express for Fort Pierre, (*Lecompt*[515] *& George*[516]) A band of cows made their appearance on the north side.

Thursday 13 — Three Wolves. An Assinneboine squaw — that was taken last summer, gave birth to a child last night — Two Men arrived with letters from Fort Pierre, out eleven days, report cattle in abundance below —

Friday 14 — Three Wolves. Put up some powder &c, to send to Fort Pierre. Light fall of snow in the evening —

Saturday 15 — Three Wolves last night. Sent two Men, with two horses, packed with powder, to Fort Pierre, Set the squaws to cut up, and dry Meat, appearance of bad weather in the afternoon,

Sunday 16 — Four Wolves last Night — Started out with two Men and two horses, to run a small band of cows on the hill — Killed one fat Cow —

Monday 17 — Two Wolves and two foxes. Sent two Men with three pack horses up to the Indian Camp —

Tuesday 18 — One Wolf — Snow storm last night — The Old Star killed a bull near the Fort, sent after the skin to make cords for my packs in the spring —

Wednesday 19 — One Wolf — The old Star Killed an other Bull, the hide was appropriated for cords — My Men arrived from the Indian Camp above, with 100 Tongues, report the arrival of four Crow Indians and one Squaw at their camp, they were attacked on their way by the Crees, and one of their party killed, the squaw was Wounded in the arm — *O. B. F.*

Thursday 20 — One Wolf — Fine pleasant day — The Old

Star left here in the evening for the Camp, being afraid to trust himself in the daytime.

Friday 21 — Light shower of rain last Night.

Saturday 22 — Two wolves last Night — One of the coldest days this year. Strong wind all day — Men Idle.

Sunday 23 — Went out on discovery.   Near the Fort discovered one Old Bull in comp.ʸ with a Cow, run them and Killed the Cow — arrived at the Fort almost frose, brought in the Meat and skin —

Monday 24 — One Wolf and two foxes — Strong North west Wind all day.

Tuesday 25 — Two foxes last Night. This Morning early the Men fired several discharges from my four Pounder, and small arms   gave them all a glass of Grog — and a *festin* of Flour, Sugar & Coffee. Saw a large band of Cows on the North side — Cold and Cloudy — Several Bulls appeared back of the Fort —

Wednesday 26 — One Wolf — Started out after breakfast to Kill Bulls to make Cords. Killed four Old Bulls and one young one, the Meat of which I brought home.
[71 Sks in Margin for this entry.]

Thursday 27 — One Wolf and one Fox — Fine pleasant day — Several hundred Buffaloes appeared on the North side. No doubt but the Yanctons are comeing up this way — if so - a good trade at this Post —

Friday 28 — Strong North West Wind — Men all idle,   set them to dress Cords for my Packs —

Saturday 29 — Three Wolves. Wind as yesterday, with snow — Cattle in all directions. Set the Men to haul timber for the Fort —

Sunday 30 — One Wolf and one Fox — Thousands of Cattle can be seen from the Fort — sent out my hunters to Kill some, went out in quest of an Old Bull — Killed one and brought home his skin for Cords. My hunters returned with the Meat of one Cow —

Monday 31 — Fine day — No News from any quarter — The end of one more Happy Year. May the next prove the same is my sincere wish .

73 Skins		Total
this	Killed 32 Rats this Month —	3423 —
month	61 Wolf	
	17 Fox	

1839   JANUARY 31 DAYS

Tuesday 1st — One Wolf — This year commences with 1,000 Buff. Robes, 300 Foxes and Wolves, and a plenty to eat. Beaver I have none, as all my Beaver hunters are *Dead*. I Killed a young Bull near the Fort — brought in the Meat and Skin —

Wednesday 2 — Sent two Men with four Mules up to the Indian Camp for meat &c &c — One of the wives of the Fort eloped this morning, a young Ree damsel of 16, regretted by us all. Killed two fat cows —

Thursday 3 — Three wolves. My Men arrived from the Indian Camp above with 250 Tongues — the Bloody Knife a Ree warrior with his Wife paid me a visit —

Friday 4 — Four Wolves & two Foxes. Sent out my hunters with three Mules — Salted Tongues — My hunters arrived with the Meat of two Cows — report as usual Cattle plenty all around us —

Saturday 5 — One Wolf — Last night we were visited by a small war party of Yanctons — Gave them something to eat, and a little tobacco &c and they departed,   say they are encamped at Canon Ball River .

Sunday 6 — Snow in the afternoon. The Bloody Knife and his Wife left here in the evening for his Camp, being afraid of the Yanctons.

Monday 7 — Four Wolves last Night,   Sent out my hunters with three Mules. A large War party of Yanctons, headed by their grand Cheif (Wan-à-ton) Paid us a visit, in hopes of getting the Scalp of the (Ree The Bloody Knife) who departed yesterday. My hunters arrived with the Meat of two Cows.

Tuesday 8 — Five Wolves.   We were up all last Night a watching the War Party,   busy tradeing with the Yanctons, as an other large band arrived to day — with Beaver, Robes, Deer skins &c &c.

Wednesday 9 — This Morning before daylight, I was awoke by several Indians out side of the Fort. I got up and made a fire, and went out to see what was going on, when I beheld the Mandan Village all in flames, the Lodges being all made of dry Wood, and all on fire at the same time, Made a splendid sight, the Night being dark — this Must be an end to What was once called the Mandan Village, upwards of one hundred years it has been standing,   the Small Pox last year, very near anihilated the Whole tribe, and the Sioux has finished the Work of destruction by burning the Village — the rest of the Tribe are scattered, some with the Minetarees, [517] and others with the Aricarees. The old Mandan squaw that was abandoned by her tribe, and that has been dead since 20 Days, was scalped by the Sioux and taken with them as a trophy to their camp —
[20 Skins in Margin for this entry.]

Thursday 10 — One Wolf — Cleared out the Retail Store, found I had traded with the Sioux 40 Robes 26lb Beaver and 100 Deer skins — Sent two Men up to the Indian Camp to inform them of the distruction of their Village by the Sioux.

Friday 11 — One Wolf — Cold Windy day — My Men not yet returned from the Camp above.

Saturday 12 — Five Wolves, My Men arrived from the Camp above — they appear to say but little about the burning of their Village, as they say they will revenge it —

Sunday 13 — Three Wolves and one Fox. Wrote letters with the intention of starting two Men in the Morning to Fort Union — Thousands of Cattle can be seen, not two Miles from the Fort —

Monday 14 — One Wolf and one Fox. Started two Men to Fort Union in quest of Powder, Ball, Tobacco &c Started out with one Man and two Mules to run a band of Cows on the North side. Killed three fat Cows, brought in the Meat and skins. Fine Weather for the season.

Tuesday 15 — Shod two horses to send down to the Sioux Camp — Mild pleasant Weather —

Wednesday 16 — Two Wolves — Put up a small equipment for the Yanctons to start in the Morning — Spring weather — thousands of Buffaloes can be seen from the Fort on both sides of the river, all travelling down —

Thursday 17 — One Fox — Started a Cart loaded with goods with three Men to the Sioux Camp, to trade Robes &c — Change in the Weather since yesterday — Cold —

Friday 18 — One Fox — One of the coldest days this Year, sent out my hunters to approach Cattle, as the hills on the North side are black with them. Two Cows —

Saturday 19 — Strong Wind from the South West — A small band of Cows crossed on the ice — Killed one fat one.

Sunday 20 — One Wolf — Light fall of snow — Started out with one Man and four Mules to run a band of Cows on the North side. Killed three Cows, the Cart arrived from below — it appears that the Sioux has moved Camp —
[18 Skins in Margin for this entry.]

Monday 21 — Warm South West Wind — snow melting fast — put up some few goods for the Rees & Gros Ventres.

Tuesday 22 — One Fox — Sent two Men with three Mules up to the Indian Camp, with a few goods &c &c — Started out after Cattle — Killed two Cows —

Wednesday 23 — Two Foxes The Weather Continues Mild. Wind S. W. Killed a Cow on the ice.

Thursday 24 — One Fox and one wolf Started out to run a band of Cows on the hill. Killed one fat Cow — Gave a whipping to my beloved wife, for not mending my Moccassins — My Men arrived from the Camp above with 180 Tongues — Cattle plenty in that Neighbourhood.

Friday 25 — Set the Men to Make Packs — An estray dog came to the Fort, suposed to belong to the Yanctons.

Saturday 26 — One Wolf — Run a band of Cows on the hill — Killed one poor Cow — brought home the skin, and Tongue.

Sunday 27 — One Wolf Killed an Old Bull near the Fort, brought in his hide for Cords.

Monday 28 — One Wolf and one Fox Snow storm Wind from the North West — The bad Weather continued all day — Arranged my dog tranes —

Tuesday 29 — The bad weather still continues Snow drifting since Yesterday — the Point of Woods opposite the Fort is full of Buffaloes — Mantá killed a Poor Cow —

Wednesday 30 — Fine day but cold — Killed a Bull in 30 yards of the Fort, Mantá killed a young heifer —*O. B. F.*

Thursday 31 — One Wolf and one Fox Weather same as Yesterday

[49 Skins in Margin for this entry.]

January I bid you *adieu* I can say that you have been one of the mildest that I have experienced, since my stay at Fort Clark, although you have held out well, as regards Cattle. May your next neighbour February prove the same —

Killed 47 Rats this Month — total 3438
37 Wolves
12 Foxes

1839 FEBRUARY 28 DAYS

Friday 1 — Two Wolves and one Fox — Put up some few articles to send to the Ree Camp —

Saturday 2 — One Fox — Sent two Men with three Mules to the Ree camp — Started out hunting — Killed two Cows and one Calf — Arrived at the Fort late in the evening — found two Yanctons arrived— they came up for me to send a Trader to trade with them, as they have a quantity of Robes &c.

Sunday 3 — One Wolf — The two Yanctons started at daylight for their Camp — Light fall of snow last Night — Strong wind all day from the North West — Snow drifting— Cattle seeking shelter in the hills.

Monday 4 — Two Wolves and one Fox — Cold day — Mantá Killed a young Bull , brought in the Meat & Skin — Charboneau arrived from the Gros Ventres, reports the arrival at that place of my Men from F. U. the traine horse not being able to draw the load, the Men *cached* the Merchandises in the Point of Woods below White River,[518] and came down to Procure a fresh supply of horses — J. Dupuis and three Men started immediately —

Tuesday 5 — Two Wolves and one Fox, Cold day. No News from any quarter, except that a Wolf Made off with a trap.

Wednesday 6 — Two Wolves and one Fox. Started out hunting, Killed three Cows — Manta also Killed two.

Thursday 7 — Three Foxes — Started out hunting with Mantá. We each Killed one Cow. Spring Weather.

Friday 8 — One Fox.   Slight shower of rain last Night.   No News from any quarter. My Men not yet arrived.

Saturday 9 — Two Wolves and one Fox — Snow — Put up a few goods for the Upper Camp — Pleasant in the afternoon —

Sunday 10 — One Wolf and one Fox. Started out hunting with one Man, and two Mules. Killed two young Bulls.

Monday 11 — Spring Weather, Wind S.W. the snow has all disappeared. Dupuis arrived from above, with the Merchandises that was left on the way from Fort Union to this place —
[23 Skins in Margin for this entry.]

Tuesday 12 — One Wolf — Set all hands to draw up a few logs that I have on the river —

Wednesday 13 — Charboneau and two Men, with four Mules

Started for the Upper Camp — Sent Dupuis and Baptiste in serch of the Yancton Camp —

Thursday 14 — Set the Men to Make packs. Dupuis arrived from below, not being able to find the Indians. Spring Weather, river riseing, Cattle moveing off .

Friday 15 — An other fine day. My Men arrived from the Upper Camp with 230 Tongues. Trade begins to be brisk in that quarter they have traded 80 Packs,

Saturday 16 — Employed the Men all day to arrange the Press, for my packs, Put up a few goods for the Upper Camp.

Sunday 17 — Set the Men to haul up some Pieces of timber from the river side, that I have had squared for the Fort —

Monday 18 — Sent three Men with four Mules laden with Merchandises to the Upper Camp, Strong South Wind since yesterday — finished erecting my Press, for Pressing Packs of Robes &c &c

Tuesday 19 — One of the warmest days, for the season of the year, that I have ever experienced in this country, the Men at Work with their Coats off.

Wednesday 20 — Three Wolves and one Fox — Thick foggy Morning Set the squaws to Cut up and dry Meat — My men arrived from the Upper Camp, with Tongues, Wolf & Fox skins —

Thursday 21 — One Wolf and one Fox — Pressed Packs 55 — A half Breed made its appearance in the Fort to day, a Girl —

Friday 22 — One Fox — Pressed Packs 21 of Robes, 6 Wolf 2 Foxes and 2 Deer skins. A band of Cows in sight.

Saturday 23 — Two Wolves — Put up a few goods for the Upper Camp — finished hauleing Wood from the bank of the river — as the water is riseing fast — finished cutting up Meat fourteen Buffaloes.
[10 Skins in Margin for this entry.]

Sunday 24 — Sent three Men with four Mules, laden with

Merchandises for the Upper Camp — Started out after break-fast to run a band of Cows on the hill — Killed two fat Cows —

Monday 25 — Strong Wind from the West all day — the Water rose one foot last Night — My Men arrived from the Upper Camp in quest of goods,   those that I sent yesterday did not last two hours,   Put up an other equipment to start in the Morning — they have traded 1500 Robes —

Tuesday 26 — Started the Men with the Merchandises for the Upper Camp, before daylight — the water rose last Night two feet — Set a Man to run Bulls — A band of Cows on the hill.

Wednesday 27 — One Wolf — Run a band of Cows on the hill, our Horses being poor, Could not Catch them. General clear Out in the Warehouse and Store.

Thursday 28 — Appearance of bad Weather — Wind from the South — Started out to run a band of Cows on the hill,   Killed one fat cow, and Wounded an other.   Sent the cart to bring in the Meat and skin — My Men arrived from the Upper Camp,   all well in that quarter.

This Month although it has been a Summer Month ends with a strong Wind from the West,   with a light fall of snow, in the afternoon.   I have traded since the departure of the Steam Boat last summer 2500 Buffalo Robes, Beaver, Otter, Wolf and Fox — and stole a young Wife, which you have been apprised of before. As yet we agree very well together.   I supose on account of haveing no young Bucks near the Fort.   However, spring is advancing and Numbers will flock in before long and then, Poor White Man, take care of your *Ribs!*

Killed 41 Rats this Month — 3479
20 Wolves
14 Foxes

1839   MARCH 31 DAYS

Friday 1st — One Wolf and one Fox — The first day of spring begins with a Strong West Wind, and Cold, which continued all day.

Saturday 2 — One Wolf. Killed two Bulls near the Fort. Màntá also Killed one.

Sunday 3 — One Wolf — Sent two Men, with Lodges to Cover the Packs at the Upper Camp. Killed two Old Bulls near the Fort —

Monday 4 — Went out on discovery,   saw Nothing but a few Bulls, Killed one. Cold day. My Men arrived from the Upper Camp — No News in that quarter — Buffaloe begins to be scarce.

Tuesday 5 — The Prairies are all on fire since Yesterday, in the direction of the Ree Camp. Set the Men to clean around the Fort — Water riseing,   haveing Nothing else to do, I set fire to the Prairies.

Wednesday 6 — One Wolf — Strong wind since three days from the West. No News from Fort Pierre since the 12th of December — the Prairies are still burning.

Thursday 7 — Wind same as yesterday, which continued all last Night. Arranged my dried Meat on the Scaffold — No News from any quarter.

Friday 8 — Light fall of rain and hale last Night — More rain at 10 A. M. which lasted all day — Saw a flock of Geese to day, the first this year. Set the Men to arrange the Saddles &c. *O. B. F.*

Saturday 9 — Cold and Cloudy — Wind from the South — The express from St Louis arrived   Old Delorme and two Men — Snow during the day —

Sunday 10 — Wrote letters, and Prepared the Express to start in the Morning for Fort Union — Mild and Pleasant in the Morning — Wind at 3 P. M.

Monday 11 — More Snow last Night, the Prairies are again

Covered with Snow — The express for above detained by the bad Weather — Killed a Bull Near the Fort, being nearly out of fresh Meat,   brought in the choise pieces — Paunche, liver, tongue, Nuts &c. &c. &c.

Tuesday 12 — The bad Weather still Continues,   Wind from the north.   The Express detained again to day by the bad Weather — it has been 19 Days out from the Little Misso [Bad River]

Wednesday 13 — The Express with six Men and two Squaws started early for Fort Union — Sent a Man up to the Indian Camp for News — A Band of Cows near the Fort — Cold day, Wind from the North — Set the Men to clean out the Fort — an other band of Cows.

Thursday 14 — Went out with one Man and two mules to run a band of Cows that was discovered last evening — came back without finding them — On our way home I Killed an Old Bull — Cold.

Friday 15 — Fine day but Windy — Wind from the West — employed the Men arrangeing the Pickets of the Fort, as they are eat off at the foundation by the Rats, and in a fair way to tumble down.   Garreau arrived from the Upper Camp — it appears that the Waters are agitated in that quarter — a Ree, accidently or by design - Killed a Gros Ventre Squaw — The latter immediately Moved Camp up the river, and at starting as is Custumary, the Gros Ventres stole several young Ree Damsals, two of which they Killed to retaliate,   the Rees are Wrothy and swear revenge, the Principal Cheifs & Warriors are for stopping, or Preventing a War between the two Nations, but the young bucks, think their Honor attacked by the Death of the two young damsals, and Nothing but revenge will satisfy them, a small War Party has already left Camp to retaliate, by stealing a few horses.

Saturday 16 — Garreau started back for the Upper Camp. Cold and Cloudy. Buffaloe are beginning to become scarce, except Old Bulls, which are in abundance all around us —

Sunday 17 — Foggy Morning, Cleared off at M. — Went out

on discovery, saw four Bulls and two Cows. Killed one Cow, and brought in all the Meat. Mantá Killed two Old Bulls.

Monday 18 — Weather same as yesterday — Cold day — No News from any quarter, two Bulls in sight.

Tuesday 19 — Cold and Cloudy all day — the Men at Work at the piquetts of the Fort —

Wednesday 20 — Bad Weather all day — Garreau arrived from above with 30 or 40 Aricaras, and 250 Robes to trade — Killed a Bull near the Fort — Prepared a Grand Feast for the Indians, Boiled Meat, Coffee & Bread — and a Kittle of Corn -

Thursday 21 — Commenced tradeing with the Indians, at 8 A. M. finished tradeing, and Indians all off Fine day but windy.

Friday 22 — Started out hunting with two Men, run a band of Bulls and Killed two, arrived at the Fort in the Afternoon — Light fall of rain. Ducks passed to day for the first time, nine days later than last year —

Saturday 23 — Strong West Wind all day — Killed a Duck to day the first this year, ordered him for breakfast —

Sunday 24 — Rain and snow last Night — Fine day — Four Bulls hove in sight, started with one Man to give them a chace. We each Killed two — they all being Poor we left the Meat, and only took the tongues and Paunches.

Monday 25 — One of the warmest days this year set the Men to Make Packs (16)

Tuesday 26 — Fine Weather — Ducks, Geese, and Swans in all directions. Sent the Men to the Lake above to Cut Wood for the Fort — River riseing —

Wednesday 27 — Had a Goose for dinner, the first this year — Finished repairing the Pickets of the Fort — The water rose two feet, ice not yet started —

Thursday 28 — Strong North West Wind all day — Water still riseing The ice in front of the Fort Made a start at 4 P. M. — Water continues riseing.

Friday 29 — Fine pleasant day — five Bulls Made an attempt to Cross the river from the North side , on reaching the shore on this side, the[y] Could not Make a landing on account of the ice, and all five were drowned. We succeeded in Cutting up one young fellow, the Meat of which was conveyed to the Fort in a Cart —

Saturday 30 — Warm South Wind. The Ice made a final start at 2 P. M Several drowned Buffaloes passed with the Ice. We succeeded in drawing to shore, an other of the five Buffaloe that was drowned yesterday .

Sunday 31 — The water rose last night four feet — the river full of ice. Went up to the lake to shoot ducks — Killed three and one *goose*. The Prairies are all on fire on the north side, the work of the Horrid tribe, that are encamped above the Gros Ventre Village .

Killed 160 Rats this Month   3639 —

1839   APRIL 30 DAYS

Monday 1 — Sent three Men up to the Indian Camp to help bring down the Skin Canoes — the river as yet full of ice,   this Month commences with 280 packs of Buff. Robes, and 12 packs of Mixed skins,   the Praries on the north side opposite the Fort are all burnt — the fire haveing reached the timber last Night —

Tuesday 2 — The ice in the river still running. Strong wind from the North West at 10 A. M —, the river clear of ice at 2 P. M —, I am in hopes that my Canoes will leave the Camp to Morrow,   Went up to the Lake, and Killed one fat goose — The Water fell to day four feet —

Wednesday 3 — At day brake we had a shower of rain with thunder towards the South, the first this year, Strong South Wind all day — More thunder in the evening towards the West — Rain

Thursday 4 — Morning calm, This Morning at 10 A. M — we were surprised by a war party of Yanctons who rushed into the

Fort unperceived,   I rushed Out with my gun, expecting at the same time to be shot down, and approached them,   they told me that they were friendly, and did not wish to harm us, that they were in quest of the Aricarees, and not the Whites,   I conducted them into my room, gave them something to eat, a few loads of Powder, tobacco &c which much pleased them,   they passed the rest of the day, with me — They were 20 in Number, Myself and one Man are the only inmates of the Fort, except 4 Squaws, the rest of My Men have not yet returned, from above —

Heavy shower of rain and hail in the afternoon — The Yanctons left here in the evening for their Camp on Canon Ball River,

Friday 5 — Cloudy, windy, rainy all sorts of my⁵ weather, Two Bulls in sight — Canoes not yet arrived —

Saturday 6 — Weather same as yesterday, wind from the north, one more long day past, and no news of my Canoes,

Sunday 7 — Rain, all day — Two Bulls near the Fort — No appearance of clearing off — Loanesome times —

Monday 8 — Foggy Morning, Cleared off at 10 A. M — Two Bulls in sight — Took a long solitary walk after the two Bulls, one of which I Killed, brought home his tongue & Nuts, The *Sun* has showen himself to day, for the first time this eight days — Strong wind from the east at 2 P. M — Thunder towards the west at 4. P. M — and at sun down a heavy shower of rain —

Tuesday 9 — Rain all last night — Strong Wind from the North all day, with rain. Canoes not yet arrived, Cleared off at sun down, prospects of fine weather.

Wednesday 10 — Foggy Morning, the rest of the day, fine and pleasant — went up to the Lake to shoot Ducks, Killed two. The water is at its lowest pitch —

Thursday 11 — Morning Calm — My Canoes arrived at 10 A. M — with 970 Robes, several wet — they have been eight days on the road.

Friday 12 — Started three Men back to the Indian Camp, to

bring down the rest of My Robes, Set two Men to Make packs, 40 — found a quantity wet — Calm pleasant day.

Saturday 13 — Shower of rain in the Morning. Strong south. wind all day — Made packs 40.

Sunday 14 — Finished Makeing packs 16 — an other fine day — Went a fishing Caught nothing —

Monday 15 — Started out early a hunting with two Men and 2 Mules,   Killed one poor cow my horse being poor,   arrived at the Fort at 2 P. M — Saw three otters.

Tuesday 16 — Strong East wind,   arranged the Meat on the scaffold, as the rats are distroying it, Wind continued all day — Mantá caught a large Sturgeon, the first fish this year — Killed five rats on the Meat scaffold —

Wednesday 17 — Wind same as yesterday — which continued all last night,   smokey weather,   had fried fish for breakfast, Sprinkled with rain in the afternoon.   Wind all day,

Thursday 18 — Shower of rain this Morning — Wind as usual all day — No News from any quarter — Canoes not yet arrived,

Friday 19 — The wind fell last night — Started Out hunting Killed two Cows and two Calves,   arrived at the Fort at 12 Oclock — Strong wind at 1 P. M —

Saturday 20 — The two skin canoes arrived at 10 A. M — with 930 Robes, left the Ree Camp on their way to this place,   report a fight between them and the Assinniboines — but None Killed on either side — a bloodless fight — and no bones broken —

Sunday 21 — Set the Men to Make packs 47 — Strong South Wind all day — rain in the Afternoon —

Monday 22 — Rain all last night,   and to day — Made Packs 50   Set the Blacksmith to work in the Shop —

Tuesday 23 — Bad weather still continues,   three Rees arrived from the Camp above, on a War excursion against the Sioux several More will arrive this evening or to morrow — Caught several fine cat fish,

Wednesday 24 — Foggy Morning — Pressed packs 70.   Enemies discovered on the hill, all on horse back, a war party of Rees arrived, on their way to the Pawnees to steal horses   42 Men's and 2 Squaws .

Thursday 25 — The war party left here last Night — Pressed packs 133 — This morning at 10 A.M. — a small war party of Sioux Made a rush on my horses and drove them all off: 11 — We pursued them 3 or 4 Miles but Could not overtake them,   We have not a horse left at the Fort, bad prospects for fresh Meat —

Friday 26 — Shower of rain last night,   Set the Blacksmith to arrange the Beaver traps, &c — *O. B. F.*

Saturday 27 — Rain all last night and today — The Ree Village not yet arrived from their wintering camp.

Sunday 28 — Moved into my summer quarters.   No News from any quarter —

Monday 29 — The water rose last night one foot,   Covered the ware houses with dirt,   &c —

Tuesday 30 — The last day of a Wet and Windy Month, Which ends in a shower of rain in the Morning, and strong Wind from the west at 10 A. M — set two Men to Make a Canoe, intending to take a trip to Fort Pierre — The water rose two feet since Morning

Killed 90 Rats this Month — total 3729

1839   MAY 31 DAYS

Wednesday 1 — Wind and rain all day — water still riseing — the two Men that is Makeing a Canoe on the North side of the river, Could not cross on account of the wind which was blowing from the West —

Thursday 2 — Fine and pleasant in the Morning — Snow at 2 P. M.   The Bloody Knife a Ree Soldier arrived from the Camp above,   he says that they will all be here to day, except the Gros Ventres and Mandans, Who have stayed behind, With the intention of Moveing to the Old Gros Ventre Village, as they

Cannot agree with the Rees — Finished Makeing the Canoe — Several More Rees arrived, the Camp will not be here untill tomorrow —

Friday 3 — The Ree Camp arrived at 8 A. M — gave them a feast, and had a talk with them which ended in Nothing, except good words, Commenced tradeing — Strong South Wind — Traded 81 Robes to day —

Saturday 4 — Strong Wind from the east, Several Mandans came down from the Upper Village, brought with them several robes, gave them a feast,   trade going on slow — 64 Robes —

Sunday 5 — This Morning haveing Nothing to do, I borrowed two horses from the Rees and Went Out to discover, saw a band of Buffaloes near the Fort, On my way home, I found the Carcasses of four of my horses that was stolen by the Sioux the 25th of last Month. No doubt in quarrelling among themselves for the seperation of the horses, they Killed them. the Indians will all go Out to Morrow to run the Buffaloe that I discovered — took an inventory of goods, as I will leave to morrow for Fort Pierre

Monday 6 — off at Day light, and arrived at Fort Pierre the 10th   found Messrs Papin & Halsey there,   Mr Picotte had left for St Louis two days before —

NOTES AND REFERENCES

NOTES AND REFERENCES

¹ Fort Clark, described by Audubon, somewhat contemptuously, as a "fort, which in general appearance might be called a poor miniature representation of Fort Pierre" (*Coues*, Elliott, *Maria R. Audubon's Audubon* and *His Journals*," vol. ii, pp. 13-14) and by Thaddeus A. Culbertson, who saw it in 1850, as "a small fort" (*Journal*, Senate Documents, Special session, 32nd. congress, vol. i, p. 115), was yet a "substantial structure" (*Chittenden*, Hiram M., *History of the American Fur Trade of the Far West*, vol. iii, p. 948) situated "on a bluff in an angle of the river and on its right bank" (*idem*), the south, or left-hand, side in ascending the stream, "55 miles above the N. P. R. R. bridge at Bismarck, N. D. (*idem*). It was built in the late spring or early summer of 1831 by James Kipp of wood cut, under his direction, the previous winter (*Maximilian*, Alexander P., Prince of Wied: *Travels in the Interior of North America*, Edition of 1843, p. 321) and built a short distance below the site of a Mandan post that he had similarly constructed for the Columbia Fur Company between May and November of 1822 (*idem*, p. 319). It is to be distinguished from the Fort Clark, to which the name of *Fort Osage* is more correctly applied — because officially so christened in 1808 (*Sibley*, George Champlin, *Diary, 1808-1811*, entry, November 13, 1808), although both places were named in honor of William Clark of the Lewis and Clark expedition, who became Superintendent of Indian Affairs at St. Louis and so continued until his death in 1838 (*Missouri Republican*, September 3, 1838; *Missouri Argus*, September 3, 1838). Yet another Fort Clark, a military post on the Illinois, was named after his brother, George Rogers Clark. For orders issued for its discontinuance, 1818, see *Letter Book of Brigadier-General Thomas A. Smith*, no. 6, p. 16, *Smith Papers*, Missouri State Historical Society).

² The other two were forts Pierre and Union, for each of which something in the nature of a description will follow in due course. See notes 12 and 24.

³ Amalgamation was resolved upon after repeated attempts to create distinct spheres of influence had proved unsuccessful. That all went well, finally, was doubtless due to the fact that Crooks and Mackenzie, being compatriots, were unhampered by personal prejudices and were disposed to be as conciliatory towards each other as was consonant with duty. More than all else, however, it was due to the fact that the Columbia Fur Company was financially embarrassed, being hard-pressed by the supply merchants. Of this situation Ramsay Crooks was nothing loath to take advantage. Extracts from his correspondence will show how matters progressed: —
(a) "Annexed is copy of what I have addressed to Mr. Lamont in your absence and although I cannot agree with you for the trade of the current year, I am still disposed to arrange for the future provided you are inclined to be moderate in your expectations for I cannot consent to abandon the St. Peters from the Travers des Sioux upwards —
"It is however next to impossible to settle such matters by correspondence and if after consulting your partners, there is a prospect of our coming

to terms, I would have no objections to meet you here or at Fort Snelling, next April, or perhaps even earlier if practicable and you desire it . . .

"Mr. Rolette has renewed his arrangements with our concern for a term of years

"I depart for St. Louis to-morrow and will see your packet delivered to Messrs. Collier & Powell.

"This letter will be confided to Mr. Graham . . .''

(Crooks to Mackenzie at Lac Traverse, *Burton Transcripts from Hoguet Collection*, New York City).

(b) (enclosure)

"I have examined very particularly the proposed arrangement for the trade of next season, so as to prevent competition with your Company from St. Croix upwards and find it so beset with difficulties that I think it best for us to take our chance of the times as we have done heretofore'' (Crooks to Mackenzie or, in his absence, Daniel Lamont, St. Peters, dated Prairie des Chiens, August 30, 1826, *idem*, pp. 204-205).

(c) "From McKenzie I have a letter of 9th January last, but their expectations are too unreasonable to permit me to hope that we can make an equitable arrangement with them; I will nevertheless try'' (Crooks to J. J. Astor, dated St. Louis, April 13, 1827, *idem*, pp. 214-216).

In similar mood Crooks wrote again about a fortnight later, when he had to report that, although Mackenzie's letter left little to hope for — he being so unreasonable — he was yet intending to do his best to end the opposition and was going up to consult with Joseph Rolette before Mackenzie should arrive. He had heard in St. Louis that "the house which supplies his concern is sick of the business and somewhat cramped in its means, but whether this be true or otherwise, it will not prevent my offering him fair terms, and if we do not agree, the negociation will only be broken off by his unreasonable pretentions'' (Same to Same, April 30, 1827, *idem*, pp. 219-220).

Astor gave full credence to the rumor that the Columbia Fur Company was being hard pressed by Collier & Powell of St. Louis (Astor to Crooks, May 25, 1827, *idem*, pp. 231-233) and encouraged Crooks in the belief that his efforts towards adjustment would not go unrewarded. Towards that view his agent was himself inclining and wrote,

(d) "With Mr. McKenzie since his arrival here, I have had a further interchange of views, and he has continued to manifest so pacific a disposition, that I entertain still stronger hopes of our becoming reconciled; some of his partners however are absent yet, and he seems inclined to await their arrival before he does anything conclusive.

"I have uniformly consulted all the four members of B. Pratte & Co., who fortunately are now assembled here, and shall act on our joint determination in regard to the terms and conditions on which we will admit Mr. McKenzie and his friends.'' (Crooks to Astor, dated St. Louis, June 8, 1827, *idem*, pp. 238-241).

On June 22nd, 1827, Crooks had every reason, as he supposed, to think that "the business with McKenzie & Co.'' was drawing to a favorable conclusion and that the "negociation will terminate in 2 or 3 days at fartherest'' (Crooks to Astor, June 22, 1827, *idem*, pp. 243-245); but another failure soon threatened and he wrote almost despairingly,

(e) "Until just before Mr. Rolette left this, I entertained the most sanguine expectations that I could come to an equitable arrangement with Mr. McKenzie but at the moment of his departure, there remained very little hope of an accommodation, and it was agreed that in three days they would hand me their ultimatum.

"The time expired yesterday, and understanding Mr. McKenzie was sick, I waited upon him but he was too unwell to talk of business, and I agreed to call again, which I have just done.

"In *addition* to all I told you, I had offered them Mr. McKenzie demands for himself an increase of $500 making his salary per annum $1500 — to retain only two of his partners in the business with him, instead of at least *three* as they to have the trade of the Poncas, also with the exclusive privilege of sending hunting parties into the Rocky Mountains if feasible, and besides all this, they asked me to employ their people in preference to our own on the Missouri & St Peters and to give Renville goods at a reasonable rate on his own account for the trade of the Lac qui Parle District.

"All this might have been conceded though the sacrifice was more than I had thought would be asked of us; but when I saw Mr. Powell on the subject of this years importations, he could not be prevailed on to accept of a less advance than *25 per cent* on the English importation and 20 *per cent* on the goods bought in the United States ! ! ! — This would cost us at least $10,000 more than we ever dreamed of and in a general consultation with B. Pratte & Co. it was unanimously decided that war was preferable to Peace on such conditions. I have done all I could (in the greatest sincerity) to become friends with our opponents and since they have refused peace on fair terms, they must take the consequences.

"I have therefore only to add that I trust you will compel Mr Aitkens to act as he ought above the Falls of St. Anthony, and I am very sure Mr. Rolette will not suffer them to triumph on the River of St. Peters."
(Crooks to Robert Stuart at Mackinac, dated St. Louis, June 22, 1827, *idem*, pp. 246-247).

(f) "Enclosed is a letter for Mr Robert Stuart which I leave open, and by which you will see all my sincere efforts to arrange with the Columbia Fur Company on equitable terms have proved abortive.

"We must now fight harder than ever. . ."
(Crooks to Joseph Rolette, June 27, 1827, *idem*, p. 248).
It was a case, seemingly, of the hour being darkest just before the dawn; for, early in July, he had his deserts: —

(g) "It affords me pleasure to inform you that after an almost useless negociation, I have, at last succeeded in agreeing on preliminaries with the Columbia Fur Company to give up their trade entirely and take a share with us in that of the Upper Missouri . . ." (Crooks to Astor, July 6, 1827, *idem*, pp. 251-252).

4 For two of the latest and best short biographical sketches of him, see *Douglas*, Walter B., *General Thomas James'* "*Three Years Among the Indians and Mexicans*," p. 273; *Marshall*, T. M., *Life and Papers of Frederick Bates*, vol. ii, pp. 16-17, *note* 128. Like Lamont, he had come from Greenock. According to his own account (Crooks to H. M. Rice, October 16, 1857, quoted in *Neill*, E. D., *History of Minnesota*, p. 291, *note*) he, too, had seen service with Robert Dickson, having gone to Mackinac as a clerk to him in 1805, Dickson's trade, at the time, being almost entirely confined to the Sioux. About two years later, or slightly earlier, he and Robert McClellan, being in St. Louis, were outfitted by Chouteau for the upper Missouri trade and were conveniently at hand when Wilson Price Hunt, under the auspices of Astor, was making his final preparations for the Astoria expedition. The connection of Crooks with that expedition, through the medium of what has come to be quite generally known as the Pacific Fur Company, would take too long to recount adequately here, were it at all relevant. Suffice it to say, that his adventures as an Astorian once

ended, he became permanently identified with the American Fur Company and, from about 1817 on, Astor's chief agent. Not the least important, by any manner of means, of the happenings of his very eventful life was his marriage, March 10, 1825, with Emelie Pratte, the daughter of Bernard Pratte and Emelie S. Labadie; for it brought him within the ranks of the influential French commercial houses of St. Louis and into immediate family relations with the Chouteau, the Gratiot, the Berthold, and the like. Then, in 1834, a significant date, as will be seen, for this study, he became, with the final retirement of John Jacob Astor, President of what to all intents and purposes was still the American Fur Company.

5 It would be idle to add to these notes a biographical sketch ever so short of the German founder of the American Fur Company, the most powerful by all odds of the earlier American monopolies, in fact, almost the only one that, in any way, compares with the gigantic commercial organizations of to-day. The recent life of John Jacob Astor, the immigrant, by Arthur D. Howden Smith, while neither exhaustive nor scholarly, is a very commendable piece of work, highly entertaining to read, strong and emphatic on some of the very things that it is the object of the present study to throw into relief. Another biography that is said to be under way will, let us hope, fill in all the gaps and give ample space to a consideration of the methods in trade that Astor and his subordinates, under his direction, everywhere employed. Vigilant Astor was, always; on occasion, he could be unscrupulous to the highest degree, halting at nothing. He, obviously, attended to the minutest details, personally, was grudging of praise, only very rarely enthusiastic. Crooks, he thought, was given to being over-sanguine (J. J. Astor to Crooks, dated Geneva, November, 1824, *Burton Transcripts from Hoguet Originals*, pp. 178-179). His way of prodding others is revealed in these extracts, a few out of many:
(a)   ''It is time that our business should be placed on a defferint footing & I hope you will have made such arrangement as will acahion less expence & Induce the Clerks & Pepol who have our property under their care to more activity & greater exertions otherwise we can not Suced . . .''   (J. J. Astor to P. Chouteau, Jr., postmarked July 8, 1829, *Chouteau Investment Company Collection*).
(b)   ''I will be glad to learn that you have bought largely of the Santa fea Beaver You know it is Genrally not so good as Ashleys Beaver but as the article is very high It will answer very well   What I sold is of the Ashly Beaver . . .'' (Same to Same, November 17, 1829, *idem*).
(c)   ''I wrote you yesterday Informing you that I had Sold 12 packs of the Ashley Beaver which has Since been weight off & I am Sorry to Say that it falls very Short in weight . . . you must have made a Mistake or there has been Some fraud Some where   light weights or the Beaver must have been put in a very Damp Place before it was weight. I wish you to Investigate the Matter it appears that what Halsey & Moore Rec'd was also Short in weight. On looking over this Beaver it is found not so good as was at first believed . . .''
(Same to Same, November 18, 1829, *idem*)
(d)   ''I now confirm what was said to you on the 18th Ulto: — viz — that such Beaver as the 17 Packs of the Ashley collection which you sent us, will not bring more than $ 6 a $ 6½ pr lb in this market, and then the dealers are generally so poor, that we hardly know who to trust — If you were not to buy the Santafee Beaver, it would nevertheless find its way here, and might fall into other hands than ours which could not fail to be

injurious, and I therefore hope you will have got it, but at a moderate price.

"..."

(Same to Same, December 3, 1829, *idem*)

6 For biographical sketches of Kenneth Mackenzie and his partners in the Upper Missouri Outfit, see notes on subsequent pages.

7 In all the secondary references to this man, under whose name the Columbia Fur Company had its legal status (*Thwaites*, R. G., *Early Western Travels*, vol. xxiii, p. 225, *note* 180), there seems a general avoidance of initials. Among the traders, listed by Agent Lawrence Taliaferro as licensed between 1819 and 1840 (*Autobiography*, Minnesota Historical Society *Collections*, vol. vi, p. 249) appears J. P. Tilton. Tilton "was sutler at Fort Gibson in 1836" (*Thwaites*, R. G., *Early Western Travels*, vol. xxiii, p. 225, *note* 180).

8 *Thwaites*, R. G., *Early Western Travels*, vol. xxii, p. 235, *note* 168; *Marshall*, T. M., *Life and Papers of Frederick Bates*, vol. i, p. 203, *note* 190.

9 The present Minnesota River.

10 The best idea of Benton can, of course, be obtained from his own *Thirty Years' View*; but, for an appraisement of his services, no better authority can, perhaps, be found than *Meigs*, William Montgomery, *Life of T. H. Benton* (1904).

11 The following letter illustrates how closely in touch with Benton Ramsay Crooks kept himself while the final doing away with the system was under consideration:
"From Mr. Joseph Rolette I have letters stating in substance what he says about the Trade, Rouse & Grignon, and the new Factor. About the Factories I had some intelligence previous, and wrote Mr Benton in consequence. An investigation is instituted in the shape of a resolution calling on the President for information, and there is no danger of the public trading houses being re-established.

"..."

(Ramsay Crooks to Samuel Abbott, January 29, 1823, *Pierre Chouteau Collection*, Missouri Historical Society). The act for the abolishment of the Factory System was passed May 6, 1822 (3 United States Statutes at Large, pp. 679-680).

12 References to the preparations made by Mackenzie for the building of this, the most important of the posts of the Upper Missouri Outfit are to be found in Laidlaw to Chouteau, August 13 and October 26, 1829 (*Chouteau Investment Collection*, Missouri Historical Society). The fort in its final shape was situated about three miles above the mouth of the Yellowstone (*Chittenden*, H. M., *History of Early Steamboat Navigation on the Missouri River*, vol. i, p. 139, *note*) at "an elevation of 1,900 feet above the sea" (*Warren*, G. K., *Preliminary Report of Explorations in Nebraska and Dakota, 1855-'57*, pp. 32-33). Travellers like Bonneville, Catlin, Maximilian, T. A. Culbertson, Palliser, and others all had interesting remarks to make about Fort Union. Denig's description of the post, dated July 30, 1843, is to be found in, *Audubon*, Maria R., *Audubon and His Journals*, edited by Elliott Coues, vol. ii, pp. 180-188.

13 South Dakota Historical *Collections,* vol. i, p. 352.

14 For an ultra-appreciative account of this man, see *Ambler,* Charles H., *Life and Diary of John Floyd.*

15 John Quincy Adams tells in his *Diary,* under date of January 18, 1821, how Monroe handed him Floyd's project to read and how his own impression was that ''There was nothing could purify it but the fire'' (*Memoirs,* vol. v, p. 238). Monroe also related to Adams a somewhat scandalous story of why Floyd was interested in Oregon. His brother-in-law had proved an embezzler of State funds and, to escape the disgrace and odium brought upon the family, various members of it, including the criminal, were anxious to migrate.

16 Some idea of Floyd's indefatigability in the matter can be got from the following congressional record:
On December 19, 1820, he moved for the appointment of a committee to inquire into the situation on the Columbia River, the settlements there, and the expediency of occupying the region (16th congress, 2nd session, *Annals of Congress,* vol. xxxvii, p. 679). The committee consisted of himself as chairman, Thomas Metcalfe of Kentucky, and Thomas Van Swearingen of Virginia. On January 25, 1821, the committee made its report and offered a bill (*idem,* pp. 945-959). The report gave what purported to be a history of the American claims to Oregon and the bill outlined a scheme of military colonization. Undismayed by his failure to overcome a prejudice against colonization and to create sufficient enthusiasm for the granting of national assistance, Floyd, December 17, 1821, called for a report on the probable expense of examining the harbors belonging to the United States on the Pacific coast and of transporting troops to the mouth of the Columbia. Although his resolution passed in the House, nothing came of it at all measuring up to his expectations. Then, after a respite and when various extraneous circumstances made the time seem especially opportune, he offered a resolution to the effect that the President should be requested to lay before the House an estimate of the expense that might be incurred in transporting the troops at Council Bluffs to the mouth of the Columbia (18th congress, 1st session, *Annals of Congress,* vol. xli, p. 478). This measure, in modified form, passed the House of Representatives (*idem,* pp. 113-157); but was lost in the Senate (*idem,* p. 1203).

17 See a communication to the *St. Louis Enquirer,* July 22, 1824 (Appendix). The *St. Louis Enquirer* was peculiarly Benton's organ and, from about 1819, he was part owner of it (Meigs, *Life of T. H. Benton,* p. 88) or, as some believed, ''half-owner'' (*Adams,* J. Q. *Memoirs,* vol. v, p. 327).

18 *Benton,* T. H. *Thirty Years' View,* vol. i, chap. 5, pp. 13-14.

19 For an insinuation of what one of Astor's methods was and evidence of the venality of Lewis Cass when Governor of Michigan Territory, see *Smith,* A. D. H., *John Jacob Astor,* pp. 200-201.

20 The leading members of the so-called ''French Company'' were Pierre Didier Papin, Gabriel Pascal Cerré, Michel Sylvestre Cerré, and Honoré Picotte. For the names of other members, see extract from a letter, Pierre Chouteau, Jr. to Kenneth Mackenzie, July, 1829, quoted by Doane Robinson, South Dakota Historical *Collections,* vol. ix, p. 113, *note* 56. In the *Chouteau-Maffitt Collection* of the Missouri Historical Society are various papers showing the amount of stock taken over by the American Fur Com-

pany according to the *Articles of Agreement* drawn up October 14, 1830. The transfers were made at the various posts where P. D. Papin and his colleagues had carried on their opposition trade, at the ''Poncas,'' at ''Eau Qui Court,'' and at White River. The transfer at Fort Tecumseh took place, October 16, 1830.

21 Agent Jonathan L. Bean was said to use this expression when addressing his Indians in order to create in their minds a prejudice against the Upper Missouri Outfit [Laidlaw to Cabanné, December 25, 1831, *Fort Tecumseh Letter Book, 1830-1832*, pp. 84-87] By implication, whenever used at this particular period, it was a term of reproach and, as such, had been cast with telling effect against the Columbia Fur Company. For Mackenzie's retort, which was published in the *St. Louis Enquirer*, July 19, 1824, see Appendix, where also can be found some citizenship data, relative to Mackenzie, Laidlaw, and Lamont, which may indicate to what extent his retort was a rebuttal. As far as the Upper Missouri Outfit was concerned, Laidlaw thought Bean was persistently hostile to him and his friends (Laidlaw to Chouteau, December 26, 1831, *Fort Tecumseh Letter Book, 1830-1832*, p. 83). He decidedly favored Narcisse Leclerc, an *Opposition* at this time. See, especially, Laidlaw to Mackenzie, February 15, 1832 (*idem*) and the following extracts from other letters of his:

(a)   ''Our Opponent Leclerc has got up this far with a few pack horses loaded; I think he will have reason to repent his folly — Father Bean it is said, employed all his means to render him every assistance possible; but I do not fear them, great as our father's power may be'' (Laidlaw to D. D. Mitchell at Fort Clark, February 15, 1832, *idem*, p. 102)

(b)   ''I observe what you say with regard to your opponent, and particularly the ill-timed interference of Father Bean; he is certainly deviating from his duty; and will I have no doubt be called to account for his conduct — If your Opponents still hold out that the goods they have under their charge belong to Bean — I would have no hesitation in telling the Indians that they are robbing them of their just rights, and selling the goods to them, that was expressly sent by Government for their annuities and presents'' (Laidlaw to P. D. Papin, February 22, 1832, *idem*, p. 111).

(c)   ''I shall rest satisfied that Master Leclerc will have no advantage over us, even at Fort Lookout, although under the wing of Father Bean'' (Same to Same, March 4, 1832, *idem*, p. 114).

22 Better known as the Rocky Mountain Fur Company, of which General William H. Ashley had been the principal organizer. For the more salient facts of its history, see *Thwaites, Reuben Gold, Early Western Travels*, vol. xxii, p. 233, *note* 163. Among the *Sublette MSS.* of the Missouri Historical Society are many interesting documents bearing upon its later development under the direction of the Sublette brothers, Thomas Fitzpatrick, and others. Only two, antedating 1827, are of much importance.

23 Tilton was the Director and, for his occupancy of the Mandan post, see Maximilian's *Travels* (*op. cit.*) pp. 318-323.

24 A fairly minute description of Fort Pierre at the time Andrew Drips was in charge, is given us by Palliser, who, travelling overland with Kipp in the early autumn of 1847, ''came opposite Fort Pierre, built on the other side of the river. We fired some shots as a signal, on which they sent boats to take us and our horses across; and we were by no means sorry to find ourselves comfortably installed in time for breakfast in the finest of the Fur Company's Stations on the Missouri. In fact, Pierre is the largest fort belonging to the F. C's traders. It consists of a large space about

120 yards square, enclosed by piles of timber 24 feet high driven well into the ground. The roofs of the stores and trading houses are attached to two of the sides, with the stables, straw yards, carpenters' and blacksmiths shops, and a dairy for such cows as may escape the marauding hands of the Indians. A flagstaff, gaily rigged, stands in the centre of the square, and the whole establishment has a most inviting look to a set of weary travellers on jaded horses, and who, with the exception of the aforesaid buffalo feast, had not fared over well for many days past'' (*Solitary Rambles and Adventures of a Hunter in the Prairies*, p. 103) Chittenden says that Fort Pierre ''was 325 by 340 feet and contained about two and a half acres of ground. . .'' (*History of the American Fur Trade of the Far West*, vol. iii, pp. 955-956). For a very detailed account of Fort Pierre as it was when first erected, see Maximilian in *Early Western Travels*, vol. xxii, pp. 317-318 and, for a ground plan of the same, *idem*, p. 319. Thwaites's editorial comments are to be found on p. 315, *note* 277.

25 According to Doane Robinson, ''Fort Tecumseh was built by the Columbia Fur Company in 1822'' and ''was located on the west bank of the Missouri, about two miles above the mouth of Bad River'' (South Dakota Historical *Collections*, vol. ix, p. 93, *note* 1).

26 In Chardon's time and certainly in his journal this stream was almost invariably called the *Little Missouri*, it being the lower of the two to which the name had been early applied. By Lewis and Clark it had been designated the *Teton* because it was in its vicinity that they first encountered the Teton Sioux. When Thaddeus A. Culbertson, the brother of Alexander, made his memorable trip to the Bad Lands of White River in 1850 he noted the fact that the Little Missouri, or Teton, River was being sometimes called ''Bad River'' (*Journal*, Senate Documents, Special session, 32nd. congress, vol. i, p. 90).

27 The United States Trade and Intercourse Law of 1796 (*United States Statutes at Large*, vol. i, pp. 469-474) was the first of its class to attempt a definition of the ''Indian Country,'' while that of March 30, 1802 (*idem*, vol. ii, pp. 139-146) was the first to contain the spirituous liquor prohibition and, for that reason, became the one always cited as fundamental by the courts, especially after the following decision had been handed down in the case of the American Fur Company vs. The United States (2 Peters, 358):

''The act of March 30, 1802, having described what should be the Indian country at that time, as well as at any future time, when purchases of territory should be made of the Indians, the carrying of spirituous liquors into a territory so purchased after March, 1802, although the same should be frequented and inhabited exclusively by Indians, would not be an offence within the meaning of the act of Congress, so as to subject the goods of the trader, found in company with those liquors, to seizure and forfeiture.''

After the passage of the Act of March 30, 1802, which had no time set for its expiration, the United States policy, in the particulars covered by it, might be said to be fixed, practically, until the law of June 30, 1834 was passed (*United States Statutes at Large*, vol. iv, pp. 729-735). The Act of May 6, 1822 (*idem*, vol. iii, pp. 682-683), amendatory to that of 1802, is, however, worthy of note, since, under it, the President might require superintendents and agents to *search* for ardent spirits and, if any found, ''all goods of the said trader shall be forfeited . . . his license cancelled, and bond put in suit.''

[28] It was set up by Mackenzie, who, thereupon, created a demand for such of their corn crop as the Mandans and Gros Ventres could spare and would part with.

[29] The bad opinion that the whites had of the Arikaras, already well developed in the time of the Lewis and Clark expedition (See *Tabeau*, Pierre Antoine, *Voyage of Régis Loisel* (in press), was fully reciprocated. For an attempt to account for their determined hostility to the whites, see *Wagner, W. F., Leonard's Narrative: Adventures of Zenas Leonard, Fur Trader and Trapper, 1831-1836*, pp. 136-137 and *note*. In the course of H. M. Brackenridge's expedition up the Missouri, he found the Rees, for the moment, disposed to be friendly. They had been previously unfriendly because their entire tribe had been held responsible by the Missouri Fur Company for the Pryor affair, which the Indians asserted had been the work of one bad chief (*Thwaites, R. G., Early Western Travels*, vol. vi, p. 127); and, even in their most hostile period, they manifested a willingness to be at peace (Major Benjamin O'Fallon to General H. Atkinson, dated Fort Atkinson, July 17, 1824). For the obstruction offered by the Arikaras to the American traders, see *Dale*, Harrison Clifford, *The Ashley-Smith Explorations and the Discovery of the Central Route to the Pacific, 1822-1829*.

[30] The departure of the Arikaras was looked for and hoped for some months before it actually took place. When Mackenzie and party, *en route* to Fort Union in the late autumn of 1830 with all the horses they could muster at Fort Tecumseh (Lamont to Laidlaw, December 13, 1830, *Fort Tecumseh Letter Book*, 1830-1832, pp. 8-10), were attacked and despoiled by the Arikaras, at whose village R. T. Holliday of the Upper Missouri Outfit was trader (Lamont to Chouteau, December 30, 1830, *idem*, pp. 14-17), the injured ones took comfort in the thought that the cowardly aggressors contemplated "quitting the Missouri" "next Spring and joining the Pawnees on the Platte (*idem*); but they failed to go. The spring came and went and summer and autumn and they were yet there. Then hope rose again; for there had been a bloody conflict between them and the Sioux in which they were worsted and Laidlaw jubilantly wrote, "The general opinion is that they will clear out for the Pawnees as soon as the weather will permit" (Laidlaw to Mackenzie, November 27, 1831, *idem*, pp. 72-76). At the time, three of the Upper Missouri Outfit employees, Picotte, Pascal Cerré, and Lachapelle, were all having dealings, much to Laidlaw's disgust, with the Arikaras at Apple River (Laidlaw to P. D. Papin, December 4, 1831, *idem*, pp. 78-79); but it was not long before the Sioux positively interdicted any such intercourse (Laidlaw to Chouteau, December 26, 1831, *idem*, p. 84). Laidlaw had been much annoyed by Lachapelle's having had foisted upon him, in the way of trade, some bad robes "that he took us in most abominably" (Laidlaw to Picotte, November 27, 1831, *idem*, pp. 70-71) and he sincerely hoped that the Sioux would drive the Arikaras from the country. They were not yet gone, however, the following February and, apparently, did not go until the autumn of 1832 (Sanford to Clark, July 26, 1833, *Indian Office Files*).

When the First United States Dragoons, under Colonel Henry Dodge, was making an expedition to the Rocky Mountains in the summer of 1835, councils were held along the Platte with both the Pawnees and the Arikaras (*Pelzer*, Louis, *Marches of the Dragoons in the Mississippi Valley*, pp. 67-70); but, from the journal of Captain Ford, it is very evident that the latter had already outstayed their welcome. "The Arikara," wrote he, "lived on the Loup River for about two years, but were so dangerous and troublesome that they were requested to return to the Missouri River, their former home" (*Pelzer*, Louis, *Captain Ford's Journal of an Expedition to the Rocky Mountains* (1835), Mississippi Valley Historical *Review*, vol. xii, pp. 550-579). The exact time of the Arikara return to their former haunts and friends can be deduced from the Fort Clark journal.

31 Their kinship with the Pawnees was generally recognized by all early travellers or sojourners among them.   To Alexander Henry the two peoples seem to have appeared so much alike that he confounded them completely, calling the Arikaras invariably the Pawnees (See, for example, *Coventry Copy of Henry Journal*, vol. i, pp. 434, 458, Canadian Public Archives, Ottawa; *Coues*, Elliott, *New Light on the Early History of the Greater Northwest*, vol. i, p. 330; and, for a possible explanation, see *Burpee*, Lawrence J., *Journals and Letters of Verendrye*, p. 335, *note*).

32 For the reasons usually assigned for Astor's retirement, in which the substitution of silk hats for beaver figures prominently, see *Smith*, Arthur D. H., *John Jacob Astor*, pp. 246-247. His decision, as communicated to his associates in trade, appears in the following:
    "Gentlemen
    "Wishing to retire from the concern in which I am engaged with your House, you will please to take this as notice thereof, & that the agreement enterred into on the 7th May 1830 between your House & me on the part of the American Fur Company will expire with the outfit of the present year on the terms express in said agreement.
                        (Signed) John Jacob Astor
                                For self & Am. Fur Co.''
(Astor to Messrs. Bernard Pratte & Co., dated Geneva, June 25, 1833, *P. Chouteau Collection*, Missouri Historical Society).
    "On the 26th August last, I addressed a letter to Messrs B. Pratte & Co. for the purpose of informing you that my father had intimated an intention of retiring from the Fur trade, that you might make such consequent arrangements as you might desire without coming to any positive conclusion. My father is now fully determined to retire from the trade as you will perceive by the enclosed letter from him addressed to your late firm . . .''
(W. B. Astor, President, to B. Pratte, P. Chouteau, Jr., & J. P. Cabanné, dated Office of the American Fur Co., New York, November 1, 1833, *idem*).

33 Besides Chardon's Fort Clark journal there is extant the fragment of another [See Appendix], which, although dated 1833, belongs, unmistakably to the following year. It was kept, as indicated, by a certain Alexander Kennedy, to whom reference was made in a letter — an extract from which is here subjoined — that Laidlaw wrote to Charles Degray, November 3, 1833 (*Fort Pierre Letter Book, 1832-1835*, pp. 34-35).   The reference was such as to imply that Kennedy was, at the time, a comparative stranger to the upper Missouri.   This would not have been said, if, in the preceding May and June, he had been keeping the books at Fort Clark, Kipp's post among the Mandans. Moreover, the subject-matter of Kennedy's journal, meagre though it be, fits in with what we know from other sources of the occurrences of 1834.   Charles Degray (Degueire?) was trading on White River, having gone there rather recently (Laidlaw to Colin Campbell, September 5, 1833, *idem*, p. 36) and to him Laidlaw communicated information about young Kennedy thus:
    "I send you a Young Gentleman the bearer of this [Mr. Kennedy] who

will keep your accounts, take care of the house when you have occasion to go out, or anything else you may have for him to do; he is a new hand and knows nothing about the trade; give him all the insight you possibly can.''

Degray, on White River, was confronted with heavy opposition trade and, in the beginning of 1834, Laidlaw, writing again to Colin Campbell, whose trade was with the ''Ogallallahs,'' at the Forks of the Cheyenne, said, ''I am much afraid that Charles Degray will be hard pushed; if you could make it convenient to pay him a visit I wish you would, and give him some of your wise counsel'' (Laidlaw to Campbell, January 22, 1834, *idem*, pp. 63-65). Whether Kennedy had, by that time already left the White River, has not been determined; but, in April, he was certainly with Kipp at Fort Clark and, to Kipp, Halsey, in Laidlaw's absence, wrote on April 30th, ''Mr Kennedy you can keep with you for the present. Mr. McKenzie when he comes down will tell you how to dispose of him'' (*idem*, p. 73). Dispose of him Mackenzie obviously did. He gave instructions to Crawford to go, when the time should come for him to leave Fort Clark, to the place where the *Assiniboine* was to be moored for the winter and there to establish a trade with the Crees and Assiniboines. Kennedy joined Crawford or, perhaps, went with him to Fort Union. Note the following letter from Hamilton to Crawford, September 27, 1834 (*Fort Union Letter Book, 1833-1835*, p. 55):

''Sundry articles ordered are packed in trunk of which A. Kennedy has the key. I propose starting the carts on Monday. Of dye stuffs a small portion sells for $1. Rifle Bell & Meat (475 lb) arrived safe   more meat pr return carts would be acceptable. J. Ram's son will bring your spare cart & A. K. ride your extra horse. I can spare A. K. for a few months or the winter if you wish to have him.

''I know Assiniboines are great beggars but the merest trifle will often content them tho' at first they ask great things.

''We know not where Jackson's camp is. Can you inform us? Francis started 17 Sept. A note for Mr. Carlisle is enclosed. I regret to hear he has adopted a line of conduct so disagreeable to you & dishonorable to himself, as he shews his cards thus early you will regulate your plans accordingly. Give him a rect. for stores he delivers up.

''Your request for any thing I can supply shall always receive my careful attention.

''You have my best wishes,

''truly yours

''J. A. H.''

Crawford did wish to have Kennedy and retained him at the mouth of Poplar River, Hamilton hoping he could ''make something'' of him (Hamilton to Crawford, October 7, 1834, *idem*, p. 55).

[34] That June eighteenth marked a change in the arrangements on the upper Missouri and, perhaps, particularly at Fort Clark may be inferred from subsequent official correspondence, of which a communication from Jacob Halsey to Chardon, dated Fort Pierre, October 1, 1834, is a specimen:

''Inclosed you will receive particulars of Stock remaining on hand at Fort Clark last Summer, shewing the price of each article; you will find it convenient when you go to make out Equipment for the Grosventres, and other Indians — You will likewise receive herewith, Invoice of Mdse deld. F. C. by Sublette & Campbell 18th June 1834 — W. P. Mays. note for $265 50/100,

Michel Bellhumers a/c in detail, a/c current between this post and F. C. and your own a/c up to June last —

By the first opportunity, I wish you would have the goodness to let me have a list of the persons in the employ of the Co. at your Post, shewing the Amt: of their Wages and the term of their engagements, this is absolutely necessary I should have, in order to make out your post a/c complete; the a/c current will shew the names of such of your people, with whose engagements I am acquainted —

I have charged your post with May⁹. note and a/c, as it is probable it will be paid at your post —

Your Invoice of Mdse: per Steam boat, shall be sent to you as soon as it is recᵈ. from St Louis, in the meantime I hope you will be able to get along without it —

I have nothing more to say to you in the way of business, and will now close by subscribing Myself

Very Truly Yours,

Jacob Halsey

35 The only evidence in support of this was obtained from excerpts in the possession of the Missouri Historical Society of the baptismal records of the old Osage Mission, which, at one time in its history, was located about where St. Paul, Kansas is to-day. From these it appears that, on May 5, 1822, the Reverend De la Croix of the diocese of St. Louis visited the Osage Mission and baptized among others the following:

"Joseph Capitaine, born in 1822, of Joseph Capitaine and Achinga. Francois Auguste Chardon" (godfather).

In the hope that additional evidence of the same sort might be forthcoming in the records themselves a visit was paid to St. Mary's, Kansas, where they are reputed now to be; but the application for them was made in vain, their present whereabouts being reported unknown.

36 In the records of St. Augustine's Church, Philadelphia, Anthony Chardon, assumed to be the father of Francis, appears as a witness to a marriage, August 15, 1804 (American Catholic Society of Philadelphia, *Records*, vol. xiii, p. 175). A man of the name was in the paper-hanging business and had a "Paper-Hanging Manufactory and Warehouse" in Chestnut Street, Philadelphia (Patrick Campbell to Mathew Carey, dated Chambersburg, Pennsylvania, September 22, 1812, *Selections from the Correspondence of Mathew Carey, idem*, vol. xi). In the Philadelphia directories from 1794 to 1833, Anthony Chardon is listed, previously to 1819, as paperhanger or paper-manufacturer and, between 1819 and 1825, as an importer of French goods in addition. In the directories from 1829 on, he is listed as "Gent." Chardon's father, whether Anthony or someone else, was alive in the winter of 1835-1836 when the son paid a visit to his aged parents after an absence of twenty years; but must have been dead at the time of Catlin's visit, which might have been four or five years subsequently. Catlin saw no occasion, at any rate, for mentioning him, while being most explicit in his references to others of the family: —

"Several years since writing the above," Catlin tells his readers, "I made a visit with my wife, to the venerable parent of Mr. Chardon, who lives in her snug and neat mansion, near the City of Philadelphia, where we were treated with genuine politeness and hospitality. His mother and two sisters, who are highly respectable, had many anxious questions to ask about him; and had at the same time, living with them, a fine-looking half-breed boy, about ten years old, the son of Monsr. Chardon and his

Indian wife, whom I have spoken of. This fine boy who had received the name of Bolivar, had been brought from the Indian country by the father, and left here for his education, with which they were taking great pains'' (*Catlin*, George, *North American Indians*, vol. i, p. 225, *note*).

[37] ''Thursday (January 8, 1835). Dull and Lonesome — Not so brisk as at this day 20 Years ago, at New Orleans.''

[38] Inasmuch as the records in both places are admittedly incomplete, it cannot be said positively that Chardon was not fighting under Jackson when he was at New Orleans in January, 1815. Indeed, the presumption is that he was.

[39] This is indicated by his sending greetings to the Berthold family as, for example, in the letter quoted of date August 20, 1820 (*note* 90); by his taking his little son to the home of Madame Berthold when in St. Louis *en route* from Fort Clark to Philadelphia in 1835 (See deposition of Pierre A. Berthold, September 1, 1851, *Bolivar Chardon Wardship Papers*, St. Louis Court House, no. 1335); by his keeping money with the Berthold firm until he transferred it in 1844 to the Pierre Chouteau, Jr. & Co. (Benjamin Clapp to Chouteau, July 20, 1844, *Chouteau-Maffitt Collection*, Missouri Historical Society); by his naming his post at *l'ours qui danse*, ''Fort Berthold''; and, finally, by his naming Pierre Alexander Berthold as executor of his estate under his will.

[40] See article, signed S.M.D. and entitled, ''Historic Homes in Missouri: The Berthold Mansion,'' in Missouri Historical Society *Collections*, vol. iv, pp. 290-294.

[41] Bartholomew Berthold married Pelagie Chouteau, sister of Pierre Chouteau Jr. See *Billon*, Frederic L., *Annals of St. Louis in Its Territorial Days*, p. 170.

[42] *Missouri Gazette*, December 27, 1817.

[43] Chardon became Maximilian's authority for the Osage speech (Thwaites, R. G., *Early Western Travels*, vol. xxiv, p. 296, *note* 268) as was Halcro for the Assiniboin (*idem*, p. 215, *note* 238), Berger for the Blackfoot (*idem*, p. 217, *note* 239), Kenneth Mackenzie for the Crow (*idem*, p. 222, *note* 242), James Kipp for the Mandan (*idem*, pp. 234-235, *note* 255), and John Dougherty for the Omaha (*idem*, p. 280, *note* 261).

[44] The fifth article of the Osage Treaty of 1825, negotiated at St. Louis, provided for land grants to the half-breeds named. There was ''one section for Francis T. Chardon'' (American State Papers, *Indian Affairs*, vol. ii, p. 588; *United States Statutes at Large*, vol. vii, p. 241). For the list of witnesses, see *idem*, p. 244.

[45] The following Ledger entries seem to indicate this:
''Chardon
1828

June 30	To Cash paid James Noble on your order		
July 17	By U. M. O. bal. of your wages as per		
	U. M. O. 1827		
	outfits & Cr.		281.97
	To bal. due you this day	276.97	

(*A. F. Co. Account Books*, Missouri Historical Society).

46 The proof of this is to be found in the subjoined extract from a letter and in certain ledger entries having reference to the account of Francis A. Chardon:

(a)   "Mr. Chardon is very anxious to get information about his Osage boy, can you obtain it and if it is practicable for him to be conveyed hither by Steam boat, please let it be done" (Kenneth Mackenzie to Pierre Chouteau, Jr., dated Fort Union, December 16, 1833, *Fort Union Letter Book*, 1833-1835, pp. 13-16, Missouri Historical Society).

(b)   1833

Mch	16	357	To Cash paid J. Fair Expenses Going after your Son	15	
June	3	215	By Osage Outfit 1832 paid them by Fair Surplus of the above $15		8.50
"	"		To paid horse hyre for Express Going after Son	10	
"	"	370	To Cash paid James Fair going to Osages	20	
Oct.	31	270	By Office " in full of the above		36.50
				45.	45.00

(*Ledger, 1831-1833 — A. F. Co., Western*, p. 45, Missouri Historical Society).

1833
June 3   45

By Francis A. Chardon paid J. Fair
Express to the Osage after Child   20.00

(*idem*, p. 369).

47 In *Accounts of Agents for Osages*, 1824-1834, *Clark Books*, Kansas State Historical Society, occur many items showing that the express most regularly employed in journeys to the Osage country was James Fair. See, in particular, pp. 96, 100.

48 Since mis-readings and consequent errors are always possible in manuscript interpretation, it would seem permissible to take the following endorsement on a promissory note found among the *Chouteau-Maffitt Papers* of the Missouri Historical Society as fair enough evidence that this son was yet alive in 1844: —

"Paid on the within note — seven hundred and thirty-four Dollars ($ 734)

May 23d / 44

Witness   is
M. Jiraud   Francis F   x   Chardon
                                                        mark

The note itself varies in the matter of the initial and, since the Osage Treaty of 1825 does likewise, there is no certainty as to what the Christian name in full really was. This is the note:

" $800   (in pencil)
            Twelve months after date we promise to pay
Francis S. Chardon the sum of Eight Hundred Dollars without discount or defalcation with Interest at the rate of Ten per cent per annum from date until paid.

Osage Nation   Pe Chouteau Jr. & Co.
    24th April 1843   Per — M. Jiraud
                                               P. M. Papin
                    cancelled"   (in pencil)

Chardon, it should be remarked, had a nephew Frank who was in the Indian country in the forties, of which the following is an indication:
''The following account for Francis A. Chardon
1840
Sept. ''delivered his nephew Frank''
(*Merchandise Ledger*, 1839-1842, P. C. Jr. Co., p. 106, Missouri Historical Society).
He was very probably a son of the man who, in the ledger account of 1836, is cited as ''your brother George'' (*P. C. & Co. Retail Store Ledger* A., 1834-1837, p. 380, Missouri Historical Society). Under date of December 12, 1838, in his journal, Chardon has a reference to ''George,'' who may have been this brother and, in some of the scribblings on outside, or covering, pages of the journal, the name, ''George,'' occurs. The Frank Chadron, the half-breed, who was at the Cheyenne River Agency in 1881 (*Hanson*, Joseph Mills, ''The Conquest of the Missouri,'' p. 416) was, conceivably, a Chardon.

[49] This Ree wife separated from him after one year of marriage (*Journal*, May 18, 1838); but soon returned (*idem*, June 25, 1838). Chardon had already provided himself with a substitute (*idem*, June 15, 1838).

[50] Jacob Halsey was a clerk, the book-keeper apparently, at the Teton post from the spring of 1829, with slight intermissions, until his death in 1842. In the opening pages of the first of the extant Fort Tecumseh journals, he has given some autobiographical data, from which it can be gleaned that he left his home (in or near New York?), June 16, 1826 and, in the company of Ramsay Crooks, proceeded to St. Louis, where he found employment with the American Fur Company and was at once sent up the Missouri River. Sickness detained him, first, at the mouth of the Kansas and, then, at the Arikara village; but he finally reached the Mandans, where he stayed until the spring of 1827. The winter of 1827-'8, he spent ''at Vermillion River'' and that of 1828-'9 at the Mandans. When spring came, he was transferred to Fort Tecumseh and, when that post was abandoned, to Fort Pierre, where, in the company of William Laidlaw, he seems to have been very congenially placed. The years they spent together, more or less, must have been convivial years and both men acquired a reputation for being very dissipated. Halsey's death, in September, 1842, was a tragic one and resulted from his having been thrown from his horse in the road not far from Liberty, Missouri, where, at the home of Laidlaw, he had been visiting. Certain details of the fatal accident, which had obviously occurred while Halsey was intoxicated, as well as Laidlaw's concern for the half-breed children he left fatherless are seen in the following letter:
'' (Copy) ''Hackberry Hall Septr. 9th 1842
''P. Chouteau Jr & Co.
''Gentlemen
''It is with feelings of the deepest sorrow that I announce to you the death of our mutual friend Jacob Halsey, who departed this life on Tuesday last, the circumstances attending his sad fate are the following. Mr H was returning from Liberty in company with Mr. Dawson & Arrott and had proceeded about a mile from town, when in the act of descending a hill Mr. H struck his horse which caused the Animal to run violently down hill, and in making a curve at the foot Mr Halsey lost his Seat and as he fell was violently dashed against a tree, the right side of his head receiving so severe a blow as to cause his death. Medical attendance was in a few minutes procured but life had fled; his body was con-

veyed to Liberty attended by many friends who deeply sympathised in our sad loss — everything that his friends could desire on such an occasion was done for him.   I was with him from his death until his burial which took place the following day.   It now becomes my duty to attend to his family. I shall make such disposition of the Children at present under my charge as he requested, there appears to be but one opinion about these Children being his legal heirs, and as such it will be my business to do all in my power for them in which I know you will gladly unite the better to enable me to do justice to his poor children.   I had intended taking out letters of administration, but as this must be done in St. Louis County, you will advise what is best as I fear his relations may endeavour to set aside the Orphans Claims, that he has acknowledged these to be his lawful children can readily be proven.   The accts of Expense attending the funeral shall be forwarded —   Mr. Kipp returned yesterday having lost some horses, he leaves again to day

Yours very respectfully
(signed)   William Laidlaw

(*Chouteau-Maffitt Collection*, Missouri Historical Society)

How Halsey's employers of the American Fur Company were likely to view the claims of these Indian children and, as a matter of fact, how they did is to be inferred from the correspondence of Benjamin Clapp with Pierre Chouteau, Jr. and, in particular, from a letter he wrote, September 19, 1842, in which these passages occur:

(1)   ''We have to day letters from Laidlaw down to 13 inst. furnishing full particulars of Halsey's death, which is in substance the same as has been communicated to you.   MacKenzie will probably administer upon the estate, as it must be done in this county — I will have copied & send herewith copy of Laidlaw's letter, which will tell the whole story — ''

(2)   ''I wrote Halsey the other day about the reported death of his Brother, & promised to furnish particulars when ascertained, but as I do not feel at liberty to send him a copy of Laidlaw's letter, you can however impart such portion of it or the whole, as you may deem best —   Will you please apprize him of such of the circumstances as may be necessary —   It is not probable that Laidlaw's views regarding the Children are quite orthodox and this part of the letter I have thought it might be improper to shew Halsey.'' (*idem*)

Kenneth Mackenzie was appointed administrator of the Halsey estate and, on December 13, 1842, he made affidavit that, so far as he knew, Stephen Halsey and two sisters, one married and one single, were the only heirs of the deceased (*Halsey Estate Papers*, formerly among the files at St. Louis Court House but now in the custody of the Missouri Historical Society).   Stephen Halsey, Jacob's brother, belonged to the American Fur Company, hence the lively regard for his interests.   Final settlement of the estate was not filed until September 11, 1848, although it was expected in 1846 and was in some way, not easily discernible, connected with the coming of P. D. Papin into the Upper Missouri Outfit as a partner (See, in connection with other somewhat obscure sources, Honoré Picotte to James Kipp at Fort Union, dated Fort Pierre, March 12, 1846, *Fort Pierre Letter Book*, 1845-'6).

Halsey's children left with Laidlaw (See Deposition of R. K. Lurtey, *Jacob Halsey Estate Papers*) were not the only ones ignored.   There were two little boys left at Fort Pierre, William and Charles Halsey, who, at the time of their father's death, were aged four and two years respectively and the younger of whom, Charles, ''son of Jacob Halsey,'' was one of several children baptized by Father De Smet at Medicine Creek, November 5, 1846 (*Notes* of Father De Smet). With the two sons of William Halsey, George and another Jacob, Miss Stella M. Drumm has had some correspondence and has elicited the information that Picotte looked out for the children when their father died. Not until they were grown, not until William had become, like his father before him, an employee of the Americon Fur Company had they the remotest idea of what their father had died possessed. Being themselves, with their mother who soon married again, left quite unprovided for, they had supposed he had had nothing. Then, one day, by the sons of another former employee, Hoskiss (Hodgkiss ?), who had been to St. Louis to enquire into his estate, they were made acquainted with the fact that Jacob Halsey had died worth forty-five thousand dollars.

Laidlaw's kindness to the Halsey children was due to several things. He was a warm-hearted man where his friends were concerned and the friendship between him and Halsey was evidently genuine. The only differences between them in the long years they were together seem to have been of a monetary nature. In the *Journals* of Pierre Chouteau Jr. & Co. are many entries showing the amounts paid out for the education of Halsey children as for that of Laidlaw. Boys of both families were at Kemper College, girls at *Vide Poche.*

[51] See entries in journal of November 17, 1838; January 24, 1839; February 28, 1839. Chardon seems to have been rather given to whipping or flogging and was, on more than one occasion, in danger of his life in consequence. See the account of how Chardon, when in temporary charge of Fort Tecumseh, had, June 8, 1830, to give a man named Amable Lacomb "a flogging" because he was not content with the amount of liquor Chardon, under the rules apparently, was willing to sell him (*Fort Tecumseh Journal*, January to June, 1830; also Audubon's account of "a rascally Indian on board [*the Omega*], who hid himself for the purpose of murdering Mr. Chardon; the latter gave him a thrashing last year for thieving, and Indians never forget such things — he had sworn vengeance, and that was enough. Mr. Chardon discovered him below, armed with a knife; he talked to him pretty freely, and then came up to ask the captain to put the fellow ashore. This request was granted'' (*Audubon and His Journals*, vol. i, p. 528). In justice to Chardon, it should be here observed that the whipping of troublesome Indians or white men was, at the time, nothing out of the ordinary. Whipping, a common form of chastisement at the time, in the army and elsewhere, was to be preferred to a too-ready resort to fire-arms. One meets with it frequently in fur-trader's journals, so that Chardon's use of his fists or of a whip was nothing exceptional. Alexander Henry, under date of April 25, 1804 (Coventry Copy of *Journal*, vol. i, p. 335) tells of giving a fearful beating to an Indian who tried to stab him with a knife.

[52] From the *Wardship Records, no. 1335* in the Court House at St. Louis, it appears that this son of Chardon's, whose full name was Francis Bolivar Chardon, was described, March 7, 1849, as of the age of sixteen years, seven months and four days. He was therefore born about August 3, 1832 and was the child referred to in a communication, unsigned, to Laidlaw at Fort Pierre, dated Fort Union, December 16, 1833, for which, see *note* 149.

In September, 1835, Chardon, having been a little over a year at Fort Clark and many years in the Indian country, decided to take a holiday for the purpose of re-visiting his old Pennsylvania home and leaving with his relatives there the little Bolivar, whom he took with him.   When, under like circumstances and with a like object in view, another trader, the noted Daniel Harmon of the North West Company, had sent his three year old son George to his own boyhood home in Vermont (*Journal of Voyages and Travels*, p. 200), the separation had proved a pathetically permanent one; for the child soon died (*idem*, p. 237) and the doubly bereft Indian mother far away grieved as inconsolably as might have done any of her white sisters.   In the Chardon case, the separation of mother and child was permanent likewise; but it was the mother that died, the child that lived. Indeed, the young Bolivar seems to have been very happy with his grandmother and to have been brought back to St. Louis only about the time of her death, perhaps because of it.   A charge against the Chardon estate shows that sometime in 1845 or early 1846, the man, Anthony C. Williamson, who was later appointed Bolivar's guardian, made a trip to Philadelphia on business for Chardon and he may have brought back to St. Louis not only the lad but a sister of Chardon's also.   According to Catlin, Chardon had two sisters at least, but of only one does there seem to be any record elsewhere.   Writing to Chardon at Fort James, afterwards Fort Berthold, February 24, 1846, Honoré Picotte said, among other things,

"You will receive a small package which your Sister gave me for you in St. Louis and which was overlooked by me when I sent up Gros-Claude & party" (*Fort Pierre Letter Book, 1845-1846*).

In March, 1846, which must have been shortly after his return from Philadelphia, Bolivar Chardon was matriculated at St. Louis University, John B. Sarpy figuring as his guardian and his father being described as a Roman Catholic (*Records of St. Louis University, 1828-1865*).   Chardon died in the late spring or early summer of 1848 and, after the term of 1848-'49, there is no record of Bolivar's attendance at the university; but, in September of the latter year, Williamson, who had been appointed his guardian by the Probate Court the previous March and bonded to the extent of ten thousand dollars, sent him to St. Vincent College at Cape Girardeau, where he stayed until April, 1850.   The following September, he started to attend Arcadia High School and was there until the end of his minority.   His guardian was discharged in September, 1852 after handing over to his ward what yet remained of his patrimony, seventeen hundred and seventy-six dollars and forty-two cents. (*Wardship Papers, op. cit.*). Possibly Williamson's wife, Harriet, may have been Chardon's sister.   In a certain property transaction, she and Bolivar were on the same side for some reason or other, too obscure to determine.   Chardon died possessed of property in Philadelphia and, if it had come to him from his deceased parents, a sister might have had a joint interest.

53 Born May 5, 1835 (See *Journal*) ; died September 21, 1837 (*idem*).

54 *Catlin*, George, *North American Indians*, vol. i, pp. 223-224.

55 *Idem*, pp. 224, 225.

56 See *Journal*.   She was buried at Fort Pierre, "the land of her parents."

57 *Church Registers*, St. Marys, Kansas.

58 Among the *Chouteau-Maffitt Papers* are the annual receipts, at least up to 1859, signed by Ellen, for the interest on five thousand dollars due to her and the two boys under the terms of Chardon's will for fifteen years.

Each year she had to be identified and, at various times, most of the men prominent on the upper Missouri, W. D. Hodgkiss, John B. Sarpy, Honoré Picotte, Alexander Culbertson, etc., ''testified on oath'' that they knew Ellen to be the ''half-breed Woman of the Sioux Nation,'' whom Chardon meant. The money was invariably three hundred dollars and paid over by the Executor, Peter A. Berthold. Beyond 1859, I took no account of the receipts.

59 *Life, Letters, and Travels among the North American Indians*, vol. iv, pp. 1286-1287.

60 All Chardon's associates on the upper Missouri, without an exception unless it may have been the Englishman, James Archdale Hamilton Palmer, had an Indian family. The story of Jacob Halsey's children has already been told (See *note* 50). In the American Fur Company papers in New York are references to Indian offspring of Kenneth Mackenzie who had been left at the Selkirk Colony in the charge of the Reverend David Jones (*Calendar*, 1836, L. B. C. 2, 432; 1838, L. B. C. 7, 204). John, who was with James Dickson, ''Liberator of all the Indians,'' (See *note 259*) was probably one of these and another, the girl who married Andrew Garrioch; but not the infant Alexander, who died some time in the winter of 1831-'32, or Owen, who was killed on a Missouri River steamboat by Malcolm Clarke (*Chittenden*, Hiram M., *Early Steamboat Navigation on the Missouri River*, pp. 233-234, *note*; *Gould*, E. W., *Fifty Years on the Mississippi*, pp. 422-427). Owen is said to have been the son of a Crow woman and born at Fort Union. He had the reputation of being one of the best buffalo hunters on the prairies (*Boller*, Henry A., *Among the Indians: Eight Years in the Far West*, p. 234) and, in that accomplishment, he resembled the Selkirk Colony half-breeds (*Palliser*, John, *A Solitary Hunter, or Sporting Adventures in the Prairies*, p. 83). For Laidlaw's condolences at the time of Alexander Mackenzie's death, see his letter to Kenneth Mackenzie, dated Fort Tecumseh, February 15, 1832 (*Fort Tecumseh Letter Book*, 1830-1832, p. 110). The debt of honor referred to in Daniel Lamont's will (See Appendix) had to do most likely with his ''Poncaw Squaw,'' for allusions to whom, see Laidlaw to Mackenzie, February 15, 1832 (*Fort Tecumseh Letter Book, op. cit.*). The Colin Lamont and the Charles Lamont of the *Chouteau-Maffitt Collection* may well have been her children. There are baptismal records for several of William Laidlaw's halfbreed offspring. One infant of four years, the child of William S. Laidlaw and a Siouse of Clay County, Missouri, was baptized on its deathbed, July 4, 1838, at the Kickapoo Mission. The baptismal record of some of Culbertson's half-breed children, the offspring of his first wife, for a further reference to whom, see *note* 145, is to be found in the register kept by Father Point. With his second wife Culbertson lived at Fort Benton, where were born to him several additional children. A daughter of his first marriage became the wife of Joseph Kipp, the missionary, for an account of whom, see the biographical sketch by Martha Edgerton Plassman in *Story of Fort Union and Its Traders*, where the claim is advanced that James Kipp took to wife, *Earth Woman*, a daughter of the noted Mandan chief, *Four Bears*. This must have been in addition to the marital connection instanced by Maximilian, for which, see *note* 80. For miscegenation at its very worst, see *Life and Adventures of James P. Beckwourth.*

61 The *bourgeois* was, technically-speaking, the manager of a trading-post; but, as a matter of fact, the term was very little used by the American companies. It originated with the North West Company and signi-

fied a partner of the company. For another view, see Chittenden, *The History of the American Fur Trade of the Far West,* vol. i, pp. 52-53. Kenneth Mackenzie, who is cited by Chittenden as an example of a *bourgeois,* was one, in effect, but he always referred to himself as Agent of the Upper Missouri Outfit and that he was, officially.

62 "Pork-eaters". This term was applied to the men who were brought on a contract basis from Montreal. On the journey, they were fed on pork, pea soup, hard bread, etc. and were dealt with contemptuously by other employees as being unused, as was supposed, to Indian life (Bonneville, p. 87; Maximilian, vol. ii, p. 25, *note* 13; F. J. Turner, Wisconsin Historical Society *Proceedings,* 1889, p. 78; J. S. Fox, Michigan Pioneer and Historical *Collections,* vol. xxxvii, p. 150, *note* 30; Lockwood, quoted by Neill, *History of Minnesota,* p. 296; Boller, p. 341). For a list of names of some of these men brought from Montreal in 1833, see *Chouteau-Maffitt Collection,* Missouri Historical Society.

63 The following extract is corroborative: "Mrs Picotte & Mrs Kipp have intimated to me their intention of Coming up in the SteamBt. I have no doubt that your Lady when she hears it, will also wish to Come, and as there is every Probability of her doing so, would it not be well for you to dispense with the Society of at least some of your present Companions" (Andrew Drips (?) to J. V. Hamilton, dated Fort Pierre, January 8, 1848 *Fort Pierre Letter Book, 1847-1848*).

64 Like David Thompson, Daniel Harmon was a very exceptional trader, morally and religiously-speaking. He refrained altogether from promiscuity. When he did, after long hesitation, cohabit with a woman in whose veins flowed Indian blood, he regarded her as his wife, even without the formality of marriage and notwithstanding the fact that, intellectually, they were, as the poles, apart. Bereavement after bereavement, however, reduced the distance between them and when, after his own conversion to Christianity, Harmon succeeded in accomplishing hers, there was no obstacle he deemed to their returning to civilization together. In the copy of his journal which was once the possession of his daughter Maria and now that of Mr. Guthrie Y. Barber of New York City and which would seem to have been a copy he sent to his relatives in Vermont, when disappointed, in 1816, in going thither himself, there is somewhat more information of the personally intimate sort than in the copy that was edited by Daniel Haskel and published in 1820. A photostat of the Barber copy is in the Dominion Archives at Ottawa and very properly so, since, in Ottawa, Miss A. Maria Harmon had her home and for years conducted with great success a first-class school for girls. It was there also that she met her death by suicide, by drowning in the Ottawa river. It is in the *Trail Makers* series that the Daniel Williams Harmon *Journal* is in its most accessible form.

65 As a basis for any biographical sketch of Kenneth Mackenzie must, perforce, be taken the account given by Richard Edwards in *Edwards's Great West,* pp. 98-101, since that, published at St. Louis in 1860, was written while the subject of it was yet alive and was, therefore, presumably, founded upon first-hand information. One item in it, however, must have escaped Mackenzie's notice since it is unquestionably an error. Kenneth Mackenzie of St. Louis could not possibly have been, as Edwards states, a nephew of Sir Alexander Mackenzie of Avoch except by marriage. The late Dr. M. S. Wade of Kamloops, B. C. made a very searching investigation

into the family history of the great British fur trader and explorer and ascertained that he had had but one brother, who died unmarried, lost at sea, and two sisters, one of whom married a Dowie, the other, a Kirkland (*Wade*, Mark S., *Mackenzie of Canada*).   According to his own testimony, Kenneth Mackenzie was born at Bracklack in Rosshire, Scotland and, in February, 1822, was twenty-six years of age so that very probably Edwards's date for his birth, April 15, 1797, is correct.   The exact date of his emigration from Scotland is uncertain.   He seems to have had some thought of going to the West Indies; but, instead, came to Canada possibly about 1818, and entered the service of the North West Company.   If the David Mackenzie of Sir George Simpson's correspondence was his brother — and he had a brother (*Calendar*, 1839, L. H. C. 9 : 9, *American Fur Company Papers*), the two ''came out to this Country on Five years Contracts three years ago from Ross-shire, the sons of a very respectable Farmer who left them some 4 or £5000 but were ruined in consequence of the badness of the times'' (George Simpson to Andrew Colville, dated York Factory, September 8, 1821, *Selkirk Papers*, Public Archives of Canada, Ottawa).   That Kenneth Mackenzie had some connection with the Selkirk Colony there seems no good reason to doubt; for he certainly left children there and, in 1831, interested himself sufficiently in the well-being of his countrymen on the Red River of the North to inquire into the prospective advantages of their removal to Missouri (Mackenzie to Governor John Miller, November 15, 1831; Mackenzie to Pierre Chouteau, Jr., November 16, 1831, *Pierre Chouteau Collection*, Missouri Historical Society).   Why or when he left the service of the North West Company is unknown.   He may have gone over to the Hudson's Bay Company on the amalgamation of the North West Company with the other corporation in 1821 and, in that event, may have been the man referred to in the following order for apprehension:

''Whereas William McLeod, Kenneth McKenzie, and James Murdoch, contracted servants of the Hon'ble Hudson's Bay Company have absconded from their service; All His Majesty's subjects are hereby requested to be aiding and assisting to the bearer hereof, Charles Gaspard Bruce in apprehending and bringing before me the said three Deserters.

''Given under my hand and seal in Fort Douglas, the 10th day of June, 1825.

''A. Bulger

''Governor of the district of Assiniboia
Rupert's Land''

(Publications of the Canadian Archives, no. 9, p. 246)

At the time this notice was posted, Kenneth Mackenzie was a resident of St. Louis and fairly on the road to full United States citizenship.   His connection with the Columbia Fur Company has elsewhere been pointed out, likewise the part he played in its disintegration by the American Fur Company.   Of the Upper Missouri Outfit that emerged he was the head, as Pierre Chouteau, Jr. was of the Western Department, of which it was a branch.   Laidlaw and Lamont were Mackenzie's assistants.   The arrangements for the disappearance of the Columbia Fur Company were all finished, practically, by 1828 and, then, Mackenzie set to work to organize the Upper Missouri Outfit, with which he continued to be identified for about ten years, although less and less prominently after his return from Europe in the spring of 1835, whither he had gone, rather unexpectedly, in the closing months of 1834.   While abroad, he studied wine-manufacture and that circumstance gave direction, apparently, to all his subsequent career.   In 1840, the early part, he bought out the interest of Pierre Chouteau, Jr. (See

Calendar, American Fur Company, L.B.C. 12: 320; St. Louis *Republican* July 1, 1840) in a commission firm that the two of them had established in St. Louis, one of the many firms subsidiary, in a way, to the American Fur Company and invited Henry H. Sibley to become his partner (See *Calendar,* American Fur Company, *Western Outfit Papers,* nos. 8629 of 1840, 10,890 of 1841) as a Forwarding and Commission Merchant. As a Wholesale Grocer and Commission Merchant, Mackenzie did business in St. Louis for several years, having close connection all the while with Chouteau and Crooks. By 1848, he had become an Importer of Fine Wines and Liquors (See *St. Louis Directories*) and, at the time of his death, April 26, 1861 (*Missouri Republican,* April 27, 1861), was conducting a wholesale liquor trade on a very large scale. His exact connection with the American Fur Company after his retirement, about 1839 (Thwaites, *Early Western Travels,* vol. xxi, p. 45, *note* 25), from the Upper Missouri Outfit it is not easy to define. That it existed seems certain. At all events, he was involved in the case in which Chouteau was suited on his bond for alleged violation of the United States trade and intercourse laws, 1846-'48. Of this a full discussion is given in *note* 248.

Kenneth Mackenzie married Mary Marshall of Tennessee, June 26, 1842 and, when he died, was survived by her and five children, Jennie, Kenneth, Marshall, Mary and Georgia, his "only heirs," so claimed the widow (See *Affidavit of Mary Mackenzie,* May 2, 1861, *St. Louis Court Records*). Another Kenneth, described as an "only son," had died November 7, 1847 (*St. Louis Reveille,* November 15, 1847).

What Mackenzie stood for in the trade of the upper Missouri is well attested by his being popularly called, "King of the Missouri," "King of the Upper Missouri," "Emperor of the West." See *note* 68.

66 No such element of uncertainty attaches itself to William Laidlaw as to Kenneth Mackenzie with respect to a preliminary residence at the Selkirk settlement on Red River of the North; for it is known in what capacity he was there and in what estimate he was held. He had been put in charge of the model farm, the Hayfield (*Oliver, E. H., The Canadian Northwest,* vol. i, p. 212), "with an expensive salary" (*Bryce,* George, *The Romantic Settlement of Lord Selkirk's Colonists,* p. 174) and was the person, who, in the very early spring of 1820, made that remarkable trip to Prairie du Chien in search of grain of various sorts that was, at the time, much commented upon (For a description of the return journey, see *Sibley,* H. H., *Reminiscences, Historical and Personal,* Minnesota Historical Society *Collections,* reprint of 1902, pp. 384-385); but he failed to give satisfaction and George Simpson, in the same elaborate report to Andrew Colville, in which he mentioned David Mackenzie, thinking of him, indeed, as a possible successor to Laidlaw, said of the latter,

"I do not know much about Laidlaw, he is thoughtless and its said dissipated and extravagant; he has certainly not done so much at the Farm as could be expected and prefers marching about the country to superintending his agricultural operations; I understand he is rather dissatisfied and inclined to return home if he does there is a young man in the service who I think would bring it to something . . ." (Simpson to Colville, September 8, 1821, *Selkirk Papers,* vol. xxiii, pp. 176-198).

With all his faults Laidlaw seems to have had qualities of the heart that endeared him to his friends and them to him. With Mackenzie, especially, he was on terms of affectionate intimacy (See, for evidence, Laidlaw to Mackenzie, February 15, 1832, *Fort Tecumseh Letter Book, 1830-1832,* pp. 103-110); but scarcely less so with Lamont, R. Holliday, J. A. Hamilton, and the rest.   He was probably his own worst enemy and, perhaps, warm-hearted and generous only with his equals.   There are indications among the many records of the Upper Missouri Outfit of positive hostility to him, at times, on the part of the *engagés* and he was a hard task-master.   The liking that he had displayed, when at the Hayfield farm, for marching about and that induced him to go all the way to Prairie du Chien for seed wheat was, doubtless, the reason for his having been almost invariably the one that went each season in search of ''pork-eaters'' and of horses.   After a time, indeed, he would appear to have spent most of his energy in the latter undertaking.   This was after Mackenzie's retirement from the Upper Missouri Outfit and after Honoré Picotte had succeeded to the post of Agent and had come to make Fort Pierre the virtual headquarters.

Like all the Scotch on the upper Missouri and elsewhere, Laidlaw had more than a fair education but it did not extend to a knowledge of the French language, which, considering how many there were in the trade to whom it was the only intelligible speech, must have been somewhat of a drawback.   He made no effort to acquire it, notwithstanding, and had been scarcely brought into close relations with Pierre Chouteau, Jr., in virtue of being in charge at Fort Tecumseh and obliged to receive reports and to send them, before he felt the necessity of saying,

''If you should at any time have occasion to address me by letters, you would confer a special favour by writing in English for I am but an in-different hand at reading French — and I am not inclined to have your letters read by other persons, especially before I am acquainted with the contents myself'' (Laidlaw to Chouteau, August 15, 1829, *Chouteau Investment Company Collection*, Missouri Historical Society).

[67] The third of this interesting Scotch trio, Daniel Lamont, is the one whose name is the least well known in the history of the Upper Missouri Outfit, possibly because he withdrew from it in 1835 and died in 1837.   Of his Scottish background and connections, however, more is known than in the case of his friends because of the self-revealings of his last will and testament.   His boyhood home was at Greenock on the Firth of Clyde, where his father, Colin Lamont, was a schoolmaster.   Like Mackenzie and Laidlaw, Lamont must have arrived in St. Louis after a more or less pro-tracted sojourn at the Selkirk Colony; for he had the same old associations and memories as his colleagues and, from one allusion to Colonel Robert Dickson that he made in a letter (*Fort Tecumseh Letter Book, 1830-1832*, pp. 8-10), it may be inferred that he had been on an intimate footing with him.   Very likely, he had gone with Dickson to the Red River at the time when that redoubtable Scot was the Earl of Selkirk's agent.

When Mackenzie returned from abroad in the spring of 1835, he found Lamont ''occupied in making arrangements for entering into a new business, and transferring his interest'' in the Upper Missouri Outfit to D. D. Mitch-ell (Mackenzie to Crooks, dated Fort Union, December 10, 1835, *Fort Union Letter Book, 1833-1835*, pp. 93-95).   The business was a mercantile one and, to conduct it, Lamont went into partnership with P. and J. Powell of St. Louis (*Daniel Lamont Administration Papers*, St. Louis Court House) under the firm name of Powell, Lamont & Co., Wholesale Dealers in Dry Goods (*St. Louis Directory, 1838-1839*).   It was not for long, sad to say, that he was permitted to be active in it; for, on January 27, 1837, when about to return to St. Louis after an absence, he was stricken with apoplexy at Fayette and died suddenly (*Missouri Republican*, February 1, 1837).

''A man in all the relations of life sustaining a most enviable reputa-tion,'' so said the writer of the obituary notice and he was probably not far wrong.   While in trade, Lamont could drive as sharp a bargain as any of his associates, yet he would seem to have been more religiously inclined than most of them.   He had been carefully brought up as a member of the Presbyterian Church and, ''tho' agreeably to the interpretation of its tenates in Missouri,'' he was not able to affiliate with it in America, he yet wished that children of his should be ''instructed'' in its doctrines and ''the utmost care'' taken in and about their ''morals and education'' (*Last Will and Testament of Daniel Lamont,* 1834 for which, see Appendix).

All the men in the prominent posts of the Upper Missouri Outfit in its earlier days had some intellectual interests and Lamont more than most. It was he, usually, who was looking out for reading matter, keeping his friends supplied, and begging more himself, sending on, even to those not immediately interested, the Greenock papers.   Between him and James Archdale Hamilton there was, seemingly, great cordiality and it was to accommodate Lamont that Hamilton consented to stay on at Fort Union when Mackenzie's absence abroad and in the east grew more and more prolonged (Hamilton to Laidlaw, dated Fort Union, December 10, 1835, *Fort Union Letter Book, 1833-1835,* p. 93).

68 Sobriquets of this sort were quite commonly applied. ''Simon M'Tavish was sarcastically nicknamed 'Le Marquis' and 'Le Premier' by the traders because of his haughty dominating manner . . .'' [*Wade,* M. S., *Mackenzie of Canada,* p. 96], Sir Alexander Mackenzie was called, ''Emperor'' (*Wallace* J. N., *The Wintering Partners on Peace River,* p. 64), also ''his all superior Great Bonaparte Mr. McKenzie'' (*Wentzel Journal, Masson Collection,* Ottawa), and Sir George Simpson, in Kenneth Mackenzie's own day, was called the ''Emperor of the North'' (*Healy,* W. J., *Women of Red River,* p. 175) For an instance of the calling Kenneth Mackenzie, ''King of the Missouri,'' see *Coues,* Elliott, *Forty Years a Fur Trader on the Upper Missouri,* vol. i, p. 65.

69 See Chardon's Fort Clark Journal.   This would seem to establish the fact that Kenneth Mackenzie was called, ''Emperor of the West,'' as well as, ''King of the Missouri.''   In speaking of John George Mc-Kenzie, who is said to have been James Dickson's Secretary of War, Miss Nute remarks that he was the son of the Emperor of the West (*Mississippi Valley Historical Review,* vol. x, p. 128) and had a deep-seated grudge against the Hudson's Bay Company, (*idem,* p. 133), the ground therefor being, a legacy duty of £500, payable after his father's death (*idem,* p. 134, *note* 16).   The Kenneth Mackenzie of the Upper Missouri Outfit, whom Chardon refers to as, ''Emperor of the West,'' did not die until April 26, 1861 (*Missouri Republican,* April 27, 1861). It is interesting to reflect, however, upon John George McKenzie's connection with James Dickson; for it would seem quite likely that Dickson's meeting with him and other Red River settlers gave a new direction to his eccentricity.   Hitherto, he had been intent upon having his revenge upon Mexico.   That Kenneth Mackenzie was vitally interested in Red River concerns is to be seen in his desire to find a way for the emigration of some of the settlers to Missouri. See *note* 65.

70 This aspect of life at Fort Union very vividly impressed Charles Larpenteur when he first became connected with the Upper Missouri Outfit, which was in 1834; but the picture that he drew of the formality obtaining was probably true only of Fort Union.   Catlin, who was there about two years before Larpenteur, had nothing to say of gradations of rank at table.

He described a dinner as if Mackenzie, Hamilton and he were alone partakers of it (*North American Indians*, ed. of 1850, vol. i, p. 21).

[71] In partial substantiation of the proofs of this in journals and travel narratives, we have the evidence of expense accounts and of the contents of trunks, the personal effects that, after death in the ''Indian country,'' were sent down to St. Louis. The ''2 Trunks from Fort Pierre'' that Mackenzie handed over, in September, 1843, ''as part of the Estate of Jacob Halsey'' had among their contents,
''1 Camlet Cloak, 2 Cloth Frock Coats, 1 Bible, 1 Prayer Book, 1 Exercises of the Closet'' (*Jacob Halsey Estate Papers, op. cit.*). Among the charges against the estate of James A. Hamilton were items of date August 26 and November 30, 1839, the former for ''altering 3 prs White pants,'' the other for ''Repairing Velvet Vest'' (*Palmer Estate Papers*, Missouri Historical Society). An order that Mackenzie made for delicacies to be sent him is another case in point. See Mackenzie to Henry K. Ortley, December 10, 1835, *Fort Union Letter Book, 1833-1835*, p. 98. Lamont's personal orders were very similar.

[72] The hospitality of trading posts was, by no means, unknown elsewhere than on the upper Missouri. Frémont, to cite only one instance, met with it in fullest measure on the Mississippi, with the Renville family (*Memoirs*, p. 36) and with Henry H. Sibley (*idem*, p. 33).

[73] There was an astonishingly large number of visitors to the ''Indian country,'' in the thirties, forties, and fifties of the last century, those travelling for sport or pleasure or general information being chiefly British. Americans who came there, as did the son of Thomas L. McKenney, hoping to like the life and to fit into it or, as did young Harrison, to get away from the trammels of civilization, were hardly visitors in the ordinary acceptation of the term and not one of any sort was a visitor, strictly-speaking, at the posts. They were all ''paying guests'' and, as *engagés* could well testify, the tariff of the ''Indian country'' was no light thing. It was heavy for all; but especially so for the lesser employees of the American Fur Company, between whom and their superiors a large discrimination was made. Of the many accounts to be found in the *Chouteau-Maffitt Collection* are some of particular interest. Take, for example, the account rendered against Catlin in May, 1832 at Fort Pierre and, in subsequent months, at forts Clark and Union, also some thirteen accounts against Paul, Prince of Württemberg, who was the first of the two distinguished visitors of royal lineage from petty German states that put in an appearance on the upper Missouri while Chardon was there. The other was Maximilian, Prince of Wied, Neuwied. The accounts against Prince Paul, with some of which Chardon had to do, were, roughly, as follows:
A bill rendered him at Fort Tecumseh, September 6, 1830, covering items from March 14 to August 31, 1830, inclusive. Among the items occur,

Augt 30	To a/c at F.T. and F.A. Chardon, 21st. Ultimo			17.51
'' ''	'' ''	James Andrews, bal. of his a/c		187.72
'' 31	'' ''	at F. Clark, August 11th.		40.25

In another document is the account had of ''John Sibile'' at the Ponca Village in March, 1830; another of things bought of the American Fur Company at the Little Cheyenne River; another at Apple River & the Arikaras. Finally, there is an account signed by F. A. Chardon and dated August 22, 1830:

"Fort Tecumseh Aug. 22, 1830

The Prince of Wertemberg .... Dr.

1½ lb Loaf Sugar	@ 1	$1. 50
2 lb Shot	1	2.00
1 Par fleche		.50
pd for making moccasins —		1.00
15 lb Biscuit	@ 50c	7.50
3 lb. Tobacco	,, 1	3.00
2 Pipes	25c	.50
2 Skeins thread	6½	.13
1 Half Axe		2.50
2 lb Grease 12½		.25
2 lb Tobacco 1		2.00
3 Pipes	25	.75
1 lb Tobacco pd Blacksmith	1	1.00

$ 22.63

F. A. Chardon

74 The officials of the American Fur Company, particularly of the Western Department and its nominal successor, seem to have been always desirous that the utmost courtesy should be extended to distinguished travellers, yet they did not encourage their own men to do anything in the way of discovery or research of any sort. Maximilian was astonished to find that their employees "seldom take any interest in scientific researches" (*Travels*, p. 246). None the less, Chardon, personally, must have had considerable interest in Natural History. Among the gifts he presented to Audubon — and there were apparently several — (*Audubon and His Journals*, vol. i, pp. 14-15) was a kit fox. Audubon says,

"We entered Mr. Chardon's room [at Fort Clark], crawled up a crazy ladder, and in a low garret I had the great pleasure of seeing alive the Swift or Kit fox which he has given to me . . . Mr. Chardon told me that good care would be taken of it until our return that it would be chained to render it more gentle . . ." (*idem*, p. 11).

Sometimes the American Fur Company seemed afraid of too much publicity being given to the "Indian country" and situations there by chance travellers. This was noticeable when permission to go was refused to C. F. Hoffman (*A Winter in the Far West*, vol. ii, p. 110) and when Catlin began to publish his letters; but, of course, the time was a critical one because of what had resulted from Nathaniel Wyeth's revelations and abuse of the hospitality that had been extended to him at Fort Union. In Catlin's case ample re-assurance almost to an extent suggestive of truckling was given. He had been ill with pleurisy or would have given it earlier.

"While in Cincinnati," he wrote, "I saw Mr. Pratt, who in conversation with me expressed some fears that my letters descriptive of Upper Missouri might excite the public attention to something like competition in the Fur trade, by inducing others to undertake in opposition to the Am. Fur Company. I have had many unpleasant feelings since, not from any expression that I *have* or *could* make, inconsistent with the friendly politeness extended to me by the Company, and which it will always afford me pleasure to acknowledge; but from the idea that I should unknowingly have been giving uneasiness to any member of that Company.

"My letters have produced much more excitement with regard to that Country than I expected, and I feel perfectly well convinced that no expressions which I have made would have the least tendency to such a result as the one suggested by Mr. Pratt.

"The high obligation which your kindness and politeness has laid me under would always dictate to me a more honest course than that, and a personal acquaintance with the toils and hazards of that Company's business would instinctively compel me to use what little influence I may have with the World, in discouraging any undertaking of the kind as inevitably ruinous to the owners.

"In one of my letters, which has not yet been published, I made some allusions to the Fur Company's trade with the Indians, and of the policy of the Government in protecting and encouraging that Institution. I do not recollect exactly what I said, but I recollect perfectly well under what *conviction* I wrote. I spoke of the vast importance of the efforts of that Company in meeting and opposing British influence which is already advancing to an alarming degree amongst the numerous & powerful tribes of Indians on our Frontier, and of securing to the U. S. a share of the Fur Trade of our own Country. I spoke also of the enormous expenditures and immense liability to heavy losses and also of the prohibition of Spirituous liquors in that Country which must inevitably result in a complete annihilation of the Company's business & even greatly jeopardize the lives of persons employed in it, if that prohibition should still be continued in force.

"Such suggestions as I did make on that subject I am sure I made from the best motives, and I am equally certain that instead of *exciting* they will go a great ways with the World in *discouraging* anything like Competition.

"The time to me Sir, has been like imprisonment in a dungeon, and I fear I shall miss (a sight) of Mr McKenzie in N. York which I would not for a great deal.

"In haste — Your Friend & Servant
"Geo Catlin"

(George Catlin to Pierre Chouteau, Jr. dated Pittsburgh, January 29, 1833, *Chouteau-Maffitt Collection*).

75 Maximilian found occasion to mention this (*Travels*, p. 304) as had Catlin the year previously, the latter seeing in Hamilton, "the cultured gentleman" and, in Mackenzie "the kind-hearted and high-minded Scotchman" (edition of 1850, vol. i, p. 21), in intercourse with whom he took great delight. Robert Campbell at the "Opposition" post was also an "agreeable" conversationalist in Maximilian's opinion, Maximilian going down at various times for a talk and to watch the building of Fort William.

76 The orders that went in every year from the individual posts are, in most cases, still extant (See *Chouteau-Maffitt Collection*). They show what the requisition for intoxicating beverages was. In some instances it was so large as to be astounding. The consumption must have been relatively great. Of course, liquor was also an article of commerce and, if sold, sold at fabulous prices and in a very diluted state. The inventory of stock belonging to the Upper Missouri Outfit, taken at Fort Tecumseh, June 25, 1832, showed the following on hand:

17	Barrels	Alcohol	595	Galls.
1	,,	Shrub	19½	,,
1	,,	N.O. Rum	35	,,
1	Qr Cask	Port Wine	28	,,
1	,, ,,	French Brandy	28	,,

At about the same time the residue at Fort Clark of alcohol alone was sixty-one gallons and, at Fort Union,

40 Barrels Alcohol
2   ''   Whiskey
1   ''   Jamaica Rum
1   ''   Shrub

A requisition for Fort Tecumseh, made in September, 1831, to come up in the spring of 1832 was for

15 Barrels Alcohol
1   ''   Good old Whiskey

and for Fort Union, which, however, failed to come,

3 Barrels Old Whiskey
1   ''   Brandy
2   ''   New Orleans Rum
1   ''   Jamaica   ''
4   ''   Shrub

The order for merchandise to be sent to Fort Union in the spring of 1833 included

30 Barrels Alcohol
5   ''   Old Whiskey
2   ''   Jamaica Rum
5   ''   Shrub
¼ Cask good Port Wine

Innumerable bills of lading are likewise extant and invoices from Irwin & Whiteman of Cincinnati.   On March 22, 1831, ''125 Barrels Whiskey and 30 Barrels Alcohol'' were shipped by the *Robert Fulton*.   There had been an endeavour to have them ''put in the best order, knowing that they are intended for a long voyage.''   Exactly a year later, were shipped ''50 Barrels Whisky making with the 74 Barrels shipped pr La Fouche 4472½ Gallons, to fill your order of 1st inst.   For this lot we had to pay ¾c which is the lowest we could procure it for, the article having risen immediately after we purchased the other lot . . .''   On April 3rd an account for ''20 Barrels Alcohol was sent and, on April 25th, the bill of lading for ''29 Barrels Whiskey per order April 12 . . .'' *Chouteau-Maffitt Collection*).

On one occasion at least, Lamont had a barrel of whiskey and other things come direct to him from Greenock (John A. Merle to P. Chouteau, Jr., dated New Orleans, April 13, 1833, *idem*).

[77] The notorious affair that resulted from the exposure made by Nathaniel Wyeth of Mackenzie's distillery at Fort Union was a case in point.   For a time thereafter great care had to be observed at the various posts against detection; but it was not for long, despite the fact that a stringent law was enacted in 1834 (*United States Statutes at Large*, vol. iv, pp. 729-735). The American Fur Company evaded and violated it in every direction. See, for example, Joseph Rolette to Pierre Chouteau, Jr. dated Prairie des Chiens, May 20, 1834 (*Chouteau-Maffitt Collection*); Hamilton to Mackenzie, dated Fort Union, November 15, 1835 (*Fort Union Letter Book, 1833-1835*, p. 59).   As usual, they charged their opponents with violations on an even larger scale than their own.   Laidlaw made wine but said that the Indians preferred the alcohol of the ''Opposition'' (Laidlaw to Kipp, dated February 24, 1834, *Fort Pierre Letter Book, 1832-1835*, p. 69).   Laidlaw, who drank so hard himself, would have denied whiskey to the men he employed because ''a man who drinks too hard'' is ''bound to neglect his duties'' (Laidlaw to Frederick Laboue, December 3, 1831, *Fort Tecumseh Letter Book, 1830-1832*, p. 77) and both he and Mackenzie professed not to be-

lieve in giving it to the Indians. They gave it, they declared, because they had to; in order to compete successfully with other traders. It was a case of grim necessity and to that way of thinking they would seem to have brought even Catlin.

78 Not on the upper Missouri but lower down and on the Mississippi, the difficulty of executing properly the trade and intercourse laws of the United States was greatly enhanced by proximity to military posts, which was always a source of extreme danger because the regular army ration included whiskey and among both officers and men intemperance was so rife as to be held accountable for the extraordinarily large number of duels and desertions that disgraced the service of the time (*Pelzer*, Louis, *Marches of the Dragoons*, pp. 2, 4, 20; *Murray*, Charles Augustus, *Travels in North America*, vol. ii, p. 86; *Hamilton*, Thomas, *Men and Manners in America*, p. 144; Willoughby Morgan to General Thomas A. Smith, dated Martin Cantonment, May 31, 1819; Same to Same, July 4, 1819, *Smith Papers*, Missouri State Historical Society). For the "frightful proportions" that the drink evil reached near Fort Leavenworth and up as far as Council Bluffs, see De Smet, *op. cit.*, vol. i, p. 171; Garraghan, G. J. (S.J.) *The Potawatomie Mission of Council Bluffs*, St. Louis Catholic Historical Review, vol. iv, p. 167.

79 One allusion to home products is illustrative of the concern felt in the matter by Laidlaw,

"The Liquor that you sent down tastes so much of Peppermint that it is not easy to say, which it is, Whiskey or Peppermint — try and get some from the same place, and put it into a clean Bottle . . ." (Laidlaw to Papin, November 20, 1833, *Fort Pierre Letter Book, 1832-1833*, p. 41).

80 The records at Ottawa show the Kipp family to have been established in the Province of Quebec, where, in the early years of the nineteenth century, various members of it, Samuel, James, Charlotte, Elizabeth, Mary, etc., were seeking land grants and one, John, was asking for a license to come to reside at Montreal (*Papers*, Office of the Secretary of State, Public Archives). One of the family must have been already there, if, as is said, James Kipp, the fur trader, was born in Montreal in 1788. When Palliser first met with him in 1847, he was "upwards of sixty years of age" (*Solitary Rambles and Adventures of a Hunter in the Prairies*, pp. 78, 82) and had been journeying annually back and forth between St. Louis and the Yellowstone for over twenty years, not even illness deterring him. See Joseph A. Sire to Messrs P. Chouteau & Co., dated Bellevue, September 2, 1844 (*Sire Log*). He would seem to have been with the Columbia Fur Company from the time of its organization or soon thereafter (*Audubon and His Journals, op. cit.*, vol. i, p. 19) and, in 1822, built for its trade a post among the Mandans (Maximilian in Thwaites's *Early Western Travels*, vol. xxiii, p. 223), "whose language," asserts Thwaites, "he was said to have been the first white man to master" (*idem*, vol. xxii, p. 345, *note* 319). Maximilian found him, indeed, an "excellent" Mandan interpreter (*idem*, vol. xxiii, p. 301) and with that tribe he formed a close connection by marrying the daughter of "Mandeek-Suck-Choppenik (the medicine bird)" (*idem*, vol. xxiv, p. 39). For his reputed marriage with the daughter of *Four Bears*, see *note* 60. With trading-post building, James Kipp's name has come to be indissolubly associated. In 1825, he built another fort for the Columbia Fur Company near the mouth of White Earth River (*Early Western Travels*, vol. xxiii, p. 228) and, after the establishment of the Upper Missouri Outfit, forts Clark and Piegan, for that concern, the former, in the

spring of 1831 and the latter, in the winter (*Chittenden, H. M. History of the American Fur Trade of the Far West*, vol. i, p. 333; Father Point's *Journal*, for which, see Appendix). To both of these Mitchell gave the finishing touches. According to Doane Robinson, Kipp also built Fort Floyd (South Dakota Historical *Collections*, vol. ix., p. 155, *note* 138), the forerunner of Fort Union. This was in 1828. He may even, if any weight is to be attached to the statement of Bad Gun, the son of the Mandan chief, Four Bears, have had something to do with the building of Fort Berthold (North Dakota Historical Society *Collections*, vol. ii, pp. 465-467).

Up to the time that Chardon assumed charge of Fort Clark, Kipp was essentially the Mandan trader and in residence there except when away building forts or conducting the boats down the river to St. Louis. When he went to the Maria River to build Fort Piegan, Mitchell took his place and, in 1833, apparently to straighten out the accounts of the post, Lamont was the superior officer at Fort Clark. How Kipp came to be transferred to Fort McKenzie because of Culbertson's disinclination to pose as a lone trader among the Blackfeet has been elsewhere told. In 1835, before going home to Canada on a visit, it would seem that he returned to Fort Clark; but, if he did so return, it was for but a very brief while. His chief responsibility for "upwards of twenty years" prior to Palliser's meeting with him was to convey the annual returns to St. Louis, going down with the boats, keel or mackinaw, in the late spring or early summer and returning overland in September (Palliser, *op. cit.*, p. 82). Between whiles he had charge of this or that post. Father De Smet, for instance, found him at Fort Union in 1841 (*De Smet, P. J. (S. J.), Letters and Sketches* in Thwaites, *Early Western Travels*, vol. xxvii, p. 149) and Audubon intimates that, in 1843, he was about to repair to Fort Alexander (*Journals*, vol. ii, pp. 69, 113), which Larpenteur, under instructions from Alexander Culbertson (*Forty Years a Fur Trader on the Upper Missouri*, vol. i, p. 162) had built in 1842 (*idem*, p. 175) to replace the recently burnt Fort Van Buren (*idem*, p. 170). In 1846, Kipp returned to Fort Union (*idem*, vol. ii, p. 244), and, with him, Larpenteur, out of employment, because of a peculiar situation that had arisen at Fort Lewis (*idem*, pp. 243-244. See also Chardon's Journal, *note* 246) spent the winter, he and his Assiniboine family. After an interval, subsequent to Chardon's death in 1848, Kipp took charge at Fort Berthold and was instructed, in 1849, to remain there (Culbertson to Chouteau, August 2, 1849, *Fort Pierre Letter Book, 1849-1850*), although the following letter shows that it had been intended that he should succeed Culbertson at Fort Pierre:

"Kipp is too good a man to be in charge of this post — his idea of the trade is good enough, but you know it requires firmness and decision of character which he has not.

"My wish was for Culbertson to remain here, and he ought to have done so, for I have no idea that he will go farther than Ft. Union — Sending Hamilton to the Crows is another wrong thing. Mr. Laidlaw ought to have been sent there — his going to Liberty for Horses will be a great loss — it will be impossible for him to get here without losing the most of them . . . Matlock is at the Vermillion awaiting Mr. Laidlaw — he says he has received $5000 to be divided out in the spring at the Vermillion between Esantees & Yanctons. Taylor is elected President . . .

"I had the misfortune . . . to lose my little Girl — Mr Picottes eldest girl 'We-ah-Wasta' also died a few weeks ago . . .''
(W. D. Hodgkiss to Andrew Drips at Fort John, dated Fort Pierre, January 30, 1849, *Drips Papers*, Missouri Historical Society).

He was yet at Fort Berthold when Kurz came there in 1851. See *Bushnell, D. I., Friedrich Kurz, Artist-Explorer* Smithsonian Institution, *Report*, 1927, p. 514.

Kipp had two or three nephews on the upper Missouri to whom he seems to have been much attached. The illness of one of them, Joseph Desautel, trader at Fort Clark, detained him at Fort Pierre in 1850 (Picotte to Culbertson, October 23, 1850, *Fort Pierre Letter Book, 1849-1850*). Meanwhile, Andrew Dawson, a Scotchman, performed Desautel's duties at the former Mandan post and, after Desautel's death, November 15, 1850, became the regular factor there (Letter of Picotte, December 4, 1850, *idem*), it being understood that ''if Mr Kipp insists on coming up,'' he can only take care of Fort Berthold'' (Picotte to Chouteau, July 20, 1850, *idem*).

Notwithstanding the slight reflection that Larpenteur seems to cast upon the character of Kipp, partly because of a partiality that he, in 1847, displayed for yet another of his nephews, Jacques Bruguière (*Forty Years a Fur Trader on the Upper Missouri*, vol. ii, p. 254), who was the Holy Ghost in Larpenteur's blasphemous grouping of the drunkards at Fort Union (*idem*, vol. i, p. 162), James Kipp would appear to have been a general favorite. For Joseph La Barge's good opinion of him, see *Chittenden, H. M., Early Steamboat Navigation on the Missouri River*, vol. i, p. 70. Thwaites says that ''He retired from the fur-trade in 1865, and settled upon his Missouri farm, which he had acquired many years before'' (*Early Western Travels*, vol. xxii, p. 345, *note 319*). The farm was near Independence and to it Palliser wended his way in 1847, when he wished to accompany Kipp on his annual return journey to the Yellowstone (*Solitary Rambles and Adventures of a Hunter in the Prairies*, p. 78).

[81] Among the fur trade papers and chiefly in the various Chouteau collections of the Missouri Historical Society are to be found several lists, complete and incomplete, of employees of the American Fur Company in the years under consideration. The most nearly complete of these lists are two, both belonging to the *Pierre Chouteau Collection, Group A* and having particular application to the Upper Missouri Outfit, the one labelled, ''Persons Employed for the Upper Missouri Outfit for the Year 1830,'' and the other, ''A list of Men to be Employed by the Am. Fur Company to Assist in the Trade with the different Tribes of Indians in the Upper Missouri and to be Transported on Board the Keel Boat Assiniboine and by Land to their Places of Destination.'' The date of the latter is 1831. The first list contains two hundred and eighty-seven names and the second, eighty-five. Supplementary lists might be held to include the numerous individual labour contracts, which, for any given year or post, are to be found filed together, as well as the comprehensive permits to remain in the ''Indian country'', which were to the lesser employees what the separate licenses were to the more important. All such were almost invariably granted by the Superintendent of Indian Affairs at St. Louis, there being only very occasional instances of mere agents arrogating to themselves this authority. The comprehensive permit is well illustrated by a document, signed at St. Louis by William Clark, March 26, 1832, and now included in the *Auguste Chouteau Collection*. From these various lists, as also from account books, considerable general information in small instalments can be obtained, as, for instance, the accepted, or usual, spelling of a name, the occupation of a man, his destination, and his wages. To illustrate this a certain portion, with some omissions, of the longer and earlier of the two lists in the *Pierre Chouteau Collection* is herewith given:

238.	John Dougherty	(Clerk & Interpreter)			Fort Union
239.	Colin Campbell	'' '' ''		600	Yanctonnas
241.	James M. Holliday	''	& Trader	315	Fort Tecumseh
242.	John McKnight	'' '' ''		450	Mandans

243.	James Kipp	,, ,, ,,	600	Fort Union
244.	Antoine Garrow	Interpreter	120	Rees
245.	Henry Picotte	Clerk & Trader	1000	Fort Union
246.	Pierre D. Papin	,,	1000	Yanctons
247.	G. P. Cerré	,,	1000	Yanctonnas
248.	Francis A. Chardon	,,	800	Sawons
250.	Saml P. Winter	,,		Fort Union
251.	Wm. H. Vanderburg	,,		Fort Union
252.	Louis Bissonnett	,,		Mandans
253.	Thomas L. Sarpy	,,	400	Ogallallas
254.	P. N. Leclerc	,,	600	Fort Union
255.	Jacob Halsey	,,		Fort Tecumseh
258.	Baptiste Daurion	Interpreter	500	Sawons
259.	David D. Mitchell	Clerk & Trader	700	Yanctonnas
260.	John Sibelle	,,	300	Poncas
262.	Emillien Primeau	,,	500	White River
264.	Richard T. Holliday	,,	500	Rees
266.	Frederick Laboue	,,	500	Honcpapas
268.	Pierre Ortubise	Interpreter	250	White River
273.	Zephire Rencontre	Clerk & Trader	450	Fort Tecumseh

82 In the *Fort Tecumseh Letter Book* there are a few letters that seem to be in the same handwriting as the bulk of the Fort Clark journal. I take it, therefore, that they were written at times when Chardon was temporarily in charge. Note, for example, Mackenzie to Pierre Chouteau Jr., July 7, 1829; Laidlaw to Same, November 2, 1829, etc.

83 The two were probably at the Forks of the Cheyenne together in the winter of 1828-'29, when Laidlaw certainly was there (*Halsey Autobiography, Fort Tecumseh Journal*, January to June, 1830). The previous spring Laidlaw was on the James River and his rumored presence there was duly reported to Chouteau by Joseph Rolette (Letter of March 10, 1828, *Chouteau-Maffitt Collection*). Under the conditions by which the American and Columbia fur companies had been amalgamated, the partners of the latter had agreed to concentrate on the upper Missouri and, in a general way, to abandon the St. Peter's, in return for which concession they were to have the exclusive right, as within the American Fur Company, to send out hunting expeditions towards the Far West and across the mountains. Rolette and Laidlaw were enemies of long standing. The Columbia Fur Company had been scarcely organized before Rolette tried, in the typical American Fur Company way, to make trouble for it with the United States Indian Office. He complained that Laidlaw was a foreigner and that he, with the connivance of Agent Taliaferro, was violating the trade and intercourse laws. Not alone rivalry in trade but Laidlaw's friendly connection with Colonel Robert Dickson had had something to do with this; for, though Dickson was now dead, Rolette could not have forgotten that it was he who had denounced him as a traitor to Britain towards the close of the War of 1812. Rolette's report to Chouteau did not deter Laidlaw from continuing to trade to the northward. Indeed, when Rolette tried himself to venture there, Laidlaw in his turn complained, saying it was an encroachment upon the reserves of the Upper Missouri Outfit. On the James River, William Dickson, who was half a Sioux himself, had established his post and Laidlaw failed to see how Joseph Rolette could go there in ''opposition'' without a license (Laidlaw to Chouteau, October 23, 1831; Same to Agent Jonathan L. Bean, October

24, 1831, *Fort Tecumseh Letter-Book,* 1830-1832, pp. 60, 60-61). For more on the same subject, see *idem,* pp. 75, 82, 84.

84 Mr. Charles Edmund DeLand asserts that ''Fort Pierre Chouteau was opened to business in June, 1832'' (South Dakota Historical *Collections,* vol. ix, p. 88) and the superscription of letters in the *Fort Tecumseh Letter Book, 1830-1832* would indicate that it was certainly occupied from about the middle of that summer. The entry in the journal, April 5, 1832, is, however, to the effect that on that day ''Laidlaw and Halsey moved up with the baggage to the new fort'' (South Dakota Historical *Collections,* vol. ix, p. 154). Fort Tecumseh was really becoming almost uninhabitable and untenable. On April 6th, it ''was nearly surrounded with water'' (*idem*) and some parts of it had had to be pulled down in February (*idem,* p. 148). When, in the early summer of 1833, Maximilian was about to land at Fort Pierre, he observed that an isolated, decayed old house was all that was left of Fort Tecumseh (*Thwaites,* R. G., *Early Western Travels,* vol. xxii, p. 316).

85 For example, he was at Fort Tecumseh and in general charge when Laidlaw was away in the winter of 1830-1831; and similarly, in that of 1832-1833, at Fort Clark, with Kipp under him. See Maximilian, *Travels,* p. 321.

86 Doane Robinson (South Dakota Historical *Collections,* vol. ix, p. 165) attempts no identification of ''Mr. Crawford'' of the Fort Tecumseh journals; but he was evidently the ''L. Crawford'' and the ''Lewis Crawford'' of the *Fort Union Letter Book, 1833-1835* and, undoubtedly, one of the old Columbia Fur Company men. For a trader of the same name at St. Joseph's, see Michigan Pioneer and Historical *Collections,* vol. xxxvi, p. 61, *note*; Wisconsin Historical *Collections,* vol. ii, pp. 120, 126; vol. iii, pp. 258, 259, *note,* 289. See post *note* 522.

87 For the uncertainty regarding the earlier history and identity of this man, see South Dakota Historical *Collections,* vol. ix, pp. 115, 117, *note* 62. Doane Robinson, however, inclines to the opinion that he was the brother of Robert Campbell, Sublette's partner.

88 Half-breed sons of Colonel Robert Dickson and namesakes of his brothers. Their mother was a Santee Sioux. For a reference to their ''uncle, a Sonte Indian,'' see *Fort Tecumseh Journal,* June 20, 1830.

89 The Holliday brothers, very prominent in the Upper Missouri Outfit in its first years, disappear from it in the early thirties and are not heard of again in its history. For suggestions as to their earlier connection with the upper Missouri, see Doane Robinson, South Dakota Historical *Collections,* vol. ix, p. 96, *note* 15. In 1830, Richard T. Holliday made a contract under which he was to receive a salary of $500. See *Chouteau-Maffitt Collection.*

90 The following letter, the only letter discovered that bears Chardon's own signature, has reference to Prince Paul: —
''Fort Tecumseh 20th - Augt 1820 [*sic*]
''Mr P. Chouteau jr.
''Sir — the Prince leaves this place to day for St Louis and can give you the news from the upper country better than Myself —
however — the Arricarees has Killed three Men belonging to Our Opponents, on their way to the Mandan's Bauche, Papiche Joe, and an other

and took from them 4 Horses laden With goods   they also stole all the Horses from the Mandan post — A canadian by the name of James Andrews descends with the prince as far as St Louis.   he Ows a balance to the Company Which I enclose to you, he is hired for three Years, and is, as I Am informed bent on running away, as Mr McKinzie this spring sent him down from the Yellow stone to this place for Horses and wrote Me word to Keep him here as I thought that he would desert from this place, I sent him back,   thinking that he would desert anyhow I thought the best way was to get what he Ows the Company and send him off —   I therefore promised him that if he would go as far as St Louis or the Bluffs With the Prince that he should be free, the Prince has promised to pay the Company at his arrival at St Louis the Balance of J. Andrews a/c $71 –72 cts   I also enclose you his private a/c from the 19th to 20th

"Lachapelle Will start for the Rees tomorrow in case there should be some difficulty in passing the Boat —

"I have Made at this place since the departure of the spring boats 140 pack, 1½ pack Beaver,   Lestant starts tomorrow for the chyenne and I expect 50 packs More —

"4 Men has deserted from this place and gone to St Louis   their Names are, A. Boileau, Rocheford, Henry White, Benture Lebrun,   they stole 3 guns   Boileau ows $170 to the Compy on this Year —   The boat (Male twins) left this place the 18th of this Month, the Others we have No News from —   Our Opponents has made as well as I can be informed 11 packs Robes and 2 packs Beaver Which they got from the white trappers at 5.50 per lb —   I am Out of Liquor, and would of taken a Barril from the Boat, but reed – orders to the Contrary which will put me back for Horses   I took from her contrary to Orders 10 (?) powder 200 lb Balls & 10 lb vermillion, as I was destitute of those articles —

"We are all in high spirits and live in hopes of doing well
"Respectfully
"Your Obedient
"F. A. Chardon"
"Compliments to Mr
Berthold and Family — "

(*Chouteau-Maffitt Collection,* Missouri Historical Society)
The foregoing letter, unrecorded in the *Fort Tecumseh Letter Book,* bears on its reverse side the following:
"Pierre Choteau Esqr
"Agent Am Fur Co
"St Louis"
"Pr. of Wertemberg"
and was evidently entrusted to Prince Paul for conveyance to St. Louis. Its date, 1820, is obviously an error and an error easily explained by the principle of association of ideas.   Chardon, having written 20 for the day of the month and being hurried or, possibly, excited over the ordeal of writing to Chouteau a semi-personal letter, wrote 20 for the year also.   In 1820 there was no Fort Tecumseh and no Prince Paul visiting in the United States.   Moreover, extant accounts against Prince Paul bear the date of August, 1830 and were made when Chardon was in charge of Fort Tecumseh (see *note* 73).   That he was in charge in July and August of 1830 is discernible from the entries of the *Fort Tecumseh Journal.*   Halsey, on July 16th,   departed with Mackenzie in the "Keel boat, Otter, bound for St. Louis," and, on the 28th., he sent a half-breed "to fort Tecumseh with a letter to Mr. Chardon."   According to Pilcher, Prince Paul was at

the Mandan villages when he himself arrived there, April 5, 1830 (*Senate Document*, no. 39, 21st Congress, 2nd session).

91 Among the *Auguste Chouteau Papers* of the Missouri Historical Society there is a record of Prince Paul's first visit to America, which is confirmed by his own narrative, *Erste Reise nach dem nördlichen Amerika in den Jahren 1822 bis 1824*, published at Stuttgart and Tübingen in 1835.

The Bishop of New Orleans, on board the steamboat *Cincinnati* from Cape Girardeau to Ste. Geneviève, wrote to Auguste Chouteau, April 29, 1823, to the effect that a fellow passenger, named Baron de Homberg, had been recognized by others as "Prince Paul de Wirtemberg, cousin germain du roi regnant" (*Auguste Chouteau Collection*).

"Einige Personen aus St. Geneviève, welche an Bord des Cincinnati mitgereist waren . . . Durch die Güte des Bischofs . . . Der General Sir Williams Clarke . . . Der General, sowie Herr Pierre Chouteau, welchem, sowie seinem Bruder, Auguste Chouteau . . . Bei Herrn Clarke machte . . . Major O'Fallon . . ."
(*Erste Reise nach dem nördlichen Amerika* . . . , pp. 171, 172).

To General Clark, Superintendent of Indian Affairs, Prince Paul applied for a passport, writing as follows:

"St louis May 5th. 1823.
"General
"My intention in Coming to the united States having for its Sole object My own instruction and particularly anxious of visiting the region of Country bordering the missoury and Columbia rivers for the improvements of botany and Natural history I have the honor to ask of your Excellency the pass ports necessary to protect me as a foreigner through those countries under the protection of the united States.

"I must here observe to your Excellency that not being aware of the necessity of being provided with a pass port for the performance of my undertaking I have left at new orleans the document which might be necessary to make me Known to you, and particularly the pass port I took in europe and which is Certified by the american Consul at homburg, under the name of baron de Hohenberg, under that name I landed at New orleans but having been Since Known by my real name of *Prince frederick Paul Guillaume* of Wurtemberg, Cousin of the reigning King, I have no further motives for Keeping the incognito. and that it might be a pledge of the Sincerity of my motives I Seal this my request with my princely Seal.

Wishing at the Same time to be Considered only as a traveller in pursuit of Scientific Knowledge under the protection of a friendly Government./.
I have the honor to be

of your Excellency

the Obt. humble Servt
frederic Paul Guillaume
Prince of Wurtemberg

"Wm. Clark Exgovernor of Missouri
and Superintendant of the
indian department./.

(Seal)
"P. S. I have with me a native German under the name of J. G. Shlape, and a Creole of this Country as a hunter of whose name I am not yet acquainted./."

The application of Prince Paul was duly reported to Washington by General Clark: —

"St. Louis May 18th 1823

"Sir

"The inclosed aplication has been made by a Foreign gentleman for a Passport to go into the Indian Country for the improvement of Botany & Natural History.   This Gentleman having convinced me of his intentions, I granted him a passport as a Botanier to pass to the upper Trading establishments on the Missouri (within the Agency of Major OFallon) with a promise to make this communication to you, and if the government does not disapprove of his passing to the Columbia, another passport will be forwarded to him.

"This Gentleman (or Prince as he may be termed) has set out to the Council Bluffs in a Boat of one of our Traders; and as I very much suspect will neither have inclination nor perseverance to go on much further. He is fond of Killing Birds and collecting plants which appears to be the source of greatest pleasure to him.

"As to political, or any other Talents which he may possess I can say but little, as they appear to be very limited.

"Please to signify to me your approval, or disapprobation of the extention of the passport this Prince of Wartemberg to the Columbia.

"I have the honor to be with sentiments of

"high respect your Mo Obt. H. Servt.

"Wm. Clark"

The Honbl John C. Calhoun
Secty. of War."

92 Hamilton was not a mere sojourner in the United States.   He died at St. Louis about February, 1840, and was laid to rest in the "Episcopal Burial Ground" there (See charges against his estate for digging the grave, building a foundation for a monument, and clearing dirt away in the lot of the Grave Yard, also for altering the tombstone, all of which were settled by J. B. Sarpy, (*Estate Papers of James Archdale Hamilton Palmer,* Missouri Historical Society).   Hamilton died intestate but possessed of considerable property, including an interest in "Half-breed Sac and Fox lands" in Iowa and capital stock in the Missouri Insurance Company (*idem*).   Pierre Chouteau, Jr. and Kenneth Mackenzie were appointed administrators of his estate, John B. Sarpy and John F. A. Sanford standing as their sureties (*idem*).   In connection with the settlement of his estate, Hamilton's family relationships were made known, principally by means of an English affidavit dated December 8, 1842, from which the following is extracted:—

". . . make oath and say that they are severally acquainted with the family and next of kin of James Archdale Hamilton Palmer late of Saint Louis County in the State of Missouri . . . Merchant, who formerly resided in England and who died as these Deponents have been informed . . . a Bachelor.   And these Deponents severally further say that the next of Kin of . . . did at the time of his death and do now consist of the following persons (that is to say),

Samuel Palmer of Chipping Norton in the County of Oxford . . ., Gentleman, the Father of the said deceased; and *Thomas Palmer* of Bourton-on-the-Water in the County of Gloucester in England, Draper;   *Henry Boswell Palmer* of Wandsworth in the County of Surrey in England, Gentleman;   *Mary Palmer* of Chipping Norton aforesaid, Spinster; *Hannah,* the Wife of John Evans of Duddeston, in the parish of Aston near Birmingham . . . Corn Dealer; *Elizabeth Wheeler* of Hook Norton in the County of Oxford aforesaid, Widow; and *Sarah,* the Wife of William

Rayner of Bayford near Hertford . . ., Gentleman, the Brothers and Sisters of the said deceased . . . and that the Mother of the said James Archdale Hamilton Palmer died in his lifetime . . .'' (*idem.*) The italics and some of the punctuation marks have been added.

93 The following notice, appearing in the Missouri *Republican* April 20, 1839, shows that, about a year before his death, Hamilton resumed his full baptismal name:

"To all persons concerned.   It is hereby notified that J. A. Hamilton is legally authorized to adopt and will hereafter use the name of J. A. Hamilton Palmer.

"American Fur Company Office, April 9th."

Why he ever surrendered it, in the first place, remains an enigma.

94 Doane Robinson makes a somewhat similar comment.   See South Dakota Historical *Collections,* vol. ix, p. 111, *note 47.*

95 Maximilian noted, in passing the mouth of the Cheyenne, that there was the place where timber had been felled for Fort Pierre.   (*Travels,* p. 165).   This was just after Laidlaw, who had accompanied Maximilian, Mackenzie, Sanford and the others of the party a little way, had set forth on his return journey.

96 This was the trader who was pillaged and killed by the Yanctonais early in January, 1836.   For a contemporary reference to this tragedy, see *Fort Clark Journal,* February 1, 1836.   The journal was then being kept by D. D. Mitchell, whose special report, June 10, 1836, on the Primeau and Deschampes massacres is to be found in the Appendix, also Sub-Agent Fulkerson's on the same subject.   For biographical data, see *note* 346.

97 For suggestions as to the subsequent fortunes of this man, see South Dakota Historical *Collections,* vol. ix, p. 112, *note 51.*   His brother married Helene Chauvin, the widow of Régis Loisel, whose two daughters married two of the Papin brothers.   For a note on the Moreau River, see *Drumm,* Stella M., *Journal of a Fur-trading Expedition on the Upper Missouri, 1812-1813*:   By John C. Luttig, Clerk of the Missouri Fur Company, p. 64, *note 99.*

98 For a sketch of John McKnight, see *Douglas,* W. B., *James' Three Years among the Indians and Mexicans,* pp. 94-95, *note* 1.

99 David Dawson Mitchell, one of the many Virginians who were to be found emigrated to the "Middle West" in the very early days, was connected with the Ioway Outfit of the Western Department in 1828 (See Contract between him and Chouteau, June 17, 1828, *Chouteau-Maffitt Collection*) and his communications from the Black Snake Hills are to be found quite numerously among the *Chouteau Investment Company Papers.* Palm was associated with him in the trade there and the two had dealings, for the most part, with the "Sauks and Foxes of the Mississippi" (See "List of Men to be Employed," dated August 30, 1828).   In passing back and forth, Lamont probably made his acquaintance and was instrumental in having him, in 1830, transferred to the Upper Missouri Outfit. In what estimation he was held is indicated by the salary he was to receive under the contract made with him, June 8, 1830 (*Chouteau-Maffitt Collection*); for, by the standards of those days, seven hundred dollars was a generous stipend.   His first winter on the upper Missouri seems to have been spent at the Yanctonais (Lamont to Mitchell, February 20, 1831, *Fort Tecumseh Letter Book,* 1830-1832, pp. 28-30) and he took charge at Fort

Clark when Kipp was called away to build Fort Piegan.   Thither he was to return, as it happened, after he had become a partner of the Outfit, in the place of Lamont, resigned.   See *notes* 67 and 406.   That was in 1836, when Chardon was on his vacation.   It was Mitchell who superintended, in 1832, the building of Fort McKenzie, the substitute for Fort Piegan, and presided there until his contract had expired and he had resolved to retire from the service of the Upper Missouri Outfit.   In 1841, he was appointed Superintendent of Indian Affairs at St. Louis and, intermittently, held that office until 1852.   In one of the intervals, he served as Lieutenant-Colonel of the Missouri regiment raised by Sterling Price for service in the War with Mexico (*Chittenden*, H. M., *History of the American Fur Trade of the Far West*, p. 388, *note*).   When in the Indian country and stationed at Fort McKenzie, Mitchell formed a connection with a woman of the notorious Deschampes family (*Coues*, Elliott, *Forty Years a Fur Trader on the Upper Missouri*, vol. i, p. 97, *note* 5); but, in 1840, was regularly married to Martha Eliza Berry, daughter of Major James Berry of Kentucky (*Drumm*, Stella M., *Magoffin Journal*, p. 174, *note* 73).   He died in 1861.   Among the many official reports that Mitchell made, good, bad, and indifferent, is one that constitutes an interesting forecast of the settlement of the ''Middle West.''   It accompanied the *Annual Report of the Commissioner of Indian Affairs* for 1842.   See *Reports on Indian Affairs, 1838-1842*, pp. 434-435.

100 *Fort Tecumseh Journal*, April 6, 1831; Lamont to Mitchell, February 20, 1831, *Fort Tecumseh Letter Book*, 1830-1832, pp. 28-30.

101 This letter was an answer to Mackenzie's of December 12, 1831, received while Laidlaw was at Crook's Point *en route* for the different posts on the Cheyenne.   Laidlaw gives many items of news, news of Thomas L. Sarpy's fatal accident; of Leclerc's having sent pack horses to White River &c; to his having sent the Dauphins & Lachanti and ''moored himself snugly along side of Lamont's Poncaw squaw;'' of ''Father Bean's assistance to our opponents;'' of Lachapelle at the Rees; and comments upon Mackenzie's wish that Picotte go to the Mandans in the spring; also of the arrangement with Fontenelle and Drips.   He sends a bundle of Greenock papers (*Fort Tecumseh Letter Book*, 1830-1832, pp. 103-110).   The Sarpy fatal accident took place, it is supposed, at the junction of Wounded Knee Creek and White River.

102 It was only by such means Mackenzie rightly thought that the difficulties, the expense, the uncertainty, incident to the peculiarities of the Missouri River, could be measurably obviated.   Thanks to Elias Rector and others, steamboats had for some years been operating on the lower Missouri (Chappell, P. E., *A History of the Missouri River*, p. 41) and, since 1823, on the upper Mississippi (*Merrick*, G. B., *Old Times on the Upper Mississippi*, p. 187).   To Henry M. Shreve, of Quaker ancestry, belongs a large mead of praise for the effort expended in developing steam navigation in western waters.

103 Mackenzie to Cabanné, dated Fort Tecumseh, June 7, 1831, *Fort Tecumseh Letter Book, 1830-1832*, pp. 40-42.   Lamont's interest in the venture had been almost as keen as Mackenzie's.   In a letter of 1830, he had expressed the hope that the experiment would be really made and, writing to Chouteau, April 28, 1831 (*Chouteau-Maffitt Collection*), after giving encouraging news of the trade, which had confirmed his anticipations, he said, ''All possible precautions are and will be taken to expedite

the Steam Boat and be assured your presence in her will be very gratify-ing.''

104 For an account of the maiden trip of the Yellowstone, the spring of 1831, see *Chittenden,* H. M., *Early Steamboat Navigation on the Missouri River,* vol. i, p. 136. She left St. Louis, April 16, 1831 and arrived at Fort Tecumseh, ''at the mouth of Bad River, S.D.,'' June 19, 1831 (Chappell, P. E., *A History of the Missouri River,* p. 44). Latrobe calls attention to the vast difference in time taken by the *Yellowstone* in going and coming. The upward voyage took from eight to ten weeks, the down-ward, ten to fifteen days. (See *Latrobe,* Charles Joseph, *The Rambler in North America, 1832-1833,* vol. i, p. 133).

105 ''I understand that old Cabanne and Pratte are quite against Steam-boating; they say it is all a 'diponce pour arien' [*une depence pour un rien?*]'' (Laidlaw to Mackenzie, November 27, 1831, *Fort Tecumseh Letter Book,* 1830-1832, p. 76).

106 It was only by the merest chance that Albert Pike was not among her passengers. He had arrived in St. Louis just as she was about to start and was strongly tempted to embark; but finally preferred a Santa Fé trading trip across the plains. The party fitted out at Independence, Charles Bent at its head (*Pike,* Albert, *Prose Sketches and Poems, Written in the Western Country; MS. Autobiography* in Scottish Rite Temple, Washington).

107 A similar journey, in 1833, was certainly made by Mackenzie on horseback. See Mackenzie to Kipp, December 17, 1833, *Fort Union Let-ter Book, 1833-1835,* p. 5.

108 *Palliser,* John, *Solitary Rambles and Adventures of a Hunter in the Prairies,* pp. 105-109.

109 His first season would seem to have been spent actually in residence at Fort Union. Various minor items of one sort or another bear witness to that, indirectly. For instance, a hunting agreement made, July 5, 1832, between Kenneth Mackenzie and a certain Johnson Gardner, a free hunter who could affix his mark only, had to do with beaver skins *en cache* on the Yellowstone River and J. A. Hamilton and Francis A. Chardon were ''to adjust and regulate the weight thereof'' (*Pierre Chouteau Collection*). A certificate, bearing date, August 6, 1832, shows they performed the duty (*idem;* also *Palmer Papers*).

110 The ''Correspondence and Journals of Captain Nathaniel J. Wyeth'' were published in 1899 in *Sources of the History of Oregon,* vol. i, under the editorship of F. G. Young. In the correspondence of the Upper Missouri Outfit, Maximilian is invariably referred to as ''Baron Braunsberg.,'' prior to Mackenzie's trip abroad. After that, writing to his erstwhile host, December 10, 1835, Mackenzie addressed him as ''Prince Maximilian de Neuwied'' (*Fort Union Letter Book, 1833-1835*).

111 For a description of this steamboat, the second for the upper Mis-souri trade, and, like the first, the *Yellowstone,* the property of the Amer-ican Fur Company, see *Coues,* Elliott, *Forty Years a Fur Trader on the Upper Missouri,* vol. i, p. 63, *note* 10. The contract for the building of the *Assiniboine* was let, October 12, 1832 (*Chouteau-Maffitt Collection*) and it was built at Cincinnati the ensuing winter (*Thwaites,* R. G., *Early*

Western Travels, vol. xxii, p. 240, *note* 179). For the cost to the owners of the *Assiniboine*, see *Chouteau-Maffitt Collection*, 1834-1835.

112 One of the first things Catlin described at any length while he was at Fort Union was this buffalo hunt in which Chardon came to grief, though not seriously. See *North American Indians*, edition of 1850, vol. i, pp. 24-28; *Donaldson*, Thomas, *The George Catlin Indian Gallery*, Smithsonian Institution, *Report*, 1885, Part v, pp. 283-286.

113 *North American Indians*, Plate 9.

114 It was on October 11th. that Maximilian decided to have his turn at hunting. Bodmer and Chardon were both of the party. "We soon proceeded on our expedition; and as we rode along, were amused by the cheerful and enterprising Chardon who had lived among the Osages, and was able to give the most authentic information respecting that people, and the Indians in general. Listening to his animated descriptions, his communications relative to the Indian languages, alternating with Indian songs and the war-whoop, we passed through the forest, then across a meadow . . . and then over a chain of hills . . .'' (*Travels*, p. 301).

115 Maximilian's itinerary is very easy to determine from his own narrative. Except when otherwise designated the edition resorted to for purposes of this work has been that of 1843 and will be found cited as *Travels*. The *Assiniboine* left Fort Pierre, June 5, 1833 (*Travels*, p. 163).

116 The post for the Crows was Fort Cass, two hundred miles up the Yellowstone (Maximilian, *Travels*, p. 188) and "2 m. below the mouth of the Bighorn'' (*Coues*, Elliott, *Forty Years a Fur Trader on the Upper Missouri*, vol. i, p. 46, *note* 10). It was built by Samuel Tulloch, who had been sent there by Mackenzie expressly for the purpose. The variation in his name, the "A. J. Tullock'' of Coues and the "Tulleck'' of Beckwourth, is difficult to account for; inasmuch as, in the correspondence of the Upper Missouri Outfit, he is always referred to by the name given here. For his own signature, Samuel Tulloch, given at Fort Union, July 21, 1834, see *Chouteau-Maffitt Collection*. When visited by Wyeth and Bonneville, Fort Cass appeared to be nothing but a mere stockade, its force, twenty men (*Irving*, Washington, *The Adventures of Captain Bonneville*, Edition of 1859, p. 344.

117 Letter of June 7, 1831, *Fort Tecumseh Letter Book, 1830-1832*, p. 44.

118 An interesting primary source for the pacification this implied and related matters has recently come to light in the manuscripts of Father Nicholas Point, S. J., the bulk of which seem to be preserved at St. Mary's College, Montreal. An effort I made to examine them personally resulted in my being informed that they were soon to be published. For so much of Father Point's account, as appears in the Appendix, I am indebted to Father Garraghan of St. Louis University, whose many kindnesses to me I have elsewhere acknowledged.

119 Laidlaw to Chouteau, December 26, 1831, *Fort Tecumseh Letter Book, 1830-1832*, p. 84.

120 *Maximilian, Travels*, p. 223.

121 The printed text of this convention, or treaty, is to be found in

Thwaites, *Early Western Travels,* vol. xxiv, p. 317. The witnesses are given as, ''Jas. Archdale Hamilton
H. Chardon''; but there was no Chardon in the Western Department other than Francis A. at the time, so the initial H is obviously an error.

122 From Laidlaw's reporting to Mackenzie that Chardon's canoe had been stolen, August 1, 1831, by men deserting (Laidlaw to Mackenzie, November 27, 1831, *Fort Tecumseh Letter Book,* 1830-1832, p. 73), it would seem he must even then have been gone.

123 Kipp had left it to go down with the furs and there was, apparently, no intention of abandoning it altogether.

124 Mitchell had built Fort McKenzie and was in charge of it at this time. He was returning after an absence and both he and Culbertson were journeying on with Maximilian. For an account of the overwhelming misfortune that Mitchell suffered on his way to the River Maria in 1832, in the loss of his keel-boat with the Blackfeet equipment, see Laidlaw to Chouteau, August 14, 1832 (*Fort Tecumseh Letter Book, 1830-1832,* pp. 130-131). The news had been brought by Catlin from Fort Union to Fort Pierre. Laidlaw feared that the disaster, in the ''untoward delay'' it would occasion, would be ''very detrimental to the infant post.''

125 He arrived September 28th. (*Travels,* p. 297). On the selfsame day, Mackenzie arrived at Fort Pierre (Mackenzie to W. B. Astor, December 16, 1833, *Fort Union Letter Book, 1833-1835,* p. 16) and began busily writing, giving, as Laidlaw assumed, ''all the country news from above'' (Laidlaw to Chouteau, September 28, 1833, *Fort Pierre Letter Book, 1832-1835,* p. 28).

126 Catlin said of J. E. Brazeau, ''a gentleman of education and strict observation, who has lived several years with the Blackfeet and Shiennes . . .'' (*North American Indians,* edition of 1850, vol. i, p. 53). For data respecting the Brazeau family of Kaskaskia, to which it is assumed this man belonged, see South Dakota Historical *Collections,* vol. ix, p. 140, *note* 114. J. E. Brazeau passed over, after a time, to the employ of the Hudson's Bay Company and was in temporary charge of Fort Edmonton when the Earl of Southesk arrived there, August 11, 1859 (*Saskatchewan and the Rocky Mountains,* p. 147). To this most fair-minded of travellers he gave ''a great deal of interesting information'' (*idem,* p. 159), much of it in verification of Catlin, for whom he was prepared to vouch as he had vouched years and years before (See testimonial, dated St. Louis, 1835, *Catlin,* George, *North American Indians,* vol. i, p. 13). He confirmed, in particular, ''all Catlin's statements about the Mandans, especially as to their customs of cruel self-torture. . .'' (*Saskatchewan and the Rocky Mountains,* p. 151). He, likewise, recounted the circumstances under which Vanderburgh met his death at the hands of the Blackfeet (*idem,* pp. 160-161) and claimed for the Sioux women a chastity that he could not ascribe to their Mandan and Crow sisters (*idem, p. 163*). Proceeding on his way the Earl of Southesk did not return to Fort Edmonton until October and considerable must have been his disappointment to find Brazeau transferred to Rocky Mountain House (*idem,* p. 268). However, at Fort Pelly, he had the great good fortune to meet, installed there, a fellow Scot, Mr. Murray, who had lived in the Indian country across the line ''for many years of his life'' (*idem,* p. 330). Murray had preceded Larpenteur at Fort Van

Buren (*Forty Years a Fur Trader on the Upper Missouri*, vol. i, p. 162), going from that doomed post to Fort Alexander (*idem*, p. 175). Of this Palliser heard when he made his acquaintance in 1847 (*Solitary Rambles and Adventures of a Hunter in the Prairies*, p. 83). It was probably more from Murray than from Brazeau that Southesk obtained his knowledge of the American fur trade, a knowledge that enabled him to draw a sharp contrast between the conditions on the two sides of the international boundary (*idem*, pp. 326-327).

127 Jean Baptiste Moncrèvier. For Hamilton's opinion of him, see Hamilton to Culbertson, May 5, 1835 (*Fort Union Letter Book, 1833-1835*, p. 76). The testimony of the *Fort Union Letter Book* is not entirely in accord with the impression of this man that Larpenteur would convey (*Coues*, Elliott, *Forty Years a Fur Trader on the Upper Missouri*, pp. 72-73, 76); but he did get into trouble in 1845, because of information that Chardon, Harvey, and others had lodged against him to the effect that, when going up with the keel boats to the Blackfeet in June, 1844, he had got drunk several times himself and had given upwards of twenty gallons of liquor to the men, whereas Picotte had ordered that not a single drop should be disposed of (A.R. Bouis to Alexander Culbertson, October 9, 1845, *Fort Pierre Letter Book, 1845-1846*). The offence lay, evidently, in the loss of the liquor, and, for that, Picotte decreed that Moncrèvier was not, after his return from his "Coutenais expedition," to be employed any more (See *note* 245). Two years earlier, when Audubon was at Fort Union, he had seen a good deal of Moncrèvier, had found him "one of the most skilful of the hunters" (Coues, *Audubon and His Journals*, vol. ii, p. 105) and had given him a commission to procure various animals for him (*idem*, p. 146). He had also found him a lucky fisherman (*idem*, p. 158). In Denig's description of Fort Union, reference is made to a "painting" on the top of the front outside gate "of a treaty of peace between the Indians and whites executed by J. B. Moncrèvier, Esq." (*idem*, p. 185).

128 Maximilian, *Travels*, p. 299. Hamilton continued in charge until Mackenzie's return, November 8, 1833 (Mackenzie to Kipp, December 17, 1833, *Fort Union Letter Book, 1833-1835*, p. 3), by which time Maximilian had not only departed for his extended stay with Kipp at Fort Clark but must have been well on his way there. He had left Fort Union October 30th. (*Travels*, p. 309; Hamilton to Kipp, October 29, 1833, *Fort Union Letter Book*, 1833-1835, p. 1) For these and other selected letters sent out from Fort Union, see Appendix. There is some reason to think that Mackenzie did not return until November 17th. See Hamilton to Laidlaw, December 10, 1835, *Fort Union Letter Book*, 1833-1835, p. 93, and Mackenzie to Ortley, December 10, 1835, *idem*, p. 98.

129 Mackenzie to Joshua Pilcher, December 16, 1833, *Fort Union Letter Book, 1833-1835*, p. 10. For this and other references to the conduct of the Opposition, see "Selected Fort Union Letters" in Appendix.

130 Of this Maximilian became convinced. See *Travels*, p. 199. He was speaking particularly of the Crees. In Mackenzie's own correspondence (*Selected Fort Union Letters, op. cit.*) will be found evidences of his trust in the Indians. Murray, although he missed seeing Clark in St. Louis, testifies to a similar affection for him (*Travels in North America*, vol. i, p. 236).

131 Mackenzie to Pilcher, December 16, 1833, *op. cit.*

[132] According to Thwaites (*Early Western Travels*, vol. xxiii, pp. 33-34, *note* 21), Maximilian was mistaken in supposing that *Rivière aux Trembles*, the one he called Martha's River and the Poplar of today, was the Martha's of Lewis and Clark (*idem*, p. 29 and *note* 16). Moreover, the Poplar was the Porcupine of Lewis and Clark (Thwaites, *Original Journals of the Lewis and Clark Expedition*, vol. i, p. 362 and *note* 1), whereas an affluent of Milk River is now called the Porcupine (*idem*) and their Martha's River, the Big Muddy (*idem*, vol. i, p. 352, *note* 1). Of it, Lewis said, ". . . This stream my friend Capt. C. named Marthas river" (*idem*, p. 352).

[133] Mackenzie to Chouteau, December 16, 1833, *Fort Union Letter Book, 1833-1835*, p. 13.

[134] Mackenzie lingered at Fort Pierre until October 24th (*idem*). His stay of three weeks (Laidlaw to Wm. Dickson, October 30, 1833, *Fort Pierre Letter Book, 1832-1835*), while it gave him an opportunity to perfect his plans, proved very irksome. He worried about Lamont's non-appearance, especially as the cholera was reported to have made "great havoc" in St. Louis (*ibid*). When he did leave he took with him every horse "that was fit for service" (Laidlaw to Colin Campbell, October 30, *idem*, pp. 31-32). Russell Farnham, who lived and died in the service of the American Fur Company, had been stricken with the cholera, dying of it, October 23, 1832 (*Darby*, John F., *Personal Recollections*, p. 166).

[135] Mackenzie to Kipp, December 17, 1833, *Fort Union Letter Book*, 1833-1835, p. 3. For the full text of this letter, see Appendix.

[136] Mackenzie to Chouteau, December 16, 1833. See Appendix.

[137] Mackenzie to Kipp, December 17, 1833. The size of the fort, as given by Chittenden, was fifty feet square (*History of the American Fur Trade of the Far West*, vol. iii, p. 961).

[138] This Fort Jackson is to be distinguished from another of the name that was built for Sarpy & Fraeb on the South Platte (See *Hafen*, LeRoy R., "Fort Jackson and the Early Fur Trade on the South Platte," *Colorado Magazine* February, 1928, pp. 9-17). Chittenden's account of Chardon's fort to the extent that it differs from Mackenzie's official and contemporary, must, perforce, be accounted inaccurate. By Mackenzie's reckoning it was placed at "about three days march" from Fort Union (Mackenzie to P. D. Papin, December, 1833, *Fort Union Letter Book*, 1833-1835, p. 9) and, in Laidlaw's phrase, it was "near Milk river," where "I presume he will go the *whole hog*" (Laidlaw to Papin, January 14, 1834, *Fort Pierre Letter Book*, 1832-1835, pp. 52-53). Whatever may have been meant by this expression, it was supposed to have originated in Virginia and to have been very popular in Jackson's day as applied to radical reformers (*Hamilton*, Thomas, *Men and Manners in America*, p. 18).

[139] There seems no doubt of this; for Chardon himself wrote that he and his companions were all "Jackson men" (*Chittenden, op. cit.* p. 961.

[140] The date of his setting out was, according to one of Mackenzie's letters, November 13th (Letter to Kipp, December 17, 1833) and, according to another, the 11th (Letter to Chouteau, December 16, 1833), that being the requisite "three days" after his own arrival.

141 See *note* 265.

142 Mackenzie to Robert Campbell, November 13, 1833, *Fort Union Letter Book, 1833-1835*, p. 2.

143 Mackenzie to Kipp, December 17, 1833, *idem*, p. 5.

144 *Smith*, Arthur D. Howden, *John Jacob Astor*, p. 245.

145 Alexander Culbertson, born 1809, was the son of Joseph Culbertson by his first marriage and grandson of Colonel Robert Culbertson. His mother, Mary Finley, was a daughter of Captain James Finley of the American revolutionary army (Letter from Mrs. Wm. A. Culbertson, Chambersburg, Pennsylvania).   Thaddeus Ainsworth Culbertson, author of the interesting report on the *Mauvaises Terres* heretofore noted, was his half-brother. An uncle, John Craighead Culbertson, who was himself engaged in the Santa Fé trade, is said to have influenced him in entering the employ of the American Fur Company in 1833 (Thwaites, *Early Western Travels*, vol. xxiii, p. 38, *note* 23); but, obviously, it would be more nearly correct to say, the Upper Missouri Outfit, for he had already had experience on the upper Mississippi, being one of the traders, listed by Lawrence Taliaferro, the ''splenetic, conceited, opinionated, but honest and incorruptible man'' (*Williams*, J. Fletcher, *Memoir of Henry Hastings Sibley*, Minnesota Historical *Collections*, vol. vi, p. 266), who ''was Indian agent at Fort Snelling from 1820 to 1841,'' as licensed between 1819 and 1840 (Taliaferro, Lawrence, *Autobiography, idem*, p. 249).   On the upper Missouri, from the very beginning of his residence there, he was identified with the Blackfeet trade.   He was with Mitchell at Fort McKenzie, going up, indeed, when Maximilian did, in the late summer of 1833, then with Kipp, and, finally, in supreme control himself at that most difficult of posts, the building of which he claimed to have completed (*Audubon and His Journals*, vol. ii, p. 188).   He married into the Blackfeet tribe, his first wife being Natawischicksina, the ''Notoesixina,'' of Father Point's *Baptismal Register*, daughter and sister of successive Blood chiefs.   About her Audubon came to have several interesting things to relate; for, when the naturalist was at Fort Union, Culbertson happened to be in charge and the three, later on in the same year, 1843, travelled in company as far down the river as Fort Pierre, where Culbertson found orders directing him to ''go to the Platte River establishment'' (*Audubon and His Journals*, vol. ii, p. 164). On his return to the Yellowstone, he ordered the destruction of Fort F.A.C., incurring thereby, perhaps and quite naturally, the ill-will of Chardon. He then built Fort Honoré, the later Fort Lewis.   For one single year, following the temporary withdrawal of Picotte from the chief direction of the Upper Missouri Outfit, Culbertson had control and resided at Fort Pierre; but the experience would seem to have been not wholly to the satisfaction of either himself or his partners.

Beyond the time of Chardon's death, it is not necessary here to follow Culbertson's fortunes.   They continued fairly exciting to the end and the story of them, largely his own reminiscences, is to be found in an article, entitled, ''Affairs at Fort Benton,'' Montana Historical Society *Contributions*, vol. iii, pp. 201-287, which, if carefully checked and all due allowance made for an old man's defective memory as well as for the very human desire to be thought the hero of every exploit recounted, is not without historical merit and value.

146 Mackenzie to Culbertson, July 8, 1834, *Fort Union Letter Book*, 1833-1835, pp. 49-50.

147 ''I had the honor to receive your letter of 10 Feby & regret that I could not avail myself of your instructions relative to Le Gros corne &c.

''I am so peculiarly circumstanced this season & my men are so dispersed it is not without difficulty that I have selected trusty men to conduct you down tho I have no men here whose term of service expires earlier than 26 Sep next & they have of course a claim on me for wages until that day.   I have explained this matter in my letter to Mr. Laidlaw & requested him to furnish you with men whose engagements will expire in July in order that the charge may be lessened, in either case I ask no more from you than I have actually to pay.   I have learnt with much pain how poorly you have fared at ye Mandans & again express my regret that I had not the pleasure to entertain you at my own table during the past Winter.   I trust your health has not suffered, in which case on your arrival in the land of plenty you can look back on your privations without pain or regret.

''It would be very pleasant to me could I utter orally my Adieus! on your leaving this inhospitable clime but I must content myself with assuring you of my best wishes that you may be blessed with health & a prosperous voyage to your Father-land.

''I enclose the acc.ts as requested,   Mr. Laidlaw will make such additions as appertain to his department & your final arrangements will be made with Mr. Chouteau in St Louis.

''Mr Hamilton begs I will present his Compts. nor would he forget Mr Bordmer to whom also I wish to be remembered.   I have the honor to remain

''Sir
''Yours very obediently''

(Kenneth Mackenzie to M. Baron de Braunsberg, dated Fort Union March 20, 1834, *Fort Union Letter Book, 1833-1835,* p. 39).

148 The preliminary movements of Chardon are largely left to inference. Curiously enough on even so unimportant a point Maximilian's narrative is fully corroborative of what is obtainable from the *Fort Union Letter Book, 1833-1835.* On April 7th, Mackenzie wrote to Kipp, ''I have been compelled to send men to Ft. Cass to bring down returns from thence,   this day I have started a Keel Bt. with 13 men for Mr. Chardon's returns, & sending also for the Baron & Pecotte I am left almost with an empty fort. I shall require Ae. Hugron to come up with H. Pecotte to make up his complement of hands . . .''   Maximilian recorded,

''On the afternoon of the 14th of April, the people whom Mr. MacKenzie had promised to send to accompany me down the river to Saint Louis, at length arrived from Fort Union.   There were, however, many others with them, among whom were Belhumeur and Mr. Chardon as leader . . . They brought us letters from (451) Fort Union, and news from Fort McKenzie . . .

''On the 15th of April, Picotte arrived with about twenty men, and had his boat laden with maize, which he was to carry to Fort Union.   They immediately set about preparing the Mackinaw boat for our voyage down the river, and Picotte set out on the 16th, notwithstanding a heavy rain. Every preparation was completed on the following day; the boat was brought to the landing-place, furnished on the deck with a spacious Indian tent covering, and all was made ready for our voyage, Mr. Chardon resolving to accompany me to Fort Pierre on the Teton River.

''On the 18th of April, at noon, the boat was loaded; and, after we had partaken of our last frugal dinner at Fort Clarke, we took a cordial farewell of Mr. Kipp . . .'' (*Thwaites, R. G., Early Western Travels*, vol. xxiv, pp. 81-82).

An incidental and petty reference to Chardon and his belongings, made a good while afterwards, is further corroborative of Maximilian. It occurs in a letter of Hamilton's dated March 3, 1835 (*Fort Union Letter Book, 1833-1835*, p. 68) and runs thus: ''As Chardon did not give up pan, cup plate &c in Apˡ I presume his a/c should be charged therewith.''

149 Although Catlin intimates that Chardon was one of those having wife or sweetheart to whom to relate hunting experiences, there is good reason for thinking that his wife was still at Fort Pierre at the time he left Fort Union. Mackenzie had written to Laidlaw, December 16, 1833, enclosing this message from Chardon:

''Mr. Chardon particularly requests you will instruct his woman & child to be at your fort in readiness to come up hither by Steam boat in Spring'' (*Fort Union Letter Book, 1833-1835*, p. 12) and, at the time Chardon went down with Maximilian, the steamboat, naturally, had not appeared. It was much too early for it. One indication, exceedingly slight however, for thinking that Chardon had some feminine taste to please at Fort Union is in a postscript to Laidlaw's letter to Hamilton, October 18, 1833: —

''P.S. Please examine whether Mr. Chardon was charged with 10 yds fancy calico, a a/c of which was sent to F.U. some time since'' (*Fort Pierre Letter Book, 1832-1835*, pp. 29-30).

150 See *Tyrrell, J. B., David Thompson's Narrative of His Explorations in Western America, 1784-1812.* Thompson, who started for the Mandan country, November 28, 1797, was a man, so strict in his own life, that he was not likely to view many of the Indian customs in any but a censorious way. To him all Mandan dancing women were courtesans (p. 234) and the total lack of chastity throughout the tribe, its curse (pp. 234-235). He was a great opponent of the liquor traffic and would never allow — the instructions of his superiors to the contrary notwithstanding — ardent spirits of any kind to be a part of his equipment. In this respect, he presented a strong contrast to a man like Charles Chaboillez, whose journal, 1797-1798 (*Masson Papers*, Canadian Public Archives, Ottawa) is truly disgusting in its allusions to liquor distribution and consumption.

151 Of Charles MacKenzie, Masson wrote, ''Unlike the generality of Indian traders, Mr. MacKenzie had a most decided partiality for the Indians, of whom, on all occasions, he made himself the apologist. His correspondence on that subject, though it would by many be considered as extreme, denotes a man of a philanthropic disposition and of strong religious convictions'' (*Masson, L. R., Les Bourgeois de la Compagnie du Nord-Ouest*, vol. i, p. 319). Yet, even MacKenzie did not sentimentalize over the red men.

152 Alexander Henry started for the Missouri River, July 7, 1806 (*Journal*, ''Coventry Copy'', Canadian Public Archives, Ottawa) and, as he drew near, remarked, ''. . . no manner of lenity can be expected from those Mandan savages, they have already given too many instances of their barbarous behaviour to white people when meeting them in the plains . . .'' (*idem*, vol. i, p. 435). This passage, be it observed, was omitted by Coues when he reproduced Henry's journal for his ''New Light on the History of the Greater Northwest.'' See vol. i, p. 317, where, if anywhere, it should appear. Of the thieving propensities of the Mandans (*Coventry Copy*, vol. i, p. 459), their disgusting habits (*idem*, pp. 448-449), the gross lack of

chastity among their women (*idem*, p. 452), at which the men connived (*idem*, p. 481), accepting one single coat button in payment, Henry had fully as much to say as had Thompson. He considered all the Missouri Indians, especially the Big Bellies (Gros Ventres), "'mercenary savages'' (*idem*, p. 598) and was nauseated by the sight of the Big Bellies eating the "'unwashed entrails of Buffalo'' (*idem*, p. 584). What would he have said had he been with Audubon and seen how successfully Culbertson and Chardon had conquered any repugnance that they, too, may once have felt, going so far as to imitate the savages?

153 This was the opinion that Pierre Antoine Tabeau, a resident trader among them at the time of the Lewis and Clark expedition, had formed. See his narrative of the *Voyage of Régis Loisel*, soon to be published by the Canadian government. It was also the opinion of Jacob Halsey. See *Fort Tecumseh Journal* under date of March 19, 1830, South Dakota Historical *Collections*, vol. ix, p. 107.

154 Henry considered the Big Bellies more hospitable but also more lascivious than the Mandans. They were given, he said, to unnatural vices (*Coventry Copy*, vol. i, p. 488).

155 *Burpee*, Lawrence J., *Journals and Letters of Pierre Gaultier de Varennes de la Verendrye and His Sons*, The Champlain Society *Publications*, pp. 1-3.

156 Some of the earliest visits of the British traders, supposing the reputed visit of James Mackay be left out of account, were made by men sent out by John MacDonell. See his journal of date, 1793-1795, Second Part (*Masson Papers* from *McGill University Collection*, Canadian Public Archives, Ottawa).

157 For the Creeks as agriculturalists see *Swanton*, John R., *An Indian Social Experiment* . . . *Scientific Monthly*, October, 1930, pp. 368-376.

158 They particularly noted the disinclination manifested by the Arikaras for indulgence in ardent spirits, Tabeau having evidently directed their attention to it.

159 "'. . . an intoxicated person is scarcely ever seen . . .'' (*Early Western Travels*, vol. xxiii, p. 277).

160 See *Forty Years a Fur Trader on the Upper Missouri*, vol. i, p. 144.

161 When Mitchell distributed liquor, Maximilian observed that serious consequences threatened (*Travels*, p. 264).

162 See Halsey to Chouteau, November 2, 1837 (*Pierre Chouteau Collection*, Missouri Historical Society). The *Missouri Republican*, January 20, 1838, published a letter, dated November 7, 1837, bearing a strong resemblance to Halsey's [Nebraska State Historical Society *Publications*, vol. xx, pp. 74-76].

163 See unsigned letter from New Orleans, dated June 6, 1838 (Translator's *Preface* in *Maximilian*, edition of 1843, pp. ix-x). This account was evidently written by someone on the spot; i.e., on the upper Missouri in 1837, possibly by Denig; but note the difference between the account and Chardon's. Chardon's was the simple, matter-of-fact registering of the daily enactment of a most awful tragedy. The writer of this letter, on the other

hand, gives a most highly-colored recital.   Note the exaggerations and note, also, the ignorance displayed.   He says, for instance (p. ix) that the Mandans ''a few miles below the American fort, Leavenworth . . .'' The ''melancholy details'' are here without a doubt and the story is vivid enough.   If the writer was giving information on the basis of what occurred at Fort Union then the Assiniboines and Blackfeet suffered even worse than did the Mandans.   Lloyd, the translator, says that the ''general correctness of the melancholy details'' has been confirmed by travellers (p. x).   For the same unsigned letter in Thwaites's *Early Western Travels,* consult vol. xxii, pp. 33-36.

164 For Mitchell's letter to Schoolcraft, January 28, 1852, giving a few meagre and unauthenticated details regarding the Mandans and the desolation occasioned by the small-pox epidemic of 1837, see *Schoolcraft,* Henry R., *Information Respecting the History, Condition, and Prospects of the Indian Tribes of the United States,* vol. iii, pp. 253-254.   Schoolcraft's own remarks are to be found in vol. vi, pp. 486-487.

165 *Coues,* Elliott, *Audubon and His Journals,* vol. ii, pp. 42-47.

166 May 6, 1839; but the entry was evidently added to later, since mention is made therein of the arrival at Fort Pierre the 10th.

167 See, in particular, *Journal, P. C. Jr. B. 1841-1852,* pp. 42, 78, 127, 262, 270, 271, 350.   On August 15, 1842 the balance of his account due him at Fort Pierre was $137.69 (p. 262) and, on August 19, 1842, he was debited for the amount of his account at Fort Clark, $74-78 (p. 271)   These are to be regarded as illustrative only.   His wife was baptized at Fort Clark in 1840.

168 Chardon was a passenger on the upward voyage of the steamboat in 1841 (See *Sire Log,* April 27 and June 3, 1841) and stopped at Fort Clark (*idem,* June 19, 1841).   When the boat arrived at Fort Clark on its return voyage, he was met with again (*idem,* June 30, 1841); but there is no indication that he went on down to St. Louis, notwithstanding that, on file in the St. Louis Court House, there is a document, showing that, on ''July 23, 1841, Francis A. Chardon conveyed to John B. Sarpy, trustee of Honore Picotte—a lot of ground & house in St. Louis—to secure unto Picotte the payment of a promissory note for $1000.''   The record shows that this was duly paid and that the ''deed of release was filed & recorded September 4, 1846.''

169 There is no reference to Chardon in the *Sire Log* for 1842; but he, nevertheless, may have been in St. Louis, although the business transaction, of which there is the following record, would not seem to have required, necessarily, his presence: —

''Saint Louis 18 August 1842

''*Dollars 5,000*

''On demand I promise to pay to the order of P. Chouteau Jun & Co. Five Thousand Dollars, Value received, payable & negotiable without defalcation or discount, and with interest from date at the rate of ten pr cent pr annum — same being for the benefit of Mr. F. A. Chardon

Wm- Laidlaw''

(*Pierre Chouteau-Maffitt Collection,* Missouri Historical Society).
The entry in *Journal B, op. cit.* shows that, on August 18, 1842, a sum

standing to the credit of F. A. C. was "transferred to the credit of W. Laidlaw by agreement & for which an int. of 10% per an. is to be allowed."
Among the papers in the *Chouteau-Maffitt Collection* is a statement from August 4, 1844 to December 19, 1850 of Laidlaw's note to Chardon. By the latter date, the amount owing was, seemingly, $10,863.20.

[170] See Entry June 28, 1844. ". . . des Maisons de Chardon" of June 16, 1843 may, possibly, have reference to the same locality or to another used under similar circumstances.

[171] Audubon's Missouri River journals, as they are called, extend from March 11 to November 6, 1843 and are to be found, in printed form, in *Maria R. Audubon's "Audubon and His Journals"* as edited by Elliott Coues, vol. i, pp. 450 *et seq.* and vol. ii to p. 195.

[172] Joseph A. Sire wrote to P. Chouteau from St. Louis, March 20, 1843 (*Chouteau-Maffitt Collection*) about Audubon "et ses Compaynons" to whom he declared he had afforded all the attention in his power short of delaying the boat. John F. A. Sanford had given him to understand that Mr. Nicollet would be of the party. Richard Smith Elliott, who had received the appointment to the Council Bluffs sub-agency from James M. Porter, Secretary of War, arrived in St. Louis, May 13, 1843 (*Notes Taken in Sixty Years*, p. 165), and met various men, connected more or less directly and prominently with the American Fur Company. From what he says the implication is that Sire was one of them; but, if he went up with the *Omega*, that could hardly have been the case. With the polite manners of all whom he did meet he was very much impressed (*idem*, p. 166).

[173] Coues, *Audubon*, vol. i, p. 524. Picotte and Chardon had come out to the boat from the Opposition post of Fort George (*Sire Log*), below "petit Fort-de Primeau," (*idem*, 1844). In 1847 (*Sire Log*, June 10th) the pickets of this post were cut down for wood for the steamboat. There had been talk of burning it down in 1845; but this was found impossible by Bouis because Two Kettle's Band was living in it. (Fort Pierre Letter Book).

[174] Coues, *Audubon*, vol. ii, p. 11.

[175] *Idem*, pp. 14-15.

[176] *Idem*, p. 12.

[177] *Idem*, vol. i, p. 529.

[178] *Idem*, vol. ii, p. 42.

[179] *Idem*, p. 28; *Sire Log*, entry, June 12, 1843.

[180] At Fort Pierre, Honoré Picotte had given Audubon a letter for Fort Union, "as Mr. Culbertson will not be there when we arrive" (Coues, *Audubon*, vol. i, p. 527). Larpenteur was also at Fort Union when Audubon and Chardon arrived (*idem*, vol. ii, p. 40).

[181] *Idem*, p. 50.

[182] *Idem*, pp. 42-47.

[183] Audubon wrote in anticipation of this jollification, "We are to have

a ball in honor of Mr. Chardon who leaves shortly for the Blackfoot Fort'' (*idem*, p. 42).

184 *Idem*, p. 50.

185 Not much documentary material has been forthcoming touching this period of Chardon's career.   At the Court House in St. Louis is one piece of some slight interest.   It is to the effect that, on October 8, 1843, at Fort McKenzie, Maria River, Joseph Howard conveyed to Francis A. Chardon a plot of ground in St. Louis.   One of the witnesses was Baptiste Thibeau.   This property Chardon reconveyed, September 3, 1846.

186 Chittenden, admitting that the date of this affair is not undisputed, nevertheless inclines to the opinion that the subjoined extract from a journal kept by one of the men at Fort McKenzie applies to it (*Early Steamboat Navigation on the Missouri River*, pp. 232-234, *note*).   If it does and the Indian Office accepts that view because E. A. C. Hatch, Indian Agent, Blackfeet Agency, in his report of July 12, 1856, seemed to do so — the date is fixed absolutely.   Hatch reported,

''An extract from the private journal of a man, now dead, who was at that time in the employ of the company, reads thus: 'February 19, 1844. Fight with the north Blackfeet, in which fight we killed six and wounded several others; took two children prisoners.   The fruits of our victory were four scalps, twenty-two horses, three hundred and forty robes, and guns, bows, and arrows.' ''

This is very different from the lurid account of Larpenteur as interpreted by Chittenden (*History of the American Fur Trade of the Far West*, pp. 373, 694-695) and by Coues (*Forty Years a Fur Trader on the Upper Missouri*, vol. i, pp. 216 *et seq.*) and of Culbertson as interpreted by Lieutenant James H. Bradley (Montana Historical Society *Contributions*, vol. ii, pp. 141-et seq.).   The account of James Stuart, worse yet (*idem*, vol. i, pp. 71-79), is not to be taken seriously.   It is so full of inaccuracies, mentioning Harvey, the desperado, if he were one, not at all and charging the entire affair with all its obloquy to Chardon alone.   Our query might be, Did Culbertson furnish him with the details for this article, ''Adventure on the Upper Missouri,'' as he did, in part, for his ''Journal'' of 1876 (Montana Historical Society *Contributions*, vol. ii, pp. 141 *et seq.*)?

187 Larpenteur, whose personal narrative (*Coues*, Elliott, *Forty Years a Fur Trader on the Upper Missouri*) has few references to Chardon and those of a somewhat depreciatory character, is yet somewhat fairer to him in this particular matter than is Chittenden, following after.   Larpenteur, to whom Chardon seemed ''a very singular kind of a man'' (*Coues*, vol. i, p. 144), unhesitatingly ascribed the worst features of the Blackfeet atrocity to Harvey, whereas Chittenden, although acknowledging that Harvey was ''the principal actor in that diabolical tragedy at Fort McKenzie'' (*History of the American Fur Trade of the Far West*, p. 694), yet declares that Francis A. Chardon, who had charge of the post, was ''almost as desperate a character as Harvey himself.''

188 This rival concern was ''Harvey, Primeau & Company, associated under the style of the St. Louis Fur Company'' (*Missouri Republican*, July 7, 1846).   In Picotte to Chouteau, dated Fort Pierre, July 15, 1850 (*Fort Pierre Letter Book, 1849-1850*) is an account of how the partnership came to be formed and an assertion that the others soon tired of Harvey and were about to desert him.   G. C. Matlock, Indian Agent on the upper

Missouri, who had once been in the employ of the American Fur Company, expressed, in his annual report, under date of September 25, 1848, the prevailing opinion about Harvey and his company.   It was in connection with a general statement about trade conditions.

"In regard to trade and the traders in my district of country, I have but little to say.   The company of P. Chouteau, jr., & Co., as it now stands under the new organization, I am satisfied with.   The company of Harvey, Primeau & Co., occupy a different position, from the fact of the serious charges which have been made against one of its members, Mr. A. Harvey, the senior partner.   The other members of this firm, in my opinion, are good men, and have the confidence of the Indians.   I have required the dismissal of many men (some of whom were principal traders) from the service of the company of P. Chouteau, jr., & Co., and Harvey, Primeau & Co., which has been done, and the greater portion of those ordered from the country have left."

189 In 1835, Hamilton, at all events, had a good opinion of Alexander Harvey.   On May 5th, he had occasion, in Mackenzie's absence, to write to Culbertson, who was, temporarily in charge at Fort McKenzie because Kipp was gone down to St. Louis, and said,

". . . I have engaged Mr Harvey for another year having a high opinion of his integrity and bravery (the latter a very desireable quality in this wild country) he professes his willingness to render himself useful in any and every way that you may direct   I hope you will find him a good aid."   (*Fort Union Letter Book, 1833-1835*, p. 76).

Lamont, apparently, subscribed to the foregoing; for he wrote the same day to the effect that Harvey was to take charge at Fort McKenzie should anything happen to Culbertson and Moncrèvier (*idem*).

190 See *note* 145.

191 See Appendix.

192 Thwaites, R. G., *Early Western Travels,* vol. xxiii, p. 70, *note* 51; Bradley's *Journal,* Montana Historical Society *Contributions,* vol. iii, pp. 237-238.   The initials, as given in the translation of Father Point's journal (See Appendix) are clearly wrong.

193 In his journal, Captain Meriwether Lewis recorded, "Cap C. who assended this R. much higher than I did has thought proper to call (called) it *Judieths* River . . . on the Missouri just above the entrance of the *Big Horn (Judith)* River . . ."   (Thwaites, *Original Journals of the Lewis and Clark Expedition,* vol. ii, p. 92) and Thwaites, the editor, commenting upon the same, says, "The Judith River, at first named 'Bighorn' by Lewis, was afterwards renamed by Clark in honor of Miss Julia Hancock of Fincastle, Va., who later became his wife.   She was but thirteen years of age at this time, and by her friends was nicknamed 'Judy'" (*idem, note* 1).   The nickname clung to her, however, and a picture of General Clark's first wife that I have seen in the possession of Mrs. Susan Maxon, a descendant of one of Lewis's half-sisters is labelled, *Judith.*

194 Although Bradley is mistaken in the dates he assigns to the various movements of Culbertson, he is probably not far wrong in saying that Culbertson had gone to "Fort Laramie" under protest and that he had been sent there because the Platte post had not been paying and the Company wanted it put on a better basis (Montana Historical Society *Contributions,* vol. iii, pp. 233-234).   Bradley further asserts that Culbertson not

only abandoned Fort F. A. C. but had it burnt, an act that Chardon never forgave (*idem*, p. 244, *note*). Larpenteur is confused as to the date of the burning of ''Fort Chardon'' (*Forty Years a Fur Trader on the Upper Missouri*, vol. ii, p. 237) as also Chittenden (*History of Early Steamboat Navigation on the Missouri River*, p. 233, *note*).

195 It must have been quite late in the year.   Culbertson, who had been at Fort John on the Platte, the later Fort Laramie, had gone to Fort Pierre and, in June, was taking temporary charge there in the absence of Honoré Picotte (Culbertson to Frederick Laboue at Fort John, June 26, 1845, *Fort Pierre Letter Book, 1845-1846*; A. R. Bouis to Honoré Picotte, August 31, 1845, *idem*).   Joseph Picotte had been sent to take charge at Fort John (Alexander Culbertson to Jos. Picotte, June 25, 1845, *idem*). The following letter offers a slight clue to the time of Culbertson's arrival at Fort F. A. C.: —

''I arrived here on the 28 Ulto, all well, . . .

''No news from the Blackfeet since Harvey's arrival.   Mr. Culbertson got up safe with his Boat, there is every appearance that he will make peace with the Blackfeet and make a good Trade — I hear from Mr Kipp, under date 4th Ulto — the Crow Boat reached her destination in Safety: there are more Buffaloe in the neighborhood of Fort Union this season than ever; but the Assiniboins will not hunt, no whiskey no trade at that place, there is no doubt if Mr Kipp had some of that article he would turn out this season upwards of 800 Packs, as it is he will make little or nothing, as I said above the Indians will not hunt except for what will procure them a little Tobacco and Ammtn.

''Mr. Chardon is with the Gros-Ventres at L'ours qui danse, fair prospects of a good trade there,   I am sorry however to inform you, that the Rees are very much dissatisfied that Mr Chardon has left them, they threaten vengeance, but as Mr Desautels is to winter with them with perhaps some goods, we may perhaps content them — Mr Kipp writes that the Hudson Bay Co. are trading Liquor in plenty with the Assiniboines for small furs, fortunately they will not trade Robes.   In this district the Indians are all settled for the winter, and every thing bids fair for a good trade, there is this drawback however, Mr Syblins people are on Riviere à Jaques opposing our Traders strongly, not only with a good assortment of goods but with Liquor which they succeed to smuggle from St Peters.   I earnestly request you to put a stop to this, the injury to the Outfit is considerable — I will leave in a few days to visit the Yancton Post and the Post on Riviere a Jacques and in two or three weeks will go to Fort John, but before I start for the latter place I will see Kenceller and buy him out as I promised if possible — The Yanctons prefer to have their goods purchased in St Louis and freighted up in the Co's Boat next Spring.   I told Maj Drips that I was willing to bring them up at whatever terms Capt. Sire thought proper to make.   I consider this an advantage to us, if we had paid the Yanctons this Season, they would not have been so industrious in their Hunt, and what few Robes they would have made would have cost us very dear . . .''
(H. Picotte to P. Chouteau Jr. & Co., dated Fort Pierre, December 7, 1845, *Fort Pierre Letter Book, 1845-1846*).

196 Chardon was at Fort Clark very early in the spring of 1845.   On this point, note the following:

''Mr Chardon sent an express to Upper Yanctonais Post in April last, the river on his arrival at oposite that place was full of drifting ice, and as he was unable to cross, he tied his letters to a tree and returned to Ft. Clark,   as soon as the weather permitted Frenière crossed the river and searched for the letters, but could not find them'' (H. Picotte to Chouteau, dated Fort Pierre, May 2, 1845, *Fort Pierre Letter Book, 1845-1846.*   See also H. Picotte to Capt. J. A. Sire of same date, evidently, although not so recorded in the letter book). It was Louis Frenière who was at the Yanctonais post. See Picott to Louis Frenière, March 12, 1846 (*idem*). When at Fort Union, he was described as ''Good Interpreter'' See List of 1830, no. 237. François Frenière and Jacques Frenière, both at the Teton River, were interpreters, likewise (*idem*).

197 He spent the summer there, was there in June, when Larpenteur passed by on his way to Fort Union (*Forty Years a Fur Trader on the Upper Missouri*, vol. ii, p. 222), and when A. R. Bouis addressed him by letter from Fort Pierre, August 17, 1845 (*Fort Pierre Letter Book, 1845-1846*).

198 At the time of the arrival of the steamboat in June, 1844, the Gros Ventres were found in council considering the construction of a fort (*Sire Log,* June 19, 1844).

199 H. Picotte to P. Chouteau, Jr. & Co., December 7, 1845, *Fort Pierre Letter Book, 1845-1846.*   For evidence of a parallel case, illustrating the way Indians resented a removal or proposed removal of a post, note the history of Fort St. John.   The factor, Hughes, and all his men were massacred (*M'Lean,* John, *Notes of a Twenty-five Years' Service in the Hudson's Bay Territory,* vol. i, pp. 234-236).   The Arikaras never went to such lengths; but, as late as December, 1847, they were still harboring thoughts of vengeance.   It was doubtful if they would let goods from Fort Pierre, destined for Fort Berthold, pass unmolested (See Letter to Francis A. Chardon, dated Fort Pierre, December 18, 1847, *Fort Pierre Letter Book, 1847-1848;* Letter to Louison Frenière, December 18, 1847, *idem*).

200 In the spring of 1846, Picotte declared himself willing to keep three men at Fort Clark.   He was writing to Chardon and said,

''Should the Rees be very much dissatisfied at Your removal I am willing to Keep up Fort Clark with three Men the Year round, if You think there is the least danger that the Steamboat will have difficulty with them in passing.   You will please send me down Garreau to meat [*sic*] the Boat here, if Garreau does not come, I will take it for granted that there is no risk —.''
(H. Picotte to Francis A. Chardon at Fort Berthold, dated Fort Pierre, March 12, 1846, *Fort Pierre Letter Book, 1845-1846*).

201 Picotte writing to Culbertson, October 23, 1850, specifically stated that this man was the nephew of Kipp, saying,

''Our Old friend Kipp came in Co. with Mr. Clark (Malcolm Clarke) and would have proceeded to take charge at Ft Berthold but the severe and dangerous illness of his nephew Mr Jas Desautel will delay him for some time longer'' (*Fort Pierre Letter Book,* 1849-1850).   ''Des Autel'' was with Chardon and Harvey at Fort McKenzie in 1843 (Thwaites, R. G. *Early Western Travels,* vol. xxix, p. 368, *note* 218), yet De Smet had occasion, in 1846, to speak of him as ''the amiable Mr. Des Autels'' (*Travels,* etc., vol. ii, p. 606).

202 In a report to P. Chouteau, Jr. & Co., March 11, 1846 (*Fort Pierre*

Letter Book, 1845-1846), Honoré Picotte, styling himself the "Agent of the Upper Missouri Outfit", reviewed these various matters and others in addition, revealing, incidentally, that the site had been agreed upon quite a while before and that Mackenzie and Sire had been conferred with.   That portion of his letter is worth quoting in full: —

"It was agreed with Mr McKenzie & Capt Sire to both of whom I spoke on the subject last year that the expences of Keeping up Fort Clark were too great and it was expedient to remove to *l' Ours qui danse,* in conformity with my instructions on the subject, Mr Chardon effected the removal with little or no trouble leaving Mr Desaulets at Fort Clark such goods only as were necessary to trade Corn as the Rees at that time had no Robes — Since then Mr. Chardon Mr Chardon [*sic*] has sent a good equipment to the Rees and Desaulet is trading with them   Some of them grumble it is true but the Case is far from being as bad as Harvey represented it to you . . ."

[203] The only reason that suggests itself for this name's being given is that it was intended as a compliment to James Kipp.

[204] One of the rare letters, containing references to Chardon's personal affairs, was written to him at "Fort James" in February, 1846 (Picotte to Chardon, February 24, 1846, *Fort Pierre Letter Book, 1845-1846).*

[205] Coues says (*Expedition of Lewis and Clark,* vol. i, p. 265, *note* 20) that it was named after the Tyrolese, Bartholomew Berthold.   Another opinion is, that it was the son, Pierre, whom Chardon designed to honor. Old Fort Berthold was burnt down by the Sioux and the edifice of the name, described by Boller (*Among the Indians: Eight Years in the Far West, 1858-1866,* p. 358) was really old Fort Atkinson.   It was at this place that Boller had his trading establishment (*idem,* p. 188).   For Fort Berthold as seen by Thaddeus A. Culbertson, see his *Journal, op. cit.,* p. 118).

[206] See Picotte to Chardon at "Fort Berthold," March 12, 1846, *Fort Pierre Letter Book, 1845-1846.*

[207] "Your two favors of the 11th & 26 Ulto have been duly recd. and Contents noted — I am pleased that you have removed to your present place and effected the same without any serious difficulties with the Rees.   I have no doubt but what we will eventually be the gainers by it" (Extract, Picotte to Chardon at "Fort James," December 18, 1845, *idem*).

[208] ". . . I am really well pleased to hear that you have removed to your present location, it will no doubt be beneficial to the Company as it is more in the Center of the Indians for whom it was built   success to you" (Extract, Picotte to Culbertson, October 9, 1845, *idem*).

[209] "I am flattered and thank you for your good opinion of me in giving my name to your Fort, but, I request you to substitute *Lewis* in the place of Honoré which is much more suitable and appropriate   by so doing you will oblige me — . . ."
(Extract, Picotte to Culbertson at "Fort Lewis," March 12, 1846, *idem*).

[210] A. R. Bouis at Fort Pierre, in temporary charge, kept the absent Picotte thoroughly informed of the movements of the *Opposition.*   In August, he reported that Cabanné had abandoned Fort Platte and that if he came up next fall it would be "with but a small outfit" (Bouis to

Picotte, August 31, 1845, *Fort Pierre Letter Book, 1845-1846*). Picotte's report of the elimination is as follows:

". . . We have bought out Messrs Pratte & Cabanne's interest at Fort Bernard on the Platte, we therefore have all the Country to ourselves, excepting Kanceller who is opposing us at this place with a small outfit . . ." (Picotte to Kipp at Fort Union, dated Fort Pierre, December 18, 1845, *idem*).

211 For original material bearing upon this expedition, see, particularly, *The Diary of James Kennerly, 1823-1826*, edited by Edgar B. Wesley (Missouri Historical Society *Collections*, vol. vi, no. i, pp. 47-97); the *John O'Fallon Papers* (Missouri Historical Society); and the *General Thomas A. Smith Papers* (Missouri State Historical Society).

212 T. L. McKenney to Daniel Brent of the Department of State, June 7, 1824, *Indian Office Letter Book,* no. 1, p. 101.

213 Although Kennerly, who was the brother of James Kennerly and of William Clark's second wife, was a resident of Missouri, he stood on the Indian Office record as coming from Virginia and Peter Wilson from Maryland. Similarly, Kennerly was officially serving the Sioux of the Missouri and Wilson, the Mandans (McKenney to Clark, November 29, 1825, *idem*, no. 2, pp. 260-261). For an interesting letter from George Kennerly to his brother James, dated Camp Manden, August 1, 1825, and conveying a very unfavorable impression of Benjamin O'Fallon, consult the *Kennerly Papers* of the Missouri Historical Society.

214 McKenney to Peter Wilson, June 17, 1824, *idem,* no. 1, p. 115.

215 Of one service he rendered, McKenney had this to say, after Wilson's death:

"An informal Treaty was entered into between the late Peter Wilson, Sub-agent on the Missouri, and the Assiniboines — informal only because he had no power to make it. The provisions are proper, and as these Indians are sometimes troublesome it is respectfully suggested whether due powers should not be conferr'd on the successor of Mr. Wilson with instructions to make a Treaty upon the same basis. I have the honor to enclose the Treaty together with the letter from Gen. Clark, which accompanied it . . ." (McKenney to Secretary Barbour, November 20, 1826, *idem,* no. 3, p. 233).

In the files of the Indian office, "Upper Missouri Sub-Agency," 1824, are some five letters, dated from "Bend of Missouri R." and addressed to B. O'Fallon, detailing Wilson's proceedings with the Indians, also some miscellaneous reports relating to his movements.

216 The circumstances of his last illness, death and burial were reported by Superintendent Clark in a letter from St. Louis, May 30, 1826: —

(extract) "He had been some time sick at the Mandans, the post assigned him and was brought down by the traders to Fort Atkinson, at which place he died on the 15th, soon after his arrival at that post. He was interred with honors of war and his papers and effects sent to this place."

G. H. Kennerly substituted for him during the time of his illness and, being his administrator, made application for his salary as sub-agent from December 1, 1825 to May 15, 1826 (Clark's "Book of Accounts of Benjamin O'Fallon, George H. Kennerly, and John Dougherty, Agents for the

Upper Missouri River, from September 1, 1822 to December 31, 1834,'' *Clark Books*, Kansas State Historical Society).

217 Barbour to J. F. A. ''Sandford,'' June 30, 1826, *Indian Office Letter Book*, no. 3, p. 136; S. S. Hamilton to Clark, June 30, 1826, p. 137.　He began at a salary of eight hundred a year and was receiving the same in 1830.　See Clark's ''Account Book for Upper Missouri River, 1822-1834,'' p. 47, Kansas State Historical Society.

218 *Thwaites*, R. G., *Early Western Travels*, vol. xxii, p. 235, *note* 171.

219 As a clerk in the office of the Superintendent of Indian Affairs, Sanford occasionally served in the field.　In 1825, he was paid for ''express'' service (See *Ledger*, p. 197, *Clark Books*, no. 20, Kansas State Historical Society).　In the same year, he drew a ''salary'' for service as an ''Interpreter,'' though how that could have been must remain a mystery (*idem*, p. 198).　Among the witnesses to the treaty with the Kansas Indians, negotiated by Clark, June 3, 1825 (7 *United States Statutes at Large*, pp. 244-247), appear Sanford and G. C. Sibley, the latter being styled ''U. S. Commissioner'' and *en route* to Santa Fé.

220 An account of the Dred Scott case, in which is set forth Sanford's connection, may be found very conveniently in John D. Lawson's *American State Trials*, vol. xiii, pp. 220 *et seq*.　Sanford's sister Irene was Dr. John Emerson's widow.

221 Pierre Chouteau, Jr. married Emily Gratiot and had three children born to him.　The eldest of these was Emilie, who became the first wife of Sanford, November 22, 1832 (*Collet*, Oscar W., *Compilation from St. Louis Cathedral and Carondelet Church Records*, vol. i (Marriages), p. 76) and who died on board the river steamboat, *George Collier*, on her trip from New Orleans to St. Louis, in April, 1836 (*Missouri Republican*, April 28, 1836).　The bereaved husband was left with an only child, a son, Benjamin Chouteau Sanford (*Collet*, vol. ''Baptisms,'' p. 232), who, eventually, married a daughter of P. A. Berthold.　Emilie Chouteau Sanford was only twenty-three years of age at her death, April 27, 1836 (*Collet*, vol. ''Burials,'' p. 102)　Like his wife, Sanford was, presumably, a Roman Catholic, since he is not listed as ''non-Catholic.''　For other biographical data relative to him and his connection with the Chouteaus, see *Beckwith*, Paul, *Creoles of St. Louis*.

222 *Lewis*, William S., and *Phillips*, Paul C., *The Journal of John Work*, p. 33 and, for repetition of the idea, Benton being designated, ''the vigorous champion of the fur trade,'' p. 36.

223 ''Your letter of the 26th inst to the Secretary of War, has been referred to this Office and in reply I have the honor to inform you that Gen. Clark has been instructed to order Major Sandford to his post without delay; and in the event of his resignation to appoint Wm. A. Fulkerson, Esqr. of St. Charles, Missouri, to fill the vacancy'' (Herring to Wm. H. Ashley, February 28, 1834, *Indian Office Letter Book*, no. 12, p. 155).

224 In his complaining and protesting letter of July 21, 1833, addressed to Superintendent Clark, Sanford somewhat melodramatically said, ''. . . the Government has not as yet paid for a *skin Lodge* to cover me (its worthy representative) or its goods. . . .'', yet, under date of August 31, 1828, he

had credited Nicolas Duran "with erecting two temporary houses at the Mandan villages, the one for the Sub-agent, the other for a Magazine for the public property." See Clark's *Book of Sanford's Accounts, Clark Books,* Kansas State Historical Society.

225 On this point, besides the direct evidence of Mackenzie to Fulkerson, December 10, 1835 (*Fort Union Letter Book, 1833-1835,* pp. 88-89) there is the indirect to be found in the travel narratives of the period, where mention is almost invariably made of Sanford's being a fellow-passenger with Mackenzie on the up-going boat.

226 Several times buffalo tongues were sent down to Sanford and it is rather interesting to observe that, in 1842, when he was a very influential person in the American Fur Company, he wrote, on one occasion, to Chouteau, saying, "What are we to do with our Buf. Tongues — not less than 16,000 this Year ! ! Cant they be sold in England — some of them at any rate. . ." (Letter of September 5, 1842, *Chouteau-Maffitt Collection*). Within the next few years, the market he had wished for must have been created; for Picotte wrote to P. D. Papin at Fort John, February 2, 1846 (*Fort Pierre Letter Book, 1845-1846*), saying,
". . . I find that some of your Traders eat up the Tongues they trade, I request you to put a stop to this. You know they are a cash article in St. Louis & should be taken care of . . ."

227 Sanford's conduct, however, was neither exceptional nor peculiar. It was quite the ordinary thing, from the beginning of Jackson's administration on, for traders to expect the Government to endorse their nefarious dealings. One letter, in particular, of Sanford's is fairly typical of the way he threw the influence of his position on the side of the American Fur Company. Extracts only can be here given:
"I had a talk with the Crows, made them a small present as usual — Gave a large sized medal to the Principal Chief (Rotten Belly). They are as friendly as ever but complain much of the Whites being permitted to trap Beaver in their Country. They say their Country is overun with Trappers who destroy every thing before them. They say, if it is not stopped it will be productive of mischief between us. I told them to wait for a while, & I would see what the Govt would do; for myself I had not the means, else the Trappers would long since have been out of their country . . .
"The Blackfeet have Killed only 18 or 20 the last winter but who they are I cant say . . . This does not surprise me at all, — as long as Whites are trapping in their Country it will be the case. The Blackfeet Chiefs have told me (SO) . . . They said if 'you will send Traders into our Country we will protect them & treat them well; but for your Trappers — Never' Since 18 Months a trading post has been established (the first that ever was) in their country where they come & trade amicably. It is the first attempt ever made by American Citizens to trade with them, and thus far has succeeded very well . . . It has been reported to me that the Traders of the Hudson Bay Co. come within our limits for the purpose of trading with those Indians who formerly traded with them — I should like to know what course I must pursue in this matter — whether take them — their property or what? It is evidently the duty of the Government to protect its Citizens from the Competition of Foreigners in their Country, particularly when the one pays an enormous duty & the other none at all.'
"As it regards the relation of the Indian Tribes or Nations towards each

other — I will only say that they are (as usual) at war with each other — & will always continue so.   They are hereditary foes and the facility with which they procure food gives them ample leisure to indulge in their hate & propensity for war.   It is as well so, as otherwise in this Country.   I once was a Pipe bearer amongst them and patched up a peace frequently (as others do sometimes & are doing) . . . Finding that it availed nothing, but that I was in a fair way to get *hammered* for my parental advice, I threw up my vocation (Pipe bearer or Peace Maker).

"The Indian Trade has not been as good this Year as the Last.

"This Comprises every thing necessary for the Government to Know — And indeed I hardly believe that any part of it was absolutely necessary — for I cannot & do not believe that she will ever Protect her citizens in that Country.   There has been too many reports of murders heretofore, for this to have any effect.   I might have enlarged this to a considerable size — But of what avail?"

(John F. A. Sanford to Gen. Wm. Clark, dated St. Louis, July 26, 1833, enclosed in Clark to Herring, August 17, 1833, *Files,* United States Indian Office).

228 Note his communications to Clark and direct to the Indian Office about his need for an interpreter, the claims of Charbonneau upon the consideration of the government, etc.   When a regular interpreter was denied him, he put in a claim for additional salary for himself on the score of having been his own interpreter.   On these matters note the following:

(a)   "With regard to Mr. Sandford's charge for his own services as an Interpreter, the Department requests, that when you transmit that officer's accounts, you would accompany them with your opinion of the propriety of allowing the claim" (Robb to Clark, August 7, 1832, *Indian Office Letter Book,* no. 9, pp. 127-128)

(b)   Sanford, writing to Clark about the curtailment of funds, his estimate having been "reduced by four hundred dollars for an Interpreter for the Mandans, Gros Ventres & Crows" and he having been informed through Clark that he must employ an interpreter by the day "when necessary & not by the year as heretofore" entered at length into reasons why an interpreter was needed and why this particular one, Charbonneau, should be retained.   "No one better than yourself, Sir, can state these services & their value" . . . . If I had have been extravagant in the expenses of my Agency, I might be disposed to submit quietly, but that not being the case, I cry out against it.

"I have at a moderate calculation (75,000) Seventy five Thousand Indians within my S. Agency.   These are divided into 8 different & distinct Nations, speaking languages radically different — & yet for all this, my *generous* Government thinks $400 ! ! ! for an Interpreter too expensive, & must be lopped off.   The value of our Indian Trade within my district of Country is Treble the Value of any other portion of our Country.   But on this subject I will stop.   In the last place it is unjust because I have paid & employed him by the Year & taken his receipts long before I knew of the existence of the order.   Having always been allowed this Interpreter, I had no reason to suppose, that I would be deprived of him.   He is indispensably necessary to me, in order to take care of any presents I may leave in that part of the Country.   I am not in the Navy Yard at Washington, where there are public magazines & guards to protect property.   But I am in the plains, & the Government has not as yet paid for a *skin-Lodge* to cover me (its worthy representative) or its goods . . ."   (Sanford to Clark, dated St. Louis, July 21, 1833)

(c) After a time, Clark was told to inform Sanford that the Secretary recognized the "necessity of two Interpreters for his widely extended Agency embracing so many different tribes of Indians speaking different languages — That the former allowance for Interpreters will be continued, and Mr. Charbourneau will be retained as one of them" (Herring to Clark, October 18, 1833, *Indian Office Letter Book*, no. 11, p. 253).

Under date of June 30, 1832, in Clark's *Book of Sanford's Accounts, 1828-1834*, it is recorded that the Sub-Agent charged the Government $37.50 for the hire of a "negro boy whom he has taken with him to attend on Indians" (*Clark Books*, Kansas State Historical Society). It was not an unusual thing, be it observed, for men in prominent positions themselves on the upper Missouri to have negroes, of status undetermined, in attendance upon them. On one occasion, Lamont's life was saved "by his negro boy" (*Fort Tecumseh Journal*, March 24, 1830) and, according to Larpenteur's version of the story of the Blackfeet "massacre" at Fort McKenzie, Chardon sought to avenge the murder of a negro (*Forty Years a Fur Trader on the Upper Missouri*, vol. i, pp. 217-218. See also *Chittenden*, H. M., *History of the American Fur Trade of the Far West*, vol. i, p. 373). This slave would seem to have been some one other than he whom, in 1837, Chardon had sent down to the Arikara village to learn the language (*Journal*, September 7, 1837); for that negro was seemingly the "Black Hawk" of subsequent usefulness (*idem*, January 13 and March 25, 1838) and the same who was manumitted by Chardon's last will and testament. See *note* 253.

229 In October, 1833, Clark had been informed that Sanford's request for leave of absence during the winter months had "been granted by the Secretary of War", who "has no doubt but Major Sandford will resume his official duties as early as practicable in the Spring, so that the public interest may not suffer by the absence of so valuable an officer" (Herring to Clark, October 14, 1833, *Indian Office Letter Book*, No. 11, pp. 244-245); but evidently some one soon saw cause for complaint and early the next year, Herring wrote further on the subject,

"It has been suggested to the Department, that the Agency of the Mandans &c at present under the charge of Major Sandford, is unnecessary — I am therefore instructed to apply to you for your opinion on the expediency of its continuance. And in expressing your views on the subject, you will please inform me, if you can, how long a portion of the year, the present incumbent has generally remained in his Agency. Information on the last point would probably much influence the Department in its decision respecting the future continuance of the Agency" (Herring to Clark, January 11, 1834, *idem*, no. 12, pp. 28-29).

230 "Complaints have been made to the Department of Indian Agents absenting themselves from their agencies frequently and for a considerable time. It becomes my duty therefore to instruct you that Major Sandford must immediately return to his post among the Mandans. It has been intimated to me that Major Sandford intended to resign his office. If therefore with the view of engaging in other business or for any other purpose that gentleman should decline going among the Indians of his Agency, you will give the appointment to William A. Fulkerson of St. Charles, Missouri" (Herring to Clark, February 28, 1834, *idem*, no. 12, p. 154).

231 For some things on the earlier history of his family, see *Bryan*, W. S. and *Rose*, Robert, *History of Missouri*, pp. 149-150.

232 William Neil Fulkerson, "non-Catholic," was married to Ellen St. Cyr Christy, November 30, 1826 *(Collet, O. W., Index to St. Charles Marriages, 1792-1863)*. He died, April 25, 1846, leaving her a widow with seven children. Chittenden says *(History of the American Fur Trade of the Far West* vol. i, p. 251), that it is said that Ashley was married four times. He married Elizabeth Christy, October 26, 1825, immediately after his return from his first success in the mountains. She lived only five years.

233 Ashley died in April, 1838 (Nebraska Historical *Publications*, vol. xx, p. 77). For a further account of him, see *Thwaites, R. G., Early Western Travels*, vol. xxii, p. 233, *note* 163; *Coues, Elliott, Forty Years a Fur Trader on the Upper Missouri*, vol. 1, pp. 6-7, *note* 10.

234 Mackenzie to Fulkerson, December 10, 1835, *op. cit.* See Appendix.

235 Letters to or from these men, showing how vitally interested they were in the matter and how anxiously they awaited news of the appointment of Andrew Drips, are to be found in the *Drips Papers* at the *Missouri Historical Society*. Some of them are in the *Chouteau-Maffitt Collection* there. A very considerable number of the *Drips Papers* or extracts from them are to be found published in South Dakota Historical *Collections*, vol. ix, pp. 175 *et seq.* For yet others, see Appendix.

236 *Davidson*, Gordon Charles, *The North West Company*, University of California *Publications* in History, vol. vii, p. 91.

237 Pilcher entered upon his duties in April, 1839. See Nebraska Historical *Publications*, vol. xx, p. 96.

238 The *Dougherty Papers* in the possession of the Missouri Historical Society contain much valuable information on this period of fur trade history.

239 T. Hartley Crawford to Dougherty, October 27, 1838, *Dougherty Papers.*

240 The bad feeling between these two men dated from the time of Colonel Leavenworth's expedition and is much too long a story to repeat here. Pilcher, a native of Culpepper County, Virginia, was a close friend of Benton and served, in 1817, as one of his seconds in the duel with Charles Lucas *(Meigs*, op. cit., p. 108). In 1833, he had been offered a special Indian sub-agency; but, having accepted appointment with the American Fur Company, was obliged to decline it (Herring to Pilcher, June 17, 1833, *Indian Office Letter Book*, no. 10, p. 436-437).

241 George C. Sibley was a staunch Whig and political friends of his recommended him strongly for the place. See Archibald Gamble, his brother-in-law, to him, July 13, 1841, *Sibley MSS.*, vol. ii, Missouri Historical Society.

242 Although Ramsay Crooks failed in this year of 1842 *(Neill*, E. D., *History of Minnesota*, p. 498) and the "*American Fur Co.* suspended in order to save creditors" *(Daily Missouri Republican*, September 26, 1842), the firm name continued to be used and is used here because that was the case. Note, however, that Chouteau and his friends, in the suits brought against them in 1846, tried to evade responsibility by arguing that no such firm as the American Fur Company was doing business in Missouri.

[243] Larpenteur seems to be the authority for much of what is reported regarding this affair. If, as seems probable, the attempt made upon his life occurred at Fort Chardon and while he was in charge of that post, Chardon himself could not have been directly involved in it. For the fullest secondary account, see *Chittenden*, H. M., *History of the American Fur Trade of the Far West*, p. 696.

[244] ''When I left this place to go down last Summer, I advised with Mr Culbertson and we thought it best to order Mr. Harvey to finish his time at this place; Harvey was sent here accordingly, but I am sorry to say that he appears to be very dissatisfied, he swears there was a plot made to assassinate him at the head of which is Mr Chardon, this I know nothing of. James Lee M. Clark and Old Berger attacked him and all three tried their best to Kill him but could not succeed, he is now going down in order to prosecute them, I have done every thing in my power to keep him until next Spring, but he is determined to go down; I also wished to re-hire him for two Years, but he declined for the present, if it is possible to come to some terms with him do so, provided he is reasonable, You may offer him the Charge of the Blackfeet Post as he informs me positively that Mr Culbertson is going down next Spring, and I Know of no other as Efficient as he is, besides I believe nothing else but the Charge of the Post will satisfy him — I wish you to Keep Harvey quiate, if he has difficuties with Some of the People in the Country he ought not to run down the Company for that reason; he has promised to speak to no one but yourself about his difficulties —'' (H. Picotte to Jno. B. Sarpy, at St. Louis, dated Fort Pierre, December 7, 1845, *Fort Pierre Letter Book*, *1845-1846*).

[245] ''It having been satisfactorily established by a recent investigation held at this office that Mr. Francis A. Chardon, one of the traders of P. Chouteau, Jr. & Co. has clearly violated the intercourse laws of the United States by directing the sale of spirituous liquors to Indians; and it having also been set forth *under oath* that three of the engages of the said P. Chouteau, Jr. & Co., namely, James Lee, Malcolm Clark, and Jacob Berger, have attempted the murder of an American citizen, Alex Harvey; you are hereby required to order the above named persons out of the Indian country forthwith. It is highly desirable that they should, if possible, be sent here, in order that they may be dealt with according to law'' (T. H. Harvey, Superintendent of Indian Affairs, St. Louis, to Andrew Drips, March 13, 1846, Indian Office *Files*).

[246] No general publicity can have been given to this order. In fact, circumstances point to its having been, although in some degree, at least, enforced, kept very secret. Apparently, to the end of his days, Larpenteur failed to understand why Picotte wanted him, in the summer of 1846, to supplant Malcolm Clark at Fort Lewis, where Culbertson had placed him (*Forty Years a Fur Trader on the Upper Missouri*, vol. ii, p. 237). Larpenteur carried to Clark a ''letter from the Company'' (*idem*, p. 240); but what its full purport may have been he cannot have known or ever suspected. Clark went away, however, but returned again in October (*idem*, p. 243)

and, much to Larpenteur's chagrin, with authority to resume his old command at Fort Lewis.   No explanation of such a strange procedure seems ever to have been offered to Larpenteur; but pecuniary indemnification he did get, when, after spending an entire winter out of employment at Fort Union (*idem,* pp. 244-245), he started down the river in the spring and, reaching Fort Pierre, had an interview with Picotte.   The situation was an extremely delicate one.   It was all-important not to antagonize employees just then who, enraged, might go on to St. Louis and tell too much, especially a man like Larpenteur, who had usually had at Fort Union the charge of the liquor shop (*idem,* vol. i, pp. 158, 161-162 &c).   Propitiated or detained all disgruntled persons simply had to be.   Larpenteur, being ignorant, and expecting to meet with a cold welcome from Picotte because he had left the Company's service, found himself smilingly received and, after a conversation that in no way accounted for why certain things had been done, his winter's expenses met, his anticipated savings, although unearned, made good (*idem,* pp. 246, 248-249, 250).

Chardon, too, went down to St. Louis in 1846.   Writing to Kipp, March 12, 1846, Picotte begged, ''Please not neglect and send me pr 1st opportunity Mr Chardons a/c at Blackfeet & Fort Union Otft 1844'' (*Fort Pierre Letter Book, 1845-1846*).   Was this in expectation of trouble on the horizon?   Possibly not; for only two days before, he had written letters to Chouteau and Sire of such import as indicates how little the injunction against liquor was bothering him: —

(a)   ''. . . Forty Barrels of Alcohol at least are required for the Upper Posts, as you are aware of the importance of getting that article in the Country I will say no more on the subject than this; if there had been some at Fort Union last year Mr Kipp would have traded 500 Packs more than he will and I have no doubt the difference (from the small quantity which was at the Blackfeet) in Mr Culbertson's trade will be equally as great, the loss as you will observe will be very great this year, let us try therefore to make it up next year and the only way to do that is for you to send us up at least 40 Barrels of that article by the Steam Boat or any other way which you may think expedient . . .'' (H. Picotte to P. Chouteau & Co., March 10, 1846, *idem*).

(b)   ''I have on several occasions conversed with you on the subject of getting alcohol in the Country and I request you particularly to manage some way or another to bring it up   Our Case is really a hard one, no alcohol no trade with the Assiniboines and Blackfeet'' (Picotte to Captain J. A. Sire, March 10, 1846, *idem*).

A little after the middle of May, 1846, Picotte sent word to Chouteau by Colin Lamont and Antoine Frenière, who were going down in a skiff, that he was looking daily for Kipp to arrive from Fort Union (Picotte to Chouteau, May 17, 1846, *idem*).   A month later he wrote again; but, in the interval, he must have received an inkling of impending disaster; for he wrote,

''Your despatches of the 4th. (received) . . . their contents certainly very much surprised me, for the present I refrain making any remarks thereon, but you will hear from me on the subject by return of Steam Boat, the letters destined for Messrs Culbertson & Chardon I have not sent as I am daily expecting the arrival of both these Gentlemen — Nothing from the Upper Country since my last'' (Picotte to Chouteau, June 16, 1846, *idem*).

Unfortunately, this was the last letter recorded in the *Fort Pierre Letter Book* for that year; but, from Larpenteur, it can be ascertained that Picotte went up to Fort Union in the steamboat (*Forty Years a Fur Trader on the Upper Missouri*, vol. ii, p. 237), carrying with him the aforementioned letter to Malcolm Clark.   On the way, he must have communicated with Kipp and Chardon; for the *Sire Log* records that they were descending the Missouri, in June, 1846, in charge of nine barges, laden with the returns.   In August, the following summons was issued:

"Missouri District, U.S.

The President of the United States
To the Marshal of the Missouri District
Greeting —

"You are hereby commanded to summon Francis A. Chardon that he be and appear before the Circuit Court of the United States for the district of Missouri at the next term thereof to be held at the City of St. Louis within and for said district on the first Monday of October next then and there to answer unto the United States of a plea that he render to them the sum of Eight hundred Dollars which he owes to and unjustly detains from them to the damage of the plaintiffs in the sum of five hundred dollars — Hereof fail not — And have you then there this writ —

"Witness the Honorable Roger B. Taney Chief Justice
of the United States the 4th day of August, A.D. 1846
"Issued at Office in the City of St. Louis
under
the seal of said Court this day & year last aforesaid.
J. O. Gamble, Clk.

(U. S. *vs.* Francis A. Chardon, no. 12, U.S. Circuit Court, Missouri District — October Term, 1846, *Record A.* 416, St. Louis).

While waiting for the term of court to begin, Chardon attended to various matters of business, re-conveying, for instance, to Joseph Howard, September 3, 1846, the plot of ground that he had negotiated for at Fort McKenzie three years before and paying the promissory note due to Picotte, to secure which, he had conveyed, July 23, 1841, "a lot of ground & house in St. Louis" "to John B. Sarpy, trustee of Honoré Picotte." At Fort Berthold, meanwhile, his place was being taken by Mr. Bruguière, by whom, on the nineteenth of September, Father De Smet, journeying downward from Fort Lewis, was "politely received and treated" (*Life and Travels*, vol. ii, p. 605).

247 The record of the Indian Office at Washington is that he was recalled, July, 1846.   From even the most cursory reading of his correspondence, much of which is in the possession of the Missouri Historical Society, from which extracts and a few entire letters have been published in the South Dakota Historical *Collections*, vol. ix, pp. 175-202, it can easily be surmised that his mission, from the viewpoint of its ostensible purpose, was an utter failure.   A sketch of Andrew Drips's life and character, appearing in a St. Louis newspaper, September 2, 1860 — he had died the day before, "aged 70 years" — stated that "He was truly one of nature's noblemen. Honest and upright in all his dealings, respected by all among the white men for his probity of character and noble qualities of heart, he was loved by the Indians, and looked up to as a father and a friend;" but how fitted he was for the post he presumed to attempt to fill in the early forties is best deduced from a remark of Charles Larpenteur, who knew him personally.   He says,

"Major Dripps was, I believe, a good, honest old beaver trapper.   He was sent to examine the trading posts, to find out about the liquor trade. He sent his interpreter ahead to let us know he was coming. On his arrival he looked in all places except in the cellar, where there was upward of 30 barrels of alcohol'' (*Forty Years a Fur Trader on the Upper Missouri*, vol. ii, pp. 416-417). To this same circumstance, apparently, Culbertson subscribes, although, according to his recollection, the alcohol was cached.

With a candor that might be mistaken for naiveté and not with entire accuracy since Drips was not agent for the Sioux exclusively, Thwaites says, referring to the American Fur Company and to the re-establishment of the upper Missouri Indian agency, ''In 1842, the company having encountered strong opposition, the federal government was prevailed upon to revive the office of Indian agent. Drips served four years as agent to the Sioux of the upper Missouri, with an annual salary of $1500. In this capacity, Drips rendered valuable service to the company . . .'' (*Early Western Travels*, vol. xxvii, p. 136, *note* 3). Therein lay the trouble. He rendered too good service. From first to last, he favored this purely private enterprise, connived at its customary and, indeed, notorious evasions and violations of the law, employed its men, notably Joseph V. Hamilton as a sub-agent, though him Mitchell soon dismissed, as his subordinates, and acted upon its suggestions, pursuing zealously, meanwhile, the Opposition. Not, however, until a change had been effected in the St. Louis superintendency, Mitchell ousted and Thomas H. Harvey appointed in his stead, did that greatly-abused Opposition succeed in bringing its grievances within the purview of the Indian Office, effectually. The period was one when Indian affairs were being very badly managed in many respects. Treaties were being made more in the interest of traders than of the government wards. For the influence exerted by Sanford, Chouteau, George W. Ewing, T. H. Benton and others, see the *Chouteau-Maffitt Collection*. Letters written by Benton to Chouteau, January 10, 22, 30, 1844 (*idem*) indicate what a keen disappointment the choice of Thomas H. Harvey must have been to them all.

Among its first effects was the cognizance given the Commissioner of Indian Affairs of the outrageous state of things on the upper Missouri. It came through the medium of a letter that F. Cutting, the trader at Fort George, a post belonging to C. Bolton, Fox, Livingstone & Co. (See Larpenteur, *op. cit.*, vol. i, pp. 174, 178, 179, 181), addressed to Superintendent Harvey, September 16, 1844 (*Upper Missouri Files* United States Indian Office) describing the Indian Agent's methods and making definite charges against him. In addition to the things already hinted at, Cutting said that Drips's interpreter, a certain Joseph Jewet (Juett?), was an employee of both the American Fur Company and the government, in receipt of a salary from both; but so also was Gabriel P. Cerré, for whose agreement with Drips, September 6, 1844, see *Drips Papers*. Cutting begged for early action in the premises and Harvey did act promptly, sending to Drips, December 26th, a copy of the charges against him, together with a letter from the Commissioner of Indian Affairs, dated the 13th.; but not until the spring did the special agent admit receiving the same and he then emphatically denied his guilt, alleging that Cutting had been ''instigated by malice and revenge; my presence at Yellow Stone in the winter of 1843 & 44, prevented him from selling spirituous Liquor to the Indians as he had anticipated, and fearing that this season might be attended with the same effect, he thought by having me taken out of the country at the approach of winter, no other agent could arrive here in time to interfere, with him'' (Drips to Harvey, dated Fort Pierre, April 6, 1845, *Drips Papers*). To a demand for a more specific rebuttal of the charges against him, the accused replied, June 1, 145, (*idem*) to much the same effect.

As a matter of fact, Andrew Drips was not at Fort Union but a very small part of the winter of 1843-'44. We know of his movements from his own records, particularly from a little memoranda book of miscellaneous jottings that is included in the collection at the Jefferson Memorial Building in St. Louis. In the very early summer of 1843, he had gone down to the settlements, notwithstanding that Picotte, hearing that he intended to go, had beseeched him not to do so, but to stay in the Indian country; for he well knew how much the ''Union Fur Co. people,'' by whom he meant Ebbitt, Kelsey, Cutting, etc., were ''using liquor'' (Picotte to Drips, April 12, 1843, *idem*). He had gone down in the company of Laidlaw, who had charge of ''four barges'' with ''ten thousand buffalo robes'', and, on May 18, 1843, Audubon, a passenger on the up-going steamboat, the *Omega*, talked with them and ''gave them six bottles of whiskey, for which they were very thankful'' (*Audubon and His Journals*, vol. i, pp. 499-500). This was doubtless a part of that liquor that Captain Sire had managed, with the assistance of Audubon, to smuggle into the Indian country, he and his crew having secreted it while Audubon engaged the government military inspectors in conversation (See *Sire Log*, May 10th., 1843; also, Coues's quotation of the passage therefrom in *Audubon and His Journals*, vol. 1, p. 479, *note* 1) or it may have been a part of Audubon's private supply. When Sir William Drummond Stewart was about to start out upon one of his expeditions into the Indian country, Mitchell had granted him a ''permit'' to take spirituous liquors for himself and party (D. D. Mitchell to Stewart, April 28, 1843, *Sublette Papers*, Missouri Historical Society) and he, communicating with William L. Sublette, May 1, 1843, had advised him ''to take along some whiskey for they are a thirsty party,'' adding that he could ''get it under his permit'' (*idem*). What Mitchell would do so readily for Stewart, he would certainly do for Audubon, whom he especially commended to the good offices of Drips (Mitchell to Drips, April 19, 1843, *Drips Papers*), particularly as it had been half-expected that Nicollet would be with him (Jos. A. Sire to P. Chouteau, March 20, 1843, *Chouteau-Maffitt Collection*). When Audubon was in partnership with Ferdinand Rozier at St. Genevieve he had himself dealt in liquor on a large scale, purchasing at Louisville, on one occasion, ''a keel-boat, with . . . 310 barrels of good Kentucky Whiskey'' (*Rozier, Firmin A., History of the Early Settlement of the Mississippi Valley*, p. 289).

In July, 1843, Superintendent Mitchell was anxious that Drips, the sleuth-hound, should get back as soon as possible to his work and wrote that ''understanding that Mr. Laidlaw would leave Liberty some where about the 1st of August, I have concluded that this will be the most favorable opportunity for you to proceed to your agency and resume your important duties . . .'' (Mitchell to Drips, July 25, 1843, *Drips Papers*). The two men left Laidlaw's farm near Liberty on August 18th. and arrived at Fort Pierre, September 4th. Ten days later, Laidlaw left for Fort Union ''with Two small Waggons & his Family'' (*Note-book, Drips Papers*. See also *Audubon and His Journals*, vol. ii, p. 165), Culbertson departing four days subsequently for Fort John. Drips, in December, made a trip to the ''Forks of Chyanne, Started for Fort Union Jany 7 . . . arrd at Fort Clark on 23d — Snow deep & Stormy continually —

Left the Mandans & Big Bellys on 28th and arrvd at Fort Union on 8th Feby.'' (*Note-Book, Drips Papers*).

If Laidlaw conducted himself this winter of 1843-'44 as he had in that of 1840-'41, when, if Larpenteur's chronology is to be depended upon, he was also at Fort Union, Drips ought to have arrived earlier and, when he did arrive, have found plenty to do. It is of that earlier winter that Larpenteur tells his objectionable Trinity story. He says, ''My being a sober man was not to my advantage, keeping me constantly in the liquor trade, and out of the charge of posts which some of my fellow-clerks took charge of, while I did all the work, and was really in charge when they got dead drunk. Mr. Laidlaw the Father, Mr. Denig the Son, and Mr. Jacques Bruguière the Holy Ghost, formed the Trinity at Union . . . and a trio of greater drunkards could not have been got together. The consequence was that the large meat trade was lost. Indians would trade robes with Mr. Laidlaw in the office, steal them back, and trade them again with Mr. Bruguière at the regular shop. The reason why Mr. Laidlaw opened trade in the office was, he said, that Bruguière got too drunk to hold out; but Laidlaw was the greater drunkard of the two'' (*Forty Years a Fur Trader on the Upper Missouri*, vol. i, pp. 161-162).

It was only to be expected that Andrew Drips's friends of the American Fur Company should rally to his defence. The method taken by Kenneth Mackenzie and John B. Sarpy indicated that they were not above resorting to a kind of legal quibble. The affidavits they made, being exactly alike, there is no need of quoting but one:

''State of Missouri   )ss
County of St. Louis)

Kenneth MacKenzie being sworn upon his oath says that he is a member of the firm of P. Chouteau Jr & Co. at St. Louis Mo. which said firm is employed in trading with the Indians on the Upper Missouri — that no such company as the American Fur Company exists in the State of Missouri — that he is acquainted with Andrew Drips Indian Agent for the United States — that said Drips is not now and has never heretofore been a partner in the firm of P. Chouteau Jr & Co — that he has not been and is not now in any manner interested with said P. Chouteau Jr. & Co. in their trade with the different Indian tribes or any or either of them in any manner way or form whatever.

Sworn to and subscribed
before me this first day
of July 1845 at St. Louis, Mo.

Geo. A. Hyde Justice of the Peace in and for the County of St. Louis State of Missouri.'' (*Upper Missouri Files*, Office of Indian Affairs).

The American Fur Company as such had, it is true, gone out of existence in 1842. Reverses had ''compelled an assignment'' (*Kelton*, Dwight H., *The American Fur Co.*, Michigan Pioneer and Historical *Collections*, vol. vi, p. 347) and the inventory had been purchased by P. Chouteau Jr. & Company of St. Louis (*Neill*, E. D., *History of Minnesota*, p. 498; *Sibley*, H. H., *Memoir* of *H. L. Dousman*, Minnesota Historical Society *Collections*, vol. iii, pp. 196-197). Of its condition, the following notice, copied from the *New York Express*, appeared in the *Daily Missouri Republican*, September 26, 1842:

''*Amer. Fur Co.* suspended in order to save creditors. The large business could not be carried on without large advances to Indians & traders. Heavy advances already made, and large stock of furs on hand & Co. is unable to sell them here or abroad on account of disastrous times. Creditors will not lose anything assures the pres. Ramsay Crooks. He is a large stockholder, having invested his entire fortune in the Co.''

And, though Andrew Drips was not, when appointed Special Indian Agent, a "partner", as Cutting had charged (Cutting to Harvey, September 16, 1844, *op. cit.*), he did, unquestionably, become one, at least of the Upper Missouri Outfit, in 1848. Indeed, he went back to his old employment almost immediately upon his dismissal from the Indian service and, in 1847, when Picotte went his rounds, visiting the various posts, was *locum tenens* at Fort Pierre (See *Fort Pierre Letter Book, 1847-1848*). The subjoined extracts of a letter show what happened next:

"We wrote you last on the 1st inst. by Constant Provost, to which letter we refer.

"Having reorganized the business to carry on the trade in the Upper Missouri for the term of Two Years, to begin from this season including the goods sent this spring by Steam Boat 'Martha', and Mr. James Kipp being one of the parties to the new arrangement, he is now on his way to Fort Pierre and will remain there untill the arrival of Mr. Alexander Culbertson who has been appointed and by contract is the Agent of Upper Misso. Outfit in the place of Mr. He. Picattel [Picotte.]

"In the new arrangement we have kept *one Share* for you, with the understanding that as the other Interested parties, (except Mr. Culbertson) you shall receive no Salary. — which, from the conversation you have had with Mr. Sarpy we suppose will be accepted. Mr. James Kipp has an equal share, Mr. W. Laidlaw one also and Mr. Frederick Laboue the same, *all* without receiving any salary — Mr. A. Culbertson of course has one Share. The last share to make up the Six Shares forming One half of the interest in the outfit is to be disposed of by Mr. Culbertson after he gets in the Indian Country.

"Mr. P. D. Papin declining to return in the Missouri as well as Mr. Picotte, we have decided that you shall have the charge of Fort John, except Mr. Culbertson should decide otherwise — This post will require a good & carefull manager and a person well acquainted with land transportation. We have thought you would fill it to advantage. When Mr. Culbertson reaches Fort Pierre, it will be then decided whether *he* shall remain there or Mr. Kipp . . .   '' . . .''

(P. Chouteau Jr. & Co. to Major And. Dripps, Fort Pierre, dated August 18, 1848, *Drips Papers*).

[248] There was some doubt as to whether a suit would lie upon the bond because the license of date, April 19, 1843, had not first been revoked. On this point note the following:

"Office Indian Affairs
April 14, 1846

"Harvey, Maj. T.H.
"St. Louis, Mo.
"Sir

"Your report on the various charges preferred against P. Chouteau Jr. & Co. together with the testimony and accompanying papers, came to hand on the 23d ulto, and your proceedings in the matter are approved and deemed highly satisfactory.

"Upon a careful examination of the testimony, I concur with you fully in the conclusions to which you arrived, and but for the introduction of other considerations which may not have been urged before you, would have had no hesitation in directing that your recommendations be carried into effect.   A number of Affidavits were affixed, however, with the view of discrediting a portion of the Witnesses and contradicting or very materially varying the facts set forth in the evidence taken by you, which being *ex parte* in their character could not be received, together with a written statement from P. Chouteau which in the opinion of the Secretary of War threw some doubt on the propriety of revoking the license of the Company without a further hearing.   It is therefore deemed best by the Secretary that the bonds be immediately put in suit & that the revocation of the license be postponed for the present.

"Some doubts having arisen as to whether Suits will lie upon the bonds under the provisions of the Intercourse law, until after the license is revoked, the Company by L. V. Bogy Esqr. their Attorney, as you will perceive by the accompanying paper, have agreed to waive any advantage that might arise from that omission on the trial, as well as all other technicalities & plead to the merits only.

"You will consult the District Attorney of the United States & if the paper signed by Mr. Bogy is not sufficient for the purposes intended, he will prepare another & have it signed, & forthwith commence suits on such bonds as will cover all the alleged violations of the Intercourse law which in your judgment can be established since February 11, 1842, the date of Mr. Secretary Spencer's order.

"W. M. (edill)"

(enclosure)

"P. Chouteau Jr. & Co., licensed traders, having been charged with introducing into the Indian Country and selling to the Indians Spirituous liquors in violation of the intercourse law, an investigation was had before Thomas H. Harvey, Superintendent of Indian Affairs, at the City of St. Louis, commencing on the 5th day of March, 1846, and the same reported to the Commissioner of Indian Affairs for his direction in the premises, accompanied with a recommendation from the said Harvey that the license of the said Company be revoked and their bond put in suit.

"And the said P. Chouteau Jr. & Co. desiring a further & more perfect examination of the said charges before they shall be deprived of the privilege of carrying on their business with the Indians, request that their license be not revoked until a trial at law be had upon their bond, and the Department placed in possession of the facts thereby elicited; and expressing a willingness to waive all and every kind of technicality, acquiesced in a speedy trial upon the merits of the case and claim no unnecessary or unreasonable delay.

"With this view and to enable the Government to bring a suit upon their bond without first revoking the license, as in the opinion of some, would be necessary under the law in question, the said Company by Lewis V. Bogy Esqr their attorney hereby expressly agrees that no advantage shall be taken on such trial of the fact that the license was not first revoked or of any other technicality not essential to a fair & full investigation & decision of the case on the merits thereof.

" (Signed) Lewis V. Bogy, Atty pr Co.
"April 1846"

249 Not only was there a special case against Chardon; but his offense was included in the complaint of the United States *vs* Pierre Chouteau, Jr., Kenneth Mackenzie, and John B. Sarpy:

"And for a further breach of said condition of the said writing obligatory, the said plaintiffs aver that the said Pre Chouteau Jr. & Co., after the making of the said writing obligatory, did at Fort Union and Fort

MacKenzie, and at the other trading posts in said condition mentioned, on the first day of May in the year 1843 and at divers other days and times between the said first day of May, 1843 and the thirty-first of March, 1844, suffer their clerk, to wit, Francis A. Chardon to sell and vend spirituous liquors (to wit, a mixture of alcohol and water capable of producing intoxication) to the Indians frequenting the said forts and trading posts contrary to the form & effect of the condition of the said writing obligatory''
(Record B, 11 & 12)

        ''In the United States Circuit Court, October Term, 1846,.
''United States of America
''District of Missouri   For the District of Missouri
    ''The United States of America complain of Francis A. Chardon of a plea that he render to them the Sum of Eight hundred Dollars which he owes to and unjustly detains from them.

    ''For that Said Defendant heretofore to wit on the first day of July in the Year eighteen hundred and forty four and at divers other days and times between said . . . and the commencement of this action . . . did sell, barter, exchange, give and dispose . . .

    ''And also that said Defendant on the first day of August in the year Eighteen hundred and forty four did introduce into that portion of the Indian Country West of the Mississippi . . . a large quantity of spirituous liquors; to wit, one hundred gallons of alcohol . . .'' (Record, A, 416)

    Among the subpoenas for the plaintiffs, it is noteworthy that, in the Chardon case, two, at all events, were dated April 26, 1848, and, therefore, subsequent to what has been held to have been the day of his death (See No. 433-1848-A405).

250 Although neither Larpenteur, who passed by in the spring (*Forty Years a Fur Trader on the Upper Missouri*, vol. ii, p. 246), nor Father Nicholas Point, who, travelling by barge from Fort Lewis to Fort Union and thence by the *Martha*, reached Westport, July 7th (See *Journal*, found by Father Garraghan in Rome), seems to have seen him, he was certainly there by August; for the ''S. Chardon, Fort Berthold,'' to whom Gideon C. Matlock wrote on the 13th., could have been no other than he. Matlock had been appointed United States Indian Agent for the upper Missouri in the preceding March and any ignorance of names he may have exhibited, was somewhat excusable. His reason for writing was to obtain certain statistical information that by a late law of Congress he was obliged to collect (G. C. Matlock to S. Chardon, August 13, 1847, *Chouteau-Maffitt Collection*). Matlock was an ex-employee of the American Fur Company and how little fitted he was to be an Indian Agent is to be seen from the opinion Larpenteur gives of his character. He was a ''drunken gambler.'' given over, at a time possibly later than this, to ''drinking and gambling'' and the keeping of ''several Mormon women'' (*Forty Years a Fur Trader on the Upper Missouri*, vol. ii, p. 416). Between Drips and Matlock had come, as Indian agent, Thomas P. Moore, another ''great drunkard,'' according to Larpenteur, ''who came up to Union in the steamer, remained 24 hours, and returned to Fort Pierre'' (*idem*). On the inside cover of the *Fort Pierre Letter Book, 1845-1846*, are two rough notes that bear out, to some extent, Larpenteur's summing up. One of them is to the effect that Colonel Moore had said, ''if he came up next spring,'' he would allow ''alcohol for Assiniboines & Blackfeet,'' the other, that ''Mr Slaughter told every one from Col Moore to Cook that I and every trader on board G. Brook were Drunk when we landed at Vermillion   I — so much so.

that he had to write my letter to some one — . . .'' For further references to Chardon at Fort Berthold in 1847, see letters written by ''H. P. per W. D. H., to Kipp, to Chardon, and to Louison Frenière, December 18, 1847 (*Fort Pierre Letter Book, 1847-1848*). In speaking of Father Point, one is reminded that, in this year of 1847, he was very much averse to extending his downward journey as far as St. Louis, being afraid that the enemies of Chouteau might compel him, to the embarrassment of himself and of his work, to testify in the case then pending. See his letter, dated, On Board the Martha, July 5, 1847, *De Smet MSS.*, St. Louis University. In 1848, that Father De Smet was wanted as a witness is indicated by the following:

''Witnesses for Plaintiffs

'' . . .

''Aug. 14, 1848. P. J. D Smith, or De Smith, a Catholic priest of whom information can be had at St. Louis University''. He was not one of those, apparently, for whom ''diligent search'' was made in vain; but, in 1847, Alexander Harvey was and then or earlier or later many another material witness.

251 On his upward journey, Palliser either made no stop at Fort Berthold or had no occasion to refer to it, yet the nature of his first allusion to Chardon would lead us to infer that he was already acquainted with him. He may, of course, have met with him at one of the other posts or simply have heard of him. At any rate, there came a time when he decided to accept Chardon's invitation to come to the ''Minitaree Fort'', an invitation that had been brought to him when he was with his ''friend, Owen Mackenzie,'' at the White River post (*Solitary Rambles and Adventures of a Hunter in the Prairies* (1853), pp. 165, 166-167, 174, 191). He got as far as Knife River, then rested a bit, then walked across the Grand Detour, ''a sinuosity in the river, forming a bend of about forty miles in length; but the chord, or, in popular words, the short cut of which is hardly fourteen'' (*idem*, pp. 191-192, 196). On April Fool's day, he reached Fort Berthold and availed himself ''of Mr. Chardon's hospitable invitation to the Fort'' (*idem*, p. 197; *Palliser*, Captain John, *The Solitary Hunter*, or *Sporting Adventures in the Prairies* (1856), p. 142.

252 (Chap. VIII) ''I found,'' writes Palliser, ''poor Mr. Chardon very ill, with a violent attack of rheumatism; but my arrival cheered him very much and what little news I could bring him of his friends at Fort Union and the White River posts, was very acceptable'' (Palliser, 1853, p. 198; 1856, p. 143). On April 6th, ''Boucharville, one of the most celebrated of the hunters and trappers of the Indian regions,'' came into Fort Berthold and Palliser, finding it possible to make some arrangement with him, ''proposed that, as soon as the ice broke up in the Missouri, we should start off on foot back to Fort Union, making nearly straight across the prairie instead of following the sinuosities of the river, as I had done in my winter journey . . . He liked the project, and so we made it a bargain . . . About this time poor Mr. Chardon became worse: the rheumatism had attacked him very severely in both legs, and he was unable to stand; but I never saw a man more patient under suffering or more grateful when any one relieved the wearisome dreary hours by sitting and talking with him'' (Palliser, 1853, pp. 198-199, 200).

''The 17th of April was a memorable day. About day-break the ice broke up on the Great Missouri river; the explosion, as the water burst the rotten mass upwards, was like distant thunder. We rushed to the high bank on which the fort is built, and from its gate watched the various sized packs of frozen blocks floating by, roaring with a splendid sound as mass after mass passed onward forcing aside all resistance and sweeping everything before it.   The ice continued to roll by for thirty hours, keeping up a continuous roar — it was a beautiful and, to me, a very novel sight.

''I now bethought myself of starting on my journey to Fort Union for my horses, and, therefore, engaged two more men to complete my party . . . We took with us a small supply of dry meat, some coffee, a little bag of biscuits which Mr. Chardon gave me, and a large quart-bottle of molasses to sweeten our coffee.. . (*idem*, p. 202)

After ''eight days' marching'' (*idem*, p. 208), Palliser and his companions arrived at Fort Union (*idem*, p. 205); but they made no long stay there and, when they set forth again, felt that Denig, who was in charge, was probably glad to see them depart; for food was scarce (*idem*, p. 207).   They proceeded up the Yellowstone, hunting and trapping as they went (*idem*, pp. 218, 223-224, 225).   Palliser even made some new clothes for himself (*idem*, p. 230).   Finally, when their camp was full of meat, which the men had spent ''all their leisure hours and most of the time while I was hunting and tailoring,'' in preserving, it seemed time ''to return down the Yellow Stone to Fort Union, there to take up the skiff that we had buried at the mouth of the river, and to row down from thence to the Minitaree Fort — about two hundred and eighty miles down the Missouri'' (*idem*, p. 235).   ''The season was now late in May'' and Palliser greatly wished ''to make another hunting trip and try'' his ''fortunes in grisly-bear hunting before the return of the American Fur Company's steamer in July'' (*idem*).

When they again reached Fort Berthold — and, although Palliser gives no date, it must have been late in May — they ''pulled into the Fort in time for breakfast, welcomed by poor Mr. Chardon, who was the bourgeois, or head manager . . .''   ''He had then been for a long time ill with rheumatism, and on my return to the Fort I found him worse.   He seemed quite to long for any one to talk to him and enliven the weary hours that he passed on his sofa hardly able to stir, so I occupied myself in making some shot, while I recounted my adventures to him, or laid plans for future expeditions.   In the evening I generally joined the Indians, and sat with the old men watching the women playing at ball, or the young men at their different games . . . The weather had now become warm, and the place was decidedly unhealthy, owing to the vile habit these Indians have of not burying their dead . . .'' (*idem*, pp. 260-261).

Continuing his retrospective narrative, Palliser says, ''A day or two afterwards poor Mr. Chardon requested me to write his will for him, which I did.   He dictated everything correctly and sensibly, and the day after signing it, died surrounded by us all, detailing to us with his last breath how some years before he had gone out after a buffalo with another man, and while passing through some willows behind his companion, his gun had gone off, shooting the latter dead at his feet.   Unfortunately they were known to have quarrelled, and were never on very good terms with one another, so that some had unjustly accused him of having designedly shot the unfortunate man; but poor Mr. Chardon's last words were, 'As I am going before my God, it was an accident.'   Poor fellow !   I felt very much cast down at his death, and as I had ever since my arrival at the Fort suffered from dysentery, occasioned by the smell of all the dead bodies about the village, I went to Boucharville's lodge, and sounded him as to his feelings upon the subject of a second hunt . . . So we finally arranged to set off next day, convey the horses across with my skiff, hunt up the little Missouri, and try the Turtle Mountains, famous for grisly bear.'' (1853, pp. 262-263; 1856, pp. 188-189).

(Chap. XI) ''As on the former occasion . . . I got well away on the opposite prairie, and once out of sight and smell of the Fort, my spirits rose, my appetite returned, and the dysentery departed.   We camped late in the evening beside a refreshing stream, which flowed through a beautiful copse, and spread our beds among the now fragrant rose-bushes; what a change from the noxious atmosphere of the Fort !   We sat long talking of poor Mr. Chardon as we smoked our pipes and sipped our coffee after supper, till one by one fatigue overcame us, and we slept soundly till dawn. . .'' (*idem*, 1853, p. 264).   On the fourth day after leaving Fort Berthold, they reached Turtle Mountain, where he had heard grisly bears were usually to be found in a great number; but to this fact he proved unable to bear testimony, it being only ''the month of June, far too soon for fruit'' (*idem*, p. 265; 1856, p. 190)

253 In due course, the steamboat, *Martha*, made her appearance at Fort Berthold (Palliser, 1853, pp. 286-287), at which point, it would seem Palliser boarded her.   He says it was then ''late in July;'' but, none the less, she reached St. Louis on the 24th (Springfield, Missouri *Advertiser*, July 25, 1848) and, on the 26th, Chardon's will was admitted to probate. According to some *MS. Notes*, prepared by Judge W. B. Douglas, Palliser appeared in the St. Louis Probate Court on the 18th and gave testimony regarding Chardon's will; but to have been able to do that he must have arrived in advance of the *Martha.*   Not until the 26th did the other witness, Edmond Rollette, give his testimony.   The will, as probated, was as follows:

''I wish to leave 5000. dollars to Manzaischata and his brother Mankezeeta, and to my wife Ellen, (a ½ breed woman of the Sue Nation) and this sum I wish to have disposed of in the following manner,   Ellen for the term of 15 years dating from my decease to have the interest of this money yearly, for the support of herself and 2 Children.   At the expiration of that time, each Boy shall receive 2000. dollars, and my Wife Ellen 1000.

I bequeathe a hundred dollars for the erection of a Tomb Stone over my departed Mother at Philadelphia.

All the rest of my property Personal and Real estate Silverware, 'et cetera' I bequeathe to my Son Bolivar at the age of 19.

All portion of that property capable of bearing Interest, to be funded for him and he shall enjoy the Interest only until he arrives at that age.

To my Negro Boy, 'Black Hawk,' I give his Liberty.

I appoint Pierre Alexander Berthold my Executor.

Fort Berthold, Minitaree Village, April 20th, 1848

F. A. Chardon

Temoins { John Palliser
{ Edmond Rollette ''

The bequest for erecting a tombstone over the remains of Chardon's mother in Philadelphia was duly attended to by A. C. Williamson, Bolivar's guardian.   See *Receipt*, September 1, 1851, *Chardon Estate Papers, op. cit.* The estate itself was quite considerable and, on it, the Executor, made the following report:

"No personal goods and chattels came to my hands as the deceased died in the Indian Country: —

"Notes and accounts.

1. Note of hand drawn by William Laidlaw; 7th August 1844, in favor of said Francis A. Chardon six years after date; for this sum of six thousand Dollars; bearing interest at the rate of ten per cent per annum; payable annually; which interest, & no part of it, as I am informed, has ever been paid.

Note	$6000.00
Interest on said note for six years, up to 7th August 1850	3,600.00
said note and interest is secured by deed of trust given by the said William Laidlaw on real estate in Clay County Missouri.	
There is due to the deceased from Messrs P. Chouteau Jr. & Co. as per their account rendered to me, 20 November 1849	3959.16
	$13,559.16

"Real Estate
A certain lot of ground with a brick house in the city of St. Louis . . . on Second Street. . . and is the same lot of ground which was acquired by the said Francis A. Chardon from Honoré Picotte and Therese his wife; by deed dated 23rd day of July 1844; and recorded in the Recorder's Office at St. Louis County in Book J no. 3, page 283.

The rents will appear from my account current.

"The foregoing constitutes all the property of the deceased which has come to my Knowledge in the State of Missouri. The deceased is said to have had at the time of his death, some real estate in the State of Pennsylvania; but as it is beyond the jurisdiction of this State; & I am not able to give a description of it, & will require to be looked after by an administrator in the State where it lies it has been considered unnecessary to say more of it in this inventory.

"P. A. Berthold

"Sworn to and Subscribed
before me this 12th day of December 1849"

(*idem*)

Laidlaw became insolvent and Chardon's estate received on his note of hand only the amount due for interest, $3487.10 (*idem*)

The subsequent fate of Chardon's negro boy, Black Hawk, history does not record. (*MS. Notes* of Judge Douglas)

254 The exact date of Chardon's decease it has been impossible to ascertain. Palliser asserts that he died the day after affixing his signature to his will. Does the date on the will signify the time of signing? Most certainly not; for, unless Palliser is very much out in his reckoning, Chardon was yet alive in May. A notice that appeared in the St. Louis *Republican*, June 1st, 1848, and in the St. Louis *Reveille*, June 5th, though interesting, is not to be taken as, in any sense, reliable on this point: —

"Died on the 20th of April last, at Fort Berthold, one of the trading posts of P. Chouteau, Jr., & Co., on the Upper Missouri river, Mr. Francis A. Chardon, after a short, but distressing illness.

"His remains were interred at Fort Pierre, on the Missouri.

"Mr. Chardon has been, for many years, one of the most prominent and distinguished traders in the Indian country, and his loss will be deeply regretted by all who knew him.

"(Philadelphia papers please copy)"

The remarkable thing is that no letters of the time, yet found, refer in any way whatsoever to his death, although it is evident from the *Fort Pierre Letter Book, 1847-1848* that, as early as May 9, 1848, Pierre Garreau had charge of affairs at Fort Berthold. The last letter in this book, sad to say, is of this date, May 9th. It is one addressed to Denig at Fort Union, mentioning the safe arrival of Culbertson and Kipp at Fort Pierre, the day before. They had come down with the returns, five mackinaw boat loads. Kipp had not been well and he, apparently, went on to St. Louis, while Culbertson remained to be a passenger on the *Martha* (Springfield, Missouri *Advertiser*, July 25, 1848). Did he linger behind for Chardon's obsequies? He is his own authority for the statement that he interred the body at Fort Pierre. For the sinking of the *Martha*, see Nebraska State Historical Society *Publications*, vol. xx, p. 172.

255 At the suggestion of Dr. H. M. Hamblin, who first discovered the Nicollet chest, and myself, its contents were transferred, some time since, from the Topographical Bureau of the War Department to the Library of Congress. They are now in its Manuscripts Division. For further information respecting the contents of the chest and the circumstances of its finding, see Mississippi Valley Historical *Review*, vol. viii, pp. 149-152 and *notes*.

256 *Sibley*, Henry H., *Memoir of Jean N. Nicollet*, Minnesota Historical Society *Collections*, vol. i, p. 153.

257 Nicollet reached Fort Pierre, June 12, 1839 (See *Report Intended to Illustrate a Map of the Hydrographical Basin of the Upper Mississippi River*, Senate Document, no. 237, 26th Congress, 2nd session, p. 41), the seventieth day out from St. Louis (*Frémont*, J. C. *Memoirs of My Life*, p. 38). Accompanied by Frémont, he had left St. Louis on board the American Fur Company steamer, the *Antelope*, June 4th (Nebraska State Historical Society *Publications*, vol. xx, p. 97). Laidlaw and Kipp were among his fellow-passengers. The provisions for his expedition had been sent on two days before (Nicollet, *Journal of 1839*, entry for April 27th) by a smaller boat, the *Pirate*, which, unfortunately, was soon reported lost (Letter of Nicollet, May 4, 1839, Topographical Bureau, *Letters Received*, vol. i, p. 348), it being one of many vessels that have come to grief on that most treacherous of streams, the Missouri. Arriving at Fort Pierre, Nicollet had found Papin and Halsey there just as had Chardon, arriving on May 10th and, from that place, June 22nd, he reported upon the progress to date of his expedition (*idem*, p. 365). His own journal for 1839, a manuscript in the War Department chest, goes only from April 21st to May 11th; but two tiny note-books carry on the story.

258There was nothing particularly worthy about Charbonneau. For the most part he shines by reflected glory, the glory that is Sacajawea's halo. For a detailed sketch, apportioning him praise and blame, as deserved, see *Drumm*, Stella M., *Journal of a Fur-Trading Expedition on the Upper Missouri, 1812-1813*, pp. 135-140. To it, as far as his character goes, there is very little to be added, except, perhaps, the specific information that is obtainable from the second part of the *Journal of John*

MacDonell, 1793-1795 (Photostats, *Masson Papers*, Public Archives, Ottawa), which was kept "at the Fort of the River qui appelle, calld by Mr— Robert Grant ~~when he built it~~ Fort Esperance—"

[1793, November] "Wednesday 6th— Five men, 5 loaded Horses, & five Dog Trains started with Goods for Mr. Grant's R.Tremblante —

found trading 1801 in (?) Lake Isle a la Crosse Peltier, Old Robert Taylor (free Man from the Missouri∧) & Tousst. Charbonneau, Gervais, and Bellair Started for the Pine Fort . . ."

[1794, February] "Saturday 1st— Sent Five men for meat — Sent for the Hunter to guide the Men to the Buffalo *Parc* who instantly answered the call —

Sunday 2nd— Cochin le noir, Pierre Fortin & Tousst. Charbonneau guided by the Hunter started en traite to the *Parc* — . . ."

[October] "Thursday 2nd— . . . Mr Grant started early next morning for the River La Coquille where Mr Peter Grants people have built a Fort this summer — This place is half way between here & Mr. Grants residence of last year about 14 to 15 Leagues over land — . . ."

[November] "Monday 10th— P. Etienne Ducharme & Tousst. Charbonneau arrived from the Fort of River La Coquille —"

"Wednesday 12th— . . . André Claude & La Buisse went to the River la Coquille with Charbonneau & Ducharme . . ."

[December] "Saurday 13th— Louis Claude & Tousst. Charbonneau returned from River La Coquille . . ."

"Wednesday 17th— La Graine &c traded & went off. Sent Charbonneau and Little Desmarais with them for a Horse I bought from Poitras adopted son . . ."

"Tuesday 23rd— . . . Pe. Desmarais & Charbonneau return'd from La Graines with the Horse they went for."

"Wednesday 31st— The five young men who arrived the two preceding days went off — Sent St. Dennis & Charbonneau with them with two Galls. Rum for Tabault & one Gallon for Chienfou's brother —"

[1795, January] "Tuesday 6th— St. & Charbonneau came from Tabault's . . ."

[March] " Tuesday 3rd— La Brie, Charbonneau, & one of Peter Grants men came from Mountain a la Basse who brought me 10 Carrots Tobacco, 7 dozn. La Knives, 12 Dozn. Small Do. . . ."

"Wednesday 4th— . . . St. Denis, Charbonneau, & St. Pierre set out for Mountn. a la Basse to court the Foutreau's daughter a great beauty . . ."

"Monday 9th— Bellair & Coquotte came from Mountain a la Basse to stay here the one having changed with Charbonneau & the other with Bedard —"

[May] "Saturday 30th— Tousst. Charbonneau was stabbed at the *Manitou-a-banc* end of the P. l. P. [Portage la Prairie] in the act of committing a Rape upon her Daughter by an old Saultier woman with a Canoe Awl

∧— a fate he highly deserved for his brutality— It was with difficulty he could walk back over the portage . . ."

259 It is rather interesting to note that in the very same month of September, 1836, when William Nourse made his report on "General Dickson"

that brought the man and his projects, real or imaginary, to the attention of the Canadian authorities (See Nourse to John Siveright, dated Sault St. Marys, September 15, 1836 (G. series, vol. 78, pp. 519-529, Public Archives, Ottawa), the Scotch traveller, James Logan, having left Edinburgh, May 30th, arrived at Sault Ste. Marie, heard of Dickson from the United States Indian agent, and made the following record:

''About a week before I arrived at this place, a person calling himself General Dickson had set out with a party of about twelve or fourteen men, in order to conquer California. Major Cobb, with whom he had frequently dined, gave me an account of his plan, which was to engage some of the most warlike tribes of the Indians. He assured the Major that he had been corresponding with some of their leaders, who only waited his arrival to bring to his aid from two to three thousand men, who would drive out the Spaniards, and, taking possession of the country, constitute it a free state with an elective government and presidency. He himself was to be chief in the first instance, and he intended to banish every white man from the state. But he was sadly deficient in the mainspring of war, being without money, and having left the Sault in debt. He had recently come from Fredericksburg, in Virginia, where he had charge of a gold mine which had not succeeded. He had been in Mexico many years ago, and when travelling there had been attacked by a party of Mexicans, who, after he and his companions had shot three or four of them, overpowered him, massacred his friend, and left himself for dead. Recovering his senses, however, he managed to reach a hut, where he recovered of his wounds. The Mexican government gave themselves no concern about the matter, and he bore them no goodwill. He had the marks of nineteen wounds on his body, which he had shown to two or three of his friends at the Sault, where he staid nearly a fortnight; and carried with him a complete suit of mail, in which he was fond of exhibiting himself. The party left the place in two canoes'' (*Logan*, James, *Notes of a Journey through Canada, the United States of America, and the West Indies*, pp. 89-90). For the international bearings of the Dickson affair, see *Nute*, Grace, *James Dickson, a Filibuster in Minnesota in 1836*, Mississippi Valley Historical *Review*, vol. x, pp. 127-140.

260 *Riggs*, Reverend Stephen R., *Protestant Missions in the Northwest*, Minnesota Historical Society *Collections*, vol. vi, p. 128.

261 And there is every reason to think that Chardon came with it.

262 The *Assiniboine* arrived at Fort Union on the 26th (Kenneth Mackenzie to P. Chouteau, Jr. & Co., June 30, 1834, *Fort Union Letter Book, 1833-1835*, pp. 48-49), having made her appearance at Fort William, where Charles Larpenteur was, June 24th (*Coues*, Elliott, *Forty Years a Fur Trader on the Upper Missouri*, vol. 1, p. 63), the very day she had reached Fort Union with Maximilian on board the year previous (Maximilian, *Travels in the Interior of North America*, edition of 1843, p. 186)

263 For information regarding keel-boats, see *Chittenden*, H. M., *Early Steamboat Navigation on the Missouri River*, vol. i, pp. 90 *et seq.*; Merrick, *Old Times on the Upper Mississippi*, pp. 185-187. A description of mackinaw boats is to be found conveniently in *Chappell*, P. E., *A History of the Missouri River*, pp. 37-38.

264 Robert Campbell of the firm of Sublette and Campbell, the late ''Opposition.'' Larpenteur refers to the preparations made by Campbell for

the departure from Fort William (Coues, *op. cit.*, vol. 1, p. 64). It was Larpenteur's intention to accompany Campbell and to return to the States; but, having been interviewed by Mackenzie, in "Mr. Campbell's room," he agreed to enter the service of the American Fur Company. His first journal, descriptive of life at Fort Union, was started September 8, 1834 (*idem*, p. 8, *note* 14). His rank was that of a clerk (*idem*, pp. 65 *et seq.*, whereas, with his recent employers, Sublette & Campbell, it had been that of a "common hand" (*idem*, p. 10), so eager had he been to get to the mountains. Not very materially had he now bettered himself, however; for the bargain with Mackenzie, "struck for one year," allowed him only wages to the amount of two hundred and fifty dollars. The "complete suit of new clothes" given in addition he apparently stood greatly in need of.

265 Fort William was the post of the *Opposition*, the name by which all competitors in trade of the American Fur Company were known, and had been built under the personal direction of Robert Campbell in the autumn of 1833, and named after William Sublette. The building was, in fact, going on while Maximilian was visiting at Fort Union and he had many an agreeable chat with Campbell (*Travels*, p. 304). For a detailed account of the building of Fort William, told, as it were, in retrospect by one who assisted in its construction, see Coues's *Larpenteur, op. cit.*, pp. 51 *et seq.* It was situated about the same distance below the mouth of the Yellowstone as Fort Union was above (*idem, note* 1). Both forts were on the northern, or left, bank of the Missouri.

On the very day of the arrival of the *Assiniboine* at Fort Union, Mackenzie wrote that he had three boats laden and would, within an hour or two, be starting himself for St. Louis. It was then his expectation that the *Assiniboine* would not be able to make the return trip before spring but would have "to remain at her present moorings" the entire winter and he wanted measures taken to protect her, presumably against both the Indians and the elements. He had had some difficulty in finding someone to take charge of Fort Union in the event of his leaving and had finally persuaded James Archdale Hamilton, the English gentleman of leisure already referred to, to take charge (Mackenzie to John Carlisle, June 26, 1834 *Fort Union Letter Book, 1833-1835*, p. 18). See also his report to Pierre Chouteau, Jr., June 30, 1834 (*idem, pp. 48-49*).

266 Samuel P. Winter. The name, Sam¹ P. Winter appears as no. 250 in the List of 1830; but he was with P. D. Papin of the French Company at his post on the Teton River in the spring and early summer of 1830. See, for evidence, *Fort Tecumseh Journal*, January to June, 1830, entries May 7th, 12th, etc. Jacob Halsey drew on Pratte, Chouteau & Co. in favor of Samuel P. Winter for beaver skins &c, delivered at Fort Pierre, October 6, 1834 (*Chouteau-Maffitt Collection*, 1834-'35), which would seem to indicate that he was then a free trapper. In 1835, Mackenzie was unwilling that Winter should be engaged for the ensuing year. "On no consideration," wrote he to Chouteau, December 10, 1835, "engage S. P. Winter or J. E. Brazeau, recent information from the Blackfeet confirms what I have long suspected, that the latter is a chip of the old block, and the former is like unto him" (*Fort Union Letter Book*, 1833-1835, pp. 90-92).

267 Kenneth Mackenzie. Because he came later in life to use this spelling of his name, it has been the one adopted here throughout, except where occurring in documentary material.

268 Sub-agent Sanford and Captain Bennett must have helped to consti-
tute this "suitte" (J. A. Hamilton to James Kipp, October 18, 1834,
Fort Union Letter Book, 1833-1835, p. 57) and, at Fort Pierre, Laidlaw
joined it (Halsey to Messrs Pratte, Chouteau & Co., October 6, 1834 (Fort
Pierre Letter Book, 1832-1835, p. 78)   Mackenzie was still at Fort Union,
July 7th; for on that day, he drew a sight draft on Chouteau in favor of
John B. Whetten (*Chouteau-Maffitt Collection*).

269 William P. May.   This man, calling himself a citizen of Missouri,
addressed Superintendent Clark from St. Louis, in August, 1826, alleging
that a party of American citizens, himself included, when returning from
an expedition to New Mexico the preceding June, had been attacked by
Kiowas, and asking that redress be sought for from the Mexican government.   Clark, October 13, 1826, wrote to Secretary Barbour on the subject
of which May complained.   It was one of the grievances piling up in the
mind of frontiersmen against the Indians generally and against Mexico.
William P. May was probably the man named May, described by Maximilian as a "beaver hunter," who boarded the *Assiniboine* with Captain
Pratte, in the vicinity of Cedar Island, May 21st., having left Fort Union
on the *Yellowstone* in March (Thwaites, *Early Western Travels*, vol. xxii,
p. 300).   He is spoken of as a "freeman" in the *Fort Tecumseh Journal*,
1830 and from the *Fort Pierre Letter Book*, p. 73 &c., it will be seen that
he was at Fort Pierre in April, 1834.   An account with him appears in
the Pierre Chouteau & Co. Ledger for 1836 (Ledger A, 1834-1837) and,
in connection with the "Rocky Mountain Outfit," in 1837 (*Account Book*,
1837-1841).   A "Mr. May of Kentucky" joined Nicollet and Frémont in
1839 at Fort Pierre, he being bound for the Red River Colony (Frémont,
Memoirs, p. 40).   He was still alive in 1843; for, apparently, he was attacked by the Indians then and his cargo seized (Lounsberry, *Early History of North Dakota*, p. 186).   According to one authority (North
Dakota Historical Society *Collections*, vol. i, p. 374), he was charged with
bringing the small-pox to the Indians of Knife River in 1837.   Among
the many references to him in the present journal, there is one, under date
of July 20, 1837, to the effect that he had just arrived there from the
Little Missouri, which would mean Fort Pierre, the direction from which
it came.   For some additional information regarding William P. May,
see James, *Three Years among the Indians and Mexicans*, and Chittenden,
History of the American Fur Trade of the Far West, p. 371.

270 This is the only place in the journal where Chardon is referred to
in the third person.   The explanation for this instance may be that Alexander Kennedy was still at Fort Clark and still the scribe.

271 By "The Village," is invariably meant the larger of the two Mandan
villages, *Matootonha*, the *Ma-too-hon-ha*, of Lewis and Clark (Coues, *Lewis
and Clark*, vol. i, p. 182) and the *Mih-tutta-hang-kush* of Maximilian
(*Travels*, page 171).   It was on the south side of the river, the smaller village, *Roop-tar-hee*, or *Ruhptare*, being on the north.   There are many descriptions available of the Mandan huts, or lodges.   Audubon's (*Missouri
River Journals*, vol. ii, p. 10) differs quite a little from Catlin's (*North
American Indians*, 1850, vol. i, pp. 81-82).   Halsey, who wintered in
1828-'29 among the Mandans, probably wrote his description for Prince
Paul of Württemberg.   It is to be found in *Fort Tecumseh Journal*, January to June, 1830.   Thwaites says that the earth lodges of the Mandans
were different from the lodges of any other Indians (*Lewis and Clark*

Expedition, vol. i, p. 219, *note* 1). See Maximilian, Plate xvi, for a view of the larger Mandan village with Fort Clark "lying before it." It was to the northwest of Fort Clark. For its destruction by the Sioux, after its desertion by the Mandans following the small-pox ravages, see this journal, January 9, 1839. For the exact site of these Mandan villages and of Fort Clark, see Libby, O. G., *Typical Villages of the Mandans, Arikara, and Hidatsa in the Missouri Valley,* North Dakota State Historical Society *Collections,* vol. ii, pp. 498-508.

272 This stream was, undoubtedly, the Maropa, or Beaver Dam (Thwaites, *Original Journals of the Lewis and Clark Expedition,* vol. vi, p. 49), referred to, in 1804, as "Rear par, or Beaver Dam R." (*idem,* vol. i, p. 183), "25 yds wide," above which was the island on which, in that day, stood one of the Arikara villages. It was there that Pierre Antoine Tabeau conducted his peltry traffic and, in his narrative, *Voyage de Régis Loisel,* soon to be published under my editorship by the Canadian government, the little Maropa is designated, the *Barriers.* How much the Arikaras were identified with the locality is obvious from the circumstance that the present Grand River of South Dakota, the *Wetarho* of Lewis and Clark, is known in various Indian languages as the Arikara River (*Mooney,* James, *Calendar History of the Kiowa,* Bureau of Ethnology *Report,* 1895- '96, p. 159). The Maropa is today called Rampart, or Oak, Creek (*Thwaites,* R. G., *Early Western Journals,* vol. v, p. 127, *note* 83). Coues says "Rampart River is about two miles above Grand River" (*Audubon and His Journals,* vol. i, p. 531, *note* 1).

273 This man is usually referred to, in this narrative as "Old Bijoux;" but, in other places, his name appears variously. In the *List of 1830,* his more correct name is given, "Louis Bissonnette" so also in the *List of 1831.* In the *P. C. & Co. Retail Store Book,* A, 1834-37, it appears as "Louison Bijoux." For biographical details regarding him, see Drumm, *Luttig's Journal,* pp. 148-149.

274 Cannon Ball River. This tributary of the Missouri falls in from the west, in the southern part of North Dakota. According to Lewis and Clark, it got its name from the number of round boulders found on its banks.

275 Confirmation of this report regarding the death of Rotten Belly is to be found in Fort Union letters of September 17, 1834 (*Fort Union Letter Book,* 1833-1835, pp. 51-54). The reference in Bradley's Journal (Montana Historical Society *Contributions,* vol. ii, pp. 181-182) is obviously to this same affair. For mention of Rotten Belly (Eripuass) see Maximilian in Thwaites, *Early Western Travels,* vol. xxii, p. 351). Maximilian was permitted to be present at the conference that Sub-agent Sanford, who had gone up to Fort Union when Maximilian did, had with this renowned Crow chief (*Travels,* edition of 1843, p. 174), and was much impressed by his appearance and demeanor.

276 The account books of the Pierre Chouteau Jr. & Co. show an Alexis Durand (Durant ?) on the upper Missouri in 1834 and in 1837-1838. They also show a Savarin Durand in 1836 and a Severin Durand in 1837. From the present journal, it is to be inferred that there was a free hunter, named N. Durant, on the Missouri who was killed in the early part of 1837. The man here meant was probably the Alexis Durant of Laidlaw's

report to Pierre Chouteau Jr., dated April 28, 1834 (*Fort Pierre Letter Book*, 1832-1835, p. 72).

277 For horse-racing among the Mandans, see Catlin, *North American Indians*, 1850, vol. 1, p. 143.

278 In Chardon's manuscript, the time of most of the individual arrivals, like this of Old Bijoux, and departures, as well as of the occurrence of significant events – e.g., deaths – , is made conspicuous by the insertion of a cross in the margin. For the most part all such crosses and other indices have had, however, to be omitted from the printed text.

279 The Bijoux Hills. For Catlin's description of the "square hills," see *North American Indians*, vol. i, p. 75 and, for their very probable identity with Maximilian's "singular hills" (*Travels*, edition of 1843, p. 182). See also *note* 414.

280 For biographical details of Toussaint Charbonneau and the more prominent facts as to his career, see Drumm, *Luttig Journal*, pp. 135-140; *Morice, A. G., Dictionnaire Historique des Canadiens . . . de L'Ouest*, pp. 64-65. His name, usually spelt Charboneau, occurs frequently in the present journal, and some revelation is made therein of his character; but nothing could be more illuminating than Laidlaw's appraisement, made with particular reference to Charbonneau's employment at Fort Clark. This appraisement is found in a letter to Kipp, dated Fort Pierre, January 14, 1834 (*Fort Pierre Letter Book*, 1832-1835, p. 57) :

"... I am much surprised at your taking Old Charboneau into favour after shewing so much ingratitude, upon all occasions (the old Knave what does he say for himself".

Maximilian found Charbonneau posing as interpreter at the Opposition post, which Sublette and Campbell had, in characteristic fashion, established in the Gros Ventre, or Minitari, villages. He had "lately quitted" (*Travels*, Edition of 1843, p. 315) the service of the American Fur Company, deserting Kipp at Fort Clark. This was in itself cause sufficient for the distrust at which Laidlaw hinted.

In Chardon's time, it could be said, as in Larocque's that Charbonneau's "usual place of residence" (*Larocque, François A., Missouri Journal, Winter 1804-5, Masson Papers*, Public Archives, Ottawa) was a particular one of the Gros Ventre villages (Maximilian, in *Early Western Travels*, vol. xxiii, pp. 229-230), where, in both periods, he seems to have been whatever the occasion called for, trader or interpreter or both. Exactly when he first went to the upper Missouri, no journal yet unearthed has divulged; but, since, while he was subject to John MacDonell's orders [See *note* 258], men were constantly being sent back and forth between Fort Esperance and the Mandans, it is safe to assume that the time finally came when he, too, was sent and was one of those that stayed, so that, before ever Lewis and Clark arrived, he was fully established near by with the Big Bellies, or Gros Ventres. He had been thirty-seven years there when Maximilian came along (*Early Western Travels*, vol. xxiii, p. 229) and forty, when Charles Larpenteur seems first to have made his acquaintance, in 1838 (*Forty Years a Fur Trader on the Upper Missouri*, vol. i, p. 141). That he was not a well-qualified interpreter for Lewis and Clark, notwithstanding it is so stated (*Thwaites, R. G., Original Journals of the Lewis and Clark Expedition*, vol. i, p. 217) is to be inferred from what Charles MacKenzie had to relate of the round-about way that the American explorers gained their information: —

". . . She (Sacajawea) understood a little *Gros Ventre*, in which she had to converse with her husband, who was a Canadian, and did not understand English — A Mulatto who spoke bad French and worse English served as Interpreter to the Captains — so that a single word to be understood by the party required to pass from the Natives to the Woman, from the woman to the husband, from the husband to the Mulatto, from the Mulatto to the Captain —" (*MacKenzie*, Charles, *Some Account of the Mississouri Indians*, pp. 34-35).

Charbonneau's engagement by the American explorers, chiefly because of his wife, is too well known to require comment. Simultaneously, for several days and with the consent, somewhat grudgingly given, of Meriwether Lewis, his services were utilized by Larocque of the North West Company (*Larocque*, F. A., *Missouri Journal*, December 6, 1805; *Thwaites*, R. G., *Original Journals*, vol. i, pp. 228-229 and *note*); in order to circumvent the trading efforts of Hudson's Bay Company men, who were also on the spot (*MacKenzie*, Charles, *Some Account of the Mississouri Indians*, pp. 12, 21). The hesitancy of Lewis was attributable to his fear lest British influence should operate to the prejudice of his own country. As the days passed and the wayfarers became intimate with each other, the Montreal traders realized that, though they were "always treated with civility and kindness," it was not possible for Captain Lewis to "make himself agreeable" to them. "He could speak fluently and learnedly on all subjects," resumes MacKenzie, "but his inveterate disposition against the British stained, at least in our eyes, all his eloquence. Captain Clark was equally well informed, but his conversation was always pleasant, for he seemed to dislike giving offense unnecessarily. —" (*idem*, pp. 32-33). As far as the lending of Charbonneau to Larocque was concerned, that was done only after the latter had given his word that he would distribute to the Indians no flags or medals and the former had been "strictly enjoined" "not to utter a word, which might any ways be to the prejudice of the United States or of any of its Citizens. . ." (*Larocque*, F. A., *Missouri Journal*, November 29th, 1804). For additional references to Charbonneau and to the somewhat equivocal situation the economic need for him created, see *idem*, November 25, 27, 28, 30; December 1, 2, 5, 10, 12, 27, 28, 31, 1804 and January 2, 14, 25, 1805.

In Miss Drumm's very detailed biographical and chronological sketch of Toussaint Charbonneau, already cited, his entire career, subsequent to the Lewis and Clark expedition, can be traced. Additional thereto might be offered information gleaned from a *Ledger of Missouri Fur Company, 1812-1817* (*Clark Books*, Kansas State Historical Society), kept, presumably, by Manuel Lisa. This book contains an account with Charbonneau, extending from August, 1812 to February, 1813. On p. 98, he is listed as attached to the "Gros Vantre Expedition, 1812" and, on pp. 106-107, where is a list of "engages," his name appears. With the first establishment of the upper Missouri sub-agency, his services as an interpreter seem to have been in requisition and the following vouchers, the originals of which are on file in the United States Indian Office indicate how continuous was his employment:

(Box 23.)

The United States
To Benj. O'Fallon, U.S.Agt for the Missouri Tribes, Dr.

. . .
1819

. . .
| July 1st. | To cash to Tousaint Charbonoe his salary as per his voucher herewith, No. 2 | 100.00 |
| July 1st. | To cash paid Tousaint Charbonoe his salary as per his voucher herewith, No. 8 | 200.00 |

Voucher 2.   The United States
    To Tousaint Charbonoe Drs.
For compensation allowed me for my services as interpreter for the Mandan & Minitary nation of Indians from the first April 1819 to the 30th of June inclusive at 400 dollars per annum $100.
    Received 1st July of Benj. O'Fallon
U.S. Ind. Agt. one hundred dollars in full of the above account.

his
Tousaint   x   Charboneau
mark

Witness
John Dougherty.

Voucher 8.   The United States to Tousaint Charbonoe, Drs.
For compensation allowed me for my services as interpreter for the Mandan & Minetary nations of Indians, from the first of July 1819 to the 31st December inclusive at four hundred dollars per annum $200.00
                                          Council Bluffs, 1st January 1820
Received of Benjamin O'Fallon, U.S. I. Agent on the Missouri, the sum of two hundred dollars in full of the above account.

his
Tousaint   x   Charbonoe
mark

Witness,
    Th. N. Kavanaugh.

The United States

                              To Tousaint Charbonoe, Dr.
For compensation allowed me for my services as interpreter, from the month of January 1820 when I set out from Council Bluffs with a message from Maj. O'Fallon to the Mandan and Minitary nations of Indians, to the 31st May 1821 inclusive $150.
                        Council Bluffs June 1st 1821.
Received of Maj. Benj. O'Fallon Agent for Indian Affairs

on the Missouri one hundred and fifty dollars in full of the above account.

his
Tousaint   x   Charbonoe
mark

Witness
    John Dougherty.

(Box 35)
    Abstract of Expenditures made by P. Wilson, U.S.S.Agent at the Grand Bend and Mandan Villages on Missouri River in the year ending the 31st of August 1825.
Aug. 24, 1825. Voucher 4.   Tusan Shabbanow, for transporting Indian presents from the lower Mandan village to the Middle Grovantes village. $10.

Voucher 4.
The United States

To Shabbanow, Dr.

1825
24th August.

For transporting goods and appropriate blanketing to P. Wilson, U.S.S. agent from the Lower Mandan Village to the Middle Grovantes village, making 4 loads @ $2.50 $10.00
    Recd Grovantes village 24th of August 1825 of P. Wilson, U.S.S.agent Ten dollars in full of the above account.

his
Tusan   x   Shabbanow
mark

(Signed Duplicate)
James Kipp.

(Box 56.)
No. 1.

The United States Indian Department
To Toussant Charbonneau, Dr.

For my services as interpreter for the Mandans, Crows, & Gros Ventres at the Mandan villages from the 1st November 1827 to the 29th February 1828 at $400 per annum $133.33⅓
    Received at Mandan Villages February 29th 1828 of J.F.A. Sanford United States sub-agent Indian Affairs one hundred & thirty three dollars 33/100 cents in full of the above account.

his
Toussant   x   Charbonneau
mark

Test
P. D. Papin.

Voucher 1.   The United States Indian Department
                  To Toussant Charbonneau Dr.
For my services as interpreter for the Mandans & Gros Ventres for the 3d & 4th Qrs of the year 1827-28 commencing the first

March & ending 31st August 1828, at Four hundred dollars per annum .... $200.

Received Mandan Villages August 31, 1828 of J.F.A. Sanford U.S.Indian Agent Two hundred dollars in full of the above account.

his
Toussant   x   Charboneau
mark

Test
K. McKenzie.

No. 4.

The United States Indian Department
To Toussant Charbonneau Dr.

For my services as interpreter for the Mandans & Gros ventres for the 1st Qr of the year 1828-29 commencing 1st September 1828 & ending 30th November at four hundred dollars per annum $100.

Received Mandan villages November 30th 1828 of J.F.A. Sanford U.S.S.Ind.Agent one hundred dollars in full of the above account.

his
Toussant   x   Charbonneau
mark

Test
K. McKenzie.

(Box 58)
No. 1.

The United States Indian Department
To Toussant Charboneau

For my services as interpreter for the Mandans & Gros Ventres in the 2d qr. of the year 1828-29 commencing 1st December & ending 28th February 1829 at $400 per annum   — $100.

Received Mandan villages February 29th 1829 of J.F.A. Sanford U.S.S.Indian Agent one hundred dollars in full of the above account.

his
Toussant   x   Charbonneau
mark

Test
K. McKenzie.

(Box 61)
Voucher 1.   Abstract B.

Received of John F.A. Sanford U.S.S.Indian Agent on the Upper Missouri one hundred and thirty three dollars thirty three cents for my services as interpreter for the Mandans and

Gros Ventres from the 1st March to the 30th June (inclusive)
at $400 per annum.

St. Louis June 30th 1829

his

Toussant   x   Charbonneau

mark

Test
Robert Scott.

(Box 64)
Voucher 1.   Abstract B.

The United States Indian Department

To Toussant Charbonneau Dr.

For my services as interpreter from the 1st October to 1st
January 1830 for the Mandan *&* Minetaree Indians at $400
per annum $100.
     Recd. Mandan villages January 1, 1830 of John F.A. Sanford
U.S.S.Indian Agent one hundred dollars in full of the above
account.

his

Toussant   x   Charbonneau

mark

Test
     D. Lamont.

(Box 81)
No. 2.   The United States Indian Department

To Toussant Charbonneau.

December 31, 1831.   For his services as interpreter for Mandan,
Minataree & Crow Indians for the quarter ending 31 December
1831 at $400 per annum   —   —   — $100.
     Received St. Louis December 31st 1831 of John F.A. Sanford
U.S.S.Indian Agent one hundred dollars in full of the above
account.

his

Toussant   x   Charbonneau

mark

Test
Joshua Pilcher.

It was the threatened discontinuance of Charbonneau's services as interpreter for the upper Missouri sub-agency that helped to arouse the ire
of Sanford.   See Sanford to Clark, July 21, 1833 (*Files,* United States
Indian Office).   In the end, Superintendent Clark was told to inform him
that the Secretary of War recognizes the ''necessity of two Interpreters
for his widely extended Agency embracing so many different tribes of Indians speaking different languages — that the former allowance for Interpreters will be continued, and Mr. Charbourneau will be retained as one
of them'' (Herring to Clark, October 18, 1833, *Indian Office Letter Book,*
no. 11, p. 253).
     Although Charbonneau is never referred to in the Fort Clark journal
as anything but a trader, he yet must have been for at least part of the
time an official interpreter.   The following communication from Fulkerson

would imply, however, that prior to its date, there had been an interval of non-employment:

"Little Missouri, July 1, 1835.
"Sir
"I have this day employed Toussaint Charboneau as interpreter for my subagency, subject to your approval or disapproval.
"Mr. Charboneau, I presume, is well known to you as he has been in your employ, and also in the employ of Maj. Sanford, whilst subagent for this post (the Mandan subagency).
"Respectfully,
"Genl. Wm. Clark   "W. N. Fulkerson,
"Supt. Indian Affairs"
"Sub Indian Agent."
"Approved — Wm. Clark."
The appointment was confirmed by the Commissioner of Indian Affairs and the salary fixed at three hundred dollars.   After Fulkerson resigned in 1838, he presented for payment the account of his interpreter; but the matter was held up until that individual, who could not yet write his name, could be communicated with through some outside channel.   With the suppression of the sub-agency, Charbonneau's official career necessarily came to an end, although he "never received notice of the intention of the Department to dispense with his services, until some time in July (1839), in consequence of the remote situation of the post."   Thus reported Superintendent Joshua Pilcher (See Letter to T. Hartley Crawford, Commissioner of Indian Affairs, August 26, 1839, quoted at length in the Appendix, pp. 140-141, to Miss Drumm's edition of the John Luttig journal, *op. cit.*), who, at the same time recounted Charbonneau's claims upon the American government for services long past and reported him as penniless, "tottering under the infirmities of 80 winters."   To his great age, Chardon bears witness.

281 This accident to Chardon is, in a sense, reminiscent of the dramatic incident described by Catlin (*North American Indians*, 1866, pp. 25-26) and pictured by him (*idem*, Plate 9), though it was a leap that Chardon took then, in 1832, and not a fall.   He had another, June 23, 1836.

282 *The Ledger*, 1831-1833, p. 244, *op. cit.*, shows an Edward Boulé employed on the upper Missouri.   The name is not uniformly spelt in the present journal, and its owner died in February 1837.   Edward Boulé was one among several men that Halsey, representing Laidlaw, recommended to the notice of Pierre Chouteau Jr.   (Jacob Halsey to Pierre Chouteau Jr., dated Fort Pierre July 9, 1832, *Fort Tecumseh Letter Book*, 1830-1832, pp. 117-121)

283 If this was A. Lacroix, note Hamilton's opinion of him in letter to Pratte, Chouteau & Co., July 18 1835 (*Fort Union Letter Book*, 1833-1835, p. 84).   Alexis Lacroix was connected with the Upper Missouri Outfit in 1837 and 1838.   In 1830, there was a Baptiste Lacroix at Fort Union.

284 See *note* 24.

285 Catlin called attention to the fact that the Mandans had so great a liking for green corn that, in their improvident way, they would sometimes eat their entire crop while it was yet immature (*North American Indians*, 1850, vol. i, pp. 185 ff).   Note his discussion of their Green Corn Dance, (*idem*, pp. 189-190).

286 Michel Bellehumeur. For some record of his commercial transactions with the Pierre Chouteau Jr. & Co. see *Ledger*, 1831-1833, p. 474 and *Retail Store Book, A*, 1834-1837, p. 164. Maximilian had occasion to make many allusions to him and Thwaites considered it likely that he was the son of Simon Bellehumeur, who "was in 1804 a North West Company's voyageur on upper Red River" (*Early Western Travels*, vol. xxiv, p. 12, *note* 3). There was also a Martin Belhumeur in the employ of the American Fur Company, connected first with the Otoe Outfit and then with the Osage. (*P. C. & Co. Retail Store Book, A*. 1834-1837, pp. 112, 434). In the present journal, Michel Bellehumeur is variously referred to as Mitchel, Michel, Bellehumeur. In the summer of 1838, he and his family took their departure for the Selkirk Colony on Red River of the North.

287 For the record of a certain B. Deguire, see letter to H. Picotte, dated Fort Union, December 15, 1833 (*Fort Union Letter Book*, 1833-1835, pp. 7-8). He was, for a while, with Tulloch at Fort Cass.

288 Pierre Garreau, the younger, is frequently spoken of by Maximilian. His brother Antoine is no. 244 in the *List of 1830*. For an account of various members of the family, including the father of these two, Joseph Garreau, their Ree mother, and their paternal grandfather, Pierre Garreau, the elder, see Coues, *Forty Years a Fur Trader on the Upper Missouri*, vol. i, pp. 125-126, *note* 11, and Drumm, *Luttig Journal*, p. 64, *note* 97. In Clark's *Book of Sanford's Accounts*, under date of September, 1828, a Joseph Garro is mentioned as Interpreter for the "Rickara," or Rees. It would seem that Antoine Garreau, who was the father-in-law of Andrew Dawson, was, at one time, in the employ of Sublette & Campbell (N. D. Historical Society *Collections*, vol. i, p. 363). At the time Mackenzie's party was robbed by the Rees in 1830, when *en route* to Fort Union, Richard T. Holliday, trader at the Ree Village, expressed grave suspicion of "Garrow" and Daniel Lamont acquiesced (Lamont to Holliday, dated Fort Tecumseh, December 19, 1830, *Fort Tecumseh Letter Book*, 1830-1832, pp. 10-11).

289 There were two, possibly, of this name on the upper Missouri, Jean Baptiste and Alexis. The spelling of the surname varies from Tabeau, Tibeau, and Thibeau in the account books of the fur company. Alexis Thiebeau is no. 233 in the *List of 1830* and no. 23 in that of 1831. In the *Fort Tecumseh Journal*, January 31, 1830 to June 13, 1830, under date of April 6th, an Alexis Tibout is "dispatched to the Little Chyenne river for the purpose of bringing down what Packs the company may have there." In the *Account Book* for 1836, Baptiste Tibeau is put down as of the Sioux Outfit.

290 Alexis Dusseau. See no. 121 of *List of 1830*. Alexis Dusseau is mentioned in a letter addressed by Laidlaw at Fort Pierre to Lamont at Fort Clark, January 10, 1833 (*Fort Pierre Letter Book*, 1832-1835, pp. 11-12) and in various other communications of the time.

291 Joseph Joyaille (Joyal) See Drumm, *Luttig Journal*, p. 88, *note* 134.

292 Jacques Molleure, who in the account books of the American Fur Company, Western Department, is listed as belonging to the Upper Missouri Outfit in 1834. See also P. C. Co. *Retail Store Account Book*, 1834-1837, p. 116. In the List of 1830, no. 206, is a Baptiste Molaire, and in the Church records of St. Louis, a person of identically the same name is given as the son of Molaire, Jean Baptiste, *dit* Lallemand.

293 Remarks like these, sometimes almost coarse, sometimes merely facetious, are to be found here and there in the present journal; also scraps of accounts, memoranda of all sorts.   They are scribbled in the heart of the text, at the end of a yearly or monthly record, and on the title-page of the different divisions of the journal.   For example,

''Time Cuts down all
  Both Great and Small
  Death says so, the old Dog
  Come on all you Boasters.''

It has not been thought necessary in most cases to include them in the printed text.

294 At about this same time Halsey at Fort Pierre was greatly concerned over the desertion of ''13 Pork eaters'' (Halsey to Laidlaw at St. Louis, August 25, 1834 (*Fort Pierre Letter Book*, 1832-1835).

295 For the damage that rats could inflict, see present journal, March 15 and April 16, 1839, and for, in consequence, the value set upon cats, Drumm, *Luttig Journal*, pp. 62-63, also the following: ''Caryon & Morin arrived on the 29 Ulto with all you sent in good order except the two Cats which were drowned in L'eau qui Court by the negligence of the Men   I think they should be made to pay well for them & I request you to send me others pr 1st opportunity . . .''   (Honoré Picotte to P. D. Papin, April 7, 1846, *Fort Pierre Letter Book*, 1845-1846).

When Maximilian reached Fort Clark, his attention was immediately called to the large number of rats infesting the place:

''. . . There were a few tame cats in the fort, but not sufficient to reduce the great number of rats.   These animals (the Norway rats) were so numerous and troublesome, that no kind of provision was safe from their voracity; their favorite food was the maize, among which they committed sad havoc; and it was calculated that they daily devoured five bushels, or 250 pounds.   There were often from 500 to 800 bushels of this corn in the loft at a time.   The rats were brought hither by the American ships; but, as yet, they have not reached the Manitari villages.   The Indians killed seven of these creatures in the prairie, which were on their route from Fort Clarke to those villages.   No rats have since attempted to visit them, but it is more than probable that they will, ere long, find their way thither'' (Thwaites, *Early Western Travels*, vol. xxiii, pp. 235-236.)   Fort Clark was not the only trading-post accursed in this respect.   In a *Journal of the Rocky Mountain Fort, 1799 (Masson Papers*, Canadian Public Archives, Ottawa) it was reported, October 20, that ''Rats eat everything they can catch.''   Henry A. Boller, speaking of Fort Clark and its neighbor, *Fort Primeau*, many years subsequent to Chardon's time, said, ''Both the forts, as well as the village itself, were completely infested with rats, to the discomfort and annoyance of all the inhabitants, both white and red.   These pests had been an importation of the Company's steamboats years before, and had multiplied to such an alarming extent that the Indians, who at first felt themselves particularly favored above their neighbors by the acquisition, had abundant reason to change their opinion'' (*Among the Indians: Eight Years in the Far West, 1858-1866*, p. 33).

296 Chardon enumerates (See this journal, March 11, 1839) the choice pieces of the buffalo.   Compare with Boller's delicacies (*Among the Indians,* p. 229).   From the journals of the Lewis and Clark expedition, one gathers that the hump, the tongue, the marrow-bones were all considered delicacies (Thwaites, *Original Journals*, vol. ii, pp. 151, 196) and the small

guts "very good" (*idem*, p. 234). Brackenridge had a longer list, the hump, tongue, marrow, tender loin, ribs (Thwaites, *Early Western Travels*, vol. vi, p. 135).

[297] More often given as Hart River. For example, see December 24, 1834, and April 23, 1837.

[298] Jean Baptiste Joncas. See no. 109 of *List of 1830*, and no. 53 of *List of 1831*, where he is designated as a boatman. The name appears also on Clark's list of 1832. From the present journal, August 15, 1837, it is fair to suppose that Jonca, or Joncas, was a half-breed Kanza Indian.

[299] Maximilian placed the three Gros Ventre villages where the Knife River joins the Missouri (*Travels*, ed. 1843, p. 178) and stated that the principal one was about fifteen miles higher up the Missouri and on the same side as the Mandan Little Village (*idem*, p. 173) Catlin visited the Gros Ventres when he left the Mandans (*North American Indians*, 1850, vol. i, pp. 185 *et. seq.* Coues says ''The three Knife River villages were permanent from 1796 at least until after 1837, when the survivors of the epidemic constituted one village on Knife River, vol. i, p. 265, *note* 20).

[300] An indication of the systematic way the trade was carried on.

[301] There is much contemporary as well as earlier evidence in support of the claim that the Mandans placed an exceedingly high valuation on the skin of the white buffalo. On one occasion, when Hamilton was in charge at Fort Union, he sent down a white skin to Fort Clark in anticipation of Mackenzie's arrival there, evidently with the idea of Mackenzie's disposing of it to advantage. He wrote to Mackenzie, on another occasion, exultingly, thus:
''Mr Crawford has traded a white cow skin & F. Deschamp has a fine white calf skin'' (*Fort Union Letter Book*, 1833-1835, p. 59); but there were evidently limits to what, in Hamilton's opinion, ought to be paid for such treasures (See Hamilton to Crawford, dated Fort Union, November 3, 1834, *idem*, p. 58). Maximilian commented repeatedly upon the veneration with which the Mandans, and also the Gros Ventres, regarded the white buffalo skin (See, especially, Thwaites, *Early Western Travels*, vol. xxiii, pp. 321-323), and Catlin narrated the special journey that a party of Mandans made to the Yellowstone in order to purchase one that they had heard the Blackfeet had for sale (*North American Indians*, 1866, pp. 133-134). Apparently, a similar sanctity attached to the white wolf skin. Alexander Ross said of it, ''The white wolf skin in season is esteemed an article of royalty; it is one of the chief honours of the chieftainship, and much used by these people in their religious ceremonies . . .'' (*Fur Hunters of the West*, vol. i, p. 64). See also Maximilian, *op. cit.*, p. 171 and, for the superstitious fear with which the Crows, contrariwise, regarded the white buffalo cow, see *idem*, p. 175. A memorandum of Chardon's on a loose sheet of his journal is as follows:

Two white cow skins (The Black Tongue)
Sold for Sixty Robes .... 60 Robes
March 20th By 40 Robes —
    '' 26 '' 8 Do

[302] By J. F. Hamtramck *a soldier* was defined as one selected ''to give efficiency to the orders of the official actions of the Agent'' (Clark's *Accounts of Agents for Osages, 1824-1834*, p. 47). For instances of

Chardon's "making soldiers for the Fort," see entries like those of April 25, 1835, May 2, 1837, etc., and for the duties of the same, see Boller, *Among the Indians*, p. 53. Atwater was of the opinion that it was customary for a chief to appoint two soldiers for the maintenance of order in each and every village (*Western Antiquities*, p. 277).

303 For initiation into the Dog Band, see Tabeau's narrative of the *Voyage of Régis Loisel* (in press) and for the badge used, see *Early Western Travels*, vol. xxiii, p. 261.

304 For an account of how these cords were made, see Wagner, *Leonard's Narrative*, p. 215, *note*. Boller says that packs of ten robes were "tied with cord cut out of a raw hide" (Boller, Henry M. *Among the Indians*, p. 283).

305 The white clay of the region (Boller, *Among the Indians*, p. 74) was useful for this purpose of white-washing, described always by Chardon as "daubing."

306 Hamilton sent by Francis and his boat the following letters:
(a) "I entrust this with my best wishes for your health and comfort to your old friend Francis who has charge of boat for St Louis, 15 men with him. Our larder is empty and having in all cases of need found you ready and willing to render assistance, I request you will furnish them with 16 bushls Corn which with the grease they have will carry them down. — The men from the Crow & Blackfoot Countries have so much news to communicate I need not put much to paper. — Mr Kipp had a safe trip of 32 days. The Crows had previous to his arrival stolen every horse from the fort. Rotten Belly was killed near the Fort: The Assiniboines have recently stolen five horses from Mr Tulloch, and the last time we sent out for meat Pellot's blonde was stolen and two horses of the Companys — I have none of your favours to acknowledge the receipt of, but trust I may ere long.
Believe me faithfully Yours
(J. A. Hamilton to F. A. Chardon, dated Fort Union, September 17, 1834 *Fort Union Letter Book*, 1833-1835, p. 53)
(b) "You will doubtless have been many days expecting to receive letters from me, but Mr Kipp having waited 26 days after his arrival at Fort McKenzie before he started the men for this place I could not send Francis away one moment earlier. I hope he will reach Fort Pierre in reasonable time but the river is so unprecedently low here he will not take charge of a loaded boat I am compelled therefore to retain a portion of last years returns. The 15 Men have agreed their Accts. — The letter addressed to Mr McKenzie, Fort Pierre, you will please retain untill his arrival, one addressed to him at St Louis you will send on pr Francis. I shall be much obliged by your forwarding the enclosed letters for England to your friend Mr Hunt, the postage to New York I will pass to credit of acct. — Mr Kipp & Mr Tulloch arrived in safety at their respective posts, but the prospect of trade is very bad at each of them. This fort has been thronged with Indians since Mr McKenzie's departure but they have nothing to trade and are too lazy to hunt and are grumbling sadly at Liquor being stopped. — Mr. Crawford paid me a visit a few days since, he says he has built a very neat snug fort 100 feet square plenty of accommodation for

Robes and wives. — Pray send me any newspapers &c you can spare by the first opportunity and believe me to be

Dear Sir
Very Truly Yours

(J. Archdale Hamilton to J. Halsey, dated Fort Union, September 17, 1834, *idem*, p. 54)

(c) "Two days since I had scarcely given my instructions to Francis to have the boat in readiness to start for St. Louis, not deeming it prudent to wait longer for the young men from Fort McKenzie, when a packet of Letters, was handed me from Mr Kipp. I send you copies herewith; prospects of trade there gloomy in the extreme, Piegans & Bloods at war to the hilt, the summer hunt only produced seven packs of beaver ! !

Mr Culbertson's letter will shew how the Crows have compelled himself and people to live on Cords Parfleche for 15 days.   Mr Brazeau's name not mentioned,   I presume he remains with Mr Kipp for the winter, — Mr Crawford has finished his fort on a more eligible spot than the one you fixed on, his equipment is made up and in part sent off. — I send you copy of a letter from Mr Tulloch   both he and Mr Kipp made their voyages in less time than might have been expected from the stage of water.   Mr Tulloch had seen none of the Crow nation at the time of his writing and could hazard no opinion regarding the trade.   Rotten Belly was killed this Summer by the Blackfeet.

The works at this place have progressed pretty regularly, the last load of hay will be brought home to day.   Manta says considerably more in quantity than last year though a good stack has been burnt, for ten days the prairies, West, North & East were burning furiously. One bastion is roofed & shingled & pointed, the other built up as high as the pickets. Luteman has made his arrangements for the Kitchen and has erected & shingled five compartments under the intended gallery —   Cattle are far away and the consumption of meat is I fancy greater than ever.   I had some difficulty in starting the Deschamps party on their hunt, they are very sanguine in their expectations. — Le enfant du fer has paid us a visit seven days march from his camp of 80 Lodges, they will all be here to trade this winter: Le Sonant Laroche & La Bras Cassé are gone to the North and tried to persuade him to go but he declined. — A few hours after you had left this place, Fr. Deschamp and Pellot arrived   the latter hoped to have been permitted to accompany you to St. Louis,   he is undecided about wintering here. —   Halcrow has hitherto conducted himself fully to my satisfaction. —   Mr Rocque was not able to start untill Aug. 28, and even then in so weak a state I fear he will never reach Red River. — I have packed up a white cow skin very carefully and addressed it to you at Fort Clark, I have traded very little except 20 beaver skins, in fact the Indians have nothing. —   The evening of your departure the young Gauché Le pelet Soldat   Le Chef que parle, Le Capot Bleu and many others arrived to see Mr Sandford   the two latter started a few days afterwards for the Crow Village and have not since been heard of, it is supposed they are killed;

Genl. Jackson is gone thither in search of them prepared for peace or War)   some young men who accompanied Le Chef que Parle stole five horses from Mr Tulloch.

The young Gauché, regretted he had not redeemed his pledge by bringing a large party to trade here on his return last spring they had all gone to the north, he will not promise again but he will do all he can: he said it went hard with him not to get his dram as heretofore on arrival: I

CHARDON'S JOURNAL AT FORT CLARK

sent him away with a glad heart but without tasting Liquor Wine. —
Almost every day small parties of Indians have visited us, some to eat,
others to beg, and many engaged in war excursions. —
On the 29th Aug there were encamped near the Fort 170 Lodges of the
Gens de Canot   40 Lodges of Les Gens des fille, & above 20 Lodges with
the General; his father and La jambe blessé with him: Le Grand Soldat
La souris qui marche & Le Chien fou are together near la bute du Sable;
they remained here some days but I had less trouble with them than I
feared; they are very reluctant members of the *temperance society*. —
Michel has got 300 barrels of coal housed & his last kiln is now nearly
ready to draw. —   Bearing in mind your conversation with Capt Bennett
regarding supplies of provisions &c for the use of the boat, I was much
surprized to receive his order (written subsequent to your conversation)
handed by Mr Carlisle requiring 6 Brls bread, 2 brls Flour, 2 brls corn and
for Sugar & Coffee in proportion. —   I could not comply therewith but
given as much as I could spare. —   M. Gravelle did not like fort Cass
quarters for his wife and has sent her back here, Jack Ram's family will in
a few days number fourteen ! ! ! —   Were you terribly oppressed with
the heat in the voyage down ? from July 29th. to Aug 7 the thermometer
rose each day to upwards of 100° & some days 105°   We have had some
furious gales since but scarcely a drop of rain: the Missouri is terribly
low; dogs walk across with the exception of the narrow channel on the
opposite shore: Francis will not undertake the charge of a loaded boat
I can send therefore only so many packs as there is a reasonable prospect
of making head way with, for particulars I refer you to the Bill of
Lading. —   It is said cattle are plenty from La R au Tremble to Les
Montagnes des bois. —   a Duplicate hereof I addressed to you at Fort
Pierre.   Anxiously hoping you will make a prosperous voyage and have
favourable weather for your return believe me ever to be
Dear Sir
Very faithfully Yours
(Signed) J. Archdale Hamilton
P. S.   The new Fort "Assiniboine" Mr Crawford says is 100 feet square
the buildings 138 feet front by 18 depth. —''
(J. Archdale Hamilton to Kenneth McKenzie Esqr, dated Fort Union,
September 17, 1834 —*idem*, pp. 51-53)

307 François Roy, or Roi, mentioned by Maximilian (Thwaites, *Early
Western Travels*, vol. xxii, p. 281).   In an editorial note to *Malhiot's
Journal*, republished from Masson's *Bourgeois*, in Wisconsin Historical So-
ciety *Collections*, vol. xix, it is stated, p. 208, *note* 98, that the name,
François Roy, was not uncommon among fur trade employees.   There was a
North West Company clerk of the name at l'Anse as early as 1801-1802.
A Francis Roy was among the Canadian *voyageurs* who volunteered for
British service, June 21, 1814 (*Prairie du Chien Papers*, 1814-1815, pub-
lished in Wisconsin Historical Society *Collections* (Madison Reprint, 1909),
volume ix, pp. 262-281. A François Roy's name appears in the "Ledger
of the Missouri Fur Company, 1812-1817,'' and also in the Pierre Chouteau
& Co. *Ledger, 1831-1833*, p. 226.   Under date of April 2nd and 5th, 1830,
Halsey refers to "Francis Roy" coming to Fort Tecumseh overland from
Council Bluffs (*Fort Tecumseh Letter Book*, January to June, 1830).

308 For the technical use of this word in the river trade, see *Drumm*, S.
M., *Luttig Journal*, p. 29, *note* 8.

309 These initials, O.B.F., that appear in the margin at intervals elude

explanation, unless, indeed, they may be made to stand, as seems likely, judging from the frequency of their occurrence, for *Opened Barrel Flour*.

310 For Maximilian's location of the winter quarters of a part of the Mandans, see *Travels*, p. 171.

311 About this time or even earlier, Chardon ought to have been in receipt of the letter that Jacob Halsey wrote to him from Fort Pierre on the 1st, asking him for particulars as to the equipment at Fort Clark, the names of the persons engaged there, etc. See *Fort Pierre Letter Book, 1832-1835*, p. 76.

312 For what constituted an *equipment*, ordinarily, see Drumm, Stella M., *Luttig Journal*, p. 78, *note* 118.

313 This "Point of Woods," so often mentioned in the present narrative, is practically located by what Chardon told Audubon of the distance he went down the river, thirty miles, to meet the steamboat in 1837. (*Audubon and His Journals*, vol. ii, p. 42-43). There is also a "Point of Woods" opposite Fort Clark which Chardon frequently mentions. It is to be identified, no doubt, with the "forest" that Maximilian remarked upon, when describing the Mandan villages, upper and lower, winter and summer, with respect to each other: —
". . . About a league below Fort Clarke the Missouri makes a bend to the east or north-east, and on this part of the bank is a rather extensive forest, in which the inhabitants of Mik-Tutta-Hang-Kush have built their winter village of sixty or seventy huts" (*Early Western Travels*, vol. xxiii, p. 234). Between this point of woods and Fort Clark, stood Kipp's post that he built for the Columbia Fur Company (*idem*, p. 223) and to the point itself it would seem that Chardon, in conference with the Mandans after their decimation by the small-pox, thought of moving its successor.

314 Distinguished in this way, it might well seem that, if still alive, Charbonneau's "lady" was Sacajawea (Sakakawea), "the woman . . . of the Serpent Nation," as Charles MacKenzie tells us, "answered the purpose of wife to *Charbonneau*" (*Some Account of the Missisouri Indians in the years 1804, 5, 6, & 7*, p. 34, Photostats, *Masson Papers*, Canadian Public Archives, Ottawa) in the time of Lewis and Clark; but, according to John Luttig, she had been dead long since, having "died of a putrid fever," December 20, 1812 (*Drumm*, Stella M., *Journal of a Fur-Trading Expedition on the Upper Missouri, 1812-1813*, p. 106). Charbonneau's "lady" was, doubtless, the particular squaw of his, who died, September 6, 1837, during the small-pox epidemic. See entry, September 10, 1837.

315 For Hamilton's report on the departure of Miller from Fort Union as soon as he had finished the bastions, see Hamilton to McKenzie, dated Fort Union, October 9, 1834 (*Fort Union Letter Book, 1833-1835*, p. 56). In Clark's list of licensed men, 1832, occurs the name of Peter Miller. A John Miller belonged to the Sioux Outfit as reported upon in August and November, 1838. Which of them, if either, this man was it is impossible to determine. He may, in fact, have been the William Miller mentioned thus by Halsey under date of May 30, 1830: "W. P. May and Wm. Miller (two freemen) arrived in a canoe from the Mandans" (*Fort Tecumseh Journal*, January to June, 1830) and the same as was meant in the following:

"I write Miller to say All's well, he has an a/c to shew what is due him should he want anything. Welsh & Ebert have beaver   try to buy it
Yours   J. A. H."
(Hamilton to Chardon, dated Fort Union, October 9, 1834, *Fort Union Letter Book*, 1833-1835, p. 56)

316 See entry November 18, 1834.

317 Knife river empties into the Missouri from the west, in Mercer county, North Dakota. Cherry creek, mentioned below in the text, is a branch of the Little Missouri.

318 John Newman was on the Lewis and Clark expedition.   For Meriwether Lewis's report of him and his conduct, see letter to Henry Dearborn, Secretary of War, dated City of Washington, January 15, 1807 (Thwaites, *Lewis and Clark*, vol. vii, pp. 355-357).   Despite his conduct, John Newman was one of those of the Lewis and Clark expedition that received a land warrant under the *Compensation Act* of May 3, 1807 (*United States Statutes at Large*, vol. vi, pp. 65-66).   From the Roman Catholic records of Pennsylvania, the following data is taken: Newman, John: Son of Walter N. and Catherine Zimmerman.   Married Olympia Dubreuil, dau. of Antoine Dubreuil and Elizabeth Paran, July 5, 1832; but, by the present journal, supposing the same person be meant, other relationships are attested.   See entries of February 25th and July 1st, 1838.   For information regarding a certain Lewis Newman who threatened to constitute an Opposition in the New Madrid country, see Benjamin Clapp to Godfrey Lessieur, March 8, 1847 (*Lessieur Papers*, Missouri Historical Society).

319 Little Missouri.   There were two rivers of this name, one below and one above Fort Clark.   To the former, Lewis and Clark gave the name of Teton after the Sioux bands of the vicinity.   When Gass's journal was first published great confusion among his readers arose from the duplication of name.   See edition of 1808, p. 77.   Almost invariably the Teton is the Little Missouri to Chardon.   It is the present Bad River. See *note* 26.

320 There was a post of the American Fur Company on Cherry River. It may have been that that he was seeking.   In the autumn of 1833, the man stationed at it was one of the Dauphins (Laidlaw to Colin Campbell, September 5, 1833, *Fort Pierre Letter Book*, 1832-1835, p. 36) and P. D. Papin had been there the winter before (Laidlaw to Papin, December 14, 1832, *Fort Tecumseh Letter Book*, 1830-1832, pp. 139-140).

321 Pierre Legris, *Voyageur*, no. 217 on *List of 1830* and no. 47 on *List of 1831*.   Of him, Hamilton wrote, "I give this to Legris who has beaver & will sell it to you as it is not in order.   Manta has left me sans permission & may give you a call.   Cattle plenty."   (Hamilton to Chardon, dated Fort Union, October 7, 1834 — *Fort Union Letter Book, 1833-1835*, p. 56).
Of Manta, who was evidently of Legris' "Suitte," Hamilton had more to say in his report to Mackenzie, "Manta declined engaging but proposed to stay & pay his debt if I would furnish proviss for voyage when his time expired.   Knowing it would then be too late for him to go down I considered he merely wanted a salvo to his conscience to save his word   You may imagine my surprise at his coming after 10 days & contending that his time was up.   I have not seen him since 1 Oct but hear he is gone down with Legris" (Hamilton to Mackenzie, dated October 9, 1834 *idem*).

The next year, when sending Legris as an express to Alexander Culbertson, who was with Kipp at Fort McKenzie, Hamilton had occasion to say, "I give this to Pierre Legris an old servant of the Compy, & a good beaver hunter who has contrived to save some money in the country, he has also paid Dupuis debt to the Coy. If they offer you beaver for sale $ 4 pr lb for well handled Spring beaver dry & well beat, is the highest price that can be given: should they wish to sell out their horses & traps I by no means wish you to treat for them . . ." (Hamilton to A. Culbertson, dated Fort Union, March 11, 1835, *idem*, p. 68).

322 Fort Pierre. See entry, January 3, 1835.

323 There were several men of this name, Villeandre, connected with the Upper Missouri Outfit. For Alexis, Auguste, and Baptiste, see *P. C. & Co. Retail Store Ledger A*, 1834-1837 and *Account Book*, 1837-1841. Under date of May 24, 1830, Halsey speaks of a certain "Joseph Villandre one of the Yellow Stone party" (*Fort Tecumseh Journal*, 1830), and there was a "Mr Villandre" on the upper Missouri as late as 1848 (Letter to Jos. Jewett, dated Fort Pierre, February 8, 1848, *Fort Pierre Letter Book*, 1847-1848)

324 Joseph Dupuis. The name occurs as no. 23 in the *List of 1830*. In the account books, under date of 1836, Joseph Dupuis is recorded as having had commercial transactions through Fontenelle and Fitzpatrick and also through Pierre Legris. Joseph Dupuis was listed as of the Sioux Outfit in September and October of 1837. A Louis Dupuis was, in 1804, an interpreter in the employ of the North West Company at Lake Népigon (Morice, p. 107)

325 Chardon had been a trader among the Saons. See *note* 81.

326 Narcisse Manta, see *Ledger*, 1831-1833, p. 446. In the *Retail Store Account Book*, 1834-1837 is the account of Narcisse Mantlia, Sioux, and also of Joseph Mantlia. Narcisse seems to have been connected, in 1836, with the Sioux Outfit and Joseph with the Otoe Outfit. A man of the name of Monta was charged with being one of the four white murderers of a Ree chief some miles below Council Bluffs in 1837 (*St. Louis Republican* June 26, 1837.

327 Of Primeau's supposed movements Halsey heard rumors. "I understand," wrote he, "that Emillein Primeau and S. N. Leclair are on their way up the Missouri in opposition to each other, we suppose they are now somewhere in the neighbourhood of the Poncaw Village." (Halsey to Messrs Pratte, Chouteau & Co., dated October 6, 1834 — *Fort Pierre Letter Book*, 1832-1835, p. 80). For biographical data concerning Emilien Primeau, see *note* 346.

328 This was the general term for any rival of the American Fur Company (Michigan Pioneer and Historical *Collections*, vol. xxxvii, p. 131, *note* 5). See also Chittenden, *Early Steamboat Navigation on the Missouri River*, vol. i, p. 59.

329 Honoré Picotte ". . . Picotte has gone to winter with the Yanctonas, Papin with the Hookpapas near the Ree Village . . ." (Extract of Letter from Laidlaw to William Dickson, October 30, 1833 (*Fort Pierre Letter Book*).

330 Kenneth Mackenzie. Others, too, besides Chardon, were beginning to wonder at his continued non-appearance. Hamilton's letters show that he had fully expected him to return promptly, and was quite unaware of his departure for Europe. As late as October 18th he thought he would appear "early in Decr." (Hamilton to Kipp, dated Fort Union, October 18, 1834 — *Fort Union Letter Book*, 1833-1835, p. 57). And Halsey was expectant also. "We have had," wrote he, "no arrival from St. Louis yet, and begin to fear Something has happened to the Gentlemen We have been looking for from thence; Otherwise it appears to me Some of them would have been here before the Present period. . ." (Halsey to Messrs Pratte, Chouteau & Co., dated Fort Pierre, October 21, 1834 — *Fort Pierre Letter Book*, 1832-1835, p. 81).

331 Another name for "surround". See *note* 355.

332 William Dickson. For references to his location at this time, see Laidlaw to E. T. Denig, dated Fort Pierre, November 23, 1834 — *Fort Pierre Letter Book*, 1832-1835, p. 83, and Laidlaw to H. Picotte, dated Fort Pierre, December 3, 1834, *idem*, p. 84. When the Upper Missouri Outfit was first organized, he had his camp on the James River.

333 Joseph Howard, described as a *voyageur* on the *List of 1830*. See no. 67. Of him, Kenneth Mackenzie wrote to Robert Campbell as follows: "One of my men deserted from my fort last night. I have reason to suppose he has taken refuge with you, his name Joe Howard, he wintered with Mr Mitchell who will present this note to you & bring back my man if at your fort. I do not claim him for his worth, for he is utterly worthless, a complete vagabond, but he is my hired servant & I am satisfied you will present no obstacles to my recovering him" (Mackenzie to R. Campbell, dated Fort Union, April 16, 1834, *Fort Union Letter Book*, 1833-1835, p. 47). Hamilton must have had a somewhat better opinion of Howard since he trusted him as a messenger. "I send pr Joe H. & P. B. tres for Mr McK. who I expect will arrive at your post abt this time . . . the men are in deep debt what you find necessary to advance them charge this post & send accts by them" (Hamilton to Chardon, dated Fort Union, November 15, 1834, *idem*, p. 59). The middle of the following January, Hamilton sent Howard and two others, Marchande and Marechal, to Crawford's post from whence they were to be despatched forthwith to Kipp at Fort McKenzie. "Joe is in debt," wrote he, "but is so fond of spending, he would never cry 'hold enough.'" (Hamilton to Lewis Crawford, dated Fort Union, January 15, 1835, *idem*, p. 66).

Joseph Howard is believed to have been the son of Thomas Proctor Howard of the Lewis and Clark expedition, although there was a man of exactly the same name with the North West Company. His mother was Genevieve Roy. On July 24, 1839, according to the records of the Old Cathedral in St. Louis, Joseph married Emelie Dubreuil, and on the following August 22nd was baptized the infant son of Joseph Howard and Margaret, an Indian woman. He was still in the service of the Upper Missouri Outfit in 1849 (Letter to Jas. Kipp, dated Fort Pierre, November 15, 1849, *Fort Pierre Letter Book*, 1849-'50).

334 Further particulars of this affair are supplied by Hamilton's report to Mackenzie, ". . . I have now to apprize you how affairs have progressed since Novr.; on the 17th of that month La Lance & L'Ours with about 80 warriors started to give battle to the Gros Ventres — on the 1st Decr. the parties met near the Village of the latter. La Lance & about

20 of his men were Killed, 16 others severely wounded found their way here in miserable plight, the remainder got to their several camps as they best could: this unfortunate coup has very much interfered with the Robe-making of the Gens des filles, Gens des roches & Gens de Canot bands, for war, war, war is their constant cry. Nor do they hesitate to declare that having lost the inducement to make robes, as they will no longer procure grog, they hunt barely for subsistence . . .'' (Hamilton to Mackenzie, dated March 29, 1835 *Fort Union Letter Book, 1833-1835*, p. 70). To J. F. A. Sanford Hamilton told further that ''La Lance was killed by the Gros Ventres after a battle in which he was taken prisoner while endeavouring to save his son's life on the 30th Novr. or the 1st Decr. last'' (Hamilton to J. F. A. Sanford, dated Fort Union, March 24, 1835, *idem*, p. 72).

Larpenteur, in his account of the affair, differs materially as to the date. According to him, the chief events happened prior to November fifteenth. See Coues, *Forty Years a Fur Trader on the Upper Missouri*, vol. i, p. 78, *note* 8.

[335] For mention of Daniel Lamont's arrival from St. Louis, see William Laidlaw to Messrs Pratte, Chouteau & Co., dated Fort Pierre, December 13, 1834 *(Fort Pierre Letter Book, 1832-1835,* p. 93) and William Laidlaw to F. A. Chardon, dated Fort Pierre, December 16, 1834, *(idem,* p. 95). It will be recalled that Lamont made his will at Fort Pierre, November 11, 1834, so it must have been on the occasion of this visit, and, perhaps, in anticipation of some disaster overtaking him at Fort Union, whither he was bound. He requested in his will ''that in event of my dying in the Civilized World or at any of the Establishments of the Upper Missouri Outfit of which I am at present a Member my Body shall be Committed to its Mother Earth from whence it came with decency but no Parade; and with the usual forms of the Scotch Presbyterian Church in which I was Baptised and in infancy reared, tho' agreeably to the interpretation of its tenates in Missouri I cannot be a Member thereof'' (St. Louis Court House *Records*) See Appendix. Lamont went on to Fort Union to take charge there during Mackenzie's absence in Europe (Hamilton to J. E. Brazeau, dated Fort Union, January 12, 1835 — *Fort Union Letter Book, 1833-1835,* p. 61). Early in 1835, Hamilton, writing to Crawford, remarked, ''You need not expect Mr Lamont for some time to come, he is comfortably housed here & I hope he has no wish to move camp'' (Hamilton to Lewis Crawford, dated Fort Union, January 15, 1835, *idem,* p. 66). Lamont had, however, already made one excursion. His movements were duly reported to the absent Mackenzie, ''. . . The river closed here on the 5 Decr. Mr Lamont & Mr Laferrier arrived here 20th Decr., they started for Fort Assiniboine 29th Decr. & Mr Lamont returned here Janry 8th. visited the Upper Fort again Febry. 15 returned here Febry 22 and started again for the same place March 20th.'' (Hamilton to Mackenzie, dated Fort Union, March 29, 1835, *idem,* 70).

[336] M. P. Laferriere, no. 14 in *List of 1831*. In the *Ledger,* 1831-1833, p. 447, and the *P. C. & Co. account book,* under date of 1834 and 1836, the initials appear reversed, ''P. M.'' For Larpenteur's allusion to this man and Coues's failure to identify him, see *Forty Years a Fur Trader on the Upper Missouri,* vol. i, p. 77 and *note* 7. Laferriere seems to have gone to live at Fort Union at about the time, in 1832, that Hamilton and Chardon went there. Previously, he, like Chardon, counted the Teton post his headquarters. In writing to Hamilton, February 12, 1833 *(Fort Pierre Letter*

Book, p. 21), Laidlaw said, ''Please remember me to Chardon and Laferrier.''

337 James Andrews. Evidently the same referred to as a Canadian, in Chardon's letter to Pierre Chouteau, dated Fort Tecumseh, August 20, 1820 (1830?). In a letter of March 3, 1835, corrective of items in Halsey's accounts, Hamilton incidentally referred to James Andrews as having been ''left at Fort Clark'' (*Fort Union Letter Book,* 1833-1835, p. 68); but the name does not occur in any list of employees examined. In the *A. F. Co. Western Ledger,* 1831-1833, p. 84, appears an account with a certain Thomas Andrews. In the ''engagements'' of 1836-1838 (*Chouteau-Maffitt Collection*), James Andrews is described as *voyageur* and interpreter.

338 For a noteworthy description of festivities at a trading post, see Alexander Henry's account of a New Year feast at his Red River post in 1801 (Coues, *Henry's Journals,* p. 162) Harmon speaks of the Indians as being actually frightened at the New Year festivities of the French Canadians (*Journal,* pp. 196-197).

339 For Maximilian's references to this dance, see Thwaites, *Early Western Travels,* vol. xxiv, pp. 48, 62.

340 Of May's whereabouts some slight information is obtainable from Laidlaw's correspondence — ''. . . Mr May has been waiting here patiently for some time past, in expectation that Newman would return and join him, but as he has not made his appearance Mr M. has given him up, and will accompany our trains as far as Wm. Dicksons, from thence to your place by whom I will forward this letter as also his account   (Laidlaw to Chardon, dated Fort Pierre, December 16, 1834, *Fort Pierre Letter Book,* 1832-1833, p. 95).

''This will be handed you by Mr Newman who leaves this tomorrow for your place in hopes of finding Mr May; he has been here for some days past, and in a pack of trouble about his *Bubbly Jock,* which he leaves in charge of P. N. Lecluc . . . I have nothing to offer you in the way of news, not having heard from any of our outposts since Mr May left here . . .

''Mr Halsey will send you a statement of Newmans a/c . . . Please tell Mr. May that his horses are both sound and well . . .''

(Same to Same, dated Fort Pierre, January 11, 1835, *idem,* pp. 101-102).

341 She-ha-ka, the same who journeyed to Washington at the time of the Lewis and Clark expedition. See Thwaites, *Original Journals,* vol. i, p. 262.

342 Laidlaw would seem to have been similarly depressed. He wrote Chardon on the 11th, ''I put this down as the most dull winter I ever passed in the Indian Country. I cannot even hear of a Buffaloe; what would I give for a month of such pleasant times as we passed at the Forks of the Cheyenne together.

''. . . I wish you would write me a long letter by the first and every opportunity . . . (Laidlaw to Chardon, dated January 11, 1835 *Fort Pierre Letter Book, 1832-1835,* p. 102).

343 Laidlaw would seem to have been not particularly pleased with William Dickson's conduct at this time. He wrote to him on the 12th in a very critical mood and hinted at the advisability of moving his camp because the Indians had moved on in search of buffalo. ''. . . your of the

31st I received yesterday, and embrace the opportunity of Mr. Newmans going to the Mandans of sending you the 2 doz. Red Stone Pipes you request . . . I regret much that you have not been a little more communicative in your last, you do not acknowledge the receipt of mine to you per Charles Primeau (perhaps you thought it not worth answering) but at all events I think you might acknowledge the receipt of the goods at least . . . I must confess this is rather a loose way of doing business, and hope that you will be a little more particular in the future —

"You give me no idea what your prospects are for trade, . . .; a person in charge of a post ought never to trust the occurrences of his post to be related verbally while he is able to write them himself.

"I am much surprised and disappointed at the same time, to learn from Charles that Emillien Primeau has opposed you so successfully, he has now got a much greater portion of the trade than I ever expected he would; considering the advantage you had over him in every respect, and after the instructions you had to push the trade so that what Furs or Robes he might get would be a loosing concern for him —   You will know that you are under no restraint with regard to prices, but to get the trade even if the returns you make should not pay the first cost of the goods, it is of no consequence so as you secure the trade; you are well aware that this is the object of the company and their positive instructions —

"I understand from Charles that the indians have nearly all left your place, and gone above on account of the scarcity of Buffaloe; if this be the case and little or no trade at your establishment, I think you ought by all means to go yourself to where the force of the trade will be, and let everything be done possible to secure it; I am in hopes that the necessity of such a step will occur to you before this reaches you . . ."

(Laidlaw to William Dickson, dated Fort Pierre, January 12, 1835 *Fort Pierre Letter Book, 1833-1835*, pp. 100-101).

344 For an interesting account of a "winter express," see *Chittenden*, H. M., *Early Steamboat Navigation on the Missouri River*, vol. i, pp. 41-42.

345 In the *Fort Tecumseh Journal, January 31 to June 13, 1830*, under date of April second, "Pierre Dauphin arrived from Little Chyenne river . . ." This seems likely to have been the man Chardon here mentions.   However, Pierre and three other men of the name of Dauphin, Constant, Alexis, and Charles were employed, in the thirties, on the upper Missouri.   The three last named were, according to the St. Louis Old Cathedral records, the sons of Jean Baptiste Dauphin and Catherine Constant, residents of Carondelet.   Constant Dauphin married Margaret Hugé, July 16, 1832.   Neither in the Roman Catholic church records nor in the P. C. & Co. account books has a trace been found of Antoine Dauphin whose name appears in Clark's list of licensed men and who was the man to whom Maximilian is supposed to have had reference (Thwaites, *Early Western Travels*, vol. xxiii, p. 67, *note* 47), although Deland seems satisfied (South Dakota *Historical Collections*, vol. ix, p. 110, *note* 44) to confound him with Pierre.   In the *Auguste Chouteau Papers* is an order of sale, 1819, with an incidental reference to "John Baptiste Dauphin and Catherin his wife."   In May, 1836, near the mouth of the White River, Constant Dauphin engaged himself to Pierre D. Papin, Agent of Pratte, Chouteau & Co., for the Sioux Outfit (*Chouteau-Maffitt Collection*, 1835-1838).   That there was a man named Dauphin among the employees at Fort Clark, at all events subsequent to June of this year, seems to be suggested by a letter that Halsey sent to Hamilton, June 20, 1835.   Dauphin was the

bearer of it from Fort Pierre but it was likely he would "stay some time at Fort Clark" (*Fort Pierre Letter Book*, p. 112).   For a Dauphin on the upper Missouri in the late forties, see Palliser, p. 180.

346 Joseph Emilien Primeau, born March 3, 1803, son of Paul Primeau and Pelagie Bissonet (Roman Catholic Church *Records* of St. Louis).   In the *List of 1830*, both Emilien and Pierre "Premeau" are numbered.   For Emilien Primeau's death at the hands of Indians, see present journal, February 1, 1836 and *note* 96; also North Dakota Historical Society *Collections*, vol. i, p. 377.   Charles Primeau of Larpenteur's acquaintance in 1845-'46 was a brother of Emilien (Coues, *Forty Years a Fur Trader on the Upper Missouri*, vol. i, p. 227).   Charles Primeau had a trading-post above Fort Clark (Lounsberry, C. A., *Early History of North Dakota*, p. 236.)

347 Beaver rivers have been so common in the west that it is difficult to identify the particular one here mentioned.   Existing maps show a small Beaver creek falling into the Missouri from the north in William county, North Dakota, and a larger stream of the same name, a tributary of the Little Missouri.   Lewis and Clark mention a Beaver river, or Lower Deer creek, a tributary of the Yellowstone; and Beaver Dam river, or the Maropa, an affluent of the Missouri.   An entry in the *Sire Log* for June 28, 1844 records the fact that "l'ancien hyvernement de Chardon" was *vis a vis* la *Riviere au Castor*.

348 Much regarding this great Mandan chief, Mah-to-toh-pa, or Four Bears, the reputed father-in-law of James Kipp (See *note* 60), develops as the journal proceeds. Catlin's very particular comments upon him should, however, be noted (*North American Indian*, vol. i, pp. 92, 145 *et seq.*) and Maximilian's (*Travels*, 1843, p. 171).   It is interesting to observe that Helen P. Clarke, daughter of Malcolm Clarke, who killed Owen Mackenzie, says, in a sketch of her father's life, that the Blackfeet Indians called him Ne-so-ke-i-o, Four Bears, because he had killed "four bears in one day" and adds, "I know he was the first man, be he white or red, who was called Ne-so-ke-i-o" (Montana Historical Society *Contributions*, vol. ii, p. 256).

349 What immediately follows constituted one of the extra pages of Chardon's manuscript.

350 The Chewah, says Coues (*Lewis and Clark*, vol. i, p. 172, *note* 45), of Lewis and Clark's day is the Apple Creek of Stevens.

351 A mistake possibly for Letant. See *note* 464.

352 Possibly Thomas Chapman.   A child was born to Thomas Chapman and Eliza Chauvin, January 6, 1839.   From the same church records of St. Louis it appears that a child of J. Chapman and Eliza Chauvin was baptized, August 16, 1837.   The same father must be meant in both cases and, since the full name is given in the one instance, it no doubt is correct.

353 When Hamilton wrote his very detailed letter to Mackenzie, March 29th, he reported, "Not a breath of news from below since Mr Lamont's arrival in December last, but I am daily expecting the return of two men who were sent down to winter with Mr Chardon" (Hamilton to Mackenzie, dated Fort Union, March 29, 1835 *Fort Union Letter Book*, 1833-1835, p. 71).   It is conceivable that Charbonneau was one of the two men sent down to winter at Fort Clark.

[354] Dominique Lachapelle. His camp was "at the Yanctonais." In the Fort Tecumseh and Fort Pierre letter books there are various references to this man and, from his intimacy with Honoré Picotte and Pascal Cerré, he might well have been an employee of the P. D. Papin concern, the French Company, so-called. In 1831, he was trading with the Rees (See *note* 30) and, when Picotte, later in that same year, went up to the Mandans, he took Lachapelle with him (Laidlaw to Mackenzie, November 27, 1831, *Fort Tecumseh Letter Book, 1830-1832,* pp. 72-76). Dominique Lachapelle had an account with the Upper Missouri Outfit in July, August, and November of 1835. He was classified as of the Sioux Outfit at Fort Clark in 1837. There was a Louis Lachapelle, whose name appears in the *List of 1831.* When Charles Augustus Murray was among the Pawnees in the middle thirties, he met with an interpreter among them whose name was, seemingly, Lachapelle and, of whom, Murray formed no good opinion (*Travels in North America* during *the Years 1834, 1835, 1836,* vol. i, p. 406). This man was probably the same as the David Lachapelle, who, being hunter and interpreter at the Arikara and Pawnee villages, was killed by the Pawnees, June 27, 1843 (Drumm, *Luttig Journal,* p. 30, *note* 12). The La Chapelle whom Maximilian met with had a Ree wife (*Travels, op. cit.,* p. 167). An André Lachapelle was on the Columbia in 1813 and killed by the Indians early in the following year (Morice, pp. 138-139).

[355] Bonneville appears to have limited the use of this expression, "surround", to a species of antelope hunting (edition of 1859, pp. 401-402); but, the following seems to define the sense in which Chardon and other traders, hunters and travellers used the term, "There had been a plan for a general 'surround,' as this species of wholesale hunting is denominated, and all was kept quiet in order to effect the object" (*Altowan,* vol. i, p. 87). See also Lewis and Clark's description, (Coues, *Lewis and Clark,* vol. i, p. 209) and Catlin's, (*North American Indian,* 1850, vol. i, pp. 199-200).

[356] According to Lewis and Clark, snow blindness was a common complaint in the winter season (Coues, *Lewis and Clark,* vol. i, p. 235) Under date of February 16, 1805, they mentioned the fact that one of the Mandan chiefs was affected by it (Thwaites, *Original Journals,* vol. i, p. 262) and Brackenridge thought it especially prevalent among the Arikaras (Thwaites, *Early Western Travels,* vol. vi, p. 123). Alexander Henry recorded March 17, 1806 (Coventry Copy of *Journal,* vol. i, p. 382), "All my people laid up Snow Blind".

[357] For the medicine dance, most probably associated with this feast, see Coues, *Lewis and Clark,* vol. i, pp. 222-223. It could be given "by any person desirous of doing honor to his medicine or genius."

[358] This may be regarded as fairly typical of the way the fur traders, out of reach of the strong arm of the law, avenged their private wrongs. The Indians, their own customs being what they were, would have thought the procedure perfectly proper, injury for injury, blood for blood; but they failed to understand why white men appealed, on occasion, to higher powers. and obtained enormous indemnities for offences that the Indians, when their relative positions were reversed, had to submit to in silence.

[359] Tabeau had a similar opinion of the Arikaras and so had Father De Smet of the Assiniboines and Brackenridge of the Osages.

[360] Michel Gravelle, no. 236 of the *List of 1830,* and, possibly, the Michel

Gravier of the account books. He was one of the two sons-in-law of Jack Rem, whose assassination by the Deschamp family led to its own destruction, a reference to which will appear later. The account books also show an Antoine Gravelle. A Michel Gravelle was among the Canadian *voyageurs*, who offered themselves for British service in June, 1814 (Wisconsin Historical Society *Collections*, Madison Reprint, 1909, vol. ix, pp. 262-281) ; a Michael Gravel married the daughter of a Menomonee chief (*idem*, vol. iii, p. 271) ; and a Michael Gravel appears in Clark's *Book of Sanford's Accounts* as being, in August, 1828, Interpreter for the Crees. Michl Gravelle was at Fort Union in 1831 when a draft was drawn there by Hamilton ("for Mr. McKenzie") in his favor (*Chouteau-Maffitt Collection*).

361 See *note* 53.

362 Lewis Crawford no doubt brought with him the following letter from Hamilton:

Fort Union March 24th 1835

Mr F. A. Chardon
                Dear Sir
                        Agreeable to your request by Mr Lamont I have sent on board the Steam Boat Sundry articles as per Invoice which will I hope reach you in safety. The trade of this post is not yet over. I am yet expecting a considerable number of Robes from the Young Gauché, the Moose Dung & Labrêume qui Marche with sundry Whips & Strays. Mr Crawford has traded 400 packs and the General above 350 packs. Mr Kipp promises 600 packs & Mr Tulloch 200. — On the 18th January your neighbours the Gros Ventres visited Pellots Camp on the Yellow Stone and took away 20 horses but on being hotly pursued they left en route 14 and eventually got off with six. Le garçon de Sonnant lately stole Halcrow's horse & one of old Deschamp's. Dr Jackson & his band have worked well this winter, Le Brechû has been encamped at the Fort since Janry 9th. — Scarcely a peace (*sic*) of Meat has been traded here this season but Pellot has left our Larder in good order. — Your old friend L enfant de fer came in last week at the head of a small band & traded near 600 Robes.
I shall have the pleasure of addressing you again next month by Mr Lamont — in the mean time believe me to be
                Dear Sir
                        Very Truly Your's
                        (signed) J. Archdale Hamilton
(*Fort Union Letter Book*, 1833-1835, p. 73).

363 On the 29th March, Hamilton wrote that he was "hourly expecting the Steam Boat" at Fort Union, "having heard that she left her moorings to day — she will not be long detained here, as all the packs are ready to be put on board" (Hamilton to Mackenzie, dated Fort Union, March 29, 1835, *Fort Union Letter Book*, 1833-1835, p. 71). She left Fort Union April 2nd (Hamilton to Samuel Tulloch, dated Fort Union, April 6, 1835, *idem* p. 73). The *Assiniboine* had wintered in the north, at the mouth of Poplar River (Chittenden, *Early Steamboat Navigation on the Missouri River*, vol. i, pp. 193-194). For Captain Carlisle's conduct in that winter of 1834-1835, see Hamilton's letters, and especially one to Mackenzie, November 15, 1834, in which he reported that Carlisle was "entirely governed by his mistress the Mulatto woman" and was leaving the steam-

boat "in a very dangerous situation exposed to ye whole force of ye current" (*Fort Union Letter Book, 1833-1835*, p. 59).

364 It had been expected that Lamont would get away from Fort Union the end of April (Hamilton to Tulloch, dated Fort Union, April 6, 1835, *Fort Union Letter Book, 1833-1835*, p. 73) or at any rate by the first of May (Hamilton to Mackenzie, dated Fort Union, March 29, 1835, *idem*, p. 70); but he was still there on the 5th, writing elaborate instructions to Culbertson and, with Hamilton and Kipp, who had already arrived there, drinking his health and wishing him the success he deserved (Lamont to Culbertson, dated Fort Union, May 5, 1835, *idem*, p. 78). There was still, apparently, plenty of liquor to be had at Fort Union, and Lamont notifies Culbertson that he is sending him "two Barrels of Alcohol and six of Wine." He warns him to make "the most of it and do not sell a single drop of it to the men, we have long since ceased to do it here; explain to the Indians that our supply of liquor would have been larger had not the Steam Boat been kept here all winter for lack of water, and consequently unable to return here in time sufficient for this Outfit, which is necessarily sent away at this early date to avoid a rencontre with the Crows. Should the Crow Indians come near you again this summer do not spare them tooth or Nail . . ." (*idem*, p. 77). The hospitality that Mackenzie had been famous for (Larpenteur, vol. i, pp. 70 *et seq.*) Lamont was more than prepared to extend. He had written to Captain Bonneville at the Wind River Mountain, ". . . setting aside all matters of business, it would afford me much pleasure to have you as my guest a few days or weeks, and I will promise you the best cheer the Country will afford . . ." (Lamont to Bonneville, dated Fort Union 8 Miles West of the Mouth of the Yellow Stone, April 6, 1835, (*Fort Union Letter Book, 1833-1835*, p. 75). This was Lamont's last winter on the upper Missouri. As elsewhere noted, when Mackenzie returned from Europe, he found that Lamont was preparing to go into other business.

365 Of their arrival at Fort Pierre there seems no definite record but Lamont, presumably, left that place the first of June (Laidlaw to Messrs Pratte, Chouteau & Co., from Fort Pierre, (no date), *Fort Pierre Letter Book, 1832-1835*, p. 110).

366 Antelope.

367 Presumably the Boneventure Lebrun, of whom Halsey wrote disparagingly to Hamilton, February 15, 1832 (*Fort Tecumseh Letter Book, 1830-1832*, p. 98), calling him "a great Black-guard;" and the Boniventure Lebrun, no. 287 of the *List of 1830*; as likewise the Bon Lebrun of Clark's List. In the present journal, the name seems, subsequently, to be abbreviated to "Venture" (e. g. October 18, 1836), to "Venture Lebrun" (e. g. November 13, 1836), and even to "Benture" (e. g. January 9, 1836, February 13, 1837, etc.). The "Bonteur" of February 11, 1836 may be yet another variation. In the *List of 1830-1831*, there is the name, "Andre Bonneture." It occurs as no. 71. There was a Bonaventure at Fort Union in 1843 (Audubon, vol. ii, p. 42), the same, no doubt, as the Antoine Lebrun who was there in 1844 (Morice, p. 174).

368 This must have been the *Yellowstone*, which left Fort Pierre on her upward journey, June 5th, 1832 (*Fort Tecumseh Journal, 1832-1833*). Kenneth Mackenzie had awaited her coming at the soon-to-be-dismantled post, Fort Tecumseh, and had finally sent down Pierre Ortubise and two

other men to inquire as to the cause of the prolonged delay (Mackenzie to the Gentleman in Charge of the Otoe Establishment, dated Fort Tecumseh May 10, 1832, *Fort Tecumseh Letter Book*, 1830-1832, p. 116). The allusion here to her arrival "this day three years" raises the question, Where at the time was Chardon? If at Fort Clark, was he there *en route* to Fort Union? Note the similarity of the entry for June 18th, in which, most certainly, the reference is to Fort Clark. Catlin was a passenger by the *Yellowstone* in 1832, and it took him three months to, cover the distance between St. Louis and Fort Union. At Fort Pierre he had painted a likeness of Chardon's wife, and he refers to her thus: "at present the wife of a white man named Chardon, a Frenchman. . ." (vol. i, p. 224), which would not indicate that he had yet met the husband. At Fort Union, he did meet Chardon, saw a good deal of him, and commented upon his going to discuss with his wife the results of a hunt. She may, therefore, have come up on the *Yellowstone*. See, however, *note* 149.

369 As elsewhere indicated this is one of the references to the Battle of New Orleans that is taken to imply that Chardon had a very personal interest in the event.

370 Hamilton, at Fort Union, was as eager for news as was Chardon at Fort Clark. He wrote to Laidlaw, "A fortnight since I sent two men to Fort Clark for news — they have not returned, nor have I received a breath of intelligence of anything that has been passing below since Mr Lamont arrived here last Christmas" (Hamilton to Laidlaw, dated Fort Union, July 16, 1835   *Fort Union Letter Book*, 1833-1835, p. 82). In similar wise he complained to Lamont, "No messenger or friendly gale has brought me a line or breath of news since your departure: a fortnight since I sent two men to Fort Clark for intelligence — they have not returned" (Hamilton to Lamont, dated Fort Union, July 17, 1835, *idem*, p. 82).

371 And so they were at Fort Union, probably because of the excessive fall of rain. Hamilton wrote, "The quantity of rain which has fallen here this season I should think is almost without precedent, the fort was quite a Lake for a month, the points of wood are deluged, grass is abundant everywhere, and Mosquitoes bad beyond all former example, the men cry out terribly and not without cause" (Hamilton to Lamont, dated Fort Union, July 17, 1835 — *Fort Union Letter Book*, 1833-1835, p. 82). Nicollet and Frémont had, in 1839, a like reason to complain of this particular pest (See Frémont, *Memoirs*, vol. i, p. 49) and Wyeth in 1833, below Bean's agency (Young, *Sources of the History of Oregon*, vol. i, p. 217).

372 "I enclose," reported Hamilton, "Bill of Lading of —— packs of Buffalo Robes pr boats Julia, Jane, Margaret & Isabella under charge of J. E. Brazeau bound for St Louis to touch at Fort Pierre &c . . . Inventories, men's Accts and so forth are addressed to Fort Pierre to be looked over. B. Bourdalone No 21. on the List, who works his passage down, came in here half dead, from a Division of Captain Bonnevilles party under Montero, who has been for the last year with 50 Men trapping & trading in the Crow Country   he tells a wofull tale the leading features whereof Mr Tulloch had previously heard from other quarters . . ." (Hamilton to Messrs Pratte, Chouteau & Co., dated Fort Union, July 18, 1835, *Fort Union Letter Book*, 1833-1835, pp. 83-84).

373 This, as seen from the letter of Hamilton's just quoted in *note* 372, was J. E. Brazeau. This man is described as a Clerk, no 12, in the *List of*

1831, where appears also a Douchoquette Brazeau. In the Account books for 1834 and subsequent years Joseph E. Brazeau's name figures repeatedly, also as the signature of a witness in engagement contracts, as does that of Charles F. Brazeau. A Nicolas Brazeau is registered in the *Ledger* for 1831-1833, pp. 323, 389. The father of some or all of these was probably Joseph Brazeau, who, according to the St. Louis Church records, married Julie Fisbac, June 11, 1812 and to whom a son, C. Brazeau, was born, October 27, 1814, the same, no doubt, referred to by Chardon, August 19, 1836. For more about J. E. Brazeau, see *note* 126.

374 William Neil Fulkerson had only just come up to the Mandans. He had been at Fort Pierre about the middle of the month and, when he proceeded on his way, May accompanied him (Halsey to Chardon, dated Fort Pierre, July 18, 1835 *Fort Pierre Letter Book,* 1832-1835, pp. 112-113). This is the first mention of the Indian Agent for the upper Missouri in the present journal.

375 Many and various are the contemporary references, like this journal entry of Chardon's, to the burning of the *Assiniboine.* For some of them, see Laidlaw to Hamilton, dated Fort Pierre, June 20, 1835, *Fort Pierre Letter Book,* 1832-1835, p. 112; Hamilton to Culbertson, dated Fort Union, September 9, 1835, *Fort Union Letter Book,* 1833-1835, p. 86; Mackenzie to Crooks, dated Fort Union, December 10, 1835, *idem,* pp. 93-95.   A very considerable portion of Maximilian's Natural History collection was on board and burnt.   Lamont duly reported the loss, and, later on, Mackenzie condoled with Maximilian.   For later accounts of the burning of the *Assiniboine,* accounts other than contemporary, see Audubon, *Missouri River Journals,* vol. ii, pp. 7-8 and T. A. Culbertson, *Journal,* p. 124.

376 Chittenden locates the scene of the disaster as at the head of Sibley Island near Little Heart River (*Steamboat Wrecks on the Missouri River,* p. 3873).

377 Justin Grosclaude, a *voyageur* (*List of 1830,* no. 166).   There are Ledger entries against him showing he was in the employ of the Upper Missouri Outfit in the late thirties as he had been in the early; but after that he must have been for a time with the Opposition.   The document here quoted shows that when he returned to the employ of the American Fur Company he was not high in the favour of Honoré Picotte, who was then its agent:—

''Justin Gros Claude the Bearer of the present was in the employ of Pratte & Cabanné and in the transfer of useless articles I had to take him, he goes to the Blackfeet as I do not wish him to go (to) the Crows he is engaged as a Trader but I have put him at the Second Tables   Please do the same thing & hurry him up as soon as possible'' (H. Picotte to James Kipp at Fort Union, dated Fort Pierre, December 18, 1845, *Fort Pierre Letter Book*).

378 No such name has been found in any of the lists of employees, account books or ledgers; but in Hamilton's communication to Tulloch of February 23rd, the following reference is made to a person who must have been the one here meant:

''. . . It is quite out of my power to send the men you require to rebuild your Fort & it is therefore my desire that you will make your arrangements to come down here in the Spring with your whole establishment as early as you think desirable to leave, of course bringing away every thing valuable.

You will not trade any more horses for I have already more than I have use for.   I send you two good hands in the place of the two lads who came down with La Bombarde . . .'' (Hamilton to Samuel Tulloch, dated Fort Union, February 23, 1835, *Fort Union Letter Book*, 1833-1835, p. 67).   Chardon gave to Audubon the use of an Alexis Bombard as a hunter. See *Audubon*, vol. i, p. 529.   See Morice, p. 138, for Alexandre Labombarde in 1885.

379 Red River of the North.

380 One gets the impression elsewhere that a ''Jackson dinner'' with Chardon was an especially good dinner, though in the present instance a ''dinner of squashes'' does not sound particularly exciting.   One must, however, remember that Chardon was living in a country where, at that period, vegetables of any kind were a rare luxury unless the traders were industrious in making a garden for themselves as had been Alexander Henry.

381 This has reference to a second section of the original journal, beginning September 12th, a separate note-book, in fact, in which the entries were made.   Although Chardon had not yet taken his departure from Fort Clark, some other person was the scribe of this part of his journal. There is internal evidence of that fact in the very marked differences in spelling and vocabulary, the use of underscorings and of such expressions as, ''sun up,'' ''breakfasted,'' etc.   Moreover, the handwriting is not what has been taken to be Chardon's.

382 This child, the younger son of Chardon and his Sioux wife, whose portrait Catlin painted, died September 22, 1837; and very probably at Fort Pierre, where Chardon had sent his ''boy,'' hoping that he would escape the infection.   The record of his death was inserted, at some subsequent time, in the journal.   That is very plainly to be seen in the original.

383 Obviously an error.   It should read ''August.''

384 There were at least two men of this name, one, Alexis Coté, born 1815 (St. Louis Church Records), and Jean Baptiste Coté, an employee for a certainty of the Upper Missouri Outfit at about this time (*A. F. Co. Western Ledger, 1831-1833*, pp. 120, 241).   See Morice, p. 71, for a Coté, no Christian name given.

385 Officially, of course, Fulkerson was agent for the upper Missouri tribes and not alone for the Mandans, although their village constituted his headquarters, if he can be said to have had any.

386 In the Fort Union letter books the name of this man is spelt Samuel Tulloch, and from a document of date July 21, 1834, in the *Chouteau-Maffitt Collection*, signed by the man himself, this would appear to be the correct form.   For other variations in spelling, see Coues, *Forty Years a Fur Trader on the Upper Missouri*, vol. i, p. 46, *note* 10.   The A. J. Tullock, referred to by Coues, as the builder of Fort Cass, was the same individual.   On this same subject, see *note* 116.

387 Possibly David Ewing.   See entry of August 16, 1835.

388 See entry of March 16, 1835.

389 It was the practice of both the British and American governments to

present medals to Indian chiefs whose influence and friendliness toward the whites marked them for such an honor. A similar practice was followed by some of the fur-trading companies.

390 This must mean the horse belonging to Aubichon (Obuchon, Hobuchon). In the *A. F. Co. Western Ledger*, 1831-1833 appears the account of Gabriel Hobuchon Philibert (p. 356) and of Edward Hobuchon (p. 352); and in the *Fort Tecumseh Journal*, under date of October 22, 1830, there is mention of Louis Obuchon. Lamont, November 23, 1830, sent a message by him to Holliday at the Arikara village (*Fort Tecumseh Letter Book*, 1830-1832, p. 5).

391 This may be the Nicholas Allquier of the Upper Missouri Outfit, 1832 (*A. F. Co. Western, Ledger*, 1831-1833, p. 172).

392 The Roop-ta-hee of Lewis and Clark (Thwaites, *Original Journals*, vol. i, p. 208; Coues, *Lewis and Clark*, vol. i, p. 183). Maximilian, in the *Assiniboine* reached *Ruhptare*, June 19, 1833 (*Travels*, p. 177). See also *note* 271.

393 Undoubtedly, by these were meant the *Sans Arcs*, or I-ta-zip-tco, who are to be found today "largely on Cheyenne reservation, South Dakota, with others on Standing Rock reservation, North Dakota" (*McGee, W. J., The Siouan Indians*, Bureau of Ethnology *Report*, 1893-1894, p. 160), although, at first glance, it might be thought that men without bows would be berdaches. For a description of berdaches and an insistence upon their differentiation from hermaphrodites, see *Dorsey, J. Owen, A Study of Siouan Cults, idem*, 1889-1890, pp. 378-379, 467, 516.

394 The only Manuel found for the upper Missouri in this period is a certain Manuel Alvary, mentioned in an order to pay, signed by Fontenelle and addressed to Laidlaw (*Chouteau-Maffitt Collection*, 1833). A son of Manuel Lisa's could scarcely have been of an age to warrant the title, "old." An Andre Pierre Lisa has an account in the *Ledger* for 1831-1833, p. 193.

395 It is possible that the word in the original text is "Crows." It might well be, and, if so, the passage would then read, "The Agent, made the 2 Crows, the Fool Chief & Little Sioux a present . . ." For Chief Two Crows, see Catlin, *North American Indians*, 1850, vol. i, p. 193 and Plate 77.

396 This may have been another informal treaty such as Peter Wilson had concluded with the Assiniboines (See *note* 215) or simply an inter-tribal affair.

397 Honoré Picotte? There were others of the name, however, on the river at about this time; viz., E. F., Gideon, Joseph. There seems also to have been a Jaidon Picotte of the Sioux Outfit in 1836. Note the reference to the return journey of "Peacot," entry September 16th.

398 Pierre Garreau.

399 The last letter in the *Fort Pierre Letter Book*, 1832-1835 is dated August 25, 1835. There seems to be no extant *Fort Pierre Journal* for the period.

400 For the "Dance of the Band of Buffalo Bulls" see Maximilian,

Travels, p. 449.   The big dance of religious significance described by Catlin in Letter no. 22 (*North American Indians,* 1850, vol. i, pp. 155 *et seq.*) must have been the bull, or buffalo, dance.   Note that James Kipp, Lewis Crawford and Abraham Bogard testified, July 20, 1833 (*idem,* p. 177) that they witnessed it in the company of Catlin.   Coues (*Lewis and Clark,* vol. iii, p. 986, *note* 8) likens it to "one of the sprees" of the Jews. It was originally intended for old men (*idem,* vol. ii, p. 221).

401 For Major Stephen H. Long's very graphic description of the Bear Dance, see his *Journal* of a "Voyage in a Six-Oared Skiff to the Falls of Saint Anthony in 1817," Minnesota Historical Society *Collections,* vol. ii, pp. 18-20.

402 This was evidently the same man, who started on the upward journey, September 2nd.   See journal entry and note to the same.   The proof that it was Honoré Picotte lies in the fact that Chardon departed with him.

403 Chardon did not show, on this occasion, such signs of a perennial thirst as Larpenteur insinuates he possessed (*Forty Years a Fur Trader on the Upper Missouri,* vol. i, p. 144).   There is no denying that Chardon was fond of intoxicating beverages and, at times, used them to excess.   Had it been otherwise he would have been a very exceptional fur trader.   The accounts of the Western Department show him charged with liquor as were others but not to any large amount.   The following are fair samples: In an account, June to October, 1830, he was charged

5 Gall. Brandy   @ $2.50
Iron Bound Keg $1.50
      Total $14.00

(*Ledger, Retail Store,* B. (April 1829-Nov. 1832) A.F.Co., Western, p. 271, Chouteau-Maffitt *Collection*).

Again, in an account against him for March, 1836, he was charged for 10 gls. old Whiskey $9.75

(P. C. & Co. *Retail Store Ledger* A, 1834-1837, p. 380, *idem*).

During the fearful ordeal through which he passed at the time of the small-pox epidemic, he being made to bear the brunt of the Indian accusation that the whites had brought the curse to them, he confessed, when almost at the end of his resources that "only an occasional glass of grog keeps me alive."   See entry, August, 18, 1837.

404 One object that Chardon had in leaving Fort Clark at this particular time was to take down the river his little son, Bolivar, then a child of about four years.   The following "depositions to prove age" are on file at the Court House in St. Louis:

(a)   "John B. Sarpy of the City and County aforesaid being duly sworn on his oath saith that in the month of October or November Eighteen hundred and thirty five Francis A. Chardon, Mr Picotte, Pierre D. Papin and Mr Halsey came to St Louis from the Upper Missouri the said Chardon bringing with him a little boy whom he said was his son the present Bolivar Chardon who then told me was about four years old the said Chardon took Bolivar on to Pennsylvania and as I was then going east they went with me part of the way

Sworn to and subscribed . . . this 1st day of September 1852."
        . . .
(b)   "Honore Picotte being duly sworn on his oath saith in the Year Eighteen hundred and thirty five on my way from the Yellowstone to St Louis I stopped at fort Clark on the Missouri where I found Francis A

Chardon and his son . . . who with others came down in company with me.''
. . .
(c) ''. . . on the first day of September in the Year 1852 also appeared Pierre A. Berthold of the City of St Louis who . . . saith that in the fall of the Year Eighteen hundred and thirty five Francis A Chardon came to St Louis from the Upper Missouri bringing with him his son Bolivar Chardon, he took said Bolivar to the house of my Mother who resided on 5th Street . . . between Pine & Olive Streets from whence he took him with him to Pennsylvania. Francis A Chardon then said that said Bolivar was about four years old that he brought him down thus young so as to have him entirely educated in civilized Society and was going to take him to Pennsylvania & leave him with said Francis A. Chardon's parents to have him educated which I believe he did. . . .''

405 This, although not quoted entire or with exactness, is from Lawrence Sterne's *Sentimental Journey through France and Italy*, from the chapter, entitled, *The Passport — The Hotel at Paris*, p. 79. After discounting, somewhat, by means of ''systematic reasonings,'' the terrors of the Bastile, Sterne saw an imprisoned English starling. Its pathetic call for release so stirred his sympathy that he expressed himself thus on the contrast between captivity, ''slavery,'' and freedom:

''Disguise thyself as thou wilt, still, Slavery ! said I — still thou art a bitter draught ! and though thousands in all ages have been made to drink of thee, thou art no less bitter on that account — 'Tis thou, thrice sweet and gracious goddess, addressing myself to Liberty, whom all in public or private worship, whose taste is grateful. and ever will be so, till Nature herself shall change — . . .''

406 The absence of Chardon would seem to have brought Alexander Kennedy back to Fort Clark, although not immediately and not again as its journalist. Mackenzie returned that fall to the upper Missouri, lingering at Fort Pierre, then at Fort Clark and walking all the way from the latter place to Fort Union, where he arrived November 17th. He had been long away, over a year, and he now found a great deal demanding his personal attention. For the time being, Bellehumuer was put in charge at the Mandan post and Kennedy sent down from the Assiniboine, to keep him company and to act as a sort of secretary (Mackenzie to Bellehumeur, dated Fort Union, November 24, 1835, *Fort Union Letter Book*, 1833-1835, pp. 87-88). No entries, however, were made in the present journal, as found, between September 17, 1835, the day of Chardon's departure, and the beginning of the next year, and, when they were made at this latter date, they were made apparently by David D. Mitchell, who had re-entered the employ of the American Fur Company, having been raised to the rank of a partner [See *note* 67], Lamont's interests being transferred to him as Lamont was leaving the trade and going into a new business (Mackenzie to Crooks, December 10, 1835, *idem*, pp. 93-95). Many things incline one to the opinion of Mitchell authorship, such as the style of composition, moralizings with some slight evidence of superior culture, the report which Mitchell made in 1836 to Agent Fulkerson on the circumstances of the Emilien Primeau murder, and, finally, certain characteristic scriblings on the outside pages of the Chardon manuscript. One of these is conclusive and the other fairly so. I give them in reverse order.

(a)   Statement of Packs at Fort Clark 1836
April 11th   14th   Pack $\times$ 1-102 Red Foxes —

————————————————————————

,,   ,, 2- 82 Grey   ,,
,,   4 Badgers
                7 Hares
                6 Red Foxes —
               85 Musk Rats
                2 Minks

————————————————————————

,,   ,, 3- 48 Wolf skins —

————————————————————————

,, — ,, 4567 each 100 Beaver — 400 pounds

————————————————————————

313 Packs Buffalo Robes   10 each

————————————————————————

1 Packton Beaver — 42 ....

==

1836
June 16 —   Recapitulation
        313 Packs Buffalo Robes 10 each is 3130 Robes
          4 Packs Beaver .... 100 each ,, 400
          1 Packton Do 42 42   442
          1 Pack Wolf Skins ....   48 skins
          1   ,,   Red Foxes — containing —   102 ,,
          1   ,,   Mix .... viz
                                    82 Grey Foxes
                                     4 Badgers
                                     7 Hares
                                     6 Red Foxes
                                    85 Musk rats
                                     2 Minks
       $ 9330.00
         1600.00
          168.00
           21.00
           51.00
           30.00
        ——————
       $ 11,200.00   Amount of Pelteries 1836
                             at Fort Clark —   D. D. M.
(b)
        Amount of Pelteries Made at Fort Clark   35 — 36 — 37 — 38
        1835 — 3270 Robes 1140   Beaver   F. A. C. — $ 13 – 800
        1836 — 3130 – ,, –   442   ,,   D. D. M. — — 10 93 7
        1837 — 3200 – ,, –   436   ,,   F. A. C. 11 126
        1838 — 2870 – ,, –   404   ,,   F. A. C. 10, 226

April 25th, Mitchell's journalistic work, assuming it was his, ceased
abruptly, and not until June did the characteristic handwriting of Chardon
reappear.   Judged by the internal evidence of chirography and orthog-
raphy, the scribe, who acted as an amanuensis for Chardon just prior to
his leave-taking, was not the same as the one who kept the journal from
January to April of the next year.   Part of the time, for a few days at

least, Mackenzie had himself been there. A series of letters reproduced in the Appendix in whole or in part, will help to fill the hiatus regarding events and conditions in the upper Missouri country. They are all from the *Fort Union Letter Book*, 1833-1835, (*Pierre Chouteau Collection*, Missouri Historical Society).

407 See *note* 387.

408 Sometimes called the Mandan lake.

409 Jean Baptiste Dufond (Defont, Defond) See the American Fur Co. account books, 1834-1838. In the St. Louis Roman Catholic Church records, the name occurs as Jn. Bap. Defond, the occasion being the baptism of a daughter born to him and a Sioux woman. Baptist Dufond appears as no. 229 in the *List of 1830*. Among the engagements for 1836-1839, he is described as ''pilot, patron, trader'' (*Chouteau-Maffitt Collection*).

410 ''Adams is a friend of Newman's, he is a stranger to me,'' wrote Mackenzie to Bellehumeur in a letter, November 24, 1835 (*Fort Union Letter Book*, 1833-1835, p. 87), ''but you may advance him 50 or 60 dollars if he has need for so much.'' There was a David Adams of Bonneville's party (Bonner's *Beckwourth*, pp. 208, 210); and a Bernard Adams at Fort Union in 1843 (Audubon, vol. ii, p. 97).

411 It was because of the uncertainty of May's wintering at Fort Clark that Kennedy had been sent down (Mackenzie to Bellehumeur, dated November 24, 1835, *op cit*).

412 Probably Pierre Ortubise (Urtubise?), who is designated a boatman in Clark's list of 1831. For Mackenzie's opinion of him, see his communication to Otoe Establishment, May 10, 1832 (*Fort Tecumseh Letter Book*, 1830-1832, p. 116). There was also a Jean Baptiste Urtibise in the employ of the Upper Missouri Outfit. See *A. F. Co., Western Ledger*, 1831-1833, p. 473, and an Ortubize, Sioux interpreter, known to Maximilian (*Travels*, p. 168).

413 For the circumstances of Emilien Primeau's death, see the report of D. D. Mitchell to Agent Fulkerson, June 10, 1836, and that of Fulkerson to Clark of slightly later date [Appendix]. When, in 1842, Andrew Drips was appointed as a Special Agent to the revived upper Missouri post, Mitchell, in his capacity of Superintendent of Indian Affairs, lost no time in seeking reparation for the Primeau outrage, upon which, as a trader of the Upper Missouri Outfit, he had reported specifically in June, 1836. On October 7, 1842, he notified Drips, whose special duties were supposed to be the destruction of the liquor traffic, that a claim for this offense of the ''Yanktonna band of Sioux on the Missouri some forty or fifty miles below the Mandan village . . . has been submitted to the Department.'' It was a claim for depredation really, since, as Mitchell informed Drips, ''It also appears that goods amounting to $776.91 — together with two horses were stolen, or destroyed by said Indians'' (*Drips Papers*, Missouri Historical Society). Drips identified, eventually, the offending band; but, having no interpreter, was unable to communicate with them (Drips to Mitchell, dated Fort Pierre, March 20, 1843, *idem*).

414 Maximilian noted some ''singular hills'' which he and his party reached after they had passed, in the *Assiniboine*, the winter village of the Gros Ventres. These hills he wrote are ''flattened at the top which are

called L'Ours qui Danse, because it is said the Indians here celebrate the bear dance, a medicine feast, in order to obtain success in the chase'' (*Travels*, p. 182). These hills were below the Little Missouri and it was at L'Ours qui Danse that Chardon selected a site for Fort James, the later Fort Berthold. See *note* 202. Maximilian's ''singular hills'' were, undoubtedly the ''square hills'' so frequently referred to by Chardon. For Dancing Bear Creek, see map accompanying Warren's *Report* of *Explorations in Nebraska and Dakota, 1855, '56, '57.* Fort Berthold is immediately opposite (*Coues*, Elliott, *History of the Expedition under the Command of Lewis and Clark*, vol. i, p. 266, *note* 21).

415 Halcro (Alcro, Alcrow). In a letter written to Laidlaw by Mackenzie, June 26, 1833, there is mentioned a J. Halcrow, who may be the man referred to in the text. Mackenzie wrote, ''Until Halcrow's Woman can join her people, please give her board and lodging in pursuance of my promise to her Husband'' (*Fort Pierre Letter Book*, 1832-1835, p. 24). The interpreter Halcro of Maximilian's acquaintance at Fort Union (*Travels*, p. 200) was no doubt the same man. See Thwaites, *Early Western Travels*, vol. xxiv, p. 215, *note* 238.

416 Rises in the foothills of the Rockies, in Montana, crosses the international boundary into Alberta, returns to Montana, and empties into the Missouri. For other names for this river, Qu' Appelle, Marais, see Cox, I. J., *Early Exploration of Louisiana*, p. 28. The neighbourhood was familiar ground to both Mitchell and Chardon. For Maximilian's description of it, see *Travels*, pp. 217, 218, etc. Laidlaw complained in 1831 that the Hudson's Bay Company had established ''all their old posts on Riviere que Appell, and are determined to annoy us as much as possible'' (Laidlaw to Chouteau, December 26, 1831, *Fort Tecumseh Letter Book*, 1830-1832, pp. 83-84). ''This is by far,'' says Thwaites, ''the largest of the Missouri's northern tributaries; it heads on the northern border of Montana, near the sources of some southern branches of the Saskatchewan, and drains all the region south of the Saskatchewan watershed'' (*Original Journals of the Lewis and Clark Epedition*, vol. ii, p. 10, *note* 1).

417 A James Dean seems to have had an account with the Upper Missouri Outfit in 1834, opened in April by the buying of leather pantaloons, white capot, saddlebags, shirts, shoes, socks, and closed in November. The St. Louis Roman Catholic Church records show a Captain James Dean, husband of Harriet Christy, baptized and buried the same day, January 6, 1839.

418 Possibly Pierre Delorme, *voyageur*. See no. 80, List of 1830. The ''D Lorm'' of March 16, 1836 and the ''Old Delorme'' of March 9, 1839 were one and the same, no doubt. For others of the name Delorme, see Morice, pp. 77-78.

419 This may be the scribe's spelling of Vallé, although an Alexis Vaille had an account in *A. F. Co., Western, Ledger*, 1831-1833, p. 150.

420 The liking that the Mandans and other Missouri River Indians had for drowned buffaloes and especially when the flesh of the same was ''high'' was remarked upon by most of the early traders and travellers. For instance, Charles MacKenzie, the companion of F. A. Larocque, wrote,

''Buffaloes and other animals are in immense numbers destroyed every winter by the Missouri Indians. In stormy weather whole droves run from the Mountains and plains to seek shelter in the woods which form the margin of the Mississouri — many of them attempting to cross when the ice is weak sink and are drowned — and in the Spring both sides of the River are in several places covered with rotten carcasses and skeletons of Buffaloes, Elks &c. — these dead animals, which often float down the current among the ice for hundred[s] of miles, are preferred by the Natives to any other kind of food:— When the skin is raised you will see the flesh of a greenish hue, and ready to become alive at the least exposure to the sun; and is so ripe, so tender, that very little boiling is required — the stench is absolutely intolerable — yet the soup made from it which is bottle green is reckoned delicious: — So fond are the Mandanes of putrid meat that they bury animals whole in the winter for the consumption of the spring'' (*Some Account of the Missisouri Indians in the years 1804, 5, 6, & 7* by Charles MacKenzie, pp. 36-37. Photostats, *Masson Papers,* Canadian Public Archives, Ottawa).

While MacKenzie seems to have had in mind chiefly the Mandans, a report from the pen of Alexander Henry of the Gros Ventres is so very nearly similar, as indicative of a taste for putrid flesh, that we may safely infer that the customs of the two tribes were pretty much the same. Henry's report is for 1806: —

''. . . This after noon I was present at the return of a party of Big Bellies a hunting excursion they had been away Eight days. They consisted of about Two hundred men and as many women who had accompanied them to attend on their Horses, dogs, and dry the flesh, all their numerous train of Beasts were heavily loaded with the spoils of such as Dried Meat, Hides, Skins, and a quantity of dried Pears and Choak Cherries. They had killed as near as I could judge about 500 animals, Buffalos and Red Deer and Cabbrie. But I did not observe amongst them that friendly sociable custom of shareing their hunt with their friends on their arrival as the Mandans did, every one kept what he brought home and appeared very precious of whatever they had; some of them invited us to their Huts to eat in expectation of receiving a bit of Tobacco, but we found it impossible to taste of any of their dried meat. It was nearly in a putrid state, the pieces would scarcely adhere together. This however is intirely to their taste and they very seldom make use of meat until it is rotten, for this purpose they always keep it in their Huts, and never expose it to the air by which means it is almost impossible for a stranger to remain indoors any time from the stench arising from such putrefied flesh. . .'' (Coventry Copy of *Journal,* vol. i, pp. 504-505, Canadian Public Archives, Ottawa; *Coues,* Elliott, *New Light on the Early History of the Greater Northwest,* vol. i, pp. 356-357).

It was not only in the Missouri that buffalo were drowned in large numbers. John MacDonell tells us that, on May 18th, 1795, after he had ''left the Forks of the River qui appelle,'' he, ''Observing a good many carcases of Buffaloes in the River & along its banks,'' began to count them and found at the end of the day that he ''had numbered when we put up at night 7360 Drowned & Mired along the River and in it — It is true in one or two places I went on shore & walked from one Carcase to the other where they lay from three to five files deep —'' (*Journal, 1793-1795,* Photostats, *Masson Papers,* Canadian Public Archives, Ottawa).

[421] White Earth River, about one hundred and forty miles above the Mandan villages (Chittenden, *History of the American Fur Trade of the Far West,* vol. iii, p. 957). Here Kipp, in the winter of 1825-1826, built

a fort for the Assiniboine trade (Maximilian, in Thwaites, *Early Western Travels,* vol. xxiii, p. 228).

422 Most likely the writer, Mitchell if it was he, departed with the boat for Fort Pierre; but, if he did, he came back again and was at Fort Clark in June, going on then with Mackenzie and the Agent by the *Yellowstone.* There is a gap in the journal of several weeks, and it is then resumed in the supposed handwriting of Chardon.

423 From this point to the entry of April 25th inclusive, the handwriting is that of the scribe of August and September, 1835.

424 Would this indicate that possibly Kipp, who knew the Mandan language and could speak it so that he was listed sometimes as Mandan interpreter, was back at Fort Clark, temporarily? That he was there for a time before going home to Canada on a visit is to be inferred from Mackenzie's letter to Maximilian, written after his own return to Fort Union. See Appendix.

425 June, 1836. At this point, the handwriting becomes again Chardon's. Did he come up with the steamboat and in Mackenzie's company? Note that there is no mention of Mitchell's arrival, although there is of his departure, June 18, 1836.

426 For details as to this affair, see Larpenteur (*Coues,* Elliott, *Forty Years a Fur Trader on the Upper Missouri,* vol. i, pp. 94 et seq. and *note* 4).

427 Was this Bazil, son of the sister of Sacajawea, and the boy, whom the Bird Woman adopted? For that Bazil's later prominence in the affairs on the Shoshone Reservation, see Lounsberry, *Early History of North Dakota,* p. 74. At Fort Union, Mackenzie had a slave named Joseph Basile (Maximilian, *op. cit.,* p. 301). For Basil in the time of Audubon, see *Journals,* vol. ii, p. 98, and for Charles Bazile, one of the pioneers of St. Paul, Minnesota, see Morice, pp. 10-11.

428 James P. Beckwourth, for whose own reminiscences, see Bonner, T. D., *The Life and Adventures of James P. Beckwourth.* It is a little odd that Beckwourth, having frequent occasion to refer to Fort Clark, at no time mentions Chardon. He associates Kipp with Fort Clark in 1825 (p. 145), "Mr. Winters" with Fort Cass (p. 187) and later, "Mr. Tulleck" (p. 251).

429 For Beckwourth's own recollection of this journey to St. Louis, see Bonner, pp. 313, 327, 333. The Bellemaire he met with at Fort Clark must have been Michel Bellehumeur, and Antoine Garro the interpreter would be Antoine Garreau (See no. 244 of the *List of 1830*).

430 Pierre Didier Papin.

431 Like Thomas D. Rice, Chardon wrote his own words here and elsewhere for Jim Crow's song, concerning which, see *Scarborough,* Dorothy, *On the Trail of Negro Folk-Songs,* pp. 125, 126, 127.

432 Maximilian observed that there was, when he was at Fort Clark, not the slightest trace left of old Fort Mandan. The channel of the river had changed since Lewis and Clark were there (*Travels,* p. 318). The Indians had probably done to it, being abandoned, what they seem to have done to all posts that traders deserted, razed them to the earth and carried

away or burnt on the spot the materials of which they had been constructed. When the employees of the American Fur Company retired from Fort Piegan in 1832, the Indians burnt it (*idem*, p. 239) and this is only one of many instances that could be given. Elliott Coues attempts to mark the site of old Fort Mandan with reference to existing topography. It was on the north bank of the Missouri, seven or eight miles below the mouth of Knife River, in what is now McLean County, while the Fort Clark of Maximilian's day and of Chardon's was a little farther down and in present Mercer County (*Lewis and Clark*, vol. i, p. 179, *note* 60). See also Thwaites, *Original Journals of the Lewis and Clark Expedition*, vol. i, p. 217, *note* 1; vol. v, p. 346, *note* 1; *Early Western Travels*, vol. xxiii, p. 233. From Larocque of the North West Company, who was near by at the time of its erection, we get our best idea of what it looked like and how impregnable it was supposed to be: —

"Sunday — 16th. [December, 1804] Arrived at Fort Mandan being the Name the americans give to their Fort, which is Constructed in a triangular form Ranges of houses Making two Sides, & a Range of amazing large Pickets; the front; The whole is made so Strong as to be almost, Cannon Ball proof. The two Range of houses, do not Join one another, but are Join'd by, a piece of fortification Made in the form of a demi Circle, that Can defend two Sides of the Fort, on the top of which they Keepe Sentry all Night, & the lower part of that building Serves as a Store, a Centinel is like wise Kept all day, walking in the Fort" (*Journal of Larocque, Masson Papers*, vol. xi, Public Archives, Ottawa).

[433] Catlin (*North American Indians*, 1850, vol. i, p. 35) says that whites sometimes posed as medicine-men. For Catlin's description of medicine-making, see *idem*, pp. 39-41.

[434] For C. Brazeau, see *notes* 126 and 373.

[435] The *Fontaine Rouge* was now "marsh covered" (Maximilian, *Travels*, p. 316).

[436] Many travellers testified to this practice. Note, for example, Harmon, *Journal*, Edition of 1820, p. 182; of 1903, p. 148; Boller, pp. 162-163; 313; Leonard's *Narrative*, pp. 271-272; Catlin, *North American Indians*, 1850, vol. i, p. 90; Bradbury, in Thwaites, *Early Western Travels*, vol. v, p. 115; Coues, *Lewis and Clark*, vol. i, p. 179. For howling as a form of mourning among the Osages, see Bradbury, *op. cit.* p. 63.

[437] A branch of the *Assiniboine*, known in Canada as the Souris. It rises in Canada, crosses the international boundary into North Dakota, returns to Canada, and joins the Assiniboine a few miles below the town of Brandon.

[438] It appears from a list attached to Chardon's journal that in 1836 on the Missouri horses were bought at prices ranging between $4.25 and $100. Out of 34 horses listed, 15 sold at the lowest figure, and only two — evidently exceptional racers or hunters — at the highest. The 34 horses cost $1330, and were sold for $1422.50 in beaver skins and buffalo robes — not an extravagant profit. For the List, see Appendix.

[439] This marks the return of the Arikaras from their sojourn among the Pawnees, their near of kin (Grinnell, George B., *Pawnee Hero Stories and Folk Tales; French Régime in Wisconsin*, Wisconsin Historical Society *Collections*, vol. xviii, p. 93, *note* 36.) They had been practically driven

away from the Missouri by the Sioux.   For a reported final bloody conflict between them and the Sioux not long before their departure for the neighbourhood of the Platte, see Laidlaw to Mackenzie, November 27, 1831, *Fort Tecumseh Letter Book*, 1830-1832, pp. 72-76.   The account of their return and of their welcome by the Mandans is interesting in view of the traditional idea that the Indians eschew all emotionalism.   For a traveller's observation to this effect, see *Cooke*, Philip St. George, *Scenes and Adventures in the Army*, p. 115.

440 Poirce.   It is more than probable that the Portra of entry, August 5, 1837, was the same man and he identical with the Poitras of John Mac-Donell's journal, second part, from which the following are taken: [1794, April] "Monday 21st.   . . . Poitras made a Pimican Trough . . ."   [November] "Thursday 27th.   Poitra's Chimney took fire . . ."   [December] "Saturday 6th   Poitras took a hunting tour but met with nothing . . ."   [1795, April] "Wednesday 29th . . . Le frêne les deux Coeurs came to sell a young Slave Girl, which, on my refusal, Poitras purchased . . ." &c. &c.   (*Journal of John MacDonell, 1793-1795*, Second Part, Photostats, Dominion Archives, Ottawa).

441 The spelling of the account books is "Pinconeau," and several men of the name figure therein — Charles, Edward, François, Laurant (Laurent?), Paschal, and Toussaint.   Most of them seem to have been of the Kickapoo Outfit.   Toussaint Pinconeau is the only one mentioned specifically as of the Upper Missouri Outfit.   Paschal Pincineau is no. 58 in the *List of 1830*.   T. Pencinneau, was passing as a free hunter in 1831; but fraternizing with the Sublette people (Lamont to Chouteau, April 4, 1831, *Fort Tecumseh Letter Book*, 1830-1832, pp. 33-34).

442 For a description of a *cache*, see Wagner, *Leonard's Narrative*, p. 67, *note*.   See also various references of Thwaites's — *Early Western Travels*, vol. vi, p. 272; Wisconsin Historical *Collections*, vol. xviii, p. 279, vol. xix, p. 214, *note* 6, vol. xx, p. 410, *note* 43; *Lewis and Clark Journals*, vol. ii, pp. 136, 137.   Note opinion that the mysterious excavations at Halley's Bluff may have been *caches* made by the Great Osages (Holcomb, R. I., *History of Vernon County, Missouri*, p. 137, *note*).

443 Baptiste Leclair, "Old Baptiste," as usually called, was for a long time the cook at Fort Clark.   His reputation was never good.   Halsey thus referred to him as early as 1832:   "Baptiste Leclair the cook who was at the Mandans, when you passed there, is said to be good for nothing, he is too great a friend to the Indians, and squanders away provisions — he offered to remain here on condition that we would allow him to take a squaw (Halsey to Pierre Chouteau, Jr., July 9, 1832, *Fort Tecumseh Letter Book*, 1830-1832, pp. 117-121.   For another name applied to him, see *note* 484.   The "Old Baptiste" that Audubon met with must have been the same man (*Journals*, vol. ii, p. 127).

444 The question arises as to whether Villeandré and Lebrun brought this liquor from Fort Union, or Alcro (Halcro?) from the Little Missouri. The incident reminds one of that told by Larpenteur (Coues, *Forty Years a Fur Trader on the Upper Missouri*, vol. i, p. 136).   In that case, however, the year was 1838, and the liquor brought by Robert Christy from Fort Union.   The Lebrun here mentioned can hardly have been Bonaventure Lebrun; inasmuch as this man went on to Fort Pierre, while, on the 18th, Venture came from the Gros Ventres.   Villeandre's companion may have

been Pierre Lebrun, who is designated a boatman both in the *List of 1830* and in Clark's list. From the account books, he was of the Otoe Outfit in 1834 and of the Rocky Mountain Outfit in 1838.

445 Michel Carrière ？ For this man, see Coues, *Audubon and His Journals*, vol. ii, pp. 136, 137; Drumm, *Luttig Journal*, p. 77. Lamont to Laidlaw, December 13, 1830 *(Fort Tecumseh Letter Book, 1830-1832, pp. 8-10)*; Laidlaw to Hamilton, January 5, 1833 *(Fort Pierre Letter Book, 1832-1835, pp. 10-11)*. A Carrière was with the Astoria expedition (Morice, p. 59).

446 Powder river flows into the Yellowstone from the south in Custer county, Montana. Clark named it Red Stone river and says that the Indian name was *Wa ha sah*. See Coues' *Lewis and Clark*, vol. i, p. 268, *note 25*.

447 All Saints' Day.

448 Bighorn.

449 Michel Carrière's initials.

450 A white Dummy and a black Dummy succumbed during the small pox epidemic.

451 Joseph Juett. In the winter of 1831-1832, Juett was sent by Laidlaw to establish a post for the Cheyennes, because they objected to trading at the same place as the Ogallalah Sioux (Laidlaw to Sarpy, December 21, 1831, *Fort Tecumseh Letter Book, 1830-1832*), with whom Juett was trading in 1833, (Laidlaw to Picotte, February 6, 1833, *Fort Pierre Letter Book, 1832-1835*, pp. 15-16). Juett's name occurs frequently in the Fort Pierre correspondence. At Fort Pierre he entered into an engagement, February 28, 1837, as interpreter, clerk, and trader with ''permission to visit St. Louis the summer of 1838'' *(Chouteau-Maffitt Collection)*, and, in the following April, articles of agreement were drawn up as between John Letrace and him, part of which was to the effect ''that the said Latrace is to winter at some of the out Posts but not at fort Pier on the Missouri'' *(idem)*. Juett was in the service of the Upper Missouri Outfit certainly as late as February of 1848 *(Fort Pierre Letter Book, 1847-1848)*.

452 The Feast of the Epiphany, or Little Christmas.

453 For the scalp dance among the Sioux, see Catlin, *North American Indians*, vol. i, pp. 245-246 and, for a sham performance of the same by Mandan boys, *idem*, pp. 131-132. A brief reference to the Osage ceremonial connected with the scalp dance is to be found in James Owen Dorsey's *Study of Siouan Cults*, Bureau of Ethnology, *Report*, 1889-1890, pp. 526-527. For a woman's scalp dance song, see *Densmore*, Frances, *Mandan and Hidatsa Music*, Bureau of American Ethnology, Bulletin 80, pp. 155-156.

Considering how greatly the so-called Blackfeet massacre has been allowed to reflect disastrously upon Chardon's character, it is well to note that he was too humanitarian to encourage the scalp dance by the bestowal of presents for its performance. See journal entry, March 3, 1837. How hideous and how suggestively cruel the scalp dance was has been well expressed by Miss Drumm in her notes to the Luttig journal. See *Journal of a Fur-Trading Expedition on the Upper Missouri, 1812-1813*, pp. 104-105, *note 153*. When Palliser reached Fort Vermillion, ''a very miserable little place,'' the Sioux, who had recently had a fight with the Otoes, were indulging in the scalp dance (*Solitary Rambles and Adventures of a Hunter in the Prairies*, pp. 96-97.

454 For Samuel Patch, the athlete, his mania for jumping, and his fatal leap from the bank of the Genesee River at Genesee Falls into the abyss below'', see Appleton's *Cyclopaedia of American Biography*,'' vol. iv, p. 669.

455 Joseph Denoyer, or Desnoyer, had an account with the Sioux Outfit in 1836.   Another man of almost identical name, Joseph Desnoyers, died at the age of fifty in 1833.   A François Denoyer was in account with the Upper Missouri Outfit in 1835 and, in the *List of 1831*, nos. 117, 118, and 124 respectively, appear the names of Joseph, Cyprian and Sylvestre Desnoyer.   According to Morice, the name is Noyon, or Desnoyers.   See p. 213.

456 Catlin rather conveys the idea that women were debarred from making medicine.   See *North American Indians*, 1850, vol. i, p. 135.

457 Chardon is here imitating or quoting Mitchell.   See Mitchell's entry, March 1, 1836.

458 Lewis and Clark mention Turtle Mountain and Turtle Hill, the former on the International Boundary, the latter on the Little Missouri river.   The Turtle Mountain referred to by Chardon, which was about 90 miles from Fort Clark, was no doubt the latter.

459 For the making of buffalo, or bull, medicine, see Boller, pp. 100 ff.

460 Kipp, it will be recalled, furnished Maximilian with fresh eggs every day.

461 This was most likely the ''Jacque Letand'' of the *Fort Tecumseh Journal*.   See entries for March 19th and 20th, 1830, South Dakota Historical *Collections*, vol. ix, pp. 107, 108.   The ''J. Letand'' of the entry for February 2, 1830 was undoubtedly the same man despite the confusion which Doane Robinson has allowed the misreading by the transcriber of a *u* for an *n* to create in his mind (*idem*, p. 95, *note* 8).

462 William Pilote ? See his account with Sioux Outfit, 1836 (A. F. Co., Western).   Under date of September 4, 1837, Chardon mentioned a man Pellot, who was probably the same person, as also of Hamilton's letter of May 17, 1835 (*Fort Union Letter Book*, 1833-1835).   In the List of 1830, occurs Alexis Pilon and also Barilla Pilette, *voyageur*.   See Morice for François-Benjamin Pillet (pp. 229-230) and for François Pilon (p. 230).

463 This was James Dickson.   For an account of him and his projects, see Introduction, *note* 259.

464 Jean Baptiste Gardepie, Baptiste Gardepie, sometimes Gardepied or even Gariépy.   For certain forms, see Larpenteur, vol. i, p. 80; Morice, pp. 118-119.   Palliser speaks of Gardépée (p. 184).   In Merrick's time there was a Joe Guardapie, a pilot on the Mississippi River (*Old Times on the Upper Mississippi*, pp. 113-114).

465 This term of reproach was often applied to the Arikaras.

466 Travellers early commented upon the fact that hanging was with

Indian women a very common form of suicide. Note, for instance, Harmon's remarks on the subject (Edition, 1903, p. 163) and Tabeau's in his Loisel narrative.

[467] Salampore was a kind of chintz popular at the period.

[468] There was an account in 1834 carried on the books of the American Fur Company, Western Department, against a certain A. Bourbonnais, which was settled in full the year following (p. 203). The St. Louis Roman Catholic Church records show a child, ''Francoise,'' born in 1816 to Augustin Bourbonnais and Victoire Constant. For an account of Augustin Bourbonnais, see Morice, pp. 45-46.

[469] Fort Van Buren ? This, the most recent of the Crow trade posts, built in 1835 at the mouth of the Tongue River, on the right bank of the Yellowstone (Coues, *Forty Years a Fur Trader on the Upper Missouri*, vol. i, p. 47, *note* 10) is very likely the one meant. Fort Cass at the mouth of the Bighorn had been built in 1832 also for the Crow trade.

[470] This was *Tchon-su-mons-ka, the Sand Bar,* a Teton Sioux, whose picture Catlin painted (*North American Indians,* vol. i, pp. 251-252 and Plate 95). The children were Francis Bolivar and Andrew Jackson. For Bolivar Chardon, see *note* 52. Chardon in thus referring to his squaw wife was but following the Sioux practice.

[471] For early and full accounts of the Dance of the Calumet, see *Jesuit Relations,* vol. li, pp. 47-49; vol. lxv, p. 121; vol. lxix, pp. 129-137. For a much more recent account, see Boller, *op cit.,* pp. 305-308.

[472] In view of the terrible calamity that was soon to overtake them, they might have been excused, those of them that survived it, if they looked back upon this omen as one of peculiar potency.

[473] The *faba minor equina,* with a fruit resembling the bean. See Maximilian's description and discussion of its use in Thwaites, *Early Western Travels,* vol. xxiii, p. 276.

[474] Were all other proof lacking, these initials would prove conclusively that Chardon and not Mitchell, as Larpenteur asserts (*Forty Years a Fur Trader on the Upper Missouri,* vol. i, pp. 123-125) — unless Coues has confounded his chronology — was in charge at Fort Clark, the spring of 1837.

[475] For the significance of ''partizans,'' see Drumm, *Luttig Journal,* p. 90, *note* 137.

[476] *Pommes des prairies,* or, as the Canadian French also call them, *Pomme blanche (Psoralia esculenta).* See Frémont, *Memoirs,* vol. i, p. 45. The name in the Dakota speech is *Tipsinna* (Neill, *History of Minnesota,* p. 506, *note* 1. For an account of the prairie turnip as a part of Pawnee diet, see Murray, vol. i, pp. 265-266.

[477] Miss Nute's investigation of the career of the ''Liberator of All the Indians'' seems to have led her to the conclusion that nothing is known as to what became of him. See Mississippi Valley Historical *Review,* vol. x, p. 135.

[478] Chardon's reason for going down is supplied by Audubon whom he told that he went down to meet the Steamboat because his young son was

on board (*Audubon and His Journals*, vol. ii, pp. 42-43).   The child must have been the little Andrew Jackson, who may have been sent down to Fort Pierre at the time the mother's body was conveyed thither in April. It is scarcely conceivable that the boy Bolivar, taken in September 1835 to Philadelphia, could be returning.   So far as can be ascertained Bolivar was never again on the upper Missouri in the lifetime of his father.

479 The son of Bernard Pratte of Pratte, Chouteau & Co.

480 Jacob Halsey was perhaps, even then inoculated with the small-pox. This was the fateful voyage in the history of steamboating on the Missouri River because of the small-pox scourge that resulted.   The journal corroborates the story that its author gave to Audubon six years afterwards (*Audubon and His Journals*, vol. ii, pp. 42-47), the only discrepancy in the two accounts being due to the fact that, in 1843, Chardon mistook the *Assiniboine* for the *St. Peter's*.

481 P. D. Papin, presumably, did not go on to Fort Union; for, among papers in the *Chouteau-Maffitt Collection* is the following: ''Pelleau is hired to the Company verbally for five hundred dollars, ten pounds of sugar twenty of Coffee and fifty pounds of flour. — this engagement begins from June the twenty first 1837, till June next 1838   Concluded and made at the Mandan on the 20th of June 1837, in presence of F. A. Chardon.
P. D. Papin''.
In further proof that Papin did not proceed with Halsey and Agent Fulkerson, there is on record a settlement of Fort Clark accounts which took place between him and Chardon at this time, and a *Recapitulation* ''Delivered to P. D. Papin, 21st June 1837, F. A. C.''
The accounts settled had chiefly to do with the Sioux Outfit.
According to Larpenteur (Coues, *Forty Years a Fur Trader on the Upper Missouri*, vol. i, p. 131) the boat reached Fort Union, June 24, 1837.

482 David Crockett, with whom because of Crockett's having been with Jackson in the Creek and First Seminole wars, Chardon may have been personally acquainted.

483 The Coquille or Musselshell River, a southern tributary of the Missouri in Montana.

484 May be the ''Soyo' (Yoho?) referred to in the following: ''We were obliged to reengage old Mayance. Bapt Leclair (otherwise called 'Soyo') would not remain'' (Halsey to Mackenzie, July 12, 1832, *Fort Tecumseh Letter Book*, 1830-1832, pp. 123-126).   See also *note* 443.

485 Audubon tells of a somewhat similar attempt to kill Chardon on the steamboat in 1843 (*Audubon and His Journals*, vol. i, p. 528).

486 Does this have reference to Chardon's attempt to recover the stolen blanket?   For the story, see Wagner, *Leonard's Narrative*, p. 41.   It was probably due entirely to the exhortation of Four Bears, whose impassioned speech against the whites, inserted here, was found with Chardon's Journal. It was made on July 30, 1837, the day of his death.   The mother of Bad Gun, a son of Four Bears, died also during the epidemic.

487 For Catlin's account of the Wolf Chief, see *North American Indians*, vol. i, p. 104.

488 Grand river empties into the Missouri from the west, in Corson coun-

ty, South Dakota. In the Lewis and Clark journals the Indian name is given as *We tar hoo.*

489 See list (Appendix) of Mandan dead that accompanied this Journal.

490 ''Dr. Sangrado'' of Le Sage's *Gil Blas,* a character made to symbolize certain peculiar medical practices of the time.

491 Antoine Garreau. For the improvement in his condition, see entry, September 7th.

492 Presumably, the little Andrew Jackson. For the inserted record of his death, see entry, September 22, 1837.

493 Pierre Detaille ? See *A. F. Co., Western,* 1831-1833, p. 438. The rendering, Pierre Detalier, occurs in the *Ledger of Mo. Fur Co.,* 1812-1817. If the same individual be meant, the adjective old would be appropriate. A Pierre Detaille, who had been at Fort Tecumseh, left that place for P. D. Papin's establishment on White River (Lamont to Papin, November 30, 1830, *Fort Tecumseh Letter Book,* 1830-1832, p. 7). For other references to him, under the name of Pierre Detaillier, see entries for June 27, and December 9, 1830, *Fort Tecumseh Journal,* 1830, and for Pierre Détayé, Morice, p. 91. For François Detaille, see Audubon, vol. ii, p. 147.

494 Evidently, Starapat (Little Hawk with Bloody Claws), the principal chief of the Arikaras (Maximilian, *Travels,* pp. 166-167) and the same as Catlin's Stan-au-pat (the Bloody Hand). See *North American Indians,* 1850, vol. i, p. 204 and Plate 82. The Arikaras had not moved away from the Missouri when Catlin passed up the river and he made a picture of their village as he saw it from the steamboat.

495 Andrew Jackson Chardon. See *note* 492.

496 The information that Schoolcraft includes in his large work on the Indians about the ravages of the small-pox among the upper Missouri tribes in 1837 he obtained, so he says, from D. D. Mitchell, who claimed to have been in the country at the time (Schoolcraft, vol. iii, pp. 253-256). Mitchell got his data second-hand in the first place and, when he reported to Schoolcraft in 1852, could not have had the lively recollection of events that might have been possible had he passed like Chardon through the awful ordeal from start to finish. Dr. Libby has advanced the idea that the very civilization of the agriculturalists among the Indians made in the end for their undoing; because a sedentary life permitted more easily the spread of the small-pox. (*The Mandans from the Archaeological and Historical Standpoint,* Mississippi Valley Historical Association *Proceedings,* vol. i, p. 62).

497 It was after he arrived at Fort Pierre that Jacob Halsey wrote his account of the ravages of the small-pox. It offers an interesting contrast to that of Chardon. Halsey's interest seems to have been mainly in the effect of the epidemic upon the fur-trade. For his report, see Appendix.

498 J. Baptiste Latress had an account with the Upper Missouri Outfit in 1834, very possibly the same as the John Latress, *Voyageur,* of the *List of 1830,* and the Jean Latresse who married Julia Duval, July 23, 1839. A Frederick Latresse had, in 1835, an account with the Otoe Outfit.

499 Intended for Hunant most likely. In the *List of 1830,* no. 278, the name Joseph Huneau is given and its owner described as a *voyageur.* In

the Church records, however, the name appears as Hunant and borne by a father and two sons, the sons being Gabriel and Joseph, born twelve years apart. Both were in a position to have accounts with the Upper Missouri Outfit in 1830. See *A. Fur Co. Ledger,* 1829-1832, pp. 165, 172.

500 This was the negro mentioned by Chardon in his will and manumitted by that instrument. See *note* 253. For the reason for sending him to the Ree Village and the proficiency gained by him in the language, see journal entry, March 17, 1838. For evidence of another negro owned by Chardon, the killing of whom by the Blackfeet is said so to have enraged his master as to have been the incitement to the massacre of February 19, 1843 at Fort McKenzie, see Chittenden, *History of the American Fur Trade of the Far West,* p. 373.

501 See Drumm, *Luttig Journal,* p. 64, *note* 98.

502 Robert Christy and Charles Larpenteur. They had left Fort Union March 22nd (Coues, *Forty Years a Fur Trader on the Upper Missouri,* vol. i, pp. 136-144). Considering the distance and all that befell them on the way down, it seems astonishing that they could have reached Fort Clark on the 25th. Robert Christy, according to Larpenteur, had come up to Fort Union in the fall for the sake of his health and was now returning to St. Louis. Larpenteur was bound for Baltimore.

503 In substantiation of this and of the impression that Chardon made upon Larpenteur, note the following with reference to the arrival and departure of these visitors from Fort Union: "... Mr. F. A. Chardon, who was then in charge, and a very singular kind of a man, entertained us in the best manner. Mr. Christy had a two-gallon keg of good whiskey, of which Mr. Chardon was so fond that he helped himself about every fifteen minutes, saying he had 'a great many worms in his throat' — to the sorrow of Mr. Christy, who found his keg so nearly empty that he concluded to make Mr. Chardon a present of what was left. We remained there two days; on the third we took leave of Mr. Chardon who, not knowing he was to fall heir to the balance of the whiskey, and not having yet destroyed all the worms in his throat, would have been glad for us to remain another day, and insisted very strongly that we should do so. I cannot say whether it was because the whiskey had been put on board before Mr. Christy made up his mind about it, that Mr. Chardon accompanied us to the boat, or whether he did so through politeness; but he felt very happy at the presentation, and hastened back to the fort in double-quick time" (Coues, *op. cit.,* vol. i, p. 144).

504 This practice, so characteristic of most primitive and of all nomadic people, has been commented upon by many travellers who had, in the early days, a chance to observe the North American Indians. Harmon speaks of it (Edition of 1903, p. 148) with respect to certain Canadian tribes; Boller (p. 84) of the upper Missouri; Isaac McCoy describes the exposure of an aged women by the Pottawatomies (*History of Baptist Indian Missions,* p. 131), a revolting sight. Forsyth offers an explanation of their callousness and want of filial affection, which, under other circumstances, was in no wise lacking. It was, he says, simply the need to consider all and everything an encumbrance that could not be easily and quickly removed from place to place. (Blair, *Indian Tribes of the Upper Mississippi Valley,* vol. ii, p. 213). Not only were the aged exposed, but the sick also (*Leonard's Narrative,* pp. 277-278). For a notable instance of the same sort of

thing among other people, see William Harvey Brown's experiences with the Matabele, who, in the uprising of 1896, left behind all their decrepit old women to fend for themselves (*On the South African Frontier*, p. 338).

505 For so-called billiard playing among the upper Missouri tribes, see Boller, *Among the Indians*, pp. 160-196; Bushnell, *Kurz, Artist-Explorer*, *op. cit.*, pp. 521-522. Pierre Antoine Tabeau, in the *Loisel Narrative*, contends that the Indian game bore little or no resemblance to European billiards.

506 He must have taken this woman to wife within a month after the death of *Tchon-su-mons-ka*.

507 It would seem to have been rather late in the day to begin the work of vaccinating. The United States Congress had passed a law in 1832 (Act of May 5, 1832, *United States Statutes at Large*, vol. iv, pp. 514-515) for extending the benefits of vaccination to the Indians, and appropriating $12,000 for the purpose, but Secretary Cass informed Agent Dougherty, May 9, 1832 (Office of Indian Affairs, *Letter Book*, no. 8, pp. 344-346), that, while one doctor, Meriwether Martin, had been appointed, and another would be, "no effort would be made . . . under any circumstances . . . to send a Surgeon higher up the Missouri than the Mandans, and I think not higher than the Aricaras." For other correspondence on the appointment of medical men, see pp. 357, 379-380, 464. Complaint was made to the Indian Office soon afterwards that Frederick Chouteau was persuading the Kaws not to submit to vaccination (Herring to Clark, February 5, 1833, *idem*, no. 10, p. 30; Same to Same, March 22, 1833, *idem*, pp. 134-135). In the summer of 1832, however, "vaccine matter with directions for the use of it" had been ordered forwarded to Fort Pierre by the Upper Missouri Outfit (*Chouteau-Maffitt Collection*) and, even in 1831, vaccine had been among the things ordered for Fort Tecumseh (*idem*). The Reverend Isaac McCoy, in his *History of Indian Missions*, p. 441, charges that, in 1831, white men had deliberately spread small-pox among the Indians of the Southwest and the Pawnees had caught the disease. Of the frightful havoc it made, John Dougherty was aware and reported it to General Clark, October 29, 1831, as McCoy did to the Secretary of War (*idem*, p. 554). For the expression of an official French opinion favorable to the deliberate spread of small-pox among the Indians, see *N. Y. Colonial Docs.*, vol. x, pp. 245-251). Wagner is of the opinion that the American Fur Company was guilty of criminal negligence in the case of the epidemic of 1837, and that their own account, based upon the showing of Halsey, E. T. Denig and Larpenteur of what occurred at Fort Union, is incriminating (*Leonard's Narrative*, pp. 44 *et seq.*).

508 A man named Vivie seems to have been killed at the time of the "Deschamps massacre" (Larpenteur, vol. i, p. 100) In the *A. Fur Co.*, *Western, Ledger* there are entries, in 1838, for Villian, Vivie, a half-breed, and Villea. For Joseph Vivier, see Lounsberry, *Early History of North Dakota*, p. 186.

509 Nicollet had come up in it as far as Fort Pierre.

510 Fort Pierre.

511 Selkirk Colony on Red River of the North. If there is justification for the belief that the Columbia Fur Company had been formed chiefly by men dissatisfied, not with the union of the Hudson's Bay and North West

companies, but with the condition of affairs at the Selkirk Colony, the employees of the Upper Missouri Outfit would have had cause to know a good deal, first or second hand, about Red River, the little settlement on it, its handicaps, and its tragedy.

512 The North West Company, as such, had, of course, gone out of existence.   Organized at Montreal in 1783-84, it absorbed the X Y Company in 1804, and was itself absorbed by the Hudson's Bay Company in 1821.

513 Unidentified.

514 For an account of how the French Canadian *charivari* was a custom brought from France and improved upon, being a sort of mockery and used when a marriage was unseemly or ill-assorted, see *Bigsby*, John J., *The Shoe and Canoe*, vol. 1, pp. 34-37.

515 Andre Lecompte, no doubt, since he had an account with the Sioux Outfit as late as 1837.   In the *List of 1830*, no. 240, is the name of Joseph Lecompte, clerk and interpreter.   A Louis Lecompte and a Narcisse Lecompte had accounts with the Upper Missouri Outfit in 1835.   For Pierre Lecompte and his attempt to deal directly with John Jacob Astor, see Morice, pp. 176-177.

516 There is some reason to think that this man, George, was a brother of Chardon's.   See *note* 48.   Chardon had an account with him at Fort Clark.   There was also one Alexander George, given in the *List of 1831*, no. 53, as *Voyageur* at Fort Union, 1830.

517 This is the first and only instance in the journal of the use by Chardon of the term Minetaree, to indicate the Gros Ventres.   Perhaps he used it here to rhyme with Aricarees.

518 White River, an affluent of the Missouri, in South Dakota.   The Bad Lands of White River, famous for their fantastic forms, are equally famous for their fossil remains.

APPENDICES

APPENDIX A.

KENNEDY JOURNAL

Journal of occurrences and transactions at Fort Clark (Mandans) Commencing the 18th May 1833[519] (1834?)

By Alex[r] Kennedy[520]

1833 (1834?)

May 18th   *Sunday* a fine clear day. — Mess[rs] M[c]Kenzie and Picotte arrived in Keel Boat Flora; they reached here early their sixth day from Fort Union. All hands bussy loading the Boat as it is intended to take down to Fort Pierre all the peltries here which she can conveniently stow. — The Chief returns of this Estab-

[519] The fragmentary manuscript, of which the following pages constitute an exact copy, is a part of the *Pierre Chouteau Collection* of the Missouri Historical Society, where it is labelled, "Fort Clark Journal, May 18, 1833 to June 18, 1834, by Alexander Kennedy." The date, 1833, is only too evidently an error, although the editors of the *Journal of John Work,* judging from their citation, p. 49, *note* 101, seem not to have detected it. The entries, if studied carefully, will be seen to be for May and June in a single year and that year should be 1834. In the margin of the original, in the middle of the entry for May 20th, the date, 1834, is, for the first time, entered. It is at the top of a new page, however, the second. The entire journal covers only four and two-thirds pages. Kennedy's entries come to an even more abrupt stop than do Chardon's. He would seem to have purposed making one on the 18th, a Wednesday, and, for some reason, did not. Chardon's journal begins where Kennedy's ends. It really begins on the 19th of June; but contains a reference to the arrival of the *Assiniboine* on the 18th. The 18th with Kennedy was a Wednesday and, from the Chardon journal, it can be easily determined that the 18th of June in 1834 was a Wednesday.

[520] I have tried, although unsuccessfully, to connect this Alexander Kennedy with the older man of the same name in the Hudson's Bay Company employ. As a matter of fact, his identity is very difficult to establish. When he first appeared on the upper Missouri, Laidlaw described him as a young man and yet unversed in the ways of fur-trading communities. He was sent to assist Kipp at Fort Clark and, when Kipp went away to take charge with Culbertson at Fort McKenzie, accompanied him or followed after him as far as Fort Union. There are a few occasional references to him in the extant *Fort Union Letter Book,* and then, from view, he disappears entirely.

lishment consist of, 180 Packs Robes each pack containing ten Robes and 588 lbs Beaver in 7 Packs each of 60 Skins, but the trade is not as yet considered at a close there being brought us daily a few Robes by the Mandans and there being still a few not yet traded at the Villages above attached to this place. Completed the lading of the Boat in the evening. —

" 19*th*   *Monday*   Early this morning Mr McKenzie took his departure for Fort Pierre;[521] the wind proved unfavourable to his progress it blowing fresh against stream most part of the day. The men variously employed about the Fort and one of them attending the Company's Horses. The presents intended for the Mandans were got in readiness for distribution, but from motives of policy were not presented untill the evening when Mr Kipp delivered them with a few words suitable and appropriate to the occasion. Mr. Bigou came up from the Gros Ventre Village for a few articles of trade which with the presents to be made that place he takes up tomorrow accompanied by Mr Kipp who does the honours of the donation in person. May the result prove favourable to the views and interests of the Company is the humble journalist's earnest desire and anxious wish, but "if wishes were horses beggers would ride" (as the old saying is) and *Chance* as it is called he is afraid will too often prodominate over certainty, but as regards this matter due time alone will decide. —

" 20*th*   *Tuesday*   Fine pleasant weather. Three men employed cutting firewood one acting mens cook and an other Horse Keeper. — The woodmen did very little, they going late to work and returning before noon. This negligence of duty may be owing to Mr Kipp's

[521] Between April 30, 1834 and August 25, 1834 there is a gap in the *Fort Pierre Letter Book*. I have been, therefore, unable to trace these happenings by means of the letters issuing from that place.

absence to day and as it is presumed not my province to command, of consequence disisted from so doing. Mr. Kipp proceeded to the Gros Ventre Village with Bigou as proposed yesterday. Lacroix came down

1834 from the Little Mandan Village and brought up all his remains of Goods and 20 Robes of which an account was taken the Trade at that Village being over for this season. Two freemen started in a peruke for Fort Pierre. In the evening Mr Kipp returned from Mr Bigou's station

" 21st *Wednesday* Continuance of favourable weather. Two Carts employed hauling home wood with which to make charcoal. The woodmen attending more to their duty to-day.

" 22nd *Thursday.* Blowing fresh down stream most part of the day but proved a fine calm evening. No variation in the employments of the men. —

" 23rd *Friday* Fine pleasant day though blowing fresh most part of the day. Early this morning Mr Bellhumeur with three men started out in quest of Buffaloe taking with them 8 Horses. Two Carts employed hauling home firewood. The trading very slack these few days past. —

" 24th *Saturday* A mild calm day. Soon after breakfast Mr. Bellhumeur and the men who accompanied him returned with very little success it appears that cattle are very scarce about our vicinity, they having seen only one small band of eight cows out of which they Killed and brought home only one. —

" 25th *Sunday* Continuance of fine weather. Nothing remarkable occured today. —

" 26th *Monday* Wind Easterly. Rained a great part of the day. We commenced taking an Inventory of the

Goods remaining on hand in the Wholesale Store. The men employed squaring timber for a corn Crib. —

„   *27th*   *Tuesday*   Wind blowing fresh from the Eastward most part of the day. Cold, disagreeable weather, and heavy rain. No work going forward to day in consequence of the inclemency of the weather.

„   *28th*   *Wednesday* Wind Continues Easterly and the weather still cold. The men employed hewing timber as before. —

„   *29th*   *Thursday*   No variation in the wind and weather. Took an account of Mr Bijou's remains of Goods. Mr Bellhumeur and two men went out in quest of Buffaloe. —

„   *30th*   *Friday*   Wind and weather as before. Early this morning Mr. Bellhumeur and the men who went out with him returned. They brought home the meat of three Cows; they say they saw very few Cattle. The men variously employed about the Fort. —

„   *31st*   *Saturday*   Wind still from the Eastward. A great quantity of Snow continued to fall the greater part of the day. The Carpenter (Boilou) making a Bedsted for Mr Kipp, the rest with the exception of the Horse Keeper were obliged to remain at home inactive as they could not work out of door owing to the badness of the weather.

June   *1st*   *Sunday*   A pleasant calm day. Nothing worthy of remark occurred to-day. —

„   *2nd*   *Monday*   Wind Westerly. fine clear weather. Alexis Dusseau and two men employed piling up wood preparatory for burning into Charcoal. Boilou at his former employment and Malliotte attending the Company's Horses. —

„   *3rd*   *Tuesday*   Wind blowing fresh from the Westward.

Boilou finished Mr Kipp's Bed. Two men employed packing Robes and Malliotte attending the horses. Mr Kipp and Mr Bellhumeur went out pegion hunting; Lacroix accompanying them. They returned in the evening with a few pegions. —

,, 4th *Wednesday* Wind Easterly a fine clear day. Mr Glaundye passed on his way down to Saint Louis. During his short stay here, he paid us a visit and remained discoursing for about two hours when he took his departure having left some Whiskey to be given to the Indians in present. — The Blacksmith and one man making Charcoal. Two Horses employed drawing the timber for the corn Crib. The Horse Keeper employed as usual. —

,, 5th *Thursday* Wind variable. Thundering and raining a great part of the day. The river rose considerably to day Nothing of consequence transpiring. — About noon two of our people who had been employed Cutting wood for the Steam Boat arrived. — They bring no news — towards the evening it cleared a little.

,, 6th *Friday* The river rose considerably yesterday but begins to fall again to day. The Carpenter employed at his trade. The rest hauling home firewood; making Charcoal, and repressing and tying Robe Packs, and one man attending the Horses. —

,, 7th *Saturday* Cool weather all day. Early this morning Mr Bellhumeur and 3 men with 9 horses started in search of Buffaloe. Two men employed sawing Logs into plank. The rest as before. —

,, 8th *Sunday* Though we had a plentifull fall of rain all last evening and night, the river continues falling. Late in the evening Mr Bellhumeur and party came home with 6 horseloads of Buffaloe meat; they saw a good many cattle.

" 9th *Monday* Another cold rainny day. The worse summer's day I have witnessed for several years. We were obliged to move every thing in the Stores and had them covered with Skins to Keep them dry. The rain penetrating through the roof in both the Stores. Mr. Kipp was also obliged to remove into the new dwelling House on account of the rain getting into his room and wetting every thing into it.

" 10th *Tuesday* Weather better to day. the employments chiefly Confined to cleaning and repressing the mischief occasioned by yesterday's rain. —

" 11th *Wednesday* Easterly Wind a pleasant cool day. Two men employed sawing Logs into Plank. Two Carts hauling home firewood. The Carpenter at his trade. The river which had been falling slowly this morning rising very rappidly this evening: How it rises & falls. — Mr Bellhumeur stowing the Goods in the retail store. —

" 12th *Thursday* Wind Easterly clear day. The employments of the men as before: About 10 Oclock A.M. Mr Crawford[522] and party arrived from Fort Pierre,

[522] Doubtless, not the Charles Crawford whose name appears as no. 51 in the *List of 1830*, but the very much less obscure Lewis Crawford, who had been with the Columbia Fur Company and shared the intimacy of others who had been, Mackenzie, Lamont, Laidlaw, William Dickson, Colin Campbell, and Kipp, an intimacy that was very noticeable even in their official correspondence and in marked contrast to the relations they sustained with the ex-members of the French Company. Although mentioned repeatedly in Laidlaw's letters, Lewis Crawford is a somewhat elusive individual. At the beginning of 1834, however, he was trading among the "Saons" and "opposing his rivals very successfully" (Laidlaw to Crawford, Janaury 14, 1834, *Fort Pierre Letter Book, 1832-1835*, pp. 53-54). It was he who appeared at Fort Clark to assist in the taking of the inventory in June, 1834 (*Kennedy Journal*, See Appendix) and he, who, in the winter following 1834-1835, was to conduct a trade at the temporary post of Fort Assiniboine (Chittenden, *History of the Fur Trade*, p. 961). Concerning the establishment of Fort Assiniboine, there is information in the Fort Union correspondence that would seem to have escaped Chittenden's notice. In the first weeks of September, 1834, Crawford paid Hamilton a visit at Fort Union and related how he had "built a very snug fort 100 feet square" with "plenty of accommodation" in it "for Robes and wives" (Hamilton

and surprized us by the information that owing to
arrangements made, the Fur Trade on the Missouri
had again become only one Company.[523] Immediately

to Halsey, September 17, 1834, *Fort Union Letter Book, 1833-1835*, p. 54).
Its location was near where the steamboat of the same name was wintering
(Hamilton to Kipp, October 18, 1834, *idem*, p. 57) and Mackenzie before
his final departure for St. Louis had deputed Crawford to establish it in
order to secure the trade of the Assiniboines and Crees (Hamilton to Car-
lisle, September 27, 1834, *idem*, p. 55). Prior to his appearance at Fort
Clark to take the inventory, Lewis Crawford was subject to the orders of
Laidlaw at Fort Pierre (Laidlaw to Crawford, February 24, 1834, *Fort
Pierre Letter Book*, 1832-1835, p, 68) ; but his salary for 1835 was charged
against Fort Union (Laidlaw to Hamilton, June 20, 1835, *idem*, p. 111) and
it was put at the princely sum of five hundred dollars. Whether or no this
Lewis Crawford was identical with the one who had been with the North
West Company and had headed a band of Canadian volunteers engaged in
the capture of Mackinac, in 1812 (Wisconsin State Historical *Collections*,
vol. xix, p. 342, *note* 82), I am not prepared to say.

[523] Evidence of this transaction is to be found in the following letter
from Kenneth Mackenzie to Justin Grosclaude, dated Fort Union, July 7,
1834 (*Fort Union Letter Book, 1833-1835*, p. 49) :
"Having bought out Sublett & Co. and understanding they have some
articles of Merchandise in cache near your fort, I hereby instruct you to
receive the same on my acct from Mr Andrew Sublett or such other Agent
as Messrs. Sublett & Co may appoint to deliver them to you at Ft. Cass.
Let them all be carefully examined and if any imperfection appears mark
it on the Inventory you will take thereof, of which let there be two Copies
with exact weights marks numbers lengths &c You will sign them both
and deliver one to Mr A Sublett and retain the other, packing up or keeping
the entire parcel of Merchandize apart untill Mr Tulloch's arrival you will
have further instructions from me respecting them.''
In the preceding winter Mackenzie had been approached by Robert Campbell and some conversation had taken place between them relative to the
buying out of the concern of the latter and his partners, the Sublette
brothers; but nothing had resulted for various reasons, one of which was
that Mackenzie wanted the *Sioux Outfit* to be included and that Campbell
was not authorized to offer; because Leclerc yet had an interest in it.
Another reason was, Mackenzie's idea "that it was not good policy to buy
out opposition, rather work them out by extra industry & assiduity''
(Mackenzie to James Kipp, December 17, 1833, *Fort Union Letter Book,
1833-1835*, pp. 2-5). Under the circumstances, the negotiations failing, it
was necessary, for a time yet, "to push on in the old way'' (Laidlaw to
P. D. Papin, January 14, 1834, *Fort Pierre Letter Book, 1832-1835*, pp.
52-53), but the dissolution of the Sublette-Campbell, or Rocky Mountain
Fur Company, had to be and was, indeed, not long in coming. It was
formally accomplished in June and, on the twentieth of June, another
Opposition emerged; for, almost simultaneously with the absorption of the
one that Robert Campbell had so ably represented, came the inauguration
of a firm composed of William L. Sublette, Milton G. Sublette, Thomas
Fitzpatrick, James Bridger, and Baptiste Jervais (*Sublette Papers*, Missouri Historical Society).

after Dinner Mr Crawford and I began to retake an Inventory or Packing account of the Company's effects at this place. —

" *13th* *Friday* Wind variable   more rain to day.   The employments going on as yesterday.

" *14th* *Saturday* Wind blowing fresh from the S.E^t. clear day.   The employments of the men hauling home firewood with two horses in Carts and cleaning out the yard.   Mr. Crawford and I continue taking the Inventory, got through the packing part of it to-day. Mr Kipp accompanied by Mr May took a ride to the Gros Ventre Village on business relative to the recent changes that have taken place. —

" *15th* *Sunday* A pleasant calm day.   River very low again.   Some Indians who had been on the other side the river in quest of buffaloe arrived; but reserved the produce of their hunt for their own consumption

" *16th* *Monday* Wind variable.   Men variously employed about the Fort.   about 2 Oclock P.M.   The men sent from Steam Boat handed a Letter to Mr. Kipp.   Soon afterwards got in readiness to return to Steam Boat with Horses and started in Company with Mr Crawford, they had only proceeded a few paces, when a heavy shower of rain obliged them to return to the Fort. —

" *17th* *Tuesday* Wind variable.   had a shower of rain in the evening.   Two Carts employed hauling home firewood.   Two men sawing Logs into plank.   The Carpenter and Blacksmith employed at their respective trades.   The Mandans complimented us with a Bull Dance; for which they received some trifling presents. —

" *18th* *Wednesday*

APPENDIX B.

EXTRACTS FROM *ST. LOUIS ENQUIRER,* July 19, 22, 1824
re Mackenzie

TO THE PUBLIC.[524]

A few years ago a company was formed composed of several active, enterprising and intelligent young Americans, for the purpose of trading with the Indians upon the river St. Peters and the Missouri. No sooner had this company engaged in its lawful and laudable enterprise, than those who claim a monopoly of the trade set themselves industriously to work to cramp their efforts and paralyze their energies by employing irresponsible individuals to assail the reputation, not only of the members of the company, but of those employed in their service, and occasionally stimulating and encouraging a temper of hostility in the Indians. Until very recently, however, the enemies of the company and its prosperity have purposely avoided putting their calumnies in a tangible shape — but the grasping spirit of monopoly could not endure the success of their last year's trade manifested by the returns made this summer. Finding that private scandal would not answer their purpose, they have ventured upon the forlorn hope of a public assault (or procured some scribbler to do it for them) in the Enquirer of the 5th inst. over the signature of "Querist", in which a persevering hostility to the company is too manifest to permit the author to protect himself behind the hypocritical pretence that he is prompted only by the interest which he feels in the prosperity of the country.

My name having been employed for the unworthy purpose of affecting the interests and destroying the reputation of worthy men, and having nothing to conceal in relation to myself and the company, I not only deem it a duty which I owe to the public, to

[524] St. Louis Enquirer, July 19, 1824. The issue of July 5th, referred to, was missing from the files from which this was taken.

the individuals concerned, and myself, to refute the impudent falsehoods insinuated in the piece alluded to, but I rejoice in an opportunity to remove every pretense which may have been set up by the assailants for their unwarrantable attacks; for that avaricious spirit of monopoly which begat their hostility will doubtless cherish it; especially as they have long since known that everything alleged or insinuated by the Querist was utterly false; but simply because I have the disposition as well as the means to satisfy the candid and impartial part of the community who may be disposed to protect. the worthy from the malice of worthless but powerful assailants.

* * * It is true that I am an alien; I was born in Scotland, which country I left and arrived in America for the first time in 1816, being then not more than twenty years of age, and was employed for some time as a clerk in the service of the North West Company, but never was either partner or agent for any British company. I left the service of the North West Company and arrived in St. Louis in February, 1822, and immediately reported myself to the Clerk of the Circuit Court, preparatory to being naturalized. I deny that I ever stated that I left the service of the North West Co. in consequence of any differences with them. I utterly deny ever having in any manner been concerned in stimulating or conducting Indians in any act of hostility against the people of the United States.

It has been insinuated by the Querist that in 1812, I embodied and led against the Americans some sixteen or seventeen hundred Indians, & in support of the charge a copy of a letter written by a Mr. McKenzie in July, 1812, is given as written by me. Unfortunately for the writer, however, I was then a lad of little more than 16 years of age, residing in Scotland, scarcely ever expecting to see America, and knew as little about Indians as Querist regards truth. That I did not come to St. Louis about the time the American government proposed to send troops up the Missouri, is evident; it being well known that the government not only had agitated the subject, but actually sent up troops on the Missouri several years before my arrival in St. Louis (in 1822). It therefore cannot be supposed that that circumstance induced my coming here; on the contrary, it is apparent that my intention always has been to become a citizen of the United States, from an attachment to its institutions; for my first act, at the very first place of my landing where it could be done, was to make a declaration of my intentions to do so, and I have already taken the second step.

It is said that "Mr. Tilton pushed a party across from his trading establishment, on Lake Traverse, to the Mandan villages, and there traded with the Arickarees" — and that "he and his party passed unmolested through Indians considered under British influence," and these facts in connection with the letter above referred to are relied on as conclusive, to prove that I have views hostile to the United States, and that Tilton & Co. are either my dupes or knaves co-operating with me in my designs. The facts, however, are, that the company obtained a license to trade not only with the Indians on the head waters of St. Peters, but also on the Missouri (the Mandans and the Aurickarees being particularly named) and Mr. Tilton at the time of obtaining his license, informed the superintendent of his intention to go to the Mandans from St. Peters, across the country, of which fact the Indian agent on the Missouri was advised. Mr. Tilton did accordingly proceed with goods from St. Peters across the country to the Mandan villages, near which he established a trading house, and traded with the Mandans — that after the Aurickarees were defeated last summer and their villages burnt, they approached the Mandans and compelled Mr. T. to abandon his establishment and retreat within the Mandan villages with his party for protection, after having one of his men murdered and some horses and other property destroyed. All trade made by Mr. Tilton with them was by compulsion, nor do I apprehend it would have been against law, or a violation of his licence if he had done so voluntarily, although it should happen not to have been to the *interest* of Querist or his employers.

The only Indians inhabiting the country thro' which Mr. T.'s party passed are the Sioux, who I believe are far from being suspected of being under British influence; on the contrary they are peculiarly hostile to them and have slain many of the colonists on the Red river. Besides there is an American Agent among the Sioux, who, as well as the military commandant at St. Peters, would long since have advised the government if they suspected any British influence to exist. But Mr. T.'s party were not suffered to proceed unmolested by the Indians; some of the Sioux objected, and threatened violence, which being disregarded they fired on Mr. T.'s party, and wounded one man so severely that he was unable to proceed, and, but for the interposition of the chief, the whole white party would have been massacred. The reason assigned by the Indians for this attack was, that they had been employed to prevent Mr. Tilton's party from going to the Missouri by a certain person concerned in a trading establishment on that river—no faith was however given to these accounts, and the party proceeded to their destination.

If anything more were required to rescue Mr. Tilton and the company of which he is a member, from the charge of being in any manner connected with a British establishment, the fact that all their outfits are obtained from American merchants at St. Louis, and their returns made and disposed of at the same place annually, would be amply sufficient. Can it be believed that a branch of a powerful British company possessing almost unlimited capital, would be permitted to make its purchases and dispose of the proceeds of their trade in an American market? This I believe has never been the practice, and is obviously not the policy, of any British company. They have always had ample means, and their goods are purchased on better terms and are of a better quality than are usually found in any American market, and especially at St. Louis. Indeed no facts are alleged against Mr. T. or any of his company, which could induce any reasonable man to believe that he had become a traitor to his country and lent himself to the advancement of British influence among the Indians.

The principal thing relied on for the destruction of the hopes of Mr. Tilton and his party . . . [This line too blurred to decipher] believe that the writer of the Querist was ignorant that no Indians under British influence resided on or near the route taken by Mr. T. in passing to the Mandan villages, nor can I suppose that the writer had any suspicion of my being the author of the letter intercepted by Gen. Hull, in 1812; because, if he felt the interest in the subject which he pretends, he must have discovered that from my appearance that I could not have been of an age to have been engaged in the expedition attributed to me, and possessing sufficient authority and influence to embody and bring into the field, under my command, a body of Indians near two thousand strong — Indians do not submit themselves to the control or command of boys. I have reason, moreover, to believe that the "Querist" had previous to the publication of his piece, been informed, on the best authority, that I was in Scotland at the date of the letter above alluded to, and for several years after — Why then, it may be asked, did the "Querist" publish these known falsehoods? I cannot suppose that my destruction alone was sought, but must believe that the design, end and aim of the author was to excite prejudice against the Company, and destroy, if possible, an association of young men, whose industry, talents and enterprise presented a formidable obstacle to the complete gratification of the grasping and avaricious spirit of monopoly of his instigators and employers. * * *

Kenneth Mackenzie.

(*Communicated.*)

Mr. Kenneth MacKenzie is informed that he has assumed too much and proved too little, in his answers to my inquiries. If he will read my letter, he will find that I have only spoken of suspicions which rested on him, and which he knows were in existence before that letter was written. His charge of falsehood, and of my being employed by the monopolists of Saint Louis are unfounded, as I shall be prepared to show. And as an American citizen, as a member of that family into which Mr. MacKenzie wishes to initiate himself, I ask him to state, in whose employment was he engaged from the time of his coming to America until he came to St. Louis?

Did he not come to St. Louis for the express purpose of forming a Company to trade with the Indians of the Upper Mississippi and Upper Missouri?

How long was he in St. Louis before he organized that Company?

Who are its members?

Did he not enter the Company as a clerk, when, in fact, he was its head?

Is he not now located in the very country in which the N. W. Company had the exclusive control over the Indians, until the location of our troops at St. Peters?

Has he not the trade of that large country, to the exclusion of all others, except those who have been long suspected to be engaged with the British Companies?

Did he not apply at the last term of the St. Louis Circuit Court, to take *final* steps, and then obtain a certificate of naturalization—and has he not expressed himself much displeased with a member of the bar who opposed it?

Has he not stated that, if he were the person who wrote the letter intercepted by Gen. Hull, in 1812, that person did no more than his duty; and, therefore, the fact of his having written that letter was no good objection to his becoming a citizen of the United States or entering into the Indian trade?

Mr. MacKenzie is again assured that the Querist has no other interest in making these enquiries than those of a citizen of the United States, who wishes their prosperity, to aid their policy and prevent an evasion of their laws. He is not engaged in the Indian trade, directly or indirectly — he is not engaged or prompted to write by any one who is.

QUERIST.

(*St. Louis Enquirer*, July 22, 1824).

APPENDIX C.

(a)

District of Missouri

Be it remembered that on the fourth day of June in the year of our Lord One thousand eight hundred and twentytwo, Daniel Lamont aged twentyfour years, a native of Greenock in Scotland and a subject of the King of Great Britain and then residing at St. Louis in the State of Missouri filed with the Clerk of the District Court of the United States for the Missouri District, a report of himself, stating that it was bona fide his intention to become a citizen of the United States and to renounce forever all allegiance and fidelity to any foreign prince, potentate, State or sovereignty whatever and particularly to George the fourth King of Great Britain &c to whom at that time he was subject, and that he intended to reside at the place aforesaid.

In testimony whereof I have hereunto set my hand and affixed the seal of said court at St. Louis the third day of July in the year of our Lord one thousand and eight hundred and twentytwo and of the Independence of the United States the fortysixth

Isaac Barton   Clerk

of the Missouri District.

(b)

Name	Age	Where Born	Country	From whence emigrated	Place of Landing in the United States	Where they intend making their future residence
Kenneth McKenzie	26	Bracklack	Scotland in the Kingdom of Great Britain	Greenock	St. Louis Missouri by the Military fort on St. Peters.	
William Laidlaw	23	Kenyledoors	Ditto	Liverpool	Ditto	Ditto
					K. McKenzie	
					Wm. Laidlaw	

APPENDIX D.

In the name of God Amen. — I Daniel Lamont of the City of Saint Louis and State of Missouri being in good health and of sound Mind, but uncertain how long these blessings together with that of life may be continued to me by the Author of my being and being anxious to make certain dispositions which come not within the jurisdiction of the Courts of the State in Case of dying intestate I do hereby Make and Publish this as my last Will and testament, no other having ever been made by me: And First I direct that in event of my dying in the Civilized World or at any of the Establishments of the Upper Missouri Outfit of which I am at present a Member my Body shall be Committed to its Mother Earth from whence it came with decency but no Parade; and with the usual forms of the Scotch Presbyterian Church in which I was Baptised and in infancy reared, tho' agreeably to the interpretation of its tenates [*sic*] in Missouri I cannot be a Member thereof: And as to such Worldly Estate as it hath pleased God to intrust me with I dispose of the same as follows: First I direct that all my debts and Funeral Expenses be paid as soon after my decease as Possible out of any Monies that may come into the hands of my Executors: Second — I direct that my dearly beloved Wife Margaret with whom I have lived in all harmony shall be and remain the Guardian of my Child or Children during Her or their Minority should it be the Will of God to spare to them so excellent a Parent; but in Case of their being deprived during their Minority by death or Marrying of her Guardianship, then and in such Case my Executors shall become their Guardians during their Minority, and I earnestly intreat their utmost care in and about the Morals and Education of my Children, and desire that they may be instructed in the doctrines and religion of the Scotch Presbyterian Church. — Third — I further direct and enjoin that the better to enable my dear Wife to fulfill her Guardianship the whole of my Personal property (except money) or such Portion thereof as she may think fit to retain shall remain in her Possession during her life; and should she not survive the Majority of her Child or Children or should she during the Minority of her Child or Children again enter into the State of Wedlock then in either Case the said Personal Property shall be disposed of and the Proceeds become a Part of my Estate: Fourth — I further direct that my Executors shall dispose of my Estate both real and Personal namely two Lots of ground fronting on the Mississippi as described in deeds now in Possession of my Wife in S^t. Louis — Ten Shares of Stock in the Missouri Insurance Company of S^t. Louis — Two Female Slaves together with my Household Furniture Plate Books and so forth (always excepting such portion of the latter as my dear Wife may think necessary to retain during her lifetime or Widowhood) as to them may seem most beneficial, and the Interest arising from such disposition shall be Paid to my dear Wife in aid of her Support and that of her Child or Children —   Fifth — And I further direct that the Sum of Two Thousand Dollars shall be paid by my Executors to my much esteem'd Friend William Laidlaw at present one of my associates in business out of the first Moneys accruing from my interest in the Upper Missouri Outfit, and which will be adjusted and paid to my Executors annually on or as soon after the first day of July as Convenient by Pratte, Chouteau and Company of Saint Louis aforesaid, until the first day of July One Thousand Eight hundred & thirtynine on which day my Contract expires — the application of said Two Thousand Dollars to be made by my said Confidential Friend William Laidlaw as agreed between us before the execution of this my last Will and over which his Control is absolute —   Sixth — And I further direct that my Brother Duncan Lamont now of Buenos-Aires but who by my invitation will probably be in Saint Louis in all next Summer, shall have the use of the Sum of Ten Thousand Dollars on his Personal security for the Purpose of enabling him to Commence business, provided he agrees to Pay to my Executors Interest at the rate of Seven Dollars per Centum per Annum during the time said Money remains in his Possession, Provided however the said loan should not exceed the time my Youngest Child shall become of Age — Seventh — And I further direct that my Executors shall annually on or before the first day of May Cause to be paid to my Father Colin Lamont Senr. Greenock Scotland my native place the sum of One hundred Dollars during his life and in event of my Mother surviving him the same to [be] continued to her, and at her death the same to be continued to my only Sister Jane during her life and at her death to revert to and become a part of my Estate. — Eighth — And I further direct that after my Executors have made Provision for the aforesaid payment to my friend William Laidlaw of Two Thousand Dollars and the aforesaid Annuity of One hundred Dollars to my Father, Mother or Sister as before stipulated, the interest arising from the residue of my Estate shall be paid over to my dear Wife during her life or Widowhood, it being expressly understood that the same shall cease in Case of her again entering the bonds of Matrimony and at her death or Marrying Provided my Child or Children are of mature age the whole amount of my Estate shall be divided equally among them, otherwise to remain during their Minority in the hands of their Guardians until they are by law entitled to demand the same — And in Case of my Child or Children dying ere they become of Age, my whole Estate always excepting the Annuity aforesaid shall be divided per Capita between the Children of my Brothers Colin & Duncan and my Sister Jane: Ninth — And I further desire that my dear Wife will consider the foregoing Provision made for her as the result of a disposition to insure her Comfort, fully convinced that it surpasses the award which the Court could allow as dowever [*sic*] in event of my dying intestate — Tenth — And I further ordain, and it is my express Will and desire that if any difference or dispute, question or controversy, shall arise concerning any feature of this my Will from my ignorance of technicalities or forms, that each difference shall be adjusted by the award of good Citizens, chosen by the contending Parties whose award shall be binding on both Parties, else the Party disposed to litigate whoever he or she may be shall be and I declare them de-

prived of all Participation in the benefits of this my last Will —
Eleventh — And I do hereby make and ordain my much esteem'd
friends Pierre Chouteau Jr. and George Collier Esquires of
Saint Louis aforesaid Executors of this my last Will and testament, feeling satisfied that they will justly Administer for and
Protect those dear ones of him who while living loved them
much —

In Witness whereof, I, Daniel Lamont, the testator have to
this my Will written on one Sheet of Paper, set my hand and
Seal this Eleventh day of November in the Year of Christ One
Thousand Eight hundred and thirtyfour at Fort Pierre near the
Mouth of the Titon River, Upper Missouri

Danl Lamont   (Seal)

Before the Witnesses who have subscribed
in the presence of each other

> Wm. Laidlaw
> Jacob Halsey.

St. Louis October 3rd 1831[525]

To the Hon. Lewis Cass
    Secretary at War
        Sir

        In answer to your letter and queries upon the Fur Trade,
dated the 9th September, I have the honor to state that my personal Knowledge & observation will enable me to answer to one
branch of your enquiries, which is the condition of the trade in
the vicinity of the Rocky Mountains and west of them.   I first
went to the Rocky Mountains to engage in the Fur Trade in
1822, and have been every year since engaged, or connected with
the business of the trade, either on the upper Missouri River, or
in the region of the Mountains.   I have twice been beyond the
mountains, and have seen all the variety of operations to which
our trade and intercourse with the Indians is there subject.   In
the year 1822 I was clerk in an expedition conducted by Immell
& Jones for the Missouri Fur Company, and was one of those
who escaped the Massacre of that party when it was attacked,
defeated & robbed by the Black Feet Indians on the Yellow Stone
river.   The circumstances of that attack shew some of our
dangers in this business, about twelve days before the attack we
fell in with the party, about thirty five Warriors, no Women or
children among them about half mounted & half on foot, with
dogs to carry their moccasins & provisions, which they pack on
the backs of the dogs as we pack horses, we were twenty nine
in number, all armed, had some goods and about twenty packs
of Furs, which we had caught, our interview was friendly; we
made them some presents & parted in the kindest manner; but
suspecting their treachery we set out for our rendezvous on the
Yellow Stone, being then on the three forks of the Missouri;

525 These and other reports similar, particularly one from Dougherty
(See *Dougherty Papers*), dated November 19, 1831, were called forth by
Secretary Cass's letter of September 9, 1831.

The twelfth day we were overtaken and ambushed at the foot of hills on the margin of the river by about four hundred of these Indians who had collected upon the information of the small party we had previously met. We were scattered half a mile along the river & had seven Killed and four wounded, and lost our Goods, furs, horses, and traps. This was my first introduction to the dangers of this trade I escaped by a run of about seven miles across a plain, pursued only by footmen, and returned at night to ascertain the extent of the Mischief, I found the Indians encamped near the ground, and made off in the dusk to provide for my own safety, and was received in a friendly way by a band of Crow Indians with which I fell in about dark the next night, of my companions two were Killed by treachery afterwards. The next Spring I was robbed by the Crows, a set of fellows with whom I had been all the winter, and treated with the greatest friendship, and made them many presents; but finding me alone they could not miss the opportunity & robbed me of every thing even powder, lead, & tobacco for my personal use. Since then I was robbed a third time & a fourth near the scene of the first, so that I know something of the dangers of the trade.

The Fur Trade in & about the Rocky Mountains is carried on both by trading goods & hunting beaver. The hunters now out I should suppose to be five or six hundred men, and are fitted out partly from Missouri and partly from Santa Fé, These are exclusive of the British who also hunt constantly *west* of the mountains & did hunt to the *east* of them until the American hunters became numerous there. The hunting is carried on nearly in the same way by all these parties. at so much per month Two or three who have capital or credit, hire the hunters at so much per month & equip them for the business. Trading is almost always united to hunting, The hunting is done with traps and beaver the principal object.

None of our American hunters ever go to the south of the main Columbia or to the North of the Latitude 49 degrees to what is considered British Ground, Nor do the British hunt there themselves. They come to our Side of the line and mean to exhaust it first, so that the treaty privilege to hunt & trade on our Side is of Great Value to them. It is universally considered unsafe to go on the country claimed by the British, and no American has ever ventured to do it, and I have no doubt would lose his life and his property if he did, All the hunting parties are on our Side of the Columbia and of latitude 49: at present I am of opinion that the Americans are taking most furs by hunting; but that the British have taken much the most in the whole country counting from the late war to the present time. The Indians in the Mountains and beyond them do not object to this hunting, which though Strange, is not unaccountable, for they do not hunt themselves for beaver, and get presents from all the hunting parties, which serve as a purchase for the privilege. Another Source of profit to the Indians is stealing the hunters horses and restoring them for a reward; an operation so common that it hardly interrupts friendship. The Indians west of the Mountains on our side of the line, were not furnished with traps to catch the beaver. North of the line they were furnished and are good trappers, of late the Indians east of the mountains & south of 49 have begun to get traps and to hunt themselves & therefore to object to White hunters. This I know to be the case with the Crow Indians, who now object to White hunters, though they did not when I first Knew them. Hunting is the only way our citizens have to contend with the British on our ground in and beyond the Mountains, their advantage in trading being so great as to put competition out of the question. They bring their Goods from Hudsons bay and from the mouth of the Columbia, without paying any duties while ours being imported through the U. States are Subject to heavy duties perhaps an average of 50 or 60 per cent. These goods are of the Same Kind being made in England, and the Indians are good judges of their quality & price; So that the difference of 50 or 60 per Cent in their Cost puts it out of the power of the American trader to compete with the British traders — the British besides their permanent posts along the line of our frontiers have temporary winter establishments on the American Side of the line, where they trade with our Indians, and nearly monopolise the trade on account of their advantages. One of these establishments is, or was lately on Medicine river, one of the Northern branches of the Missouri, falling in above the falls.

The principal tribes of Indians in the region of the Rocky Mountains & their Vicinity, with their disposition &c are as follows: 1st the most numerous are the Snake Indians of which I know three great bands, the Shoshawnees, the Ietans and the Camanches; and many other Smaller bands. Many of these go by a name which signifies Root digger, because they live by digging roots, and are wretchedly poor, miserable & theiveish. They have no horses, no traps, no guns, and depend for safety upon hideing, & for subsistence upon roots, berries, insects, reptiles and such game as their mode of life & bows and arrows enable them to Kill. There are a great number of these bands, all in the Mountains, where they stay for shelter, seldom comeing in the plains except to steal, at which they are Wonderfully expert, They are the most miserable human beings I ever saw; ignorant to the last degree, superstitious in the extreme, destitute of every thing necessary to even Indian comfort, but appear to be perfectly contented with their situation, and will not avail themselves of the means in their power to better their condition.

2nd The Blackfeet are the most dangerous warlike & formidable, they go in larger bodies than other Indians, and are well armed with guns, chiefly obtained from the British, these Indians are trappers, having been supplied with traps by the British & learnt the art from them, They have been always hostile to the citizens of the United States & trade almost exclusively with the British. They reside principally on the bend of the Sascatchiwine & make constant excursions for hunting & plunder on the waters of the Missouri.

3rd The Flatheads inhabit the south branches of the Columbia and have always been friendly to the Citizens of the U. States. They are not very numerous, say about five hundred families. They have never Killed or robbed our Citizens, This is their boast, they proclaim it continually, like the Chicasaws did formerly & in fact we always feel safe among them. Some Americans have been living with them for many years & have families among them.

4th Crows about 500 families say 1000 Warriors; live on the Yellow Stone & roam along the foot of the Mountains. They are theives at home and abroad, and spare no chance to rob us, but never Kill. This they frankly explain by telling us that if they killed, we would not come back, & they would lose the chance of Stealing from us. They have no Shame about stealing & will talk over their past thefts to you with all possible frankness & indifference. The best trade with them is in getting horses from them to carry on other operations. These horses are chiefly stolen from the Spaniards. They raise but few themselves. They have a great many mules and horses. I suppose I have seen ten thousand horses & mules feeding at their Village. The children are learnt to ride from their earliest age. The infant is often secured on a board, which is hung on the horse horn of a saddle and the horse turned loose to follow, as soon as it can sit up it is tied on a saddle, & the horse follows. At four years of age they will ride alone & guide the horse; this both male & female; Sex makes no difference; and all become first-rate riders.

5. Arapahoes & Gros Ventres; they are the same people, Speak the same language & have about 1200 Warriors. They inhabit the country from the Santa Fee trail to the head of the Platte. The Gros Ventres are from Fort de Prairie a British post on the SasKatchiwine, and are very inimical They harrass the Santa Fee traders & those engaged in the Fur Trade.

With respect to the value of the furs obtained by hunting in the region of the Rocky Mountains, I understand that the returns of this year are & will be as follows:

1st Soubletts Company about $ 40,000
2nd Dripps & Fontenelle about 30,000
3rd a detachment from the American
     Fur Company   30,000
4th Two Companies of American
     Citizens fitting out from
     Santa Fee making their
     returns to St. Louis about 50,000

I left the head of the Colorado of the West where it issues

from the Rocky Mountains on the 18th of July last and arrived at St. Louis the last of August. At the time I left the Mountains, the above was understood to be the amount of the hunting or trapping branch of the business in and beyond the Mountains. The trade in furs robes &c is not included and will be better answered by others.

With respect to the loss of lives, I will only Speak of those Killed since I have been engaged in the fur trade, and in the part of the country [which] was the scene, or nearly so of my own operations.

In 1823 forty three persons were Killed from the Arikeras to the Mountains. About twelve of these were in General Ashley's employ & seven with me at the defeat of Immell & Jones. The next year 8 men were Killed at one time by the Snakes on the waters of the Columbia, who were in the employ of Provost & Leclerc. Same year eight of Robidoux men were Killed by the Camanches. Every year since the deaths have amounted to ten, fifteen, or twenty, except the present year, of which I only Know of 4 being Killed, two of Dripps & Fontenelle's men who were Killed just before I left the mountains. And Mr. Smith & Mr Winter, the first at the head of a party and the last a clerk of Mr Soublette. The two latter were Killed on the Santa Fee trail by the Camanche Indians.

The furs are diminishing, and this diminution is general & extensive. The beaver may be considered as exterminated on this Side of the Rocky Mountains; for though a few beavers may be taken, yet they are not an object for any large investment. Along the foot of the Rocky Mountains & down the water courses which issue from them & in & beyond the mountains, they are yet in sufficient numbers to make it an object to hunt & trap them. But they are greatly diminished. The permission which was given to the British after the late war to trade on our own country has been most liberally used, and the country trapped over and over again. Young ones of Six months old, the dams never being spared. At present the trappers are only gleaning where the British have been reaping. If the country was allowed to rest a few years, it would be replenished; but the treaty which

grants the privilege to the British tends to the ravageing of the
Country as both parties do all they can to make the most out of
the present time.

The improvement & protection of the trade requires two things
to be done, both of which are in the power of the United States,
and are called for by every consideration of interest and human-
ity.   The first of these things are to put the American trader on
a footing with the British trader by releasing his goods from
duties, & the next would be to secure him against danger of
murder and robbery by equipping the frontier military posts
with horses; so that the Soldiers instead of being Stationary on
the frontiers, could visit the whole tribes of Indians, and demand
and take satisfaction for the depredations they commit.   These
two measures which the federal government could so easily adopt,
would in my opinion put the Fur trade on a footing to compete
successfully with the British.   And if the Government wishes
the hunting and trapping discontinued they ought surely to stop
it first on the part of the British; and then the most effectual
way for stopping it on the part of our own citizens would be to
enable them to substitute trading for *trapping,* to do which the
duties on Indian goods would have to be abolished, so that the
American and British trader would be on a par as to the cost of
of their goods

I have the honor to be Sir

Respectfully

Your Obt Sert

William Gordon

St. Louis October 27, 1831

To Genl William Clark
   SuP Ind Affairs
      Sir

      In answer to your queries relative to the Fur Trade, I
have the honor to state that my personal Knowledge and observation will enable me to answer only a part of them my operations

in the business having been chiefly confined to the Upper Missouri and in the Rocky Mountains.

The number of trading posts on the Missouri above the Council Bluffs, which are maintained and kept up during summer amounts, I believe, to only six or seven. These are the principal depots,'' whence a great number of wintering posts are established, and called in again in the spring, at the termination of the winter's trade —

These principal depots have generally an investment in goods, say to the amount of from fifteen to twenty thousand dollars, and the branches which they establish temporarily are given an amount, ranging from five hundred, to two and three thousand dollars — Woolen goods of coarse fabric, such as blue and red strouds, Blankets &c constitute the principal and most costly articles of trade — they are almost exclusively of English manufacture, and tho' coarse, are good — the Indians are good judges of the articles in which they deal, and have always given a very decided preference for those of English manufacture — knives, guns, powder, lead and tobacco are also among the primary articles, some of which are of American and some of English manufacture — *Whiskey,* tho not an *authorized* article, has been a principal, and I believe a very lucrative one for the last several years, tho I consider it as deleterious in its effects generally as regards the welfare of the Indians, and dangerous in the hands of unprincipalled men, who might by possibility be engaged in the trade —

Of the first cost of the goods, I think it unnecessary for me to say any thing, as that can be ascertained from others better calculated to give you the information you desire.

The goods are exchanged for Buffaloe robes and beaver *skins,* and at the place of exchange would give to the trader a great ostensible profit upon the primary cost, say from 200 to 2000 per cent — The real profits, however fall far short of even the Minimum stated, owing to the very heavy expenses which the trader has to incur in carrying on his business — The expenses incidental to the prosecution of the fur trade are immense and far beyond those of any other business that American citizens are engaged in according to the amount of capital employed, hence many are deterred from engaging in it that would otherwise do so.

Not only does the trader have to supply himself with the number of hands which ought to be necessary to carry on his business, but he has in most instances to have two or three times that number to serve as a protection to himself and property — this unnatural expenditure has to be bourne by the indians as it produces the necessity of selling to them at much higher rates, when it is of no advantage to the trader — The only means which suggest itself to me to correct this evil would be the Federal Government to adopt some more efficient means for the protection of the fur trade than has heretofore been done, and from my intimate acquaintance with the extensive region of country to which these remarks are applicable, I feel warranted in presenting to you my views of what I would consider efficient protection — For this purpose there should be five or six hundred U. S. troops stationed somewhere in the interior of the Indian country, and the nearer the base of the Rocky Mountains the better — those troops to be efficient should be mounted — footmen can do no good against the indians of that country, who are always mounted and can evade Infantry without subjecting themselves to the least inconvenience — An arrangement of that kind would have a most salutary effect upon the interests not only of the white trader but of the Indian himself because at present the intercourse between the parties depends but too often for profit to their relative strength; taking alternate advantages of each other — hence a spirit of mutual bad feeling obtains, alike injurious to both parties —

By affording this or some other adequate protection to the trade, an additional number of persons would be led immediately to engage in it, and the consequence would be that the unnecessary expenses of the trader would be reduced — and the profits if not so great would be more certain, and benefiting a larger number of persons —

In those districts where the American has to compete with the British trader, the latter occupies a very great and striking advantage over the former, owing to the privilege he enjoys of introducing his goods free of duty, while the former pays a duty of from 40 to 60 per cent on almost all the principal articles.

The number of men at each of the principal posts amounts to from 15 to 20 and at the temporary wintering posts to from 3 to 6 — dried or fresh buffaloe meat constitutes the almost exclusive article of provision, and is mostly procured of the indians.

The diminution of furs in the Upper Missouri and in the Rocky Mountains is general and extensive, and has been very great since my first adventures to those countries ten years ago — indeed to the east of the mountains they are not any where in sufficient quantities to authorize the expense of an expedition exclusively in search of them — The Buffaloe robe trade is perhaps in a more flourishing condition than at any former period, and promises I think to continue valuable for many years —

The foregoing remarks contain all the information I am able to afford you, touching the subject of your queries, and is respectfully submitted —   I am

> Your Most Ob^t
> Servant
>
> Wm. Gordon

APPENDIX F.

Mr Ja^s Kipp   Fort Union Dec 17
    Dear Sir

H^y. Morrin & the men under his charge made a long trip not arriving here until 29 Nov being so long absent I was fearing some accident had happened to them.   I was glad to get your letter of the 15 Nov although much disappointed that the long looked for express from St. Louis was not forth coming, however before breakfast on the 9 Dec the express arrived.   I thank you for your promptitude in forwarding it and now very particularly request that not an hours unavoidable delay may interfere with the progress of my packet for Fort Pierre & St. Louis, every hour is of consequence and after all with every exertion I fear my letters will not reach St. Louis in time for my purposes but I rely on every effort being made to effect my wishes The extraordinary state of the weather (for even the river here flows smoothly on like Spring) prevents my compliance with your wishes in sending Mdze & Stores, so soon as trains can travel I will endeavor to supply all your wants not forgetting the bitters for your Stomach's sake.   I have not Sugar to supply my table until Spring but I will spare you a little.

I shall write to Baron Braunsberg and though I cannot let him have H^y. Morrin I will arrange to supply him with men in time for his descending the river.   I am very sensible that a good deal of trouble is laid on your shoulders by the Baron's arrangement to winter with you, as you observe he is a fine old gentleman and I much regret that I have not his company for the winter myself.

I arrived here safe & well on the 8 Nov. and have experienced a continued succession of fine weather since that day: on the 13 Nov Mr Chardon started with a snug equipment & 20 men in boat to build and winter near la rivière au tremble,   he writes me that he has a comfortable fort ab^t 80 f^t. square called by him Fort Jackson,   the Indians are visiting him regularly and giving him abundance of provisions, his prospect of making robes is far more cheering than mine: Cattle are far off   it takes my hunters 6 or 7 days to send in a supply of fresh meat and the Assiniboins are poor, poor beyond any thing ever known on this river, horses they have none, their dogs they have eaten & a large portion of the Indians have not killed cattle sufficient for their own clothing.

Our opponents are not idle, they have opened a house near Mr Chardon.   Deschamp's three hopeful sons are in their employ, and are very active, they have sent Glenday & a Mr Vasquez to the Crows, they are giving a blanket for a robe, and have already partially dressed several Indians.   You know that I have hitherto abstained from this procedure but I suppose I shall be driven to it in my own defence and if I begin I will do it well.   I expect a good many Crees to trade here this winter, M Gravell is engaged as interpreter.   Should cattle even yet visit us in numbers as they once did there are Indians enough on the river for me to make a respectable quantity of robes notwithstanding the opposition I have to compete with.   I am well pleased that Pecotte kept Ortubise to winter with Crawford and hope they will do well.

I would wish Bellehumer to be at one of the Indian villages for even with the utmost industry & exertion on our part our opponents contrive to get both beaver & robes that should come to us: I am informed that Durand has a pack of beaver & a great many robes, if true, 'tis pity, that with his small means he should do so much

You astonish me by one observation in your last letter, "The interest of the Company suffering by your not having Sc^t, Ch^{fs} Coats & G^r Bl^{kts}."   You know they are waiting for you at Apple River & even if you had no horse both you & I remember the time when two men could carry on their backs as many Chiefs Coats & blankets as would supply your immediate wants.   I cannot bear to hear or read the word "impossible" applied to business affairs especially when of so easy accomplishment. —

You inform me that Bapt^e. Deguire is employed by you, having passed an engagement with Mr. Pecotte; when he left Fort Cass in Sept last, he was indebted to A. F. C^o $ 205.04 & engaged to deliver two horses he had to bring him down on his arrival here, however he sold his horses to Sublett C^o for $ 80 and never shewed himself here at all, Keep your eye on him.

Our opponents are almost without horses & are offering such unusual prices to the Indians even for horses they know to have been stolen from the Mandans or Gros Ventres that I wish you to keep your Indians on their guard for in consequence of the opposition my power of restraining the Assiniboins is at an end and as soon as Winter sets in they will endeavour to make a haul.

I do not expect our opponents will make any considerable number of robes at Fort William as was to be expected the Assiniboins rushed towards them at first but having spied out the nakedness of the land they have nearly all returned to their old allegiance.

You know the sorrel horse, white face, which I rode up, called Steam boat, he is a pleasant riding horse, & has already proved himself one of the best buffalo horses I have, I am told he is 9 or 10 yrs old, and though I should very unwillingly part with him, if Bellehumer cannot get an American horse to suit him at Fort Pierre where they have a good collection or if he prefers said Steam boat he shall have him in the Spring at $ 120.

Please send me acc^t. of advances to L'Ange Guerir who came up with H^y Morrin.

A few days after my arrival Mr. Campbell called upon me to ascertain if I was disposed to buy their Company out, but as he could not sell the Sioux outfit in which Leclèrc had a share until Spring, moreover being unwilling that Leclèrc should prior thereto be privy to any transaction we might enter into and more especially as it was your opinion in which all my old respected clerks on the river concurred, that it was not good policy to buy out opposition, rather work them out by extra industry & assiduity, I was somewhat indifferent to Mr. Campbells proposition & after two interviews the negotiation broke off. I trust I am not unreasonable in expecting that all my experienced &

faithful clerks will justify by the results of the Spring the correctness of their opinion. —

Our opponents must get some robes but it is my wish that it should be on such terms as to leave them no profit.

I have been very unfortunate with my dogs this Summer and am unable to procure a single one from the poor Assiniboins. I must look to you to secure me a few trains by the time I send down.

I send you a little Calomel and hope when obliged to be used it may always be efficacious.

Fr. Croteau an engagée is privileged to accompany the express to St. Louis,   on his arrival there he will be free & on paying his debt to the A. F. Co. of $ 107.

Signed   K. McK.

To Mr Jas Kipp   17 Dec 1833

After filling one sheet some fresh ideas occur to me on commencing a second: the fact is I want much to see you and consult you about some matters that I cannot well put on paper & it strikes me you could at this season make the trip in a short time & be hardly missed from home, Belhumer I presume you may safely place in charge.

I send you down one extra man P Gaboleau to return with you & you will bring two more men with dogs & trains to supply yourself with Mdze & stores such as you want & I can spare   in addition to the dogs necessary to carry down your goods you must contrive to bring me at least 6 more or all you can.   Every day after Jany 1 I shall be looking for your arrival   could it be practicable for you to pass New Years day with me it would afford me much pleasure   at all events the sooner I see you the more agreeable.

Mr Hamilton desires his respects & will be happy to greet your arrival in conjunction with your friend & well wisher & who always has pleasure in subscribing himself Yours very truly

Signed K McKenzie

Acc^{ts} Le Brun — Denoyer, J. Papin Fr Delorme & Calomel $ 1.

Fort Union 29 Oct 1833

Mr. Ja^s Kipp,
  Dear Sir

    You were doubtless apprized by Mr. McKenzie that it was very probable the Baron Braunsberg with Messrs. Bordmer & Drydapple would pass the winter at your fort, this will be handed you by the Baron & I am satisfied he will receive every attention in your power to render him. I have endeavoured to persuade him to pass the winter here but he is so anxious to gain information relative to the Mandan's & Gros Ventres thro' your means that he cannot wait for it until Spring. If Mr McKenzie on his way hither before this reaches you allow me to request you will make such arrangemnts for the Baron's comfort as the nature of your establishment will allow, he will require men to conduct him down stream in the Spring but hereon you will receive instructions during the winter Hugron Beaugard & Beauchamp will remain with you until further orders & you can no doubt find them work to do, the latter has generally attended on the Baron to make his fire carry water &c. Hy Morrin & L Vachard you will send back after a day or two rest unless you are expecting dispatches from below & wish to keep them to (be) the bearers thereof for a few days longer. I send you statement of the Men's a/c's, if Morrin or Vachard take any thing at F^t. C. charge it to this post handing me particulars on their return. Mr. Chardons Comp^{ts}. I beg to assure you of my best wishes & am &c   J. A. H.

    The Baron is charged in a/c with the boat, will you have it looked after during the winter that it may serve him in the Spring. I send you list of prices to be charged Baron B. other things in like proportion on his departure send copy of his a/c to Ft. Pierre handing him duplicate   Make any purchases you can in accordance with his wishes of the Indians & charge him a reasonable price.   Please supply him with what he applies for if you can.   J. A. H.

K. McKenzie Esqr.   Fort Union 30 Oct 1833
    Dear Sir
    On 5th Inst. I wrote you by Dubreuille, & sent letters from Mr Mitchell & Mr Tulloch if they reached you, in course, you will be prepared to find Baron B. at Ft. Clark.   The Baron looks to you to find men to take him to St. Louis in Spring he paying their wages as also from Ft. McK. to Fort Clark.
    I have no partars of Morrin's engagement,   Mr. M. relies on his being back with him & Vachard also.   I send Hugron to accommodate the Baron as he complained much of his first crew also Beauchamp who acts as servant & Beaugard a simple harmless fellow who is terribly haunted with fear of dying without confession & being buried in unconsecrated ground.   I have furnished a fresh boat.   I send you duplicate of the Baron's a/c. M. Gravelle & the Deschamps are returned from hunting   we have only 100 1b Beaver from them; Mr. Campbell has engaged the 3 Deschamps for one year at $ 1500 salary.   Le Vache Blanche Le fils des Gros Français Le Jamb blesse & L'Ours have been here but nothing to trade   they have crossed the river to hunt,   Le Brechu's with Gens de Canot are on head of White Earth R Le Manguer d'hommes on R au tremble & have cattle. Le Gauche is gone to the North with 100 lodges.   Le Sonnant came in to beg dogs & horses   he has two lodges with him, no peltries.   On 10th Ins. Duchaine deserted with Durocher who arrived the preceding day.   On 14th Miller deserted   he had tried for 10 days to persuade Maloney & Holmes to go with him. The work progresses tolerably well but having lost the boat the supply of stone is very scant.   Hunters have killed cows once only since you left.   A copy of Mens a/c is enclosed to Mr Kipp.

You will of course direct the men whether to remain or return here.   Yours truly

J. A. H.

Mr H. Picott   Fort Union Dec 15 1833
     Dear Sir
     The express which I had long waited for with so much anxiety reached me on the 9th Inst. just one month after my arrival;   for the promptness with which you accelerated its progress accept my thanks.
The tin Smith arrived here Nov 29,   he is a good workman   I shall find him a most useful artisan.
     It was some cause of regret that adverse winds had prevented you reaching Apple River at the time I passed but the detail of your arrangements and the result of your exertions since your arrival are so satisfactory that it is evident no additional remarks from me were necessary as a spur to your laudable efforts if the interests of the A. F. C. are as well looked after at every other post as yours the Opposition of Messrs. Sublett & Co. will not be very detrimental to our interests.   On my arrival Mr Campbell called on me proposing to sell out their interest on Missouri river at all the posts above the Sioux but Leclerc having a share in the Sioux outfit he could not sell the interest therein until Spring.
     I have so much confidence in the support I receive from my old & tried clerks that I was very indifferent to Mr Campbells proposition & after two or three interviews the negotiation terminated   if we are to be opposed on the river it will be more honorable to break up a formidable Company like our present opponents by dint of extra industry & long tried experience than for them to abandon the trade from other circumstances   at this station which they call Fort William they have a heavy outfit – more ammunition & tobacco than I have alcohol & wine — and an expensive establishment of clerks & men.   They have sent a

small equipment to the Crow Camp & another to oppose Mr Chardon who is stationed at Fort Jackson a few days journey above this place,   the Indians naturally visited their establishment at the outset but hitherto they have had nothing to trade and I believe I shall lose very few of my old friends,   My trade at this post I fear will be very limited but Sublett & Co. shall have much less, if health & vigour be spared me.

Since my arrival there has been a continued succession of fine clear weather and the river still remains open but when the winter commences & the ground is well covered with snow I will contrive to send you some whiskey.

With respect to your visiting St. Louis in the Spring, I do not at this moment see any insuperable objection thereto and know that I would suffer some personal inconvenience to comply to the requests of those who do their utmost for my interest, but as unforeseen circumstances may arise between this and the Spring I am sure you will excuse my not promising absolutely but you shall however hear from or see me in time for you to make your arrangements.

With respect to the boat to convey your peltries you shall also hear from me with full instructions.

Will you ascertain from your Indians if they are desirous to have a permanent fort, if so I will build a good fort near the old Mandan Villages & will do all I can to please them, inform me fully hereon.   You will please write to me by every opportunity as you have hitherto done giving me all the information which reaches you of our opponents mighty deeds ! ! as well as your own proceedings with your Indians relative to Soldiers & endeavors to get robes I prescribe no limit but your own discretion   my object as you know is to prevent the robes going past us.   I am convinced all you do will be done to the best of your judgement.

B. Deguire whom I understood you engaged is indebted to A. F. C. $ 205 $\frac{4}{100}$, he promised Mr. Tulloch at Fort Cass to deliver his two horses on his arrival here, but he sold them to Sublett Co for $ 80 & pocketted the money, and came not to Ft. Union   I rely on your using every exertion to forward the express without delay to Fort Pierre for I much fear the St. Louis letters will not reach their destination in time for my purpose.

M. Baron de Braunsberg   Fort Union Dec 15th 1833
    Sir

I beg to acknowledge the receipt of your letter by Hy Morrin bearing date Nov 15th and assure you it has cause of great regret to me that our travelling arrangements so clashed as to prevent our meeting   had I been so fortunate as to have arrived here before your departure I think I should have prevailed on you to have given me your company for the Winter and although at any place in this wild country you must have suffered some privations I would have endeavoured to have made them less sensible than at any post not under my immediate personal control.   If the fates have so ordained that we do not meet again in the Missouri territory I do hope at no distant day to renew the acquaintance in your own country for I shall ever cherish the most agreeable reminiscences of our last Summer's intercourse.

With respect to your arrangements for the Spring I will find you men to convoy your boat down stream but I cannot promise you Hy Morrin as he is about to make the voyage to Fort Mc-Kenzie and cannot be down in time to answer your purpose, but I trust you will be fully satisfied with such men as I shall appoint to conduct you.   Although the winter has not yet commenced, no snow having fallen, for a month past not a single gale of wind, & the river flowing as smoothly in front of the fort as in the month of May, yet though it tarry it will come.   I shall then renew this pleasure and in accordance with your request will furnish you my bill of charges.   I have no prospect of visiting Fort Clark this winter but Mr Hamilton tells me he invited you hither if you find the voyage practicable and to me there appears no insurmountable difficulty, allow me to assure you of a

hearty welcome and that your visit will be considered an honor
conferred on

                                Sir

                    Your very obedient Servant

                        Signed   K. McKenzie

—————————

Mr Joshua Pilcher   Fort Union 16 Dec 1833
    Council Bluffs
        Dear Sir
            You will long ere this have heard of my visiting Fort
Pierre in the month Sept where for several weeks I anxiously
awaited the arrival of Mr Lamont with my letters & Invoices &c
from S^t. Louis   My patience being exhausted & having the fear
of a winter voyage before me, I directed my course hither leaving
Fort Pierre Oct 24 and arriving here Nov 8 — the long looked
for letters consigned to Mr Lamonts care did not reach me until
the 9th Ins. and I much fear unless extraordinary attention is
paid by my people on the river my present express for St. Louis
will not reach its destination in time to answer my purpose.
I know Sir I can rely on your diligence when it reaches your
post to forward it by trusty men in the most expeditious manner,
it is of very great importance that it reach Mr Chouteau with
the least possible delay.   I have been very busily but very un-
profitably occupied with Indians since my arrival here, very few
of my old friends will leave me but my opponents are not want-
ing in exertion, they have a large assortment of Mdze abundance
of Alcohol in barrels which came up the Missouri independent
of what came via the Mountains & down the Y Stone — and wine
highly charged with Spirits no lack — That the partiality or
laxity of the Government officers should allow them to pass an
unlimited quantity of Alcohol for they have abundance at all
their Sioux posts and by their extreme rigor carry away every
drop over which we had control not leaving us enough to moisten
a hair of our heads, will surely justify us in making a complaint:

be the laws good or bad they were enforced against the A.F.C. and ought in like manner to be enforced against others engaged in the same trade & at or near the same stations — Could I hope for the pleasure of a visit from you I could regale you with a glass of genuine Fort Union wine; it is such as you would not sneeze at.

Notwithstanding the great pretensions and formidable preparations of our opponents I think I can say with great truth there may be great cry but very little wool at their station near me they must lose money and my information from every other post tends to the same conclusion. Mr Campbell proposed to sell out to me I prefer that they should try their powers & finding their chance of success hopeless be compelled to withdraw.

You know the nature of opposition & that Indians will try new traders but all that are worth having will stick to their old friends, saying the new people are only come for a day. I give a blanket for a robe and other things in like ratio.

There has hitherto been no cold weather here, nor any fall of snow, & the Missouri is still open, in consequence thereof Buffalo Keep so far out in the plains that though Indians are numerous, as they have neither horses or dogs, robes will be very scarce.

The Baron Braunsberg spent a month in the Black feet country, passed some weeks here on his return and is now at Fort Clark where he will pass the winter he has made a valuable & interesting collection of objects in Natural history & Mr Bordmer has been very industrious in making drawings of the peculiarly interesting scenery of the upper country with a great number of Indian portraits, the Baron expresses himself greatly *interested* with his voyage, he expects to reach your post early in May if not before —

I shall expect a long letter from you by the upward express, and I trust we shall meet again next Summer.

I hope you will be able to furnish me with a good supply of corn in the Spring or my wine oats will be idle. I beg Dear Sir to assure you of the esteem of Yours truly

Signed K. McKenzie

P. Chouteau Jr Esqr   Fort Union Dec 16 1833
    Dear Sir
    My last letters from ~~this place dated 17 Sept and supple~~
~~mentary thereto~~ from Fort Pierre entrusted to care of Mr. E.
L. Patton, I ~~trust~~ presume reached you safely in due course.   I
remained at F^t. Pierre anxiously waiting the arrival óf Mr
Lamont until 24 Oct: when the rapidly advancing season compelled me to commence my journey hither.   I arrived here Nov
8. and three days afterwards sent a boat with good equipment
up Stream under charge of Mr Chardon to establish a trading
post as near to Mouth of ~~Milk R~~ R au Lait as the ice then running fast in the river would permit him to proceed,   after 10
days heavy work he came to anchor on this side La R^re au tremble
where he has built a ~~fort & called~~ fort & named it Fort Jackson
~~& is to this time doing a better trade than at this~~
I ~~found~~ considered it peculiarly desirable to establish a wintering post west of this partly for the convenience of the Indians
who frequent that section of country ~~and who have often com~~
~~camp~~
~~plained that in comeing hither from their hunting grounds they~~
~~had to pass several successive~~ and as this season no Buffalo can
be found in any other ~~direction~~ quarter there was good prospect
of securing more robes but principally with a view of ~~annoying~~
compelling our opponents to divide their forces and the principle
of divide & conquer has often been verified: they have sent up
a small equipment under Mr Geness to try their powers against
Mr Chardon but hitherto without any success.
    A few days after my arrival Mr Campbell visited me to make a
proposition to sell out to the A. F. C^o. all the interest of Sublett
& Co in each & every trading post established by them from the
Sioux upwards with the exception of their stock of Alcohol
Brandy & other spirituous liquors: Leclere having a share in
the Sioux outfit Mr Campbell could not negotiate for the sale
hereof until next Spring: I deliberated one night on the terms
submitted by Mr Campbell which were too preposterous to
have been acceded to under any circumstances and especially

contemplating
~~considering~~ the advantage our standing in the Country ought
to give us with the Indians; some consideration being also
made for our hard earned experience in the Indian trade and
further the inclination I felt to try the spirit & tax the exertions
of our expensive establishment of clerks & traders who were
unanimously of opinion that they could drive our opponents from
the field, determined me to ~~abandon~~ decline making an offer to
Mr. Campbell even on terms that might have served our purpose.
resolved
Nor do I regret having so ~~determined~~ for altho' as was natural,
the Indians flocked at first to the New house   all who are
valuable have returned to their old allegiance and if cattle
are Killed and robes dressed I shall have my full share: I am
prepared and expect to pay a good price for them but I am no
prophet if Mr Campbell does not find in the Spring his returns
very unequal to the amount of his expenditure: the statements
I have received from the Onkpapa, Yanctona & Mandan posts are
very gratifying inasmuch as the exertions of Mess. Papin & Picott
at the former have more than counterbalanced the advantage our
opponents possessed in being abundantly supplied with Alcohol,
and at the latter ~~post~~ the Indians are all for us: ~~Old Charbon-~~
~~neau cannot~~   The Gros Ventres are very much scattered this
winter but they express themselves so delighted by some unlooked
for kindness shewn a large war-party (comprising their principal
men) who visited this fort last Summer that we have secured
their interest.

I have no news from Crow or Black feet posts since my last:
The Crows are wintering on Wind river, I have a trader with
them; Mr Campbell has also sent out an equipment there & I
hear Fitzpatrick & Cᵒ were to winter in that country: The
Baron Braunsberg arrived at Fᵗ. Union a few days after my
departure for Ft. Pierre & moved forward again down stream a
few days prior to my return: he will pass the winter at Fort
Clark, and take the earliest opportunity in the Spring to proceed
to St. Louis.   I will send you the bill of charges against him to
the time of his leaving Fort Clark, any subsequent expences in-

curred by him at the lower posts will be handed you from thence. I much regret that circumstances prevented my further intercourse with so interesting a companion.   I understand the Baron is highly gratified with his visit to this country and I trust the public will some day have an opportunity of judging how judicious & indefatigable his researches have been relative to the manners & customs of the natives, in procuring an extensive collection of objects in Natural history hitherto unknown or undescribed, a vast number of new plants a ponderous cargo of mineralogical specimens & a portfolio rich in Indian portraits and the peculiar and unrivalled scenery of the Upper Missouri.

I send you herewith, an order for Mdze &c requisite for Fort Clark to be packed & Invoiced as before, also a copy of the order I sent by Mr. Patton for Mdze &c for this post & a supplementary Order for further articles absolutely necessary; as the trade here has not commenced it is impossible to say what my expenditure may be but as I am determined to have the robes I know it will take a great quantity of Amm^n. Tobacco &c

I will give explicit instructions for the Inventories to be rendered from Fort Pierre in the mode you desire.

I congratulate Mr Cabanné on the amicable arrangement of Leclerc's and hope he will not suffer much in pocket how much soever he may have been annoyed in mind pending the transactions.

The returns of this year I hope and have reason to expect will be larger in quantity & better in quality than last season.

With respect to the Mountain affairs upon the present arrangements I cannot look for profit; last Spring Mr. Fontenelle was empowered by me to make certain propositions to Milton G Sublett & Co and communicate the result to me here:

I received a letter from Mr Fontenelle but he was wholly silent on the subject: Mr M. G. Sublett arrived here, had seen Mr Fontenelle but nothing passed on this point: I have good reason to believe he would willingly have entered into some arrangements with me, but it was as necessary for him to consult his partners as for me to know if Mr Fontenelle had abandoned the views suggested & recommended to him in the Spring, thus a chance has been lost of relieving ourselves of a dead weight or perhaps of turning the scale in our favor.

My thanks are poor payment for your care & attention to my interest relative to my buildings. I have nought else to render you. I pray you accept them, they are sincere.

The Invoices and Acc^{ts}. have only received a cursory glance but I beg to make one or two observations:

N. W. Guns in packing a/c are priced 19/– Bt charged in Invoice 21/6. . . .

Mr Chardon is very anxious to get information about his Osage boy, can you obtain it and if it is practicable for him to be conveyed hither by Steam boat, please let it be done.

I could not with any propriety send off my winter express until I received the long looked for letters by Mr Lamont and though late in the season, having urged extraordinary dispatch at all the posts I hope it will reach you in due time, my order is large but I cannot prudently reduce it, and of some articles I fear I may yet be short. To the supplementary order I have appended some remarks which I beg may be regarded. Mr Hamilton desires his respectful remembrances. Accept Dear Sir the assurances of respect & esteem of

Your friend & Ser^t.

Signed K. McK.

Do not load Steam boat too much as I must have 2 or 300 bush corn from C Bluffs. F^t. U. & F^t. C. goods must be first placed on board the S. B. Goods for Sioux post if too weighty must remain in part to follow in Keel boat which will be time enough for lower trade. Our manufactory flourishes, we only want corn enough to be able supply all our wants the quality is *fine* but the yield from Mandan corn is small. You will surely contrive to send Alcohol to Bluff for Sioux trade; it is hard that people with so limited means should have an advantage over us. Campbell has not traded of every kind 5 packs. Fitzpatrick, Capt. Stewart robbed by Crows.

[K. McKenzie]

Fort Union 16 Dec 1833

W. B. Astor Esqr. Pres^{dt} Am^n Fur C^o.

Dear Sir

I have the honor to receive your polite & friendly letter of the 26 Apl last, on my arrival at F^t. Pierre on the 28 Sept.   In consequence of the formidable appearance our opponents presented at their various stations on the river and particularly near the mouth of the Yellow Stone two miles below this place I judged it prudent to visit our various posts this fall that by my personal instructions & advice I might in some degree counteract the plans of Mr Sublett & his partners and inspire our several clerks and traders with zeal & energy to drive them from the field.

Dr. McKenney accompanied me on my return to this place we arrived on the 8th Novr. and much as I am inclined to respect him as a man and value him as a companion candor compels me to say that I fear it is beyond my power to convert him into a good Indian trader, his walk in life, his knowledge of the world, his pursuits & habits and the bent of his mind & inclinations appear to me calculated to disqualify him for the petty detail of our trade which although en masse it may some seasons present an imposing appearance on paper, is made up of so many trifling transactions as tend to disgust all who are not at a comparatively early age initiated into its mysteries.   there is no scope here nor at any post on the river for the fair exercise of his talents, and the drudgery of an inferior clerk would ill comport with his character & views neither could I in consonance with my own feelings, see him in such situation   he seems by nature formed to command though I do not question at the same time his willingness to obey :   In his medical capacity such has been hitherto the salubrity of this climate, no one post could furnish him on the average a patient a month :   salts, castor oil, & essence of peppermint are our usual specifics and it requires but little skill in administering them : in cases arising from amatory passions the remedies are equally simple & in all cases not too long neglected are efficacious.   I am thus explicit that no disappointment may be felt if after a fair trial of this western wild Dr. McKenney should find his own expectations were raised too high. Rest assured I will do all in my power to promote his views that personal respect, regard to your recommendation and the high estimation in which I hold your father and the late Superintendent of Indian affairs can unitedly present to claim my attention, and the result we must leave to time & circumstances.

With respect to the trade of the Upper Missouri I have reason to expect that our returns will somewhat exceed in quantity those of last year, but they will cost us dear, our opponents are well supplied at all their trading posts with Alcohol & wines highly charged with Spirit, whereas our Steam boat was minutely searched & every drop taken from her, and we have only to depend on the extra exertions of our traders the standing we have with the Indians & our hardly earned experience to countervail the decided advantage liquor gives our opponents, hitherto I am happy to say our success has fully equalled my expectations.

In reply to your kind enquiries after my health and progress I beg to say that I have been happily free from sickness except of a slight nature, that I had an agreeable journey to St. Louis and after remaining there 110 [?] days placed my self on board the Assiniboine on the 10 April but in consequence of the unprecedented low stage of water did not arrive here until June 26.

Though tardy in my acknowledgements of the very many polite attentions I received from you in New York I feel assured you will not question the sincerity with which I now tender the respect & friendly reminiscences of Dear Sir

Yours very obediently

Signed K. McKenzie

Mr P. D. Papin   Fort Union Dec 1833
    OnKpapa post
        Dear Sir
            The express which reached me the 9th Inst brought me your letter for which I thank you   On every occasion which

presents itself it is very pleasant to me to receive communications from my confidential traders and at this time more especially when our opponents are doing their utmost and as you justly observe by their possessing Alcohol they have a great advantage over us which can only be met by such extra experience as you possess & the extra exertion I know you will use. On my arrival I declined negotiating with Sublett on their proposition to me to buy them out, judging it better that the unanimous opinion of all my old & tried friends should be justified by what I consider my self will be the result of our combined exertions to compel them to withdraw on finding their chance of success to be hopeless: they are very active here but hitherto with no better results than at the other stations on the river and they will find what few robes they do trade will cost them dear: they have sent an equipment to the Crow Village & another to oppose Mr Chardon who is stationed at Fort Jackson about three days march above me; they have abundance of Mdze. & a long list of clerks & men.

Hitherto the trade here has been inconsiderable but I have confidence in my Indians and if cattle can be found I shall have robes.

I hope it will not be long before I have another of your letters to acknowledge and please to bear in mind that all information about your own trade or the proceedings of your opponents will be very acceptable.

My express for St Louis is I fear too late in leaving this place, spare no exertion to accelerate its progress on its reaching you.

[K. McKenzie]

Fort Union June 30th 1834

Pierre Chouteau Junr Esqr:
  Agent Amer. Fur Co.
    Saint Louis
      Dear Sir

        This will be handed you by John Mogan who I send down in charge of a Keel boat, and Batteau laden with Robes &c.

shipped to your address, for particulars of which I refer you to the Memorandum herewith.

After much difficulty the Assiniboine reached here on the 26th. inst. The June rise has not yet made its appearance, but we are now in daily expectation of it; indeed if it does not come soon, I shall begin to despair of it altogether.

The Crow returns fell short 200 Packs of what I wrote you in the winter I expected would be made there; this arises from my having been wrongly informed on the subject by the Clerk at that post.

I scarcely expect to be able to go down in the Steam Boat, and it is quite doubtful whether I will be able to leave this place at all, till I can find some person to take my place; my presence here this year is more required than it was before —

Inclosed you will receive a statement of the accounts of the men now going down. Some advances may perhaps be made them at Fort Pierre; if so Mr. Papin (who is in charge there) has instructions to notify you on the subject —

I send back two men sent up in the Assiniboine, as they are perfectly useless to me, and have done little or nothing on board the boat since she left Saint Louis. Their names are Louis Flourant and Jules Traca — Jean Letup is indebted to the Co. $ 157. $\frac{50}{100}$. I send you his note for that amount which perhaps you will be able to Collect —

I have nothing more to communicate at the present moment, and will close with my best wishes for your health and happiness.

Believe Me Ever
Yours Most Truly
(Sign'd)   K. McKenzie

Fort Union July 8th 1834

Mr. A. Culbertson
    Dear Sir

In the spring I had the pleasure to receive your letter pr Mr Mitchell and much wish an early arrival of the Steam Boat had enabled me to give you a more prompt reply, but this year we have had more difficulties to contend with than any former season and I much fear she will be compelled to winter here.

Your precautionary measures respecting the Fort were very judicious: in this country it is always requisite to be on the alert, for danger or disaster comes when least expected. Mr Kipp has charge of your trunk or Box from the Lower Country; Mr. Mitchell having resolved on visiting old Virginia, in consequence of your mistrust of your powers, I have been compelled to take Mr. Kipp from the Mandan post to assume the charge of Fort McKenzie: you saw but little of him when passing Fort Clark but I feel convinced you will pass your winter very agreeably with him, he is moreover acquainted with most of the leading Indians in your district, and well known and respected by the men in the Company's employ; and should the Indians throng you the coming season as you are sanguine enough to hope and expect, you will find great relief in the main burden's resting on older Shoulders, while I am confident you will render every possible, and very efficient aid.

I thank you for your forethought in apprizing me of the probability of the Gens du Sang wintering with you and have regulated the equipment accordingly, the men made the trip in nine days.

In reply to your enquiry respecting horses kept by Clerks or men in the Company's employ, my rule has been hitherto to permit them so to keep them on condition of my using them to aid in supplying the Fort with meat, and should any person possessing a horse object thereto I should not hesitate in making a charge for the guard and care of him — Hoping to hear of your wellfare at your earliest convenience I am Dear Sir

Very Truly Yours
(Signed)   K McKenzie

Fort Union July 26" 1834

Mr. John Carlisle
   Sir

    I have three Boats laden and in an hour or two I start for

St. Louis. I leave this to be handed to you by Mr. Crawford; In my anxiety to make the most prudent and judicious arrangement to protect the Steam boat during the winter, as there is every probability she will be compelled to remain at her present moorings, I made my arrangements to build a fort near her station, and very naturally calculated that the men under your charge would assist me in so doing, satisfied that their comfort would be essentially promoted thereby : I also proposed using the Fort when completed as a trading house for the Indians of that district; but I am informed your men are resolved to be independent of me, to take care of the boat without aid from me to build a fort and house for themselves, and at all events to render no assistance to my people. Now I wish you to state candidly and fairly the real facts in a letter to Mr. Hamilton whom I leave in charge of this place and whose proceedings will be guided by the information you give   at the same time I wish you to understand that I have no desire to establish a trading post near the boat, but if any of my people are there I must provide them with the means of trading with the Indians; if your men persist in their present plans and think they are right in so doing, I will have nothing to do with them.   Perhaps I am misinformed   I hope such will prove to be the case.

Believe yours truly
(signed)   K. McKenzie
Agt. U. M. O.

Fort Union 10th Decr 1835

Major Fulkerson
    Ind^n Ag^t
        Dear Sir

For several years past on my return to this post from my visits to St Louis or Fort Pierre, I have been always accompanied by Mr Sandford, and the Indians of this District have then regularly received their presents from the U. S. Government, but this season after after [sic] an unusually protracted absence returning alone, and without any thing to give away my situation for the past three weeks has been any thing but agreeable, and not without great sacrifices have I been able to keep the Indians in any approach to good temper; they cannot or will not discriminate between their traders and the Government, and those Chiefs especially who have been peculiarly noticed or have been to Washington City say their great Father assured them they should never want for ammunition & Tobacco, so long as they traded on this side the lines, and behaved well to the Whites, nor can they believe their great father would tell a lie.   I have therefore the odium of keeping back their presents.   I never was an advocate for large and indiscriminate distribution of presents; a good and industrious Indian may be encouraged to greater exertions by a well timed gratuity, but when all receive alike, every good effect is destroyed and the nation claims as a right what was intended as a boon.   I annex you a statement of Sundry articles left by Mr Sanford to be distributed after my departure last year, and during his month residence here he must have dispensed nearly an equal am^t. to the Gens de Canot and some bands of Crees; you will at once perceive how utterly impossible it is for me to be equally profuse; and may hence imagine what I have to endure from the disappointed and of course discontented red Skins.

This place is barren of news.   I arrived here on the 17th Novr. having walked all the way from the Mandans, (because it was impracticable to ride) the winter has set in exceedingly early (20th Oct^r) and with unusual rigor.

I shall look forward with pleasure to meeting you & Mrs Fulkerson at Fort Pierre next Spring, and remain

···(Signed)   Kenneth McKenzie

· · ·

Fort Union 10th Decr 1835

J. B. Cabanne Esqr
    Dear Sir
        This will be accompanied by my usual express for St Louis and with your friendly aid I trust it will reach its destination in

good season. Your kind attentions to me have been so constant and of so decided a character, that although I cannot sufficiently thank you I shall never cease to think of them. My trip from your place to Fort Pierre was very pleasant but from thence forward, I had a great deal of trouble. The Boat with Outfits for the Upper trade had left Fort Pierre before my arrival. I had therefore to take charge of some very essential articles for the Yanctona trade, and what with carts breaking down and horses giving out, I made but very slow progress, and on my getting a little above heart river I found the boat ice-locked, the landing and securing the cargo detained me some time: I was obliged to remain many days at the Mandans to make arrangements as far as practicable to baffle our opponents: I did not reach this place untill the 17th Nov^r. (having walked the whole distance from the Mandans) and find my Indians in such bad humour; from being disappointed of their customary Government presents & the uncertainty of obtaining liquor for their Robes, that nothing short of almost profuse liberality on my part will induce them to make peltries, "No liquor no trade" is prevailing sentiment with the Assiniboines, and I am now more than ever convinced that no trading can be done without it here. I know I may rely on a continuance of your kind exertions to assist me herein, and with such a friend in need, I feel perfectly at my ease. — I have written Mr Chouteau to engage Martin Dorion, but if you will take the trouble you are much more likely to effect it for me.

I leave the entire arrangement to you. I cannot at present say whether he will be wanted at this post or with the Sioux, but I presume it would be immaterial to him. I should wish him to come up in the Steam Boat in the Spring. — Accept my assurances of respect & esteem and believe me ever to remain

Dear Sir

Very Truly Yours

(Signed)   Kenneth McKenzie

Fort Union Dec[r] 10th 1835

Mess[rs] Pratte Chouteau & Co.

Dear Sirs

I did not arrive here untill the 17th Nov[r]. having been upwards of six weeks making the trip from Port Pierre.   You are
aware that a portion only of the Outfit for this post was forwarded from Fort Pierre in July, arriving here in September,
the remainder with the exception of such articles as were retained for the trade of the lower posts were forwarded in September with the Outfit for the Yanctona :   the Boat was taken by
the ice near heart river where the Cargo was landed and proper
measures taken for its protection. —   It is a mortifying reflection after spending so much money in Steam boats the whole
Summer should be too short to transport goods from St Louis to
this place, and that this Company should be subject to the derision of our pitiful opponents, inasmuch as with all our ap-
pliances and means to boot we could advance no further than
heart River with the Outfit for our winter's trade; it is true the
winter has set in with great force unprecedently early this year,
but there is no excuse for our being thus taken by surprise.   I
send herewith order for Fort Union & Fort Clark Outfits for next
year, and rely on your exertions to fulfil it to the letter :   in addition thereto the Tobacco & Liquor at C. Bluffs must come to
this post, there is also a box of beads some Iron & perhaps some
other things remaining at the Bluffs but having left the packing
acc[t]. at Fort Pierre my memory will not serve me to particularize
them, but be they what they may, with the exception of Liquor
& Tobacco they should be deducted from the present order.   The
order for this place may appear large, but by no means unnecessarily so when I inform you that but little more than half
the equipment of this year came hither; Beads, Guns, Lead,
Powder &c were required at Fort Pierre :   Cloth, Blankets &c at
Fort Clark and moreover I have been compelled to send Tobacco
from hence for the Mandan & Sioux trade.   I fear the Steam
Boat cannot bring the Cargo for this place, Fort Clark, Fort
Pierre, & the Agents goods in addition, I therefore suggest your
starting a Keel Boat as early as possible with the Outfit for Fort

Pierre, it can easily make the trip in good season for their trade. You are aware I have no Keel boat for the Blackfoot Outfit of next year and must therefore have one towed up by the Steam boat. The number of men on this establishment is considerably reduced this year at the four posts there are in all but 84 and of these I cannot depend on more than 20 remaining with me, since the Sale of Liquor has been stopped they save their money and no doubt will go down to spend it.

I shall require fifty men to be engaged for next season for this upper trade; they must be good, likely men, not ignorant useless boys, who are mere cumberers of the ground, should such come I will send them back instanter; nor can high wages be afforded now it is almost a cash charge to the Outfit. I must again caution you about such unreasonable advances to the hands, it is a direct temptation or premium to be indifferent, independent & faithless. — I shall require a Carpenter, old Luteman would answer very well on moderate (wages), he is slow but sure — I shall also want a Blacksmith, Please send my boy Prince. I am anxious you should engage Martin Dorion. I cannot say at present whether he will be wanted for this post or the Sioux, of course it will be immaterial to him which post he winters at. If Mr Halsey does not return to this Country (of which he will apprize you) I shall require a Clerk for Fort Pierre and one for this place, they must be good accountants, fully competent to the charge of a set of Books, if Mr Halsey returns one will suffice. With respect to traders I can give you no instructions, I believe Mr Culbertson will go down, Mr Tulloch & Mr Laferriere will probably remain, but verily I will not tempt them by the offer of high salaries. On no consideration engage S. P. Winter or J. E. Brazeau, recent information from the Blackfeet confirms what I had long suspected, that the latter is a chip of the old block, and the former is like unto him.

I have never been able to ascertain what advances were made to the Manyer du Lards of 1833, please furnish me therewith, C Marion, D. Jabotte & Fr. Landry are all that are at this post . . . I have no later news from Blackfeet post than was communicated by Mr Hamiltons letter of Sepr. 10th by H.

Pecotte. — Mr Tulloch was putting up his new fort near the mouth of the Rosebud on the 30th Octr, no subsequent intelligence. I found on my arrival that the post established last year called Fort Assiniboine was kept up Mr Laferriere in charge. I cannot safely hazard an opinion on what quantity of peltries my District may yield this season; last year these upper Indians received from the Government 1000 lbs Tobacco 40,000 Balls & powder 75 doz Knives besides Cloth Blankets &c &c and getting nothing this year they are careless and indifferent and say they are without Tobacco & Ammunition and consequently cannot go out to hunt; I verily believe if I were destitute of Liquor I should not trade a hundred packs of Robes. — Pray be careful in sending good Tobacco, that which came up in 1834 I cannot even give away, & trading it is out of the question. I find I shall want a man for the Blackfeet post who is able to build boats, a professed carpenter is not required, you will please attend to this . . . Two hundred or more lodges of Crees who traded here last year are gone to the North, they did not like the wine of last season but if we will give them whiskey, they will come and see us again. Le Gens de Gauché have been at the North all fall, about 150 Lodges are just returned but they have not a Robe dressed or a skin in camp, nothing but liquor will keep these Indians to us, in fact without it it is a mere waste of time and money to keep up this post. There must be some mistake in 3 pst Wt Blkts of this year at such an advance on former prices the quality ought to be maintained but these are the meanest I ever saw in 1833 we had better blankets at 9/— stg. blankets we well know are much advanced but not a hundred p.ct.

Fort Union Decr 10th 1835

Ramsey Crooks Esqr
    Dear Sir

    Could I but fancy myself seated opposite to you by your own comfortable fireside with a bottle of your excellent port on a small table between us, we should see the bottom of it before I had recounted to you half my adventures "by flood & field" since we parted last summer but abandoning the flights of fancy and coming down to sober reality, I am alone in a smoky room, the thermometer 15 below zero, and although my ink is not frozen, my pen will neither move so nimbly, nor my ideas so freely as I could desire, when writing to my good friend Ramsey. I think I told you of my mortification when I (was) appealed to in the old country respecting the falls of Niagara, to be obliged to confess I had not visited them. I congratulate myself on having lived to see this most sublime of natures works. — I am not going to weary you with a description of what many may attempt but no one can adequately perform, words may convey ideas but they often fail to pourtray feelings; you have been there and I doubt not felt as I did, how utterly impossible it is for language to do do justice to the scene. At Cincinnati the news of our disasters recorded in the Columns of a newspaper, of the loss of our un-insured Steam Boat first reached me, (on this subject, especially the total disregard of our interests by our Agents, I shall have more to say to you on an other opportunity) to say "it was forgotten" is poor satisfaction for the loss of thousands! Misfortune never comes alone, and news of loss upon loss met me on my arrival at St. Louis the 17th of July, but a truce to gloomy reflections — What will you say at my neglecting to write to you during a whole month that I remained in St. Louis? You will know it was not from want of inclination: how shall I excuse myself; first Mr Lamont was occupied in making his arrangements for entering into a new business, and transferring his interest in this, to our friend Mitchell; second, Mr. Laidlaw was on a sick bed and really very ill, I had consequently a good deal on my hands; and further, knowing of your absence from home, I delayed from day to day until the hurry of my departure fairly prevented my writing to you at all: well, say you, enough of apology and let us proceed. I left St Louis by Steam boat for Council Bluffs, where I procured horses and came on to Fort Pierre, Mr. Laidlaw unwilling to leave his bones in St Louis gave his Physician the slip, took the Stage to Independence, furnished himself with horses, and riding post came up with me at the Vermillion trading house whence we proceeded to Fort Pierre, while there I made arrangements for Mr Mitchell to take out an equipment to Laramie's Fork on the river Platte, to trade with the Sioux and Chayennes, a fine Buffaloe Country, and where Sublett & Co established a post last winter. The Steam Boat from St Louis this summer came no higher than Fort Pierre, although there never was a finer stage of water than at the time she arrived there, but there was no person on board to direct the self-willed Captain & no one at Fort Pierre to enforce his proceeding to this place, the consequence has been, that after all the Money we have expended on Steam Boats, our boat with outfit for the upper posts was taken by the ice a little above Heart River where I found her ice-locked on the 20 Octr. I was detained a considerable while in seeing her cargo landed and property secured, but at length reached the Mandans, where we have opposition again this year, and but for the circumstance of our opponents boat being taken by the ice far below ours, it must have extended to this place and I still expect that during the winter I shall have to contend with them at one or two of the Indian camps. — I arrived here the 17th Novr. having walked and lead my horse the whole distance from Fort Clark. They told me in St Louis that the Crow post was abandoned, I was well pleased to find a new equipment was sent thither and another to the post established last year near the spot where the Steam boat Assiniboine wintered. It is impossible at this time to form any idea of this seasons returns returns Cattle are tolerably abundant and the prospects fair at the several posts, I shall be satisfied if this post equals last year from whence there were shipped 4100 lbs. Beaver Skins, 1970 packs Robes 4000 fox Skins 9000 Rats &c &c though unfortunately so small a portion thereof got to market. Eleven of our oldest Clerks & Interpreters have left the service this summer and no new ones have been engaged to fill their places I have had some difficulty in supplying the different posts efficiently, I have not much fear of our doing quite as well without them, and we are certainly releived of some very heavy salaries. — And now my good friend, being fixed in my winter-

ing ground I must take my leave of you untill the next express
for St Louis, in the mean time you have my ardent wishes for
your health happiness, & prosperity.   Please to present my respects to Mr Whetten and if he will do me the favour to consider
himself a letter in my debt, I shall feel very much obliged to him.
I have room only to assure you My Dear Sir, that I am ever
most faithfully & cordially Your's &c &c

signed   Kenneth McKenzie

Fort Union 10th Decr. 1835

To His Highness Prince
  Maximillian de Neuwied
    Sir
        Flattering myself that sometimes when your thoughts
wander to the Banks of the Missouri they may linger for a moment at Fort Union I embrace the opportunity of the usual
winter express to St Louis to apprize you that I found the Fort
in statu quo on my arrival here the 17th Ult^o.   Mr. Kipp has
left Fort Clark for Canada, Mr. Hamilton who was my locum
tenens during my long absence is wintering with me, and the
beauties of the Rhine & especially the hospitalities of Chateau de
Neuwied are frequent subjects of our conversation;   I shall
ever retain the most agreeable reminiscences of your polite attentions, and regret that I can only return you my poor thanks.
Mr Lamont apprized you of the loss of our Steam boat last spring
with your several cases of animals & birds on board, collected
with so much toil and trouble!   Your loss is irreparable, I sincerely regret it and should feel happy could I in any way supply
the defficiencies thus created in your valuable collection of
Natural History.   Our Cargo of furs &c destroyed was of very
considerable pecuniary value, from sixty to eighty thousand Dollars, a total loss, no part being insured.   My voyage across the
Atlantic was as agreeable as a good ship with experienced Captain, sumptuous fare, and pleasant Company could possibly
render it.   On my way out to St Louis I visited that most

sublime of natures works, the falls of Niagara, but what pen can describe so magnificent a scene, and still less the feelings excited by a contemplation thereof. — I reached St Louis July 17th. and after a month's sojourn commenced my voyage to this place, which occupied three months, the winter set in with great force unusually early the Missouri was closed on the 23rd Octr. Since my arrival I have been pretty constantly occupied in "talks" with the red Skins, a great contrast to the very agreeable manner in which my time was passed at this period of last year, in fact my rambles in Germany, France and England yielded me so much delight, I am anxious for a repetition of the like enjoyment. You will please command my services in this country or in the U. States in any way they can be available. I make tender of my best wishes for the continuance of your health & vigor to enjoy the many good things of this life which surround you, and have the honor to be,

Sir
Your Highness's
Most Obedt & Very humble Servant
signed   Kenneth McKenzie

Fort Union 10th Decr 1835

Henry K. Ortley Esqr
    Dear Sir
    Various untoward circumstances occurred to protract my voyage so that I did not arrive here until the 17th Ulto fully a month later than I contemplated. I am however in good health & vigor and ready for a hard winter's campaign if my Indians will but crowd in their peltries upon me until I cry "hold, enough." None of the luxuries of life having found their way into my cellars or stores during my absence, and the Stock I left there being considerably diminished, I must request you to put up for me sundry articles as pr annexed order, have them carefully packed in boxes marked with my name, and sent on board the Steam Boat when she starts for this place, Pratte Chouteau

& Co will pay your Bill on your presenting it to them. Some people find pleasure in contrast but you can readily immagine (*sic*) how dull this place must appear, after my gay and busy life with its ever varying & always interesting scenes of the last twelve months. I know not when we shall meet again, the sooner the better say I, and until the day arrives, may you be as happy and prosperous as you can desire, is the sincere and ardent wish of

Your friend &c &c

(Signed)   Kenneth McKenzie

Order for Sundry Articles to be shipped by H. K. Ortley Spring 1836 pr Steam boat Addressed to K. Mc Kenzie Fort Union.

10 Gallons best french Brandy
  ,,   ,,   ,,   Hollands Gin
1 Doz ½ pint bottles Capers
½ ,, Qrt   ,,   best Katchup
10 lbs Almonds in shell
1 Box Fr. Plums
½ Bush^l Pearl Barley
1 Box Herrings
A Budget of newspapers
1 Box Segars

APPENDIX G.

REPORTS[526] ON PRIMEAU AND DESCHAMPS MASSACRES.

Fort Clark, Mandan Village,
June 10th, 1836

Majr. Fulkerson,

Sir.

In compliance with your request I will endeavor to furnish you with a plain and succinct statement of the *facts* respecting the murder of Mr. E. Premeau — by the Yanktona band of Sioux Indians during the last winter.

Premeau had left his trading house — situated about 15 miles above the old Arickarah Village with several trains loaded with merchandize — destined for the Mandans and Assiniboine Indians. He proceeded on without any dificulty to a place called the old Mandan Village about 20 miles below Heart River; he was here met by a party of Sioux returning from the neighborhood of the Mandans where they had very recently suffered a most disastrous defeat from the Gros Ventres.

After making many threats — and telling him he should not proceed further up the River, alledging as a reason that he had kept back information which would have enabled them to escape the late massacre; They took forcible possession of his horses, and commenced pillaging amunition Tobacco &c. after doing much mischief, and making many threats they returned to the camp a few miles above. Premeau followed in the course of the day and arrived late in the evening at a trading house occupied by Pierre Ortibise, a clerk in the employ of the Co. He requested Ortibese to aid him in recovering the stolen horses, which he readily promised to do; early next morning one of the Indians who appeared to have been a leader among the pillaging party — made his appearance at Ortibeses house, by the offer of a liberal reward Premeau prevailed on him to again restore the horses,

526 From photostats at Jefferson Memorial Building, St. Louis.

which he stated were concealed 8 or 10 miles below — Premeau and the Indian left the house in company with the avowed purpose of bringing in the horses. It afterwards appeared they had not went more than a mile from the house, when the Indian shot P^e. dead — and after stripping him of his clothes &c, buried him in the Snow and returned to the camp. It was near two days before his melancholy fate was known to either whites or Indians, the Murderer in the mean time fled from the Missouri, and found refuge in a camp of his own tribe, at *Coteau de praires,* about 120 miles from the Scene of the cold blooded murder.

There were many contradictory reports at the time relative to the melancholy affair but after a careful examination and comparison of the whole — the facts recited were such as above stated; The true cause of this outrage is difficult to ascertain, perhaps the best reason will be found in the well known character of the Indians on the Upper Missouri — treacherous, revengful, and vindictive. The slightest injury — real or imaginary, that an Indian may have sustained will often remain locked in the inmost recesses of his heart, and perhaps deeply revenged many years after.

There never has been a year during my residence on the Upper Missouri — but that whites have been killed without any cause being assigned — But a brief history of the situation of this band during the last winter will suffice to Show the feelings by which they seem to have been actuated —

The whole of the Yanktonas, together with a large band of Sowans collected on the Missouri last fall below the Mandans — throughout this whole range of Country no Buffalo had been seen for several months so that the Indians were soon reduced to a state of Starvation. Their only prospect for relief was from the Mandans and Gros Ventres — whom they knew had plenty of corn — about the first of January the Sioux commenced moving up, and soon assembled in the neighborhood of the Mandan village — So long as the Sioux had wherewith to barter for corn the two tribes mingled together in peace and harmony, but the Mandans and Gros Ventres being keen traders took advantage of the suffering condition of the Sioux — and by usurous extortions soon reduced them to such a state of poverty and distress as compelled them to leave the river, nothwithstanding the extreme rigor of the weather, in search of Buffalo. A camp of 150 Lodges, principally Sowans left the Mandan Village on the 9th of January and proceeded up Knife River. On passing the Gros Ventres Village they stole a quantity of corn and beans, leaving at the same time a fiew blankets, knives, tobacco &c by way of payment. This being a large party was suffered to pass unmolested; they were followed the next day by a camp consisting of 45 lodges of Yanktonas who took up their quarters for the night a fiew miles below the Gros Ventre Village, they struck their tents next morning at day light and commenced their ill-fated march up knife river — On ascending the hills a short distance from their late encampment, they found themselves completely surrounded by a large party of Gros Ventres and Mandans (of the little Village) — weakened by coald and hunger, and destituted of arms or amunition they were unable to make but a weak defence — nearly the whole party, men, women and children, were indiscriminately butchered — The loss of the Sioux is said to have been 150 killed and 43 women and children prisoners, 8 or 10 young men saved themselves by flight and were the first to bring the news to the fourt — After telling their melancholy tale, one of the Young Sioux deliberately fired at a Gros Ventre boy in the Interpreters room — Old Charbono, made a narrow escape two balls having passed through his hat — this daring attempt at revenge made in presence of a large number of Mandans, who immediately flew to arms determined to exterminate a small band of Sioux on the opposite side of the River — but after a short consultation they agreed to spare them on account of their wretched situation — such an act of magnanimity is rarely to be met with in the annals of Indian history, and reflects the highest honor on the Mandans — they advised the Sioux to move off as quickly as possible for fear of a second attack from the Gros Ventres this friendly advice did not require to be repeated — the Sioux immediately struck their lodges and commenced moving down the river — during this march many perished with coald and hunger, and the sufferings of the whole camp were such as none but Indians could have borne — It was Whilst in this melancholy condition that they fell in with Premeau and his party — perishing with coald and hunger — burning with a thirst for revenge, and completely reckless of consequences. Moderation or good behaviour could scarcely have been expected from them.

Any other Information that I may be able to furnish on this subject—shall at any time be cheerfully given.

Respectfully

Your Obdt Sevt &c

David D. Mitchell

Maj. W. N. Fulkerson
 U. S. S. Ind. Agt.
  For Mandans &c

—————

Genl. William Clark
 Super Intendent Indian Affairs
  Saint Louis.

Sir. . . I have the honor to submit the following report relating to the affairs of the Mandan Sub-Agency, U. Mo. during the year ending 30th of September 1836.

Since my last annual report, all has not been so peaceful and tranquil in this quarter as could have been wished. But little violence however has been offered by the Savage towards the Whites, — what was, was of an aggravated nature. From their indomitable spirit of revenge, and their eager thirst for war; considerable blood has been shed among themselves.

On the 9th of January last a camp of about 150 lodges, principally *Sowans,* left the neighborhood of the Mandan village in search of Buffalo: — they proceeded up knife river, a stream which passes by the Gros Ventres Village; and in passing the Village stole a quantity of corn &c, leaving however at the same time a fiew blankets, knives, tobacco &c, by way of payment, but nothing like a sufficient compensation. This being a large party was suffered to pass unmolested. They were followed the next day by a camp of the Yanktona band of Sioux consisting of about 45 lodges, who took up their quarters for the night a fiew miles below the Gros Ventres Village. They struck their lodges next morning at day light, and commenced their illfated march: they had proceeded but a short distance from their encampment, when they found themselves completely surrounded by a large party of the Mandans (of the little Village) and Gros Ventres — Weakened from cold and hunger, and almost destitute of arms and ammunition, they were able to make but a feeble defence nearly the whole camp, men women and children were indiscriminately butchered, or made prisoners; the loss of the Sioux it is supposed, was not less than 150 killed and about 43 women and children made prisoners. On the retreat of those who escaped the scalping knife, about 20 miles below heart river they met with Mr. Premo, a trader, on his way with several trains laden with Merchandize for the Mandans Gros Ventres and Assinnaboine Indians; whom, by threats, they endeavored to prevent from proceeding further, alledging as a reason that he had kept back information which would have enabled them to escape their massacre — And finally robbed him of his horses, and pillaged him of amunition, tobacco, and various other articles, and after doing much mischief, returned to a trading house occupied by Mr. Ortabise, a clerk to the fur company. Premeau followed after, and arrived there late in the evening — next morning, one of the Indians who appeared to have been a leader among the pillaging party, came to the house where Premeau was, when by the offer of a liberal reward, he prvailed on him to restore the horses again, which he stated were eight or ten miles below. Premeau and the Indian left the house for the avowed purpose of again getting the horses. It afterwards appeared they had not gone more than a mile before the Indian shot Premeau in the back with two balls — stripped him of very thing he had on, — buried him in the Snow — and returned to the camp. It was two days before his melancholly fate was known. The murderer in the mean time fled from there and found refuge in an other camp of the same tribe at the Coteau de prairie, about 120 miles from the scene of his cold blooded murder. He has since, I understand gone over to the Mississippi to Wah-na-tah's band for protection.

Last July, I endeavored to procure the release of the prisoners from the Mandans and Gros Ventres, to restore them again to their tribe, but, (with one single exception) they refused to liberate them, unless paid for the corn stolen by the Sowans, with whom, they considered the Yanktonas connected; the exception was an elderly female who had been made prisoner by one of the principle chiefs of the Gros Ventres tribe; she was delivered up by him, without hesitation; and I having no way of taking care of her, and being satisfied that her life was every day in danger whilest she remained here, I paid thirty dollars to have her conveyed to the little Missouri, a distance of about 400 miles, where she might remain in safety, and in a short time be restored to her tribe, and drew a requisition on Majr. Brant for the payment of the same; This, however, I should not have done, had I received yours of the 28th June last prior thereto — but at that time, from her defenceless and miserable condition, I thought myself justified in doing it. The circumstances relative to those two melancholly affairs have been more minutely detailed by me to you in my letter of the 30th June last, and the communication which accompanied it.

On the 2nd day of June last two war parties of about 25 each, of the Gros Ventres tribe, went to revenge the death of some of their friends on the Assinnaboines, and after an absence of about 20 days returned to their village having found only one lodge, and that at the mouth of the Yellow Stone, which they fired on in the night, killed two of the Assinnaboins and a Cannadian who was in the lodge with them.

On the 25th of June last, an unpleasant occurrance took place at the mouth of the Yellow Stone, at Fort Union,   Among the whites and a family of half breeds at that place from North Red River, Selkerks settlement; It was a family of 6 or 7 Strong, athletic young men; who always acted in concert, and effected their purposses by force — It was a treacherous quarrelsome family, and one that every American and half breed held in awe;

as none knew when they were safe from their treachery. It appears they made the Onset themselves upon the whites by firing into a crowd of them indiscriminately, and as far as I could learn, without any just provocation, in the night time, and without any suspicion of their intentions, only to revenge the death of their father who was killed about twelve months ago by a half breed from the same country of themselves. Their fire killed a very efficient & meritorious half breed, also from North Red River. The whites and the balance of the half breeds, being so provoked and so much exasperated, at such an unprovoked assault, arose in mass against them, with a determination of extinguishing the whole family, and insuring greater safety among themselves for the future, which they succeeded in through the course of the day, not saving even the mother — a small lad I believe only escaped, who fled into the fourt, where he was protected by Mr. K. McKinzy. who was in charge of it; they however were not exterminated without blood shed on the part of the whites; a Cannadian of the party was severely wounded, and an Assinnaboine Indian who had also joined them was killed.

Late in the night of the 5th of July last, five of the Yanktonas, came to the Mandan Village to revenge in part the death of some of their friends, murdered last January; and after prowling about for some time, to no purpose, came to the fourt gate & knocked, where I had some talk with them, and without admitting them in the fourt; gave them a fiew twists of tobacco, some powder and balls, and advised them to desist in their adventure, and leave; which they did without doing any mischief.

I have distributed the greater portion of the presents allotted to my agency among the Mandans and Gros ventres, because they have emerged much further from those indolent habits, which characterize the Savages in this region, and have turned their attention to the cultivation of several of the prime necessaries of life, and because they are in perfect amity with the U. S. and I have felt desirous of Stimulating them in their active exertions to provide for their wants, and to retain their friendly relations with us —

The Assinnaboines and Crees, who have regularly received

presents from the Government, I am informed are becomeing very much dissatisfied at not having them still sent to them as usual. The traders state that it is not without sacrafices, they have been able to keep them in any approach to good temper, that they cannot, or will not, discriminate between their traders and the Government, and that they thereby have the odium of keeping their presents back. None of these Indians have ever visited this post since my arrival here, nor indeed do I conceive it would be safe for them to do so, consequently have never received a present from me. I went to the Yellow Stone this summer to see them, they had left for their hunting ground before my arrival, so I had to return without being able to have any talk with them. These Indians at least once a year visit the English at the North, where, they say, they receive large presents from the English Government, which probably causes them to be much more dissatisfied with us than they probably otherwise would be. From Statements made to me, it seems it would not be difficult to alienate them from us altogether. A fiew presents however separately for them, would, I have no doubt, have great effect in sustaining our friendly relations with them. An equal distribution of the fiew presents now allotted to my Agency among them, the Mandans and Gros Ventres and the other Indians which occasionally visit this post, would be an utter loss of the good intended to be produced by them.

The Rickarees are still residing on the river Platte. There is a talk of them returning to the Missouri River again, — It is to be hoped however, that they will remain where they now are, as this Country has been sufficiently stained with blood, shed by their treachery. It is reported here that they have committed some murders this Summer where they now are, as to its correctness however I cannot say, but from their notorious thirst for blood, I think it very probable. There are several families of that tribe, residing among the Mandans, and with whom they have intermarried, among which I distributed separately considerable of the presents. They appear much dissatisfied at the course pursued by their tribe, and say they left them in consequence of their treacherous conduct.

By your letter of the 10th of February last, I was required to afford immediate notice to Genl. Gains and also to yourself of any design which I might perceive on the part of the Indians connected with my Agency to make excursions into, and to attack the citizens of the Mexican States. I am happy to inform you that I have seen nothing which has rendered a notice of the nature there adverted to necessary.

No infringement of the Law regulating trade & intercourse among the Indian tribes has come to my knowledge, consequently no seizures have been made.

In answer to a circular received from the War Department, directed to the Superintendent of Indian Affairs, Agents and Sub Agents, dated May 1835 — requiring from them, immediately after the 30th of September in each year, complete abstracts to be prepaired of all licenses granted for trade with the Indians, in the Indian country, I have only to reply, that so far as regards myself in this respect none have ever been granted by me —

A complete list of all persons in the employ of the Indian Department within my Agency, has been made out, and accompanies this report.

There are no schools established within this Sub Agency — Neither are there any farmers or mechanics employed; therefore I have nothing to report on these two heads.

Statistical returns have been prepared in obedience to the Circular above referred to, and accompanies this report, showing as near as I have been able to ascertain, the numbers of the respective tribes, the number employed in the chase, agriculture and mechanics respectively. This Circular came to hand at so late a period, that I have not the time to furnish so full and accurate a return, as I should like to have done, as I had never until then investigated that matter perhaps so attentively as I ought to have done. It shall be more attentively attended to in the future.

I have drawn requisitions on Majr. J. B. Brant Mill. Dist Agt. Ind. Dpt. since the first day of October last, for the pay of Sub Agent, Interpreter, and expenses accrued &c the sum of $1092.-50/100.

The estimated sums required to defray the expense of this Agency for the comeing year, is put down at $1725 — the same as heretofore. A statement exhibiting the sums required under each spacific head of expenditure also accompanies this report.

Since the Commencement of this report I have been informed from information upon which I can rely, that the murders above referred to have been committed by the Rickarees and within the bounds of the Sioux Sub Agency.

I have the Honor to be

Sir Your Most Hble Servant

Wm. N. Fulkerson,
U. S. Ind. Sub. Agt.

APPENDIX H.

REPORT ON SMALL-POX EPIDEMIC.

Fort Pierre Novr 2d 1837.[527]

Mess. Pratte Chouteau & Co. St. Louis.

Gentlemen

When the Steam boat St. Peters left Fort Union in June last for St. Louis you are no doubt aware that I was afflicted with the small Pox. I did not have the disease in its most malignant form though it was far from being light — however thank God I have escaped the disease but my constitution has received a severe shock.

Fifteen days after I was taken sick a second case of this detestable pest made its appearance in the fort, and a few days afterwards there was 27 persons ill with it in the fort out of which number 4 proved fatal — during the prevalence of the malady the Assiniboines were continually coming in. I sent our Interpreter to meet them on every occasion, who represented our situation to them and requested them to return immediately from whence they came however all our endeavours proved fruitless, I could not prevent them from camping round the Fort — they have caught the disease, nothwithstanding I have never allowed an Indian to enter the Fort, or any communication between them & the Sick; but I presume the air was infected with it for a half mile without the pickets — the weather was unusually warm & the stench so great that those who had long before had the malady, were more or less Indisposed I lost but one of my men by the Small Pox (Bte Compton) the other deaths were squaws —

Among the Indians it is raging with the greatest destruction imaginable at least 10 out of 12 die with it. I do not know how many Assiniboins have already died as they have long since given up counting but I presume at least 800 and of the Blackfeet at

[527] *Pierre Chouteau Collection, idem.*

least 700, it was introduced to that nation by a Pied noirs who embarked on the St. Peters at Little Missouri. The Mandans have all died except 13 young & 19 old men. The Gros Ventres hitherto have escaped the worst by remaining in the barge but I hear it has now attacked them also. At the Crow post the disease was raging but there were no Indians near. The loss to the company by the introduction of this malady will be immense in fact incalculable as our most profitable Indians have died. Mr. Mc-Kenzie had drawn a great many of the Northern Indians to the Missouri, they were disposed to work well Buffalo were & are still in the greatest abundance but there will be few Indians to hunt them — of what will be the result of the U. M. O. trade this season I can form no idea, perhaps it will pay expenses but of this you can judge as well as myself. My only hope is that the cold weather will put a stop to the disease but this is mere conjecture. You are aware that all diseases introduced to the Indians by the whites must have a tendency to make them malicious, we consequently have something to fear. Up to the time of my departure from Fort Union the Assiniboins had behaved very well, they have stolen but 2 horses but they have lately been making threats of a serious nature. Le vieux Gauche band was the first to take the disease and it spread to every lodge in the camp. The old man has burnt his flag and vows vengence on the Fort. A double gate has been fixed with a trading house between where the transactions with the Indians are carried on, none but the chiefs enter the fort, a regular guard is kept up, our only apprehension is for the horses & cattle. Of horses there were after Mr. Mitchel's arrival 120, and perhaps every one will be stolen before Spring & for certain the Indians will not trade any. The Small pox has not yet made its appearance here but we hear it has broke out in the Sowan Band, of whom many have died but there is more discipline among the Sioux and we hope the disease will not be so fatal as with their neighbors.

Mr. Papin is much occupied sending equipments to such bands as are at present free from the disease, he begs you will excuse his not writing. About the end of December you probably will hear from us again. Mr. Mitchell will send an express as soon as he hears from Fort McKenzie & Fort Vanburen.

Regarding Mr. Laidlaw's claim of $2500 from me I deny the fact let him shew the clause in the Agreement if it exists, my engagement was to pay him by yearly instalments in such sums as I could find it convenient.

I only arrived here yesterday from Fort Union and Hope Mr. McKenzie will pardon my not writing.

Pray send some Vaccine matter had Mr. Mitchell brought some thousands of lives might have been saved.

On hand at					
Ft. McKenzie	200	packs robes	8	packs Beaver
Ft. Union	35	"	1	"
Ft. Clark	40	"	3	"
Ft. Pierre	20	"	½	"
Ft. Vanburen	10	"	½	"

Your obed Servt

Signed Jacob Halsey

APPENDIX I.

1 Le Couteau l'aune

½ Bandé

  Les 4 Ours

  Les 2 Coeurs

  Brother

  Brother

  L'enfant Chefe

  Sussé

  Chefe Avèuglés son

  L'homme de Medicine

  Celui qui tient laisseau Brassé

  The 2 Hearts Son in Law

  La Grosse Citrouile

  Brother of L'enfant Chefe

  Barbé Baiteur

  Brother

  Le Chefe des Loupes

  Le Coeur D'Ours

  La peau du ventre

  The Wolf Cheifs son

  La tete de portepique

  La Grosse Noisseau

  Brother of Sussé

  Balle dans le Coup

  Capitaine Marloe

  L'Ours fou

~~½ Bandés Son~~

3 Plumes Brother

  Kipps Brother in Law

  The Crow Belts Son

  Tobaccos Son

  Durants Brother in Law

  The Pheasant

~~Le Biquolo~~

  Les Cheveulé

  The 4 Men's Son

Le Vieux Sioux

Son

L'oreille

Gros Soldat

Le Yancton

Les Yeux D'Ours

Jacez

Le Vieux Boeuf

Les 3 Plumes

La Lodge

Cotillion de femme

Boeuf Malin

Son in Law

Tabac

32

Manuels Son

Do. Nephew

Le Foureau de Fleche

Casseur des Vitres

Baullion

50 Les Grande doigts

Le Garçon du partizan

Les Bras Fleurie

Le Garcon de Petit Brave

The Chicken hawks head

,, ,, Son in Law

The Fozen Foot

Les 2 Corbeau

The Frozen Foots Son

Manuel

Son of L'eau dans la pin

59

Little Village

Le Fort

Plusieurs des Corbeau

Brother of 4 Turtles

La peaux de Vache Blanche	The Forts Son
He that runs in the Middle	Do Do Do
Dummy White	Do Do Do
Le Loupe fou	La Langue Noir
Le petit loupe a Moulle	Son of Foin de Loupe
Les Yeux de Loupe	4 Turtles
Son in law of Grosnoisseau	The Iron Eyes

70

Dummy - Black	Le Gras de Pense
L'ours qui revient	Le Beaufrere a Baptiste
Son of Old Sioux	,, Do ,, Do
Porteur de Viande	The Little Swan
Coulotte Blanche	La bande des chein de Prairie
L'eau dans la Pine	L'arc des Corbeau
The Bulls Neck	Le Colteur
Son of L'homme de Medicine	The Big Shoe
,, ,, Corne de Boeuf	Foin de Loupe
Brother of Le Chefe fou	Chaudiere Cassé

Celui qui Boucante Castor   Yellow Tail

Les Sept Cheveau   ,,   Son

                                                  ,,   Son

                              Son of Foin de Loupe

                              Le Coeur Mort

                              Le Fire

                              The Squaw Killer

                                   ,,   ,,   ,,   Son

                                   ,,   ,,   ,, Brother in law

                         Brother in law of Gras de pense

                         Son of Celui qui attacks les fleche

                         ,,   ,,   ,,   ,,   ,,   ,,   ,,

                         Son of Grande Cottillion

APPENDIX J.

EXTRACT FROM FATHER POINT'S JOURNAL[528]

Voyage in a Barge on the Missouri from the Fort of the Blackfeet to the Fort of the Assiniboines,

22 May [1847]. I wish to speak of Fort McKenzi [McKenzie],
which of all the forts of the Blackfeet has lasted the longest, and
of Fort Pegane, the first which the Whites built in the Blackfeet
lands. As the history of this last is bound up with the history
of a pacification long desired and all the more desirable as before
that time all the whites who fell into the hands of the Blackfeet
were so many men who fell beneath their blows, you will allow
me to pause here a moment.

It was only in the spring of 1831 that peace was concluded.
It came about in this wise (I put forward nothing which has not
been certified to me by trustworthy witnesses). There was at
that time at Fort Union a Canadian who is still living and who
was chatting with me this morning. This brave trader, having
already spent twenty-one years in the forts of the North to which
the Blackfeet used to go to trade, had frequent occasion to speak
to the headmen of the nation and had retained enough of the
language to understand them and be understood by them. As
he joined to this two-fold knowledge a very conciliatory character, his bourgeois, who at that time was Mr. McKenzi, asked
him whether he felt himself courageous enough to go and bring
to the Blackfeet the good tidings of which there was question for
so long a time. To so honorable a proposal Berger answered
finely and, in spite of the winter, and accompanied by four other
Canadians no less devoted than himself, and furnished with
presents for the Blackfeet, he set out having no other desire than
to die as a man of honor or to fulfill the noble mission with which
he had been charged. They were all on foot, obliged to travel

on in the snow and in quest of a sort of men which they particularly wished to keep away from.   Judge now of their hardships and courage.   They proceeded on without meeting any other living beings except the animals of the desert for forty long days; but on the fortieth and at the very moment of reveille a war-party suddenly made its appearance.   "We are lost," say Berger's companions; "but it is all the same, we must fight." "No," answers their brave leader, "we did not come here to fight, leave the matter to me," and he advances alone to meet the enemy.   It was a Pegane party composed of 17 men.   What was his joy to recognize in the partisan one Assapoke by name to whom he had quite recently rendered a service.   Among the Indians, as I have already remarked, a favor done is never thrown away.   Here is an instance.   The calumet was smoked and presents were made; but their quality or quantity not measuring up to the hopes they had entertained some of the malcontents took it upon themselves to add to the presents, together with a good part of the booty of the deputation, all the weapons except one belonging to the deputies, which thing did not of course quite suit the latter.   But what after all could be done?   Happily, God, Who holds in His hands the hearts of men, disposed the robbers, as it were in spite of themselves, to listen to reason and the partisan, who bore no resemblance to them, succeeded by agreement or force in having all due restitution made.   This done, they set out on their way and a few days later, namely, on March 5, they arrived with flag unfurled at a camp of Peganes who had, for chief, one Stematone.   There is no need of saying whether at their appearance (Ms. illegible) of the headmen or whether the presents offered were well received. As to persons and propositions, the former were listened to with interest and the latter accepted on one condition, to wit, "that everything would be according to representations," for at that time still distrust on the part of the Blackfeet for the traders went so far that they believed only with great difficulty in the sincerity of the traders' words; but this time the latter gave so many excellent proofs [of their sincerity] that the hardest [among the Indians] to be convinced joined with the others and all offered to conduct the peace-makers back to Fort Union, whether to defend them from attack on the way or to confirm more solemnly the alliance that had been made. After twenty days of rest and festivities Berger and his companions took up the trail back to their fort followed by 92 Indians (braves) and 32 squaws. On leaving they had said: ''we shall be here May 15 at the latest; if at this time we have not arrived, it will be because things did not turn out as was hoped.'' Now this date had already passed and they had not returned. ''What has become of them?'' their friends began to say to themselves, ''what has become of them? Oh, they most likely have been massacred like so many others.'' Such were the melancholy thoughts which the delay was giving rise to and which were shared by almost the entire fort, when the cry was raised, ''here are our men- here are our men!'' Judge of the joy on all sides when they reappeared at the head of so numerous a company, all bearing themselves well, without fear or reproach, and with the flag of victory in their hands. In particular the burgeois, whose honor and interest were at stake in the affair and who, moreover, was gifted with an excellent heart, did not know how to express his own joy. Amid jubilations and rejoicings of every sort peace was confirmed to the great satisfaction of all and it was resolved that at the opening of the fair season men in sufficient numbers would leave to go and build a fort in the Blackfeet lands, a resolution which was put into effect. The fort built by order of Mr. Makenzi and under the direction of Mr. Keep [Kipp] was called Fort Pegane, in honor of the first Blackfeet who had made an alliance with the whites, a token of delicate deference which does honor not less to the wisdom than to the modesty of their [sic] founders. This fort having been burnt by a party of Bloods [hommes du Sang], who apparently were not aware of the intentions [of the builders], orders were given to build a second one a little higher up and this one [McKenzie] which received the name which the first should have borne, prospered until 1844, at which juncture reasons of prudence dictated its removal. Apparently the vicinity of the Judith River [rivière dite de la Judée] coupled with the beauty of the environs tempted more than it ought to have done the persons commissioned to discharge the business; for experience having proved that these advantages as well as others which they thought they saw in that locality did not counter-balance the grave inconvenience of offering too many opportunities to enemies, one year after its construction Fort J. F. C. [F. A. C.], otherwise called the Judith Fort, was transferred further up. This gave birth to Fort Louis [Lewis], which, as we have seen, after having achieved a long career in a short time, gave itself a successor in the fort now in process of construction and called Fort Clay. Not to omit anything that belongs to the ancient history of this journal, I must place in the neighborhood of Fort Louis [Lewis] and of Fort J. F. C. [F. A. C.], two forts of the opposition set up in 1844 which, as well as all those lower down, lasted scarcely longer than the span of a springtime. What shall we say of the thousand and one fortresses built of the Blackfeet? In this region they are sown like the grass of the field, only they have not its duration. Most frequently the morning destroys or abandons what the evening before has set up. So in these lands perhaps more so than elsewhere, in spite of foresight, skill, courage (nothing of all this is lacking in the bourgeois of the company) it is true to say, "we have not here a lasting city." We saw that the longest-lived of all, Fort Makenzi, lasted scarcely three lustres [fifteen years]; but as it was to commerce, what Fort Louis [Lewis] was to Religion, honor to its ashes!

APPENDIX K.

Additional Letters from the *Drips Papers*

The following letters or extracts of letters will illustrate the close relation existing between the Indian service and the American Fur Company. The first is from the pen of John F. A. Sanford, who, after he had become identified with the American Fur Company, had retained his connection with the Indian service by accepting, for a season, an appointment at Fort Gibson. On June 11, 1842, he addressed the Commissioner of Indian Affairs ''with respect to the appointment of an Agent to reside in the Indian Country for the purpose of suppressing the Whiskey,'' and endorsed Superintendent Mitchell's recommendation of Andrew Drips. This Crawford duly acknowledged, July 2nd, whereupon Sanford wrote to Drips, then near Westport, a ''Private'' letter, saying, July 10th,

''. . . From this you will perceive that every thing goes as we could wish it, & I hope that in a few days, you will be in possession of your Commission & Instructions. In the meantime, however, I would advise you to say nothing about it, as it might probably defeat in some measure some of the objects, which we wish to accomplish, when we urged the appointment — My principal object, in addressing you now, is to call your attention to the fact, that within a few days from this time several expeditions (for trade) will leave this place & the Frontiers for the Platte, Arkansas & Missouri Rivers; and as the principal & sole object of your appointment, is to exercise a surveillance over the Traders & put a stop to the introduction of spirits & liquor into the Indian Country, would it not be well enough for you to keep an eye upon the movements of these Expeditions & apprise Cummins of anything you may learn in relation to their time & place of departure. Maj. Mitchell has written a *strong letter* to Cummins, reiterating former instructions & giving new ones, in relation to these particular land Expeditions — *We want our Expeditions (Bent StVrain & Co.)* to undergo the same rigid investigation, & ordeal, that the others are subjected to — We are in earnest about this matter & are willing and anxious to aid in putting a stop to it.   John Sybil leaves here in a few days on board the Edna — I am sure he has or will attempt to take liquor & he will try to evade an investigation either by taking some circuitous route or possibly by sending his liquor on a head to some point & await him — It is said, that he intends getting off the Boat at Fort Osage — See to it — I hope that you will not fail to obtain all the information possible & give it to the Agent, who will be instructed to make a thorough search after they have got fairly into the Indian Country. 'An Ounce of prevention, is better than a pound of Cure,' and if you can succeed in putting a stop at the Commencement you will have but little difficulty hereafter.   There is a large Opposition going up the Missouri & I trust that your efforts & our own, will forever put an end to Whiskey traffic in the Sioux Country.

"Do not let any of these Expeditions give Cummin's the slip. For the part, that you take in this matter you can (confidentially) apprise Cummins of your expectations regarding the appointment to an agency & of the sole object in creating the Agency — This will be a sufficient apology, if any is required, for your zeal in the matter. You will have quite as much as you can do this Winter, in visiting Sioux traders & the Platte. As soon as you can get your commission would it not be well enough for you to have some communication with Miller at the Bluff, relative to the best & most efficient mode of examining all expeditions passing that way.

"Heretofore, *we traders,* have never thought the Gov^t in earnest when they spoke about Liquor — I hope you will teach us now that it is no longer a jest.

"Very truly

"yr frnd

"J. F. A. Sanford"

The commission for Drips was not forthcoming and Sanford,

while somewhat anxious himself, wrote, on September 3rd., to reassure him,

". . . The Department have certainly been very dilatory in complying with their promises, yet I do not despair. Your nomination I learn has been before the Senate for a long time, and the reason of its not being confirmed, is, that there are many other matters & appointments that have precedence in the Senate Calendar . . ." [*idem*]

Other important men, including Pierre Chouteau Jr. himself, connected with the firm of Pierre Chouteau Jr. and Co., were concerning themselves in the matter. September eighth, Crawford notified Drips of his appointment, sending the letter with his commission enclosed in care of Mitchell; but before it reached Drips, Benjamin Clapp wrote him. This was on the twelfth of September. Congress had then adjourned, as Clapp informed Drips, but no news had come of his appointment, "altho every assurance had been given that it would be made, and we still think the commission will be forthcoming.

"Meantime, as the money for the Indians, at Marais des Cynes has gone up, & you may be of service to our Outfit there, you had probably join Mr. Giraud at once — and if your appointment shall come forward, it shall be sent immediately to Mr. Cyprian Chouteau, who will be instructed by us to forward it to you by express & at our expence.

"We cannot abandon the belief that your appointment will yet be made, tho' the delay is provoking — but it is of a piece with all public business at Washington in these degenerate days —

"We are glad to know that the Woman purchased had reached you & proved satisfactory."

[*idem*]

John B. Sarpy, in the temporary absence of Clapp, wrote to Drips twice within four days, on the fifteenth of September and then again on the nineteenth, the reason for which is very plain from the letters. In the earlier of the two, Sarpy acquainted Drips with the fact that his commission had at last arrived, having come in a communication addressed to the superintendent on the sixth; but no instructions had come to Mitchell and, therefore, it was not yet possible to say whether or no Drips's presence would be required in St. Louis, the signing of a bond being evidently to these highly trained business men a not very important matter in the absence of positive instructions from Washington. They wanted to profit by the services of Drips as a trader up to the very last moment. Sarpy had some instructions of his own to give, however.

"I take this early mode," wrote he, September 15th., "of apprizing you of this fact, in order that you may hold yourself in readiness for prompt action.

"I would strongly recommend that (the) appointment, as also your movements, until fairly under way & beyond the frontier settlements, be kept as quiet as possible, as a knowledge of these things in advance, might be the means of such intelligence reaching the Indian Country as would in a measure defeat the good intended by your movements &c.

"In advance, I beg to tender you individually my best aid in promoting your views in the Country, and to assure you that our people in the Country will render you all the assistance, & co-operate with you in all their power — When at their posts or in their neighborhood I desire that you will make yourself at home with them — But in this particular I will write more fully when I know of the course which you will be instructed by the authorities to pursue in the Country —
"..."

[*idem*]

In his letter of the nineteenth, Sarpy wrote to the same effect that Mitchell did, the selfsame day, that Drips must qualify in person. He should come on to St. Louis "with as little delay as practicable," so said Mitchell, and Sarpy, "You will therefore lose no time in coming down." The duties ahead, Mitchell reminded him, were bound to be "arduous."

INDEX

Note: Roman numerals refer to the Historical Introduction, which in the original edition began on page xv. Arabic pagination has not been changed.

INDEX

Arikara River, *note* 272. See Grand River.

Arikaras, departure of, for the Platte, xviii, *n o t e s* 30, 494; character of, xxxiii; Chardon's acquaintance with, not limited to the five years of his journal, xxxiv; take possession of abandoned Mandan villages, xxxiv; Audubon conducted to the village of, xxxv; resentful of Chardon's desertion of them, xxxvii, *notes* 195, 199; a few arrive from the Sioux camp, 44; seven or eight squaws of the, married to Saons have disappeared, 50; twenty-four, arrive at Fort Clark, 80, *note* 439; are welcomed by Mandans, visit the Gros Ventres, 80; Mandans wish to keep their corn for, 83; said to be moving toward Fort Clark, 86; band of sixty, arrives at Fort Clark from camp on one of the forks of Little Missouri, 88; leave Mandan village to visit the Gros Ventres, 88; return from visit to the Gros Ventres, 89; Chardon feasts and counsels with, 89; seven, arrived at Fort Clark and report that the camp will not appear there until spring, 91; Chardon has great expectations with respect to trade with, 97; band of, arrives at Gros Ventre camp on Little Missouri, 98; at Fort Clark start for camp on Little Missouri, 100; said to be encamped at Turtle Mountain, 101; several, arrive at Fort Clark bringing with them six horses stolen from Yanctons on headwaters of Cannon Ball River, 102; no news from, since March 2, 1837, 104; two, arrive at Fort Clark and report their tribe encamped on Knife River, 105; Gros Ventres report that a small band of, has been killed by Yanctons on Knife River, 106; said to be encamped within 40 miles of Fort Clark, 107; prairie fire in the direction of camp of, 108; five, leave Fort Clark for camp of, 108; Mandans set out to meet their friends, the, 109; Gros Ventres dance the *Calumet* to the, 109; Chardon invited to a feast at camp of, 109; Chardon gives a feast to, 109-110; trade with the, begins, 110; twenty lodges of, go to the Gros Ventres, others take up their quarters with the Mandans, 110; making their medicine, 110; Dog Band of, gives dance at Fort Clark, 111; Chardon counsels with chiefs of, respecting proposed war with Saones, 112; war party of, leaves for Yancton camp, 112; soldiers of, start up to the Gros Ventres to whip those who robbed Newman, 113; several families of, start for below, 114; war party of, starts out to war against the Yanctons, 114; war party of, finds Yancton camp near the Cheyenne River, 116; Mandans and, arrive with dried meat, 117, 118; war party of, and Mandans sets out in search of Yancton camp, 119; war party of May 31st returns without making a *coup*, 119; give dance at Fort Clark, 120; war party of, sets forth against the Sioux, 120; Chardon coun-

sels with, and Mandans respecting proposed removal of Fort Clark, 120; the old village of, 122, 384, *note* 272; Mandans and, start out to make dried meat, 123; pose as the protectors of the whites against the enraged Mandans, 123; speech of Four Bears to the Mandans and, 124-125; several, leave the Mandan village and pitch their lodges out in the open prairie, 126; all go down to the Island, 126; war party of Gros Ventres and, reported "used up" by Saones, 127; accused by the Gros Ventres of making threats against the whites, 127; making medicine for their sickness, 127; some, have had dreams, 127; some of war party of, and Mandans, returning from attack upon Sioux lodges at the mouth of White River, are taken sick at Grand River, 128; one of the, takes drastic measures to effect a cure of small-pox, 130; one of the, kills self and attempts to kill his wife, 131; the band of, to which murderer of Cliver belonged, smokes the pipe of peace with Chardon, 132; one of the, tells his mother to dig his grave, 132; several, are yet encamped at the Point of Woods taking care of the sick, 135; two, that have been with the Saones on Cannon Ball River arrive at Fort Clark, 136; Mandans and, cross the river in quest of buffalo, 136; Gros Ventres steal horses of, 138; daily fatalities among, from small-pox, 138; that were with the Gros Ventres are on their way to the Mandans, 139; Chardon counsels with, 139; start out after fresh meat, 139; several lodges of, cross the Missouri River to winter with the Mandans, 139; give a dance at Fort Clark, 140; party of, sets out to steal horses from the Gros Ventres but is made to return by chiefs, 140; all move down to the Point of Woods opposite the little lake to take up their winter quarters, 140; are busily engaged in dancing the scalps of three Sioux, 142; eighty to one hundred, visit Fort Clark on their way out buffalo hunting, 142; Hunant, arriving from the camp of, reports cattle in abundance, 145; three, arrive at Fort Clark from the camp above, 145; several, arrive at Fort Clark from the camp below, 146; Chardon sends his boy (negro) to village of, 146; two, appear at Fort Clark from camp above and report arrival there of forty Gros Ventre lodges, 147; Garreau and Co. start down to the lower camp of, 150; several, come up from below on their way to upper camp, 150; moving up from below, 153; Chardon feasts and counsels with, 154; start out to make dried meat on Knife River, 154; Chardon gives a feast to forty old women left behind by, 154; war party of, about to go against the Sioux, dances the war dance at Fort Clark, 156; returning from dried meat excursion, report three war parties out against the

mor of their intending, 391; declares he has never issued a single trade license, 392; has seen no evidence of any disposition on the part of his Indians to invade Mexico, 392; no infringement of the Trade and Intercourse Law has come to the knowledge of, 392; Clark instructed that, in the event of Sanford's resignation, is to succeed, *notes* 223, 230; marriage and death of, *note* 232; engages Charbonneau as his interpreter subject to the approval of Superintendent Clark, *note* 280; is agent for other tribes of the upper Missouri besides the Mandans, *note* 385; makes a present to Two Crows, the Fool Chief, and Little Sioux, *note* 395; the report made by Mitchell to, helps to establish Mitchell authorship of a portion of the Fort Clark journal, 384-387, *note* 406; proceeds to Fort Union at the time Halsey does, *note* 481.

Gaboleau, Pierre, 356.
Gaines, General Edmund P., 392.
Gamble, Archibald, *note* 241.
Gamble, J. O., *note* 246.
Gardepie, Jean Baptiste, negotiates at the little Mandan village a peace between the Mandan chiefs and the Chippewa, 104; starts for the North, 104; arrives from the North with 200 muskrats and 50 lbs. beaver, 127.
Gardner, Johnson, *note* 109.
Garraghan, G. J. (S. J.), x, work of, cited, *notes* 78, 250.
Garreau, Antoine, 5, 6, 12, 18, 19, 26, 33, 43, 72, 77, 79, 80, 90, 95, 99, 101, 102, 104, 118, 120, 121; avenges the killing of John Cliver, 128-129; nephew of, dies at the village, 132; Chardon's interpreter, falls sick, 133, *note* 491; improvement in condition of, 135; goes out in quest of lost horses, 141, 142; visits of, to the Arikara camp, 149, 150, 153, 170, 171, 188, 189; turns his wife off for infidelity, 154; on the list of 1830 as interpreter for the Arikaras, *note* 81; is to be sent down by Chardon to meet the boat, *note* 200; doubtless the "Antoine Garro" of Beckwourth, *note* 429.
Garreau, Joseph, *note* 288.
Garreau, Pierre, senior, *note* 288.
Garreau, Pierre, Junior, 20, 27, 45, 48, 58, 64, 74, 76; has charge of affairs at Fort Berthold, *note* 254.
Garrioch, Andrew, *note* 60.
Gass, Patrick, journal of, cited, *note* 319.
General Jackson, 24, *notes* 33, 306, 362.
Genesee Falls, *note* 454.
Genesee River, *note* 454.
Gens de Canot, 358, 374, *notes* 306, 334.
Gens de Gauche, 378.
Gens des Fille, *notes* 306, 334.
Gens des Roches, *note* 334.
Gens de Vieux Gauche, 395.
Gens du Sang, 372, 403. See also Blood Indians.
George, Alexander, *note* 516.
Gervais, ——, *note* 258. See also Jervais.

Giraud, M. 407, *note* 48.
Glaundye, ——, 327.
Glenday, ——, 354.
Gordon, William, reports of, on the fur trade, 343-352.
Gould, E. W., work of, cited, *note* 60.
Graham, Richard, *note* 3.
Grande Cotillon, 400.
Grand River, 82, 128, 134, *notes* 272, 488.
Grant, Peter, *note* 258.
Grant, Robert, *note* 258.
Gratiot, ——, *note* 4.
Gratiot, Emily, *note* 221.
Gravelle, Antoine, *note* 360.
Gravelle, Michel, 30, 57, 354, *notes* 306, 360.
Gravier, Michel, *note* 360.
Green Corn Dance, *note* 285.
Greenock, birthplace of Lamont and of Crooks, *notes* 4, 67; Lamont imports whiskey, etc. from, *note* 76; Laidlaw sends to Mackenzie a bundle of papers from, *note* 101.
Grinnell, George B., work of, cited, *note* 439.
Grosclaude, Justin, 38, *notes* 52, 377, 523.
Gros Ventre Expedition, *note* 280.
Gros Ventres, character of, of the Missouri, xxxiii; acquaintance of Chardon with, not limited to the five years of his journal, xxxiv; Chardon prepares to winter with, xxxvii; feast given to some, under *Par Fleche Rouge*, 9; fight between, and the Sioux, 9-10, 162-163; battle between, and the Assiniboines, 16, 86; Chardon accompanies Lamont as far as, 17; arrival of Bijoux from, 18; arrival of Molleure from, reporting starvation, 19; Chardon visits, 30, 69, 105, 173; war party of, goes against the Yanctons, 32, 111; give a dance, 37; Agent Fulkerson prepares to distribute presents to, 44; Little Dog Band of, dances at Fort Clark, 45; squaws from Fort Clark go to, to dance, 47; Agent Fulkerson and Chardon with Sioux and Mandans go to, to ratify the treaty, 47; report that Assiniboines have attacked the, 49; attack the Yanctonais, 52; Charbonneau to aid, in moving their goods to their summer village, 54; visit Fort Clark, 60, 156, 159; dance in the Mandan village, 61; feast given to, 61; some, and Mandans of the little village come to settle in lower Mandan village anticipating an attack from the Sioux, 72; join Mandans in the ceremony of crying and cutting for the dead, 74; Andrews prophesies an attack of, by Assiniboines and Crees, 76; Boulé returns to Fort Clark from, 78, 91; Arikaras go on a begging expedition to, 80; Mandans and, prepare for war against the Yanctons, 80-81; idea of war abandoned because, have changed their minds, 81; a Saon Indian arrives at, to trade a white cow skin, 83; Pinconeau brings news that the Assiniboines are preparing for war against,

route for Baltimore, *note* 502; allusions of, to the small-pox epidemic necessarily reflect upon the Amer. Fur Co., *note* 507.

La Souris Qui Marche, *note* 306.

La Tête de Porc-épic, 397.

Latress, Frederick, *note* 498.

Latress, Jean Baptiste, sent with letters to Fort Pierre, November 28, 1837, 142; in company with Villeandré arrives at Fort Clark with the express from St. Louis, 155; possibly the Jean Latresse who married Julia Duval in 1839, *note* 498

Latrobe, Charles Joseph, work of, cited, *note* 104.

La Vache Blanche, 358.

Lawson, John D., work of, cited, *note* 220.

L'Eau dans la Pin, 399.

Leavenworth, Colonel Henry, *note* 240.

Le Barbé, Batteur, 397.

Le Boeuf Malin, 398.

Le Bras Cassé, *note* 306.

Le Brechû, 358, *note* 362.

Lebrun, Antoine, *note* 367.

Lebrun, Baptiste, 152.

Lebrun, Bonaventure, 34, 35, 44, 58, 65, 83, 85, 88, 90, 94, 99, 100, 102, 104, 109, 110, 111, 112, 119, 138, 152, *notes* 90, 367.

Lebrun, Pierre, *note* 444.

Le Chef des Loupes, 397.

Le Chien Fou, *notes* 258, 306.

Leclair, Baptiste ("Old Baptiste"), 83, 109, 122, 150, 185, *notes* 443, 484.

Leclair, S. N., *note* 327.

Leclerc, Narcisse, *notes* 21, 101, 523.

Leclerc, P. N., *notes* 81, 340.

Le Coeur d'Ours, 397.

Le Coeur Mort, 400.

Lecompte, Andre, 178, *note* 515.

Lecompte, Joseph, *note* 515.

Lecompte, Louis, *note* 515.

Lecompte, Narcisse, *note* 515.

Lecompte, Pierre, *note* 515.

Le Coup de Boeuf, 32.

LeCouteau l'Aune, 397.

Lee, James, xliii, *notes* 244, 245.

L'Enfant Chef, 397.

L'Enfant du Fer, *notes* 306, 362.

Le Fils des Gros Français, 358.

Le Fort, 126, 398, 399.

Le Frene les Deux Coeurs, *note* 440.

Le Garçon de Petit Brave, 398.

Le Garçon du Partizan, 398.

Le Garçon de Sonnant, *note* 362.

Le Gauche, 23, 148, 358, *note* 306.

Légris, Pierre, 13, 14, 16, *notes* 321, 324.

Le Grand Soldat, 398, *note* 306.

Le Gros Corne, *note* 147.

L'homme de Medicine, 397, 399.

Le Loupe Fou, 399.

Le Manguer d'hommes, 358.

"*Le Marquis*," *note* 68.

Leonard, Zenas, narrative of, *notes* 29, 436, 486, 504, 507.

L'Oreille, 398.

L'Ours, 358, *note* 334.

L'Ours Fou, 397.

L'Ours Qui Revient, 399.

Le Pelet Soldat, *note* 306.

"*Le Premier*," *note* 68.

Le Sage, Alain René, work of, cited, *note* 490.

Les Grande Doigts, 398

Les Montagnes des Bois, *note* 306.

Le Sonant Laroche, *note* 306.

Le Sonnant, 358.

Les Sept Chevreaux, 400.

Lessieur, Godfrey, *note* 318.

Lessieur Papers, cited, *note* 318.

Le Vieux Boeuf, 398.

Les Yeux d'Ours, 398.

Les Yeux de Loupe, 399.

Letand, Jacques (Letant? Lenfant? Lestant?), 24, 102, 103, *notes* 90, 351, 461.

Letrace, John, *note* 451.

Letup, Jean, 371.

Lewis and Clark Expedition, *notes* 26, 29, 132, 153, 158, 193, 205, 271, 272, 274, 280, 314, 318, 333, 341, 347, 350, 355, 356, 357, 392, 414, 458, 488.

Lewis, Meriwether, observation of, and Clark regarding the sobriety of the upper Missouri tribes, xxxiii, *note* 158; remark of, concerning the name, Martha, as bestowed by Clark upon the present Big Muddy, *note* 132; entry in journal of, respecting the naming of Judith River, *note* 193; bitterly prejudiced against the British, *note* 280; report of, of John Newman and his conduct, *note* 318.

Lewis, William S., work of, cited, *notes* 222, 519.

Le Yancton, 398.

Libby, O. G., work of, cited, *notes* 271, 496.

"Liberator of all the Indians," See James Dickson.

Liberty, *notes* 50, 247.

Lisa, Manuel, *notes* 280, 394.

Lisa, André Pierre, *note* 394.

Little Cheyenne River, *notes* 73, 289, 345.

Little Heart, River, *note* 376.

Little Lake (Mandan Lake?), 52, 53, 81, 85, 93, 94, 133.

Little Missouri River (Bad River?), See Bad River and Teton River.

Little Missouri River, 13, 54, 61, 65, Boulé, coming from the Gros Ventres, reports cattle abundant near, 94; news is brought that a band of Arikaras has arrived at the Gros Ventre camp on, 98; the Arikaras at Fort Clark start out for the camp on, 100; the Mandans start out to make dried meat on, 101; the boats from Fort Union are wind bound at, 117; the Gros Ventres have horses they stole at, 120; all but ten lodges of the Gros Ventres are scattered along, 145; Palliser decides to hunt on, *note* 252; Beaver River, a branch of, *note* 347; Maximilian's "singular hills" and, therefore, *l'ours qui danse* a little below, *note* 414; Turtle Hill near, *note* 458.

Little River, 85, 98, 122, 128, 158, 170.

Little Sioux, 47, 131, *note* 395.

Little Swan, 399.

Liverpool, 338.

Lloyd, H. Evans, *note* 163.

Logan, James, work of, cited, *note* 259.

of, 366; unless the June rise of, soon
makes its appearance Mackenzie will
despair of it altogether, 371; the boat
is ice-locked in, 375, 380, 382; it is
to be hoped the Arikaras will never
return to, 391; Fort Clark located on
a bluff in an angle of, *note* 1; Palliser
crosses, opposite Fort Pierre, *note* 24;
Fort Tecumseh on the west bank of,
note 25; Arikaras propose leaving, *note*
30; Halsey is sent up, *note* 50; Mackenzie's position with respect to the
trade of the upper, *note* 65; hospitality
extended at posts of upper, not peculiar, *note* 72; Prince Paul desirous of
visiting countries bordering on the
Columbia and, *note* 91; peculiarities of,
and steamboating, *note* 102; Stuart's
article, on, *note* 186; Matlock in
charge of Indian affairs on the upper,
note 188; letters from the bend of,
note 215; Kipp and Chardon are said
to be descending, June, 1846, with
nine loaded barges, *note* 246; the Commissioner of Indian Affairs is informed
of the outrageous state of things on the
upper, *note* 247; fur trade for region
of the upper, is re-organized, *note* 247;
Palliser walked across the grand detour of, *note* 251; Palliser is waiting
for the break-up of the ice in, *note*
252; "Pirate" is lost on, *note* 257;
Fort Union and Fort William both
situated on the northern, or left, bank
of, *note* 265; approximate date at
which Charbonneau first went to, *note*
280; the boats brought the rats to the
upper, *note* 295; location of the Gros
Ventre villages on, *note* 299; bend of,
about a league below Fort Clark, *note*
313; a "Villeandre" on upper, as late
as 1848, *note* 323; Primeau and Leclair are on their way up, in opposition
to each other, *note* 327; several men
of the name of Dauphin were employed
on the upper, *note* 345; Beaver Creek
flows into, *note* 347; Picotte, Papin,
Chardon, Halsey, and Bolivar Chardon
travel down, to St. Louis, *note* 404;
Mackenzie returns to the upper, *note*
406; hiatus in record of the country
of, is filled partly by letters from Fort
Union, *note* 406; buffalo seek shelter in
the woods which border, *note* 420;
course of, changed between the time of
Lewis and Clark and that of Maximilian,
note 432; cost of horses on, *note* 438;
Bolivar Chardon never again on upper,
in the lifetime of his father, *note* 478;
a fateful voyage in the history of steam-
boating on, because of the small-pox
epidemic that resulted, *note* 480; the
Coquille, or Musselshell, a southern
tributary of, *note* 483; the Grand, or
Arikara, or We-tar-hoo, enters into,
from the west, *note* 488; Arikaras had
not yet moved away from, when Catlin
passed up, *note* 494; no surgeon to be
sent up, higher than the Mandans,
note 507; White River an affluent of,
in South Dakota, *note* 518; not possible
to determine when Kennedy first appeared on, *note* 520.

Mitchell, David Dawson, first winter of,
on the upper Missouri, xxvii, *note* 99;
is *en route* for Fort McKenzie, xxx;
withdrawing from the employ of the
Upper Missouri Outfit, xxxi; information is imparted to Schoolcraft by,
xxxiv, *notes* 164, 496; becomes Superintendent of Indian Affairs at St.
Louis, xli; is interested in the revival
of an agency on the upper Missouri,
xli; is supported in his political as-
pirations by Benton, xlii; is hand-in-
glove with leading men of the Amer.
Fur Co., xlii; rides up to the Gros
Ventres and gives a feast, 61; enjoys the luxury of a glass of milk at
Fort Clark, 62; sells a white buffalo
robe to Wounded Face, 63; visits the
Gros Ventre village, 64, 66; is preparing to leave Fort Clark for Fort
Pierre, 65; gives a feast to the Mandan villages and makes a speech four
hours in length, 66; is a passenger
with Mackenzie and Fulkerson on the
steamboat leaving Fort Clark for the
Yellowstone, June 18, 1836, 69; arrives
at Fort Clark, *en route* for the Yellowstone, 139; Chardon sends letters to, at
Fort Union, 152; vaccinates the Gros
Ventres who arrive unexpectedly at
Fort Union, 162; Chardon and, journey
together overland from Fort Pierre to
Fort Clark, 171; leaves Fort Clark for
Fort Union, October 16, 1838, 171; is
going back to Virginia, 372; Lamont
is transferring his interest in the Upper
Missouri Outfit to, 379, *notes* 67, 406;
Mackenzie sends, to Laramie's Fork to
trade with the Sioux and Cheyennes,
380; had, brought some vaccine matter
thousands of lives might have been
saved, 396; letter to, from Laidlaw,
note 21; gives the finishing touches to
forts started by Kipp, *note* 80; is
listed as a clerk and trader among the
Yanctonais, *note* 81; biographical
sketch of, *note* 99; builds Fort McKenzie, *note* 124; loses the entire Blackfeet equipment, *note* 124; Culbertson
with, at Fort McKenzie, *note* 145; Maximilian apprehensive that bad results
will come from the distribution of liquor
by, *note* 161; orders the dismissal of
J. V. Hamilton, appointed by Drips an
Indian sub-agent, *note* 247; permits
Sir William Drummond Stewart to take
spirituous liquors into the Indian country, *note* 247; is anxious for Drips to
return to his duties, *note* 247; Joe
Howard, who wintered with, is a de-
serter, *note* 333; is in charge at Fort
Clark during the absence of Chardon,
note 406; the writer of a portion of
the Fort Clark journal, *note* 406; takes
advantage of his own superintendency
and of Drips's special agency to seek
redress and indemnity for the Primeau
outrage, *note* 413; a passenger on the
"Yellowstone," June, 1836, *notes* 422,
425.

Missouri Argus, cited, *note* 1.
Missouri Fur Company, Immell & Jones
of, 343; holds the Arikaras responsible